Radio Speakers

ALSO BY JIM COX
AND FROM McFARLAND

Rails Across Dixie: A History of Passenger Trains in the American South (2011)

American Radio Networks: A History (2009)

The Great Radio Soap Operas (1999; paperback 2008)

This Day in Network Radio: A Daily Calendar of Births, Deaths, Debuts, Cancellations and Other Events in Broadcasting History (2008)

Sold on Radio: Advertisers in the Golden Age of Broadcasting (2008)

The Great Radio Sitcoms (2007)

The Daytime Serials of Television, 1946–1960 (2006; paperback 2010)

Music Radio: The Great Performers and Programs of the 1920s through Early 1960s (2005; paperback 2011)

Mr. Keen, Tracer of Lost Persons: A Complete History and Episode Log of Radio's Most Durable Detective (2004; paperback 2011)

Frank and Anne Hummert's Radio Factory: The Programs and Personalities of Broadcasting's Most Prolific Producers (2003)

Radio Crime Fighters: More Than 300 Programs from the Golden Age (2002; paperback 2010)

Say Goodnight, Gracie: The Last Years of Network Radio (2002)

The Great Radio Audience Participation Shows: Seventeen Programs from the 1940s and 1950s (2001; paperback 2009)

Radio Speakers

*Narrators, News Junkies,
Sports Jockeys, Tattletales, Tipsters,
Toastmasters and
Coffee Klatch Couples Who
Verbalized the Jargon
of the Aural Ether from the
1920s to the 1980s*

A Biographical Dictionary

Jim Cox

McFarland & Company, Inc., Publishers
Jefferson, North Carolina, and London

The present work is a reprint of the illustrated case bound edition of Radio Speakers ... —A Biographical Dictionary, *first published in 2007 by McFarland.*

LIBRARY OF CONGRESS CATALOGUING-IN-PUBLICATION DATA

Cox, Jim, 1939–
Radio speakers : narrators, news junkies, sports jockeys, tattletales, tipsters, toastmasters and coffee klatch couples who verbalized the jargon of the aural ether from the 1920s to the 1980s— a biographical dictionary / Jim Cox.
p. cm.
Includes bibliographical references and index.

ISBN 978-0-7864-6086-1
softcover : 50# alkaline paper ∞

1. Radio broadcasters—United States—Biography—Dictionaries.
I. Title.
PN1991.4.A2C69   2011   791.4402'8092273—dc22   [B]   2006034217

BRITISH LIBRARY CATALOGUING DATA ARE AVAILABLE

© 2007 Jim Cox. All rights reserved

No part of this book may be reproduced or transmitted in any form or by any means, electronic or mechanical, including photocopying or recording, or by any information storage and retrieval system, without permission in writing from the publisher.

Front cover photograph © 2011 Photodisc

Manufactured in the United States of America

*McFarland & Company, Inc., Publishers
Box 611, Jefferson, North Carolina 28640
www.mcfarlandpub.com*

With profound esteem
for all my grandchildren—
each one flaunting
a delightful personality

Jessica Alexander
Brandon Alexander
Jordan Elizabeth Lowe
Hannah Lynn Cox
Caroline Rose Reed
David Aaron Cox
Sophie Gayle Reed

Contents

Acknowledgments viii

Preface 1

THE DICTIONARY 5

Appendix: More Who Spoke Radioese 323

Bibliography 331

Index 333

Acknowledgments

Before launching into the daunting task of amassing the copious details on celebrated individuals who were regularly ushered into our homes and lives via the aural airwaves, my data-gathering was expanded significantly: realizing my personal limitations, I enlisted a trio of old time radio hobbyists with confirmed track records in meticulous and tenacious research. The threesome—Claire Connelly, Derek Tague and Jim Widner—were up for a challenge that was to result in preservation of some little known facts about a great many extraordinary personalities.

While the final text was written by me and much of the raw data resulted from my digging, voluminous portions of this matter were collected by those intrepid, unflappable volunteers. For ten months, in fact, the four of us labored harmoniously, locating and processing vast sums of obscure information. We kept in touch almost daily, especially when the records from multiple sources conflicted or were difficult to find. On at least one occasion it took weeks—and a surfeit of intense investigation—to determine if a particular subject was *one* man, *two* or perhaps *three*! (It turned out that there were three under the same given name and surname working concurrently in show business, although only two were in radio. Separating them wasn't easy, given that the incidents in their lives were intermingled in a plethora of earlier texts.) I'm quite proud of Claire, Derek and Jim, and gratefully acknowledge their profuse and worthy contributions.

A couple of other resourceful individuals added scores of biographical details to the mix: Gary Mercer and David Schwartz. Furnishing hard-to-find notations, they raided personal stashes and out-of-the-way resources to turn in facts and anecdotes that added sparkle to the metaphors. I'm thankful for their unselfishness in sharing so much and so often.

There are more than two dozen additional individuals whose assistance made a tremendous difference in the quality of the finished product. I'm pleased to acknowledge their participation: Philip Blumenthal, Frank Bresee, Jess Cain, Chris Chandler, Camilla Clocker, Bob Cockrum, Ed Fleming, Fred Foy, Jack French, Danny Goodwin, Martin Grams Jr., William Harper, Debby Barrett Hatic, Michael Hayde, Irene Heinstein, Mike House, Laura Leff, Tim Lones, Elizabeth McLeod, Charles Niren, Jim Nixon, David Pollock, Terry Salomonson, Buck Saunders, Ron Sayles, Michael Shoshani, Paul Urbahns, Barbara Watkins and Stewart Wright.

In addition, I wish to thank a steadfast troupe of friends who underscore and support all we authors do in maintaining vintage audio history. They are some of the long-suffering editors of various old time radio newsletters and nostalgia publications; their efforts often go unheralded. They have helped me many times and I'm gratified to call them my comrades: Bob Axley, Bob Burchett, Steve Darnell, Jack French, Jay Hickerson, Ken Krug, Patrick Lucanio and Robert Newman. A special tip of my hat goes to Tom Heathwood and Walden Hughes, a couple of pals who persist in perpetuating old time radio through contemporary on-the-air expressions.

My cheering section, led by Sharon Cox, permits me to toil at this pastime that is so invigorating to me. I'm exceedingly grateful for her support in these quests.

Finally, I'm also thankful to the OTR community at large, which gives me plenty of reasons to perpetuate the material. They make it fun and purposeful and my life is enriched substantially by their encouragement. Thanks, one and all!

Preface

This dictionary of radio broadcasters proffers an assortment of species. Collectively they are defined by assignment that typifies the aural airwaves in the medium's popular golden age (traditionally late 1920s to early 1960s). Because some of the network programming that originated during the epoch lingered for a couple of decades beyond the golden age, however, prominent figures during those extensions are highlighted, too. The inclusions persist until virtually all of the chain-fed series stemming from the earlier period eventually played out.

The register is populated by both a limited and a broad spectrum of personalities who dignified the airwaves with their recurring intonation. It is circumscribed by the fact that most of the individuals cited enacted specific spoken functions. In the preponderance of cases, rather than being authentic *performers* in the normal sense of the word—as actors, singers, comedians, instrumentalists and comparable artists (although some exceptions exist among the most versatile)—the celebrities recognized herein are more likely to be *orators* instead: people who talked directly to their listeners instead of being overheard, for example, in a pretense or an exhibition of skill, talent or ability. The key responsibilities of such individuals were often to communicate, inform, establish or improve knowledge, understanding or feeling among listeners. With no mediator required between spokesmen and listeners, the broadcasters expressed their thoughts directly to anyone tuning in. In so doing, some developed distinctive delivery styles that were instantly recognized by a particular show's fans.

While a few individuals defy classification, most radio speakers fall into at least seven subgroups that share common traits and thus may be readily distinguished again and again. With descriptive colloquialisms appearing in parentheses, the composition embraces Announcers (Narrators), Newscasters (News Junkies), Sportscasters (Sports Jockeys), Showbiz Reporters (Tattletales), Consultants (Tipsters), Masters of Ceremonies (Toastmasters) and Husband-and-Wife Dialoguers (Coffee Klatch Couples). Most of the people you will encounter on these pages may be classified in at least one of those categories and a fair number turn up in multiple breeds.

They were, in a sense, speakers of the house—albeit, electronic style.

All of them spoke *Radioese*, a term we have coined to describe their jargon, to wit: *the vernacular articulated on the ether that is applied to communicating essential details for the listener's awareness and potential improvement or response.*

A more descriptive characterization of these seven peculiar designations follows:

• There were Announcers, sometimes nicknamed Narrators, who generally introduced series and kept the fans apprised of what was happening as a feature progressed. They helped their hearers form mental pictures in the Theater of the Mind.

• There were Newscasters of several

stripes—Reporters, Commentators, Analysts, Correspondents and Anchors—sometimes called News Junkies. They dispatched the headlines and current events and frequently interpreted what it all meant to the listeners' lives.

• There were Sportscasters of multiple varieties—Interviewers, Scoreboard Reporters, Play-by-Play Announcers, Color Commentators—and they were sometimes branded as Sports Jockeys. Their enthusiasm for the athletic competitions they covered was contagious among the legions of zealous fans they lured.

• There were Showbiz Reporters, too—often referred to as Gossips or Rumormongers, dubbed Tattletales on occasion, who divulged seamy, sordid, scandalous tidbits from behind the scenes of the studios and entertainment palaces and in the personal lives of legendary luminaries. Not coincidentally, their revelations were timed to scoop their rivals, whose prestige rose and fell with how soon and how much they divulged to a salivating public.

• There were self-help Advisors and Advice Consultants in a diverse assortment of fields (beauty and grooming, consumer purchasing, cooking, family concerns, financial planning, gardening, health, home improvement, psychology, relationships, and so on). These Tipsters offered practical solutions to dilemmas experienced by real people and simplified some of life's frustrations in the process.

• There were masters of ceremonies who presided over games, panels, puzzles, quizzes, musicals, talent parades, variety shows and a myriad of added features. The moderators might be christened the Toastmasters of radio—hosts who normally introduced the acts to follow while exuberantly participating in exchanges with their casts, contestants and guests. Among other things, these key figures motivated the studio and home audiences to rally on cue.

• There were binary breakfast blabbers, conjugal domestics who—over a steaming pot of java—chatted at the day's start regarding all sorts of minutiae. A form that the Coffee Klatch Couples—as they were sometimes labeled—fostered in the nation's largest city proliferated elsewhere. Soon bacon-and-eggs gabfests turned up in manifold radio markets across the land.

With only a few exceptions, all of these individuals appeared as themselves, supplying exacting information that their audiences used in appreciating explicit circumstances. *Radioese* could be dubbed as the language they employed in achieving their objectives.

When I embarked on this odyssey, I intended only to include announcers. It didn't take long to discover, however, that an infinite number of those announcers, interlocutors and narrators on network and syndicated radio performed copiously in capacities superseding mere announcing: they were also actors, vocalists, instrumentalists, commercial spokesmen, panelists, writers, directors, and producers, among countless designations—some carrying many supplementary responsibilities. Beyond that, a profuse lot crossed over into newscasting or sportscasting while a handful were scandalmongers, advice-givers, stars and chatterboxes at one and the same time. It would have been difficult to classify them purely into single categories, for indeed hundreds performed such a myriad of duties as to demand no less than an asterisk alongside their designations. As a result, the inclusion criteria for this book were broadened to incorporate people from many disciplines.

A total of 1,161 performers are documented herein, including 569 in the text and another 592 appearing in the Appendix. While this volume may or may not be the most extensive in total number represented, it does offer substantially more comprehensive content about its subjects than earlier books. The entries feature most of the prominent air-life "speakers" of radio from the 1920s to the 1980s. The Appendix furnishes an extensive list of obscure and lesser figures, but still contributors to the medium. The majority of people within these pages have not been profiled (at least, extensively) in other works. I hope that the resulting volume is a windfall for the intensive researcher and for the avid hobbyist and casual reader as well, a volume that will be referred to again and again in the years ahead.

The dictionary does not purport to include every single announcer, newscaster, sportscaster, showbiz reporter, advisory counselor, master of ceremonies or chatty duo who broadcast in the time period under study. That's an impossible feat. But great pains have been taken to turn over each stone within the author's purview to uncover every legitimate candidate that could be found. For those who were missed, a sincere apology is extended. The intent was to include every qualified individual; omissions are as disappointing to me as they are to you.

From the outset, accuracy was the overriding concern. While presenting an entry in depth and with objectivity is important, being right has always outweighed every other aim. That is not to intimate that every fact that follows is 100 percent correct and cannot be challenged, but to affirm that the information was meticulously checked against a variety of responsible, habitually trustworthy sources to make it as nearly perfect as possible. If there are mistakes, the author assumes full responsibility. Such failures are matters of the head and not the heart.

The announcers of radio, in particular, were often unheralded heroes of the series on which they appeared. They were critical to the success of thousands of audio features, yet the actual people who filled their pivotal roles have been (to our knowledge) the dominant focus of just one text released in the last three decades: Ray Poindexter's brief citation, *Golden Throats and Silver Tongues* (River Road Press, 1978). From the start, it has been my aim to build upon that foundation. The passage of time has netted numerous additional sources and employed a technology that was not available only a few years ago. Documentation on many announcers has been expanded while details on scores of others were obtained for the first time.

Data in the entries that could be substantiated include dates of birth and death and locations; sundry governmental sources were the chief providers of this information. While resolute attempts were made to locate the information on every name, lamentably, some defied detection after many searches or could not be authenticated or simply could not be identified separately from identical names with similar work histories. Documented radio programs on which the individuals worked are included. Their specific assignments on those shows are cited along with the years or approximate years of their service. If no category is specified (e.g., actor, newscaster, writer, etc.), it may be assumed that a personality was the announcer on a listed series.

In determining the show dates, meanwhile, the final arbiter for the preponderance of cases (although not quite all) was *The Third Revised Ultimate History of Network Radio Programming and Guide to All Circulating Shows* by Jay Hickerson (2005). That reference by and large appears to be more accurate, reliable and comprehensive than any other source available at the time the present work was underway. Some of the periods of a performer's service on given series are indicated by "ca." for *circa*, meaning approximate dates. The imprecise periods were not, however, casually selected; a complex formula based on assorted factors was applied in determining those periods. While most are probably fairly dependable, be aware that—without the availability of specific show documentation—there can be no absolute guarantees that the estimated dates are valid.

In addition to a multiplicity of Internet websites far too numerous to list, nearly a dozen published volumes were especially helpful again and again by offering some perspectives and anecdotal material that

PREFACE

inspired part of the substance of this dictionary. Included are the works of Frank Bresee and Bobb Lynes, Tim Brooks and Earl Marsh, Frank Buxton and Bill Owen, Stanley Cloud and Lynne Olson, Thomas A. DeLong, John Dunning, Irving E. Fang, Wesley Hyatt, Alex McNeil, Luther F. Sies, and Vincent Terrace. For specific titles, see the bibliography.

The networks recognized in this chronicle are the American Broadcasting Co. (ABC), which had earlier been the NBC Blue chain and was separated from NBC by the Federal Communications Commission in 1943 to repair a real or imagined monopoly of the airwaves, becoming ABC in 1945; the Columbia Broadcasting System (CBS), which was launched in 1927 as the Columbia Phonograph Broadcasting System, becoming merely "Columbia" the following year and subsequently CBS; the Mutual Broadcasting System (MBS) with origins dating to 1934; and the National Broadcasting Co. (NBC), which was founded in 1926 with dual webs, the Red and the Blue, and which retained the Red after the Blue was spun off, thereafter identified by its call letters. In addition, there are a handful of smaller regional hookups represented; the Don Lee chain which operated in several Western states is possibly the most extensive and impressive, although there were many others identified by locality served. Individuals who appeared on syndicated series are also documented.

This book likely will not be the ultimate text to be compiled about the personalities within its pages. Until such time as a true successor arrives, may the work endure as a satisfying recompense to historians and hobbyists alike by supplying the gaps that have existed for too long about the lives of these people, those powerfully influential spokespersons who might have talked softly but who carried a big shtick.

THE DICTIONARY

They spoke radioese. Some individuals performed specific tasks in addition to or in lieu of being the announcer of a radio series (e.g., actor, comedian, director, host, interviewer, master of ceremonies, musician, newscaster, panelist, producer, quizmaster, sportscaster, vocalist, writer, commentator, et al.). In most cases, there was only one duty per person per show although there were exceptions. When a personality had multiple responsibilities, the extra duties have been so noted wherever possible. If such notations are not present, it may be assumed that an individual was a show's announcer, interlocutor or narrator. Some programs had more than one person performing a specific function—most of them one at a time—and a person may have appeared on a particular series for only a portion of its run.

ADAMS, WILLIAM PERRY. b. May 9, 1887, Tiffin, Ohio; d. Sept. 29, 1972, New York, N.Y. *Announcer, Emcee.* **Series:** *Abie's Irish Rose* (actor, 1942–1944); *The Adventures of Mr. Meek* (actor, 1940–1942); *Big Town* (actor, ca. 1951–1952); *Cavalcade of America* (actor, mid 1930s–late 1940s); *The Collier Hour* (actor, 1927–1932); *The Gibson Family* (actor, 1934–1935); *The Heinz Magazine of the Air* (1936–ca. 1937); *Let's Pretend* (host-narrator-commercial spokesman, 1943–1954); *The Light of the World* (actor, 1940s–1950); *The March of Time* (actor, 1930s–1945); *Pepper Young's Family* (actor, ca. 1939–1940); *Rosemary* (actor, ca. late 1940s); *Roses and Drums* (actor, ca. 1932–1936); *Saturday Night Serenade* (1936–1941); *The Story of Mary Marlin* (actor, ca. 1930s, ca. 1940s); *These Are Our Men* (actor, 1944–1945); *Valiant Lady* (actor, ca. early 1940s); *Wayside Cottage*, aka *House By the Side of the Road* (actor, 1934); *Your Family and Mine* (actor, 1938–1940); *Yours Truly, Johnny Dollar* (actor, 1950s). **Aphorism:** *It's way up in flavah ... it's way down in cost ... it's pa-lenty smooth!*

It was Bill Adams' original intent to become an attorney when he enrolled at Heidelberg College in his hometown but before long he switched his interests to music and hoped to become a professional vocalist someday. He transferred to Cincinnati's College of Music. While in school he became part of a stage act during a local engagement featuring renowned Shakespearean thespians Edward Sothern and Julia Marlowe, a married couple. Adams was such a hit then that—following his graduation in 1912—they hired him as a permanent member of their touring troupe, with Adams signing a long-term contract. His duties included acting, stage managing and eventually directing. His newfound luck ultimately took him to Broadway where he appeared with John Barrymore in 101 performances of *Hamlet*. Many other stage productions kept him busy.

Fifteen years after he completed his formal training, radio had become a reality. Adams was on the scene, readily accessible, capable and accustomed to performing before audiences (especially those in theaters and studios), and he quickly became a natural for the new wave of amusement sweeping the nation. If he didn't predate network radio, he was active in it virtually from its start. A source claims that he inaugurated the role of

"Uncle Henry" on the *Collier Radio Hour* in 1926—the same year NBC was formed—although other scholars believe the series itself wasn't launched until 1927. (He could have done so on a local series, of course.) At any rate, Adams maintained that character's part on the NBC Blue chain to 1932, making him one of the pioneers of on-the-air broadcasting. He was to become an even more famous uncle about a decade after he portrayed the first one.

In the meantime, in the 1930s and early 1940s he offered a convincing portrayal of U.S. President Franklin Delano Roosevelt in occasional appearances before the microphones of *The March of Time*. Adams' impersonations were believably authentic sounding, even though as a dyed-in-the-wool Republican he didn't care for the figure he inspired on the ether. While all of this was going on, his authoritative, grandfatherly voice was turning up in a plethora of daytime serials, mostly in supporting roles, although for two years he played the lead in *Your Family and Mine* in the late 1930s. But it was when he was tapped to play that "other" uncle that he became adoringly typecast by millions of the nation's adolescents and thereby memorable to a generation of juveniles spiraling toward their teens.

"Uncle Bill" Adams opened his most famous show, *Let's Pretend*, exclaiming: "Hel-looooo, Pretenders!" A wildly enthusiastic studio audience seasoned with precocious youngsters shot back: "Hel-looooo, Uncle Bill!" He soon inquired: "How shall we travel to Let's Pretend?" and a member of the cast replied something like, "Let's take a tugboat today." The sound effects technician was waiting for the cue and suddenly the din of a tugboat swept the whole gang off on another adventure to fantasyland. Uncle Bill narrated a fairy tale recited by members of a young thespian entourage corralled by director Nila Mack.

At appropriate intervals, Adams whipped up enthusiasm for the sponsor's product, Cream of Wheat breakfast cereal. He often made a game of it to the fanciful delight of the shrill-voiced kids in the broadcast theater. Some members of the cast sang the familiar Cream of Wheat song ("Cream of Wheat is so good to eat, And we have it every day; We sing this song, it will make us strong, And it makes us shout hooray!"). And Uncle Bill would deliver repetitious lines in his deepest basso profundo at the close of every commercial, accompanied by a whistle going up and sliding down the scale: *It's way up in flavah ... it's way down in cost ... it's pa-lenty smooth!* "If you were inventing an Uncle Bill you could not have found a better type than Bill Adams," observed former Let's Pretender Arthur Anderson. "Bill was also the delight of the ad agency and the Cream of Wheat people. You could not help but trust what he told you about Cream of Wheat ... was the absolute truth."

In addition to appearing in 1963's made-for-TV movie *East Side, West Side*, Adams also turned up in a quintet of theatrical motion pictures: *Sweet Surrender* (1935); *The House on 92nd Street* (1945); *I Am a Camera* (1955); *Odds Against Tomorrow* (1959); and *The Hustler* (1961). In several of those films he was uncredited.

AGRONSKY, MARTIN. b. Jan. 12, 1915, Philadelphia, Pa.; d. July 25, 1999, Washington, D.C. *News Commentator.* **Series:** *The ABC Morning News* (newscaster, 1944–ca. 1956); *Emphasis* (newscaster, 1960); *NBC News on the Hour* (newscaster, 1960).

A critic summarized the newsman's role in a pithy statement: "Agronsky was an extremely liberal news commentator during his entire career." Another source identified him with a handful of resolute journalists who "rarely, if ever, faltered in the impossible task of trying to keep McCarthy and his ilk honest." (Wisconsin Republican Senator Joseph McCarthy was accused of recklessly perceiving Communists at the highest levels of government during the 1950s Cold War.) Meanwhile, as Agronsky addressed national radio audiences with his commentary, he was simultaneously newscasting for local outlets WMAL in Washington, D.C., and WABC in New York City.

Educated at Rutgers University, he received a journalism medal in absentia in 1942 for widely acclaimed feats. Following graduation several years earlier, Agronsky joined the editorial staff of *The Palestine Post* in Jerusalem, Israel, continuing more than a year. At the same time he was a correspondent for *The Christian Science Monitor*, International New Service (INS) and *Newsweek* magazine. He returned home briefly and embarked for Italy, where he pursued a series of articles for *Foreign Affairs* magazine, followed by a stint with the Paris bureau of INS. Next came freelance reporting in Spain on behalf of *The Chicago Tribune* and *The London News-Chronicle*.

By February 1939 Agronsky was in England, where he spent several months freelancing for *Time* magazine. The exposure greatly widened and influenced his perspectives, grounding him for the important work that lay ahead. He earned still more name recognition as a freelance newspaper stringer in Geneva, Switzerland, while concurrently reporting for NBC as early as December 1939. The following May Agronsky joined that web's permanent staff of foreign correspondents, shifting to multiple far-flung sites including Ankara, Turkey, in 1941. A biography of war scribes recalled his experience there: "Two fierce competitors among the journalists were [CBS's Winston] Burdett and Martin Agronsky of NBC. Both worked day and night collecting information from diplomats, foreign agents, and anyone else who might have facts. Burdett and Agronsky were, a colleague said, 'busy cutting each other's throats.'"

Subsequently stationed in Singapore, Agronsky fiercely competed with CBS's Cecil Brown. In 1942, NBC dispatched Agronsky to the headquarters of Gen. Douglas MacArthur, considered a peerless responsibility. The next year, the newsman transitioned to NBC's Blue network (renamed ABC a short time later) as a commentator.

Agronsky was a transitional broadcasting figure, shifting into television to emerge as one of the medium's foremost journalists during its earliest decades. He questioned contemporary newsmakers for the ABC series *At Issue* in 1953–54. During the 1957–58 season he interviewed newsmakers on *Look Here*, a live NBC Sunday afternoon public affairs program. It was considered NBC's answer to CBS's engaging *Person to Person* with Edward R. Murrow. In 1961 Agronsky joined a repertory company of contributors on NBC's *Today* show, intermittently interviewing Washington notables. He hosted *This is NBC News* in 1962–1963, a Sunday afternoon half-hour in which he coordinated data supplied by overseas NBC reporters via live, taped and filmed presentations.

Agronsky anchored *The CBS Saturday News*, a weekly half-hour early afternoon affair, in 1964–1965. From 1965 to 1969 he moderated CBS's venerable newsmaker-interview feature *Face the Nation*, joining a line of distinguished hosts, among them Stuart Novins, Howard K. Smith, George Herman, Leslie Stahl and Bob Schieffer. From 1971 to 1976 he presided over *Martin Agronsky: Evening Edition*, a daily PBS analysis of current events offering conversations with newsmakers and journalists produced at Washington's WETA-TV. In 1973 and again in 1980 Agronsky hosted the PBS series *Great Decisions* focusing on world affairs, a single issue per week.

In 1975 he officiated on the PBS feature *Agronsky at Large*. By the following year he was headlining the syndicated *Agronsky & Co.*, a weekly news show aired on *The Washington Post–Newsweek* commercial stations as well as many PBS affiliates. The program was so influential that President Ronald Reagan reportedly called up when he disagreed with something he heard there. "It was really the granddaddy of all the modern talking-heads pundit shows," a modern critic claimed, "albeit a lot more civilized than we see today." When Agronsky bowed out of the popular series in 1988, it was re-titled *Inside Edition* and became a tabloid information entry hosted by Bill O'Reilly and later by Deborah Norville. Agronsky retired after almost a half-century in electronic journalism, achieving one of the most durable tenures in the breed.

ALEXANDER, BEN. b. May 26, 1911, Goldfield, Nev.; d. July 5, 1969, Hollywood, Calif. *Announcer, Actor, Emcee.* **Series:** *The Anniversary Club* (master of ceremonies, 1940s); *The Baby Snooks Show* (actor, 1946–ca. 1951); *Brenthouse* (actor, 1939–1940); *Dragnet* (actor, 1952–1957); *The Edgar Bergen and Charlie McCarthy Show*, aka *The Chase and Sanborn Hour* (1940–1941); *Everyman's Theater* (1940–1941); *Eyes Aloft* (1942–1943); *The Great Gildersleeve* (actor, 1946–1947); *Heart's Desire* (master of ceremonies, 1946–1948); *I Love a Mystery* (actor, 1939–1944); *It Happened in the Service* (host, 1942–1943); *It's a Living* (host, 1948–1949); *Lady Be Beautiful* (master of ceremonies, 1946); *Little Ol' Hollywood* (master of ceremonies, 1939–1942); *The Martin and Lewis*

Show (actor, ca. 1949–1950); *This Moving World* (newscaster, 1939); *The New Old Gold Show* (1941–1942); *Red Ryder* (1942–?); *This Is Judy Jones* (actor, 1941); *Watch and Win* (master of ceremonies, 1940s).

While an announcer and an actor in a myriad of aural venues, Alexander gained momentum as a veteran host of audience participation and human-interest features. He was one of a handful of Hollywood celebs routinely replacing Jack Bailey when the august emcee was away from *Queen for a Day* on radio and TV. He was only five years old in 1916 when he debuted in an uncredited role in the Hollywood film *Each Pearl a Tear*. Before he abandoned the silver screen at 32 in 1943, Alexander played in 81 full-length mostly B-movie features, occasionally in major roles. Among those flicks: *Little Orphan Annie* (1918); *Penrod and Sam* (1923); *All Quiet on the Western Front* (1930); and *Shall We Dance* (1937).

His performances before the cameras were good practice for his achievements later. Yet the University of California and Stanford trained thespian fully intended to become a radio official. By the time he got to that medium in 1935, nevertheless, he was aware that being in front of the mike offered more lucrative incentives. As he amassed assets, Alexander diversified, prospering by purchasing a string of auto dealerships, funeral homes and gas stations. In 1943 he temporarily left his civilian duties to serve with the U.S. Naval Air Corps.

His most memorable role was portraying Sergeant Joe Friday's (Jack Webb) sidekick, Officer Frank Smith, of the Los Angeles Police Department on *Dragnet*. Alexander maintained the part on NBC Radio for five years (1952–1957) and on NBC-TV for seven seasons (1952–1959). A video critic termed the show "probably the most successful police series in the history of television." Another textwriter confirmed: "He brought the show decided comic relief.... Frank became the most human member of the small cast." A radio historian labeled Alexander "a paunchy police detective ... dependable and courageous under fire ... [and] a perpetual worrywart," adding: "He fretted over his disputes with his wife Fay; he fussed over his pills and was always concocting some exotic recipe. Frank became such a vital part of the show that when he was wounded in a two-part story and his life hung in the balance, fans reacted with thousands of letters."

In addition to *Dragnet*, Alexander turned fading radio opportunities into multiple stints on the tube. In 1950–1951 he presided over *Party Time at Club Roma*, a 13-week outing on NBC that began as a quiz and stunt feature and ended as a talent competition. For 18 months in 1960–1961 he hosted the ABC daytime game show *About Faces*. Simultaneously in 1960 he appeared as a recurring panelist on the ABC primetime game show *Take a Good Look* moderated by Ernie Kovacs. Not surprisingly, from 1966 to 1969 Alexander capped his career playing a cop in an ABC crime drama, *The Felony Squad*.

ALLEN, EDWARD. *Announcer.* **Series:** *Backstage Wife* (1935–1936); *The Hometowners* (1945–1947); *Meet the Meeks* (1947–1949); *Tom, Dick and Harry* (ca. 1936–early 1940s).

By the mid 1930s Edward Allen was on the staff of Chicago's WGN, a member of a quartet of influential radio stations that formed the Mutual chain in the summer of 1934. As an announcer and newscaster, he was tapped to narrate one of the earliest soap operas of prolific producers Frank and Anne Hummert—*Backstage Wife*—premiering over WGN and MBS on August 5, 1935. In a commercial campaign aired on the aural series and in supporting print ads, Allen urged listeners to "do as your dentist does when you go to him—use powder!" The commodity was Dr. Lyon's tooth powder, then the largest selling brand in the country.

Allen transferred his loyalties to Chicago rival station WMAQ, an NBC affiliate, in the early 1940s, where he picked up multiple network assignments. By the late 1940s he was also presiding over a couple of local disc jockey features on weekday mornings and afternoons at WMAQ.

ALLEN, HERB. b. Dec. 24, 1913, San Francisco, Calif. *Announcer.* **Series:** *Dear John* (ca. 1944); *The Guiding Light* (1947–1949); *The Hardy Family* (1949–1950, 1952–1953); *I Want a Divorce* (1940–1941); *People Are Funny* (ca. 1940s); *Sherlock Holmes*; *Woman from Nowhere* (actor, 1944).

As 1938 opened, Herb Allen presided

over an unusual Sunday afternoon feature on San Francisco's KFRC simply titled *Listen*. The quarter-hour program focused on reviews of radio shows, no matter what the originating station or network, while removing identifications of outlets and chains. It was scripted by KFRC press agent Pat Kelly and delivered by Allen. *Variety* observed: "Kelly's copy is well written, and Allen's reading is snappy, smooth and easy on the ears." After assessing what was aired in the previous week, Allen offered responses to listeners' questions to end each installment.

In addition to his radio work, in 1948 Allen was instrumental in launching a competitive juvenile stunt series, *Hail the Champ*, over KLAC-TV in Hollywood. Not only was he occupied by its production, he emceed the contest-centered show involving a trio of adolescents on dual teams seeking to become the "Champ of the Week." When the show moved to Chicago in September 1951, it originated at WENR-TV and was aired by three Midwestern stations. By December the series advanced to the full ABC-TV network with Allen still hosting. In late 1952 Howard Roberts replaced him and the program design was franchised to local stations in 1953. Later, Allen produced *The Johnny Carson Show* on CBS-TV (1955–1956) and was associate producer of *The Bob Crosby Show* on NBC-TV (1958).

ALLEN, MEL (born Melvin Allen Israel). b. Feb. 14, 1913, Birmingham, Ala.; d. June 16, 1996, Greenwich, Conn. *Sportscaster, Announcer*. **Series:** *The Army Hour* (1944); *The Chesterfield Supper Club* (1946–1947); *Command Performance* (1940s); *Duffy's Tavern* (1940); *Kitty Foyle* (1942–1944); *The Mel Allen Show* (host, 1939–1940, 1949–1950, 1953–1954); *Monitor* (co-host, 1961–1963); *The Saturday Night Swing Club* (late 1930s); *Sports Daily* (host, 1953–1955); *This Day is Ours* (1938–1940); *Truth or Consequences* (1940–?); *White Owl Sports Smoker* (1947–1948). **Aphorism:** *How about that!*

Mel Allen didn't intentionally start out to be what he ultimately became—one of the nation's best recognized, most respected and durable sportscasters. He loved baseball and was a sports columnist during his undergraduate years at the University of Alabama, from which he earned a bachelor's degree in 1932 and a law degree in 1936. When Allen operated Alabama's public address system during the fall gridiron season in 1935, a Birmingham radio station hired him as a part time sports announcer. And when CBS talent scouts heard his coverage of a gridiron match between rivals Alabama and Tulane in 1936, they signed him to a $150-a-week contract. Allen joined the network's New York announcing staff and never spent a day in court practicing what he trained himself to do.

Within three years the versatile Southern interlocutor was covering major league baseball games of the New York Giants and Yankees. While Allen's talents were also divided between introducing audience participation fare, musical features and soap operas, he had unmistakably entered a phase that would ultimately dominate his life's direction. He interrupted his plans to serve with the U.S. Army in 1943 at Fort Benning, Ga., and the following year at Armed Forces Radio in New York City, where he appeared on sportscasts that were transmitted overseas by shortwave. In 1946 he went to work for the Yankees exclusively.

Allen rose to icon status when, in 1939, he was named the voice of the New York Yankees. His classic trademark signature following each home run—*How about that!*—was adopted by legions of fans as part of their American vernacular. Another call that became synonymous with him was *going ... going ... gone!* He was entrenched at his post until 25 years later when the Yanks yanked the props from under him in favor of Phil Rizzuto, who continued for three decades as their spokesman. Despite it, team owner George Steinbrenner said at Allen's passing: "Mel Allen meant as much to Yankee tradition as legends like Ruth, Gehrig, DiMaggio and Mantle." Allen became a fixture on World Series broadcasts, too, along with handling Rose Bowl coverage and occasional trackside at Kentucky Derby races. He covered kick-off events, sports roundups, All-American awards banquets and games of the week. A recipient of numerous honors, Allen and colleague Red Barber won the initial award for broadcasting excellence that was named for baseball commissioner Ford C. Frick.

On television Allen presided over *NCAA Football* (1948, 1951–1954), *College Basketball*

(1949), *Notre Dame Football* (1949–1950), *NCAA Basketball* (1950), *Sports Spot* (1951–1954), *Jackpot Bowling* (1959–1960) and a syndicated 30-minute series, *This Week in Baseball* (1977–1996). Nevertheless, looking back on his career, he acknowledged that he enjoyed radio more than television. "On radio you could choose your direction, but on television you always had these earphones on, with the director telling you they were going to cut away to some cheesecake in upper right field or a mother holding a baby," Allen shuddered.

AMECHE, JIM (born James Amici). b. Aug. 6, 1915, Kenosha, Wis.; d. Feb. 4, 1983, Tucson, Ariz. *Announcer, Actor, Emcee.* **Series:** *The Adventures of Ellery Queen* (actor, 1940s); *The Amos 'n' Andy Music Hall* (1957–1959); *At Home with Faye and Elliott* (1946); *Big Sister* (early to mid 1940s); *Broadway Matinee* (host, 1943–1944); *Grand Central Station* (actor, 1940s); *Grand Hotel* (actor, 1937–1938); *Grand Marquee* (actor, 1946–1947); *The First Nighter* (actor, ca. 1930s–1940s); *Here's to Romance* (1943–1945); *Hollywood Open House* (master of ceremonies, 1947–1948); *Hollywood Playhouse* (actor, 1939–1940); *Jack Armstrong, the All-American Boy* (actor, 1933–1937); *Love Story Theater* (actor, 1946–1947); *Lux Radio Theater* (actor, late 1930s–early 1940s); *Manhattan at Midnight* (host-actor, 1943); *The Mercury Summer Theater* (actor, 1946); *The Naval Air Reserve Show* (host, early 1950s); *Philip Morris Playhouse* (actor, early 1940s); *Romance, Rhythm and Ripley* (1945); *The Saturday Morning Vaudeville Theater* (host, 1941–1942); *Silver Eagle, Mountie* (actor, 1951–1955); *Terry Regan, Attorney at Law* (actor, 1938); *The Texaco Star Theater* (actor, 1940s); *Welcome Travelers* (1947–1954); *What's New?* (interviewer, 1943–1944); *Win Your Lady* (co-host, 1938).

Jim Ameche's national radio exposure was foreshadowed by a couple of juvenile adventures in which he played the lead. The first, *Jack Armstrong, the All-American Boy*, maintained one of the most enduring tenures of all pubescent programs, persisting in its original and extended versions for 18 years. His already famous actor-brother, Don Ameche (Dominic Felix Amici, whose strong suit was acting, not announcing), summoned the 17-year-old sibling to tryouts for the role of Jack; he urged him to get to Chicago promptly from their ancestral home in Kenosha, Wis., where eight offspring of an Italian immigrant father were raised.

Jim won the coveted namesake part, an astonishing launch to his chosen profession with no experience. It paid him $59.50 weekly for five live episodes performed twice daily at the peak of economic fallout during the Great Depression. (Conversely, Jim's annual radio earnings were estimated by *The Milwaukee Journal* in 1943 at something between $25,000 and $40,000; it wasn't a particularly shabby haul compared with about $3,000 he was getting when he went into radio a decade earlier.) "Nobody ever knew I was on the show," he allowed. "There was an unwritten law against revealing who played Jack." Yet a journalist writing in 1975 gathered aptly: "In the 1930s, radio was king and Jack Armstrong, the All-American Boy, was its prince." Ameche ended his network radio career a couple of decades later portraying the lead in another adolescent adventure, *Silver Eagle, Mountie*. Between those high water marks he gallantly shifted back and forth between acting and announcing duties in a variety of venues.

For several years he introduced a daytime serial by ever so slowly spelling out the sponsor's brand name, hyphenated by lengthy and deliberate pauses between letters while he enunciated. Following an advertising trademark triple-note bird whistle, the bassy-voiced Ameche—still in his mid 20s—confirmed: "Rinso presents ... *Big Sister*." A tower clock struck the first four notes of the Westminster Chimes and Ameche bellowed: "Yes, there's the clock in Glen Falls town hall telling us it's time for Rinso's story of *Big Sister* ... brought to you by the new ... soapy-rich ... Rinso ... R ... I ... N ... S ... O." It was one of the most excruciatingly dawdling openings in radio and therefore incredibly unforgettable to anyone who heard it repetitiously in those days.

In the summer of 1957 Ameche hosted the NBC-TV dramatic anthology *Festival of Stars*, a program comprised altogether of repeats from *The Loretta Young Show*. That was Ameche's only ongoing video acknowledgment. He also earned a single credit in the movies that year, appearing as Alexander

Graham Bell in *The Story of Mankind*. As his national radio stage began to fade, Ameche—like some of his contemporaries—became a disc jockey. For 11 years he held forth on Chicago radio, boasting a two-and-a-half-hour daily stint over WJJD at the peak of his performance. He persisted with a weekday morning program over New York's WHN from 1963 to 1969. Finally growing weary of big city life, Ameche moved from Gotham to Encino, Calif., in 1970. After two decades of putting it off because he was "too busy," he launched a long-planned Ameche Academy of Broadcasting, an educational institute situated at 3875 Wilshire Blvd. in neighboring Los Angeles.

But soon afterward he was in Nashville where life was pleasantly laid back and where he recorded lots of commercials for distribution to stations all over the nation. By 1975 Ameche permanently settled in Tucson, Ariz., joining KCEE-AM and FM as a DJ. His brother and oft-admitted "inspiration," Don, seven years his senior—who introduced him to radio and starred as *The First Nighter* and emcee of *The Chase and Sanborn Hour* with Edgar Bergen and Charlie McCarthy as well as pursuing a film and TV acting career—had retired from entertainment at nearby Scottsdale, Ariz. Jim battled cancer for two years. Don died a decade after Jim, on Dec. 6, 1993.

ANDERS, BILL. *Announcer.* **Series:** *Broadway is My Beat* (1949–1954); *Mr. Aladdin* (1951); *That's Rich* (1954).

ANDERSON, BOB. *Announcer.* **Series:** *The Lone Wolfe* (1948–1949).

Bob Anderson portrayed Aeneas MacLinahan on NBC-TV's *Wichita Town* in the 1959–1960 season.

ANDERSON, ORVAL. *Announcer, Emcee, Newscaster.* **Series:** *Darts for Dough* (host, 1944–1947); *Defense Attorney* (1951–1952); *Hollywood Star Playhouse* (ca. 1951–1953); *The Man from Homicide* (1951); *ABC News* (newscaster, 1960).

Before being a co-creator of *Darts for Dough*—a game combining physical skill and mental dexterity, which he launched in 1943 over Dallas's WFAA—Orval Anderson paused at Orlando's WDBO as a sportscaster (1939) and New Orleans' WWL as a newscaster (1940).

ANDRE, PIERRE. b. Nov. 25, 1899, Duluth, Minn.; d. July 21, 1962, Evanston, Ill. *Announcer.* **Series:** *Arnold Grimm's Daughter* (ca. 1938–1942); *Backstage Wife* (ca. 1936); *Betty and Bob* (1932–ca. 1938); *Captain Midnight* (1940–1949); *The Carters of Elm Street* (1939–1940); *The Couple Next Door* (1937); *The Great Gunns* (1941); *Harold Teen* (1941–1942); *How's the Family?* (1953); *Little Orphan Annie* (1931–1940); *The Romance of Helen Trent* (ca. late 1930s–1944); *Sky King* (1946–1947); *Tena and Tim* (1944–1946).

Pierre Andre was educated at the University of Minnesota, became a newspaperman in 1920 and published his own paper at Virginia, Minn., from 1923 to 1925. He broke into radio at Duluth's WEBC in 1926 but gave it up six months later to return to print journalism. He ultimately deserted the latter in 1928 when he was hired by KSTP in St. Paul. In 1930 he affiliated with Chicago powerhouse WGN; he joined NBC in 1936 and departed by the early 1940s to become a freelance announcer. Andre originated one of the first remote dance band broadcasts, *The Midnight Flyer*, from Chicago's venerated Blackhawk Restaurant. In 1942 he was interlocutor for WGN's *Music That Endures* featuring guest vocalists backed by a live orchestra conducted by Henry Walker.

Andre introduced numerous programs originating in the WGN studios for the Mutual network following that web's 1934 formation. Sometimes he was engaged to preside over prominent series of competing national chains that aired from the Windy City. Many of those network features were soap operas and juvenile adventure thrillers produced by the seemingly inexhaustible creatives Frank and Anne Hummert. In 1936 Andre announced a transcribed *Rubinoff and His Violin* over Chicago's WLS, spotlighting celebrated concert virtuoso David Rubinoff. In 1945 the announcer went to Hollywood where he temporarily affiliated with the recently established ABC network, formerly the Blue chain.

In regard to Andre's announcing performances, a radio historiographer asserted, "His delivery was truly one of a kind." He may have had "the best remembered voice" in the entire cast of *Captain Midnight*, the reviewer stated. Over the midnight pealing of a bell and the rush of an aircraft, his opening signature intoned: *"Cappp-taaiinnMidnight! Broughttoyoueveryday ... MondaythroughFriday ... by the makers of Ovaltine!"* As each episode left the ether, Andre bade the captain's Secret Squadron a vigorous, retreating "Happ-e-e-e-e lan-n-n-dings!"

For another of Andre's interlocutory charges, a different chronicler lamented: "What remains most memorable about the show was announcer Pierre Andre peddling gotta-have Little Orphan Annie mugs that now fetch exorbitant prices at collectible shows: 'Hey, boys and girls, you'll want to get your Orphan Annie Shake-Up Mug for chocolaty shakes and malts! Yessir, real shaker-uppers, kids!'" He put it so electrifyingly that no middle class kid in America could afford to be without one. Confirmed a media historian: "Announcer Pierre Andre has to be considered an important factor in the show's appeal to that age group; he had the youngsters hanging upon every word.... Wander [the firm that made Ovaltine] should erect a monument to Andre ... atop one of the Swiss mountains whence the idea for Ovaltine supposedly came."

Andre appeared as a dancer in a trio of films: *Tangier* (1946), *The Gay Cavalier* (1946) and *My Wild Irish Rose* (1947). He was also the uncredited announcer of the 1954–1956 CBS-TV version of *Captain Midnight* that later returned to the small screen in syndication as *Jet Jackson, Flying Commando*.

On May 18, 1962, two months prior to his death, Andre co-hosted a two-hour broadcast celebrating WGN's 40th anniversary. He was then headlining the 90-minute weekday afternoon *Pierre Andre Show* over the station. A 1962 sales promotion flyer boasted that he was "one of the outstanding commercial men in the industry, consistently delivering high adult women composition." He'd come a long way from shilling for shake-up mugs.

ANDREWS, WILLIAM JOHN. b. April 5, 1905, Oakland, Calif.; d. May 2, 1985, Contra Costa, Calif. *Announcer.* **Series:** *One Man's Family* (1932–1940s).

William J. Andrews' initial fascination with radio during his high school days was purely scientific. Following graduation, he enrolled at the Western Radio Institute, a radio operator's training ground that opened at the Hotel Oakland in 1921. Its avowed purpose was to prepare students in electronic theory so they could qualify as a ship's radio operator. Andrews' aptitude and initiative made an impression and he was selected as a student instructor and technician. At the same time, he capitalized on his interest in ethereal transmissions by landing a job as a radio specialist at Oakland's Montgomery Ward emporium. Recognized for his authoritative ability, he was given responsibility for replying to local and long distance mail order requests about radio receivers. Those inquiries often pertained to how the sets operated or asked for help in what to do when they didn't function properly.

In 1924, when a vacancy occurred at Western Radio Institute, Andrews was appointed announcer and engineer, and virtually ran the school's one-man station, KLX. A historian acknowledged: "Andrews the technician would operate the transmitter and associated equipment, and Andrews the announcer would introduce live remote programs from the studio. And, when the station was off the air between 7:00 and 7:30 each evening, Bill Andrews the reporter would compile the 7:30 newscast." The news, incidentally, was received in Morse code over a telegraph line. The increased exposure produced fan mail for him, too, something he hadn't experienced previously.

As a sidelight, Andrews was also a sportscaster, announcing the Oakland Oaks baseball games. Remaining in the studio, he relayed a game's progress to listeners as the on-site scorekeeper telephoned him with updates every half-inning for the nearby games at the Oaks' home stadium at Emeryville or the Seals' stadium at San Francisco. Scores from "away" ballparks in Los Angeles, Portland and Seattle were telegraphed to KLX. "Andrews relayed the results to the audience as they came into the studio.... If there was nothing to say, he would simply remain silent, frequently for over a minute."

Following the inauguration of the National Broadcasting Company in 1926, a handful of stations in the far West coalesced to form the NBC Pacific Coast Network. The fledgling group's on-air personalities included "actors, musicians, or generally whomever was available," a historian recalled. William Andrews was among the individuals "borrowed from a local station." In 1928 he joined the new cluster as its first full time announcer. At its peak the group employed 17 announcers. In 1933 he was appointed chief announcer of the NBC Pacific Coast Network. Decidedly industrious, Andrews was writing promotional copy for local concerns as an avocation.

His transition to NBC and its San Francisco affiliate, KGO, out of which it operated, put him in a strategic position when journalist Carlton E. Morse left *The San Francisco Chronicle* in 1929 to author dramatic productions for KGO audiences. By 1932 they included Morse's most enduring family tale, *One Man's Family*. Andrews was selected as the epic drama's spokesman; from its inception, he remained with it for many years. The show was to be his singularly celebrated one. Ironically, in a 137-page paperback Morse published in 1988, *The One Man's Family Album: An Inside Look at Radio's Longest Running Show*, all the on-air personalities were introduced with photographs and insightful text except Andrews and his dual successor announcers—Ken Carpenter and Frank Barton—surprisingly downplaying their noteworthy contributions.

ANSBRO, GEORGE. b. Jan. 14, 1915, Brooklyn, N.Y. Announcer. **Series:** *The American Album of Familiar Music* (commercials, 1930s–1951); *The Avengers* (1945–1946); Big band remotes—Charlie Barnet, Xavier Cugat, Jimmy Dorsey, Tommy Dorsey, Eddie Duchin, Benny Goodman, Gene Krupa, Guy Lombardo, Glenn Miller, Chick Webb, et al. (ca. mid 1930s–mid 1940s); *Chaplain Jim, U.S.A.* (1942–1945); *Cliff Edwards Show* (1944–1948); *Coast to Coast on a Bus* (boy soprano, 1927–1930); dance remotes for the Dorsey brothers, Eddie Duchin and more (mid to late 1930s); *Easy Aces* (1936); *Esso News* (1938–1941); *Ethel and Albert* (1944–?); *FBI Washington* (1965–1989); *Home Sweet Home* (1934–1936); *Let's Dance* (1934–1935); *Lowell Thomas and the News* (1943–1944); *Manhattan Maharajah* (1951–late 1950s); *Manhattan Merry-Go-Round* (commercials, 1930s–1949); *Mr. Keen, Tracer of Lost Persons* (substitute and commercials, 1938–1941); *Mrs. Wiggs of the Cabbage Patch* (1936–1938); *Omar the Swingmaker* (1937–mid 1940s); *Pick a Date with Buddy Rogers* (1949–1950); *Singo* (1944); *Sammy Kaye's Sunday Serenade* (1943–1944); *Waltz Time* (commercials, 1930s–1948); *What Makes You Tick?* (early 1950s); *When a Girl Marries* (ca. 1953–ca. 1954); *Young Widder Brown* (1938–1956). **Aphorism:** *I have a lady in the balcony, doctor.*

"Ansbro simply did his job in a crisp, polished, workmanlike way for as many shows as required his services—soaps, comedies, detective dramas," a contemporary radio historian affirmed.

Breaking into radio at age 12 on Milton Cross's *Coast to Coast on a Bus* (a series identified under several monikers), George Ansbro became an NBC page and tour guide at 16. Three years beyond, in 1934, he was classified as a "junior" announcer. He attended Manhattan College for a year but left it to work in daytime radio. His absorbing journey through the medium's golden epoch is recalled in compelling detail in an autobiography, *I Have a Lady in the Balcony: Memoirs of a Broadcaster* (McFarland, 2000). During the early years of the 21st century, a tall, imposing, affable Ansbro continued to attend the annual Friends of Old Time Radio conventions that beckon hundreds of vintage hobbyists in Newark, N.J., every autumn. He and casts composed of celebrities and neophyte thespians still appeared in staged reenactments of the serials and dramatic features that he and others introduced many decades earlier.

Ansbro gained some TV exposure across his long career, too. In the mid 1940s he performed in some sporadic 6 P.M. experimental newscasts. In primitive fashion compared to modern techniques, he merely sat before a camera and read copy torn from a teletype machine. There was no film to accompany it nor were there commercials "because there was practically no audience," Ansbro attested. "When I had finished the newscast, my clothes could have been wrung out, the lights were that hot." Before the 1940s passed, he was paired with John Charles Daly (of *What's My Line?* fame on

CBS) for a daily ABC-TV newscast at 7 P.M. Ansbro not only introduced the respected ex–CBS newsman (who on Dec. 7, 1941 was first in informing the world that the Japanese had struck Pearl Harbor), he delivered live commercials for Pontiac automobiles. During the 1953–1954 TV season, Ansbro was one of four roving announcers on ABC's *Dr. I.Q., the Mental Banker*, a popular earlier radio show. Dr. I.Q., portrayed by Jimmy McClain, routinely switched to Ansbro to ask a contestant in the audience a question for which silver dollars were awarded for right answers. It gave Ansbro opportunity to deliver the inimitable line that all America seemed to be quoting: *I have a lady in the balcony, doctor.*

In the mid 1940s, when the Federal Communications Commission ordered NBC's Red and Blue chains to be separated, Ansbro was aligned with the Blue web, which subsequently became ABC. Under terms of the separation, he was allowed to continue narrating *Young Widder Brown*, a Red network (NBC) daytime serial. For 18 years he prevailed there, surpassing the tenures of all other announcers on a single soap opera, as well as all other cast members on *Young Widder Brown*. He once clarified that venerable soap opera as "eighteen years of the most excruciating radio torture ever devised by [producers] Frank and Anne Hummert." At his retirement in early 1990 at age 75, Ansbro ended 59 years in the industry, the last employee still in service with dual ABC and NBC affiliations.

ANTHONY, ALLEN C. b. Aug. 5, 1906, Buffalo, N.Y.; d. May 11, 1962. *Announcer.* **Series:** *Dr. I.Q., the Mental Banker* (1939–1950); *Dr. I.Q. Jr.* (1941, 1948–1949); *Inner Sanctum Mysteries* (1950–1951).

Allen C. Anthony left Columbia University with an undergraduate degree in journalism and a graduate degree in law, the latter acquired merely for a foundation in "logical thinking." He was a short story writer for a while; his fiction turned up in *Redbook* and other periodicals. Even after he no longer wrote professionally, he still churned out an average of 10,000 words monthly to remain in practice, intending to write again full time in retirement. Anthony launched a radio career at a Jacksonville, Fla., station in 1928. From there he moved to WLW, Cincinnati; WHAS, Louisville; WCAU, Philadelphia; and KWK, St. Louis. He was program director and chief announcer at KWK when he quit to be radio director at Grant Advertising, Inc.

His was a classic case of an announcer becoming identified with one firm's commodities to the extent that he wasn't remembered for anything else. Anthony was so effective in proffering the confections of candy-maker Mars, Inc. that it spread his effusive commercial pitches over at least a trio of well-received aural series. He routinely wrapped his plugs in convincing metaphors like "creamy nougat" and "delicious chocolate." As Bugs Beagle on *Dr. I.Q. Jr.*, Anthony told tales littered with factual mistakes. Kids who spotted the blunders were prizewinners. In his early days at the advertising helm of *Dr. I.Q.*, Anthony was still chief announcer at KWK, St. Louis. Each week he commuted by air to the program that was making him famous, logging an estimated 75,000 miles in six months. Unfortunately for him, there were no frequent flyer clubs then in existence.

ANTOINE, H. JON (TEX). b. April 21, 1923, Texas; d. Jan. 12, 1983, New York, N.Y. *Announcer.* **Series:** *The Adventures of Frank Merriwell* (late 1940s); *The Eternal Light* (1944–?); *The Jane Pickens Show* (ca. 1951–1952).

In October 1948 WNBT's television operations in New York City were integrated with those of WNBC Radio. WNBC became the NBC flagship TV station, responsible for programming its own local features. Cartoonist Tex Antoine delivered weather forecasts on the "new" station.

ARCHINARD, PAUL. b. April 1899, Paris, France. *Correspondent, Newscaster.* **Series:** *NBC News* (1934–1946).

Moving to the United States in 1904, Paul Archinard returned to his homeland in 1918 as a U.S. Army serviceman during World War I. Later that year, he was in private business in Paris for American firms to 1926, the last six years with Montgomery Ward worldwide purchasing offices. Returning to the United States in 1927, he remained until he joined NBC as Fred Bate's assistant in London in 1934. In 1935 the network dispatched Archinard to Paris as its correspondent in the French capital. He was an NBC newscaster from 1942 to 1946.

ARLEN, MARGARET (born Eleanor Hines). b. ca. 1917, Edenton, N.C. *Emcee, Commentator.* **Series:** *Margaret Arlen* (hostess-interviewer, 1943–1952).

Mary Margaret McBride was the most successful and perhaps the original star of a subgenre of radio series in which a woman presided over an early talk show. Those programs were often conducted by a hostess using an assumed name. In McBride's case, she didn't have the stomach for passing herself off as somebody else, and—only a few weeks after her long-running feature began on May 3, 1934, on New York's WOR, subsequently picked up by Mutual—she abruptly halted the charade by revealing that she wasn't "Martha Deane" with lots of grandchildren; she wasn't even married and had no kids or grandkids! Nevertheless, a new pattern was established in radio and it became commonplace for stations and networks to adopt certain names and apply them to their feminine chatterboxes.

The month after Tar Heel broadcaster Eleanor Hines joined CBS in New York, she was substituted for *Adelaide Hawley's Women's Page* (which had aired from Sept. 25, 1939 to Nov. 12, 1943). Beginning Nov. 29, 1943, Hines became identified on the air as "Margaret Arlen"—a web-owned house name in the vein of McBride/"Deane" (and others). She conducted celebrity interviews and dispensed cooking, child-rearing and household advice in quarter-hour portions five mornings a week for nine years (to Aug. 19, 1952). Announcer Harry Marble introduced her daily tête-à-têtes.

Eleanor Hines was a graduate of Meredith College, Raleigh, N.C. One of radio's pioneering feminine newscasters, her broadcast journalism career took off at nearby Goldsboro's WCBR. With some experience under her proverbial belt, she returned to Raleigh and aired over both WPTF and WRAL before moving to CBS in October 1943.

ARLINGTON, CHARLES. *Announcer, Newscaster.* **Series:** *The Count of Monte Cristo* (late 1940s); *Mutual News* (newscaster, late 1960s–ca. 1970s); *Tarzan* (1951–1953); *The Voyage of the Scarlet Queen* (1947–1948).

Charles Arlington was a staff announcer at Los Angeles' KHJ in the early 1940s. Afterward, he was news director of that city's KFWB for a decade beginning in 1958. Arlington subsequently shifted to Burbank's KBBQ, where he provided regular news feeds over MBS.

AVERBACK, HYMAN J. b. Oct. 21, 1920, Minneapolis, Minn.; d. Oct. 14, 1997, Los Angeles, Calif. *Announcer, Actor.* **Series:** *The Adventures of Maisie* (actor, 1945–1952); *The Adventures of Philip Marlowe* (actor, late 1940s–ca. 1950); *The Bob Hope Show* (1948–1950); *Broadway is My Beat* (actor, ca. 1949–ca. 1954); *Crime Classics* (actor, 1953); *Hollywood Calling* (1949–1950); *The Jack Carson Show* (1948–1949); *The Jack Paar Show* (1947); *Suspense* (actor, early 1950s); *Let's Talk Hollywood* (1948); *The Lineup* (actor, early 1950s); *Presenting Charles Boyer* (actor, 1950); *The Ray Noble Show* (1948); *Richard Diamond, Private Detective* (actor, late 1940s–early 1950s); *The Saint* (actor, 1951); *The Sealtest Village Store* (1947–1948); *Sweeney and March* (1948); *Take It or Leave It* (1949–1950); *Tales of the Texas Rangers* (actor, early 1950s); *The Whistler* (actor, late 1940s–1950s).

Raised in Los Angeles, the son of Russian immigrants, Hy Averback moonlighted as an announcer and writer at local stations KHJ and KMPC during his high school years. The experience launched a lifelong career branching into multiple dimensions. Completing a stint with the U.S. Army during the Second World War, Averback was assigned to the Armed Forces Radio Service. On his return he acquired an announcing slot with KFWB in Los Angeles, his voice thereafter beamed across the nation as he introduced headliners Jack Carson, Bob Hope, Jack Paar and a myriad of other entertainers and series.

Film critic Leonard Maltin observed that many performers managed to lead double lives, acting on some radio shows while announcing on others. "When he was making top dollar as a 'name' announcer in Hollywood," said Maltin, "Hy Averback gladly worked for scale [minimal payments approved by the radio actors' union] in the supporting cast of *The Lineup*." He did so in a lot of added dramatic series, too.

Averback used his experience as an audio performer to consequently catapult himself onto the silver screen and television. He appeared in eight motion pictures: *Because of Eve* (1948); *Cry Danger* (1951); *Francis in the Navy* (1955); *The Benny Goodman Story* (1955); *Four Girls in Town* (1957); *How to Succeed in Business Without Really Trying* (1967); *Where Were You When the Lights Went Out?* (1968); and *I Love You, Alice B. Toklas!* (1968). He also produced several feature length movies, including *Where Were You When the Lights Went Out?* (1968); *The Great Bank Robbery* (1969); *Suppose They Gave a War and Nobody Came?* (1970); and *Where the Boys Are* (1984).

On the small screen Averback turned up in the casts of *The Jack Benny Program* (1950–1964); *Tonight* (1955); *NBC Comedy Hour* (1956); and *Our Miss Brooks* (1956). He announced for vocalist Tony Martin in Martin's mid 1950s NBC-TV entry. In successive decades, Averback concentrated on producing and directing TV series: *The Real McCoys* (1957–1963); *Mrs. G Goes to College* (1961–1962); *Ensign O'Toole* (1962–1963); *Burke's Law* (1963–1966); *F Troop* (1965–1967); *McCloud* (1970); *The Don Rickles Show* (1972); *M*A*S*H* (1972—for which he was twice nominated for an Emmy); *Needles and Pins* (1973); and *At Ease* (1983). He directed one or more episodes of 21 television series and produced 10 series. He also produced 15 TV movies and a TV miniseries (*Pearl*, 1978). Among his made-for-television films were *Columbo: Suitable for Framing* (1971); *Columbo: A Stitch in Crime* (1973); *Topper Returns* (1973); *The Love Boat II* (1977); *The Night Rider* (1979); and *The Last Precinct* (1986).

AVERY, GAYLORD JAMES. b. July 6, 1918, Minnesota; d. March 11, 1996, San Francisco, Calif. *Announcer*. **Series:** *Gangbusters* (ca. 1950s); *My Son Jeep* (1955–1956).

Gay Avery was on the air on Omaha's WOW in the 1930s and 1940s before moving to KFAB, Lincoln, Neb., as a newscaster between 1946 and 1948. He was one of 10 men picked to introduce *Gangbusters* over its long radio run (1935–1957). After a turn on *My Son Jeep* over a nationwide hookup, Avery seemed to vanish from the national radio scene.

He wasn't done yet, however, for he persisted as a staff announcer at CBS through the 1960s. It's his voice, in fact, that introduces the syndicated reruns of *The Honeymooners* classic 39 shows. Jack Lescoulie was the original interlocutor there but the opening was re-cut for subsequent distribution to local stations and cable networks. Avery was also the announcer on the CBS-TV series *The Entertainers* (1964–1965).

BABBE, OWEN MILLER. b. Dec. 19, 1916, Council Bluffs, Iowa; d. June 25, 1996, Mason City, Iowa. *Announcer*. **Series:** *The Adventures of Sherlock Holmes* (1940s).

Leaving Council Bluffs High School, Owen Babbe earned a music degree at the University of Iowa. Yet he initially pursued radio as a career, becoming an announcer in the environs of Hollywood, Calif. for a decade. His assignments included newscasting at Los Angeles' KMTH in 1939 and Beverly Hills' KMPC the following year. He was one of a half-dozen announcers tapped for *Sherlock Holmes* during that series' long run (1930–1956).

At mid century Babbe divorced himself from his profession to launch a new one for which he had been educationally equipped. Returning to his native Iowa, in 1950 he opened Jones Piano House in Fort Dodge. His entrepreneurial success was extended a dozen years later to a second store in Mason City. Babbe managed the dual operations until he retired in 1984.

BACH, ALWYN E.W. b. Jan. 28, 1898, Springfield, Mass.; d. unknown. *Announcer*. **Series:** *Around the World with Libby* (ca. late 1920s, early 1930s); *Heel Hugger Harmonies* (1931–1932); *Enna Jettick Melodies* (1928–1933); *The Lehn and Fink Serenade* (ca. late 1920s, early 1930s); *Luden's Novelty Orchestra* (1931–1932); *Real Folks* (1928–1932); *Stars of Melody* (ca. early 1930s).

In the mid 1920s, Alwyn E.W. Bach (who applied the first name and both initials in references) was one of several staff announcers whose voices emanated from WBZ, then transmitting from Springfield, Mass. (The station went on the air in 1921. In March 1931 WBZ was relocated to Boston. At that juncture, the remaining Springfield outlet was re-lettered WBZA.)

In November 1926, meanwhile, WBZ joined the NBC network for its inaugural broadcast and became an affiliate of the chain. Some of its announcers, among them Thomas Shaw Young and eventually Bach, too, became groundbreaking interlocutors for the fledgling web. (Bach was designated WBZ's senior announcer for a brief while following NBC's launch.) Subsequently, in 1930 Bach was distinguished by the American Academy of Arts and Sciences by receiving the group's Good Diction Award, bestowed annually.

BAILEY, JACK. b. Sept. 15, 1907, Hampton, Iowa; d. Feb. 1, 1980, Santa Monica, Calif. *Emcee, Announcer.* **Series:** *The Adventures of Ozzie and Harriet*; *Comedy of Errors* (quizmaster, 1949–1952); *County Fair* (master of ceremonies, ca. 1945); *Duffy's Tavern* (1940s); *Glamour Manor* (1944–1945); *Meet the Missus* (master of ceremonies, 1944–ca. 1945); *Movie Quiz* (quizmaster, 1945); *Potluck Party* (master of ceremonies, 1944); *Queen for a Day* (master of ceremonies–writer, 1945–1957); *Silver Theater* (ca. 1943–1944); *Stop That Villain* (co-host, 1944). **Aphorism:** *I'd like to make EV-ery woman a queen EV-ery day!*

Jack Bailey was a man who parlayed his opportunities into full-fledged star status. While a collegian he pursued acting with the Ralph Bellamy Stock Co. In his early years in show business he played in a jazz band, ran a tent show and barked for a couple of world's fairs—preliminaries that were to hold him in good stead for what was to be his *real* life's work. He broke into radio at WHO in Des Moines. That was followed by a string of West Coast radio opportunities: KFSD, San Diego, where he rose to chief announcer; KEHE, Los Angeles, in 1937; San Diego's KGB as chief announcer; and Hollywood's KHJ in 1942. During that epoch he was a disc jockey on the West Coast's Don Lee Network.

In 1939–1940 Bailey earned additional compensation for voiceovers on Donald Duck cartoons screened in cinema palaces. His specialty was the animated character Goofy. As Bailey subsequently announced multiple prominent national radio series, his ability from pre-radio days to work a crowd resurfaced. In 1944 he was presiding over various audience participation series, a niche he filled quite naturally and for which destiny seemed to have prepared him.

The resolutely jocular announcer-turned-star reached the pinnacle of his success when he took over the helm of the tear-jerking reality show *Queen for a Day* and became—as a pundit characterized him—"radio's favorite male sob sister." The feature that turned his name into a household word plucked women with hard-luck stories from the studio audience and showered them with boatloads of gifts. They competed with three or four others of similar fate, each one recounting a miserable plight before an animated audience that was electrified by every appalling and sorry detail. Bailey could project the most wretched of life's unfortunates onto a fleeting pedestal before exuberantly signing off the show with the memorable idiom: *I'd like to make EV-ery woman a queen EV-ery day!* At its peak the radio series was so popular it was reincarnated into a televersion, playing from 1956 to 1964, during which it briefly became the top-rated daytime show. Across 19 years Bailey crowned more than 5,000 queens.

The emcee had already performed on the tube by the time his epic series reached it. While starring in the aural version of *Queen for a Day*, he concurrently hosted two more primetime video game shows—*Place the Face* (1953–1954) and *Truth or Consequences* (1954–1956). In later years he played supporting roles on *Daniel Boone*, *Emergency*, *Gunsmoke*, *The Monroes* and a few other trendy TV narratives. Bailey appeared in road companies of *Hello, Dolly* and *How to Succeed in Business Without Really Trying*, too.

BAKER, ART (born Arthur Shank). b. Jan. 7, 1898, New York, N.Y.; d. Aug. 26, 1966, Los Angeles, Calif. *Announcer, Emcee.* **Series:** *Art Baker's Notebook* (host, 1950); *The Bob Hope Show*, under varied monikers (ca. late 1930s); *The Dinah Shore Show* (1953–1955); *The Grouch Club* (1939); *Hedda Hopper's Hollywood* (1939–1942); *Hollywood in Person* (host, 1937–1938); *Meet Joe Public* (host,

1943); *Never Too Old* (host, 1945); *People Are Funny* (master of ceremonies, 1942–1943); *Portraits of Life* (commercial spokesman, 1936); *Pot o' Gold* (West Coast quizmaster, 1939–1941); *Pull Over, Neighbor* (master of ceremonies, 1939); *Sing, America, Sing* (host, 1939).

After singing in his high school glee club in Philadelphia, Art Baker continued his musical preparation with a prominent Chicago voice coach and became a gospel singer. He signed as an understudy at the Chicago Opera Co. as World War I broke out. On his 20th birthday he enlisted in the U.S. Army, where he became a machine gunnery instructor. While overseas he often conducted audience sing-alongs for the troops. On his return to America, Baker sang in an evangelistic choir and a barbershop quartet. He attempted a myriad of business ventures, too, including valet parking, hauling gravel and selling oil burners.

Baker pursued acting and was a professional toastmaster in Hollywood. In the mid 1930s in Los Angeles he lectured about the stained glass windows depicting "The Last Supper" at Forest Lawn Cemetery and delivered commercials for the firm on CBS's *Portraits of Life*. On one such occasion, Leonard Maltin recalled, a little girl declared, "My grandma lives in Forest Lawn," followed by a syrupy-voiced Baker adding: "Yes, your loved ones will live forever at Forest Lawn." That line "made us throw up in the control room" said the series' writer, Jerome Lawrence. Baker was soon narrating *Tapestries of Life*, also underwritten by Forest Lawn, on a Los Angeles radio outlet, his earliest permanent show.

Next came the first of a wave of audience participation features, *Reunion of the States*. Baker's highly touted "voice of sincerity" led to added openings as a commentator and interviewer, including his own show, *Art Baker's Notebook*, in 1938. It originated over Los Angeles' KFI and remained on the ether for two decades. "His homespun philosophy was so much enjoyed by West Coast listeners, it wasn't long before his show was syndicated coast-to-coast, lasting for over a decade," confirmed media historian Frank Bresee. By 1939 Baker was hosting a game-oriented series, *Pull Over, Neighbor*, for rising producer John Guedel.

By being in the right place at the right time, Baker gained the first shot as master of ceremonies for Guedel's debuting 1942 stunt program *People Are Funny*. It followed in the wake of Ralph Edwards' stupendous reception with *Truth or Consequences* a couple of years earlier. (Edwards had previously been a busy radio announcer, too.) At *People's* inception, Art Linkletter appeared on the air alongside Baker for a few weeks. Linkletter previously assisted Guedel in deriving many of the show's initial pranks.

Guedel actually preferred the more gregarious Linkletter as emcee. But NBC would have none of it. After the show's premier, it was obvious that something was amiss. In late 1943 Guedel abruptly replaced Baker with Linkletter. Baker subsequently sued Guedel and lost. *People Are Funny* lasted to 1960 on radio and ran from 1954–1961 on TV. Linkletter also had the good fortune of headlining yet another Guedel production, *House Party*. The weekday audience participation marathon aired between 1945 and 1957 on radio and from 1952 to 1970 on TV. Linkletter's dual series turned his name into a household word in millions of the nation's homes while Baker was soon forgotten as the debuting host of *People Are Funny*.

Baker flourished in his own extensive primetime TV series, however. From 1950 to 1958 he steered the audience participation feature *You Asked for It* (debuting as *The Art Baker Show*), originally over Dumont Television and later on ABC-TV. In 1958 he hosted a fleeting Saturday night game show, *The End of the Rainbow*, on NBC-TV. Perhaps his best assignment on the small screen was to present the weekly ABC series about a winsome sorceress, *Bewitched*, starring Elizabeth Montgomery (1964–1972)—a sitcom that's still available in infinite repeats on cable systems today.

Baker, who presided over a local show on KECA in Los Angeles from 1948 to 1949, found yet another career in Hollywood motion pictures. Between 1937 and 1966 he acted in supporting roles of 51 full-length films, among them: *Abie's Irish Rose* (1946); *The Farmer's Daughter* (1947); *Daisy Kenyon* (1947); *State of the Union* (1948); *A Southern Yankee* (1948); *Walk a Crooked Mile* (1948); *Any Number Can Play* (1949); *Only the Valiant* (1951); *Voyage to the Bottom of the Sea*

(1961); *Young Dillinger* (1965); and *The Wild Angels* (1966).

BAKER, DONALD. b. Feb. 26, 1903, Ontario, Canada; d. Nov. 12, 1968, Hollywood, Calif. *Announcer, Instrumentalist.* **Series:** *The Columbia Workshop*; *Information Please* (1938–1940); *My Best Girls* (organist, 1944–1945); *Pursuit* (1949–1952); *Sing for Your Dough* (organist, 1942–1943); *Strike It Rich* (1947–1950); *This Day is Ours* (music composer, 1938–1940).

A multitalented Don Baker could not only enunciate properly, he could play a mean keyboard, demonstrating his talent at the studio console for a couple of network radio features (a sitcom and an audience participation show). He accompanied theater bands on piano at the start of his show business career in 1923–1926. From 1926 to 1928, Baker was organist at the Rialto and Rivoli theaters in New York. He was employed by London's Sidney Bernstein Theater in 1933–1934 and followed it with a year as a staff musician at WOR Radio in New York (1934–1935). Baker was organist at New York's Paramount Theater from 1935 to 1948, a period overlapping some of his network gigs.

In yet another dimension, in 1948–1949 he appeared on a weekly five-minute question-and-answer primetime series over CBS-TV labeled *Sportsman's Quiz*. Bernard Dudley posed sports-related questions proffered by viewers and Baker replied with correct responses. Baker joined CBS Radio in 1943 in New York and transferred to Hollywood in 1949, where he was affiliated with KNX, the network's owned-and-operated outlet. During his lengthy tenure at KNX he was an announcer, producer, director and operations supervisor. His passing was the result of a stroke that occurred on election night a week earlier while he was on duty at KNX.

BAKER, EUGENE LOCK. b. Jan. 11, 1910, Portland, Ore.; d. Aug. 14, 1981, Burbank, Calif. *Announcer, Vocalist.* **Series:** *Family Theater*; *The First Nighter*; *Golden Days of Radio* (1949–early 1950s); *Houseboat Hannah* (ca. late 1930s–1941); *Knickerbocker Playhouse* (1939–1942); *Lum and Abner* (1944–1945); *Midstream* (1939–1941); *Queen for a Day* (ca. 1950s); *The Quiz Kids*; *Songs of a Dreamer* (vocalist, 1942–1944).

Gene Baker was a boy soprano and as a youngster John Charles Thomas was his idol. Growing up, Baker hoped to become a respected vocalist, too. But he didn't want to take any chances so he studied debating and dramatics as well as voice. At 16 he auditioned at a Portland radio station and was soon on the ether singing and announcing. He cemented the deal by marrying the station manager's daughter!

In 1940 he acquired a quarter-hour syndicated series that eventually went to the Blue network three times a week for 18 months. There simply weren't that many announcers who could heist a few tunes as well as speak well. He also sang in public appearances with New York's Columbia Symphony Orchestra. Over his professional career Baker maintained local radio stints in Portland, Ore. (KEX), Chicago and Los Angeles (KHJ), as a disc jockey at the latter address. Most of his national series occurred during his sojourn in Chicago.

BALDWIN, BILL. b. Nov. 26, 1913, Pueblo, Colo.; d. Nov. 17, 1982. *Announcer.* **Series:** Big Band Remotes (late 1930s); *The Edgar Bergen and Charlie McCarthy Show* (1950–1957); *Golden Days of Radio* (early 1950s); *Here's Morgan* (ca. 1950); *The Jack Kirkwood Show* (early 1950s); *The Mario Lanza Show* (1951–1952); *Night Editor* (1940s).

Bill Baldwin got into radio by first being a master of ceremonies and vocalist for a walkathon; that was a Depression-era dance marathon that persisted until one couple from among scores that began it was still standing following countless hours on a dance floor. When a radio announcer didn't show up on a 1936 occasion at Casper, Wyo., Baldwin was pressed into service. An agent of WOW, Omaha, Neb., was present and introduced him to Omaha officials. Baldwin was hired as an announcer but was sent to a five-month apprenticeship at KSSC, Grand Junction, Colo., before joining WOW. In Grand Junction he read news dispatches into a microphone from the current issue of *The Christian Science Monitor*. At WOW he gained an interview with the Vatican's papal secretary. Their live exchange occurred in—of all places!—the men's room of the Omaha airport.

In 1937 Baldwin became, in his own words, "king of the band remotes" at Chicago's WGN, where he was on the air for the fledgling MBS network. "At night I would do all the band remotes starting at 6:00 and finish up at 1:00 in the morning," he told interviewer Chuck Schaden. "Every other half-hour I had a show." A typical weeknight schedule began with dinner music at the Blackstone followed by music from the Palmer House, then the Blackhawk and the Drake, returning to the Palmer House and signing off at the Blackhawk. In the daytime Baldwin presided over other shows and pitched for Marshall Fields department stores and still more concerns and commodities.

Baldwin's career in radio carried him to many parts of the country. From Chicago he moved to KWKH, Shreveport, La.; then to KOIL, Omaha; in December 1938 to KFSO, San Francisco; in 1940 back to KOIL, Omaha; that same year to KDYL, Salt Lake City; in 1941 to KFWB, Hollywood, Calif.; back to San Francisco's KGO in 1942 and the Blue network as the chain's San Francisco news director, taking him overseas with the U.S. Navy from 1943 to 1945; freelancing in San Francisco to 1949; and back to L.A. in July 1949 where he appeared in the movie *Champion*. Baldwin subsequently read Coca-Cola commercials on *The Edgar Bergen and Charlie McCarthy Show* and did the same on several other series.

In the mid 1950s—as his big network radio series neared the finish line—Baldwin introduced *The Bob Cummings Show* on NBC-TV (1956–1959). Concurrently, between 1957 and 1959 Baldwin was the interlocutor for NBC-TV's *The Thin Man* crime series starring Hollywood actor Peter Lawford. In the 1960s he was the welcoming voice on NBC's animated cartoon *The Flintstones* (1960–1966). And from 1962 to 1971, producer Paul Henning allowed Baldwin to use his name on the air to announce the arrival and departure of *The Beverly Hillbillies* on CBS-TV, something few of his colleagues were permitted.

BALINGER, ART. b. Feb. 4, 1898, California; d. January 1980, Alhambra, Calif. *Announcer*. **Series:** *Here Comes McBride* (1949); *Here's Morgan*, aka *The Henry Morgan Show* (1949–1950); *Mr. and Mrs. North* (ca. late 1940s–ca. early 1950s); *The Philip Morris Playhouse* (1948–1949); *The Roy Rogers Show* (1951–1955); *This Is Your Life* (1948–1950).

In 1949 Art Balinger was pitching commercials for Studebaker automobiles on an early Buster Keaton TV series. By 1955 he joined a stock company of thespians on NBC-TV's *Dragnet*, often appearing as a Los Angeles police captain. He continued until the series ended in 1959, returning on the same basis when a subsequent series of the same show ran on NBC-TV between 1967 and 1970. In the meantime, Balinger turned up acting in supporting roles on multiple TV series: *Adam-12*; *Code Red*; *Ellery Queen*; and *77 Sunset Strip*.

BALL, DONALD I. b. Feb. 8, 1904, Block Island, R.I.; d. Jan. 7, 1974. *CBS staff announcer*.

Don Ball followed his daddy into business as a hotelier following his graduation from Brown University. The studios of radio station WCAH were housed in the lodging property Ball managed in Columbus, Ohio. On one occasion, an act failed to arrive at the studios by air time and Ball was pressed into service as a substitute. He received such favorable reaction from listeners to his appearance that he left the profession he had trained for to enter broadcasting. Ball eventually landed at WABC in New York, the flagship station of the fledgling Columbia chain, as a staff announcer. That opportunity in the 1930s thrust him before the CBS microphones before long in a similar capacity.

BANGHART, CHARLES KENNETH. b. Sept. 11, 1909, Paramus, N.J.; d. May 25, 1980, Delray Beach, Fla. *Announcer, Newscaster, Emcee*. **Series:** *Archie Andrews*; *Author Meets the Critics* (1947–1948); *Best of All* (1954–1955); *Biography in Sound* (1955–1958); *Encore* (1952–1953); *Home is What You Make It* (1944–1948); *Katie's Daughter* (1947); *The Ken Banghart Show* (host, 1947); *Kenneth Banghart and the News* (newscaster, 1946–1949); *Lora Lawton* (1940s); *Meredith Willson's Music Room* (ca. 1940s); *News Game* (quizmaster, 1954); *Parallel* (communicator, 1957–1960); *The Private Files of Rex Saunders* (1951); *Proudly We Hail* (1947–1948*)*; *RCA Victor Show* (1945–1949); *Robert Q.*

Lewis (1945); *The Robert Shaw Chorale* (1948); *So Proudly We Hail*; *The Telephone Hour* (ca. 1940s); *When A Girl Marries* (1940s); *The World's Great Novels* (1944–ca. 1948).

Growing up in New York City, Kenneth Banghart became a successful businessman, employed by travel agency Thomas Cook & Sons, rising to East Coast manager and head of the firm's Washington, D.C. office. He left his post in 1942 to become an announcer at D.C. NBC outlet WRC and significantly increased his visibility with that network in successive years. Meanwhile, during World War II he narrated U.S. Navy instructional films. On the ether Banghart announced programs in multiple genres and was especially identified with news, initially on radio (1946–1949) and then in video.

With John Cameron Swayze as the NBC Radio anchor, Banghart was one of a handful of floor reporters at the 1948 political conventions, the last covered exclusively by radio. In 1953 he was a commentator on NBC-TV's *Gillette Summer Sports Reel*. He was a disc jockey in 1957 at New York's WRCA Radio. Banghart also acted in regional theater productions and co-produced several plays at the Olney (Md.) Theatre Summer Playhouse, among them *A Dash of Bitters*. Resigning from NBC after two decades, in 1962 he joined WCBS Radio, the flagship station of the Columbia Broadcasting System, where he finished out his broadcasting career.

BANNON, JIM. b. April 9, 1911, Kansas City, Mo.; d. July 28, 1984, Ojai, Ventura, Calif. *Announcer, Actor.* **Series:** *The Adventures of Nero Wolfe* (1946); *The Eddie Bracken Show* (narrator, 1945, 1946–1947); *The Edgar Bergen and Charlie McCarthy Show* (late 1930s); *The Great Gildersleeve* (1941–1942); *I Love a Mystery* (1943–1944); *The Joe Penner Show* (1938–1940); *Silver Eagle, Mountie* (actor, early 1950s); *Stars Over Hollywood* (early 1940s); *The Zane Grey Theater* (actor, ca. 1947–1948).

After graduating from Rockhurst College in Kansas City, Mo., Jim Bannon's radio career was baptized in adjacent Kansas City, Kan., with KCKN. He soon transferred to KMOX in St. Louis and, in 1937, to KEHE in Hollywood, Calif. By September that year he was working for Los Angeles' KHJ, a Mutual outlet. In December he shifted to KFI, Los Angeles, through a connection with radio (and later TV) actress Bea Benaderet, who became his first wife. (They divorced in 1950. Bannon and his second wife, Barbara Cork, 23 years his junior, also divorced.) Meanwhile, by June 1938 he was announcing for both Edgar Bergen and Joe Penner.

Columbia Pictures released a trilogy of *I Love a Mystery* films in 1945. Jim Bannon, who had delivered the Oxydol commercials for Procter & Gamble Co. during the radio dramas, replaced Michael Raffetto as Jack Packard. Raffetto was reportedly too diminutive for the part.

From 1954 to 1955 Bannon acted in the role of Mitch Fredericks on the NBC-TV daytime soap opera *Hawkins Falls*. During the 1955–1956 television season he appeared in a major role in the fleeting CBS juvenile series *The Adventures of Champion* starring the celebrated mount of legendary cowboy singer Gene Autry. Bannon returned to the CBS cameras in 1959–1960 to host a weekday 30-minute soap opera anthology, *For Better or Worse*. His autobiography, *The Son That Rose in the West* (Devil's Hole Printery, 1961), is a detailed account of his fascinating climb in big time broadcasting.

BARBER, WALTER LANIER (RED). b. Feb. 17, 1908, Columbus, Miss.; d. Oct. 22, 1992, Tallahassee, Fla. *Sportscaster, Announcer.* **Series:** *Baseball Quiz* (co-host, 1943–1944); *Broadway Matinee* (1943–1944); *Hear It Now* (sports commentator, 1950–1951); *Monitor* (sports interviewer, ca. 1955–ca. 1966); *The Old Gold Program*, aka *The Old Gold Show*, aka *The Old Gold Comedy Theater* (sportscaster, ca. 1943–ca. 1947); *Pepper Young's Family* (commercial spokesman, mid 1950s); *The Red Barber Show*, aka *Red Barber's Club Room*, aka *CBS Presents Red Barber* (host-interviewer, 1946–1950); *Schaefer Star Revue* (1945–46). **Aphorism:** *Oh-ho, doctor!*

Red Barber's initiation into broadcasting came late in 1928 while he was a student at the University of Florida. At a professor's insistence, he read a paper over the noncommercial campus radio station, WRLT. The paper's title was "Certain Aspects of Obstetrics." By March 4, 1930, Barber agreed to become a part time announcer at WRLT at $50 monthly following the station manager's persistence. After the station's sportscaster departed, Barber was asked that fall to broadcast the school's football games. Early in 1931 he aired the all-day Florida State High School Basketball Tournament. That year his salary increased to $75 monthly. When the station's chief announcer quit, Barber was named successor and his salary doubled. Before long he was announcing at a local commercial station, WRUF, Gainesville.

In 1934 he signed with Cincinnati's WLW to call the Cincinnati Reds games at $30 weekly over WLW's 5,000-watt sister station, WASI. He hadn't witnessed a major league game until he called his first one! Barber (often referred to throughout his career as "the old redhead") was the play-by-play announcer for the Reds on WASI from 1934 to 1937 and WLW from 1937 to 1938. On May 24, 1935, he called baseball's first after-dark game. In October that year he covered his first World Series for the Mutual Broadcasting System (MBS). There would be many more to follow. In the off-season Barber broadcast regional football games usually involving the University of Cincinnati or Ohio State University. On New Year's Day 1937 he aired the Villanova-Auburn football game for MBS from Havana, Cuba. It was emblematic of the diverse assignments coming his way in that epoch.

Moving to New York in 1939, he was linked with the home team at Ebbets Field—the Brooklyn Dodgers (1939–1953). Most of those games aired over WOR or WHN. Although Barber had a pronounced Southern drawl that remained with him for life, Dodger fans warmed up quickly to his laid-back delivery. On Aug. 26, 1939, Barber called the first telecast of a major league baseball game between the Dodgers and the Reds. By 1941 he was earning $15,000 annually for baseball coverage and a similar sum for a daily sports show and commentary for Pathé News. A syndicated sports column he wrote appeared in hundreds of newspapers across the U.S. He was also getting 500 fan letters weekly. Sometime after the Dodgers left Gotham for L.A., Barber associated with the New York Yankees. In 1966 he retired from active sportscasting with the club.

During his career Barber materialized in lots of unexpected places. He was a "guest expert" on radio's *Information Please* on at least four occasions in the mid 1940s; he appeared on the prestigious *Radio Hall of Fame* in that same era; and sometime between the inception of CBS-TV's *Sunrise Semester* in 1963 and its demise in 1982, he was one of thousands who signed up for a college course.

Barber materialized at least one other place that few might have anticipated. After pushing Camay, "the soap of beautiful women," for two decades, in the mid 1950s Procter & Gamble Co. expanded its scope on the durable daytime serial *Pepper Young's Family* to include more commodities from an extensive line of its household goods. Listeners were suddenly confronted with pitches for Joy dishwashing liquid, Tide detergent and—wonder of wonders—sportscaster Red Barber plugging Fluffo shortening! The idyllic connection that he supposedly maintained with millions of housewives appeared uncanny. In one spot he gushed over a homemaker's prize-winning cake recipe made with Fluffo. Barber added to her "amazing results" description with avowals like "that's the stomp-down truth," seemingly designed to reassure the listeners of its validity. No matter, it was a hoot to hear a play-by-play announcer affirming the merits of cooking grease.

For nine years he presided over his own television series, *Red Barber's Corner* (at varying times under other monikers—*Red Barber's Clubhouse, Peak of the Sports News*) on CBS-TV (1949–1955) and NBC-TV (1955–1958). During part of the run the program filled time between the end of boxing matches and the 11 P.M. news. Interviews with sports figures, sports scores and features on athletes and athletics comprised the format. The show was simulcast on radio and TV in 1950. Barber announced telecasts of NCAA football contests in the early 1950s and early 1960s on various networks. And in 1951 he co-hosted CBS-TV's *Take Another Look* in which films of NCAA football games were re-screened.

Barber's memoir, *The Broadcasters* (Dial, 1970), is an informal overview of sportscasting and some of the key individuals who contributed to it in his epoch. In 1978 he and sportscaster Mel Allen became the first with airlife careers to be included in the National

Baseball Hall of Fame. In 1960 he won a George Foster Peabody Broadcasting Award for completing six decades in the breed. For many years until his death he commented on the current sports scene on National Public Radio's *Morning Edition* every Friday.

BARNES, PATRICK H. b. ca. 1898, Sharon, Pa.; d. June 9, 1969. *Announcer, Emcee.* **Series:** *I'll Never Forget* (1940); *Let's Be Charming* (1943–1944); *Those Good Old Days* (1942–1943, 1944); *Musical Cruise,* aka *Benny Meroff's Revue* (1933–1934); *Pat Barnes* (host, 1931–1932); *Pat Barnes and Barbara Show* (co-host, 1950); *Pat Barnes Barnstormers* (host, 1937–1938); *Pat Barnes in Person* (host, 1935–1936); *Pleasure Island,* aka *Guy Lombardo and His Orchestra* (1934–1935).

Pat Barnes was on hand almost from radio's inception, at least as a commercial venture. He launched his career over reputedly the world's first station, Pittsburgh's KDKA, in 1921, only a short time after it went on the air. Within four years he was chief announcer at Chicago's WHT and by 1927 manager of the station. Barnes produced and performed in his first transcribed series while there, *Henry Adams and His Book,* one of the earliest recorded shows on the ether. Barnes transitioned from WHT to the Windy City's WGN and WENR; in the 1930s he went to New York City and affiliated with WOR, WINS and WNBC while headlining a handful of network features.

After his radio gigs ended, Barnes relocated to Milwaukee in 1954, becoming public affairs director at WISN-TV. He was still there when he died 15 years later.

BARRETT, RAY. b. Sept. 1, 1907, New York City, N.Y.; d. Jan. 16, 1973, Ft. Lauderdale, Fla. *Announcer, Newscaster.* **Series:** *Monitor* (interviewer and newscaster, mid 1950s–ca. 1960s); *Talent Search, Country Style* (1951).

After being in vaudeville for three years, teaching English and public speaking in New York City and working for transcription outfits and in commercial movies, Ray Barrett joined WDRC Radio, Hartford, Conn. By May 1941 he was the station's chief announcer, earning $65 weekly while also copywriting and hosting a couple of daily DJ features. He performed in summer stock as a sideline. Barrett entered the U.S. Army Air Corps in 1941 and upon his return joined NBC in New York. As a staff announcer he filled a myriad of assignments to retirement in 1967, when he moved to Ft. Lauderdale. He continued working in commercials and film in Florida.

In between horse races on 1950's *Trotting Races* live over NBC-TV from New York's Roosevelt Raceway, Barrett and sportscaster Bill Stern conducted quizzes. Their contestants, summoned from a studio audience, filled the time between main events. In 1953 and 1955 Barrett was a commentator for NBC-TV's primetime *Gillette Summer Sports Reel.* In the late 1950s he appeared on *The Gillette Cavalcade of Sports* on that network, a series commonly referred to as the Friday night fights (boxing matches). He introduced live prestige dramas on NBC-TV's *Robert Montgomery Presents* (1950–1957) and occasionally acted in its narratives as well as on that chain's *Goodyear Playhouse* (1951–1960). In 1965 Barrett faced one of his greatest professional challenges when he and Merrill Mueller presided over a four-hour radio marathon, broadcasting without scripts during the infamous blackout that blanketed the Northeast.

A journal critic cited Oct. 4, 1957, as the apex of Barrett's broadcast career, however. It was the day the Russians launched Sputnik I. "An ardent space travel student, Barrett went on NBC-TV to fill in substance and background detail lacking in the sketchy reports issued by the Soviet Union, a task few broadcasters were capable of at that time," the pundit sanctioned.

BARRY, JACK. b. March 20, 1918, Lindenhurst, N.Y.; d. May 2, 1984, New York, N.Y. *Announcer, Emcee.* **Series:** *Daily Dilemmas* (host, 1947–1948); *It's the Barrys* (actor, 1953); *The Joe Dimaggio Show* (host, 1949–1950); *Juvenile Jury* (moderator, 1946–1951, 1952–1953); *Life Begins at Eighty* (host, 1948–1949, 1952–1953); *So You Think You Know Music* (1940s); *Special Investigator* (1946–1947); *Stars and Starters* (host, 1950); *Uncle Don* (early 1940s).

Starting in radio over WTTM, Trenton, N.J., Jack Barry transferred to New York's WOR where he announced a juvenile-oriented show for *Uncle Don* (Carney). At

WOR Barry formed a lifelong partnership with producer Dan Enright; together they developed many television series across several decades. With Barry as host, the duo initially teamed together for *Juvenile Jury*. A TV incarnation of the popular feature prevailed on NBC and CBS from 1947 to 1955 and in syndication in 1970. *Life Begins at Eighty*, created by Barry & Enright Productions, followed with a TV run from 1950 to 1956 that touched the NBC, ABC and Dumont chains.

The inspired twosome, Barry and Enright, collaborated on legions of subsequent TV features, primarily for networks but a few were in syndication. On most occasions, Barry was the master of ceremonies; at other times, the pair simply produced a show for broadcast. Their efforts included: *The Faith Baldwin Theatre of Romance* (1951); *Wisdom of the Ages* (1952–1953, Barry hosting); *Back That Fact* (1953); *Winky Dink and You* (1953–1957, Barry hosting); *The Joker's Wild* (1972–1975, 1976–1984, Barry hosting; 1984–1986, Bill Cullen hosting); *Blank Check* (1975); *Break the $250,000 Bank* (1976–1977, Barry hosting); *Way Out Games* (1976–1977); *Joker! Joker!! Joker!!!* (1979–1981, Barry hosting); and *Play the Percentages* (1980).

Barry was an emcee of NBC-TV's *Tic Tac Dough* in the late 1950s. He was also quizmaster for NBC's *High Low Quiz* (1957) and the first host of that net's *Concentration* (1958), which he and Enright created. In the same epoch he emceed *The Big Surprise* and *Twenty-One* (1956–1958), two TV quiz shows tainted by scandal when contestants revealed that producers had supplied some of them with answers to questions in advance, thereby juicing up the shows' ratings. Those series were promptly withdrawn. Barry, *Twenty-One's* creator and host, did not work again in national television for a decade following U.S. Senate investigations. A published report noted that both he and partner Enright acknowledged later "what they did on the quiz shows may have been wrong morally, but not illegal."

He initiated *You Don't Say* as a local game show in 1962 in Los Angeles on KTLA-TV—it subsequently became a popular network feature conducted by Tom Kennedy (1963–1969, 1975). In the intervening years, Barry owned an FM radio station in Redondo Beach, Calif. Although he created the game show *Everybody's Talking* that aired on ABC-TV in 1967, he got no credit for it, a lingering response of his alleged involvement in the quiz show imbroglio. He returned in 1969 as host of an ill-fated ABC game show, *The Generation Gap*, and was quizmaster of that web's *The Reel Game* in 1971. In the meantime, he owned and operated the Barry Cable TV system in Los Angeles and, with Enright, purchased other cable systems around the country. Together they produced a few theatrical films, including *Private Lessons*.

BARRY, NORMAN. b. Jan. 19, 1909, St. Louis, Mo.; d. Dec. 25, 1997, Chicago, Ill. *Announcer, Sportscaster, Newscaster.* **Series:** *Dan Harding's Wife* (late 1930s).

Norman Barry attended Ohio State University and left a job as an accountant in 1930 to become an announcer at Chicago's WIBO when friends told him he had an excellent telephone voice. He was a spokesman for some experimental television broadcasts during the WIBO tenure. By 1931 he was also writing and producing programs for Army and Navy air maneuvers. Not long afterward Barry left his regular broadcasting post to freelance as a straight man on the vaudeville stage and assist Ben Lyon and Bebe Daniels in a radio act while pursuing other entertainment venues. Barry appeared in movie trailers and also performed at Chicago's Terrace Gardens with Don Irwin's Orchestra as a bass baritone vocalist.

Returning in 1933 to WIBO as a sportscaster, a short time later he affiliated with NBC Radio (April 1934). Barry's radio career centered on a series of Windy City outlets where he frequently delivered local news and sports roundups. From 1939 to 1942 he was a newscaster for two of Chicago's foremost stations, WENR and WMAQ. In 1954 he again brought the scores to waiting ears tuned to WMAQ. According to a 1935 NBC press release, Barry was "heard on many network programs," although publicists and radio historiographers failed to document them. As scores of network programs originated in Chicago during radio's golden age, nonetheless, it isn't a stretch to believe that Barry had many opportunities.

BARTELL, HARRY. b. Nov. 29, 1913, New Orleans, La.; d. Feb. 26, 2004, Ashland, Ore. *Actor, Announcer.* **Series:** *Adventures by Morse* (actor, 1944–1945); *Amos 'n' Andy* (actor); *Broadway is My Beat* (actor, 1949–1954); *California Caravan* (actor, 1947–1952); *The Casebook of Gregory Hood* (ca. 1946–1951); *The Cavalcade of America* (actor, ca. early 1940s); *The CBS Radio Workshop* (actor, 1956–1957); *The Charlotte Greenwood Show* (actor, 1944–1946); *Columbia Presents Corwin* (actor, 1944); *Crime Classics* (actor, 1953–1954); *A Date with Judy* (actor, 1940s–ca. 1950); *Dear Abby* (1962–ca. 1974); *Defense Attorney* (actor, 1951–1952); *Dr. Christian* (actor, 1940s–1950s); *Dragnet* (actor, 1952); *The Eddie Cantor Show* (actor, ca. 1940s–ca. 1950s); *Escape* (actor, 1947–1954); *Fort Laramie* (actor, 1956); *Frontier Gentleman* (actor, 1958); *The Green Lama* (actor, 1949); *Gunsmoke* (actor, 1952–1961); *Have Gun, Will Travel* (actor, 1958–1960); *Hollywood Star Playhouse* (actor, 1950–1953); *I Love a Mystery* (actor, 1940s); *Let George Do It* (actor, late 1940s–early 1950s); *Lux Radio Theater* (actor, 1940s–1950s); *The Man Called X* (actor, ca. mid 1940s–early 1950s); *The Modern Adventures of Casanova* (actor, 1952); *My Favorite Husband* (actor, late 1940s–early 1950s); *The New Adventures of Nero Wolfe* (actor, 1950–1951); *The New Adventures of Philip Marlowe* (actor, ca. 1947–1951); *Nightbeat* (actor, 1950–1952); *On Stage* (actor, 1953–1954); *Raffles* (1942–1943); *Red Ryder* (actor, 1940s); *Rogers of the Gazette* (actor, 1953–1954); *Romance* (actor, 1952); *The Saint* (actor, 1950–1951); *Sherlock Holmes* (early 1950s); *Silver Theater* (early 1940s); *The Six Shooter* (actor, 1953–1954); *Suspense* (actor); *Tales of the Texas Rangers* (actor, 1950–1952); *This Is Your FBI* (actor, ca. 1945–1953); *Yours Truly, Johnny Dollar* (actor ca. 1950s–1962).

Of the 45 network radio series listed for Harry Bartell, he was an announcer on only four of them, performing as a thespian on the remainder. "I never considered myself an announcer," he said. "I sort of played an announcer as an actor." But these numbers were only the tip of the iceberg, according to radio historian Stewart Wright, who estimates Bartell appeared in more than 10,000 radio performances on at least 182 series. That places him near the forefront in capacity among his contemporaries. Bartell participated in several radio stock companies, thereby was a supporting figure in a myriad of features. Often identified with western roles, he played in crime and romance dramas, too. He once allowed, "Live radio was stimulating and horribly challenging. You were working without a net."

Bartell launched his profession in the early 1930s in Houston, where he performed in brief aural film adaptations. It was a prelude to what he would be doing on *Lux Radio Theater* in future years although the compensation wasn't at the same level: in Houston he received only a couple of 25-cent movie tickets for his efforts. Moving to the West Coast in 1937, he was a disc jockey and staff announcer and concurrently acted at the Pasadena Playhouse. In 1942 he appeared in a CBS West Coast crime drama, *Raffles*, five nights weekly, his first network venture.

He acted in 77 TV series, including highly popular productions like *Dragnet, Get Smart, Gunsmoke, I Love Lucy, Laramie, Perry Mason, Peter Gunn, Richard Diamond—Private Detective, The Twilight Zone, The Untouchables* and *The Wild Wild West*. On the side Bartell co-wrote a couple of *Gunsmoke* scripts while working as a professional photographer, frequently capturing network show rehearsals on film for permanent preservation.

In June 2003 at Seattle—a few months before his death—Bartell was roasted and toasted by the Radio Enthusiasts of Puget Sound during the group's annual showcase. He had performed there often in reenactments of dramas in which he appeared many years earlier. On that occasion, admiring fans signified his long-term impact on vintage broadcasting.

BARTLETT, THOMSON. b. July 11, 1914, Milwaukee, Wis.; d. Sept. 6, 1998, Wisconsin Dells, Wis. *Emcee, Announcer.* **Series:** *News and Rhythm* (ca. 1940–1941); *Welcome Travelers* (master of ceremonies, 1947–1954).

A pundit once characterized Tommy Bartlett's laid-back style as unique, one of the "most able and least offensive" human-interest emcees.

A high school dropout, as a youth Bartlett was fascinated by hearing people talking over the airwaves without the benefit of wires connecting their voices to his crystal set. At 14 he started announcing for his hometown's WISN. His first "role" was that of a barking dog. At 17 he joined Chicago's WBBM. At 20 he was announcing seven soap operas daily. An interviewer, writing in 1997, allowed: "He introduced and encouraged talk radio and he developed a mystical name for himself. His fans, mostly bored housewives, had imaginary affairs with the man whose voice delivered their dreams." In 1936 he presided over WBBM's *Meet the Missus* and *The Missus Goes to Market*, local audience participation series, a genre that would ultimately become his most widely celebrated life's work. In 1939 he took over a CBS program, *News and Rhythm*, on which he introduced tunes by Carl Hohengarten's Orchestra. He interrupted his career plans to serve with the U.S. Army Air Corps in Europe during World War II.

Returning following the war, Bartlett was increasingly persuaded that people generally like to talk about themselves. "If people would take time out to know about other people, to really learn what makes them tick, then all people would be all right," he declared. He catapulted his belief into a popular daytime radio feature that eventually went to television. Every weekday morning prior to broadcast, *Welcome Travelers* dispatched a cadre of scouts to Chicago train, bus and airline terminals to pluck potential guests passing through those venues on their way to somewhere else. The novelty of their adventures, told before a live studio audience, captured the imagination of listeners who tuned in everywhere. Occasionally a celebrity, perhaps Bob Hope or Ronald Reagan, appeared before Bartlett's microphone, in addition to plenty of common folk.

The tube version persisted from Sept. 8, 1952 to July 2, 1954 on NBC and from July 5, 1954 to May 6, 1955 on CBS. At that juncture the latter web pulled the rug from under Bartlett. The human-interest series abruptly left Chicago and opened the next week in New York City with a revised format—then a quiz show—and singer Jack Smith hosting. The game was altered a few months later, a co-host added (Pat Meikle) and the moniker revised to *Love Story*. The whole affair was canceled five months after that, having lost all residue of Bartlett's premise and most of its audience.

Meanwhile, in 1950 Bartlett narrated a radio remote from the Chicago Rail Fair. The broadcast booth was adjacent to an exhibit for Cypress Gardens, a Florida attraction boasting daily water-ski shows. That encounter led Bartlett to develop his own Midwestern ski show at Wisconsin Dells, Wis. His venture, Tommy Bartlett's Ski, Sky and Stage Show, Robot World and Exploratory, lured thousands of summer fun-seekers.

BARTON, FRANCIS C. (FRANK). b. Sept. 17, 1903, Chicago, Ill.; d. Jan. 11, 1995. *Announcer, Actor.* **Series:** *A Day in the Life of Dennis Day* (ca. early 1950s); *Dr. I.Q., the Mental Banker* (roving announcer, ca. 1940s); *The James and Pamela Mason Show* (1949); *Official Detective* (actor, ca. late 1940s–early 1950s); *One Man's Family* (ca. 1950s); *Open House* (actor, 1941).

After 32 years, Frank Barton retired from NBC in 1974. On his final day, he was a guest on Tom Snyder's *Tomorrow*, then originating from Burbank, Calif., following *Tonight*.

BARUCH, ANDRE. b. Aug. 20, 1908, Holland; d. Sept. 15, 1991, Los Angeles, Calif. *Announcer.* **Series:** *The American Album of Familiar Music* (ca. 1930s); *The Andrews Sisters Eight-to-the-Bar Ranch* (1944–ca. 1945); *Bobby Benson and the B-Bar-B Riders* (mid 1930s); *Dr. Christian* (1938); *Exploring the Unknown* (1945–1948); *The FBI in Peace and War* (1952); *Guy Lombardo Time* (ca. 1930s, 1940s); *Just Plain Bill* (1932–ca. 1936); *The Kate Smith Show* (1936–1945); *Leave It to the Girls* (ca. late 1940s); *Linda's First Love* (ca. 1940s); *Little Orphan Annie* (1930s); *Marie, the Little French Princess* (1933–1935); *Mark Warnow Orchestra* (1935); *Myrt and Marge* (ca. late 1930s–ca. early 1940s); *My Son and I* (1939–1941); *Second Husband* (1937–1946); *The Shadow* (1947–1949); *Stoopnagle and Budd* (1935); *Your Hit Parade* (1936–1947); *Your Song and Mine* (1948).

Andre Baruch arrived in the United States as a pre-teen and in due course attained permanent citizenship. He earned a bachelor's degree in 1929 at Columbia University. Afterward, he studied art for a year at the Pratt Institute and at Beaux Arts School in Paris. During World War II—as a major in the U.S. Army Signal Corps stationed in North Africa—he was assigned to the Armed Forces Radio Service. He had long before established himself as a major network interlocutor. A pianist, when he went to audition at CBS in New York in 1932, he inadvertently fell into the wrong line and was given printed names of composers from abroad to read aloud. That resulted in his being hired as a radio announcer and ultimately refocused his career. He covered band remotes and baseball games early and later became the commercial voice of U.S. Steel. For 22 years he was a leading spokesman for the American Tobacco Co., appearing on several Lucky Strike cigarette series on radio and television.

Baruch hosted *Masters of Magic* in 1949 on TV; he appeared the following year on video's *Shoppers Matinee*; and he introduced the top songs of the week on *Your Hit Parade's* NBC-TV run (1950–1957). Furthermore, he recorded newsreel voiceovers that played in cinema houses for many years across the country. The cosmopolitan Baruch was fluent in seven languages—English, French, Spanish, Italian, Dutch, Flemish and Portuguese.

In 1955 Baruch and his wife and business partner Bea Wain, a *Your Hit Parade* vocalist, attempted to revive the aura of that legendary program via a disc jockey series (*Mr. and Mrs. Music*) over WMCA Radio in New York. Consequently, the pair collaborated on an extensive run of transcribed syndicated features, summoning the *Your Hit Parade* tunes that actually appeared on the air while featuring original singers and accompanists. Each segment echoed the song charts of a given week and year. The countdown linked with the earlier programs held modern listeners at rapt attention until the number one tune was revealed. In the 1970s the couple also conducted a talk show over WPBR Radio at Palm Beach, Fla.

BATE, FREDERICK B. b. Nov. 13, 1886, Chicago, Ill.; d. Dec. 25, 1970, Waterford, Va. *Newscaster.* **Series:** *NBC News* (1932–ca. 1940s).

Fred Bate began living in Europe in 1912 when he went abroad to study art in Paris. During World War I he served in the U.S. Army's Ambulance Corps. He was employed by the Reparations Commission in Vienna (1919–1921) and Paris (1921–1930) and was employed for two years by the Paris branch of an American banking concern. Bate joined NBC in September 1932 as the network's European representative. One of his primary duties was to facilitate the exchange of radio programming across the Atlantic Ocean. In doing so he assisted foreign nations in acquiring and choosing American programs for rebroadcast over their own radio systems while doing the same for American listeners. Parenthetically, he was stationed in London as he boarded the *Queen Mary* in 1936 for its maiden voyage to New York.

Returning to his post, Bate was designated NBC's bureau chief in London. According to documentation, at NBC during the 18-day Munich crisis "At least 460 newscasts were logged.... Fred Bate and Max Jordan, and enlisted newspaper correspondents, came up from overseas during all hours of the day and night." A source observed: "NBC's man in London, Fred Bate, noted that the British government went to extraordinary lengths to make certain that neither network [NBC and CBS] was shown favoritism and that both were given equal access to all reports, but Bate said there was one aspect that set apart the networks' reports. 'The difference was that CBS had something we didn't have—Ed Murrow.'" Murrow and Bate were friends, despite the professional rivalry. But, according to a couple of Murrow biographers: "It was a fierce, cutthroat game. Alarms had gone off at NBC when Murrow was first sent to London. Between 1937 and 1939 NBC's European representatives—Fred Bate in London and Max Jordan in Basel, Switzerland—were under orders to do everything they could to stymie Columbia. On March 16, 1937, NBC's John F. Royal, based in New York, alerted Bate that Paul White [head of CBS News operations] was soon to sail for Britain to help Murrow capitalize on the coronation of King George VI by drumming up a 'publicity showing' for CBS. Bate must engineer a better showing for NBC, and in case he didn't understand the stakes, Royal spelled them out: 'Don't let's be too ethical about the way we handle this show.... After the Coronation is all over we cannot have ... Mr. Sarnoff [RCA chairman, of

NBC's parent firm] yelling at us as to why we didn't get certain publicity.'"

NBC's offices were knocked out in December 1940 during a German bombing raid on London and Bate was wounded but survived. In February 1942, after the U.S. entered the war, he was summoned to New York for reassignment as director of the chain's short-wave broadcasts. He retired from NBC in 1949. From 1950 to 1954, under a Ford Foundation grant, he assisted in promoting educational TV.

BAUKHAGE, HILMAR ROBERT. b. Jan. 7, 1889, LaSalle, Ill.; d. Jan. 31, 1976, Washington, D.C. Commentator. **Series:** *Baukhage Talking* (commentator, 1937–1953); *Four Star News* (commentator, 1939–1940); *The National Farm and Home Hour* (commentator, 1932–1937); *News form the Nation's Capitol* (commentator, 1939–1940). **Aphorism:** *Baukhage talking.*

Hilmar Robert Baukhage opened his news commentaries with *Baukhage talking*. One radio history branded him "the consummate professional journalist, much in the mode of [Hans V.] Kaltenborn. A man who never used his first name, either on the air or in his personal life, Baukage [sic] tried to present an accurate, evenhanded view of current events. He was widely respected for his objectivity." Intimates called him "Buck." At the peak of his popularity, 545 stations broadcast his daily program. Another source acknowledged: "He was considered by many people in broadcasting to be the originator of the casual, down-to-earth news-reporting style that became so popular on the airwaves and is still being used by many newscasters."

He was academically prepared with a literature degree from the University of Chicago combined with further study at European institutions of higher learning: Bonn (1911), Kiel (1912), Jena (1912), Freiburg (1913), the Sorbonne (1913). Returning to America in 1914, he joined the Associated Press in Washington, D.C., assigned to the State Department and embassies. He left it to take a post with a precursor of *Life* and *Look* magazines, *Leslie's Illustrated Weekly*, soon emerging as assistant managing editor. Shortly before World War I ended, Baukhage joined the coast artillery and was sent to Europe as a reporter for *Stars & Stripes*, the Army news journal. Returning in 1919, he gained employment in sales and promotion with a newly founded Consolidated Press Association. That led him to become the syndicate's bureau chief in Washington, San Francisco and Chicago. He also wrote extensively for *The United States Daily* and *The United States News*, ancestors of the *U.S. News & World Report* for which he would be a scribe four decades later.

Baukhage launched a broadcasting career in 1932 on a midday program, *The National Farm and Home Hour* produced by *The United States News*. On the show he delivered five-minute commentaries. After five years he made a seamless transition to his own news analysis series from Washington, D.C. At the same time he penned a column for the North American Newspaper Alliance and one later for the Western Newspaper Union consortium. A few years hence he inaugurated broadcasts from the White House. For the first time, on Dec. 7, 1941, he persuaded President Franklin D. Roosevelt's press secretary, Steve Early, to add a microphone to the executive mansion's newsroom. That afternoon Baukhage aired reports to NBC listeners of the Japanese attack on Pearl Harbor. In April 1945 his live reportage of Roosevelt's funeral merited a special recognition from the National Headliners Club as the year's best domestic broadcast. On yet another occasion *Radio Life Magazine* certified him as "the most 'listenable' commentator on the air."

Over the years Baukhage was variously associated with a couple of major Washington, D.C. outlets, WMAL and WRC, while serving as NBC's Washington correspondent. Starting in August 1948, he and Jim Gibbons co-anchored ABC-TV's pioneering ongoing newscast, *News and Views*. The groundbreaking quarter-hour at 7 o'clock persisted on six nights a week to April 1951.

Baukhage left radio in 1953 when a new leader at MBS claimed his salary was excessive and a quarter-hour news commentary was too long. Baukhage began writing again—initially an investment column for *The Register*, a newspaper of the Army, Navy and Air Force; and a column for *U.S. News & World Report* (1963–1967). Also in the 1960s he appeared on broadcasts of *Pentagon Reports*, a weekly series produced by the Armed

Forces Radio Network for American troops abroad.

Assessing Baukhage's broadcast career, a biographer wrote: "His politics were generally middle-of-the-road. Listeners regarded Baukhage as an informed, objective commentator who considered all sides of a controversial matter before commenting on it.... He kept himself informed by reading widely and by interviewing top political and military figures."

BAXTER, GEORGE. b. Dec. 13, 1904, Paris, France; d. Sept. 10, 1976, New York, N.Y. *Actor, Announcer.* **Series:** *The Career of Alice Blair* (actor, 1939–1940); *Grand Central Station* (ca. 1940s).

George Baxter's true claim to fame occurred in the form of celluloid—theatrical and television. Between 1929 and 1960 he appeared in 36 motion pictures while from 1954 to 1960 he turned up in dramatic roles on a dozen TV series, including: *Space Patrol* (1954); *The Adventures of Wild Bill Hickok* (1956); *Jane Wyman Presents the Fireside Theater* (1956); *Richard Diamond, Private Detective* (1957); *Dragnet* (1957); *The Life and Legend of Wyatt Earp* (1957–1958); *Goodyear Theater* (1958); *Letter to Loretta* (1958); *Sergeant Preston of the Yukon* (1958); *Maverick* (1958); *The Twilight Zone* (1959); and *Tightrope* (1960).

Among Baxter's movie credits, mostly of the B-film variety, were: *The Careless Age* (1929); *The Right to Love* (1930); *A Woman Commands* (1932); *Miss Fane's Baby is Stolen* (1934); *The Great Flirtation* (1934); *Restless Knights* (1935); *I Live My Life* (1935); *Son of Billy the Kid* (1949); *The Flying Saucer* (1950); *The Damned Don't Cry* (1950); *Tea for Two* (1950); *The Sword of Monte Cristo* (1951); *Scaramouche* (1952); *The Purple Mask* (1955); *The First Traveling Saleslady* (1956); *The Ten Commandments* (1956); and *The Purple Gang* (1960).

BEATTY, MORGAN. b. Sept. 6, 1902, Little Rock, Ark.; d. July 4, 1975, St. John's, Antigua and Barbuda. *Commentator, Emcee.* **Series:** *Military Analysis of the News* (commentator, 1942, 1945–1948); *Monitor* (co-host, 1956–1960); *News of the World* (commentator, 1946–1967).

Most historiographers readily identify Morgan Beatty as a conservative commentator, clearly to the right of center. Yet while he drew one of two long-running prestige assignments at NBC News, especially after Lowell Thomas left for CBS (the other being *Kaltenborn Edits the News*), Beatty's career was glossed over by most documentarians and entirely missed by some. Based on those findings, he seemingly didn't receive the respect he earned and there really isn't a satisfying explanation. For at least 21 years he had a weeknight quarter-hour where he delivered and assessed the world's current events. Only a handful of electronic journalists gained that much exposure to place an indelible imprint on American ears.

While in high school in Little Rock, Beatty launched a reporting career with a hometown newspaper. In succeeding years he was a print and wire service correspondent, ultimately rising to high levels within the ranks of the Associated Press. He gained widespread visibility by reporting a Mississippi flood for the Associated Press in 1927. Eyewitness accounts that emerged while he blanketed European capitals on the eve of World War II—including a couple of years spent in London—placed him in high esteem. Furthermore, he compiled the first extensive map of the continent's western front; because his data was so authentic, U.S. War Department officials included its details in strategy planning.

Hired by NBC in 1941, Beatty represented the chain in Washington, D.C., while reporting locally over WRC and WMAL. Within five years (some sources say three) he was editing and commenting on NBC's daily roundup of important global events, *News of the World*. Later, from 1969 to 1975, he wrote and taped five commentaries every week for the syndicated AP feature *NewsBreak*.

For six weeks in 1952 Beatty delivered a quarter-hour Saturday afternoon wrap-up of current events from Washington on NBC-TV's *Morgan Beatty*. He anchored a nightly quarter-hour news roundup over the Dumont Television network in 1954–1955, unmistakably one of the final features on the web before it folded. In 1955 Beatty interviewed human-interest figures, live or on film, with fascinating stories to share on NBC-TV's *People*, a Sunday afternoon half-hour entry that persisted for eight weeks.

BECK, JACKSON. b. July 23, 1912, New York, N.Y.; d. July 28, 2004, New York, N.Y. *Announcer, Actor.* **Series:** *The Adventures of Superman* (announcer and actor, 1940–ca. 1951); *Believe It or Not* (actor, ca. 1930s, 1940s); *Big Sister* (actor, ca. late 1930s–early 1940s); *Brownstone Theater* (actor, 1945); *The Busy Mr. Bingle* (actor, 1943); *By Popular Demand* (1938); *Calling All Cars* (actor, 1930s); *The Casebook of Gregory Hood* (actor, ca. 1949); *Casey, Crime Photographer* (actor, 1940s); *The CBS Radio Mystery Theater* (actor, 1970s, early 1980s); *The Cisco Kid* (actor, 1942–1945); *Cloak and Dagger* (actor, 1950); *The Clyde Beatty Show* (1950–1952); *Columbia Presents Corwin* (actor, 1944, 1945); *Creeps by Night* (actor, 1944); *Dangerously Yours* (actor, 1944); *Death Valley Days* (actor, ca. mid 1930s–mid 1940s); *Dimension X* (actor, 1950–1951); *Doc Barclay's Daughters* (actor, 1939–1940); *Easy Aces* (actor, ca. 1930s, 1940s); *The FBI in Peace and War* (actor, 1940s–1950s); *Five Minute Mysteries* (actor, 1946); *Grand Central Station* (actor, ca. 1940s); *Happy Island* (1944–1945); *Highroads to Health* (1959); *Hop Harrigan* (actor, 1940s); *The Jack Pepper Show* (actor, 1944); *Joe and Ethel Turp* (actor, 1943); *The Joe Dimaggio Show* (actor, 1949–1950); *Life Can Be Beautiful* (actor, ca. 1940s); *The Life of Mary Sothern* (actor, late 1930s); *The Man Behind the Gun* (1943); *The Man I Married* (actor, early 1940s); *The March of Time* (actor, ca. 1930s–early 1940s); *Mark Trail* (1950–1951); *Matinee Theater* (actor, 1944–1945); *The Milton Berle Show* (actor, ca. 1940s); *The Morey Amsterdam Show* (actor, 1948–1949); *Myrt and Marge* (actor, ca. 1930s); *The Mysterious Traveler* (actor, 1943–1952); *Mystery in the Air* (actor, 1947); *Mystery Theater* (actor, 1940s); *On Broadway* (actor, 1937–1938); *Philo Vance* (actor, 1948–1950); *Popeye the Sailor* (actor, 1935–1936); *Quick as a Flash* (actor, ca. mid 1940s–ca. early 1950s); *The Robert Q. Lewis Show* (actor, ca. 1950s); *The Shadow* (actor, ca. 1940s); *Society Girl* (actor, 1939–1940); *This Day Is Ours* (actor, late 1930s–1940); *The Timid Soul* (actor, 1941–1942); *Tom Corbett, Space Cadet* (1952); *The Witch's Tale* (actor, 1930s); *A Woman of America* (actor, 1943–1946); *Words at War* (actor, 1943–1945); *You Are There* (actor, 1947–1950); *Yours Truly, Johnny Dollar* (actor, 1960–1962); *X Minus One* (actor, 1955–1958).

Of the 58 network radio series documented for Jackson Beck, he acted in all but about a half-dozen, where he was the announcer, indicating a strong propensity for dramatic panache. He was the son of silent film thespian Max Beck so he came by it naturally. Allan Sloane, who contributed to the scripting of *The Man Behind the Gun*, claimed Beck's voice was "an instrument" and "he had a narrative skill that was unmatchable."

From his childhood in Far Rockaway, N.Y., Beck recalled: "In 1923 I was about ten years old. After my father brought home our first radio, word got out and not only neighbors but even strangers from nearby towns started coming to our house. We used to go to bed fairly early and often people were coming to our door so late that they were waking us up. On Sundays they came in very large numbers. Finally we had to put up a sign 'Don't come in.'"

Following high school Beck worked as a department store detective and elevator operator. There he overheard the accents of patrons with Italian, Grecian, Russian and other native tongues, proving invaluable for his life's work. By 1934 he was on the air, beginning with New York's WINS and WHN and moving to other metro outlets. The following year he and Paul Daniels wrote, produced and acted all the roles of a quarter-hour sustaining series, *Danny and August*, over New York's WBNX Wednesdays at 12:15 P.M. It wasn't uncommon for one or two people to pursue multiple tasks for a radio show at that time. Danny, a policeman on a beat, bought a paper each week at his pal August's newsstand. After the pair read the headlines, they turned the current events into narratives. Fifteen years hence, in December 1950, again on a New York outlet (WNEW), Beck introduced a debuting weekly narrative, *Radio History of the War*, aka *A History Book Wired for Sound*, which he announced weekly thereafter. By then he had established a profitable sideline of providing voiceovers for transcribed commercials for both radio and television.

Thinking back to his humble audio

beginnings, Beck allowed: "Announcers always went for the middle–American hard 'r.' It took me years to learn it, and when I did I got more work. When I was a child and grew up in New York, I didn't know 'r' was in the alphabet. I called my mother 'mutha' because that's the way my family spoke. And when I found it was necessary to roll your r's, or hit the r accent, emphasize the r, that's when I started to make a buck."

Beck participated on one of TV's first panel shows, *Charade Quiz*, on the Dumont network from 1947 to 1949. Later, for a decade the former radio man enjoyed one of the most durable runs as a video interlocutor, introducing one of the new medium's premier dramatic anthologies, *The U.S. Steel Hour* (1953–1955 on ABC and 1955–1963 on CBS). His penchant for acting shifted seamlessly into a host of tube-borne juvenile cartoons, too.

While Beck was the announcer for *Tom Corbett, Space Cadet*—which appeared between 1950 and 1955 successively on all four television webs (CBS, ABC, NBC, Dumont)—he provided voiceovers for the following animated series for the little tykes: a syndicated *Popeye* feature (1960–1963); NBC's *King Leonardo and His Short Subjects* (1960–1963); CBS's *Tennessee Tuxedo* (1963–1966); and *Batman* (1968–1970). Beck narrated one of his longrunning radio series for TV, too—*Superman*. From 1966 to 1969 it was reincarnated as a CBS cartoon. Reprising their radio voices were Bud Collyer (Clark Kent) and Joan Alexander (Lois Lane). More than a quarter-century after their premier on the ether, the old gang was together again. Beck also narrated NBC's 1978 weekly documentary about medical practitioners, *Lifeline*. In the summer of 1983 PBS reran it.

He was present at the organizational meeting of the American Federation of Radio Artists (AFRA) in July 1937, a coalition in which he took an active part. AFRA was the forerunner of the American Federation of Television and Radio Artists (AFTRA); Beck was not only elected to that body's national board of directors but became the organization's vice president. In due course he received the George Heller Gold Lifetime Membership Card Award for unremitting contributions to the union.

BECKER, SANFORD GEORGE. b. Feb. 19, 1922, New York, N.Y.; d. April 9, 1996, Calverton, Long Island, N.Y. *Actor, Announcer.* **Series:** *Backstage Wife* (1950s); *The Columbia Workshop* (mid 1940s); *Hilltop House*; *Life Can Be Beautiful* (actor); *Now Hear This* (actor, 1951); *The Shadow* (1951–1953); *Stepping Out* (1950); *Take It or Leave It* (ca. late 1940s); *Treasury Agent* (actor, 1947–1948); *Young Doctor Malone* (actor, 1947–1960).

Sandy Becker left WBT, Charlotte, in 1942 to serve in the U.S. Navy. He was formally discharged in 1948 although he returned to broadcasting earlier.

When his most memorable radio series faded—he portrayed the title character Jerry Malone in *Young Doctor Malone* during its final 13 years on the air (1947–1960)—Becker provided voiceovers for a trio of TV juvenile cartoons: *King Leonardo and His Short Subjects* (1960–1963); *The Underdog Show* (1966–1968); and *Go Go Gophers* (1968–1969). From the mid 1950s to the late 1960s he also hosted several local daily series on New York television outlets WABD and WNEW, some appealing especially to the small fry.

BEEMER, BRUCE BILL (BRACE). b. Dec. 9, 1902, Mount Carmel, Ill.; d. March 1, 1965, Oxford, Mich. *Actor, Announcer.* **Series:** *The Challenge of the Yukon*, aka *Sergeant Preston of the Yukon* (actor, 1941, 1953–1955); *The Lone Ranger* (announcer, ca. late 1930s–1941; actor, 1941–1956). **Aphorism:** *Hi-yo Silver!*

Such an adventurer was Brace Beemer that, at 14, he enlisted in the U.S. Army, becoming the youngest soldier in the American Expeditionary Forces during World War I. It was emblematic of the part he was to characterize over the long haul of his professional life.

A radio historiographer suggested it might have been H. Allen Campbell, a financial guru at Detroit station WXYZ in the 1930s, who—more than anyone else—was responsible for formation of the Mutual Broadcasting System. He prompted it by selling three more important outlets (Chicago's WGN, Cincinnati's WLW, New York's WOR) on the enormous value of *The Lone Ranger*. Campbell also discovered Brace Beemer reading poetry over an Indianapolis station. He had been a staff announcer and actor there since 1922, during commercial radio's incubation. Summoned to Detroit in 1932, Beemer became the interlocutor on WXYZ's legendary series, and briefly played the lead in *The Challenge of the Yukon*.

When Earl Graser, who portrayed the Ranger for several years, died in an automobile crash in 1941, Beemer was suddenly swept into the role he had been introducing for a few years. As a result, in millions of American homes his name and that unmistakable voice became synonymous with the West's most celebrated mythical crimefighter. At the peak of his career, he toured fairs and rodeos across America adorned with the trappings of his infamous role. Yet surprisingly, he was never involved with the subsequent movie or television incarnations that evolved from the series.

Unfortunately Beemer's distinguished voice worked against him after the final live broadcast of *The Lone Ranger* in September 1954 (there were repeats aired on network radio for two more years). He was unable to get back into radio because sponsors thought he sounded "too much like *The Lone Ranger*," which of course he did. After retiring, he devoted his time to raising racehorses on his Oxford farm outside Detroit. The legendary "masked rider of the plains" suffered a fatal heart attack at 62.

BELL, JOSEPH. b. July 13, 1912, California; d. March 1987, Centralia, Mo. *Announcer, Actor, Director.* **Series:** *The Big Guy* (actor, 1950); *Big Town* (director, ca. late 1930s–1940s); *The Bishop and the Gargoyle* (director, 1936–1937, 1940–1942); *The Collier Hour* (actor, 1927–1932); *David Amity* (actor, 1950–1951); *East of Cairo*, aka *Echoes of Cairo* (director, 1930); *The Gulf Headliners*, aka *The Will Rogers Show* (1933–1935); *House in the Country* (producer, 1941–1942); *My True Story* (actor, 1940s); *The New Penny* (actor, 1935–1936); *The Orange Lantern* (director, 1932–1933); *The Right to Happiness* (actor, ca. late 1930s–1940s); *Sherlock Holmes* (ca. early 1930s); *Twenty Thousand Years in Sing Sing* (interviewer, 1930s); *Uncle Jim's Question Bee* (1936–1939, ca. 1940–1941); *X-Minus One* (actor, 1955–1958).

BENNETT, BERN (born Bernard Blume). b. Oct. 19, 1921, Rochester, N.Y. *Announcer.* **Series:** *Rock 'n' Roll Dance Party* (1956); *Winner Take All* (ca. 1946–1952).

Bern Bennett joined CBS in New York as a staff announcer on May 1, 1944. In the late 1940s he became the announcer on radio's *Winner Take All*, following it to CBS Television in 1948 (to 1950). In 1950 he presented the musical competition *By Popular Demand* on CBS-TV. Other television announcing duties from New York, all on CBS: *Beat the Clock* (1950–1958), *The Steve Allen Show* (1952), *The Phil Silvers Show*, aka *You'll Never Get Rich* (1955–1959) and *To Tell the Truth* (1956–1960).

In 1960 Bennett transferred to Los Angeles and was the final CBS staff announcer in that city. "For almost 60 years he was the voice of CBS," a West Coast media observer affirmed. His voice filled legions of network billboards promoting upcoming CBS features. Bennett's permanent announcing assignments on CBS-TV included *The Clear Horizon* (1960–1961, 1962); *The Verdict is Yours* (1960–1962); *Your Surprise Package* (1961–1962); *The Danny Kaye Show* (1963–1967); and *The Jonathan Winters Show* (1967–1969). From 1962 to 1999 (an aggregate 38 events) Bennett introduced the *Tournament of Roses Parade* on New Year's Day. For years he ushered in two venerable daytime serials, *The Young and the Restless* (1973–2003) and *The Bold & the Beautiful* (1987–2004). He had been with CBS 59 years when he retired from full time duty in 2003.

BENSON, COURTNEY. b. Nov. 4, 1914, Vancouver, Canada; d. Feb. 5, 1995, Mount Kisco, N.Y. *Actor, Announcer.* **Series:** *Adventure Theater* (actor, 1977–1978); *Backstage Wife* (actor); *Big Sister* (actor); *Big Town* (actor); *The Cavalcade of America* (actor, ca. early to mid 1940s); *The Falcon* (actor, ca. 1940s); *Gangbusters* (1946–1948); *Lux Radio Theater* (actor, ca. 1940s); *Suspense* (actor); *Tennessee Jed* (1945–1947); *The CBS Radio Mystery Theater* (actor, 1970s–ca. early 1980s); *Theater Five* (actor, 1964–1965); *Wendy Warren and the News* (actor); *Young Widder Brown* (actor).

Courtney (Court) Benson received a law degree from the University of Toronto but made his livelihood in the performing arts. At 16 he portrayed an Indian (a Native

Canadian?) on a Calgary radio station, his first part on the ether. At 22 he aired hockey games for the Canadian Broadcasting Company. Between 1941 and 1945 he took time away from a promising career to go to Europe as a captain in the Canadian infantry during World War II. By 1946 he and his actress-wife Grace Matthews, a Toronto native, broke into New York radio. That year they became staples in a plethora of soap operas and crime dramas. (She was Margot Lane on *The Shadow* from 1946 to 1949 and played the leads on *Big Sister, The Brighter Day, Hilltop House, Soldier's Wife* and *The Story of Dr. Susan*. She gained a recurring role on *Just Plain Bill*, appeared in *The CBS Radio Mystery Theater* and, in 1968–1969, won a supporting role on CBS-TV's *The Guiding Light*.)

Benson, meanwhile, earned running roles on TV's *Young Mr. Bobbin* (1951–1952); *First Love* (1955); *The Doctors* (1960s); *The Edge of Night*; and *The Guiding Light*. He appeared in the movie *Dirtymouth* in 1970 and narrated industrial and educational films as an avocation.

BILLSBURY, RYE (born Michael Rye). *Actor, Announcer.* **Series:** *The Cisco Kid* (ca. 1940s–1950s); *The First Nighter* (actor, ca. 1952–1953); *Heartbeat Theater* (actor, ca. 1956–ca. 1960s); *Jack Armstrong, the All-American Boy* (actor, 1943–1944); *Ma Perkins* (actor); *Meet Millie* (actor, 1951–1954); *Tales of the Texas Rangers* (actor, 1950–1952).

Although Rye Billsbury starred as "Mark Dillon" on a tryout tape for *Gunsmoke* recorded on June 11, 1949, the audition performance was never aired and when the show at last went out over the ether on April 26, 1952, it was without Billsbury as "Matthew Dillon." Nevertheless, he was linked with a couple of legendary western features on radio. Even better, he secured a place for himself in a plethora of animated TV series.

Under his own moniker, Michael Rye, the actor made a mint out of voiceovers for the small fry: *The Lone Ranger* (1966–1969, CBS, in which he played the lead); *Hot Wheels* (1969–1971, ABC); *Sky Hawks* (1969–1971, ABC, again the lead); *Super Friends* and similar monikers (1977–1983, 1984–?, ABC); *Scooby and Scrappy-Doo* and similar monikers (1979–1981, 1983–?, 1985–1986, ABC); *The Super Globetrotters* (announcer, 1979–1980, NBC); *The Smurfs* (1981–?, NBC); *Spider-Man* (1981–1982, NBC); *The Incredible Hulk/Amazing Spider-Man Hour* (1982–?, NBC); *Super Friends* (1984–1985, ABC); *The 13 Ghosts of Scooby-Doo* (1985–1986, ABC); *The Gummi Bears* (1985–1989, NBC; 1989–1990, ABC); *The Super Powers Team—Galactic Guardians* (1986, ABC); *The Flintstone Kids 'Just Say No' Special* (1988, ABC); *Tale Spin* (1990–1994, syndication); *The Pirates of Dark Water* (1991–1992, ABC); plus several more.

Rye also turned up in a quartet of full-length motion pictures: *Two Lost Worlds* (1951, using the Michael Rye moniker); *Hands of a Stranger* (1962); *Cougar Country* (1970, as the narrator); and *The Nativity* (1986, in multiple voiceover roles).

BINGMAN, FRANK. b. April 9, 1914, Athens, Ohio; d. Aug. 21, 1988, Warrenton, Va. *Announcer, Actor.* **Series:** *The Abbott and Costello Show* (1940s); *The Cavalcade of America* (actor, 1940s); *Hollywood Players*, aka *The Cresta Blanca Hollywood Players* (1946–1947); *The Jack Benny Program* (commercial spokesman, ca. 1937–1941); *The Joan Davis Show* (actor, 1940s–ca. 1950); *My Friend Irma* (ca. late 1940s–early 1950s); *Straight Arrow* (1948–1951).

Although he expected to pursue a career in electronics, Frank Bingman was awarded a scholarship to Cincinnati Drama School upon his high school graduation. There he acted and created sets which projected him into radio where he played small roles (one gained him $5 for five words!). Bingman performed in dramatic narratives over Mutual's WLW from 1934–1937 and as an announcer at WKRC, a CBS affiliate. His wife, Madelyn, an early disc jockey and possibly the first of her gender in the breed, maintained a two-hour morning show over WKRC during their Cincinnati hiatus.

Moving to California in 1937, Bingman took a couple of staff announcing jobs—KHJ, Hollywood (1937–1939), and KFI, Los Angeles' NBC affiliate (1939–1941). Following a stint with the U.S. Signal Corps in the Pacific Theater during World War II, he sought work in electronics, his first love. When that didn't happen, he returned to the airwaves, becoming a disc jockey and interlocutor for a myriad of comic and drama series. Bingman quit radio in 1954 and opened a hobby shop. But he soon left it to return to broadcasting, eventually becoming a local TV news director.

He retired from full time responsibilities in 1972, confining himself to occasional weekends in 20th Century–Fox trailers (he announced coming attractions in theaters for 13 years, his steadiest employment) and made brief appearances in TV series. Bingman ultimately moved to Warrenton, Va., and became part of its community theater. In 1986 he was critically acclaimed as Henry Drummond in *Inherit the Wind*.

BIVENS, WILLIAM C. b. March 24, 1915, Wadesboro, N.C.; d. Jan. 15, 1984, Charlotte, N.C. *Announcer.* **Series:** *The Fred Waring Show*, under multiple appellations (1942–1949); *The Harry James Show* (1943–1944); *Vox Pop* (1943–1944).

Bill Bivens broke into radio at age 12 at WRBU in Gastonia, N.C. (which subsequently became Charlotte's WSOC). He moved to Greenville, S.C., next, where he rose to chief announcer at WFBC by the time he was 18. That same year, 1933, he went to the CBS outlet in Washington, D.C., WJSV, and occasionally subbed for Arthur Godfrey on his *Sundial* early morning DJ program. From 1937 to 1941 CBS sent Bivens to its 50,000-watt chain owned-and-operated affiliate in Charlotte, WBT. Afterward he settled in New York City, acquiring network announcing status with a handful of shows. He was soon prominently identified with the Harry James and Fred Waring orchestras. In 1965 Bivens returned to his native Tar Heel roots, finishing his broadcasting career at WBT-FM (later renamed WBCY). He retired in 1968 and became the inaugural director of the news center at Central Piedmont Community College, an institution that he had assisted in establishing.

BLAINE, JAMES RALPH (born James William Bunn). b. Dec. 26, 1924, Greenville, Texas; d. March 18, 1967, Wilton, Conn. *Announcer, Actor, Emcee.* **Series:** *Criminal Casebook* (actor, 1948); *Get Rich Quick* (1948); *Ladies Be Seated* (master of ceremonies, late 1940s); *The Lanny Ross Show* (1949–1950); *Superstition* (1948–1949).

Jimmy Blaine not only could speak but could also heist a tune, and did so regularly on television. After winning a local talent contest in 1947, he moved to New York City where he joined WNEW Radio as a singer. Soon he became a featured vocalist for *Stop the Music*'s 1949–1952 ABC-TV run. Meanwhile, he occasionally showed up in the cast of NBC-TV's *Howdy Doody Show* (1947–1960). Blaine introduced comic Jackie Gleason in an early television vehicle, *Cavalcade of Stars*, on Dumont Television (1949–ca. 1952). He announced *The Speidel Show*, aka *The Paul Winchell and Jerry Mahoney Show*, on NBC-TV in 1950. For a month that same year he interspersed hosting with his singing on a Dumont game-and-variety feature, *Hold That Camera*.

The host-vocalist presided over a music discussion series, *Jimmy Blaine's Junior Edition*, in 1951 on ABC-TV featuring tunes for teens. He was emcee of a fleeting ABC-TV variety series, *The Billy Daniels Show*, in 1952. Blaine was master of ceremonies for that chain's *Music from Cedar Grove*, aka *Music from Meadowbrook* (1953, 1956). He introduced the infamous mentalist, Joseph Dunninger, on *The Dunninger Show* in 1955 (NBC-TV) and 1956 (ABC-TV). Between 1957 and 1960, he announced Hanna-Barbera's initial network animated cartoon show on NBC-TV, *Ruff and Reddy*. Forming Jimbo Productions, he penned a couple of special entries for ABC Radio, 1965's *Let's Keep Christmas* and 1966's *Sing Out for Uncle Sam*. Blaine died of a heart attack at age 42.

BLAIR, FRANK. b. May 30, 1915, Yemassee, S.C.; d. March 14, 1995, Hilton Head Island, S.C. *Announcer, Emcee.* **Series:** *Helen Holden, Government Girl* (1941–1942); *Monitor* (co-host, 1955–1959; host, 1964–1966).

When Frank Blair was an infant, his family moved to Walterboro, S.C. and then to nearby Charleston. He quit pre-med studies in 1935 to join a Southern stock company which led him into radio that year with Charleston's WCSC. Before 1935 ended he took a newscasting post at WIS, Columbia, the state capital. Two years hence he was at Greenville's WFBC as program director. Within a few months in late 1937 Blair left his native Palmetto State to accept a job at WOL,

Washington, D.C., which came replete with network announcing opportunities for MBS. He interrupted his airtime during World War II to serve with the U.S. Naval Air Corps beginning in 1942.

Blair's most widely recognized contributions to broadcasting were in television, not radio. In the summer of 1951 he hosted *Heritage*, an hour-long cultural series focused on music and art telecast live by NBC from the National Gallery of Art in Washington. For more than two years during 1951–1953, he moderated a weekly half-hour roundtable discussion from the nation's capital, *Georgetown University Forum*, on the Dumont television network. It featured faculty and guest experts dialoguing on a variety of contemporary topics. From 1963 to 1965 Blair delivered the news that was especially tailored to youngsters on *Sunday*, a 60-minute NBC news-and-information series. But unequivocally, his most memorable coup was as the weekday newscaster on NBC's *Today*, a slot he filled for 22 years, 1953–1975, setting the pace for early morning headline dispatches then and now. In that epoch he worked alongside anchors Dave Garroway, John Chancellor, Hugh Downs, Barbara Walters, Frank McGee and Jim Hartz. After he left, Blair co-hosted *Over Easy* with Hugh Downs in 1980–1981, a daily half-hour PBS televised public affairs presentation aimed at seniors.

Born near the water and wedding a coastal South Carolina girl from Beaufort, Blair and family—including seven children—maintained a strong interest in boating which they practiced regularly at Irvington, N.Y. His memoir, *Let's Be Frank about It*, was published in 1979. The devout Southerner wrote: "It became painfully obvious to me that network announcers had no regional accents. I knew that if I were to get ahead in radio, I would have to sound as if I came from nowhere in particular." *The Beaufort Gazette* declared that Blair began his successful career in radio and television "with absolutely no hint of a Southern accent." He retired to Hilton Head Island. Behind his façade of suits, ties and white shirts worn while delivering the day's headlines had always beat a heart tinged with humor. On his final *Today* appearance in 1975, asked where his native hamlet of Yemassee got its name, Blair replied: "It's an Indian word. When they were trying to figure out what to call their new settlement, a tribal leader mused pensively, 'Well, yemasee here.'"

BLOCK, MARTIN. b. Feb. 3, 1903, Los Angeles, Calif.; d. Sept. 19, 1967, Englewood, N.J. *Announcer, Disc Jockey.* **Series:** *The Chesterfield Supper Club* (1944–1947); *Chesterfield Time* (1943–1944); *Kay Kyser's Kollege of Musical Knowledge* (ca. 1940s); *The Martin Block Show* (host, 1954–1961); *Pepper Young's Family* (ca. 1950s); *Your Hit Parade*.

A media website asserted: "Announcer Martin Block was the first radio disc jockey to become a star in his own right." A biographer opined: "Many radio people feel he was to radio what Bing Crosby was to recording—the first to introduce an intimate, personal style rather than a disembodied voice of authority." Block presided over a local show whose fame went national. *Make Believe Ballroom* on New York's WNEW debuted on Feb. 3, 1935, and persisted to Jan. 1, 1954, frequently consuming three-and-a-half hours of daily airtime. It proffered the fantasy that a quartet of big bands was playing tunes in a crystal-chandeliered venue while the show actually emanated from a simple radio studio adorned with a couple of turntables, a microphone and a DJ. "Block working off cued transcriptions makes a corking emcee," assessed *Variety*. "Block carries out the illusion with style.... Voice, personality, dance-orchestra knowledge all impress."

Credit for originating the concept went to Al Jarvis, a West Coast DJ who for years ruled the airwaves over Los Angeles' KFWB and KLAC. Around 1932 he played discs under the sobriquet *The World's Biggest Make Believe Ballroom*. Meanwhile Martin Block, Jarvis's junior assistant at KFWB, left L.A. in late 1934 to pursue his fortune in Gotham. Block had broken into radio a short time earlier, reading commercials on a Tijuana, Mexico, station. Block and Jarvis later appeared in a 1949 motion picture about their industry, *Make Believe Ballroom*. Block and more than two dozen contemporaries also turned up in the 1951 full-length theatrical feature *Disc Jockey*, capitalizing on a charmed nation's fascination with their profession.

Sponsors of Block's *Make Believe Ballroom* estimated that he sold $750 million worth of goods. With national syndication of his show's concept in 1940, by the end of World War II Block was carrying home $22,000 a week. He gained such widespread notoriety that numerous major market chains sent DJs to New York to learn his formula and to try to replicate his feat. When WNEW moved into new facilities on Fifth Avenue, a simulated ballroom—including chandelier and black linoleum—was added for exclusive origination of Block's show.

In June 1947 he returned to California, recording his WNEW programs a few days before they aired. Near Encino, he bought a small ranch, yet continued to influence disc jockey programming on dual coasts and in the markets in between. According to one reporter, nevertheless, "Angelenos considered him an obnoxious, arrogant, know-it-all New Yorker and tuned him out by the millions." In the fall of 1948 he returned to Gotham to take advantage of budding horizons in television. From 1948 to 1950 he announced *The Perry Como Show* on NBC-TV. Block simply wasn't cut out for television, he quickly discovered, and again concentrated on his opportunities for awhile at WNEW Radio.

When ABC signed him to spin discs 23 hours a week in 1954 on its WABC New York outlet—a contract that included a daily network show—Block was paid $250,000 annually, a princely sum for mere platters and patter. Newspaper ads touted: "It's that old Block magic, only now there's more of it, at a new time, new spot on your dial." For 15 months (1956–1957) during his extensive ABC Radio run, Block also presided over a daily namesake half-hour variety series on ABC-TV, *The Martin Block Show*. After the network radio run ended in 1961, the master of turntables transitioned to New York's WOR, spinning discs until his death six years later. Two decades beyond that, in 1988 he was inducted into the Radio Hall of Fame. In Block's way, perhaps more than anybody else, he had earned respect for DJs everywhere.

BOLTON, JOSEPH REEVES, II. b. Sept. 8, 1910, Flushing, N.Y.; d. Aug. 13, 1986, Santa Monica, Calif. *Announcer.* **Series:** *The 1937 Radio Show* (1937); *Go Get It,* aka *Melody Treasure Hunt* (co-emcee, 1941–1943); *Uncle Don* (1939–1940).

Joe Bolton is one of many announcers credited with working beside *Uncle Don* (Carney), a New York-based juvenile series carried by WOR from September 1928 to February 1949, with a year as an MBS feature. Although Bolton's own show business career was diversified, much of it was devoted to adolescents. From his teens he performed with a jazz band in and around New York City. When the group disbanded, he formed another duo, "The Two Man Band," which not only made public appearances but also played on New York radio. He left the band after WOR hired him in 1928 as an announcer.

Subsequently, in the early 1930s Bolton began a cross-country trek that carried him first to CBS in New York followed by stations in Philadelphia, Sioux Falls, S.D., and Los Angeles. He also turned up as sportscaster in a plethora of movie theater newsreels. Returning to radio following service in the U.S. Army during World War II, Bolton took a post as broadcasting director of the U.S. Office of War Information in Washington. Presently he made his way back to New York to work for WOR a second time, then moved to nearby WNEW.

In the mid 1950s everything changed. Bolton appeared as "Officer Joe" on the debuting local kids' TV series *The Clubhouse Gang* in 1955. It was a role he was to be identified with for 17 years. A year after the series ended in September 1957, Bolton (as "Officer Joe") was back on WPIX-TV hosting *The Three Stooges* films. He was soon taking the character out of the studio for personal appearances, too. *The Three Stooges Funhouse* lasted from 1958 to 1961. Bolton as "Officer Joe" presided over *The Dick Tracy Cartoon Show* (1961–1963) followed by *The Mighty Hercules Show, The Felix the Cat Show* and *The Little Rascals Show* on WPIX-TV. He also appeared in a couple of movies during the period: *Stop! Look! and Laugh!* (1960) and *The Outlaws is Coming* (1965). His kids' series ended in 1972 but Bolton stayed on at WPIX-TV as an announcer for four more years, retiring in 1976 to the warmer climes of California. In his final decade he taught broadcast history while enrolled as a student at a southern California university.

BOND, DAVID FORD. b. Oct. 23, 1904, Louisville, Ky.; d. Aug. 15, 1962, St. Croix,

U.S. Virgin Islands. *Announcer.* **Series:** *Alias Jimmy Valentine* (1938–1939); *American Melody Hour* (commercial spokesman, 1941–1948); *Backstage Wife* (mid 1940s–1953); *Believe It or Not* (ca. 1930s); *Cities Service Band of America*, and analogous monikers (1930–1953); *College Prom* (1935–1936); *The Collier Hour* (ca. 1929–1932); *David Harum* (1936–1951); *Easy Aces* (1941–1945); *Just Plain Bill* (ca. 1930s); *The Kraft Music Hall*; *Lora Lawton* (1943–1950); *Manhattan Merry-Go-Round* (1932–1949); *Monday Merry-Go-Round* (1941–1942); *Nona from Nowhere* (1950–1951); *Orphans of Divorce* (1939–1942); *Stella Dallas* (ca. late 1930s–ca. mid 1940s); *Your Family and Mine* (1938–1940). **Aphorism:** *Keep it clean with Energine!*

One of the foremost announcers of radio soap opera, Ford Bond maintained a rapid-fire staccato delivery that could be instantly recognized. He was the exclusive commercial spokesman and narrator for a trio of serialized melodramas underwritten by B.T. Babbitt (Bab-O, Babbitt's Best, Lycons and other brands). Exuding a distinct tremolo along with a deep base timbre, Bond dispatched a compelling urgency to buy. "Compare grease-dissolving Bab-O with your former lazy cleanser," he'd petition. "Then see if you could ever go back to any less modern method!" He typically spelled the name of the sponsor's flagship commodity: "Beeee-aaaa-beeee (long pause) ohh-hhh!" adding: "Put it on your marketing list. To save extra steps, get *two* cans—one for the bathroom, one for the kitchen!"

Having begun singing at age five, by seven, young David Ford Bond was a tenor in a boys' choir. With eight sons and no daughters in the family, the Bonds actually produced enough boys for their own homegrown choir! Ford, the third son, became a boy soprano at Christ Church Cathedral in Louisville. During the same period he was taking piano and violin lessons. At 14 he started singing professionally, traveling many places to perform before audiences. His inaugural radio appearance occurred at 17 on July 19, 1922, when he sang over hometown station WHAS. Following his graduation from Louisville's Male High School, Bond went to Chicago for further voice training and vocal engagements, and earned a degree from the University of Chicago.

After performing on some other stations, young Bond accepted a full time spot at WHAS as head announcer, musical director and general program manager. He maintained some concert gigs as a sideline. As he entered radio professionally, he also decided to drop his first name (David) and be known merely as Ford Bond from that time forward. In late 1929, at the age of 25, he joined the announcing staff at NBC in New York City. Before long he aired as a freelance announcer over the CBS and MBS chains, too.

For 23 years Bond held broadcasting's most durable sponsor-announcer connection as the commercial voice of the Cities Service Oil Co. In the same epoch he appeared numerous times every week on programs packaged by producers Frank and Anne Hummert for Sterling Drugs Inc. (including brand names Bayer, Dr. Lyons, Energine, Haley's, Phillips and an extensive line of health, beauty and personal care aids). A quivering *Keep it clean with Energine!* was possibly Bond's most potent idiom, becoming a part of the vernacular of many savvy Americans as a consequence of his repetitious use of the phrase on multiple musicals, crime detective dramas and serialized narratives.

In 1942 he formed Ford Bond Productions, commonly packaging and distributing transcribed features to as many as 300 radio and television stations. Meanwhile, capitalizing on the voice training of his youth, he joined a lecture circuit. He also became a radio and television consultant to the political campaigns of Gov. Thomas E. Dewey of New York and President Dwight D. Eisenhower. Married to concert soprano Lois Bennett, Bond developed a resort hotel, Estate of Good Hope, in the Virgin Islands after leaving radio in 1953.

BOONE, FOREST E. *Commercial Spokesman.* **Series:** *Information Please* (commercial spokesman, ca. 1940–1944); *The Jack Benny Program* (commercial spokesman, 1944–1955); *Your All-Time Hit Parade* (commercial spokesman, 1943–1944); *Your Hit Parade* (commercial spokesman, ca. late 1930s/early 1940s–1953).

Tobacco auctioneer F.E. Boone of Lexington, Ky. was one of two celebrated commercial spokesmen (the other, L.A. "Speed" Riggs) for the American Tobacco Co. and its flagship product, Lucky Strike cigarettes, featured on a handful of memorable shows during radio's golden age. Boone was engaged by the firm's president, George Washington Hill, a man exhibiting a savvy predilection for applying innovative marketing and sales techniques sufficiently ahead of his contemporaries. Hill set high standards in broadcast advertising and promotion. Doubling Boone's annual salary as an auctioneer to $25,000, Hill directed him to repetitively chant (a Hill advertising trademark, incidentally) during a couple of 90-second commercials on all the Lucky-sponsored broadcasts. Using a monotone style, Boone rolled out a rapid-fire spiel that couldn't be easily deciphered but was spectacular anyway: *Hey TWENTY NINE nine nine nine nine nine, roundem roundem roundem roundem roundem, am I right at thirty thirty thirty thirty thirty thirty thirty thirty thirty thirty THIRTY ONE thirty one thirty one one one one one....* Boone continued until he inevitably arrived at the number 38—all of this reminiscent of real tobacco auctions. Habitually, he finished with the cry: *Sol-l-l-d to A-merican!*

Following the sound of a clicking telegraph, announcer Basil Ruysdael or one of his colleagues concluded the inimitable sales pitch: "From men who know tobacco best ... it's Luckies, two to one!" An authoritative voice put in: "LS/MFT ... LS/MFT ... Lucky Strike Means Fine Tobacco!" To increase the commercial's effectiveness, LS/MFT was added to the bottom of every Lucky Strike pack and carton. It quickly became a part of the American vernacular, reinforcing the pains of Boone and Ruysdael.

Boone ultimately transitioned from aural-only broadcasting to video, appearing in the same sponsor's missives on the extensions of the shows American Tobacco underwrote in radio (*The Jack Benny Program* and *Your Hit Parade* were foremost). There an auction setting was filmed as a backdrop for the infamous plugs that had been ringing in listeners' ears for years. Boone and his peers were sometimes credited for ushering in relatively novel methods of broadcast commercials in that day. Not only did they sell cigarettes by the billions, their marketing skills evolved into a noteworthy byproduct that is still cited by students of modern advertising techniques.

BRADLEY, TRUMAN. b. Feb. 8, 1905, Sheldon, Mo.; d. July 28, 1974, Los Angeles, Calif. *Announcer.* **Series:** *The Dinah Shore Show* (1942–1943); *The Drene Show*, aka *The Don Ameche Show* (ca. 1946–1947); *Easy Aces* (actor, 1932–?); *The Ford Sunday Evening Hour* (1932–1938); *The Frank Sinatra Show* (1944–1945); *The Hinds Honey and Almond Cream Program*, aka *The Burns and Allen Show* (1939–1940); *Hollywood Playhouse* (1940); *Jack Armstrong, the All-American Boy* (ca. mid 1930s); *The Lady Esther Screen Guild Theater* (1942–1947); *The Prudential Family Hour of Stars* (1948–1950); *The Raleigh Cigarette Program*, aka *The Red Skelton Show* (1941–1944); *The Royal Gelatin Hour*, aka *The Rudy Vallee Show* (ca. late 1930s); *Shirley Temple Time* (1939); *The Story of Mary Marlin* (ca. mid 1930s); *Suspense* (1943–1947).

As a youth Truman Bradley won a statewide debating championship. He subsequently attended Missouri State Teacher's College on a scholarship for three years and studied forensics at Kansas City School of Law. He left school to sell electric ware for Westinghouse at a salary of $500 weekly. His Kansas City friend Goodman Ace, of radio's *Easy Aces*, meanwhile, urged him to try the stage. Bradley gave up his lucrative career in 1927 and was quickly subdued by the footlights. After entering vaudeville, he toured with the Henry Duffy Players for a while. A year hence he migrated to Hollywood to run his sister's publishing business.

Still stage struck, however, he launched a radio career in 1929 at Hollywood's KMTR, although his tenure there was brief. Colleague Harry Von Zell persuaded him to follow him to New York City where—in 1930—CBS hired Bradley as a staff announcer. Moving to Chicago in 1932, he joined CBS affiliate WBBM as an announcer and newscaster and was soon introducing and acting in a myriad of nationally heard series.

One of his major radio assignments was announcing *The Ford Sunday Evening Hour*, which originated weekly in Detroit. By late 1939 CBS reported that Bradley had racked up 39,000 miles making round-trip excursions by air between Chicago and Detroit (on propeller-driven planes and sans frequent flyer clubs, no less!). At the same time Bradley was writing, producing, announcing and acting in multiple shows and working in executive positions, too. As a sideline, in 1937 he and his sister Elene purchased a cosmetics manufacturing concern. Returning in 1940 to the West Coast, he picked up newscasting responsibilities at Los Angeles' KNX. He left Red Skelton's program in February 1942 for a tour in the U.S. Army but was on the job with Skelton again by October of that year.

Between 1938 and 1952 Bradley appeared in 37 motion pictures, mostly B-movies but also a couple of box office superlatives. They included *Young Dr. Kildare* (1938); *Northwest Passage* (1940); *Murder Among Friends* (1941); *Lone Star Ranger* (1942); *The Horn Blows at Midnight* (1945); *I Wonder Who's Kissing Her Now* (1947); *Call Northside 777* (1948); and *Fighter Squadron* (1948). He played a radio announcer or was the narrator in no fewer than 10 of those 37 cinematic features. From 1955–1957 Bradley introduced the syndicated TV anthology *Science Fiction Theater*, majoring on UFOs, space survival and psychic phenomena.

BRANDT, LYNN. *Sportscaster.* **Series:** *NBC Sports.*

Lynn Brandt was an NBC college football play-by-play sportscaster in 1937. From 1938–1942 he was a combination news-and-sports reporter at dual Chicago outlets WENR and WMAQ.

BRANDT, MELVILLE S. b. June 18, 1919, Brooklyn, N.Y. *Announcer.* **Series:** *The Adventures of Frank Merriwell* (1947–1949 and replayed on some stations in syndication in the 1970s); *Monitor* (co-communicator, ca. 1957–1958); *When a Girl Marries* (1947–ca. 1951).

Educated at Brooklyn College and Columbia University as a speech major and drama society participant, Mel Brandt played in summer stock with the Caravan Theatre. His intent to open on the Broadway stage was interrupted when he enlisted in the Army in February 1941. For the next three-and-a-half years he was an announcer on the Office of War Information's *Voice of America* broadcasts produced in Iceland. While touring Scandinavia with the Army, he performed in *Angel Street* and *Heaven Can Wait* at the Copenhagen Royal Theatre.

Returning home, Brandt was a freelance actor in radio and television until one day in 1947 when he reported to an agency for an audition. Mistakenly, the officials thought he was trying out for an announcer's job. When he didn't object, Brandt was hired to narrate NBC Radio's daytime serial *When a Girl Marries*. "That led to all the breaks I've had so far," he disclosed a decade afterward.

Brandt was in the cast of the continuing romantic drama *Faraway Hill*, a weekly primetime series that appeared on the Dumont "network" (then consisting of just *two* stations, in New York City and Washington, D.C.) for 12 weeks in 1946. While not many people witnessed that embryonic exhibition, it possessed many of the elements that were to characterize video soap opera in the years ahead. Between 1955 and 1957 he was the "voiceover" announcer for NBC-TV's *Producers' Showcase*. From 1957 to 1958 Brandt was the "story editor"-host of the NBC-TV weekday drama anthology *Modern Romances*. It was Brandt's voice the fans heard delivering the opening epigraph of NBC's *From These Roots* weekdays between 1958 and 1961: "From these roots grow branch, leaf and flower ... children of the sheltering earth, ripening into the tumult of the seasons ... generation unto generation." From 1962 to 1975 his dulcet tones echoed behind the chain's Peacock symbol, reminding viewers that "The following program is brought to you in living color on NBC."

Meanwhile, Brandt announced the video version of *The Bell Telephone Hour* (1959–1968) and the *G.E. College Bowl* (1963–1967), both NBC productions. He narrated an NBC-TV documentary for children, *Animal Secrets*, in 1966–1967 and again in 1968. And in 1981–1982 he was the announcer on the web's *Saturday Night Live*. Brandt was elected president of the New York chapter of the American Federation of Television and Radio Artists (AFTRA) in late 1965. In mid 1967 he assumed the presidency of the national body. In retirement, Brandt moved to New Port Richey, Fla.

BRANDT, SAM. *Announcer.* **Series:** *We Deliver the Goods* (1944).

In a show about heroism during battle exhibiting the U.S. Maritime Service's Merchant Marines, Boatswain Mate Second

Class Sam Brandt announced while radio actor Howard Culver was "your Maritime narrator."

BRECKINRIDGE, MARY MARVIN. b. 1905, New York, N.Y.; d. Dec. 11, 2002, Washington, D.C. *Correspondent.* **Series:** CBS *News of Europe* (correspondent, 1939–1940); *World News Today* (correspondent, 1940).

Enumerating her incalculable avant-garde endeavors over a lifetime, a eulogist at the memorial service for Mary Marvin Breckinridge compared the intrepid journalist to the original Eve, contemplating the Apple of Life and thinking to herself, "Why not?" It seemed appropriate, considering where she had been.

The only feminine member of "the Murrow Boys," translating into gargantuan recognition among golden age newscasters, Breckinridge is so distinguished because of "historical accuracy," according to Murrow Boys biographers Stanley Cloud and Lynne Olson. They profiled 11 reporters (10 men and Breckinridge) who comprised an elite coterie of professionals appointed by CBS chief overseas correspondent Edward R. Murrow to tell the developing Second World War story for the chain. When he hired her, she was an American socialite, then 33. Breckinridge was assigned to Amsterdam with the admonition: "When you report the [Nazi] invasion of Holland, or I report the invasion of England, understand the situation. Don't say the streets are rivers of blood. Say that the little policeman I usually say hello to every morning is not there today." Cloud and Olson submitted, "Pictures in the air were what Murrow wanted. He himself painted them brilliantly." He taught his minions to do so, too.

At first glance, Breckinridge appeared an unlikely candidate for such a responsible post. She came from affluence, even being introduced to the British monarch while a debutante. She proved to be much more than a dim-witted social butterfly, nonetheless. Her folks instilled in her a desire for adventure and travel. Prior to the First World War she journeyed to Europe thrice; when it ended, she went to China and Japan. She attended a dozen schools before enrolling at Vassar College and wasn't expelled from any, her mother proudly noted!

Breckinridge graduated from Vassar in 1927 with a degree in modern history and languages. While there she joined others to form the National Student Federation, becoming its president. That body embraced collegians all over America to foster global communications among academics seeking to boost peaceful prospects. Ed Murrow was elected the group's leader in the third year following Breckinridge's term, thus they became friends before she became one of the Boys. She exhibited leadership qualities naturally, meanwhile. Her great grandpa was ex–U.S. VP John C. Breckinridge, a Kentucky Democrat who was his party's candidate for president against Abraham Lincoln. Her maternal grandpa was tire tycoon B.F. Goodrich of Ohio. Her background, therefore, was vested in prestige and social prominence.

The year following her college graduation, Breckinridge became an aviatrix, the first of her gender to be certified in Maine, where her family owned a vacation retreat. Subsequently, she was a horseback courier for the Frontier Nursing Service (FNS), the earliest association of U.S. nurse-midwives, launched by her cousin, also named Mary Marvin Breckinridge. At that point the aviatrix—demonstrably unconventional to a fault—labeled herself "Marvin" to distinguish between them. The sobriquet stuck and some persisted in referring to her by that moniker throughout her life. Working for the FNS, she served in isolated stretches of the Appalachian Mountains in eastern Kentucky. FNS contributed significantly to decreasing by roughly 70 percent the maternal rate of death in the territory.

Requested by her cousin to go to New York in 1930 to learn cinematography so a FNS capital-raising flick could be produced, Marvin was independently tutored by a proficient motion picture photographer. After a few lessons, she put on a one-woman show: she wrote a script, gave directions for operating hand-cranked cameras and specified details for lighting while riding on horseback in excess of 600 miles for the finished product. The superb, poignant silent documentary, *The Forgotten Frontier*, about the nurses and gratified mountaineers they assisted, is still screened at exhibitions where the accomplishments of distaff moviemakers are showcased. The American Film Institute cited it as a historic classic.

Breckinridge was introduced to domestic politics as an intern in the Washington congressional office of Arizona Democrat Isabella Selmes Greenway, her cousin and godmother. While a secretarial assistant to Jouette Shouse, chair of the executive committee of the Democratic National Committee, Breckinridge met a foreign service officer from Dayton, Ohio, Jefferson Patterson, a bachelor 15 years her senior. Patterson, an heir to the National Cash Register Co. fortune, was even more affluent than she. He would become her spouse in time.

The next challenge Breckinridge set for herself was learning still photography through a year-long course at a New York institute founded by sophisticated camera connoisseur Clarence White. The encounter refocused her life into photojournalism. She did well, soon selling text and accompanying illustrations to *Life, Harper's Bazaar, Junior League, Town & Country, Vogue* and similar periodicals, including several metropolitan dailies. With multiple assignments in hand, she sailed for Europe in July 1939, intending to be away for six weeks. News reached her that Hitler's troops had crossed the border into Poland while she was at Lucerne, Switzerland. The Lucerne Music Festival she had gone to cover for *Town & Country* was suspended and all the other events she had commitments for were cancelled. Her original mission evaporated overnight.

Breckinridge went to London, anticipating getting out of Europe as quickly as possible. But she had second thoughts. "It now seems foolish to run away from the most interesting thing that I could be doing on earth right now," she wrote her mom, who was anxiously awaiting word back in America. Considering what was happening around her, it was relatively easy for Breckinridge to line up replacement magazine work. After all, she was then in the world's global hot spot. Having met Ed Murrow a few years before through the National Student Association, she looked him and his wife Janet up in London. Murrow was so intrigued with the magazine assignments she had acquired, he asked her to appear on CBS and share some of her experiences with the home audience. She did so on at least three occasions at his beckon.

Cloud and Olson reported, "Murrow didn't touch her script." Unknown to her, he had asked the CBS brass in New York to be listening. She displayed "a natural radio voice—strong, clear, and confident, with an upper-class American accent ... cool and self-possessed.... Unlike her male counterparts, Breckinridge never showed any nervousness about broadcasting," the authors affirmed.

Murrow liked her third performance so much that he proffered a job as a CBS correspondent in Amsterdam, The Netherlands. Breckinridge accepted. As a matron of high society, her appointment seemed out of character to some, including news chief Ed Klauber, Murrow's boss, who along with CBS owner-chairman William S. Paley even had male secretaries. Klauber thought some of Murrow's hires were eccentric yet he didn't oppose him. "Give the human side of the war, be honest, be neutral and talk like yourself," Murrow urged as she departed for Amsterdam.

Said Cloud and Olson, "Breckinridge was adept at taking complex issues and translating them into human terms as Murrow wanted.... Even the bastards in New York were forced to agree that Breckinridge was a success." Murrow wrote to her a few weeks into her appointment, "Your stuff so far has been first rate. I am pleased, New York is pleased, and so far as I know the listeners are pleased. If they aren't, to hell with them!"

Working alongside CBS's Tom Grandin in Amsterdam, Breckinridge made some side excursions to Norway, Belgium and Germany. In Germany she substituted briefly for William L. Shirer, another Murrow Boy, while he was absent from regular duty. She also had occasion to renew her friendship with Jeff Patterson, by then a U.S. diplomat based in Berlin. Their friendship developed into romance. She returned to Amsterdam and—six months after arriving in The Netherlands—she literally escaped only two days ahead of the Nazi army. CBS put her to work again at her next stop, Paris. But she wasn't there long, for she and Patterson had matrimony in mind. Her final CBS broadcast on June 5, 1940 was about a French farming hamlet and the war's influence on its residents. That done, she boarded a train for Berlin, cabling CBS: "Farewell Columbia. Have enjoyed working with you." The pair wed at the U.S. embassy in Berlin on June 20, 1940.

Breckinridge had tempted fate on at least three occasions, seemingly having a penchant—and constitution—for it. She left Lucerne on the last train out after Nazi forces invaded Poland; she fled Amsterdam on the last train out of there in the nick of time; and she caught the last train from Paris immediately prior to France's collapse. Following her marriage, the U.S. State Department said it would be "unseemly" for her to write journalistically in the delicate prewar and wartime climate. She fully acquiesced to her husband's career, although there were indications she would have preferred continuing to cover Europe for print media and CBS. ("I liked it more than any job I ever had," she said.) It wasn't to be. For 18 years she and her husband traipsed the world on State Department assignments.

After his 1958 retirement, they moved to Washington and resided in an old mansion in the capital's fashionable Massachusetts Heights section. At her memorial service in the 21st century, ex-congressman Clarence J. Brown Jr. (R-Ohio), stated: "Born to the silk of the wealth and historic reputations of two of America's great families and married into another, Mary Marvin Breckinridge Patterson might well have lived a life of private ease without any social significance or notable accomplishment." After becoming a grand dame of Washington society, she continued looking beyond herself. She wrote and photographed and shared her work with others while the two of them served on numerous boards, frequently of charitable and philanthropic persuasions. They held Kentucky Derby parties at their Washington home to benefit the Frontier Nursing Service.

Following his death in 1977, she began giving away real estate and exclusive art they had collected around the globe. Their estate at York, Maine, was gifted to Bowdoin College, which established the Breckinridge Public Affairs Center. She signed over their 544-acre Point Farm in Calvert County, Md., to the state of Maryland, the largest single bequest it has received. From it the state created Jefferson Patterson Park, a historic, environmental and archeological site. Her accomplishments are chronicled in the 1982 biography by Ann Denton Behlen, *Mary Marvin Breckinridge Patterson: From Career Broadcaster to Career Diplomatic Wife*. It satisfies the question she expressed again and again to herself: "Why not?"

BRECKNER, GARY C. b. Nov. 10, 1891, Illinois; d. June 25, 1945, Redlands, Calif. *Announcer*. **Series:** *Al Pearce and His Gang* (1930s, 1940s); *The Army Hour* (ca. 1942–ca. 1945); *Breakfast in Hollywood*, aka *Breakfast with Breneman*, aka *Welcome to Hollywood* (ca. 1943–ca. 1945); *Gateway to Hollywood* (1939); *Hollywood Startime* (host, 1944); *Jimmy Fidler in Hollywood* (ca. 1930s); *Laugh with Ken*, aka *The Ken Murray Show* (ca. 1936, ca. 1937); *Maxwell House Coffee Time* (ca. 1937–1945); *PDQ Quiz*; *The Phil Baker Show* (mid to late 1930s); *What's On Your Mind* (1936).

A cavalry captain in the First World War, Gary Breckner returned to pursue a show business career, touring on the stage with music comedy stars. In 1928 he entered radio as a sportscaster, becoming one of the earliest individuals in that arena. He turned up in multiple dial settings on Los Angeles radio—KHJ (1932), KNX (1936), KMPC (1940), KNX (1940). Rejected for service during the Second World War, Breckner nevertheless joined the U.S. War Department as a civilian, coordinating transmissions from multiple sites on *The Army Hour*. He succumbed to death at 53, the victim of injuries sustained in a vehicle accident.

BRICKERT, CARLTON. b. May 14, 1890, Martinsville, Ind.; d. Dec. 23, 1943, New York, N.Y. *Announcer, Actor*. **Series:** *Abie's Irish Rose* (actor, 1943); *The First Nighter* (1930s, early 1940s); *Joyce Jordan, Girl Interne*, aka *Joyce Jordan, M.D.* (actor, ca. late 1930s–ca. late 1940s); *Lum and Abner* (ca. mid 1930s–1938); *Portia Faces Life* (actor, early 1940s–1943); *Show Boat*, aka *The Maxwell House Show Boat* (actor, 1940–1941); *The Story of Mary Marlin* (actor, 1934–1943); *A Tale of Today* (actor, ca. 1936–ca. 1939); *Thurston, the Magician*, aka *Howard Thurston, the Magician* (actor, 1933); *Treasury Star Parade* (announcer-actor, 1942–1943); *Way Down Home* (1938).

From about 1896 to 1902 Carlton Brickert (intermittently identified by leisure documentarians as Carl Brickert, Carlton Brickett and Carl Brickett) and his family lived in England where the youngster was a boy soprano in a choir. Returning to the U.S., at Indianapolis' Shortridge High School he produced, directed and starred in Shakespeare's *Othello*. It was an indication of where he would invest his life. He acquired scholastic training successively for a year each at Cornell and Butler universities and Marion (Ind.) Normal School but quit before finishing in favor of the footlights. Brickert's initial professional stage engagement was with a Syracuse, N.Y. stock company at age 21. He established himself in the theater as a stage manager and actor. On Broadway he became a leading man to stage luminaries Mary Boland, Olga Petrova and Florence Reed. For two years he played opposite Lenore Ulric in a record-breaking run of *Kiki*. He starred in a triumphant production of *White Cargo* that persisted for 85 weeks.

In his mid twenties Brickert went into motion pictures, appearing in a half-dozen flicks: *The Half-Million Dollar Bribe* (1916); *A Million a Minute* (1916); *Daughter of Maryland* (1917); *The Embarrassment of Riches* (1918); *The Rider of the King Log* (1921); and *You Are Guilty* (1923). He landed a contract with NBC in 1932 and—following an audio run with *Lum and Abner* on the Blue network—joined the staff of NBC, Chicago, in 1938, winning acting roles in several daytime serials. At 53 he died from a heart attack shortly after returning to his home after rehearsing for an ongoing role in *Abie's Irish Rose*.

BRIGGS, DONALD P. (born Lester B. Sprawls). b. Jan. 28, 1911, Chicago, Ill.; d. Feb. 3, 1986, Los Angeles, Calif. *Actor, Announcer.* **Series:** *The Adventures of the Abbotts* (actor, ca. 1945–ca. 1947); *The Adventures of Frank Merriwell* (actor, 1934); *The Army Hour* (co-producer, 1942–1945); *Betty and Bob* (actor, 1932–ca. 1940); *City Desk* (1941); *Columbia Workshop*, aka *Twenty-Six by Corwin* (1941–ca. 1947); *David Harum* (actor, ca. 1940s); *Dick Daring's Adventures*, aka *Dick Daring, a Boy of Today* (actor, 1933); *The FBI in Peace and War* (actor, ca. 1944–ca. 1958); *The First Nighter* (interlocutor, ca. late 1940s); *Girl Alone* (actor, ca. mid 1930s); *Grand Hotel* (actor, ca. 1930s–ca. mid 1940s); *Hilltop House* (actor, ca. late 1930s–1941); *Martha Webster* (actor, 1941); *Masquerade* (actor, 1935); *Mr. Feathers* (actor, 1950); *Mr. Keen, Tracer of Lost Persons* (actor, ca. 1946–ca. 1948); *Musical Memories*, aka *It Can Be Done*, aka *Welcome Valley* (actor, ca. 1932–ca. 1938); *Perry Mason* (actor, ca. 1945–1947); *Portia Faces Life* (actor, ca. 1940s); *The Sheriff* (actor, ca. mid 1940s–ca. early 1950s); *The Story of Bess Johnson* (actor, 1941–1942); *What's My Line?* (1952–1953).

Don Briggs' career in show business sprang from a serious football accident when he was a three-letter athlete in a Chicago high school. All strenuous sports were barred from his extracurricular school activities. He subsequently joined the school's dramatic club and grabbed the lead in every production during the remainder of his school career. Upon graduation he accepted a post selling bonds with a leading local brokerage firm. He also joined the Goodman Repertory Co. and was soon concurrently appearing on the professional stage.

During his first two-week vacation from the sales spot, he took a vaudeville engagement in Milwaukee. Briggs entered radio in 1931, dividing his time between his LaSalle Street clients, radio studios and the stage. By 1935 he appeared in 97 radio shows monthly. As the broker was ordering him to choose between trading and entertainment, Briggs received an offer he couldn't refuse—in Hollywood films.

Between 1936 and 1976 he turned up in 37 motion pictures, largely of the B-movie variety. Some of the titles included *The Adventures of Frank Merriwell*, in which he reprised a title role he played on radio (1936); *Show Boat* (1936); *After the Thin Man* (1936); *Captains Courageous* (1937); *All-American Sweetheart* (1937); *Blondes at Work* (1938); *The First Hundred Years* (1938); *Mr. Chump* (1938); *The Hardys Ride High* (1939); *Unexpected Father* (1939); *Men Against the Sky* (1940); *Dr. Kildare Goes Home* (1940); *The Wheeler Dealers* (1963); and *W.C. Fields and Me* (1976).

When he had had enough, having been typecast as a suave, sinister villain—the only kind of role he could get—Briggs turned his back on Hollywood and left the West Coast to return to a plethora of radio broadcast opportunities seemingly awaiting him in New York. Broadway, summer stock and touring companies also beckoned. Eventually, there was television, with Briggs acting in *Cameo Theatre*, *Pulitzer Prize Playhouse*, *Robert Montgomery Presents*, *Studio One*, *Suspense*, *Tales of Tomorrow*, *The Web* and other dramas.

BRINKLEY, JOHN D. (JACK). b. Nov. 30, 1907, Oxford, N.C.; d. Aug. 8, 1972, Chicago, Ill. *Announcer, Actor.* **Series:** *Aunt Jemima* (ca. 1930s, 1940s); *Betty and Bob* (1930s); *Caroline's Golden Store* (actor, 1939–1940); *The Couple Next Door* (actor, 1936); *Judy and Jane* (1932–1935); *Kitty Keene, Incorporated* (ca. 1939–ca. 1941); *Ma Perkins* (actor-announcer, ca. 1930s, early 1940s).

Jack Brinkley broadcast over the Yankee network in New England at the start of his ethereal career, finding radio work at WTIC, Hartford, Conn., and WINS, New York. Afterwards, he permanently set up shop in Chicago in 1932. He joined WLS there as an announcer and freelanced on Chicago-originated series of both CBS and NBC. *Variety* suggested that he remained an on-air presence in the Windy City until 1952, although he may have persisted longer. Brinkley was a prominent Windy City disc jockey and interlocutor when he wasn't announcing or acting on a handful of chain-fed audio series.

BROKENSHIRE, NORMAN ERNEST. b. June 10, 1898, Murcheson, Ont., Canada; d. May 4, 1965, Hauppauge, N.Y. *Announcer, Emcee.* **Series:** *At the Sign of Green and White* (host, 1930); *Ceco Couriers* (1928–1930); *The Chesterfield Show* (1933); *Detect and Collect* (1945–1946); *The Eddie Cantor Show* (ca. 1930s); *Elsa Maxwell's Party Line*; *The Gulf Headliners* (1935); *Hawaiian Shadows* (1929); *Hollywood Star Playhouse*, aka *Hollywood Star Showcase* (1950–1951); *The Johnny Morgan Show* (actor, 1946); *La Palina Smoker* (1929–1930); *Major Bowes' Original Amateur Hour* (ca. 1940s); *Music That Satisfies* (1932); *Nehi Program* (host, 1931); *The Norman Brokenshire Show* (host, 1945); *Society's Playboy Hour* (1932); *The Theatre Guild on the Air*, aka *The United States Steel Hour* (1945–1953); *The Three B's* (1934); *Uncle Don* (ca. 1940s). **Aphorism:** *How do you do, ladies and gentlemen. How DO you do?*

Irreverent radio comic Henry Morgan recalled from a lengthy stint at New York's WOR that one of his assignments was to cover for Norman Brokenshire, an imbiber who "forgot to leave the bar at 21 in time to announce his own program." Brokenshire (often shortened to "Broke" by colleagues) was one of a handful of interlocutors who fashioned signature greetings for the ether. He signed on his shows with a lusty *How do you do, ladies and gentlemen. How DO you do?*

He took credit for "inventing" the daytime serial. While on the air on New York's WJZ about 1924, Broke presided over a variety half-hour for which—as luck would have it—all of the intended talent arrived late, after the show was already on the air. Not to be defeated, the innovative host spied a book of short stories in the studio and began to read it aloud. When the entertainers showed up, they interrupted his finish and he put the book away. In successive days legions of perturbed listeners implored the station to request that Brokenshire conclude the tale. Out of that scenario the announcer insisted he was the father of an as-yet-unnamed performing art, a story meted out in installments. It would be a while, of course, for the critics to dub the practice *soap opera*. Not many within the industry agreed with his allegation, either.

An itinerant pastor's son, Brokenshire emigrated from Canada to the U.S. where he graduated from Arlington High School, Boston, in 1915. In 1918 he joined an artillery unit of the U.S. Army, although World War I ended before his training was completed. Subsequently he solicited support for Near East Relief part time and took a full time post with the YMCA at Ft. Totten, Long Island. He studied two years (1920–1922) at Syracuse University on a YMCA scholarship. He accepted an advertising job but was soon fired from it. In 1924 Broke auditioned as an announcer at New York's WJZ and was among a handful of candidates hired at $45 weekly.

He was one of two reporters (the other, Graham McNamee, for rival WEAF) to broadcast the very first presidential inaugural ceremonies in 1925 from Washington. Broke aired his eyewitness account of Calvin Coolidge's installation for WJZ and coincidentally inserted his own name in the proceedings several times, even spelling it for his audience to impress it on them. He followed that with a sojourn at WRC, Washington, a WJZ sister station; was master of ceremonies for the Miss America pageant in 1926 which he broadcast over WPG, Atlantic City; and briefly became a freelance announcer, departing the WJZ fold where he was earning $65 every week.

After unsuccessful attempts at producing talent programs, he joined WFBH in New York (soon renamed WPCH) at $125 weekly. In 1927 the station fired him for excessive reliance on the bottle. He took a job in vaudeville imitating radio in his act and was promptly fired from it for the same reason. Next, Atlantic City officials lured him as their chief spokesman; he frequently aired "direct from the steel pier" over WPG. A short time later, in 1929, Broke was broadcasting over Philadelphia's WCAU. He made such a favorable impression that he was moved up the line to New York's WABC, the flagship CBS station, and thereby to CBS itself. He finally made the first of several triumphs over alcohol in 1932 when readers of *The New York Mirror* voted him "King of the Announcers" in a personality poll.

In September 1933 comic Ed Wynn picked Brokenshire as guest announcer for gala ceremonies launching the Amalgamated Broadcasting System. The web of 14 outlets dissolved within a brief span, nonetheless. In 1935 Broke joined the announcing staff at NBC. When he went on a road assignment to Cincinnati that October, he started drinking heavily prior to airtime. Attempting to read a commercial, he crumbled and was instantly fired. By 1937 he was occasionally heard over New York's WOR. He returned to Washington, D.C., that year and launched a morning show over WMAL that competed favorably against WJSV's morning disc jockey, Arthur Godfrey.

Unfortunately, after suffering injuries in a vehicle crash, Broke hit the bottle again. He acquired newscasting duties at New York's WNEW in 1941. Two years later he joined Alcoholics Anonymous at Forest Hills, N.Y. Temporarily returning to WMAL in Washington, by 1944 he moved to WBYN in Brooklyn, N.Y.

He was appearing on limited radio programming in 1945 while addressing units of Alcoholics Anonymous in scattered settings. Yet despite his checkered history, surprisingly Broke was invited to appear before officials of the U.S. Steel Corp. to be considered as the announcer for a prestigious series of Broadway dramas that they were about to inaugurate on radio. He was selected for *The Theatre Guild on the Air*, a program that continued for eight years, initially on ABC and later on NBC. Said *The New York World-Telegram*: "Norman Brokenshire, long absent from big-time radio ... still has a fine, easy way of announcing, mercifully lacking in the phoney [sic] exuberance we have too much with us these days."

During the same era, Broke aired locally over New York's WNBC, hosting a couple of DJ series—*The Norman Brokenshire Show* (1947–1948) and *Brokenshire Broadcasting* (1949). He finally won his battle against alcohol addiction, turning up as a guest on an ABC-TV series *The Comeback Story* (1953–1954), in which George Jessel and Arlene Francis interviewed subjects who had conquered misfortunes and re-ordered their lives.

In August 1948 Broke made his TV debut over NBC with a single-shot appearance on *Dress Rehearsal*. A critic labeled it "the best show" of the series. He announced a primetime game show, *Battle of the Ages*, in 1952 over the Dumont network, pitting children and adult celebs against one another. Home improvement was the thrust of a 30-minute Saturday night ABC-TV series that he emceed. *The Better Home Show* (1951–1952) was inaugurated locally in New York before going to the network. There, Dick and Doreen Wilson played Broke's neighbors, assisting him with simple residential repairs and other projects for the do-it-yourselfer.

In 1952 Broke moderated ABC-TV's *Four Square Court*, a half-hour feature wherein ex-cons donning masks dialogued about their criminal histories, rehabilitation and futures. State parole board officers appeared on the same panel. A pundit attested that it might have been the only time TV starred the criminals in an ongoing series. Before retiring from show business, Broke made a final foray into television, hosting yet another home repair entry. This one, in syndication, was titled *Handyman* and it was distributed to purchasing stations in 1955.

At his death he was freelancing with a couple of Long Island radio stations, WPAC,

Patchogue, and WBIC, Bay Shore. Until a short time before that, he also owned a Port Jefferson, Long Island, newspaper.

BROWN, CECIL B. b. Sept. 14, 1907, New Brighton, Pa.; d. Oct. 25, 1987, Los Angeles, Calif. *Newscaster.* **Series:** *CBS News* (foreign correspondent, 1940–1942); *Cecil Brown and the News* (newscaster, 1942–1956, mostly with a daily series at times supplemented by multiple broadcasts); *Kate Smith Speaks* (newscaster, 1942–ca. 1944); *NBC News* (foreign correspondent, 1958–1962); *Sizing Up the News* (newscaster, 1945–1947).

After attending Case Western Reserve University and graduating from Ohio State University in 1929, Cecil Brown pursued manifold avenues in journalism. He took a post as an International News Service reporter in Europe in 1937. "Embarking on a career of high adventure," according to a profiler, Brown became a war correspondent for CBS in January 1940, stationed in Rome. Fascists dispatched him from the city in 1941 when he displayed a "hostile attitude" to the regime in power. Nevertheless, he filed accounts as one of the legendary (Ed) "Murrow Boys," reporting from Cairo, Singapore, Syria, Turkey and Yugoslavia. Notably, a biography of *The Murrow Boys* stated: "Although Murrow had hired Brown, they were never as close as Murrow and the other Boys were to one another.... Overwrought and strident much of the time, Brown hardly fit the statesmanlike image that Murrow preferred."

Colleagues believed Brown perished when the Japanese sank the British battleship *HMS Repulse* off the coast of Malaya in December 1941. But he resurfaced not only to provide an eyewitness account of the disaster and his ensuing rescue but to also retell his encounter in a 1942 Random House best-seller, *Suez to Singapore*. His broadcast of that event, incidentally, earned for him a coveted George Peabody Award. He cabled his wife at home: "Health reasonably satisfactory. In October, the Air Force crashed me. In November, an Army truck plunged over a hill with me. In December, the Navy tried to sink me. Since no additional branches of the force remain, don't worry about the indestructible Mr. Brown."

Despite the fact that *Newsweek*, *Life*, *Collier's* and other periodicals were clamoring for his stories, Brown incensed British officials in Singapore. He infuriated them with blistering and relentless attacks over their alleged incompetence, so much so that they banished him from the local airwaves. In early 1942 CBS had no choice but to remove him, sending him to Australia. In June 1942 Brown acquired Elmer Davis's vacated timeslot on CBS in New York. Following a dispute with his bosses over airing editorial opinion in newscasts, he abruptly departed CBS in 1943 and told the press he was censored. Early the following year he joined the Mutual Broadcasting System (MBS), where he persisted as one of that chain's foremost newscasters, maintaining a weekday program for much of his broadcast tenure. Later, Brown joined NBC and then became its bureau chief in Tokyo from 1958 to 1962. He subsequently taught English at California State Polytechnic University. Before his career ended he directed news and public affairs at Los Angeles' KCET-TV.

A profiler assessed Brown as "a liberal and a supporter of racial integration in the days when it was not popular to favor integration.... Like most commentators who were liberal on domestic matters, Cecil Brown was an internationalist on foreign affairs, opposing moves toward isolationism."

BROWN, JIM. b. ca. 1927; d. Nov. 30, 2004. *Announcer.* **Series:** *Give and Take* (1945–1953).

BROWN, ROBERT VAHEY. b. Dec. 7, 1905, New York, N.Y.; d. Feb. 14, 1988, Lexington, Ky. *Announcer, Director, Producer.* **Series:** *American Women* (producer, 1943–1944); *Auction Quiz* (auctioneer, 1941–1942); *Backstage Wife* (ca. 1936–ca. early 1940s); *Ben Bernie, the Old Maestro*, aka *The Ben Bernie War Workers' Program* (ca. early 1940s); *The Breakfast Club* (1936–1941); *Dear Mom* (director, 1941); *The First Line* (producer-director, ca. early 1940s); *Girl Alone* (1936); *Ma Perkins* (1933–?); *Myrt and Marge* (producer-director, 1931–1932, 1937–1942); *The Night Club of the Air* (1937); *Quicksilver* (1939–1940); *Service to the Front* (producer-director, 1944–ca. 1945); *The Singing Story Lady* (1931–1941, 1945); *The Story of Mary Marlin* (ca. 1934–?); *This Amazing America* (quizmaster, 1940); *Vic and Sade* (1932–1940).

Born of Canadian parentage in New York City, by the time he was 10 Bob Brown had already lived in a half-dozen municipalities. At eight he sang in the choir of widely known evangelist Billy Sunday. While cultivating musical interests, he pursued civil engineering for two years at the University of Buffalo, then worked in that domain for the U.S. Engineering Corps a couple of years. In 1925 Brown was hired by Buffalo's WGR with announcing, directing and program continuity responsibilities, soon rising to chief announcer and studio director. Moving to Cincinnati's WLW three years later, he took charge of its announcing staff, wrote dramas and produced shows. He was the inaugural host of *Moon River*, a popular late-night music and poetry-reading feature that aired over WLW from 1930 to the late 1940s. Having never gotten a love for singing out of his system, meanwhile, Brown went back to school for further study at Cincinnati College of Music.

In 1932 he transferred to Chicago where he joined the announcing staff of NBC, thereby principally introducing daytime serials and primetime dramatic fare and quiz shows. In addition to his network assignments, Brown co-hosted the *WBBM Nutty Club*, a Saturday midnight celebrity outing premiering in 1935 that was broadcast from the Windy City's Grenada Club. When television emerged, he presided over a 1949 ABC-TV entry, *Science Circus*. In that final foray into network aircasting, he played an absent-minded professor who offered scientific experiments and stunts before a live studio audience.

BROWN, THEODORE DAVID. b. May 5, 1921, Collingwood, N.J.; d. March 20, 2005, Martin, Fla. *Announcer, Emcee.* **Series:** *Bulldog Drummond; The Gold and Silver Minstrels* (1946–1947); *The Great Talent Hunt* (1948); *The Joe DiMaggio Show* (1949–1950); *The Lawrence Welk Show*, aka *The Lawrence Welk High Life Revue* (host, 1949–1951, 1952–1953, 1955–1957); *Monitor* (host, 1970–1972); *The Phrase That Pays* (quizmaster, ca. 1954–1955); *The Saturday Night Revue* (1946); *Stop Me if You've Heard This One* (ca. 1947–ca. 1948); *Under Arrest* (ca. early 1950s); *A Voice in the Night* (1946).

Ted Brown got his first taste of broadcasting when the master of ceremonies failed to show up at a dance and Brown took his place. He attended Roanoke College in Salem, Va., and joined the U.S. Army Air Force during World War II. As a tail-gunner in a B-17 bomber, he was shot down over Germany and spent 15 months as a prisoner of war. From 1948 to 1956 disc jockey Brown presided over the daily *Ted Brown Show* on New York's WMGM. He spent time spinning records at Gotham's WNEW (1962, 1972–1989) and WNBC (1970) and at WVNJ, Oakdale, N.J. (1996), when a stroke sidelined him. He died of complications from it nine years later.

Brown appeared on several television series. For the run of NBC's daily adolescent charmer *The Howdy Doody Show* (1947–1960), Brown performed steadily as Bison Bill. In 1949 he hosted the Dumont network's juvenile series *Birthday Party*. He was master of ceremonies for the short-lived ABC stunt series *The Greatest Man on Earth* in 1952–1953. And in 1959 he presided over the ABC game show *Across the Board* that focused on contestants solving crossword puzzles.

As a final fling in network broadcasting, Brown was a popular segment host of NBC's marathon weekend radio service *Monitor* near the finish of that show's enduring run. He occupied the air chair from 2 to 6 P.M. Sundays for a couple of years in the 1970s. The program's biographer termed Brown "brash, opinionated and off-the-wall." Accordingly, Brown "could be a wild man at times on the air—[delivering] ad-libbing outrageous remarks, breaking into a foreign accent, and occasionally driving *Monitor* producers crazy because his ravings would put the broadcasts well behind-time.... At any point while his microphone was on, Brown would, and could, deviate from his script to get a laugh." At his passing *Monitor* cohort Jim Lowe allowed: "He was a major talent, with a keen sense of the ridiculous." Brown left the air at the end of his radio shift with "Put on the coffee, mama. I'm coming home."

BROWNING, CHARLES. d. 1988. *Announcer.* **Series:** *Terry and the Pirates* (1937–1939, 1941–1942, 1943–1948).

The song "I've Been Everywhere" applies in announcer-disc jockey-newscaster

Chuck Browning's case. Here's a dossier on the local stations he worked for after his sole network series was withdrawn: WFIL, Philadelphia (1966); CKLW, Detroit (1966); WMCA, New York (1968); KFRC, San Francisco (1969); KHJ, Los Angeles (1970); KRUX, Phoenix (1971); KUPD, Phoenix (1972); KCBQ, San Diego (1972); KGB, San Diego (1974); WMYQ, Miami (1975); Warner Brothers-Capricorn Records, Los Angeles (1976); KFI, Los Angeles (1980); WHBQ, Memphis (1981); KFRC, San Francisco (1984); KTSA, San Antonio (1986).

BROWNING, DOUGLAS. b. Oct. 16, 1910, Norwood, Ohio. *Announcer*. **Series:** *Communism—U.S. Brand* (1948); *The Doug Browning Show* (host, 1954); *Ed East and Polly* (ca. 1943–1944); *Go for the House* (1948–1949); *Ladies Be Seated* (1944–?); *Music Tent* (1955); *The Old Gold Hour*, aka *The Paul Whiteman Show* (ca. 1930s, 1940s); *On Stage America* (1947–1948); *The Sea Hound* (1942–1944, 1946–1947, 1948, 1951); *S.R.O.* (1953); *Stop the Music!* (ca. 1954); *Terry and the Pirates* (ca. 1937–ca. 1948).

After leaving the University of Cincinnati, Doug Browning tried at least a half-dozen jobs—telephone operator, telephone engineer, ambulance driver, grocery clerk, soda jerk, oil station attendant. As a sideline he took parts in local venue dramas as his schedule allowed. In 1934 he tried radio announcing and found it to his liking. Five years afterward he left Cincinnati's WLW for the NBC Radio staff in New York City.

Much of his tenure in Gotham was devoted to introducing a handful of respected audience participation series. He also maintained a long-running tenure on the juvenile adventure serial *Terry and the Pirates*. That was "a show of its time," according to one pundit, "when announcer Douglas Browning sold his product almost as a national duty ('Uncle Sam wants you to keep strong!'). In Browning's lingo, 'robistitude' was what a kid got from eating Quaker Puffed Wheat; 'marvolious' was what those 'shot-from-guns' cereals were."

Browning's solo expedition into television didn't pan out, however. In 1951 he moderated a premiering ABC celebrity panel show, *Q.E.D.* The following week Fred Uttal, who had also acquired a portfolio in radio, replaced him permanently. By the early 1960s, Browning was situated in a less urbanized America, serving WKAZ, Charleston, W. Va., as night engineer.

BRUNDAGE, HUGH E. b. Jan. 17, 1915, Montana; d. March 31, 1972, Los Angeles, Calif. *Announcer*. **Series:** *Academy Award Theater* (1946); *Aunt Mary* (1942–1951); *The Burl Ives Coffee Club*, aka *God's Country*, aka *Wayfaring Stranger* (1941–1942); *Heart's Desire* (1946–1948); *Junior Miss* (1948–1950); *The Old Fashioned Revival Hour* (ca. 1940s); *Sound Off* (ca. 1943–1944, ca. 1947–?).

In 1936 announcer Hugh Brundage left KRKD for KEHE; the following year he moved to KHJ. All three stations were in Los Angeles. In 1939 he was cast in an obscure part in the movie *Mr. Smith Goes to Washington*. Brundage took time out from his ethereal pursuits in 1942 to serve the U.S. Coast Guard as an apprentice seaman. As his network-broadcasting career began to dim, Brundage was on the air at KDAY, Los Angeles, in 1957. He went over to KMPC, Los Angeles, in 1964 as news director; he was news anchor at KTLA-TV, a station owned by singing cowboy-entrepreneur Gene Autry in 1965–1966; and Brundage returned to KMPC in his previous capacity in 1966, remaining until his death six years hence. Counting the brief interval on TV, he worked at a half-dozen stations in a single metropolitan area, one of only a handful of broadcast announcers to serve as many outlets in a solo market.

BRYAN, GEORGE. b. June 9, 1910, New York, N.Y.; d. June 27, 1969, Stamford, Conn. *Announcer, Newscaster, Vocalist*. **Series:** *The Aldrich Family* (1940s); *The Armstrong Theater of Today* (newscaster, 1940s); *Arthur Godfrey's Talent Scouts* (1946–1956, with TV simulcast 1948–1956); *Catch Me If You Can* (1948); *CBS Presents Red Barber*, aka *Red Barber Sports* (1946); *CBS Weekly News Review* (1947–1948); *The Dixieland Music Shop*, aka *The Camel Caravan*, aka *The Bob Crosby Show* (1939); *The Helen Hayes Theater* (1940–1942); *Hit the Jackpot* (1948–1949, 1950); *It's Always Albert* (1948); *Let's Pretend* (1940s); *The Life of Riley* (1941); *Mr. Chameleon* (early 1950s); *Mr. Keen, Tracer of Lost Persons* (relief announcer, 1954); *National Amateur Night*

(1936); *The News from Europe* (1940); *The Peter Lind Hayes Show* (ca. 1954–1955); *Road of Life* (ca. 1950s); *So You Think You Know Music* (1940); *Songs by George Bryan* (host-vocalist, 1946); *We, the People* (1940s).

At 26 George Bryan won a first award in a match for tenderfoot narrators—the prize being an opportunity to announce for 20 weeks the radio talent series *National Amateur Night*. As a consequence, he was soon working at WGAR and WKBW, both in Buffalo, N.Y. By 1940 he joined CBS in New York as a staff announcer, an assignment that lasted 28 years except for wartime service. He was a second lieutenant in the U.S. Army Air Corps starting in 1942. Upon his return in 1946, Bryan—also a composer and vocalist—hosted his own quarter-hour syndicated tune-filled series that same year. He exhibited yet another dimension on Oct. 30, 1951 when his play, *Navy Blue*, starring Robert Cummings, Santos Ortega, George Petrie and Kenny Delmar, was produced on the *Cavalcade of America*.

On Dec. 26, 1949, Bryan became the instant "star" of *Arthur Godfrey's Talent Scouts*, then simulcast over CBS Radio and Television, when the namesake master of ceremonies was delayed in traffic. Until Godfrey showed up, Bryan conducted interviews with talent scouts and presented their "finds" as if the Old Redhead was on the scene, acquiring 10 of the proverbial 15 minutes of hoped-for fame in anybody's life in one performance!

BRYANT, GEOFFREY. b. Oct. 11, 1906, Houston, Texas. *Actor, Announcer.* **Series:** *Aunt Jenny* (actor, late 1930s, 1940s); *Central City* (1938–1941); *City Desk* (actor, 1941); *Death Valley Days* (actor, 1930s, 1940s); *Just Plain Bill* (actor, ca. 1930s–1940s); *Meyer the Buyer* (actor, mid 1930s); *Mr. District Attorney* (ca. 1939–?); *Mystery in the Air* (actor, ca. 1945, ca. 1947); *This is Your FBI* (actor, 1945–?).

Geoffrey Bryant performed on stage in New York and London and with a stock company that appeared at multiple venues. His stage theatrics prepared him for radio, where Bryant was both a thespian and an interlocutor on network series.

BUCK, LOUIS. b. May 10, 1910, Bessemer, Ala.; d. May 18, 1971, Nashville, Tenn. *Announcer.* **Series:** *The Checkerboard Fun Fest* (1945); *Grand Ole Opry* (1939–1946); *Opry House Matinee* (1945–1946); *Sunday Down South* (1940–1941, 1942).

Louis ("Cousin Louie") Buck was hired by WDOD, Chattanooga, Tenn., in 1936. Two years later he joined Nashville's WSM, where he was an announcer, newscaster and sportscaster and where he presided over several important musical features. He has been cited as one of the *Grand Ole Opry's* initial trio of pure announcers—including men who announced but carried no added duties with the durable program. (Others were David Cobb and Jud Collins.) The plum assignment of Buck's longstanding engagement categorically was to introduce the country music and comedy acts on the weekly network half-hour portion of the *Opry*. It was a task he joyfully fulfilled for seven years until Grant Turner was tapped to replace him. The 30-minute segment was the only one of the marathon live broadcast stage show that was scripted and rehearsed.

Afterward, Buck departed Music City for Atlanta's WAGA for a couple of years. Upon his return to Nashville he rejoined the *Opry* (multiple non-network portions) and ultimately became WSM's sales manager, a post he occupied at the time of his death. In 1956 he appeared with several local artists on an ABC-TV live special aired from Nashville, *Country-Western All-Stars*. Buck was a small time librettist, too, penning the lyrics of a handful of country tunes. Hank Snow recorded Buck's *Your Locket is My Broken Heart* and Red Foley recorded his *Loafin' on a Lazy River*. It was also Cousin Louie Buck who—in 1949—accidentally acquired the coveted distinction of presenting the legendary performer Hank Williams to an *Opry* crowd during the singer's initial visit. That's a trivia fact that has been almost overlooked by the fans. Virtually overnight Williams became a country music icon after his early appearances in Nashville's Ryman Auditorium. He continued to perform there for a couple of years.

BUELL, BRUCE NORTON. b. April 10, 1919, Santa Ana, Calif.; d. April 23, 1996, Los Angeles, Calif. *Announcer.* **Series:** *California Caravan* (1947–1952); *Mystery is My Hobby* (1947–1951).

For many years Bruce Buell was a fixture at KFAC in Los Angeles, where he was a disc jockey playing classical music. A critic wrote: "Bruce Buell and the rest of the stellar announcers of the Golden Age [at KFAC] left an indelible impression."

BURDETT, WINSTON MANSFIELD. b. Dec. 12, 1913, Buffalo, N.Y.; d. May 19, 1993, Rome, Italy. *Correspondent.* **Series:** *CBS News* (correspondent, 1940–1978); *CBS World News Roundup* (correspondent, 1940–1978); *The World Tonight* (correspondent, 1956–1978).

Although not directly hired by CBS's chief newsman Edward R. Murrow, Winston Burdett was among nearly a dozen of the web's overseas reporters who came to be popularly identified as "Murrow Boys." A Harvard summa cum laude Romance languages intellect who finished his formal education in three years, Burdett was in Oslo as a stringer. In 1939 he fed stories of culture and films to *The Brooklyn Daily Eagle* (a paper which would qualify him for an Overseas Press Club recognition after his 1959 reportage of the death of Pope Pius XII). Concurrently, he was a correspondent for Transradio, a minor wire service. Burdett impressed CBS's Norwegian stringer, Betty Wason, a woman being forced out by sexual discrimination, a common practice. Then 24, Burdett was hired at her initiative.

Reporting from Oslo, he impressed Murrow. The young protégé possessed an innate ability to scoot around the continent with the Nazis in hot pursuit. They soon sent him packing in Oslo and he migrated to Stockholm. From there he transitioned to Moscow, then Rumania where the Nazis literally expelled him. He tried Yugoslavia and was expelled again. Ankara was his next outpost. There he and NBC's Martin Agronsky sparred competitively in journalistic pursuits. Of Burdett's work, a reviewer observed: "A frequent criticism made of Burdett was that he sometimes blurred the lines between reporter and analyst without warning his listeners."

All of this occurred before America entered the war. An account of his subsequent experiences appears in a provocative chapter of *The Murrow Boys* (Houghton Mifflin, 1996), including his revelation that he was a Communist and a Soviet spy before joining CBS. In 1951 Burdett was summoned from Rome to New York. Following explanations of his *past* affiliations, he was assigned to the United Nations as a CBS correspondent and remained there for four years. When he decided to go public with his life's story in 1955, he named other journalists who had been Communists, also, resulting in the firing of several *New York Times* reporters. Burdett lost the respect of multiple colleagues. In 1956 he was banished by CBS to Rome. "He was told that he would have every opportunity to reestablish himself there, in exile, but with the clear understanding that he had forfeited whatever chance he had of becoming a big-name correspondent in New York or Washington," according to one account. He was based in the Italian capital as a CBS reporter until he retired in 1978, and continued living there to his death.

"Over the years," that assessment concluded, "a whole new generation of viewers grew up and became ardent admirers of his reporting from Rome, without ever knowing the circumstances that had sent him there in the first place." The authors of *The Murrow Boys*, meanwhile, were just as gracious: "For pure intelligence, Winston Mansfield Burdett was the best of the Boys. Frail and handsome, considered a comer at CBS after the war, he wrote beautifully and had what others described as a 'photographic memory.' He could memorize a script in a single reading and speak flawlessly on the air, even when he had to ad-lib.... Burdett was an anomaly in the increasingly cutthroat and cynical world of broadcast journalism."

BYRON, WARD. b. June 2, 1910, New York, N.Y.; d. Feb. 4, 1996. *Announcer, Director, Producer.* **Series:** *Bughouse Rhythm* (creator, 1936–1937); *The Chamber Music Society of Lower Basin Street* (commentator, ca. 1950, 1952); *The Chesterfield Supper Club* (director, ca. 1940s); *The Fitch Bandwagon* (producer, 1938–ca. 1944); *The George Jessel Show* (director, 1937–1938); *The Philip Morris Follies of 1946* (producer, 1946).

Ward Byron transferred his penchant for producing radio shows to television in the early 1950s. He wrote and produced Paul Whiteman's *TV Teen Club* on ABC in 1950. He was responsible for yet another trio of short-lived video series: *Daydreaming with Laraine* (Day) on ABC (1951), *The Frances Langford–Don Ameche Show* on ABC (1951–1952) and *Night Editor* on Dumont (1954).

CALLAGHAN, JACK. *Announcer, Director.* **Series:** *The Breakfast Club* (commercial spokesman for General Foods, ca. 1940s, 1950s); *The Quiz Kids* (director, ca. 1940s or early 1950s).

In 1940 Jack Callaghan was a newscaster and announcer at WKAR, East Lansing, Mich.

CALMER, EDGAR (NED). b. July 16, 1907, Chicago, Ill.; d. March 9, 1986, New York, N.Y. *Newscaster, Writer.* **Series:** *Backstage Wife* (writer, ca. 1930s); *CBS World News Roundup* (correspondent, 1940s–ca. 1950s); *Ned Calmer and the News* (newscaster, 1943–1944); *World News with Robert Trout* (correspondent, 1952–?); *You Are There* (reporter, 1947–1949).

From 1927 to 1934 Ned Calmer was getting his feet wet as a reporter and foreign correspondent with a couple of major metropolitan dailies, *The Chicago Tribune* and *The New York Herald-Tribune*. During part of that epoch he was enrolled at the University of Virginia. For six years (1934–1940) Calmer, based in New York City, was foreign news editor of the French Agence Havas newsgathering bureau. Hired by CBS in 1940, he was employed as an electronic journalist with that network for 27 years.

Calmer was assigned as a war correspondent with the U.S. Armed Forces in Europe in 1944–1945. There may have been a tinge of resentment in his observation on one occasion that the "Murrow Boys" (a cadre of foreign correspondents appointed by CBS's chief newsman, Edward R. Murrow) "worked for Murrow first and CBS second." Calmer, who wasn't in that perceived elitist deputation, was among a handful of reinforcements CBS dispatched overseas, including John Charles Daly, Douglas Edwards and Robert Trout. Nonetheless, as the allies invaded France on D-Day on June 6, 1944, Calmer assured CBS listeners that the beaches along the Normandy coast were "smooth and easily approachable."

For six weeks in 1950 he interviewed newsmakers, politicians and entertainers on the CBS-TV weekly quarter-hour primetime series *In the First Person*. Calmer became the newscaster on one of CBS-TV's early (and many) responses to NBC-TV's *Today*, titled *Good Morning* in 1956–1957 hosted by Will Rogers Jr. with Pamela Good as the show's weathercaster. Furthermore, he made sporadic appearances on several other groundbreaking television series: *CBS Views the Press, See It Now* and *You Are There*.

An avid author as well as a broadcaster, he penned multiple works of fiction and was characterized by one reviewer as "a novelist of striking ability." His accounts often recalled his own experiences as a newsman. Under pseudonyms he wrote *Beyond the Street* (Little, Brown, 1934) and *When Night Descends* (Farrar & Rinehart, 1936). Nine subsequent works, however, were issued under his own name: *The Strange Land* (Scribner, 1950); *All the Summer Days* (Little, Brown, 1961); *The Anchorman* (Doubleday, 1970); *The Avima Affair* (Doubleday, 1973); *Late Show* (Doubleday, 1974); *Madam Ambassador* (Doubleday, 1975); *The Peking Dimension* (Doubleday, 1976); *Bay of Lions* (Arbor House, 1980); and *The Winds of Montauk* (Seaview, 1980). Calmer retired from CBS in 1967 at age 60, in fact, to concentrate on his writing.

While it seems inconsistent with the focus of his lifelong pursuits, the fact remains there is compelling documentation by some trustworthy sources intimating that Calmer—for a while, at least—penned dialogue for one of radio's most popular daytime sagas from the wares of the profuse producers of sunshine stories Frank and Anne Hummert—*Backstage Wife*. (It aired from 1935 to 1959.) If correct, Calmer is the only American news broadcaster known to have subsidized his income by churning out melodrama focused on beleaguered housewives.

CAMPBELL, ROBERT MAURICE. b. Feb. 16, 1922, Detroit, Mich.; d. May 1981. *Announcer.* **Series:** *Out of the Deep* (ca. 1945).

Robert Campbell launched his show business career on radio and the stage in Detroit, interrupted by service in the U.S. Coast Guard during the Second World War. Following his discharge, he produced and directed Broadway plays. Getting into television, Campbell was producer-director of ABC-TV's *All-Star News* in 1952–1953.

CANHAM, EDWIN D. b. Feb. 13, 1904, Auburn, Maine; d. Jan. 3, 1982, Guam. *Newscaster, Commentator.* **Series:** *Canham Views the News* (commentator, 1948); *Edwin Canham Sports* (1951); *Headlines and Bylines* (correspondent, 1937–1938); *Monitor Views*, aka *Christian Science Views* (host-commentator, 1945–ca. 1959).

Edwin D. Canham (sometimes identified as Erwin D. Canham) launched his network career airing nine-minute news summaries over CBS in the late 1930s. Becoming the Washington bureau chief of *The Christian Science Monitor* subsequently, he was that body's radio spokesman during weekly stints over ABC and NBC from the mid 1940s through most of the 1950s.

Canham was an executive of the Christian Science church, filling its presidency in 1966. He became the newspaper's editor-in-chief. In Boston he joined a panel for a local TV show, *Starring the Editors*. Retiring in 1975, he maintained residences at Cape Cod, Mass. and on the Pacific island of Saipan.

CANNON, JOHN. b. May 17, 1906, Chicago, Ill.; d. June 22, 2001, Cologne, Germany. *Announcer, Actor.* **Series:** *City Hospital* (1951–1958); *Jack Armstrong, the All-American Boy* (actor, ca. late 1940s–1950); *The Will Rogers Show* (1951).

John Cannon was more important to show business than his brief network radio resume hints. Not only was he the voice of Fox Movietone newsreels screened in cinema houses across the land in the 1950s, he was elected president of the National Academy of Television Arts and Sciences in 1976. For a quarter-of-a-century, he served the NATAS, supervising its daytime Emmy awards and the annual Emmy awards presentations until his death by heart attack while he was vacationing in Europe.

Also in the 1950s, Cannon introduced a half-dozen premier television series every week: *The Colgate Comedy Hour* (NBC); *I've Got a Secret* (CBS); *Strike It Rich* (CBS); *Studio One* (CBS); *You Are There* (CBS); and *Your Hit Parade* (NBC, CBS).

CARLIN, PHILLIPS. b. June 30, 1894, New York, N.Y.; d. Aug. 27, 1971, New York, N.Y. *Announcer.* **Series:** *The A&P Gypsies* (ca. 1920s); *Broadway Hits* (1935–?); *The Chilquot Club Eskimos* (ca. 1920s); *Dixie Circus* (1929–1930); *The Goodrich Silvertown Orchestra* (1926–1928); *Major Bowes' Original Amateur Hour* (ca. late 1930s); *Palmolive Hour* (ca. early 1930s); *Roxy and His Gang* (ca. 1927–ca. 1930).

Phil Carlin was recognized for his elocution skills as early as P.S. 65 in New York City and afterward in debate competitions at DeWitt Clinton High School. Still later he won prizes for oratory at New York University. A pioneer announcer at WEAF starting at $50 weekly in 1922, Carlin originally introduced *The A&P Gypsies* in 1923, a true aural pioneer. The following June he assisted Graham McNamee in reporting from a "rambunctious, free-wheeling, drawn-out" Democratic Convention staged at the old Madison Square Garden in New York City. After no candidate corralled enough votes to win the nomination, 16-hour-day sessions ran into a second week. In the fall of 1925 the McNamee-Carlin team (referred to as the "WEAF twins") aired the action of major collegiate football games. Together they broadcast the first NBC coast-to-coast event on Jan. 1, 1927, the Rose Bowl game from Pasadena, Calif., with Alabama opposing Stanford. The pair, along with J. Andrew White and Ted Husing, emerged as the nation's initial "sportscaster" legends.

WEAF (Red network) and WJZ (Blue network) became NBC's flagship outlets when the web organized in late 1926. The chain touted Carlin as "the voice with a smile." In addition to his announcing duties that frequently included band and sports remotes, Carlin was appointed an assistant to the vice-president in charge of programming for the nationwide hookup. In 1935 his responsibilities were altered; he became manager of sustaining programs. He presented Dorothy Lamour in her initial audio outing in 1935 and gave Dinah Shore her inaugural network exposure in 1939.

By 1942 he was the Blue (later ABC) network vice president in charge of programs. He introduced *Breakfast at Sardi's* to the airwaves in 1942, a weekday series that became better known as *Breakfast in Hollywood* a year afterward. From 1944 to 1949 Carlin was vice president in charge of programs for the MBS chain. He worked in television between 1949 and retirement in 1964.

First Use of the Famous NBC Chimes, an internal document of the web, credits an inspired Carlin with the notion of employing chimes to distinguish NBC programming on the ether. The original chimes, incidentally—purchased for just a few dollars from Lesch Silver Co. on Dec. 22, 1926, after NBC was only five weeks old—set in motion an identifying audio symbol that persisted throughout the radio network's viable run. Today it is a service mark of the succeeding television network, actively maintained by its present corporate owners, NBC Universal.

A 1950 NBC press release reflected that chief engineer Oscar B. Hanson, musical director Ernest La Prade and announcer Phillips Carlin "each had a hand in the development of the present-day three-note signal." Contemporary researcher Michael Shoshani, who developed a website dedicated to the history of the chimes, asserts that "Carlin is mentioned most likely because the idea of using the chimes is credited to him." When the three-note sequence was adopted, seven-, five- and four-note progressions had been attempted and abandoned. The famous three-note series, G-E-C, became one of the most familiar sounds repetitively heard in American households coast-to-coast at the close of every NBC five-minute, quarter-hour, half-hour and hour-long program for over seven decades.

CARNEGIE, DALE. b. Nov. 24, 1888, Maryville, Mo.; d. Nov. 1, 1955, Queens, New York, N.Y. *Instructional commentator.* **Series:** *Little Known Facts about Well-Known People* (self-help advisor, 1933–1935, 1937–1938, 1945); *How to Win Friends and Influence People* (self-help advisor, 1938); *Interesting People* (self-help advisor, 1943–1945).

Dale Carnegie turned an idea into a gold mine: tell people how to build better relationships by interacting positively with other human beings, guaranteeing sensational outcomes. He made a mint out of his theory when followers flocked to it, eager to hear what apparently only a few had thought out for themselves. The organization Carnegie left behind continues to rake in colossal sums from concerns and individuals seeking *How to Win Friends and Influence People.* That's the title of the founder's most famous bestseller (Simon & Schuster, 1936), dubbed the original modern self-help volume. "Smile, be friendly, never argue or find fault, or tell a person he is wrong," a pundit summarized. Among other tomes: *Public Speaking and Influencing Men in Business* (Kessinger, 1931); *How to Stop Worrying and Start Living* (Simon & Schuster, 1944).

Carnegie grew up in poverty on a Missouri farm. While still milking the cows at 4 A.M. daily, he attended State Teacher's College, Warrensburg, Mo., and following graduation, he peddled correspondence courses to homesteaders. Later he sold lard, bacon and soap for Armour & Co. in suburban Omaha, Neb. So incredibly flourishing were his results that his geographic district quickly became Armour's sales frontrunner. He honed the principles he developed there, turning them into self-improvement, salesmanship and corporate training courses, pioneering a new American industry.

To popularize his newfound entrepreneurial pursuits, Carnegie went on radio, where he offered counsel to listeners impoverished by the Great Depression. He helped many rebuild the self-confidence and determination they had lost, stirring their imaginations to realize dreams that had seemed beyond reach at that low period in the nation's history. With the exception of about five years, Carnegie was on the air continuously from the early 1930s until the mid 1940s, beamed to the country by NBC, CBS and MBS at diverse periods.

In the obituary it prepared for him, *The New York Times* condensed Carnegie's advice for successful living into two of his maxims: "Forget yourself; do things for others" and "Cooperate with the inevitable."

CARNEY, DON (born Howard Rice). b. 1897, St. Joseph, Mich.; d. Jan. 14, 1954, Miami, Fla. *Actor, Announcer, Emcee.* **Series:** *The Adventures of Terry and Ted* (narrator, 1937–1939, 1943–1948); *Don Carney's Dog Chats* (host, 1933); *Friendship Town* (actor, 1932); *Let's Dance* (1934–1935); *Main Street Sketches* (actor, 1927–?); *Romance Isle* (actor, 1928–1929); *Uncle Don* (host, 1938–1939).

A circus acrobat in his early teens, at 15 "Don Carney, the Trick Pianist" was a successful act on the vaudeville circuit. Onstage he not only played and sang but also stood on his head to maintain audience intensity. That was long before the thespian playing him, Howard Rice, turned up as an announcer at New York's WMCA Radio in December 1925. After a brief while he transferred to WOR, where he literally made his fortune (in excess of $90,000 annually by 1934) in a 19-year run as Uncle Don, persisting to 1947. The series for tykes was carried by MBS only one year, but—according to a radio historiography—Rice "established the pattern for later children's shows." He played piano, sang, told stories, noted birthdays, scolded youngsters for bad habits and lobbied the moppets to join membership clubs. On Sunday mornings, he read the comics to his fans.

Uncle Don invented mythical characters that espoused popular concepts with grownups for their juveniles, like performing household chores, cultivating good manners, caring for one's health, developing good study habits, etc. He also inspired good works among older folks. In 1945 he launched the nonprofit Uncle Don Institute of Child Guidance and Recreation, a fraternity fostering solutions to delinquency and recreational difficulties among youngsters.

Rice (as Carney) worked with local parents who literally had him say things to specific adolescents. Legend has it that on one occasion a boy's parents were beside themselves over little Johnny's foul-mouth. They worked hard to help him overcome it. When improvement occurred, Johnny was tuned in to Uncle Don one day and heard him say: "Johnny, your parents are so proud of you for not swearing any more. Look behind the radio and you'll find a special present for you." The precocious youngster did so and retrieved a wrapped gift. "How in the hell do you think he knew that was there?" he inquired of his bewildered elders. Howard Rice also devoted much of his career to repudiating a story that circulated about him that—following one performance while thinking the mike was turned off (though it wasn't)—he bellowed: "There! Maybe that'll hold the little bastards!" Rice was convinced that some rivals in the industry who hadn't done as well as he perpetuated malicious gossip about him, including that tale. It was a well-known fact that the showman imbibed regularly. Once, after having a few drinks, he walked down the street and was recognized by a young fan that rushed into his arms. He swept her up and she kissed him. "I love you, Uncle Don," said the little girl. "You taste just like daddy!"

Rice wrote and recorded eight albums of "Uncle Don" songs that sold in excess of a million copies. He also participated in a myriad of creative WOR shows that were never carried by a network. *New Deal on Main Street*, beginning in 1933, was one. It was a serialized narrative of rural life. Some of the episodes provided an opportunity for the cast members to play old-fashioned tunes as they focused on the brass band rehearsals in the folksy neighborhood community. Ultimately, in 1948 Rice left New York for warmer climes, joining Miami Beach's WKAT. He was still conducting a weekly children's show for that station at the time of his passing.

CARPENTER, KENNETH L. b. Aug. 21, 1900, Avon, Ill.; d. Oct. 16, 1984, Santa Monica, Calif. *Announcer.* **Series:** *The Bing Crosby Chesterfield Show* (1949–1952); *Command Performance* (1940s); *The Edgar Bergen and Charlie McCarthy Show* (mid-late 1940s); *The General Electric Show* (1952–1954); *The General Electric Theater* (1953); *The Great Gildersleeve* (1942–1945); *The Halls of Ivy* (1950–1952); *The Kraft Music Hall* (1935–1949); *The Life of Riley* (1945–1949); *Lux Radio Theater* (mid to late 1940s–ca. 1955); *Meet Corliss Archer* (1940s, 1950s); *One Man's Family* (1940s); *Packard Mardi Gras* (ca. 1937–ca. 1938); *The Passing Parade* (ca. 1930s, 1940s); *Philco Radio Time* (1946–1949); *This is Bing Crosby* (1948–1949, 1950); *Three Sheets to the Wind* (1942); *Truth or Consequences* (1950s).

Ken Carpenter worked for a boatload of prestigious series and people. His voice was one of the most distinguished and resilient among those introducing network radio programs during the medium's golden age. While he is perhaps best remembered for his enduring ties to crooner Bing Crosby, Carpenter was the easily recognized interlocutor of Edgar Bergen and Charlie McCarthy, *The Great Gildersleeve, Lux Radio Theater* and added musical, comedic and dramatic fare. In 1930 he launched a network career over KFI in Los Angeles, working for NBC as opportunities arose. He had some history in broadcasting at Peoria, Ill., and some experience in advertising before traveling to the West Coast in 1929. Seeking an advertising post, he was given a radio tryout at KFI instead. After announcing the Rose Bowl game in 1935, Carpenter was suddenly in demand for programs carried nationwide. In 1936, when NBC opened its Hollywood studios, he was hired as a staff announcer, persisting there to 1942, when he became a freelance announcer and worked shows on all the major chains.

Carpenter often aired sporting events: football games and the Santa Anita handicaps, plus some major Hollywood events. While announcing at the Cocoanut Grove in 1932 he met Bing Crosby. Ultimately, he was to become Crosby's permanent announcer on no fewer than a quintet of radio series: *The Bing Crosby Chesterfield Show*, *Kraft Music Hall*, *The General Electric Show*, *Philco Radio Time* and *This is Bing Crosby*. He was one of only three individuals that Crosby invited to go with him when the singer terminated his contract with NBC's *Kraft Music Hall* in 1946. Crosby subsequently struck out for San Francisco and ABC, where he went on the air with *Philco Radio Time*. (The other "indispensables" retained were bandleader John Scott Trotter and engineer Murdo MacKenzie.) Carpenter, meanwhile, remained on the *Kraft* show, too, for another three years with succeeding hosts including a couple of years with singer Al Jolson. He had started on *Kraft* a year before Crosby arrived, in fact, with bandleader Paul Whiteman. Therefore, his tenure on the one show was about 14 years.

Carpenter was tapped to announce the *Lux Video Theatre* dramatic anthology on television. It ran from 1950 to 1954 on CBS and from 1954 to 1957 on NBC. During the summers of 1955, 1956 and 1957, Carpenter also hosted the series in addition to handling announcing chores. He was responsible for announcing and delivering commercials during a season of a Ford-sponsored hour-long TV program in the 1950s (there were several). In 1958–1959 he handled the same for *Milton Berle Starring in the Kraft Music Hall*, a half-hour NBC-TV feature. Carpenter provided voiceovers for legions of video commercials, too.

CARSTENSEN, VERN. b. May 24, 1914, Clinton, Iowa; d. April 28, Riverside, Calif. *Announcer, Director, Producer.* **Series:** *Box 13* (announcer-director, 1948–1949); *The Damon Runyon Theater* (producer, 1948–1949).

While enrolled at the University of Iowa, in 1936 Vern Carstensen began announcing for Iowa City's WSUL Radio, getting an early jump on life as a broadcaster. After college he moved to WHBF, Rock Island, Ill., and by 1938 he joined NBC in Chicago.

CARTER, HAROLD THOMAS HENRY (BOAKE). b. Sept. 28, 1903, Baku, Azerbaijan; d. Nov. 16, 1944, Hollywood, Calif. *Newscaster, Commentator.* **Series:** *Boake Carter and the News* (1933–1938, 1940–1944). **Aphorism:** *Cheerio!*

Controversy surrounded Boake Carter's birthdate just as it followed him throughout an abbreviated life. Born in southern Russia while his father was a British petroleum agent, he claimed to have arrived in 1898 and 1901. A Carter biographer speculated that September 1903 was more probably the actual date, amplifying: "Carter apparently figured he would make a better impression if he were older ... and if his father had a British diplomatic career." At 15 young Carter joined the British Royal Air Force coast patrol. He may have attended Christ College at Cambridge but records don't support his claim. He arrived in the U.S. and situated with his father in Philadelphia. The younger Carter pursued journalistic interests and took a job as a rewrite editor on *The Philadelphia Evening Bulletin*. In time he moved to rival paper *The Philadelphia Daily News* as a reporter. By 1939 he penned a syndicated column and had already authored several books.

Turning 27 in 1930, Carter added radio to his reportorial repertoire, becoming a newscaster for WPEN in the City of Brotherly Love. He exhibited a distinctively British inflection evident throughout his ethereal career. ("He could roll his R's with the best of them," said a source.) Officials at Philadelphia's CBS affiliate, WCAU, soon noticed him. In 1931 Carter began reporting from the offices of the *Daily News* with a couple of five-minute weekday newscasts over WCAU. The following year he leaped into the national spotlight by covering the kidnapping of the Lindbergh baby. That catapulted him into full time reporting for WCAU in July 1932. In January 1933 the Philco Corp. began underwriting a CBS daily newscast with Carter delivering the headlines. Considered "America's most popular commentator" according to two news historians, he persisted for five years. Then General Foods took over the spot and carried him for six months. Riding the peak of fame, the ultraconservative was fired from his $150,000 job when he "stepped on too many toes and ... criticized the administration of Franklin D. Roosevelt too often and too harshly." One of Carter's book titles may have said it all: *I Talk As I Like* (Dodge, 1937). There was speculation that CBS president William S. Paley was afraid his star newsman was about to cripple his network with government intervention and investigation.

Reviewing the aforementioned 1937 text two years after its release, an article titled "What's Happened to Boake Carter?" published in the fanzine *Radio Guide* allowed that the book dealt with "the headaches with which I [Carter] have battled in the last eight years, promoted solely from intolerance of Mr. Average Man." Carter stated that when John Q. Citizen didn't approve of his opinions, he blanketed commercial sponsors with "the intolerance of threats to destroy their business." In the interest of freedom of reporting, Carter pled for listeners to refrain from similar actions and requested advertisers and radio stations to disregard demands for censorship.

In 1939 Carter airmailed discs of his commentaries to 25 stations in hopes of returning to the national airwaves. It didn't happen for a while. In late 1940 he joined MBS, broadcasting for several sponsors until his untimely demise from a heart attack four years later. His newscasts originated at KHJ in Los Angeles by then. Speaking of the shift to Mutual, a spokesman suggested: "He seemed more compatible with its open-ended talk features."

A radio historiography recalled an interesting sequence that originally brought Carter to WCAU's awareness: "WCAU needed a man to broadcast a rugby match, and Carter was qualified.... The radio station then engaged him to simulate 'live' coverage of an Oxford-Cambridge boat race. He had been a member of a rowing team in England. During the boat race, he spoke from the radio studio, using newspaper accounts of the real contest and crowd noise effects. It created the image that he was reporting from the bank of the Thames River." In that era, it was not unusual to employ pretense in radio to cause listeners to accept that what they were then hearing were live events.

In a lengthy tribute following his passing, *The New York Herald-Tribune* observed: "Boake Carter was one of the most controversial figures in radio, and his millions of listeners during the last decade were perhaps evenly divided among friends and enemies. He was an editorialist of the air and violently partisan in his comments on government, labor or any other issue before the public." In a scathing rebuke of Carter as an undisciplined, unprepared newsman, *The Murrow Boys* (Houghton Mifflin, 1996) authors Stanley Cloud and Lynne Olson suggested that he rarely knew "what was happening in the world." They further allowed, "He needed help in clarifying what was and was not important in the day's news." CBS gave it to him in the form of reporter Larry Lesueur, who "consulted" with him regarding what was newsworthy. Colleague Robert Trout remarked, "Nobody ever had the faintest idea what he [Carter] was doing, where he'd get his news." Cloud and Olson conjectured: "How, Boake Carter's critics wondered, could such an unschooled, untalented impostor hoodwink the American people into believing what he said on the air?" Irving E. Fang intimated in *Those Radio Commentators!* (Iowa State University Press, 1977) that Carter "may have been insane when he died." In *Air Time: The Inside Story of CBS News* (Harper & Row, 1978) by Gary Paul Gates, surprisingly, Carter—CBS's star journalist throughout the 1930s—isn't even mentioned.

CARUSO, CARL. b. Jan. 11, 1917, Boston, Mass. *Announcer.* **Series:** *A.L. Alexander's Goodwill Court* (director, ca. 1936–1937); *The Adventures of Leonidas Witherall* (1944–1945); *Bandwagon Mysteries* (ca. 1940s, early 1950s); *Bobby Benson's Adventures*, and multiple similar monikers; *High Adventure* (ca. 1950, 1953–1954); *My Friend Irma* (1947–ca. late 1940s); *The Mysterious Traveler* (ca. 1940s); *Rogue's Gallery* (1945–1946, 1947, 1950–1951); *The Shadow* (1949–1951).

Carl Caruso—who began his broadcast career at Boston's WBZ—was one of a trio of individuals presiding over the short lifespan of the hour-long giveaway show *Cut*, soon modified to *Spin the Picture* on Dumont Television in 1949. In 1953 he returned to the small screen as an offstage—and at times intimidating—voice on the fleeting ABC audience participation series *Back That Fact*. He was employed by ABC for two decades, 1963–1983.

CASE, NELSON. b. Feb. 3, 1910, Long Beach, Calif.; d. March 24, 1976, Doylestown, Pa. *Announcer.* **Series:** *The Adventures of the Thin Man* (early 1940s); *Against the Storm* (ca. 1940–1942); *Ask-It Basket* (ca. 1940–1941); Big band remotes (1930s); *Big Sister* (ca. 1950–1952); *Carefree Carnival* (1933–1934); *Charlie and Jessie* (1940–1941); *Crime Doctor* (1940–1942); *Criminal Casebook* (1948); *The Dave Garroway Show* (ca. late 1940s–early 1950s); *The Edgar Bergen and Charlie McCarthy Show* (ca. 1940s); *The Ed Sullivan Show* (ca. early 1940s); *Ford Theater* (1948–1949); *Hilda Hope, M.D.* (1939–1940); *The Hour of Charm* (1936–1939); *Johnny Presents*, aka *Philip Morris Playhouse* (commercial spokesman, 1938–ca. 1940s); *Kate Hopkins, Angel of Mercy* (ca. 1940–1942); *The Ken Murray Show*; *The Lanny Ross Show* (ca. 1940s); *Life Can Be Beautiful*; *Lone Journey* (early 1940s); *Lowell Thomas and the News* (1934–1941); *Marriage Club, Inc.* (1939–1941); *My True Story*; *Mystery of the Week* (ca. 1946–1947); *The NBC Symphony Orchestra* (1953–1954); *The New Carnation Contented Hour* (1946–1948); *Road of Life* (1952–ca. 1955); *The Sky Blazers* (1939–1940); *The Story of Mary Marlin* (ca. late 1930s–ca. early 1940s); *Wheatenaville Sketches* (1932–1933); *Youth Versus Age* (1939–1940). **Aphorism:** *Ninety-nine and forty-four one hundredths percent pure. It floats!*

In high school Nelson Case, son of the publisher of *The Long Beach Sun*, was active on the school newspaper staff. He was a baritone soloist and local dramatic thespian, too. An assignment to pursue a feature on Long Beach's KFON Radio so entranced the youngster that—at 15—he sold himself to the station manager as an occasional vocalist. At 16 pianist Case formed his own instrumental outfit and performed regularly on KFON. In 1927, at 17, he moved to rival station KGER; it hired him as a combination announcer-singer.

Still 17, he became the senior announcer, vocalist and orchestra leader at KFI, Los Angeles. At that juncture he paused for station identification—enrolling at William and Mary College. After graduation, in 1931 he joined the NBC announcing staff in San Francisco. By the following year he was on the air at KGO, the local NBC affiliate, with a quarter-hour on which he sang. Moving to Radio City in New York in 1934, Case introduced Lowell Thomas on nightly newscasts as well as the big band remote shows of Wayne King, Guy Lombardo and Ray Noble.

Before long he was introducing Johnny Rovetini, who uttered the infamous line ringing in Americans' ears for many years: "Callllllll for Phillllip Morraisseeee!" Case preceded Rovetini's spiel with: "And here comes Johnny now, stepping out of thousands of store windows to greet you!" Shifting gears temporarily, in 1942 Case went overseas with the U.S. Naval Air Corps. From his strategic vantage points along the warfront he dispatched firsthand accounts to NBC listeners back in the U.S.

One scholar termed Case "the original 'soft-sell' announcer." The venerable, mellow-toned narrator of daytime serials was long linked with Ivory soap through appearances on multiple showcases. His rhapsodic timbre connected with listeners and netted him instant voice-identification with "the most famous soap in the world." Ivory maker Procter & Gamble Co. paid Case to convince soap opera addicts of the commodity's attributes without resorting to high-pressure, hard-sell tactics. He unpretentiously reminded his audience that the brand was *ninety-nine and forty-four one hundredths percent pure. It floats!* When *Big Sister* left the air at the end of 1952, Case remained behind, plugging Ivory to the fans of *Road of Life* that inherited the time period just vacated. It was a tribute to Case's soft-spoken efficacy as P&G's chief Ivory spokesman. Invariably he precipitated the newly installed washboard weeper's familiar theme with an unpretentious billboard. Gently, preceding the familiar Tchaikovsky theme, he'd state matter-of-factly: "*The Road of Life*, compliments of Ivory soap." His soothing reverberation compared favorably with the adroit, philosophical CBS commentator Charles Osgood in successive decades dispatching humorous rhyming couplets.

In subsequent years, in addition to providing voiceovers for TV commercials, Case performed more functions on the tube. He hosted a dramatic anthology featuring original teleplays concerned with topical issues, *Armstrong Circle Theater*, during the series' inaugural season on NBC (1950–1951). He took over hosting duties of Dumont TV's *What's it Worth?* in the 1952–1953 season, a feature appraising art and antiques. That same season he co-hosted a similarly themed Dumont panel show, *Trash or Treasure?* Its title was altered to *Treasure Hunt* in April 1953. Case presided when a group of reruns was screened on an NBC-TV weekly anthology, *Summer Playhouse*, in July and August 1954. For six months he was the interlocutor of CBS-TV's *Road of Life* in 1954–1955; the Ivory-backed serial used the same scripts as the by-then transcribed radio version but aired at another time and was performed live. For six weeks in the summer of 1956 Case introduced pilot episodes of half-hour comedies that the viewers might anticipate seeing that fall (although none of them made it into permanent berths). Case's show was called *Sneak Preview* and it ran on NBC.

CHAPPELL, ERNEST (CHAPPIE). b. June 10, 1903, Syracuse, N.Y.; d. July 4, 1983, North Palm Beach, Fla. *Announcer, Newscaster, Emcee.* **Series:** *The Adventures of Ellery Queen* (1942–1944); *Amos 'n' Andy* (substitute announcer, 1940); *Are You a Genius?* (quizmaster, 1942–1943); *The Atwater Kent Hour* (producer, 1930–1931); *Between the Bookends* (1945–1949); *The Big Story* (1947–1955); *Campana Serenade* (ca. 1939–1940); *The Campbell Playhouse* (1939–1941); *The Campbell Room*, aka *Hildegarde* (1946–1947); *The Chamber Music Society of Lower Basin Street* (cast, ca. 1940s, early 1950s); *Edward R. Murrow and the News* (1945–ca. late 1940s); *The Fabulous Dr. Tweedy* (1946–1947); *Headlines with Ernest Chappell* (newscaster, 1938); *George Jessel's Jamboree* (1938); *The Mercury Summer Theater of the Air* (1946); *The Mercury Theater on the Air* (ca. 1938–ca. 1939); *Musical Mock Trial* (ca. 1938–1940); *Quiet Please* (host-producer, 1947–1949); *The Song of Your Life* (1940–1941); *That They Might Live* (1943–1944); *Thirty Minutes in Hollywood* (1937–1938); *True Story Hour with Mary and Bob* (producer, 1932).

After earning a degree from Syracuse University in 1925, Ernest Chappell intended to go into show business as a vocalist. But he was hired by hometown station WFBL as program director and announcer and that turned his plans into unexpected directions. In 1927—at just 24 years of age—he moved to Rochester as manager of WHAM, the local NBC Blue network voice. Not long after, the rising broadcaster took over programming for a quartet of regional outlets owned by a Buffalo media firm. While still in his twenties, in 1930 he started overseeing the production of some national radio series.

Chappell represented American Tobacco's Pall Mall cigarette brand for 17 years. He was the vendor's chief spokesman on its important *Big Story* broadcasts nearly half of that time and appeared on several other series supported by Pall Mall. Meanwhile, he tutored Eleanor Roosevelt for her abiding radio appearances (including her own show). During the 1939 New York World's Fair, Chappell officiated at the very first televised beauty competition. In 1940 when regular *Amos 'n' Andy* interlocutor Bill Hay suffered a heart attack, Chappell filled in until Hay was on his feet. Later, Chappell announced *Eyewitness to History* on CBS-TV (1960–1963) as well as that chain's early TV coverage of a myriad of presidential appearances.

CLANEY, HOWARD. b. April 17, 1898, Pittsburgh, Pa.; d. April 1980, Charlotte, N.C. *Announcer.* **Series:** *Amanda of Honeymoon Hill* (early 1940s); *The American Album of Familiar Music* (ca. 1930s, 1940s); *America's Town Meeting of the Air* (ca. late 1930s, 1940s); *Backstage Wife* (ca. 1950s); *Borden Special Edition*; *The Canada Dry Program*, aka *The Jack Benny Program* (1933); *Information Please* (1938–ca. early 1940s); *The Lucky Strike Hour*, aka *The Lucky Strike Dance Orchestra* (1933); *The NBC Symphony Orchestra* (ca. late 1930s–ca. early 1940s); *The Metropolitan Opera Auditions of the Air* (1935–1945, 1948–ca. 1958); *Mr. Chameleon* (ca. early 1950s–1953); *Stella Dallas* (ca. 1954–1955); *Waltz Time* (ca. 1930s, 1940s).

Howard Claney enrolled at Carnegie Institute of Technology, a college recognized for training engineers. But Claney didn't share those sentiments—he was concerned about drama, painting, sculpture and architecture. He eventually found the Art Institute of Chicago to his liking. Later, while in New York City, one day he accompanied an actor chum to a Broadway booking agency. On that occasion, out of the blue Claney was signed for a role in *A Man of the People*, opening the door for future productions. In the 1920s he appeared in noteworthy shows like *Cyrano de Bergerac*, *Juno and the Paycock* and *Liliom*. He joined the dramatic staff at NBC in addition and, in 1930, became a network announcer.

A gifted painter and watercolorist, Claney augmented his income by conducting one-man shows at prestigious art galleries. He studied painting in London in 1938 and—having previously joined the announcing staff of New York's WEAF, the flagship station of NBC's Red chain—he offered listeners at home eyewitness reports by short-wave radio, giving vivid descriptions of gathering war clouds. Prolific freelance program packager Frank Hummert used him steadily on his plethora of musical, serial and crime detective features. NBC Artists Service touted the nasal-toned Claney as "an expert in selling, psychology, and blessed with an air personality which strikes a note of genuine sincerity into his excellent delivery."

CLARK, HARRY. b. April 17, 1913, Providence, R.I.; d. Feb. 28, 1956. *Announcer, Newscaster, Actor.* **Series:** *Backstage Wife* (1935–ca. early 1940s); *CBS News* (newscaster, 1944–1947); *The Columbia Workshop* (1940s); *The Parker Family* (1939–ca. early 1940s); *The Second Mrs. Burton* (ca. late 1940s–ca. 1950s); *Skyline Roof* (1946); *Stoopnagle and Budd* (actor, ca. 1930s, 1940s).

After his network life faded, in 1952 Harry Clark joined WVOM in Boston as a sportscaster, signifying yet another dimension for the former announcer-actor-newscaster.

CLOSE, UPTON (born Josef Washington Hall). b. Feb. 27, 1894, Kelso, Wash.; d. Nov. 13, 1960, Guadalajara, Mexico. *Commentator, Newscaster.* **Series:** *Close-Ups of the News* (commentator, 1942–1944); *Events and Trends of the Week* (newscaster, 1941–1942); *News of the World* (correspondent, 1941–1944); *World News Parade* (newscaster-commentator, 1944–1945, 1946–1947).

Josef W. Hall studied at Washington Missionary College and received a bachelor's degree in 1915 from George Washington University. During the Japanese invasion of China from 1916 to 1919, he lived in China's Shantung province, serving in the U.S. Legation espionage service. He also penned a few articles for the Shanghai *Weekly Review*, invariably ending them with the signature "Up Close." That was to indicate where he was situated in relation to the battle raging. The editor ran the phrase as the author's name and Hall liked it so much, he turned it into "Upton Close."

Afterward, he acquired multiple posts: he became a newspaper correspondent in China, Japan and Siberia; he advised Chinese student revolutionaries; he was foreign affairs chief in the regime of Gen. Wu Pei-fu; and he became an explorer for both the National Geographic Society in Asia and the League of Nations. Typhoid fever intervened in 1922, however, and sent him packing; by then virtually an invalid, he returned to the U.S. to recover. Following a recuperation period, he joined the faculty of the University of Washington as a lecturer on oriental life and literature. During this epoch, in 1924 he appeared on radio for the first time, with Lowell Thomas, another globetrotter with whom he shared common interests. The pair established themselves as radio's first lecturers.

Close left the University of Washington in 1926 to return to the orient as director of the annual American Cultural Expeditions to the orient. From 1926 to 1935 he led hordes of business professionals, instructors and students to the Far East, India, Russia, the Middle East and Europe. After that lengthy experience he went home to America but quickly left for Mexico. By 1936 he was in Newark, N.J., offering his perspectives to listeners of WOR.

During his lecture years Close was also writing extensively. Ultimately he contributed to seven volumes on Asian and world affairs: *In the Land of the Laughing Buddha* (Putnam, 1924); *Outline History of China* (D. Appleton, 1926, co-authored with Herbert H. Gowen); *The Revolt of Asia* (Putnam, 1927); *Moonlady* (Putnam, 1927); *Eminent Asians*

(D. Appleton, 1929); *Challenge* (Farrar and Rinehart, 1934, updated and re-released in 1942 as *Behind the Face of Japan*); and *The Ladder of History* (Macmillan, 1945, co-authored with Merle Burke). "Nothing was slapdash about these books," Irving Fang surmised. "They were fat with pages and carefully researched." Several combined the author's personal adventures and his political observations.

Anyone familiar with Close's voice could recognize it in Fox Movietone newsreels. Occasionally he substituted on the air for his pal Lowell Thomas. He appeared intermittently, in fact, on several NBC newscasts between 1934 and 1941. By the spring of 1941 the network hired him as its expert on the Far East and assigned him a quarter-hour timeslot on its Red network on Sunday afternoons and on its Blue chain on Wednesday evenings.

"The next two years saw Upton Close at the peak of his national popularity," declared Fang. "By this time the thrust of his messages had changed. Instead of the old relatively objective analysis of events in the Pacific, he now lashed out at President Roosevelt, at liberalism, at Britain, and at Russia. Liberals responded by accusing him of being isolationist, anti–British, pro–German, anti-labor, and anti–Semitic." Even as this trend was occurring, in 1944 NBC published a history of its news operations with a ringing endorsement of its Far East authority, offering a photo and compelling biography recounting the newsman's diverse accomplishments, concluding with: "Currently heard from Hollywood, Close's NBC broadcasts are notable for their authentic interpretation of events in the Orient."

Nevertheless, Close became an outspoken ultraconservative who so angered management of not one but *two* networks that he might have been dismissed by the second had he not quit. He was relieved of his duties at NBC in December 1944 and subsequently left MBS little more than two years beyond in February 1947. A pundit succinctly characterized his beliefs by then: "The grand secret of Close's point of view is not hard to discover. Whatever happens, he is against it."

He wasn't hostile to everything, of course, although he took plenty of potshots at organized labor, American allies and the United Nations on a hit list that routinely surfaced on the air. During the Second World War, Close strongly advocated concentrating the battle on Japan, thereby seemingly letting Germany off the hook, at least until Japan was vanquished. All of it ran afoul of liberal groups, which threatened to boycott his NBC sponsor, pen and pencil manufacturer Sheaffer Co. When he was terminated from that chain, he protested vociferously that it was provoked by Communist inducement, a charge NBC president Miles Trammel promptly refuted.

Close voluntarily left broadcasting in early 1947 and never returned as an active participant. He moved to Mexico in retirement and was killed 13 years later when his car collided with a train.

COLE, FREDERICK B. b. ca. 1915, Hingham, Mass.; d. Dec. 20, 1964. *Announcer*. **Series:** *Double or Nothing* (ca. 1940s); *Ethel and Albert*, aka *The Private Life of Ethel and Albert* (1940s); *The Strange Dr. Karnac* (1943).

Frederick B. Cole isn't to be confused with Fred Cole of the same era, one of the busiest network sound effects technicians in the 1940s and 1950s. While *that* Cole was responsible for many of the resonances echoing from numerous dramatic programs, his most memorable one was probably the voice of the penguin in the Kools cigarette commercials. But Frederick B. Cole used *his* voice exclusively in his work.

From 1947 to 1960, his network years then history, Frederick B. (Fred) Cole joined WHDH in Boston, the same local station then enjoying the services of comedians Bob (Elliott) and Ray (Goulding). At WHDH Cole—by then a disc jockey—presided over the *Carnival of Music*. In the early 1950s, Bob & Ray's careers were headed the other way; having been "discovered" by the major chains, they gained momentum and national exposure by relocating in New York City.

COLE, GRADY. d. 1979. *Announcer, Emcee*. **Series:** *Carolina Calling* (host-announcer, 1946–1949); *Carolina Hayride* (announcer, 1944–1945); *Grady Cole and the Johnson Family* (host-announcer, 1950–1951); *Grady Cole Show* (host, 1951–1953).

Grady Cole was a Carolina radio institution. Arriving in Charlotte—the centrally situated "Queen City of the Carolinas"—in

1929, he became a listening habit with people all over those dual states and as far as 50,000-watt WBT reached beyond. Initially hired to read the weekday news at noon followed by the stock market reports, by April 1930 Cole was a full time staffer at the CBS owned-and-operated affiliate: CBS held title to WBT for 16 years, from 1929–1945. In addition to his midday chores, the basal-toned announcer became the station's widely acclaimed morning man; he broadcast from 5 to 9 A.M. until retirement more than three decades hence in 1961. Writing in *The Charlotte Observer*, columnist Bob Quincy allowed that Cole's voice "sounded like a lawnmower in a gravel pit."

WBT quickly began to develop its own identity, creating a myriad of live programming features, a large segment of that staged before studio audiences like bigger metropolitan stations in New York, Chicago and Los Angeles did. Reflecting its strategic position in the rural belt, one of WBT's earliest trademarks was a plethora of country music acts (The Carter Family, Arthur Smith and the Crackerjacks, The Rangers Quartet, others). By 1944 Cole presided at a mammoth barn dance, *Carolina Hayride*, in the city's Armory Auditorium on Saturday afternoons featuring the station's roster of pickers and singers. Beginning in December 1944, CBS picked up a segment of the live show, beaming it to the nation. In 1946 the chain opted for another Charlotte-originated country-western series, *Carolina Calling*, which ran for a few weeks on Saturday morning, then for more than three years on Sunday morning. Once again Cole was at the mike introducing assorted performers.

When that entry departed, WBT was already feeding the network a program of harmonizing featuring pianist Larry Walker and the Johnson Family Singers. Walker and station announcer Kurt Webster were the group's interlocutors until Cole was appointed in 1950. Almost two years later they went separate ways and CBS offered its audience the quarter-hour *Grady Cole Show* with his homespun humor weekday afternoons. "Mr. WBT," as Cole was known locally, became a familiar presence to CBS listeners for a decade between the mid 1940s and mid 1950s. "As announcer, disc jockey, farm editor, weather reporter, news commentator and general entertainer, he was incomparable," wrote Kenneth M. Johnson, a member of the Johnson Family Singers, in a memoir of that entourage's entertainment pilgrimage. "Grady was an incessant talker, but a mild and mellow man whose warmth was contagious. He provided a forum for our family and the opportunity for us to develop."

Some time after Cole died in an automobile accident in the summer of 1979, the city of Charlotte erected a daunting downtown 3000-seat civic center accommodating multiple sport and leisure activities including concerts, festivals, trade shows, auctions, basketball and meetings. They decided to name it the Grady Cole Center for a man who pioneered broadcasting across the two Carolinas.

COLLINGWOOD, CHARLES CUMMINGS. b. June 4, 1917, Three Rivers, Mich.; d. Oct. 3, 1985, New York, N.Y. *Correspondent, Newscaster.* **Series**: *CBS World News Roundup* (correspondent, 1942–1945, 1948, 1949); *Charles Collingwood and the News* (newscaster, 1946, 1947, 1949–1952); *This Is London* (correspondent, 1941–early 1940s); *World News Roundup* (correspondent, ca. 1942–ca. 1952).

Charles Collingwood spent much of his early years in Washington, D.C. In 1939, on the precipice of World War II—aided by a Rhodes scholarship—he went to England to study at Oxford, intending to enter international law. He revised his plans with the inception of war, turning his focus to journalism instead. At 23, in 1940 he signed with United Press and was situated in London. The following March he was hired by CBS newsman Edward R. Murrow, who was assembling a team of foreign war correspondents ("the Murrow Boys") of which Collingwood was to be a crucial player. So enamored was he with his broadcast news coach, in fact—arguably the best in the business—that he acknowledged later he wanted "to write like Ed and sound like Ed. I wanted to *be* Edward R. Murrow."

While making solid contributions to his new profession, Collingwood was described by an observer as "imposing, dashing, and a lady-killer." He reported during the war from London and North Africa. One source certified his coverage from the latter region as "patented, careless ease." A media historian noted—throughout his career—Collingwood scored notable scoops by an almost uncanny ability to "catch the turn of events" just before they broke. In 1943 he won a George Foster Peabody Award of excellence for his reportorial efforts.

After the war he married Hollywood movie actress Louise Allbritton. For a year (1946–1947) the Collingwoods lived in Los Angeles while she played major roles in two movie comedy hits, *The Egg and I* and *Sitting Pretty*. Collingwood, meanwhile, was a daily newscaster and analyst for local CBS affiliate KNX. He also reported sporadically for his network. Returning east, he became CBS's first United Nations correspondent. Near the end of the 1940s he began covering the Truman White House. Before Truman was out of office, however, Collingwood took a leave of absence from his employer to become a special assistant to Averell Harriman, director of mutual security in Washington.

Coming back to CBS in 1953, Collingwood found that radio had been supplanted by television. "Of all 'Murrow's boys,'" a pundit affirmed, "Collingwood came the closest to being ideally suited for television. He was, in many ways, a more fluent and polished broadcaster than Murrow himself, and ... he had all his mentor's on-air urbanity, and then some.... He was movie-star handsome.... He ... was very bright and serious and had sound reportorial instincts.... He was a natural for TV journalism."

All of Collingwood's ongoing TV gigs were on CBS. He was soon substituting for Douglas Edwards as anchorman for his evening quarter-hour, forerunner of *The CBS Evening News*. In 1951–1952 Collingwood moderated an ephemeral discussion series from Washington, *The Big Question*, which weekly focused on a major issue of domestic or international import. He was a guest participant on the 1953 forum *Youth Takes a Stand*. From 1953 to 1955 he narrated *Adventure*, an educational series for kids. He inherited Ed Murrow's *Person to Person* (1959–1960, 1961) as his supremely admired tutor departed CBS. In 1962–1963 Collingwood anchored a weekly primetime news analysis feature, *Eyewitness to History*. He hosted *Portrait*—interviews with prominent figures from entertainment, political and other public-eye venues—in 1963. He presided over *Chronicle*, a CBS documentary on arts and sciences, in 1963–1964.

When Collingwood was passed over for Walter Cronkite as Doug Edwards' nightly replacement in 1961, followed by Harry Reasoner's appointment as Cronkite's primary sub, the durable newsman negotiated with ABC about being its chief anchor. Ultimately he decided to continue at CBS, however. "He decided he would rather remain a semistar at a first-class network than become the headliner at an inferior one," an assessor confirmed. "The pull of the old Murrow tradition exerted its force on Collingwood." In 1964 he prevailed on CBS to send him to London as chief foreign correspondent (a job once held by Murrow). For several successive years he reported from the British Isles and other newsmaking hot spots around the globe. He retired from CBS in 1982.

COLLINS, FRED. *Announcer.* **Series:** *Best Plays* (ca. 1952–1953); *The Big Guy* (1950); *The Chase* 1952–1953); *Crime and Peter Chambers* (1954); *Dimension X* (announcing sporadically in 1950–1951); *Dr. Sixgun* (1954–1955); *My Son Jeep* (1950s); *Radio City Playhouse* (ca. 1949–1950); *Spend a Million* (1954–1955); *Top Secret* (1950); *Wanted* (narrator, 1950); *X-Minus One* (1955–1958, 1973–1975).

Fred Collins launched his life in broadcasting over WASK in Lafayette, Ind.

On June 24, 1973—16 years after the network finale of *X-Minus One*—NBC dug out its transcriptions for a test to see if contemporary listeners would embrace radio drama a second time. The scheduling was self-defeating; the series appeared monthly, intermittently on Sundays or Saturdays, hardly a blueprint for building a consistent flock of followers. Collins pleaded with those tuning in to urge local stations to carry it. But mired in a plethora of sports events and news bites, not enough fans did. After a resilient effort the reprise died on March 22, 1975.

COLLINS, JOSEPH MARTIN (TED). b. Oct. 12, 1899, New York, N.Y.; d. May 27, 1964, Lake Placid, N.Y. *Announcer, Emcee, Newscaster.* **Series:** *The Kate Smith Show,* and multiple added monikers (personal manager, producer, co-host and newscaster on numerous Smith series, 1931–1964).

According to one opinion, "[Ted] Collins, a one-time announcer and Columbia Records scout, kept [Kate] Smith at arm's length from the public, securely wrapped in patriotic bunting." He was singularly responsible for packaging her all-embracing voice and down-home style for records, radio and television, mediums in which she soared from the 1930s to the 1960s.

Collins, a Columbia Phonograph Co. executive, caught Kate Smith's show one night in August 1930 at the Apollo Theater. So enamored with her was he that he became the first to see her budding possibilities while visualizing elevated opportunities for himself. Initially he asked Smith to record vocals for the label he managed. Simultaneously, he was astute enough to realize that problems lay directly ahead for the recording trade. Wary consumers were seeking to survive a Depression-epoch collapse of the national economy, offering them little in the way of discretionary spending for the foreseeable future.

At that fortuitous juncture, radio was experiencing a wildly enthusiastic reception. Once listeners purchased a receiver, its costs for providing home entertainment were generally negligible. The possibilities that radio, and Kate Smith, presented did not escape an enterprising, entrepreneurial Collins. He offered to become her personal manager, arranging bookings, overseeing finances, handling promotion as well as legal aspects and logistics of appearances. "You do the singing and I'll fight the battles," he told her. "We'll split the profits equally."

It was a good deal for her, as she was then still undiscovered by all but limited audiences, and profitable for him. Most managers received less than a fifth of their clients' incomes as a fee, some considerably less. Collins took half. Smith was impressed by Collins' sincerity and believability. The two shook hands. Their alliance turned out to be a good supposition for both, one never put into writing but which extended to Collins' death nearly 34 years later. He was her business partner and co-hosted many of her ensuing broadcast series that continued every day or week for many years.

COLLYER, CLAYTON (BUD) (born Clayton Johnson Heermance Jr.). b. June 18, 1908, New York, N.Y.; d. Sept. 8, 1969, Greenwich, Conn. *Announcer, Actor, Emcee.* **Series:** *Abie's Irish Rose* (actor, ca. 1944); *The Adventures of Superman* (actor, 1942–1950); *The Benny Goodman Show*, under various monikers (ca. late 1930s, early 1940s); *Big Sister* (1940s); *Break the Bank* (host-announcer, 1945–1955); *By Popular Demand* (1938); *Cavalcade of America* (1940–1943); *Chick Carter, Boy Detective* (actor, ca. 1943–ca. 1945); *Chips Davis, Commando* (actor, 1942–1943); *The Goldbergs* (ca. mid 1930s–ca. 1945); *The Guiding Light* (1940s); *High Places* (actor, 1944–1945); *Hillbilly Heartthrobs*, aka *Heartthrobs of the Hills*, aka *Dreams of Long Ago* (actor, ca. 1935–ca. 1938); *House in the Country* (1941–1942); *Joyce Jordan, M.D.* (actor, ca. late 1930s–ca. early 1940s); *Just Plain Bill* (actor, ca. 1930s, 1940s); *Kate Hopkins, Angel of Mercy* (actor, 1940–1942); *Kitty Foyle* (actor, 1942–1944); *Life Can Be Beautiful* (actor, ca. 1940s); *Listening Post* (ca. late 1940s); *The Man I Married* (actor, ca. 1940–1942); *Mary Small* (1944–1946); *On Your Mark* (quizmaster, 1948–1949); *The Philip Morris Playhouse* (actor, ca. 1939–ca. 1944); *Pretty Kitty Kelly* (actor, 1937–1940); *Quiz of Two Cities* (mid 1940s); *The Raleigh Room*, aka *Hildegarde* (1945–1946); *Road of Life* (1937–ca. 1951); *Shoot the Moon* (quizmaster, 1950–1951); *Silver Theater* (actor, ca. 1937–ca. 1942, ca. 1943–ca. 1944); *Stage Door Canteen* (ca. 1942–ca. 1945); *The Story of Mary Marlin* (ca. 1940s); *Terry and the Pirates* (actor, 1937–ca. 1939); *Three for the Money* (master of ceremonies, 1948); *Times a-Wastin'* (quizmaster, 1948); *Truth or Consequences* (1940–ca. 1945); *Winner Take All* (master of ceremonies, late 1940s); *Young Widder Brown* (actor, 1938–1940). **Aphorism:** *Duz does everything!*

Intending to become an attorney, Bud Collyer equipped himself at Williams College and Fordham University for a career that barely happened. Having received a bachelor of laws degree from Fordham and practiced for a couple of years, he altered his life's course after he discovered that radio performers earned more than attorneys. In his undergraduate years his weekly income for singing over New York's WABC, then the CBS flagship station, was $85; not bad for a time when the nation was suffering the pangs of absolute financial collapse. Before long Collyer was earning really "big dough"—$135 a week—from 30 broadcasts each week! By then he had also performed in a Broadway production of *The Fields Beyond* and realized that his heart was positively in show business.

For many years he appeared as the chief spokesman for Procter & Gamble's Duz, a leading washday detergent in the 1930s, 1940s and 1950s. In that capacity he constantly reminded listeners "Duz does everything!" on *The Goldbergs, The Guiding Light, Road of Life* (he introduced it daily as "the Duz program"), *Truth or Consequences* and several more. He was finally linked to no fewer than 16 open-ended (without conclusion) radio soap operas, seven as announcer and nine as a thespian (he played the masculine lead in five of the latter group). But the busy actor-announcer didn't conclude with that. He contributed to many more series, extending his show business career to eventually become a master of ceremonies-quizmaster-panel moderator of substantial standing. Getting his feet wet in radio quizzes and stunt games, he was poised to make a leap to television at a propitious moment. There, dropping "Clayton," which he had often been identified by in radio, for "Bud," he became one of the new medium's most visible audience participation entertainers.

On the tube Collyer presided over a dozen primetime and daytime interaction features: *The Missus Goes a-Shopping* (1948); *Winner Take All* (1948–1950); *Break the Bank* (1948–1953, plus a 1953 daytime version); *Talent Jackpot* (1949); *Beat the Clock* (1950–1958, plus a 1957–1961 daytime version); *Say It with Acting* (1951); *Masquerade Party* (1952); *On Your Way* (1953–1954); *Quick as a Flash* (1953–1954); *Feather Your Nest* (1954); *Number Please* (1961); and *To Tell the Truth* (1956–1967, plus a 1962–1968 daytime version). Between 1966 and 1969 he reprised his *Superman* radio role for the small fry, providing voiceovers for an animated video incarnation. He was the voice of Batman for *The Batman-Superman Hour*, another cartoon entry, in 1969–1970. With at least 52 broadcast series to his credit, Collyer was one of the busiest performers in show business.

He was also a tireless worker in the American Federation of Radio Artists. He was president of the New York chapter for a while and—in 1948 and 1949—was elected the body's national president. During the Cold War in the middle of the 20th century, Collyer played a key role in exposing (blacklisting) performers suspected of maintaining Communist or Nazi sympathies. While exhibiting peacemaking and mediating tendencies, he nonetheless made few apologies for his outspoken tough stand, one that ultimately cost some entertainers their livelihoods. His cause was embraced in places but it resulted in many unsettled nerves elsewhere.

COMBS, GEORGE HAMILTON, JR. b. May 3, 1899, Lee's Summit, Mo.; d. Nov. 29, 1977, West Palm Beach, Fla. *Commentator.* **Series:** *George Hamilton Combs News and Commentary* (news analyst, 1937–1971); *Think Fast* (panelist, 1949–1950).

George Hamilton Combs was a multiplicity of professional people: an attorney, politician, bureaucrat, electronic journalist and author. After graduating from the public schools of Kansas City, he attended the University of Missouri and the University of Michigan, served in the U.S. Navy (1918) and graduated from the Kansas City School of Law (1921). From 1922 to 1924 Combs was an assistant prosecuting attorney in Missouri and was elected as a Democrat to the U.S. Congress in 1926, serving a single term (1927–1929). He did not run for a second term but moved to New York City in 1929, resumed his law practice and in 1931 became special assistant to the New York state attorney general.

While in Gotham, Combs became news director of radio station WHN. He founded Radio Press International, a global newsgathering agency, and authored a few books—among them, *Himmler Nazi Spider Man: The Man After Hitler* (McKay, 1942). In 1936 he was appointed director of the National Emergency Council by President Franklin D. Roosevelt. From 1937 to 1971 Combs was a liberal radio news analyst, war correspondent and writer, speaking on the NBC Blue, ABC and MBS networks and—between 1952 and 1961—on television, too. He capped his career as chief United Nations correspondent and news commentator for the Mutual Broadcasting System (1961–1971).

CONOVER, HUGH. b. March 27, 1915, Washington, D.C.; d. Sept. 27, 1992, Morgan Hill, Calif. *Announcer.* **Series:** *Amanda of Honeymoon Hill* (ca. mid 1940s); *Big Sister* (ca. late 1940s, early 1950s); *The Right to Happiness* (ca. 1940s, ca. 1950s).

In 1935 Hugh Conover left WIS, Columbia, S.C., for WJSV, Washington, D.C. where—between 1939 and 1941—he was a newscaster. He interrupted his network radio career in 1944 to report to the U.S. Army, serving in the last months of the Second World War.

CONSIDINE, ROBERT BERNARD. b. Nov. 4, 1906, Washington, D.C.; d. Sept. 25, 1975, New York, N.Y. *Announcer, Newscaster.* **Series:** *The Fred Waring Show* (ca. 1930s, 1940s); *On the Line with Considine,* aka *Headline Hunters* (1947–1968, 1971–ca. 1975); *Monitor* (interviewer-commentator, ca. 1968–ca. 1971).

Educated at George Washington University's night school, Bob Considine became a journalist quite by accident. He was working as a messenger at the U.S. State Department when he played in an amateur tennis tournament that was covered by *The Washington Herald.* The rag misspelled his name and he complained, informing officials he could do a better job than they. He was promptly hired as a sports reporter and soon branched into drama and editorial writing.

With a reputation being built on print journalism and a syndicated column ("On the Line") beginning in 1933, Considine added radio news to his portfolio in 1932, broadcasting nightly for then-employer *The Washington Post.* A decade later, in 1941–1942, he was a sportscaster for New York's WNEW Radio. Not long afterward he presided over his own quarter-hour Sunday evening series aired nationally. His popular radio show *On the Line with Considine* was named for his enduring column in *The New York Daily Mirror* and scores of other papers. He was still penning it when he died, 42 years after its inception.

From 1951 to 1954, *On the Line with Considine* appeared on NBC-TV, and in the summer of 1954 on ABC-TV. During those quarter-hours the host read news headlines, offered intermittent comments and interviewed a well-known figure about a relevant topical point. In 1955 he was a panelist on the live ABC-TV quiz *Who Said That?* Considine was a recurring guest on the NBC-TV series *Tonight! America After Dark* that replaced Steve Allen's *Tonight* in 1957. Sometimes he was called on to narrate dramatic presentations on CBS-TV's *Westinghouse Desilu Playhouse* (1958–1960).

Considine authored, co-authored or edited 25 books, including biographies of Jack Dempsey, Armand Hammer, Robert L. Ripley, Babe Ruth and Toots Shor, plus *General Wainwright's Story, MacArthur the Magnificent* and *Thirty Seconds Over Tokyo.* He also penned an autobiography released in 1967. He wrote a half-dozen movie scripts: *The Babe Ruth Story; The Beginning of the End; Church of the Good Thief; Hoodlum Empire; Ladies Day;* and *Thirty Seconds Over Tokyo.* A few months prior to his death the New York chapter of Sigma Delta Chi, the Society of Professional Journalists, cited Considine as one of 10 superior practicing pressmen.

CONTE, JOHN. b. Sept. 15, 1915, Palmer, Mass. *Announcer, Actor, Vocalist.* **Series:** *Al Pearce and His Gang* (ca. 1930s, 1940s); *The Baby Snooks Show* (late 1930s, early 1940s); *Big Town* (ca. 1940s); *The Burns and Allen Show* (1938); *Command Performance* (ca. 1942–ca. 1950); *The Gulf Screen Guild Show,* aka *The Gulf Screen Guild Theater* (1939–1942); *Guest Star* (ca. 1940s); *It Happened in Hollywood* (co-host, 1939–1940); *The John Conte Show* (host, 1953); *Mail Call* (ca. 1942–ca. 1950); *Maxwell House Coffee Time,* aka *The Frank Morgan Show* (1944–1945); *MGM Screen Test* (1944); *My Good Wife* (actor, 1949); *Passing Parade* (1937–ca. 1938); *Radio Hall of Fame,* aka *Philco Radio Hall of Fame* (actor, 1943–1946); *Screen Guild Theater* (1939); *Screen Test* (1944); *Sherlock Holmes* (actor, late 1930s–1940s); *Silver Theater* (1937–1942); *Teentimers Club* (host, 1946–1947, 1948); *Treasury of Music* (host, 1955).

John Conte began his career as a simple radio announcer. Ultimately he would invade the legitimate stage, motion pictures and television, too. He worked his way up the radio ladder to chief announcer for CBS in Hollywood before leaving to be a freelance announcer in 1937. Conte performed in road shows and multiple California little theater productions, including the Pasadena Playhouse. On Dec. 30, 1936, he announced a 90-minute dedication program signifying the launch of the combined Mutual-Don Lee network, originating at Los Angeles' KHJ. On that occasion artists appearing on remotes from across the nation included Mary Bryan, Mae Clarke, Nadine Conner, Norman Field, Thomas Lee and Paula Winslowe.

Conte interrupted a successful career in 1945 when the Army drafted him. Within a year he was back on the ether and also was the singing star of Broadway musicals by Richard Rodgers and Oscar Hammerstein II, like *Allegro* and *Carousel*. Within a short while he was turning up on the home screens as a recurring personality. Most of his showcases had musical themes and occurred in the 1950s (except as noted) over NBC-TV. Between 1950 and 1954 he vocalized sporadically on *Your Show of Shows*. In 1950–1951 he hosted his own quarter-hour on Tuesday and Thursday evenings, variously known as *Van Camp's Little Show*, as *John Conte's Little Show* and as *The Little Show*. On most outings the star was paired with a visiting feminine vocalist but occasionally there were other guests. During the same season Conte costarred with Martha Raye in the madcap tune-filled romp *Anything Goes* on the live *Musical Comedy Time*. In the mid 1950s on *Max Liebman Presents* Conte performed with Anne Jeffreys, Brian Sullivan and Edward Everett Horton in a production of *The Merry Widow*.

He won a bit part in the CBS soap opera *Woman with a Past* (1954). From 1955 to 1958 he hosted *Matinee Theater*, an ambitious anthology presenting a new, live, hour-long drama every weekday afternoon in color. In 1959 Conte hosted a 39-week syndicated television series titled *Mantovani* featuring Annunzio Paolo Mantovani and his orchestra. His final widespread TV performing effort, also syndicated, *The Best of the Post* (1960–1961), was a dramatic anthology based on narratives from *The Saturday Evening Post*. After that Conte managed KMTR-TV at Palm Desert, Calif., where he also conducted a video talk show. He purchased KMIR-TV at Palm Springs, Calif.

Between 1932 and 1964 Conte appeared in 14 mostly B-movies: *The Crowd Roars* (1932); *Campus Confessions* (1938); *Our Neighbors, the Carters* (1939); *Each Dawn I Die* (1939); *Indianapolis Speedway* (1939); *Unmarried* (1939); *Invitation to Happiness* (1939); *Confessions of a Nazi Spy* (1939); *Thousands Cheer* (1943); *Lost in a Harem* (1944); *Nobody Lives Forever* (1946); *The Man with the Golden Arm* (1955); *Trauma* (1962); and *The Carpetbaggers* (1964). In the first eight of those, Conte portrayed an uncredited radio announcer, narrator or reporter. He met his first wife (1944–1947), actress Marilyn Maxwell, on the set of *Lost in a Harem*.

In 1953 while working in New York City the multitalented man with the affable personality presided over a 45-minute late afternoon *John Conte Show* on WABC Radio, then CBS's flagship station. Conte crooned some fan favorites ("Side By Side," "How Do You Speak to an Angel?," "S'Wonderful" were typical), intermingling them with an assortment of recorded discs by popular artists. "It's a pleasant setup that warrants sponsor attention," *Variety* proclaimed.

COOK, LOU. Announcer. **Series:** *I Fly Anything* (1950–1951); *Jay Stewart's Fun Fair* (1949); *Mr. President* (1947–1953); *Starr of Space* (1953–1954).

COOPER, EDWIN. b. ca. 1920; d. Aug. 14, 1961. Announcer, Actor. **Series:** *The Milt Herth Trio* (1938–1939, 1942, 1946); *RFD America* (1947–1949); *The Silver Eagle, Mountie* (early 1950s); *The Texaco Star Theater* (actor, early 1940s).

CORNELL, JOHN. Announcer. **Series:** *Just Plain Bill*.

John Cornell was a newscaster at Cincinnati's WSAI in 1942.

COSTELLO, JOHN PATRICK MICHAEL JOSEPH (JACK). b. May 31, 1908, Sauk Centre, Minn.; d. September 1983. Announcer. **Series:** *The Adventures of the Falcon* (ca. 1950–1952); *Battle of the Sexes* (ca. 1938–ca. 1944); *Battle Stations* (1943); *The Bob and Ray Show* (ca. 1951–ca. 1953); *Carson Robison's Buckaroos* (ca. 1938–ca. 1940); *The Falcon* (1943); *The Fitch Bandwagon* (ca. late 1930s, 1940s); *Helpmate* (ca. 1941–ca. 1944); *The Johnny Morgan Show* (ca. 1943, ca. 1946); *Just Plain Bill*; *The Ken Banghart*

Show (1947); *The Leopold Stokowski Show*; *Mr. Keen, Tracer of Lost Persons* (1951–1952); *Now Hear This* (1951); *Portia Faces Life* (ca. 1940s–ca. early 1950s); *Pot o' Gold* (1939–1941); *Stars in Khaki 'n' Blue* (1952); *Stella Dallas*; *The Stradivari Orchestra* (ca. 1943–ca. 1945); *These Are Our Men* (1944–1945); *Treasury Salute* (1945–1946); *Vacation with Music* (1946); *Vox Pop* (1937–ca. 1939); *What Would You Have Done?* (1940); *Where Have You Been?* (1954–1955); *Words at War* (1943–1945); *X Minus One* (ca. 1955–ca. 1958).

After graduating from Sauk Centre High School in 1926, for a year Jack Costello worked alongside his dad in a family construction concern. In 1927 he relocated to St. Paul where he was a cook at the St. Francis Hotel and a night clerk at the Minnesota Club while pursuing studies in journalism, history and English at the University of Minnesota. During that sojourn, *The St. Paul Pioneer Dispatch* hired him as a $25-a-week reporter. Costello, in the interim, was rejected after applying for an announcer's slot at KSTP Radio without experience. But in June 1932 a station at Grand Forks, N.D., KFJN, did hire him and KSTP welcomed him to its staff one year later.

On a visit to New York City in the summer of 1935, Costello auditioned at NBC. Making the leap to Radio City in February 1936, he joined a cadre of KSTP staffers who had done or would do the same—Pierre Andre, Tom Breen, Roger Krupp, Pat Murphy and George Watson among their number. During his early years there Costello penned a weekly column titled *From Main Street to Broadway* and peddled it to community and county seat newspapers for a dollar an installment. Later, he flirted with motion pictures, briefly appearing in a 1947 release, *The Shocking Miss Pilgrim*, and narrating the 1955 film *Amalfi Way*.

In the meantime, underscoring the legendary status that Americans afforded some of their radio announcers during the medium's heyday, in 1939—only three years after he joined NBC's interlocutory staff—Costello was recognized by the denizens of Sauk Centre as one of their favorite sons. On that occasion, a dossier of his professional achievements to that date and a sketch of the revered hometown hero were signified by a permanent display in the hamlet's local library.

Costello was Bishop Fulton J. Sheen's announcer on a couple of televised series that extended to a dozen years—*Life Is Worth Living* (1952–1955, Dumont; 1955–1957, ABC) and *The Bishop Sheen Program* (1961–1968, syndication). In 1952 Costello also introduced the fleeting NBC-TV game show *What Happened*, an imitation of CBS-TV's popular *I've Got a Secret*. Regrettably, *What Happened* (and some of Costello's video fame with it) lasted just three weeks while *Secret* persisted for 15 years before padding its portfolio with a syndicated embodiment! He returned to the NBC-TV studios to announce the daytime serial *Young Doctor Malone* (ca. 1958–ca. 1963). Costello retired from the network in 1976.

COTT, TED. b. Jan. 1, 1917, Poughkeepsie, N.Y.; d. June 12, 1973, New York, N.Y. *Announcer, Emcee, Director*. **Series:** *Major Bowes' Original Amateur Hour* (ca. 1942–1945); *Music You Want* (1941–1943); *The Pause That Refreshes on the Air*, aka *Coca-Cola Hour* (master of ceremonies, 1947–1949); *Society Girl* (director, 1939–1940); *So You Think You Know Music?* (master of ceremonies, 1939–1941).

Ted Cott broke into broadcasting as a 16-year-old youth, announcing for a Brooklyn outlet. WNYC, a city-owned station, subsequently offered him $150 per month to announce for it while also being its director of drama. It took nine years for the Civil Service Commission to decide he was unqualified for the job; when it did, he moved to WNEW, earning $600 a month! Before long CBS's *Major Bowes' Original Amateur Hour* was paying him $1,500 monthly!

During his stint at WNEW, Cott was involved in developing a game show requiring a quartet of competitors and focusing around knowledge of composers and classical music, *So You Think You Know Music?* CBS added it to its lineup; later, it appeared within NBC's *Schaefer Revue*. Cott became an NBC vice president in 1950 and general manager of the chain's New York radio and television affiliates; he held the same responsibilities for the Dumont television network and its Gotham station before that operation folded in the mid 1950s. For many years the International Academy of Television Arts and Sciences has presented an annual Ted Cott Award to a board member who has contributed appreciably to the academy.

In its issue of Oct. 19, 1953, *Time* magazine wrote: "NBC last week dropped a $5,000,000 blockbuster in the form of 28 new or revamped radio shows. The man tossing the bomb (target: public apathy about radio) is NBC's go-getting Vice President Ted Cott, 36, who arrived at the 'Magic 28' after three weeks of all-out celebration with his NBC associates."

COURTNEY, ALAN. b. Nov. 29, 1912, New York, N.Y.; d. Sept. 16, 1978, Miami, Fla. *Announcer, Disc Jockey, Emcee.* **Series:** *Courtney Record Carnival* (disc jockey, 1947–1950); *The Gloom Chasers*, aka *Stoopnagle and Budd* (host, 1938–1939); *The Korn Kobblers* (1942–1943, 1946–1947).

Alan Courtney became a DJ at 17 and was still at it three decades later. In between a few stints on network radio, Courtney offered WOV, New York, listeners *Do You Know the Answer?* in 1942. The feature presented a combined news and quiz format involving him randomly telephoning area residents to ask questions for prizes about current events. He subsequently added a three-hour-long local DJ series, *The 1280 Club*, to his weeknight schedule. In 1948 he presided over *The Alan Courtney Show*, a live weekday half-hour at noon over New York's WNEW that included the Ray Ross Orchestra and vocalist Marilyn Towne.

Having also appeared in the 1930s on New York's WMCA and WOR, Courtney left Gotham in 1948 for the warmer climes of south Florida. Over the next three decades he was a disc jockey and later a controversial and patently stormy Miami radio telephone talk show host. His actions netted job shifts between WGBS, WQAM, WIOD and WINZ, the latter station his employer at the time of his demise following a bout with hepatitis.

The New York World-Tribune reported an amusing incident in 1939 surrounding Alan Courtney: "One day an attractive young woman came to him and told him she wanted to sponsor his program on a nationwide network. She said that her father manufactured men's clothing, that she was running the business, and that she wanted this big air show. Mr. Courtney paid small heed to her, but the next day she telephoned him from the office of a network sales manager—a big, important man in radio. The dickering went on for three months. A contract was drawn up and notarized. By its terms Mr. Courtney was to be paid $2500 a week. He was to broadcast six days a week for three years and there were no cancellation clauses in the agreement. In addition he was to get a month's vacation with pay each year. It was a lovely contract.

"The big, important radio man carried on most of the negotiations with the young woman, taking her to dinner, driving her around in his big car, taking her to the theater and playing up to her generally. Mr. Courtney had a Brooklyn telephone number for the young woman and had talked to her a couple of times. Then one day he called her number and another woman answered. Courtney asked about the girl, and the strange woman said: 'Yes, certainly she lives here. She's my maid. She's not real bright, but she's a good maid.'"

CRAVENS, KATHRYN C. b. Oct. 27, 1898, Burkett, Texas; d. Aug. 29, 1991, Burkett, Texas. *Newscaster, Commentator.* **Series:** *Kathryn Cravens Broadcasts the News* (1945); *News Through a Woman's Eyes* (1936–1938, 1940s).

Kathryn Cravens was born the daughter of a country doctor whose mom was the postmistress of their rural Texas town. As the little girl jogged along the roads with her dad on his visits to patients on neighboring farms, she dreamed of becoming an actress. Even then her instinct to "get the story" was being nurtured. When she returned home in the evenings she recounted to her mother vivid and dramatic details of the sick people her father had helped that day. Following high school graduation, the young woman studied at Kendall College (now the University of Tulsa), Kansas City's Horner Institute of Fine Arts and St. Louis's Morse School of Expression.

The first feminine radio commentator on a national hookup, Kathryn Cravens launched her career at 15 as a 20th Century–Fox motion picture actress. After eight years of performing on the silver screen in silent films under the alias Kitty O'Dare, in 1929 she began acting in dramas that she wrote aired by KWK, St. Louis. She also recited narratives and vocalized and performed Negro dialect on the air. Cravens later transferred to the local CBS affiliate, KMOX; she was subsequently dubbed the "Voice of St. Louis" because she appeared on four programs daily. "Her flair for interpreting current events, for doing interviews with the great and near-great, in a way that had a special significance for feminine listeners, soon put her on a coast-to-coast CBS network," a pundit acknowledged. CBS introduced her to a national audience from New York City in 1936. After her show's run ended in 1938, she wrote newspaper columns and features. New York's WNEW returned her to the ether in 1941.

With no background in news, Cravens didn't focus on accepted news disseminating principles and practices. Instead of approaching her assignments by answering who, what, where, when and why, she dwelled on the sentiments of those involved in the stories she reported. Cravens elaborated to *Radio Guide*: "How does it feel to be the mother of a murdered boy, of one to be executed that night? ... how does it feel to survive flood and misery? ... to be America's most notorious shoplifter? ... to be mayor of a great city, a congressional lobbyist, a famous playwright, a war-torn cripple, a flophouse bum?" Pontiac automobiles underwrote her 18-month-long CBS series.

In 1942 she launched *Kathryn Cravens Broadcasts the News* over WNEW, where it ran until Mutual added it under the previous title. Her persistence might indicate that she conformed to more conventional news delivery styles as time transpired. *Radio Mirror*, one of the most popular fanzines, commented in September 1945: "It was inevitable that as soon after V-E Day as the Army would accredit a woman radio correspondent for broadcasts from Europe, she would be the first woman to receive such accreditation.... It was because, as an actress, she always wanted to rewrite and improve the scripts she was assigned to act, that Kathryn Cravens became radio's most outstanding woman commentator."

That periodical concluded: "Before she flew to Europe this spring [1945] she had already scheduled interviews with a number of important personages including General DeGaulle, Bernard Shaw, and the Pope. But her main purpose was to get a picture for American women of how the common people of the liberated—and the conquered—countries of Europe are managing in the wake of Nazi devastation, such vital but humdrum problems as feeding their families, caring for their children's health, recreation and cleanliness, keeping themselves dressed and alive. Her job is to report a 'woman's angle' on living conditions amid the chaos of a catastrophic war—a chaos that American women have been protected from."

Cravens furthermore interviewed President and Mrs. Franklin D. Roosevelt, Herbert Hoover, Walter Huston, Gloria Vanderbilt, J. Edgar Hoover and many other distinguished personalities across her pithy broadcast career. During the two years she was on CBS she racked up 50,000 air miles in pursuit of story material for her show. Cravens wrote a novel, *Pursuit of Gentlemen*, published in 1951. In 1962 she retired and literally returned to her ancestral home in Texas, where she died 29 years later.

CROSBY, LOUIS. b. 1914, Lawton, Okla.; d. Jan. 27, 1984, Australia. *Announcer, Actor, Producer.* **Series:** *The Bob Hope Show* (1942–?); *Double or Nothing* (producer, ca. 1940s, early 1950s); *Gene Autry's Melody Ranch* (1940–?); *Hollywood Playhouse* (ca. 1937–1940); *Law West of the Pecos* (actor, 1944); *Lum and Abner* (1943–1944); *The Risë Stevens Show* (1945); *The Roy Rogers Show*, aka *Happy Trails* (1944–ca. 1955).

In 1935 Lou Crosby left KVOR, Colorado Springs, Colo., for KNX, Hollywood, Calif. There he met and wed Rachel Mendenhall (actress Linda Hayes) and became the father of future actress Cathy Lee Crosby. The family (including three daughters) appeared in a 1950s local TV show in San Francisco, *The Crosbys Calling*. Crosby ultimately joined ABC-TV's *The Lawrence Welk Show* as announcer in the early 1960s and remained with it for a decade. He resided in Australia during the last 11 years of his life.

CROSS, MILTON JOHN. b. April 16, 1897, New York, N.Y.; d. Jan. 3, 1975, New York, N.Y. *Announcer, Emcee.* **Series:** *The A&P Gypsies* (ca. 1927–1936); *America's Town Meeting of the Air* (ca. 1940s); *Betty and Bob* (1930s); *Bughouse Rhythm* (ca. 1937); *The*

Chamber Music Society of Lower Basin Street (1940–ca. 1944); *The Chicago Civic Opera*; *Coast-to-Coast on a Bus* (host, 1927–1948); *Don't Forget* (1939–1940); *General Motors Concerts* (ca. 1929–ca. 1937); *Information Please* (ca. 1940s); *The Jeddo Highlanders*; *The Lucky Strike Music Hall* (ca. 1934); *The Magic Key* (late 1930s); *Melody Highway* (1952–1953); *The Metropolitan Opera* (host, 1931–1975); *The Metropolitan Opera Auditions on the Air* (ca. 1940s, 1950s); *The Milton Cross Opera Album*; *Musical Americana* (1940–1941); *Musicomedy*, aka *Silver Summer Revue* (1948); *The New York Philharmonic Symphony* (host, ca. 1940s, early 1950s); *Piano Playhouse* (ca. 1945–ca. 1952); *Raising Your Parents* (1936–1937); *Roxy and His Gang* (ca. 1930–1931); *The Slumber Hour*; *This is Your FBI* (ca. 1946–1947). **Aphorism:** *Good afternoon, opera lovers from coast to coast.*

No voice is better identified with the durable Metropolitan Opera broadcasts than that of Milton J. Cross, who for more than four decades introduced the prestigious weekly concerts. As the opera's permanent host-commentator, he was present at its inception on Dec. 25, 1931, and eventually was branded "the voice of the Met." With a home audience of 12–15 million faithfully tuning in, Cross became one of the most listened-to men in America. He stayed at his post until his death more than 800 airdates later, missing only two performances, both at the passing of his wife in February 1973. For about $80 in salary, Cross broadcast from box 44 in the Met's grand tier. As each recital was about to begin, he routinely advised listeners: "The house lights are being dimmed. In a moment, the great gold curtain will go up."

Cross studied at the Damrosch School of Musical Art, his background training and interest pointing him toward a professional career in the field. He was a soloist in several Manhattan churches and toured the nation with the Paulist Choristers. Radio fascinated him early and at 24 he was hired by station WJZ on Sept. 15, 1921 as a soloist. Soon—for $40 a week—he was narrating, reading comic pages to kids, singing and providing his own accompaniment via a player piano.

Broadcasting from a tiny booth off the station's women's room, he aspired to still greater summits, coveting a career for himself in music. But he was unsuccessful. A critic dubbed him "a failed tenor." Cross persisted in radio—*speaking* instead of singing—and eventually announced-hosted a myriad of fan favorites. Several of his series were enduring. In 1929 the American Academy of Arts and Letters conferred its highest diction honors on him, signifying his impact on broadcasting quite early in his career.

On the Met airdates he filled in the color around the music. He exhibited a colossal knowledge of story line scenarios and easily conveyed to home audiences images of the sets and cast backgrounds. "Cross was a veritable talking playbill who synopsized convoluted plots and provided biographical notes, between-acts trivia, and an intermission quiz with celebrity opera buffs," a pundit affirmed. *Time* magazine characterized him as a "huge, humble, bestectacled music-charmed announcer, whose cultured genuflecting voice seems to come straight from NBC's artistic soul." A historian submitted: "His resonant voice was an instrument in itself, one that produced a burnished announcer-profundo sound." Another added: "His diction was near-flawless. His pronunciation of difficult names was accurate and sure."

Cross also had the ability to keep from taking himself—and his music—too seriously. On *The Chamber Music Society of Lower Basin Street* he poked fun at the stuffed shirts identified with the highbrow fare. He literally let his hair down as he pulled off a joke on those restrained lords and ladies. On *Chamber* Cross "added humor with nothing more than his presence," an observer suggested. He was also responsible for stimulating an interest in music among legions of the nation's adolescents through several aural series, particularly the long-running *Coast-to-Coast on a Bus* that he steered for two decades.

For two-and-a-half months in 1952, ABC-TV carried a primetime version of *Metropolitan Opera Auditions of the Air*. With Cross hosting, it permitted the viewers a rare glimpse into intense competition for a few spots at the Met.

CROWLEY, MATTHEW D. b. June 20, 1905, New Haven, Conn.; d. March 10, 1983, Clearwater, Fla. *Actor, Announcer.* **Series:** *The Adventures of Superman* (actor, 1940s–ca. 1951); *The Ask-It Basket* (1941); *The Beatrice*

Lillie Show (actor, ca. 1935–ca. 1937); *Buck Rogers in the 25th Century* (actor, mid 1930s); *Dick Tracy* (actor); *Dimension X* (actor, 1950–1951); *Flashgun Casey,* aka *Casey, Crime Photographer* (actor, 1943); *Hop Harrigan* (actor, 1940s); *John's Other Wife* (actor, late 1930s); *Jungle Jim* (actor, 1935–ca. 1938); *Keeping Up with Wigglesworth* (1946); *Mark Trail* (actor, 1950–ca. 1951); *Myrt and Marge* (actor); *Perry Mason* (actor, 1940s–ca. early 1950s); *Pretty Kitty Kelly* (1937–1940); *Road of Life* (actor, 1937–1939).

A versatile performer who exhibited ease in handling announcing and acting chores, Matt Crowley ultimately invested his life in network radio in a couple of genres—juvenile adventure series and soap operas. Determined in his youth to become an actor, he trained in dramatics at Yale University. Then he appeared in a Broadway run of *The Front Page.* Nothing occurred following an initial radio audition in 1932. It was two years hence, while performing in Broadway's *Lady of Letters,* he was asked to portray the lead role in a radio dramatization of *The Broken Wing.* Crowley was subsequently summoned to play the lead in the radio adaptation of *Clear All Wires.* A myriad of narratives followed and he also soon found himself playing a stooge to actress Beatrice Lillie. A plethora of daytime fare tailored for homemakers and the juvenile set wasn't long in coming, expanding Crowley's talents both as an actor and announcer.

CUBBERLY, DAN S. b. Jan. 6, 1917, Colorado; d. Oct. 6, 1991, Mendocino, Calif. *Announcer.* **Series:** *Fort Laramie* (1956); *Frontier Gentleman* (1958); *The Judge* (1952); *The Line Up* (1950–1953); *Night Watch* (1954–1955); *Romance* (ca. 1956–1957); *Whispering Streets* (1959–1960); *Yours Truly, Johnny Dollar* (1951–1954).

Dan Cubberly launched his broadcast career as a newscaster, initially for KGY, Olympia, Wash. (1938), and then for KOY, Phoenix (1940).

CULLEN, WILLIAM LAWRENCE. b. Feb. 18, 1920, Pittsburgh, Pa.; d. July 7, 1990, Los Angeles, Calif. *Announcer, Emcee.* **Series:** *Arthur Godfrey Time* (ca. mid 1940s); *Casey, Crime Photographer* (ca. mid-late 1940s); *Catch Me If You Can* (master of ceremonies, 1948); *Danny O'Neil and His Guests,* aka *The Danny O'Neil Show* (1945–1947); *Fun for All* (co-host, 1952–1953); *Hit the Jackpot* (quizmaster, 1948–1949, 1950); *Hollywood Jackpot* (1946–1947); *It Happens Every Day* (1951–1953); *Monitor* (host, 1971–1973); *The Patti Clayton Show* (1945–1946); *Quick as a Flash* (quizmaster, 1949–1951); *The Road Show* (host, 1954); *Stop the Music!* (master of ceremonies, 1954); *This is Nora Drake* (1947–1951); *Walk a Mile* (quizmaster, 1953–1954); *Winner Take All* (quizmaster, 1946–ca. late 1940s).

After a bout with polio at 18 months of age that left him with a decided limp the remainder of his life, plus an automobile accident in his teen years that laid him up for nine months, Bill Cullen decided he would become a physician. Entering the University of Pittsburgh as a pre-med student, he quit after the money ran out. He took a job at his father's tow truck garage and amused the help with imitations of radio announcers. Reaction was so affirming that in 1939 he tried out at 250-watt WWSW and won a non-paid post working six hours each evening. A couple of months later he was added to the paid staff as a newscaster-announcer, proving—as he said later—"Radio was the one place that a ham like me ... could limp and still get a job."

A radio historiographer positioned Bill Cullen as the "emcee of more game shows than any entertainer." He couldn't have been much off the mark due to the wealth of quiz, stunt and panel shows Cullen moderated, presided over and announced in two mediums—nearly three dozen over his lifetime. By 1941 he was hired by the legendary Pittsburgh 50,000-watter KDKA and was soon doing man-in-the-street interview and game show features beside producer Walt Framer, later of *Strike It Rich* fame. A new bug had bitten Cullen. In 1943 his salary reached $250 weekly. He was able to resume his studies at the University of Pittsburgh and earn a bachelor's degree. In 1944 he set off for New York City and soon established multiple network connections.

One of Cullen's early duties in Gotham was to narrate a premiering soap opera, *This Is Nora Drake,* and deliver home permanent commercials there. The affable man with the horn-rimmed glasses and elfin grin couldn't be enclosed with a microphone for long, however. His enthusiasm for work came off as contagious and he was soon in front of crowds at a plethora of audience participation shows. In the mid 1950s Cullen conducted a morning wake-up show over New York's WNBC. For a while timidity from his polio limp prevented him from embracing video. But shortly after mid 20th century, he was on the weekly *I've Got a Secret* panel on CBS-TV, a gig that extended for 15 years (1952–1967) and thrust him into national visibility.

For the rest of his career Cullen habitually turned up on a surfeit of televised series, on most as a game show emcee: *Give and Take* (1952); *Matinee in New York* (1952); *Winner Take All* (1952); *Who's There* (1952); *Why?* (1952–1953); *Quick as a Flash* (1953); *The Bill Cullen Show* (1953); *Name That Tune* (1954); *Bank on the Stars* (1954); *Place the Face* (1954–1955); *Down You Go* (1956); *The Price Is Right* (1956–1965); *NBC Sports in Action* (1966); *Eye Guess* (1966–1969); *Three on a Match* (1971–1974); *Winning Streak* (1974–1975); *Blankety Blanks* (1975); *Pass the Buck* (1978); *The Love Experts* (1978–1979); *Chain Reaction* (1980); *Blockbusters* (1980–1982); *Child's Play* (1982–1983); *Hot Potato* (1984); and *The Joker's Wild* (1984–1986). Cullen was a textbook example of how so many of TV's earliest entertainers across virtually every genre were equipped for their tasks by their educations in an aural medium.

CULVER, HOWARD. b. June 4, 1918; d. Aug. 5, 1984, Hong Kong. *Actor, Announcer.* **Series:** *The Adventures of Ellery Queen* (actor, 1948); *The Adventures of Philip Marlowe* (actor, 1947, 1948–1950, 1951); *Chandu the Magician* (1948–1950); *The Croupier* (actor, 1949); *Defense Attorney*, aka *The Defense Rests* (actor, 1951–1952); *The Gallant Heart* (actor, 1944); *Gunsmoke* (actor, 1952–1961); *Have Gun, Will Travel* (actor, 1958–1960); *Make-Believe Town, Hollywood* (actor, 1949–1950); *Mystery in the Air* (actor, 1947); *The Sears Radio Theater*, aka *The Mutual Radio Theater* (actor, 1979–1981); *Straight Arrow* (actor, 1948–1951); *Strange Wills*, aka *I Devise and Bequeath* (actor, 1946); *We Deliver the Goods* (host-narrator, 1944); *The Whistler* (actor, ca. late 1940s–1955). **Aphorism:** *Kaneewah, Fury!*

According to one scholar, on *Straight Arrow* Howard Culver "gave a robust performance, modifying his voice as he changed from [rancher Steve] Adams to Arrow, much as Bud Collyer seemed to grow as he changed from Clark Kent to Superman." The Arrow's summons to his waiting palomino mount "Kaneewah, Fury!" exploded out of an echo chamber, resplendently magnifying the reverberation, underscoring that the great one was in command to right the wrongs proffered by treacherous schemers.

Culver played the hotel clerk, Howie Uzzell, on CBS-TV's *Gunsmoke* for two decades, 1955–1975. Following the network radio era, in the meantime, Culver was a newsman at KLAC, Los Angeles, between 1965 and 1969 and did the same at KGIL also in the City of Angels from 1969 to 1974.

CUNNINGHAM, BOB. *Announcer, Director.* **Series:** *The Crime Files of Flamond* (1953, 1956–1957); *The Peabodys* (1946–1947); *Welcome Travelers* (director, 1947–1954).

In 1937 Bob Cunningham was program director at Omaha's KOIL. By 1939 he was a newscaster and announcer at Chicago's WBBM, the local CBS affiliate, and was soon elevated to announcer supervisor. He departed in 1944 to become a U.S. Navy lieutenant. In 1948 Cunningham announced *Speak Your Mind* over Chicago's WGN, a nightly quarter-hour on which listeners were urged to express their thoughts on topical issues. The program's host was Paul Harvey; two years elapsed before Harvey bowed on a network hookup with his long-running news and commentary program.

For two months in 1949 Cunningham played an on-camera director on NBC-TV's primetime drama *The Crisis*, which lasted only three months altogether. When *Welcome Travelers* added an NBC-TV weekday run from 1952 to 1954, Cunningham moved with it, becoming the show's co-host. On radio—as director—he was responsible for making the final selections of individuals in the studio audience who were to be interviewed on the live show by host Tommy Bartlett.

CUTRER, THOMAS CLINTON (T. TOMMY). b. June 29, 1924, Tangipahoa Parish, La.; d. Oct. 11, 1998. *Announcer.* **Series:** *Grand Ole Opry* (1955–1957).

Thomas Clinton Cutrer (nicknamed T. Tommy) spent his early youth anticipating a career as a boxer or a professional football player. While engaged in playing the latter sport in high school, a bruise he sustained resulted in osteomyelitis—an infectious inflammatory bone disease that often ends in death. Although his life was spared, young Cutrer was confined to bed for eight months. As he lay there he tuned in the radio and adopted a new mission in life: to become a broadcaster when he could resume normal activities. His first on-air job, at 18 (about 1942), was at WSKB in McComb, Miss. From there his career moved swiftly as the neophyte announcer gained experience at a whirlwind pace, successively moving from one station to another throughout the lower Mississippi delta and adjacent area—in five states. Including McComb's WSKB, across the next decade Cutrer turned up at 15 radio stations: WDSU, New Orleans, La. (where he lasted just two weeks before being canned); WNOE, New Orleans; WJXN, McComb, Miss.; WJDX, Jackson, Miss.; WSLI, Jackson; KARK, Little Rock, Ark.; WMC, Memphis, Tenn.; WREC, Memphis; KXYZ, Houston, Texas; KLEE, Houston; KNUZ, Houston; KPLC, Lake Charles, La.; KCIJ, Shreveport, La.; and finally he reached the holy grail, WSM, Nashville, Tenn.

As a sideline, an enterprising Cutrer formed his own band in which he played drums. During the early 1950s the troupe recorded several single jukebox tunes and gospel numbers on the Capitol, Columbia, Dot, Mercury, Million and RCA Victor labels. They also cut records especially for the Air Force and Army. En route from Little Rock to Nashville in 1953, Cutrer lost his left leg, the result of an automobile mishap, which also ended his peripheral venture as a drummer.

WSM brought him to Nashville permanently in 1954 to preside over the *Opry Star Spotlight*, a combination DJ and interview show that aired for an hour before the station broadcast evening ball games. Cutrer was soon assigned as an interlocutor for some of the *Grand Ole Opry* segments, becoming commercial spokesman for Martha White flour, Pet milk and other commodities that purchased half-hour and quarter-hour portions of the live stage show. At the same time, he provided Ace gasoline commercials for a half-hour syndicated series, *The Cisco Kid*. Cutrer remained with the *Opry* on Saturdays and the live *Friday Night Frolics* stage performances that preceded it for a decade—until 1964. While he was never the principal announcer on the 30-minute NBC network portion of the show (which ended in 1957), he pinch-hit on occasions when the permanent man, Grant Turner, was out of pocket. The readers of *Billboard* magazine voted Cutrer the nation's top DJ in 1957 and he was elected to the Country Music DJ Hall of Fame in 1980.

When he departed from the mother church of country music, Cutrer bought a Jackson, Miss. radio station, WJQS, which wasn't one of those for which he worked earlier. Continuing to exhibit talent as a businessman, the entrepreneurial entertainer subsequently purchased Kentucky Fried Chicken outlets in a trio of Texas cities: Bryan, Killen and Temple. He also put together a syndicated radio show for mass distribution that he hosted, *Music City, U.S.A.* For a year he presided over a local early morning television series, *Nashville Scene*.

Cutrer eventually landed in politics. After he was beaten by Al Gore Jr. in the Democratic primary in 1976 as both ran for U.S. Congress from Tennessee, he received Gore's backing for a state Senate seat in 1978 and won it. Cutrer vacated the seat in 1982 to become a field rep for the International Brotherhood of Teamsters. Four months following his death, the Volunteer State's Senate adopted a resolution honoring Cutrer for his multiple achievements.

DAHLSTEAD, DRESSER. b. Sept. 19, 1910, Springville, Utah; d. April 20, 1998, Las Vegas, Nev. Announcer. **Series:** *Death Valley Days* (ca. 1930s, 1940s); *The Fitch Bandwagon* (ca. 1939, 1940s); *Hollywood Tour* (1947); *I Deal in Crime* (1946–1947); *I Love a Mystery* (ca. 1939–ca. 1940s); *I Love Adventure* (1948).

Radio announcing provided the capital for Dresser Dahlstead to attend college. He worked his way through the University of Utah while at an Ogden station. In 1931 he went into full time radio in San Francisco; a year later he signed with NBC's announcing staff in the City by the Bay. Those NBC auditions were legendary. "If you could pass that test, you could do anything on the air," an industry observer asserted. Dahlstead recalled his own "cattle call" tryout when the network was seeking a couple of announcers. "They did everything that you can imagine to throw you," he allowed. "They gave you a whole list of names of composers—foreign names—titles of songs that you had to go through. They'd stand you in a studio and say, 'OK, describe the studio.' ... I think it took a week of weeding out ... and it finally wound up that I was one of the two."

DALY, JOHN CHARLES, JR. b. Feb. 20, 1914, Johannesburg, South Africa; d. Feb. 25, 1991, Chevy Chase, Md. *Newscaster, Emcee.* **Series:** *CBS is There*, aka *You Are There* (correspondent, 1947–1949); *Continental Celebrity Club* (host, 1945–1946); *Report to the Nation* (correspondent, 1942, 1943–1945); *The Spirit of '41* (host, 1941); *What's My Line?* (moderator, 1952–1953); *The World Today* (reporter, 1941, 1943–1948).

Not to be confused with the radio actor John C. Daly who portrayed *Fu Manchu* and other dramatic roles, John Charles Daly began his career as a newsman and ended it as one of early television's most admired game show hosts. Indeed, he established a reputation in dual arenas. For legions who watched *What's My Line?* on CBS-TV for 17 years (1950–1967) he was the affable, impish, urbane panel moderator consummate. (The show was also aired on CBS Radio for a year.) But most of those fans forgot that it was his voice that first told them that the Japanese attacked Pearl Harbor on Dec. 7, 1941, or that President Franklin D. Roosevelt died on April 12, 1945. And no one outside the industry knew he tutored Douglas Edwards for greater responsibility, preparing him for a post that would one day be Daly's most formidable competition as the two newsmen sought viewers on rival evening network telecasts.

Born in South Africa, John Charles Daly lost his dad there, an American geologist, while the boy was still young. Subsequently his mom took the family to Boston. In 1930 John completed high school at Tilton (New Hampshire) Academy. He entered Boston College the next year but a lack of funds cut his formal training short. Daly accepted various jobs while performing avocationally with the Peabody Players. In 1935 he worked in Washington, D.C., but returned to Boston where he gained some radio experience at WLOE.

Daly's big break arrived when he signed with CBS in 1937 at Washington's WJSV and accompanied FDR some 150,000 miles as CBS's White House correspondent. He was assigned to cover the political conventions in 1940 and then became a special events reporter for his chain. When Robert Trout went to London in 1941 to relieve Edward R. Murrow, Daly was tapped as reporter for the evening news program *The World Today*. He covered the Army in training camps as they conducted war games, fodder for broadcasts of *The Spirit of '41*. For about 15 months in 1943–1944, Daly also reported from overseas—London, North Africa, Sicily, Malta, the Middle East and South America. He appeared on CBS's V-E Day programming and in due course covered the Nuremberg Nazi war criminal trials.

In 1949 Daly jumped ship, joining ABC News where—four years later—he was named vice president in charge of news, special events, public affairs, religious and sports programming. In the fall of 1953 he also became the network's anchorman for its weeknight televised quarter-hour newscast. The following year he received a Peabody Award for distinguished radio and TV news coverage. He was also given an Emmy the same year (1954) by the National Academy of Television Arts and Sciences as best news reporter/commentator. A perceptive scribe observed, "For the remainder of the 1950s Daly was the virtual personification of ABC News." That news series concluded in 1957 but the network resumed its newscasting a year later, presenting an early evening report at 7:15 Eastern Time hosted by Don Goddard and a late evening edition at 10:30 anchored by Daly.

Daly resigned from ABC News near the end of 1960 and focused his creative energies on CBS's *What's My Line?* Toward the close of that decade he devoted a year as director of the Voice of America. He had enjoyed almost a dozen other TV gigs earlier, predominantly of an audience participation, quiz or panel motif: *Riddle Me This*, aka *Celebrity Time* (panelist, 1948–1950, CBS, ABC); *The*

Front Page (actor, 1949–1950, CBS); *The News and Its Meaning* (host, 1950, CBS); *We Take Your Word* (wordmaster, 1950–1951, CBS); *The March of Time* (host, 1951, ABC); *It's News to Me* (moderator, 1951–1953, CBS); *America's Town Meeting* (moderator, 1952, ABC); *Open Hearing* (host-moderator, 1954, ABC); *Who Said That?* (moderator, 1955, ABC); *The Voice of Firestone* (host-narrator, 1958–1959, ABC); and *Real TV* (host, syndicated).

What's My Line? producer Gil Fates wrote in his portrait of the enormously popular broadcast feature: "John thought of himself first and foremost as a newsman.... The fact that the public thought of him first and foremost as the moderator of television's most successful game show did not make him happy. I think the greatest disappointment in John Daly's life was that somebody else beat him to being Edward R. Murrow. But there could be only one Murrow in a generation, so John had to settle for fame and money."

DAVID, DON. b. March 22, 1905; d. Feb. 22, 1977, Punta Gorda, Fla. *Announcer.* **Series:** *Clara, Lu 'n' Em* (ca. 1942); *Coronet Quick Quiz* (1944–1945).

DAVIS, ELMER HOLMES. b. Jan. 13, 1890, Aurora, Ind.; d. May 18, 1958, Washington, D.C. *Commentator, Newscaster, Correspondent.* **Series:** *Elmer Davis* (commentator, 1953–1955); *Elmer Davis and the News* (newscaster, 1939–1942, five minutes weeknights; 1939–1940 and 1941–1942, 15 minutes three nights weekly; 1940–1941, 15 minutes Saturday evenings; 1945–1946, 15 minutes Sunday afternoons and Monday and Tuesday nights; 1946–1953, 15 minutes weeknights); *The Kate Smith Hour* (newscaster, 1940–1941); *This is London* (correspondent, early 1940s).

Hailing from the Hoosier State, Elmer Davis graduated magna cum laude from Franklin College there in 1910, then became a Rhodes Scholar to Queen's College, Oxford, with an ambition to teach ancient history. After returning to America he decided on writing instead. In New York City in 1909 he found work editing a small periodical, *Adventure* magazine, which paid him $9 weekly. The following year he became a reporter for *The New York Times*, a job he would hold for a decade. In 1921 he wrote a history of that celebrated publication. He resigned in 1924 to do freelance writing, becoming an acclaimed author of short stories for *Harper's, The New Yorker* and *The Saturday Review of Literature*, as well as novels, a livelihood that sustained him throughout the 1930s.

Meanwhile, a few times he dabbled unsuccessfully in radio. Finally, CBS news chief Paul White—impressed by Davis's writing—hired him on Aug. 23, 1939, to replace H.V. Kaltenborn, who had been reassigned to Europe. Overnight Davis became one of the most popular newscasters of that era. *Radio Guide* pontificated that he possessed "an Oxford brain and an Indiana twang that reeked of neutrality" which was "exactly the kind of homey down-to-earth manner needed in a moment of crisis." In 1941 Davis, too, was sent to England for a while. In June 1942 he left his annual CBS salary of $53,000 to become director of the Office of War Information where he oversaw a staff of 3,000 until the bureau was eliminated in 1945. He also conducted a weekly quarter-hour news broadcast beginning in March 1943 that was beamed by all four webs.

After his OWI service, Davis joined ABC and relinquished full time broadcasting in 1953 when his health began to fail. For two years between 1953 and 1955 he offered opinions on politics and topical issues each week, nevertheless. For nearly three months in 1954 the program, labeled simply *Elmer Davis*, was carried by ABC-TV on Sunday afternoons, transcribed and the audio portion replayed on ABC Radio the same evening.

A pundit assessed Davis's journalistic pursuits as "rational, straight-from-the-shoulder ... especially during times of great calamities and national disasters." Dubbed "a horse-sense liberal," Davis still "brought an incisive, analytical mind to the air." While he admitted he never conquered mike fright, his deadpan, soothing voice was rarely perturbed.

DAWSON, STUART V. d. Oct. 4, 1958, Evanston, Ill. *Announcer.* **Series:** *Backstage Wife* (ca. mid 1930s).

Stuart Dawson sang over Chicago's WHT in 1927 and the following year was announcing on WIBO in the Windy City. But most of his career was spent in executive positions. In time he was program director of the CBS Radio central division. Following that he became radio director of two major advertising agencies in Chicago—Young & Rubicam and Foote, Cone & Belding. Dawson was active in radio and television packaging thereafter and moved from Chicago to Las Vegas in 1953. At the time of his death he was vice president of Point of Sale, a Las Vegas advertising agency.

DEAN, JAY HANNA. b. Jan. 16, 1910, Lucas, Ark.; d. July 17, 1974, Reno, Nev. *Sportscaster.* **Series:** *Dizzy Dean* (host, 1948, 1951); *Game of the Day* (sportscaster, 1953–1955); *The Kate Smith New Star Revue* (sportscaster, 1934–1935).

Dizzy Dean's mom died when he was just three; his pop, meanwhile, was an itinerant sharecropper. Dean returned from a stint with the U.S. Army to take a job with a Texas gas utility where he pitched for his employer's scrappy sandlot baseball squad. Professional scout Don Curtis happened to witness the right-hander's fastball and signed him to a contract in the minor leagues. Dean advanced rapidly to the majors, playing with the St. Louis Cardinals (1930, 1932–1937), the Chicago Cubs (1938–1941) and briefly with the St. Louis Browns (1947). In 1941, when he couldn't cut the mustard any longer, he retired from the game and went into broadcasting. Singer Kate Smith had given him national exposure in the field in 1934 when he delivered sports summaries on her show. The idea appealed to him and he remembered it when his playing days ended. "I ain't what I used to be," he said, "but who the hell is?" Dean had been the National League's most valuable player in 1934 and was elected to the Baseball Hall of Fame in 1953.

One of the most colorful players-turned-broadcaster, Old Diz depicted the games he worked perfectly. In doing so, he contributed continuous homespun humor by taking editorial license with the mother tongue. For example, he would interject errant expressions such as "He slud into first," "They throwed him out at third" and "The runners had to go back to their respectable bases." He signed off the radio *Game of the Day* reminding listeners, "Don't fail to miss tomorrow's game!" Dean's lexis was informative and amusing although it raised the ire of linguistic purists. He was, in fact, the bane of English teachers across the land. One complained about his use of the term *ain't* on the air, citing it as a poor example to the nation's youngsters. He read the teacher's note to his listeners, and responded thusly: "A lot of folks who ain't sayin' *ain't* ain't eatin'. So Teach, you learn 'em English and I'll learn 'em baseball."

His wit and animated butchering of acceptable dialect resonated with most of the fans. He built on—rather than countered—his image as a none-too-bright country boy as a method of entertaining followers. "The good Lord was good to me," he allowed. "He gave me a strong right arm, a good body and a weak mind." A critic observed: "Even if 'Old Diz' sometimes suffered with his syntax, he still was more informative, interesting and entertaining than most other players who followed him on radio and television."

On his namesake quarter-hour NBC Radio series in the summer of 1948, Dean appeared in his inimitable, frequently ungrammatical style and answered questions sent in by the listeners. The show was followed three years later by a syndicated sports interview feature which he also headlined.

Dean was the play-by-play announcer on local television for the New York Yankees baseball team during the summers of 1950, 1951 and 1952. Having already carved out a comfortable niche for himself in front of the cameras as well as rapport with the fans, he was picked to host the *Game of the Week* on national television for 13 successive summer seasons. The Saturday afternoon feature debuted on ABC in 1953–1954 and was telecast on CBS thereafter (1955–1965). The video medium's premier showcase for professional baseball, *Game of the Week* took the sport into geographic territory where games were heretofore ignored. The series was blacked out in cities like Chicago, New York, Philadelphia and Washington that boasted major league teams and in places within 50 miles of game sites to encourage in-person attendance.

Nevertheless, a devoted viewer base resulted in the distant and rural areas with no professional baseball in their neighborhoods. Aside from the game, Dean may have been the main attraction. His garbled grammar amused legions of loyalists who appreciated his laid-back style. Joining him at mikeside were Buddy Blattner (1953–1959) and Pee Wee Reese (1960–1965). When the series shifted to NBC-TV in 1966, becoming known as the *Baseball Game of the Week*, Dean was out and replaced by Curt Gowdy, who persisted with Reese, although the jargon was raised several notches. An era was over in baseball coverage.

A Dizzy Dean Museum honoring the player-sportscaster was subsequently established in Jackson, Miss. Today a private group operates Dizzy Dean Baseball, Inc., an organization with an avowed purpose "to provide a recreation outlet for as many youth as possible with emphasis being on local league play rather than tournament play." The program is open to youngsters aged 5–19 regardless of gender, religion, race or color.

DELMAR, KENNETH H. b. Sept. 5, 1910, Boston, Mass.; d. July 14, 1984, Stamford, Conn. *Actor, Announcer.* **Series:** *Cavalcade of America* (actor, ca. late 1930s–ca. 1953); *Columbia Presents Corwin* (actor, 1941, ca. 1944, 1945); *The Court of Missing Heirs* (actor, 1946); *The Danny Kaye Show* (actor, 1945–1946); *The Fred Allen Show* (announcer, actor, 1945–1949); *Funny Side Up* (actor, 1959); *Guest Star* (actor, ca. 1943–ca. 1962); *The Henry Morgan Show* (actor, 1949–1950); *Hollywood Jackpot* (master of ceremonies, 1946–1947); *The Jack Benny Program*; *Jungle Jim* (ca. late 1930s–ca. 1954); *The Lux Radio Theater* (actor, ca. late 1930s–ca. 1955); *The March of Time* (actor, late 1930s–1945); *The Mercury Theater on the Air* (actor, 1938, 1946); *Mystery Theater* (actor, ca. 1943–ca. 1948); *The RCA Victor Show*, aka *Music America Loves Best* (1945–ca. 1949); *The Theater Guild of the Air*, aka *Theater Guild Dramas*, aka *U.S. Steel Hour* (actor, 1943–1944, 1945–1953); *The Shadow* (actor, ca. late 1930s–ca. 1954); *Twenty-Six by Corwin* (actor, 1941); *Your Hit Parade.* **Aphorisms:** *Somebody, ah say, somebody knocked?*; *That's a joke, son, that's a joke!*

Growing up, young Kenny Delmar toured the nation in the vaudeville act of his mother and aunt. He also played a child star in silent movies, among them *Orphans of the Storm* in 1921. By the late 1930s he was in radio playing police commissioner Weston on *The Shadow* and in a trio of roles on the classic Orson Welles *Mercury Theater* 1938 Halloween eve airing of *The War of the Worlds*—the latter possibly the most famous radio broadcast of all time. Other series beckoned and he developed not only as a straight actor but also as an announcer and especially as a comedian. Delmar's most famous role was Senator Beauregard Claghorn, the blowhard Southerner who was a pivotal resident of Allen's Alley on *The Fred Allen Show*; he also simultaneously doubled as announcer for the same series. His *That's a joke, son, that's a joke!* was emblematic of that windbag figure from Dixie and offered a rollicking good time for Allen and his listeners. Delmar concurrently starred in the 1947 motion picture *It's a Joke, Son!* He appeared in a few other films. His last was *Strangers in the City* in 1962.

As Claghorn, he repeated everything. *Somebody, ah say, somebody knocked?* ... *Claghorn's the name, Senator Claghorn, that is!* A pundit wistfully recalled, "What followed was a gush of southern superlatives, during which Allen struggled to get his question of the week asked and answered. Claghorn drank only from Dixie Cups; he never went to the Yankee Stadium, danced only at the Cotton Club, and ate only the part of the turkey that was facing south. By the end of his first month on the air (a total of perhaps five minutes of air time) people across the country were mimicking his voice. Commercial firms turned out Claghorn shirts and compasses (the needles always pointed south, son); Delmar cut two Claghorn records."

Delmar was featured as the "teacher" (presiding official) in a short-lived weekly revue, *The School House*, in 1949 over Dumont Television. Some others in that illustrious cast whose names soon would be going up in lights were Russell Arms, Wally Cox, Buddy Hackett and Arnold Stang. Later, Delmar provided voiceovers for a veritable cornucopia of video cartoons, among them: *King Leonardo and His Short Subjects* (1960–1963, NBC); *Tennessee Tuxedo and His Tales* (1963–1966, CBS, ABC); *The Adventures of Hoppity Hooper* (1964–1967, ABC); *The Underdog Show* (1966–1968, CBS); and *The Go Go Gophers* (1968–1969, CBS). Delmar also narrated CBS's *The Beagles* (1966–1967).

DENTON, ROBERT (born Robert D. Butts). b. March 12, 1910; d. Jan. 30, 1990. *Announcer.* **Series:** *Best Plays* (1952–ca. 1953); *Dimension X* (ca. 1950–1951); *The Eternal Light* (ca. 1940s); *Let's Play Reporter* (host's assistant, 1943); *The Marriage* (1953–1954); The NBC Symphony Orchestra (ca. late 1940s); *The Robert Merrill Show* (1945–1946).

DIXON, ROBERT R. b. April 11, 1911, Stamford, Conn.; d. Aug. 22, 1998, Bethel, Conn. *Announcer, Emcee.* **Series:** *Cinderella Inc.* (master of ceremonies, 1946–1947); *Dimension* (1962–); *Edward R. Murrow and the News* (1950s); *Hobby Lobby* (ca. 1945–1946); *Larry Lesueur and the News* (late 1940s, early 1950s); *Life Can Be Beautiful* (late 1940s, early 1950s); *Perry Mason* (late 1940s, early 1950s); *Rhythm on the Road* (host-announcer, 1954, 1955); *Rosemary* (ca. early 1950s); *Who Dun It?* (master of ceremonies, 1948).

At about 12 years of age, Bob Dixon began traveling every summer with his dad to work on various ranches, often in Montana. For his livelihood Bob's pop drove a stagecoach between Pound Ridge, N.Y. and Stamford, Conn., a line owned by *his* father. Bob was exposed to Western lore early, something that was to influence his life forever. While at Springfield (Mass.) College, from which he graduated in 1935, young Dixon acted on WBZA Radio. He jumped from one job to another for a half-dozen years—salesman, mountain guide, construction worker, laundryman, stock actor, magician—before joining WHYN, Holyoke, Mass., in 1941 where he "did a little of everything." He moved to WTAG, Worcester, Mass., a short time later and by 1944 settled at New York's WOR as a staff announcer.

In 1949 Dixon performed in costume on the weekly ABC-TV children's feature *The Singing Lady*. He also appeared in the ongoing cast of *Holiday Hotel*, a 1950–1951 musical revue on ABC-TV set at the Holiday Hotel in New York City. Meanwhile, "Sheriff Bob" Dixon hosted a poorly financed late afternoon rival to NBC-TV's popular adolescent entry, *Howdy Doody*. Dixon presided over *Chuck Wagon* on CBS-TV from 1949 to 1951, presenting western films, chatting with sporadic guests (Little Grey Wolf, an American Indian, on one occasion; newsman Edward R. Murrow on another in Murrow's allegedly inaugural TV appearance) and conducted simple quizzes. Dixon instructed the 35,000 youngsters who registered with his "posse" how to build a campfire, cautioned them about water safety, told them how to interpret weather signs, guided them in the care and treatment of animals, and showed them how to tie a diamond hitch. "I'm much more interested in helping kids learn how to do the things they like to do than I am in playing the almighty adult," acknowledged "Sheriff Bob."

At the time a newspaper columnist affirmed: "Dixon has been knee deep in Western lore since he was knee high.... He regrets having to leave the range around New Canaan [Conn.] every morning to pursue his big-city career as a free-lance announcer." Another critic described him as "a tall, rangy man in authentic Western gear and with a resonant twang that fairly shouted Wyoming." Still another journalist characterized him as "easily the most authentic cowboy ever to come out of Connecticut." Several mornings weekly, before commuting to New York, Dixon mounted the Palomino pony he kept at his ranch and rode for an hour. Eventually he marketed his own line of western apparel, something not many radio announcers could lay claim to. After his CBS-TV show faded, Dixon continued performing for the buckaroos in a local New York television series along the lines of his network feature.

Edward R. Murrow's appearance on Dixon's *Chuck Wagon* allowed the two men to form a permanent friendship. Within a year Dixon was tapped as Murrow's radio announcer and he also got the nod to do the same for Murrow's important CBS-TV documentary *See It Now* (1951–1958). As Murrow lay dying from brain cancer in New York Hospital in 1965, he summoned Dixon to his bedside to help him leave the hospital so he could die at his own Connecticut home. Dixon assisted in nursing Murrow through the final days of his illness. When Dixon, himself, died 33 years later, an obituary writer classified him as "Edward R. Murrow's best friend."

DIXON, TOM. b. ca. 1915. *Announcer.* **Series:** *The Billie Burke Show*, aka *Fashions in Rations* (ca. mid 1940s).

Over an enduring career in Los Angeles radio, Tom Dixon was employed by a quartet of area stations—KHJ (1939–1943), KFAC (1946–1987), KUSC (1987–1989) and KKGO (1989–1998). He retired in May 1998 at age 82.

DOBKIN, LAWRENCE S. b. Sept. 16, 1919, New York, N.Y.; d. Oct. 28, 2002, Los Angeles, Calif. *Actor, Announcer*. **Series:** *The Adventures of Ellery Queen* (actor, 1947–1948); *The Adventures of Nero Wolfe* (actor, 1950–1951); *The Adventures of Philip Marlowe* (actor, 1948–1950); *Broadway is My Beat* (actor, 1949–1954); *The Damon Runyon Theatre* (actor, 1950–1951); *Escape* (actor, 1947–1954); *The Eternal Light* (actor); *Fort Laramie* (actor, 1956); *The First Nighter* (actor); *Frontier Gentleman* (actor, 1958); *The Green Lama* (actor, 1949); *Gunsmoke* (actor, 1952–1961); *Have Gun, Will Travel* (actor, 1958–1960); *The Judge* (actor, 1952); *Lux Radio Theater* (actor, ca. late 1940s–mid 1950s); *The Man from Homicide* (actor, 1951); *The NBC University Theater* (actor, 1948–1951); *Nightbeat* (actor, 1950, 1951–1952); *One Man's Family* (actor, ca. late 1940s, 1950s); *Rocky Jordan*, aka *A Man Called Jordan* (ca. 1947, 1948–1950, ca. 1951, ca. 1952–ca. 1953); *Rogers of the Gazette* (actor, 1953–1954); *Romance* (actor, 1950, 1951–1953, ca. 1954–ca. 1957); *The Roy Rogers Show*, aka *Happy Trails* (actor, 1944–1945, 1946–1947, 1948–1955); *The Saint* (actor, 1950–1951); *The Six-Shooter* (actor, 1953–1954); *Suspense* (actor, 1940s–ca. 1962); *Yours Truly, Johnny Dollar* (actor, 1949–1960).

Of 27 radio series scholars have documented for Larry Dobkin, he acted in 26 and announced only *Rocky Jordan*. Dobkin played in the half-hour CBS-TV sitcom *Mr. Adams and Eve* in 1957–1958. In 1988 and 1989 he appeared as Gen. George S. Patton in the ABC-TV miniseries *War and Remembrance*.

DONALD, PETER. b. June 6, 1918, Bristol, England; d. April 30, 1979, Ft. Lauderdale, Fla. *Actor, Announcer, Writer*. **Series:** *The Benny Goodman Show* (cast, 1939–1940s); *Can You Top This?* (humorist, 1942–1951, 1953–1954); *The Children's Hour*, aka *Coast to Coast on a Bus* (ca. 1930s, 1940s); *Columbia Presents Corwin* (actor, 1941, ca. 1942, ca. 1945); *County Fair* (writer, 1945–1950); *The Fred Allen Show* (actor, 1945–1949); *The Grummits* (actor, 1934–1935, 1936–1937); *Into the Light* (actor, 1941–1942); *The Lady Next Door* (1930–1935); *Manhattan at Midnight* (actor, 1940–1943); *The March of Time* (actor, ca. 1930s–ca. 1945); *Melody Lane with Jerry Wayne*, aka *The Jerry Wayne Show*, aka *Gulf Spray Presents* (announcer, actor, 1942–1945); *The Peter Donald Show* (host, 1947); *Philco Radio Hall of Fame*, aka *Radio Hall of Fame* (actor, ca. 1943–ca. 1946); *Second Husband* (actor, ca. 1936–ca. 1946); *Stella Dallas* (actor, ca. late 1930s, 1940s); *The Story of Mary Marlin* (actor, ca. 1935–ca. 1945); *Talk Your Way Out of It* (host, 1949); *Terry and the Pirates* (actor, ca. 1937–ca. 1939, ca. 1943–ca. 1948); *Treasury Star Parade* (actor, 1942–1944); *Your Family and Mine* (actor, 1938–1940).

One of radio's great dialecticians, Peter Donald was born into the Scottish vaudeville team of Donald & Carson, which carried him to Broadway in 1928 to perform in Noel Coward's *Bittersweet*. He soon portrayed Tiny Tim in a radio adaptation of *A Christmas Carol*. Donald was an early regular on *The Children's Hour* hosted by Milton Cross. A graduate of the Professional Children's School in New York in 1936, he is probably best remembered for two roles—playing himself as the quipmeister on the long-running *Can You Top This?* in which he recalled many dialects to fit each jest, and as Irishman Ajax Cassidy, one of the permanent residents of Allen's Alley on *The Fred Allen Show*.

In the summer of 1948 Donald and a half-dozen other comedians vied to permanently host NBC-TV's debuting *Texaco Star Theater*, a slot that ultimately went to Milton Berle. On CBS-TV's *Prize Performance* in summer 1950, Donald was a panelist as youthful artists trotted out their talent. That same summer he was an occasional star of the drama and variety series *ABC Showcase* on that TV network. He was also a panelist on ABC-TV's *Can You Top This?* in 1950–1951 featuring all of the radio cast. In the summer of 1951 Donald was master of ceremonies for *The Ad-Libbers*, a CBS-TV celebrity panel improvisation show. He was a panelist on the Dumont TV game show *Where Was I?* in 1952–1953. Donald furthermore hosted *Masquerade Party* on ABC-TV from 1954 to 1956.

After radio ebbed he was an avid voiceover performer on TV commercials and narrated industrial film documentaries. He also appeared on radio and television shows in south Florida. His death resulted from stomach and throat cancer, possibly a twist of irony for such a renowned and matchless dialectician.

DONALDSON, DANIEL JONES (aka Charlie Warren). b. March 11, 1915, St. Louis, Mo.; d. Dec. 1, 1991, Chapel Hill, N.C. *Announcer.* **Series:** *Auction Quiz* (1941–1942); *Can You Top This?* (commercial spokesman, 1940s–1948); *Clara, Lu 'n' Em* (ca. 1942); *Kitty Keene, Incorporated* (ca. 1939–early 1940s); *Little Herman* (1949); *Ma Perkins* (ca. 1939–early 1950s); *Musical Millwheel* (1941–1942); *Radio Reader's Digest* (ca. 1940s–1948); *Road of Life* (ca. early 1940s); *The Trouble with Marriage* (1939).

Unable to settle on a course for his life, Dan Donaldson enrolled at St. Louis University where he pursued both law and medicine. At the end of seven years he went into radio, having paid his tuition by announcing at the school station, WEW. When a pal bet him that he couldn't get a "real" radio job, while vacationing in Chicago in 1939 Donaldson surprised them both on his initial try by nabbing a spot narrating a couple of network daytime serials!

During the long run of *Ma Perkins*, he was one of two announcers (the other, Marvin Miller) appropriating the pseudonym Charlie Warren to avoid a sponsor conflict. The homilies that the homespun, golden-throated, mellifluous-sounding Donaldson dispatched on that narrative often perfectly matched the scene of a laid-back Rushville Center, for sure a misplaced moniker for a Midwestern hamlet. He would take an incredibly well-written monologue penned by wordsmith Orin Tovrov and make it his own, exclaiming matter-of-factly in one episode: "And so ... the whole family is deeply concerned about Fay. And though Ma expresses her deep faith in Fay ... is Ma concerned too? Well, Fay *does* see Andrew White and ... Fay finds words on her tongue which surprise even Fay ... tomorrow." Who could resist? Deeply devoted aficionados *had* to know what the darling of the Perkins family would say to Dr. White—there wasn't much chance they'd be missing tomorrow's episode, thanks to Orin Tovrov's metaphors and Dan Donaldson (er, Charlie Warren's) superlative delivery.

Donaldson/Warren promised the listeners a great deal as he transitioned from a commercial for Oxydol (*"Seeing is believing!"*) to each day's episode. Recapping the previous action, he would state something like: "Well, today we'll hear Ma express herself on this very important matter." His abstract at the close of the previous day's installment would have told listeners the same thing, only in different words. Sometimes in those summaries he would get even bolder as he enticed the audience to stay with the show: "On Monday, Fay considers the proposal of marriage, while Shuffle [Shober, Ma's business partner and best friend] wonders about those ulterior motives ... and there's that matter of the missing funds from the charity ball. We've got lots to listen for in the days just ahead." Donaldson's directives were compellingly urgent; listeners caught up in the narrative could hardly refuse him.

DOUGLAS, DON (born Douglas Kinleyside). b. Aug. 24, 1905, London, England; d. Dec. 31, 1945, Los Angeles, Calif. *Actor, Announcer.* **Series:** *The Black Castle* (announcer-actor, all roles, 1942–1944); *Kelly's Courthouse* (actor, 1944); *Scattergood Baines* (actor, ca. early 1940s).

Don Douglas appeared in a single theatrical release, 1937's *Headin' East*. His career abruptly ended when he died at 40 following an appendectomy.

DOUGLAS, HUGH. b. Aug. 3, 1915, Illinois; d. Sept. 1, 1993, Los Angeles, Calif. *Announcer.* **Series:** *The CBS Radio Workshop* (ca. 1956–1957); *The First Nighter* (ca. 1940s, early 1950s); *Have Gun, Will Travel* (1958–1960); *Hollywood Soundstage* (1951–1952); *Romance* (ca. 1955–1956).

Hugh Douglas was a newscaster at Chicago's WCFL in 1945. Four years later he was a disc jockey at the same station, presiding over *Tops in Town*.

DOUGLAS, PAUL FLEISCHER. b. April 11, 1907, Philadelphia, Pa.; d. Sept. 11, 1959, Hollywood Hills, Calif. *Announcer, Emcee, Actor.* **Series:** *Abie's Irish Rose* (actor, ca.

1942–ca. 1944); *Buck Rogers in the 25th Century* (ca. 1930s); *The Burns and Allen Show* (1938–1939); *The Chesterfield Supper Club* (1944–?); *Chesterfield Time*, aka *Moonlight Serenade*, aka *The Paul Whiteman Show* (1937–1939), aka *The Glenn Miller Show* (1939–1942); *Chesterfield Time*, aka *Pleasure Time*, aka *The Fred Waring Show* (1939–1944); *Command Performance* (1942–?); *The Community Sing*, aka *Summer Hotel*, aka *The Gillette Community Sing* (1936–1937); *Country Club of the Air* (1936); *Court of Human Relations* (ca. 1935–ca. 1939); *Dial Douglas* (sportscaster, 1941); *Earl Wilson's Broadway Column*, aka *It Happened Last Night* (1945); *Easy Aces* (ca. 1940s); *The Fred Waring Show* (ca. 1930s, 1940s); *Irene Beasley*, aka *The Zerone Program*, aka *Dupont Zerone Jesters* (1936–1937); *Jack Armstrong, the All-American Boy* (ca. late 1930s); *The Jack Benny Program* (1930s); *Meyer the Buyer* (actor, mid 1930s); *Paul Douglas, Sports* (1936, 1940); *Pick and Pat* (late 1930s); *The Saturday Night Swing Club* (ca. 1936–1937); *Star for a Night* (master of ceremonies, 1943–1944); *The Town Crier* (1930s); *Treasury Star Parade* (co-host, 1942–1944); *The True Story Hour with Mary and Bob* (1932).

After graduating from West Philadelphia High School where he was prominent in athletics and dramatics, Paul Douglas was active in little theater during the two years he was a student at Yale University. He left it to play professional football with the Frankford (Pa.) Fighting Yellow Jackets. His experience was brief. Entering radio in Philadelphia in 1930, he became one of the medium's best-recognized sports announcers, airing Saturday afternoon football games.

In addition to previously listed series, for a while in the 1930s Douglas also hosted *The Horn and Hardart Children's Hour*, aka *The Children's Hour* over New York's WABC. While Douglas's was a local show, it ran on a major station that beamed it to much of the Northeast for three decades, so it had the "feel" and influence of a more powerful series. In that regard it projected the host's name beyond a limited geographical community, adding some of the perceived glitz of a big time network feature, even though a regional chain of automat delicatessens underwrote it. A pundit described Douglas's introduction of another series for the small fry, stating that he would "shout into an open piano": *Buck Rogers in the 15th Cen-tur-EEE ... eee ... eee. The Sporting News* named him the best baseball commentator of 1942, recognizing one of several dimensions he filled in radio.

Douglas performed in a sketch on the May 9, 1946, premier of *Hour Glass*, an NBC-TV variety series, which established a pattern for what was to follow—in the show's life as well as his own. For example, he starred in *Casablanca* during the *Lux Video Theater's* long 1950s run on CBS-TV and later on NBC-TV. In 1953 he co-starred with Lee Grant in *Justice* on ABC-TV's *Plymouth Playhouse*. Douglas presided over the NBC-TV summertime film anthology series *Adventure Theatre* in 1956 and 1957 (the second year featuring reruns from the first year). He joined a rotating company of 10 actors that performed in filmed dramas on NBC-TV's *Goodyear TV Playhouse* between 1958 and 1960.

Nevertheless, Douglas is undoubtedly best recalled for his work in motion pictures. He appeared in 30 flicks between 1935 and 1959. Critic Leonard Maltin proffered: "The most successful—and complete—transition from the airwaves was made by Paul Douglas. Douglas was on the CBS staff for many years, though his bombastic personality never won him any popularity contests among his colleagues. An introduction to playwright-director Garson Kanin led to his casting in the Broadway comedy *Born Yesterday* [1946], in which he played the rough-hewn, self-made business tycoon Harry Brock. It was a tailor-made part, and the play's huge success led Douglas to Hollywood and a long starring career in such movies as *A Letter to Three Wives* [1949], *Angels in the Outfield* [1951], and *Executive Suite* [1954]. He never gave radio a backward glance." Other memorable films: *It Happens Every Spring* (1949); *Clash By Night* (1952); *The Solid Gold Cadillac* (1956); *Beau James* (1957); and *The Mating Game* (1959).

The stage production of *Born Yesterday*, incidentally, persisted from 1946 to 1948 for 1,024 performances. It was an opportunity that Douglas almost missed. Playwright Kanin searched high and low for "a Paul Douglas type" thespian to play the lead. Two days before rehearsals began—with no sign of luck—Kanin's wife, Ruth Gordon, suggested that he try to get Douglas. Kanin called the radio announcer-actor and gave him a chance to read the lines. The part was his on the spot and critics hailed Douglas on opening night as "the stage find of the year." He subsequently toured the nation in 1954–1955 in the starring role in *The Caine Mutiny Court Martial*. By then well into movies, Douglas died of a heart attack at the peak of his cinematic career.

DOWD, DONALD M. b. March 22, 1905, Philadelphia, Pa.; d. Feb. 21, 1977, Punta Gorda, Fla. *Announcer, Host.* **Series:** *ABC Mystery Time* (host, 1957–1958); *Black Night* (host, 1951); *The Breakfast Club* (1943–1955); *Club Matinee* (ca. 1937–1943); *Here's to Veterans* (ca. 1947–ca. 1950s); *Hot Copy* (ca. 1943–1944); *In Care of Aggie Horn* (1941–1942).

In 1924 Don Dowd matriculated at Pennsylvania State College, intent on becoming a physician. After two years of pre-med studies, enlivened by track and wrestling competitions, the young Dowd decided on another route to lifelong satisfaction—singing. He entered Ohio University in 1927 to pursue a bachelor of music degree. Working at odd jobs while in school, as his time permitted Dowd took part in dramatics, edited the school yearbook and launched a professional career in radio—although he was unaware of it at that juncture—by singing and announcing on a Mansfield, Ohio, station. Radio, he discovered, could offer the capital he needed to finance added voice training, and he returned to the mike at every opportunity given him. By the time he graduated in music he had changed his mind again, deciding to invest his life in broadcasting. He was soon on the air at a hometown station.

In 1933 Dowd transferred from Philadelphia's WLIT to Cincinnati's WLW, the latter outlet already a major Midwest audio powerhouse. By 1934 he was featured on his own vocal music program, *Don Dowd*. He was also one of possibly a dozen narrators of the popular late night series *Moon River* that was heard by millions of Americans during an epoch in which WLW operated at 500,000 watts (later reduced to 50,000). In 1934 Dowd left the station to join NBC in Chicago. That gave him national exposure for more than two decades, including a simulcast of the legendary early morning audience participation feature *The Breakfast Club* over both ABC Radio and TV between 1954 and 1955. There the intended doctor-turned-vocalist-turned-announcer was frequently a comic foil to the show's enduring lighthearted master of ceremonies, Don McNeil.

Dowd was employed by ABC for an aggregate 27 years—1943–1956 in Chicago and 1956–1970 in New York.

DOWNS, HUGH MALCOLM. b. Feb. 14, 1921, Akron, Ohio. *Announcer, Emcee.* **Series:** *Doctors Today* (1947–1948); *The Dave Garroway Show* (1947, 1949–1950); *It's Our Turn* (host, 1948); *Monitor* (co-communicator, 1955–1959); *RFD America* (1949); *Surprise Serenade* (1949); *Woman in White* (ca. 1944–1948).

When he was two, Hugh Downs' family moved to Lima, Ohio. A few years later money was tight in the post–Depression era but he managed to attend Bluffton College for a year on a public speaking scholarship (1938–1939). He returned to Lima to begin a job hunt. Turned down several times, one day at 18 a despondent Downs was sent by his mother with an empty jug to the local milk depot to get it refilled. Radio station WLOK was next door to his destination so he popped in for a tryout as an announcer. He won a part time spot at $7.50 weekly with the possibility of future full time work. The year was 1939. Had Downs not gone for the milk he might never have entered broadcasting.

Two years later he left WLOK to join Detroit's WWJ as program director and be a part time student at Wayne University (1940–1941). He interrupted his professional life in 1942 when Uncle Sam beckoned him to the Army. Returning in 1943, Downs joined WMAQ in Chicago. He was on the fast track to national exposure. In the late 1940s he announced one of the most powerful local features to advocate civil rights for Negroes, WMAQ's *Chicago Defender*, heard weekly between 1948 and 1951. He became the announcer on NBC-TV's *Kukla, Fran and Ollie* juvenile puppet series in 1949, extending into the early 1950s.

Downs was tapped as announcer-narrator of the daily live production of the NBC-TV soap opera *Hawkins Falls* in 1951, beamed from Chicago. He remained in that post for about three years. He also introduced the NBC public affairs entry *American Inventory* (1951–1955). By early 1952 he was appearing as a vocalist on *The Bunch*, an NBC weekday half-hour variety series. By 1954 he was in New York with NBC's *Home* show where he remained as announcer and sidekick to Arlene Francis until the show left the air in 1957. During that period Downs completed his formal education at Columbia University (1955–1956).

His activities in the visual medium were legion, including many guest appearances and several of the more enduring variety: *The World at Home* (announcer, 1955); *Caesar's Hour* (announcer, 1956–1957); *The Arlene Francis Show* (cast, 1957–1958); *The Tonight Show* (announcer-sidekick, 1957–1962); *Concentration* (master of ceremonies, 1958–1969), and a nighttime version of the same series (1961); *Today* (host, 1962–1971); *Not for Women Only* (co-host, mid 1970s); *Over Easy* (host, 1977–1980; co-host, 1980–1981); and *20/20* (host, 1978–1984; co-host, 1984–1999). A source assessed: "An easy-going, warm if placid TV announcer and personality, Hugh Downs was certified by the *Guiness* [sic] *Book of Records* in 1985 as having hosted more hours on TV than anyone else in the history of the medium."

Downs developed an abiding interest in science that led him to graduate studies in gerontology and the presidency of the National Space Society. He became chairman of the board of directors of Raylin Productions, Inc. in 1960; was special consultant to the United Nations on refugee concerns from 1961 to 1964; and later chairman of the U.S. Committee for UNICEF. After retiring in the Phoenix area, he taught at Arizona State University. He is the author of nearly a dozen books.

DOWNS, WILLIAM R, JR. b. Aug. 14, 1914, Kansas City, Mo.; d. May 3, 1978, Bethesda, Md. *Correspondent, Newscaster.* **Series:** *Bill Downs and the News* (newscaster, 1937, 1944, 1948, 1957); *CBS World News Roundup* (correspondent, ca. 1942–ca. 1962); *World News with Robert Trout* (correspondent, 1952).

Bill Downs aspired to a journalism career early in life and never wavered. He was sports editor of his high school newspaper and managed the paper at Wyandotte College for two years. At the University of Kansas, where he enrolled in 1933 for his final two years of undergraduate study, a cohort signified him as "the best and most prolific writer and reporter in the whole university." At a critical point in resuscitating a faltering *Daily Kansan*, that school's journal, Downs was appointed managing editor and received credit for turning the paper back to profitability. After his graduation, United Press hired him for its Kansas City bureau along with a fellow Kansan, Walter Cronkite. A short time later, Downs moved to the Denver bureau and then to New York.

In 1941 he received the wire service's plum assignment, the London bureau, covering the war. He crossed paths with CBS's Edward R. Murrow there. In the fall of 1942 Murrow made him an offer he couldn't refuse: $70 weekly and an expense account as CBS's Moscow correspondent. Bill Downs was to be one of the legendary "Murrow Boys" for a couple of decades.

In 1945 the National Headliners Club presented an award to Downs for "a vivid account of the surrender of German Armies in North Germany, Holland, and Denmark to English forces in Hamburg." That year he covered the surrender of Japan and the following year the atom bomb tests off Bikini Atoll in the Pacific. In 1950 he received an Overseas Press Club award for coverage of the Berlin blockade and airlift.

The one assignment Downs really enjoyed after the war—Rome—came to an abrupt end in 1956 when an exiled Winston Burdett was sent there and Downs returned to the U.S. He was given a daily five-minute radio news summary in 1957 that didn't last long. Then he went to the State Department but was miscast there. He resigned from CBS in March 1962, expecting to be a novelist for the remainder of his life. But the publishers weren't buying his fiction and he was forced to return to the air, becoming a second-echelon reporter in the Washington bureau of ABC News in November 1963. He remained there for the duration of his working life. Downs covered the swearing-in that same month of President Lyndon B. Johnson in the wake of John F. Kennedy's assassination, perhaps his most notable encounter with ABC.

DOYLE, JAMES. b. Oct. 4, 1910, St. Paul, Minn.; d. July 1, 1980, Lynnwood, Wash. *Announcer, Newscaster.* **Series:** *The Abbott and Costello Show* (1940s); *The Andy Devine Show* (ca. 1940s); *Dr. I.Q., the Mental Banker* (roving announcer, 1940s); *The Great Gildersleeve* (1949–1950); *Hollywood Mystery Time* (1944–1945); *Jim Doyle and the News* (newscaster, 1944); *The Louella Parsons Show* (ca. 1940s, 1950s); *Melody Roundup* (1944, plus 1942–1949 on AFRS); *Rogue's Gallery*, aka *Bandwagon Mysteries* (1945–1946); *The Wizard of Odds* (1949–1954).

Jim Doyle became a staff announcer for KHJ in Los Angeles in 1937, moving to NBC in the same capacity in 1940. Afterwards, he was a freelance announcer. A member of Pacific Pioneer Broadcasters, Doyle relocated near Seattle later in his career, accepting the post of executive secretary of the local office of the American Federation of Television and Radio Artists from 1966 to 1977.

DRAKE, GALEN (born Foster Rucker). b. July 26, 1906, Kokomo, Ind.; d. June 30, 1989, Long Beach, Calif. *Commentator, Newscaster.* **Series:** *The Galen Drake Show* (host-commentator, 1953–1956); *Housewives Protective League* (commentator, 1950s); *Mutual News* (newscaster, 1960s–ca. 1971); *This is Galen Drake* (commentator, 1944–1960s).

His Hoosier heritage notwithstanding, Galen Drake was raised in Long Beach, Calif. and grew up aiming to become a performing vocalist and impresario. He acquired a few opportunities to sing and conducted the Southern California Symphony briefly. Surprisingly, however, he abandoned his musical dreams to pursue law and medicine at the University of California Los Angeles. To help him finance his tuition, young Drake (still known as Foster Rucker then) took a part time job announcing at his hometown radio station in Long Beach, KFOX. In the meantime Los Angeles radio personality Fletcher Wiley intersected with him in 1939 and invited him to join the KNX staff to host a laid-back chat series he (Wiley) was then handling. The idea clicked, appealing so much to Drake, in fact, that whatever notions he had harbored for law, medicine and music evaporated entirely. He determined to concentrate on the ether instead.

His network run was preceded by a couple of years as a CBS West Coast commentator (1942–1943). During the early 1940s he presided over a couple of weekday talk stints over KNX for the regional audience, too. In 1944 he left it all behind to journey across the country and premier a brand of philosophical chatter from New York that would fairly well be viewed as something entirely new on the nation's airwaves. At that juncture he adopted the pseudonym Galen Drake. And he was good enough at the task he set for himself to persist for about two decades on three major chains (ABC, CBS, MBS) at varying times, occasionally on more than one web simultaneously.

His colorful, folksy gabfest aimed at the homemakers in the 1940s and 1950s spawned a plethora of similar shows in local markets. In a one-on-one conversational style Drake dispatched household, child-rearing and cooking tips while relating some spellbinding tales. He spoke with such candor that his audience could hardly turn away. Drake maintained a weekday quarter-hour from 1944 to 1950 and a five-minute daily show from 1953 to 1958. During most of the era he also broadcast for another quarter-hour or a full hour on weekends. Other performers on the 60-minute Saturday show included singers Stuart Foster and Betty Johnson and The Three Beaus and a Peep quartet backed by Bernard Leighton's orchestra. Olin Tice announced.

In the 1950s Drake delivered his homespun philosophy to New York listeners in still more WOR weekday appearances, as he had done at KNX a decade earlier. For four months in 1957 he presided over *This is Galen Drake* on Saturday nights, a half-hour on ABC-TV aimed at children. Drake persisted as a storyteller, something he did well on radio, while heisting an occasional tune, introducing songs by vocalists Rita Ellis and Stuart Foster and interviewing guests. Among the latter coterie were puppeteer Bill Baird and many others with appeal especially to youngsters.

After his radio format fell out of favor with the masses, Drake persevered as a newscaster at MBS in the 1960s. On Oct. 17, 1960, he launched a 10-year program over WOR intending to read the entire Holy Bible aloud. He lived almost three more decades, eventually succumbing to lung cancer.

DRAKE, RONALD. *Announcer.* **Series:** *The Burns and Allen Show*, aka *The Grape Nuts Program* (1937–1938); *The Edgar Bergen and Charlie McCarthy Show* (ca. 1937–ca. 1938).

The week after guest Mae West erupted with some very provocative lines on *The Edgar Bergen and Charlie McCarthy Show* in December 1937, Ronald Drake expressed the allegedly first ever on-air apology for a network broadcast. Bergen later recalled: "We got into all sorts of trouble. The network apologized, [sponsor] Chase and Sanborn apologized and I went and hid for a week. The net result was our ratings went up two points so we weren't really too sorry."

DREIER, ALEX. b. June 26, 1916, Honolulu, Hawaii; d. March 13, 2000, Rancho Mirage, Calif. *Correspondent, Newscaster, Commentator.* **Series:** *Alex Dreier News and Comments*, aka *Dreier Comments*, aka *Skelly News*, aka *Alex Dreier, Man on the Go* (newscaster-analyst, 1942–1943, 1944–1945, 1951–1956); *NBC News* (correspondent, 1941–ca. 1957); *This Fabulous World* (host, 1946).

Raised in San Francisco, Alex Dreier studied political science at Stanford University, receiving a degree in 1939. While subsequently covering Berlin for United Press Features in 1941 he joined NBC News. During a year in that city he found increasing Nazi resistance to his reporting. The Gestapo rigorously scrutinized his activities. Coincidentally, a day before the Japanese bombed Pearl Harbor, Dreier fled Berlin (on Dec. 6, 1941) very likely escaping detainment that other American journalists remaining behind were subjected to following the U.S. declaration of war.

Drier arrived in New York City early in 1942 and soon launched a commentary series on NBC. In October of that year he journeyed to London to relieve Robert St. John at NBC's British outpost. In so doing, he persisted in reporting the war news and observations from both sides of the Atlantic as the battle raged on. Returning to America sometime later, he was assigned to NBC in Chicago and by 1944 was appearing on national news programs and also airing local newscasts daily over the Windy City's WMAQ. His assignments in the 1950s and 1960s were broadened to include farm and rural news reports.

Dreier not only maintained a quarter-hour NBC newscast weekdays at 8 A.M. for five years (1951–1956), he furthermore gained the virtually unthinkable: he acquired a second daily newscast at 7 P.M. that overlapped some of that era (1953–1956). It was an indication of the esteem by which he was regarded at NBC during the period.

The news commentator possessed an uncanny ability to make fairly accurate predictions, among them: he correctly foretold the Allied invasion of North Africa during the Second World War while missing the date of Germany's surrender by just four days; he prophesied that Harry S Truman [sic] would be elected president in 1948 when the odds-on favorite was Thomas E. Dewey; he presaged Dwight D. Eisenhower's electoral voting outcome within two of the total tally in 1952.

Dreier was card-by-card commentator for *Championship Bridge*, shown on ABC-TV in 1959–1961 and in syndication for another 26 episodes in 1961–1962 with Charles Goren hosting. The program was filmed in Chicago. Dreier was later a regular in the cast of the 1969 ABC-TV comedy variety hour *What's It All About, World?* The show was hosted by Dean Jones and produced by Saul Ilson and Ernest Chambers, who were also responsible for *The Smothers Brothers Comedy Hour*.

When his broadcasting career started to fade, Dreier launched a new one acting in bit parts in a half-dozen motion pictures: *The Boston Strangler* (1968); *Chandler* (1971); *The Carey Treatment* (1972); *The Loners* (1972); *Lady Cocoa* (1975); and *Invisible Strangler* (1981). In addition, he played parts in a trio of made-for-TV movies: *Sweet, Sweet Rachel* (1971); *This Week in Nemtim* (1972); and *Murdock's Gang* (1973). For a decade—from the late 1960s to the late 1970s—Dreier was a character actor in numerous television series, too, including installments of *Cowboy in Africa*; *Hart to Hart*; *It Takes a Thief*; *Land of the Giants*; *Love, American Style*; *Mannix*; *The Name of the Game*; *O'Hara, U.S. Treasury*; *The Smith Family*; *Toma*; and more.

Extending his influence even further, Dreier was chairman of the board of the Annenberg Center for Health Sciences and a director of the Eisenhower Medical Center, both headquartered at Rancho Mirage, Calif.

DUDLEY, BERNARD. b. ca. 1878; d. October 1964. *Announcer.* **Series:** *A.L. Alexander's Mediation Board* (1943–?); *The American Forum of the Air* (ca. 1947–1948); *Big Town* (1948–ca. 1952); *The New York Philharmonic Orchestra* (ca. 1943–ca. 1947); *The Pause That Refreshes* (1944); *Starlight Serenade* (1944, 1945); *This Is Hollywood,* aka *The Hedda Hopper Show* (1946–1947); *Treasure Hour of Song* (ca. 1944–1945); *We Love and Learn* (1944); *Yours for a Song,* aka *Conti Castille Show* (host, 1948–1949).

Bernard Dudley asked the questions and Don Baker supplied the answers on CBS-TV's weekly five-minute *Sportsman's Quiz* in 1948–1949. It's believed to be Dudley's only continuing network video series.

DUDLEY, RICHARD ALLEN (born Casper Bernard Kuhn Jr.). b. April 22, 1915, Louisville, Ky.; d. Feb. 2, 2000, Lancaster, Pa. *Announcer.* **Series:** *The Aldrich Family* (ca. 1940s, early 1950s); *Archie Andrews* (ca. 1940s, early 1950s); *Believe It or Not* (1947–1948); *Colonel Humphrey Flack* (1947); *My Silent Partner* (1949).

Dick Dudley, whose full adopted moniker was Richard Allen Dudley, was reared in Tennessee and initially appeared on a juvenile radio series over Nashville's WTNT when he was only 11 (1926). He moved to New York City in 1938 and pursued various lines of work before becoming an NBC page. In 1940 he was promoted to staff announcer for the chain. In that capacity Dudley was among a handful of interlocutors thrust before the microphones on Dec. 7, 1941, to provide early news about the Japanese attack on Pearl Harbor.

Two years later, in 1943, he was drafted and assigned to London as a program director for the Armed Forces Radio Network. Dudley entertained the troops as master of ceremonies for live shows involving bands, vocalists and ensembles. Upon his discharge, he returned to announcing duties at NBC, continuing some 40 years after he began there, until retirement.

While also performing national radio assignments, Dudley presided over *Rockabye Dudley,* a nightly DJ series on New York City's WNBC, the flagship station of the National Broadcasting Co., in 1948–1949. He was one of a quartet of fleeting masters of ceremonies for the NBC-TV musical variety feature *Village Barn* in 1949. In the 1950s he introduced televised concerts of the NBC Symphony Orchestra conducted by Arturo Toscanini. During that decade he announced on *Today* and substituted for Don Pardo on *The Price is Right* on the video network. Furthermore, he introduced *Bob and Ray* during a portion of their NBC-TV run (1951–1953).

DUNBAR, RUSS. *Announcer.* **Series:** *The Adventures of the Falcon* (ca. 1940s); *The Mysterious Traveler* (ca. 1940s); *Snow Village Sketches* (narrator, 1936–1937, 1942–1943, 1946).

After his network programming faded, Russ Dunbar took up residence at New York's WOR. In 1951 he introduced WOR's weekly *Heatherton House* on which baritone Ray Heatherton—an NBC vocalist two decades earlier—interviewed guests.

DUNHAM, DICK. b. Feb. 26, 1916, New York, N.Y. *Announcer, Newscaster.* **Series:** *As the Twig is Bent* (1941–1942); *Dick Dunham and the News* (newscaster, 1945–?); *The Falcon* (1940s); *Katie's Daughter* (1947); *Madeline Carroll Reads* (1943); *Molle Mystery Theater* (1943–1948); *One Man's Destiny* (host, 1945–1946); *Policewoman* (1946–1947); *Rose of My Dreams* (1946–1948); *The Strange Romance of Evelyn Winters* (1944–1948); *We Love and Learn* (ca. 1943–1944).

Until 1942 Dick Dunham was a newscaster and announcer at Baltimore's WITH. That year he relocated in New York. Within three years he was a newscaster at CBS, having already been assigned to several network gigs on CBS, NBC and MBS. By 1944 Dunham also became the voice of Sweetheart soap, plugging the commodity repeatedly on a multiplicity of aural features into the early 1950s.

DUNNE, FRANK. *Announcer.* **Series:** *True Detective Mysteries.*

In 1940 Frank Dunne was a newscaster at WTAG, Worcester, Mass.

EASTMAN, CARL. b. ca. 1907, New York, N.Y.; d. Jan. 16, 1970, New York, N.Y. *Actor, Director, Announcer.* **Series:** *Abie's Irish Rose* (actor, 1942–1944); *The Adventures of M. Hercule Poirot,* aka *Mystery of the Week* (director, 1945, 1946–1947); *The Adventures of Nero Wolfe* (ca. mid 1940s); *The Big Story* (actor, ca. 1947–ca. 1955); *Brave Tomorrow* (actor, 1943–1944); *Cavalcade of America* (actor, ca. late 1930s, early 1940s); *Famous Jury Trials* (director, ca. 1940s); *Gangbusters* (actor, ca. 1930s, 1940s); *Life Can Be Beautiful* (actor, ca. late 1930s–1940s); *The March of Time* (actor, ca. 1930s, 1940s); *McGarry and His Mouse* (actor, 1946, 1947); *The MGM Theater of the Air* (actor, 1952); *Mrs. Miniver* (actor, 1944); *Perry Mason* (director, ca. 1940s); *Renfrew of the Mounted* (actor, 1936–1937, 1938–1940); *Rosemary* (producer-director, ca. late 1940s); *The Shadow* (actor, ca. 1930s–1950s); *This Small Town* (actor, 1940–1941); *Under Arrest* (actor, 1946, 1947, 1948–1954); *We Love and Learn* (director, 1940s); *Woman of Courage* (actor, ca. 1939–1942).

Carl Eastman attended Townsend Harris Hall High School with some pretty heady names of the future, among them Ben Grauer, Harold Hubert, Ken Roberts and Everett Sloane. After further studies at Columbia University, young Eastman joined his father at L.S. Rothschild, planning a future on Wall Street. The Great Depression and an absorbing interest in the performing arts redirected the young brokerage salesman into radio, however, which he joined in 1933. As radio's fortunes ebbed a couple of decades later, Eastman entered the personal management arena, specializing in commercial talent. Some of his clients included Mason Adams, Dane Clark, Joyce Gordon, Carleton Hence, Don Morrow, Arnold Moss, Joe O'Brien and Santos Ortega.

EASTON, JOHN. b. July 10, 1918, New York, N.Y.; d. April 10, 1984, New York, N.Y. *Announcer.* **Series:** *The Adventures of Maisie* (1945–1947, 1949–1952); *The Great Gildersleeve* (ca. 1940s, 1950s); *Let George Do It* (1946–1954).

While John Easton dabbled in radio, he earned the bulk of his income by unremittingly jumping into broadcast advertising. Over a successful career in the field he wrote and produced radio and television commercials for an extensive line of personal, household and industrial commodities. Some of the brand names Easton plugged were Arnold (bread), Avon, Beechnut (coffee), Betty Crocker, Buick, Dentyne, E.I. Dupont, El Producto, General Motors, Ipana (toothpaste), Johnson & Johnson, Reynolds (metals), Tareyton, Texaco and U.S. Steel.

EDWARDS, DOUGLAS. b. July 14, 1917, Ada, Okla.; d. Oct. 13, 1990, Sarasota, Fla. *Newscaster, Announcer.* **Series:** *Answer Please* (1958–?); *CBS World News Roundup* (correspondent, 1945–1946; anchor, 1946–ca. 1948); *Douglas Edwards and the News* (newscaster, ca. 1958–1988); *The Green Hornet* (relief announcer, 1938–1940); *The Lone Ranger* (relief announcer, 1938–1940); *Wendy Warren and the News* (newscaster, 1947–1958).

Spending part of his childhood in Silver City, N.M., many years later Doug Edwards acknowledged that he was "transfixed by broadcasts I could bring in from faraway places" on a crystal radio set. At 15 he was on the air on WHET, a 100-watt station at Troy, Ala., that he depicted as put together "with rubber bands, high hopes, and great spirits." While he formally trained at the University of Alabama, Emory University and the University of Georgia—initially in medicine until a pervasive allure of broadcasting led him into journalism—Edwards accepted announcing and newscasting posts at a succession of stations: WAGF, Dothan, Ala. (1935); WSB, Atlanta (1936); WXYZ, Detroit (1938); WSB again, as assistant news director (1940); and in 1942—at 25—he joined CBS in New York, his employer until he retired April 1, 1988.

While he went to CBS in the capacity of staff announcer, he was soon developing as a network newscaster under the tutelage of John Charles Daly, a man who would be his underdog rival for TV news-watchers a decade hence. He took over Daly's CBS broadcast duties in 1943 when the latter was assigned to North Africa. For a few months before the close of World War II, Edwards was attached to Edward R. Murrow's London staff but was never dubbed one of the renowned "Murrow boys," largely due to the lateness of his arrival. He was CBS's Paris bureau chief after the war in the days leading to the Nuremberg trials. He followed that with an extended assignment in the Middle

East before returning to America in June 1946. He soon became the anchor of the *CBS World News Roundup*.

Afterwards, for nearly a dozen years, one of Edwards' unique tasks was to dispatch a three-minute capsule edition of the current events weekdays at noon at the start of CBS Radio's soap opera *Wendy Warren and the News*. The serial's heroine (played by actress Florence Freeman) portrayed a journalist who then delivered "news reports from the women's world" immediately following Edwards' headlines. Integrating news into a mythical storyline added an aura of realism to the narrative that similar fare only rarely approached.

Edwards inaugurated a weekend CBS-TV newscast in 1947 and covered the political conventions in 1948. (Newsman Larry Lesueur preceded Edwards' debut on CBS's flagship station, WCBS-TV in New York.) That same summer the chain tapped him to anchor the nation's first nightly network newscast, *CBS TV News*, renamed *Douglas Edwards with the News* in 1950, indicating his widespread recognition by then. (While NBC's John Cameron Swayze led the competition into the nightly newscast arena, it didn't happen until 1949.) "It wasn't an easy decision for him [Edwards] to make," wrote a biographer, "in fact his initial reaction was to say no to the offer. Television was considered unworthy for serious journalists, a sideshow and dead end, by many in broadcasting and print. Not only that, but Edwards would have to give up the substantial additional income which radio advertising provided to announcers. [The debuting TV news show was without sponsorship.] It took Frank Stanton, the president of CBS, to convince him that, far from being a dead end, television was the wave of the future."

"The truth is," pontificated Gary Paul Gates, a chronicler of CBS News, "that [Walter] Cronkite and all the other TV anchormen who have come along since are the direct descendants of Douglas Edwards." Gates continued: "For fourteen years, from 1948 to 1962, Doug Edwards was the face and voice of CBS on its evening news show. In fact, his critics, then and later, would argue that he never was anything more than that: an announcer masquerading as a journalist, a mere 'reader' with no background or training in news. But it was unfair, ... to suggest that Edwards simply jumped into television straight out of an announcer's booth.... He had seized every opportunity along the way to establish himself in news." After the coaxial cable linked all of the nation's TV watchers in September 1951, the pioneering journalist introduced his daily quarter-hour newscast with "Good evening, everyone, from coast to coast." In 1955 he won a George Foster Peabody Broadcasting Award for his reporting.

Edwards simultaneously hosted *The Eyes Have It* over New York's WCBS-TV beginning in 1948, a program that segued into an early network quiz-audience participation series, *Celebrity Time*, not long after. In 1953 he was an interviewee on the panel discussion show *Youth Takes a Stand* on CBS-TV. Edwards presided over CBS-TV's *State of the Nation* (1953); *Masquerade Party* (1953); and *Armstrong Circle Theater* (1957–1961). In the summer of 1960 he hosted *F.Y.I. (For Your Information)*, a weekly CBS-TV public affairs entry. From 1979 to 1988 he introduced a weekly 30-minute interdenominational religious feature on CBS-TV, *For Our Times*. Notwithstanding, his daily radio newscasts continued until his retirement. He also maintained a five-minute weekday newscast on CBS-TV from April 16, 1962, to May 30, 1980, at shifting times (in sequence at 3:55, 3:25, 4:25, 12:25, 11:54 and 10:55).

Shortly after his retirement, Edwards told a reporter for *The New York Times*: "Next to my family and friends, broadcasting is my great love, a romance I've carried on for more than 50 years. Where else are you going to satisfy your natural curiosity, be privy to the great events of your time, be a disseminator of information to a vast audience, be a conduit by which your fellow human beings understand the world?" His papers are housed in the Douglas Edwards Archives at St. Bonaventure (New York) University.

EDWARDS, RALPH LIVINGSTONE. b. June 13, 1913, Merino, Colo.; d. Nov. 16, 2005, West Hollywood, Calif. *Emcee, Announcer, Actor.* **Series:** *Against the Storm* (ca. 1939); *A Dream Comes True* (1948–1949); *The Gospel Singer*, aka *Edward McHugh* (1938); *The Gumps* (mid 1930s); *The Heinz Magazine of the Air* (1936); *The Horn and Hardart*

Children's Hour, aka *The Children's Hour* (host, mid to late 1930s); *Life Can Be Beautiful* (1938–ca. 1939); *Major Bowes' Original Amateur Hour* (1936–1939); *Musical Mock Trial*, aka *The Ben Bernie Show* (1938–ca. 1940); *The O'Neills* (1938); *Our Gal Sunday* (ca. 1937–?); *The Phil Baker Show* (ca. 1935–1938); *Radio Hall of Fame*, aka *Philco Radio Hall of Fame* (actor, 1930s); *Renfrew of the Mounted* (1936–1937); *Road of Life* (ca. 1937–?); *Stoopnagle and Budd* (1936); *These Are Our Men* (actor, ca. 1944–ca. 1945); *This is Your Life* (creator-host, 1948–1950); *Town Hall Tonight*, aka *The Fred Allen Show* (ca. late 1930s); *Truth or Consequences* (creator-master of ceremonies, 1940–1951, 1952–1954); *Vic and Sade* (ca. 1940s); *The Whistler* (actor, ca. 1940s). **Aphorism:** *Aren't we devils?*

Ralph Edwards broke into radio when he wrote a short play while a high school junior. It aired over KROW, Oakland, Calif., in 1929. The station manager subsequently hired him as a part time writer, actor and announcer. During his collegiate days at the University of California in nearby Berkeley, Edwards worked concurrently at KROW and San Francisco's KPRC. On campus he appeared in nearly every little theater production. Enamored by the pull of burgeoning network radio, following his 1935 graduation, Edwards thumbed his way to New York City where he lined up several radio auditions. Before long he was appearing on *Renfrew of the Mounted* and *Stoopnagle and Budd*. When CBS held tryouts for a staff announcer, Edwards competed against 69 other aspirants—and won. Instantly his voice was heard introducing 45 shows weekly.

Wrote critic Leonard Maltin: "It was Ralph Edwards' friendly, warm, personal approach to commercials on daytime soap operas that all but revolutionized announcing in the late 1930s. Rather than reading the advertising copy strictly as written, he would ad lib and embellish, injecting conversational punctuation along the way, as if speaking casually—and personally—to each female listener."

Edwards shared an apartment near WABC Radio in those days with a couple of other rising radio legends, Mel Allen and Andre Baruch. The shows Edwards appeared on provided him with a more than comfortable living in post–Depression America. By then his annual salary exceeded $50,000 and he was convinced he was introducing more commercial programs than anybody else. Yet he was a malcontent. "I didn't want to be just an announcer," he disclosed. Having probed the successes of those who rose to the forefront of broadcasting careers, Edwards was convinced that performers who developed unique program styles gained eminence among radio's affluent purveyors. The best of all possible worlds, he decided, would be to prove himself as an innovative program producer. Such an opportunity might allow him to concentrate on only one or two primary properties rather than running from show to show throughout the workday.

Learning that one of radio's major underwriters, Procter & Gamble, was seeking a novel concept for a primetime feature, Edwards put together a stunt-filled half-hour based on an old parlor game that his family played at home during his youth. He called it *Truth or Consequences*. For several decades it captured the imagination of millions of Americans in dual mediums. Weekly he conducted hilarious antics that called for contestants to be embroiled in zany exhibitions, invariably causing the studio audience to convulse in raucous, uncontrollable laughter. Then Edwards squealed into a microphone: *Aren't we devils?* The show's popularity may not have been eclipsed until a successive Edwards-inspired human-interest foray, *This is Your Life*, appeared on radio and television. In the 1950s his own production company was churning out multiple video entries and making his $50,000 salary in the 1930s look like a pauper's stash.

Truth or Consequences premiered on TV in 1950 and lasted one season. It returned to the tube from 1954 to 1956 and again from 1957 to 1958. A weekday televersion ran almost continuously from 1956 to 1965, nonetheless. By then Edwards was immersed in *This is Your Life* and relinquished *T or C*'s hosting duties to Jack Bailey, Steve Dunne and Bob Barker. Edwards tried twice to revive *T or C* in syndication, each time unsuccessfully, with Bob Hilton as emcee in 1977–1978 and Larry Anderson and Murray Langston in 1987.

Meanwhile, the entrepreneurial spirit of Ralph Edwards wasn't done yet. *This is Your Life*, the first of the reality shows, aired for a couple of years on radio in the late 1940s, then it sprung to TV in 1950 where it persisted in primetime to 1951, returned from 1954 to 1956 and again from 1957 to 1958. A daytime incarnation ran from 1956 to 1959 and 1959 to 1965. It appeared in syndication from Ralph Edwards Productions in 1966–1975, 1977–1978 and 1987–1988. Other Edwards ventures: *It Could Be You* (1956–1961, most of that time in weekday and primetime versions); *Place the Face* (1953–1955); *Crosswits* (1975–1980, 1986–1987); and *The People's Court* (1981–1993, 1997–). In the early years of the 21st century, several days a week Edwards—then in his nineties—stopped by the Hollywood offices of Ralph Edwards Productions that he maintained for many years.

ELLIOT, WIN (born Irwin Elliot Shalek). b. May 7, 1915, Chelsea, Mass.; d. Sept. 19, 1998, Norwalk, Conn. *Announcer, Emcee, Sportscaster.* **Series:** *The Betty Crocker Magazine of the Air* (1954); *County Fair* (master of ceremonies, ca. 1945–1950); *Fish Pond* (quizmaster, 1944); *Guest Star* (1947–1949); *Gunsmoke* (1953); *Heinz Magazine of the Air* (1936–1938); *Juvenile Jury* (ca. late 1940s, early 1950s); *Musical Mysteries* (master of ceremonies, 1944); *One Man's Family*; *Payroll Savings Plan* (ca. mid to late 1940s); *Quick as a Flash* (quizmaster, 1947–1949); *Sports Central USA* (host, late 1960s–early 1980s); *Stars for Defense* (ca. 1957–ca. 1962); *Walk a Mile* (quizmaster, 1952–1954); *Willie Piper*, aka *Tales of Willie Piper* (1946–1948).

While majoring in zoology at the University of Michigan, Win Elliot looked for a class to complete the final credits he needed to graduate. He decided on communications, where a professor urged him to pursue a career in sportscasting. He took a job at Detroit's WJR while honing his skills. After a subsequent stint at WMEX, a low-powered Boston outlet, he transferred to a Washington, D.C., station as a local staff announcer. In a short while he was added to Baltimore's WFBR where he had the opportunity to write, produce and be master of ceremonies of a daytime variety show, *Club 1300*. The experience helped Elliot develop as an audience participation host and brought him to the attention of emcee Ralph Edwards, who was riding *Truth or Consequences* to national prominence at that moment.

At Edwards' pending induction into the Armed Services, he told Elliot, "You're the best we've auditioned to replace me." Elliot didn't get the nod to temporarily step in at *Truth or Consequences*, nevertheless, due in large measure to the fact he was an unknown quantity beyond his regional turf. Edwards assured him that he would "do something" for Elliot "as soon as I can" anyway. Hollow thoughts? When Edwards was consequently deferred by the draft board, he made good on his promise, passing Elliot's name along to the Blue chain. The latter was soon hosting a couple of fleeting New York–based network entries, *Musical Mysteries* and *Fish Pond*, the latter an amateur talent competition. That brought him to the forefront and—after a brief stint in the U.S. Merchant Marines—Elliot was soon in charge of multiple broadcast stunt features.

After he became known as a radio commodity, Elliot segued into television as the master of ceremonies for a quintet of game shows: *It's in the Bag* (1950–1951); *On Your Account* (1953–1954); *Tic Tac Dough* (1957–1958); *Win with a Winner* (1958); and *Make That Spare* (1961–1962). He announced NBC-TV's debuting *Fireside Theater* for eight weeks in 1949. In between gigs, from 1953 to around 1957, he introduced the CBS-TV daytime serial *Valiant Lady* and sporadically doubled as an extra in its cast.

He earned sizeable credentials as a TV and radio sportscaster. Elliot's sports roundups were ongoing CBS Radio features from the 1960s into the 1980s, with a special accent on boxing, hockey and horseracing events. He anchored pre- and post-game features during World Series on radio. In four nonconsecutive seasons in the 1950s and 1960s he covered the New York Rangers hockey team from Madison Square Garden over Gotham's WMGM and WINS. Concerning his televised sportscasts, a critic summarized: "Elliot had a flair for the dramatic, but was still able to pinpoint what the viewer needed to know."

ELLIOTT, LAWRENCE K. b. Aug. 31, 1900, Washington, D.C.; d. July 27, 1957, Port Chester, N.Y. *Announcer, Newscaster.* **Series:** *The Alan Young Show* (ca. mid 1940s); *The American Melody Hour* (1942–ca. mid 1940s); *Barry Cameron*, aka *The Soldier Who Came Home* (1945–1946); *The Bob Hawk Show* (1940s–ca. early 1950s); *Boston Blackie* (1940s); *The Fred Allen Show*, aka *The Texaco Star Theater* (1940s); *Front Page Farrell* (1940s, ca. early 1950s); *Headlines and Bylines* (newscaster, 1938); *Mr. Keen, Tracer of Lost Persons* (1943–1951); *The Music of Andre Kostelanetz*, aka *The Pause That Refreshes*, aka *Music Millions Love* (1940s); *Rose of My Dreams* (1946–1948); *Saturday Night Bondwagon* [sic] (1942–1944); *The Strange Romance of Evelyn Winters* (1944–1948); *Treasury Star Parade* (1942–1944); *Your Song and Mine* (1948).

Larry Elliott's foray into radio was totally unscripted. While selling cars for an automobile dealership, he developed a flair for singing. For five years, strictly as a sideline, he took voice lessons, unsure what he would do with his budding artistry. At about the time he sold a car to a local WJSV radio official, the auto dealership failed and Elliott was tossed out on his ear. Taking pity on him, the radio man offered him an announcing spot at his CBS affiliate. The year was 1932, at the height of the country's economic slump.

Elliott was soon newscasting at WJSV and by the mid 1930s was appointed CBS's chief White House reporter. He also substituted sporadically for Arthur Godfrey when the Old Redhead failed to appear at the start of *Sundial*, his local early morning disc jockey program, long before Godfrey became a national institution. Elliott once advised the early risers in that listening audience: "If you're silly enough to get out of a nice warm bed at this ungodly hour, it's your fault. Don't expect me to entertain you. I'm tired, too!" Paradoxically, in October 1938 he left the capital to become a CBS staff announcer in New York and soon launched his own early morning program, *The Rising Sun Show*.

As a freelance announcer Elliott turned up on numerous radio features, from drama and comedy to music, quiz and variety shows. He was the official voice of the U.S. Treasury on *Saturday Night Bondwagon* and *Treasury Star Parade*, pitching war bonds wrapped in the banner "Millions for Defense." Elliot was the most durable and therefore most familiar announcer for broadcasting's longest running detective drama, *Mr. Keen, Tracer of Lost Persons*. In the 1940s he was the daily interlocutor for multiple soap operas. Those who knew him intimately said Elliot had "more hobbies than anyone else in radio." His favorite pastimes were making pipes for smokers and gardening at his Scarsdale and later Port Chester, N.Y., residence.

In 1956, the year before a heart attack abruptly ended his life at age 56, Elliott launched a video acting career by appearing on NBC-TV's *Kraft Theater*.

EMERICK, ROBERT E. b. Dec. 9, 1915, Tacoma, Wash.; d. June 1, 1973, San Diego, Calif. *Announcer.* **Series:** *Bobby Benson and the B-Bar-B Riders* and similar monikers (ca. late 1940s, early 1950s); *Mr. Feathers* (1949–1950); *The Mysterious Traveler* (ca. 1948–ca. 1952); *Scattergood Baines* (1949); *Scout About Town* (ca. 1946, 1947); *Special Agent* (1948); *Top Secrets of the FBI* (1947).

Bob Emerick launched his ethereal career in California at stations in San Francisco and Los Angeles before moving to New York in 1948. He was on the staff of WOR Radio in Gotham for several years and then joined ABC-TV. Emerick was a commercial spokesman for copious advertisers in dual mediums. He also narrated manifold television documentaries and motion pictures. From 1971 to 1973 he was director of speech and drama at Litchfield (Conn.) Preparatory School. Although he lived in Litchfield, he was vacationing in San Diego when he succumbed to a heart attack at 57.

ENGLE, HOLLAND E. b. April 26, 1907, Wheeling, W. Va.; d. March 24, 1988, Oakland, Calif. *Announcer, Emcee.* **Series:** *Ladies Fair* (emcee's assistant, 1950–1954); *Quiz of Two Cities* (occasional regional announcer, 1944–1947); *Variety Fair* (host, 1946).

Holland Engle got his start in radio in 1921, predating almost every other successful announcer. A versatile entertainer, in 1948 *Radio Mirror* reported that his assignments included not only announcing and being a master of ceremonies, for "he also sings, plays the piano, acts, and writes." On a DJ series he might introduce a record featuring a number played on the piano by him and also composed by him!

By 1942 Engle took up permanent residence at Chicago's WGN, often as a newscaster. WGN, in fact, subsequently publicized him as "Dean of American Newsmen in Broadcasting." WGN supplied much of Engle's income between his brief respites on national webs aired from the Windy City. In 1949 he presided over an early morning quarter-hour weekday DJ series, *Today's the*

Day. A reviewer labeled it "a cheerful wake-up program of music, time, temperature and news on a sustaining basis."

EVANS, FRANKLYN. *Announcer.* **Series:** *Pat Novak for Hire* (ca. 1949–1950).

Franklyn Evans (spelled Franklin by at least one source) was heard from coast to coast even before his brief stint on national radio. In 1941 he was a newscaster at WDNC, Durham, N.C. By 1945 he was a sportscaster at San Francisco's KPO.

EVANS, RICHARD L. b. March 23, 1906, Salt Lake City, Utah; d. Nov. 1, 1971, Salt Lake City, Utah. *Announcer, Commentator, Producer.* **Series:** *Music and the Spoken Word from the Crossroads of the West*, aka *The Mormon Tabernacle Choir* (narrator-spokesman, producer and director, 1930–1971).

Richard Evans, who delivered "the spoken word"—a weekly three-minute homily—for one of the world's most respected choral groups from its inception on CBS until his death four decades later, was a general officer of the Church of Jesus Christ of Latter Day Saints for much of his adult life. Evans was hospitalized with a viral infection of the central nervous system for a period of time before his demise, according to *Variety*. J. Spencer Kinard succeeded him as the voice of the famous program. Lloyd Newell followed Kinard in 1990.

FALKENBURG, EUGENIA LINCOLN (JINX). b. Jan. 21, 1919, Barcelona, Spain; d. Aug. 27, 2003, Long Island, New York, N.Y. *Commentator, Sportscaster.* **Series:** *Leave It to the Girls* (panelist, 1945–1949); *Meet Tex and Jinx* (1947, 1948).

Glamour girl Jinx Falkenburg and her spouse, Yale alumnus-scholar Tex McCrary, became the final duo in a trilogy of celebrated New York couples that debuted on the ether with venerated early morning audio shows. In the 1940s and 1950s those breakfast chat features radiated from Gotham for hundreds of miles along the Eastern seaboard. Dubbed by a journalist "Mr. Brains and Mrs. Beauty," the McCrarys (as *Tex and Jinx*, originally *Hi Jinx*) followed in the train of broadcasting innovators Ed and Pegeen Fitzgerald (*The Fitzgeralds*)—who initiated the subgenre—and another connubial twosome, newspaper gossip columnist Dorothy Kilgallen and radio actor Richard Kollmar (*Breakfast with Dorothy and Dick*).

Falkenburg, meanwhile, was a movie actress in the early 1940s "though never a very good one," she stressed, as well as a swimming and tennis aficionado. Her airtime exposure was limited when she linked with McCrary in 1946 on WEAF Radio (which was renamed WNBC and WRCA by the time their program ran its course in the late 1950s). Yet she was already an American icon in the tradition of the eminently stellar Hollywood legend Grace Kelly, who arrived a few years later. Millions knew Falkenburg's form and figure for she possessed a face and body that adorned the slick covers of more than 200 popular periodicals.

She wed *New York Daily Mirror* reporter John Reagan (Tex) McCrary in 1945 when he wooed her following a newspaper interview and a subsequent whirlwind romance carrying them overseas—he in the U.S. Army Air Force and she a performer for the armed forces. Her image was also captured on a postage stamp commemorating the USO. Her lack of higher education presented no difficulty as they shared professional careers. McCrary branded his bride "the most intelligent uneducated person I know." Despite that, a critic reported that some of their celebrity interviews turned out to resemble "press releases." He elucidated: "From a conversation with Walt Disney, for instance, Jinx breathlessly reported that he loves his work."

McCrary's and Falkenburg's breakfast radio series was easily adaptable to the newer medium of television. In early 1947 NBC-TV experimented with formats by offering them as part of a Sunday evening quarter-hour labeled *Bristol-Myers Tele-Varieties*. A reviewer confirmed, "The McCrarys were naturals for TV, ... with their combination of friendly chatter, interviews, and features." That summer the network awarded the couple an exclusive Sunday night half-hour under the moniker *At Home with Tex and Jinx*. They moved to CBS-TV for six months in 1949 with 30 minutes on Monday nights under the title *Preview with Tex and Jinx*. The two presided over *The Tex and Jinx Show* (initially *Closeup*) for a year in 1957–1958 on NBC-TV's daytime lineup. Meanwhile, on Sept. 2, 1951, Jinx Falkenburg was a guest panelist on the CBS-TV game show *What's My Line?* For a few weeks in 1958 she was a panelist on the stunt show *Masquerade Party* on the same network. She also filled a guest panelist chair on that web's *I've Got a Secret*.

Eugenia Lincoln Falkenburg was nicknamed Jinx by her mother. She was born in Spain while her native American parents lived there, her dad being employed by Westinghouse Corp. The family was transferred to Chile when Jinx was two. During her early teens she became a swimming champion in that country and, subsequently, a tennis champion after they moved to Brazil. She turned 16 when the family relocated in California. Her statuesque figure led to a modeling contract with the Powers agency and ultimately projected her into movies. Before joining with Tex McCrary in their own radio series, Jinx Falkenburg appeared in guest spots on shows headlined by entertainers Eddie Cantor, Bing Crosby and Bob Hope. She and sportscaster Bill Stern covered the national singles and doubles tennis matches from Forest Hills in 1942. Although she could neither sing, dance nor act well, she performed in Al Jolson's Broadway musical *Hold On to Your Hats*.

An outspoken Republican, Falkenburg raised tons of cash for the party and in 1954 was named to lead its women's division. She and McCrary co-wrote a column carried by *The New York Herald Tribune*. She left radio in 1958 due to hepatitis but he persisted there for two more years. Between 1935 and 1946 she appeared in 23 mostly B motion pictures. Among them: *Big Brown Eyes* (1936); *Nothing Sacred* (1937); *There Goes My Heart* (1938); *The Lone Ranger Rides Again* (1939); *Two Latins from Manhattan* (1941); *Lucky Legs* (1942); *Sweetheart of the Fleet* (1942); *Two Senoritas from Chicago* (1943); *She Has What It Takes* (1943); *Cover Girl* (1944, in which she appeared in a cameo as herself); *The Gay Senorita* (1945); *Tahiti Nights* (1945); *Talk About a Lady* (1946); and *Meet Me on Broadway* (1946). In the 1980s the McCrarys split but maintained an amiable rapport for the remainder of their lives. Ironically, Tex McCrary died less than a month before his ex.

FARREN, JACK. b. Nov. 17, 1922, New York, N.Y.; d. June 25, 1997, Los Angeles, Calif. *Announcer.* **Series:** *Under Arrest* (ca. late 1940s).

Jack Farren began his show business career as a radio announcer in New York City before switching to television in the early 1950s. His first production efforts there included *Howdy Doody* and *Winky Dink and You*. Much later Farren became an executive producer with Barry & Enright Productions and still later with Goodson-Todman Productions. He produced TV movies including *Mafia Princess* (1986) and *Fatal Judgment* (1988) and a single feature film, *Fuzz* (1972).

FARREN, WILLIAM ANTHONY. b. Sept. 1, 1900, Albany, N.Y. *NBC staff announcer.*

After two years at Annapolis and two years in pre-legal studies at Georgetown University, William Anthony Farren went to work for a Washington, D.C., newspaper. During that sojourn he organized a radio quartet of wounded war veterans and stepped in when they needed a bass vocalist. The station manager liked his voice and put him on the air regularly reporting a couple of daily sportscasts. In 1933 Farren went to New York and then to a Boston station to cover prizefights, baseball and football games. Returning to New York in 1936, he became an NBC staff announcer at Radio City.

While on a hunting and fishing trip in the bush country 90 miles north of Ottawa, Canada, Farren discovered an island with a lake on it in the Madewaska River. Surprisingly, the island didn't appear on Canadian maps. Following a dominion government-backed survey, the island was officially given Farren's name. He acknowledged that his most treasured memory from radio, meanwhile, was an interview with Admiral Richard Byrd following the famous explorer's return from his initial expedition to the South Pole.

FARRINGTON, FIELDEN. b. July 4, 1909, Michigan; d. July 1977, Bayville, N.Y. *Announcer, Newscaster, Writer.* **Series:** *The Armstrong Theater of Today* (ca. 1940s); *CBS News* (newscaster, 1947–1948); *The CBS Radio Mystery Theater* (writer, 1974–1976); *Edward R. Murrow and the News* (domestic headlines reporter, 1944); *The Ford Summer Theater* (1939, 1940, 1941); *The Green Hornet* (1936–1939); *Just Plain Bill* (ca. late 1940s, early 1950s); *News and Views from the Show*

World (1940); *News of the World* (newscaster, 1941); *Our Gal Sunday* (cowcatcher and hitchhike commercial spokesman, 1950); *The Romance of Helen Trent* (1944–1960); *Theater Five* (writer-announcer, ca. 1964–1965); *We Love and Learn* (ca. late 1940s, early 1950s); *World News Today* (ca. 1940–ca. 1945).

Before and after he was a durable network announcer, Fielden Farrington was first and foremost a writer. After decades of introducing soap operas and other fare, he chucked it all to return to his first love and made something of a name for himself in that scene, too. Farrington broke into broadcasting as a writer in 1929 and in a short while found himself in front of a WXYZ microphone in Detroit as a staff announcer. That put him in place in 1936 as the debuting interlocutor for *The Green Hornet*, a dramatic juvenile adventure series originated by WXYZ for the Mutual network. In 1939 Farrington moved to New York and joined CBS, where he soon introduced a plethora of ongoing series.

When the last of them left the air in June 1960, Farrington had long grown weary of broadcasting, feigning "perpetual boredom." In yet another dimension of his multitalented proficiency, he developed into an adept author of science fiction and crime dramas for anthology series aired beyond radio's golden years. In that connection, for *The CBS Radio Mystery Theater* alone he penned more than a score of original audio plays. He also turned into a novelist of some repute, releasing *A Little Game* (Walker & Co., 1968) and *The Strangers in 7A* (D. McKay Co., 1972). *The Strangers in 7A* was subsequently developed into an *ABC Movie of the Week* then re-released as a feature-length film starring Andy Griffith, Michael Brandon, Ida Lupino and Suzanne Hildur.

Nevertheless, Farrington is undoubtedly best recalled by millions of homemakers for the 16 years he introduced one of daytime's most beleaguered heroines searching for love through many a midlife crisis. Each day, between the hums and strums of Stanley Davis plucking on a ukulele to the strains of "Juanita," Farrington offered the serialized narrative to addicts with a familiar, albeit substantial epigraph: *And now The Romance of Helen Trent, the real-life drama of Helen Trent who—when life mocks her ... breaks her hopes ... dashes her against the rocks of despair—fights back bravely ... successfully ... to prove what so many women long to prove in their own lives: that because a woman is thirty-five—or more—romance in life need not be over; that the romance of youth can extend into middle life ... and even beyond.* If Farrington said it once, across the 16 years he presented her he must have said it over 4,000 times. And poor single Helen was still, well, single—but only 35—when it ended, her captivating tale having been heard for 27 years!

FENNEMAN, GEORGE. b. Nov. 10, 1919, Beijing, China; d. May 29, 1997, Los Angeles, Calif. *Announcer, Actor.* **Series:** *Dragnet* (1949–1957); *Gunsmoke* (commercial spokesman, 1954–1957); *I Fly Anything* (actor, 1950–1951); *On Stage America* (ca. 1947–1948); *Pat Novak for Hire* (1949); *Pete Kelly's Blues* (1951); *Too Many Cooks* (actor, 1950); *You Bet Your Life* (1947–1956).

In 1945 George Fenneman switched from San Francisco's KGO to the Hollywood staff of ABC. It was a constructive move: as a result, it seemed he would spend his career under the auspices of one man, Jack Webb, for whom he broadcast three aural series, two of them also in video incarnations. But long before he was finished with the ether, Fenneman rode the coattails of a zany comedian to instant recognition in his own right—and once again, in dual mediums.

Among the many innovations that Jack Webb's *Dragnet* ushered onto the ether was the appearance of *two* announcers, Fenneman and Hal Gibney. Their voices bounced back and forth, complementing one another as they contrasted, giving the show's opening greater power than either could have provided alone. On graphically wicked outings, Fenneman offered a preliminary announcement: "This story is for you, not your children," yet another unique characteristic of that series.

Forty-two men auditioned for the announcer's role on radio's debuting *You Bet Your Life* in 1947. Fenneman was picked on the spot. Cited by a radio historian as the "eternal straight man," Fenneman became the "ideal foil" for emcee Groucho Marx. Another historiographer branded Fenneman "Groucho's good-natured whipping boy," certifying him "as mild-mannered as

Groucho was ill-mannered." In selecting Fenneman, Guedel affirmed: "Right away, I felt the contrast. George was the guy on the top of the wedding cake. They were the odd couple." Marx relentlessly bullied the soft-spoken announcer although Fenneman never took it personally. "At the beginning I was young and resilient, and I didn't have the good sense to know I was being insulted," the suave, debonair Fenneman acknowledged. "It was part of the character he was building for me that became wonderfully salable in years to come. I'd have to be a clod to badmouth the man who made it possible."

In a 1987 interview Fenneman granted: "I pinched myself regularly to make sure that a kid who planned to be a schoolteacher could find himself on the same stage with one of the master wits of all time." In addition, the reruns of the NBC-TV version (1950–1961) of *You Bet Your Life* that Marx and Guedel shamelessly peddled after the show left the air brought the famed announcer a tidy $100,000 in residuals for doing *nothing*—seven times what he earned while he was working! He also hosted a trio of short run video series: *Anybody Can Play* (1958, ABC); *Your Surprise Package* (1961–1962, CBS); and *Your Funny, Funny Films* (1963, ABC).

Fenneman pursued a career in movies, too, mostly with bit parts or as a narrator. Between 1951 and 1971 he was featured in nine motion pictures, among them: *Ocean's Eleven* (1960); *How to Succeed in Business Without Really Trying* (1967); and *Once You Kiss a Stranger* (1969). Eight years following Fenneman's death, *The Naked Monster* was released with Fenneman narrating (2005).

FERGUSON, FRANKLYN. b. Aug. 10, 1902, Texas; d. Sept. 1969, Tampa, Fla. *Announcer.* **Series:** *Big City Serenade* (1952); *The Breakfast Club* (1948–1951); *Faultless Starch Time* (1948–1953); *The Hoosier Commentator*; *Jack Armstrong, the All-American Boy* (1945); *The Tom Mix Ralston Straight Shooters* (ca. late 1940s, early 1950s); *The Quiz Kids* (1948–1951).

Franklyn Ferguson got into radio in 1933 in his native Texas as program director for the Southwest Broadcasting System. Two years hence he became chief announcer at a Grand Rapids, Mich., station. Still in radio, he moved to Detroit and then to Chicago. He eventually turned to acting when television came along, playing Gus Broeberg in *My Friend Flicka* on CBS (1956–1957) and NBC (1957–1958). Ferguson was Judge Gurney in the NBC western *Temple Houston* (1963–1964). He also appeared as Eli Carson in primetime's *Peyton Place* (1964–1969, ABC) and on the daytime reprise *Return to Peyton Place* (1972–1974, NBC).

FIDLER, JAMES M. b. Aug. 24, 1900, St. Louis, Mo.; d. Aug. 9, 1988, Westlake, Calif. *Commentator.* **Series:** *Hollywood on the Air* (screen gossip reporter–film reviewer, 1933–1934); *Jimmy Fidler*, aka *Jimmy Fidler in Hollywood*, aka *Your Hollywood Reporter* (screen gossip reporter–film reviewer, 1933–1934, 1935–1940, 1941, 1942–1950, 1951, syndicated into the 1970s); *Musical Romance* (screen gossip reporter–film reviewer, 1934). **Aphorism:** *Good night to you—and I do mean you!*

Jimmy Fidler (who in the 1930s autographed publicity photos as "Jimmie" but applied "Jimmy" in later years, and whose surname is incorrectly spelled "Fiddler" by a few historians) arrived in Hollywood purportedly with intents of becoming an icon of the silver screen. Drifting into journalism following the First World War, in 1920 he edited *The Hollywood News*. Multiple sources affirm he also acted in a handful of silent films under the pseudonym James Marion but, alas, informed cinematic chroniclers unequivocally state that—to date—no such credits can be substantiated.

He performed a couple of cameos in 1938, in *Garden of the Moon* and *Personality Parade*, and appeared in and was the subject of 1947's *Screen Snapshots No. 5*. That's all. Eventually realizing he wasn't destined for idol worship in celluloid, Fidler discovered different methods of connecting with an industry he adored. He signed on as Sid Grauman's publicity manager and established his own hype mill as a press agent for the studios and stars. Yet his enterprise was one of the casualties of the collapsing stock market in 1929 and he turned elsewhere for sustenance.

Fidler decided to write about the burgeoning film trade in fanzines and newspapers next. In doing so, he capitalized on the juicy tidbits in people's lives by ferreting out little details they would just as soon not see reported. He worked tenaciously and the results built him a reputation. Ultimately, he devised a syndicated newspaper column which—at its peak in 1950—ran in 360 journals nationwide. His developing talent allowed him to habitually contribute Hollywood gossip to Fox Movietone newsreels screened in theaters before the regular motion picture features.

The newly acquired notoriety led him to a continuing radio gig in 1933 on *Hollywood on the Air*, where he divulged inside information about the business and its heretofore respectable celebrities. He was breaking new ground and he would persevere on the air for at least four decades (historiographer Roger C. Paulson claims Fidler persisted to 1983; if so, he was an ethereal fixture for five decades). Nevertheless, radio gave him name recognition with millions of Americans; at his peak, he was heard by at least 20 million listeners via 500 radio stations, and some estimates indicate he had 40 million in his audience.

The reputation he created was, nevertheless, dubious. "He was hated by those he wrote about," said Paulson. "Fidler had a lot of the bitchy Rona Barett in him," Gerald Nachman contended, and possessed "an opinionated mouth." Frank Bresee pontificated: "Unlike Hedda Hopper and Louella Parsons, who treated Hollywood and the stars with respect, Hollywood columnist Jimmy Fidler was considered radio's most threatening menace to movies and movie people. He called bad movies 'stinkers' and had a rating system never before equaled: four bells for a top film, one bell for a stinker! He read open letters to the stars from his 'little black book'; condemned them for their 'bad' deeds." John Dunning saw him as "one of the nation's most controversial figures" and—while maintaining that Fidler worked in the shadows of Hopper and Parsons—insisted "he was more feared by some studios and stars than either." (His 1945 Hooperating of 13.4 was double that of Hopper.) Fidler's blunt, caustic assessments, offering amusing invective to listeners, simply did not set well with the studios. He was literally banned from the backlots, screenings and soundstages. He was also frequently on outs with the luminaries of the silver screen who were infuriated by his disclosures about the intimate details of their personal lives. None of it had an intimidating effect on him; instead, he redoubled his efforts to gather still more choice morsels.

Fidler relied on a divergent corps of industry insiders and observers to feed him material, a pattern copied from his radio-columnist hero, Walter Winchell. He adopted the newsman's ethereal style, too, dispatching as many as 3,000 words in a quarter-of-an-hour in rapid-fire, staccato fashion. Author Gerald Nachman referred to him as "the brash, Winchellesque Jimmy Fidler" and it would have been difficult to miss the similarity as the West Coast tattletale mimicked the master's "scoop-crazed mentality."

With an annual income topping $250,000, Fidler attracted some of the most respected names in the business as announcers. He was introduced by Gary Breckner, Ken Carpenter, Hal Gibney, Ken Niles, Bob Sherwood, Maurie Webster and Don Wilson. Signing off his shows, his farewell sounded like a threat: *Good night to you—and I do mean* you! "He was imbued with a moral fervor against divorce and similar shady doings among the movie crowd," wrote Nachman. Radio critic John Crosby compared him to a small-town blue-nosed biddy, clucking over failed marriages and inebriated spouses.

Fidler turned up in 1952 with Hollywood gossip news for viewers of CBS-TV's *Morning News*. He subsequently hosted NBC-TV's primetime anthology series *Hollywood Opening Night* (1952–1953) featuring many of the people he had long talked about on the air and in his columns—John Hodiak, Dorothy Lamour, David Niven, Gloria Swanson, Franchot Tone and multitudes of others. The show held the distinction as the first live dramatic production to originate from the West Coast, at NBC's just completed Burbank studios. Fidler began each program in a "theater" lobby and invited the TV audience to join him within to witness half-hour plays. It was reminiscent of a radio theme from decades earlier when Mr. First Nighter invited patrons inside "the little theater off Times Square." Jimmy Fidler had—in possibly some faint sense—finally become the thespian that had eluded him three decades earlier.

FITZGERALD, ED. b. 1898, Troy, N.Y.; d.

March 22, 1982, New York, N.Y. *Commentator.* **Series:** *The Fitzgeralds* (co-host, 1945–1947).

In 1940 Ed and Pegeen Fitzgerald instated a format in New York radio that was to pervade the national airwaves and prosper well beyond the confines of Manhattan. Indeed, it would become a certifiable minor breed among aural aircasts. *Breakfast with the Fitzgeralds*, reduced to *The Fitzgeralds* in a short while, was the first breakfast hour gabfest featuring a conjugal couple as hosts in the nation's largest city. In its original expression it began on WOR and persisted there for five years to 1945. At that juncture the principals went over to challenger station WJZ, flagship outlet of the newly commencing ABC chain (which had been NBC's Blue network until 1943). For a couple of years Ed and Pegeen's early morning chatter was beamed nationally, although it never developed a huge fan base beyond its original geographic territory. After the ABC deal folded, in 1948 the duo returned to WOR where they lasted until Ed's death in 1982. Thereafter Pegeen revisited the ether as a solo act for a few more years.

Like some of the other binary breakfast blabbers, *The Fitzgeralds* was expanded from a weekday 40-minute bacon-and-eggs timeslot, eventually invading the steak-and-potatoes hour (*Dinner with the Fitzgeralds*) three nights weekly. It also offered a 30-minute Sunday morning performance. Some other couples doing similar features transferred to afternoon or evening spots, too, vacating their premiering morning trysts altogether. The point worth noting, however, is that *the form*—and not always the time period established by the pioneering Fitzgeralds—caught on elsewhere. For a while in the 1940s and 1950s, the blueprint flourished in Gotham and in lesser-sized metropolitan radio markets across the country. At one point it was said to have 78 imitators, although a critic observed that at its worst the model "degenerated into little more than a saccharin parade of commercials without much information or entertainment provided for listeners."

A handful of New York stations beamed a plethora of competitive husband-and-wife early morning talk show brigades to the far reaches of the upper Eastern seaboard. One couple became a thorn in the sides of *The Fitzgeralds*, both locally and beyond. Ed and Pegeen conducted a particularly intense, ongoing feud with Dorothy Kilgallen and Richard Kollmar of WOR's *Breakfast with Dorothy and Dick* (1945–1963). They probably got as much as they gave in return. "Neither liked the others' shows, and sniping was frequent from both sides," cautioned a pundit. "Kilgallen considered the Fitzgeralds vulgar and coarse; the Fitzgeralds called Dorothy and Dick upper-crust dilettantes."

In addition to the Kollmars, another well-recognized New York couple, newlyweds Tex McCrary and Jinx Falkenburg, added coffee pot chatter to the airwaves between 1946 and 1959 over WEAF (renamed WNBC and WRCA later) as *Tex and Jinx*. To their credit, however, they attempted to remain above the fray that was carried out between Ed, Pegeen, Dorothy and Dick; the McCrarys preferred to devote their time to noble ideas, guests and features. There were other wedded couples that came along to institute their own variations of table talk shows, too, although none became as prominent in the venue as the aforementioned. Among them were WMCA's Andre Baruch and wife Bea Wain and WABC's/WCBS's Peter Lind Hayes and spouse Mary Healy.

Fitzgerald, who could be acerbic-tongued, not only lashed out at his broadcast rivals but frequently at his own wife, putting her down on the air. With the exception of the commercials, their show was totally spontaneous. He exploded before listeners when she confessed that she had checked his pockets and snitched a dollar without his knowledge. "Fitzgerald was probably the most unpredictable of all the morning husbands," wrote a historian. Sometimes their live disagreements were quite animated. On the other hand, "Much of the time they were suspiciously lovey-dovey." Their show originated at their East 36th Street apartment.

Before getting into radio, Fitzgerald was a West Coast newspaperman working for dailies in Seattle, Los Angeles and San Francisco. Three years after wedding Margaret Worrall, Fitzgerald joined KFRC Radio. From 1933 to 1936 he adjusted to the microphone as emcee of *Feminine Fancies*. When WOR hired him around 1936, Fitzgerald introduced a literary feature there, *Book Talk*,

Back Talk and Small Talk. He also conducted an all-night show, *Almanac de Gotham*. Meanwhile, after applying an Irish derivative of her name, by 1939 his spouse joined him as a WOR broadcast personality with *Pegeen Prefers*. The two worked together while reporting from the 1939 New York World's Fair. Within a few months, the inspiration of the husband-wife breakfast feature emerged.

FITZGERALD, MARGARET WORRALL (PEGEEN). b. Nov. 24, 1904, Norcatur, Kan.; d. Jan. 30, 1989, New York, N.Y. *Commentator*. **Series:** *The Fitzgeralds* (co-host, 1945–1947).

A couple of years after her husband, Ed Fitzgerald, passed in early 1982 and their long-running aural series left the ether—by then aired in late evening hours—Pegeen Fitzgerald, in her mid seventies, returned to the WOR microphone as a solo act. She persisted there and later at WNYC between 1984 and April 1988. In 1940 the Fitzgeralds inaugurated an innovative design in local New York radio in which husbands and wives chatted around the breakfast table weekday mornings, sometimes introducing guests and presenting special features. Several major New York outlets adopted the premise, offering their own couple teams. *The Fitzgeralds* was also carried briefly on a nationwide hookup.

Pegeen and Ed Fitzgerald were wed in San Francisco in June 1930. At the time he was a theatrical press agent while she was an advertising copywriter and fashion emporium coordinator. He got into radio with KFRC in 1933 and three years hence they were in New York, where he went on the air for WOR. Pegeen soon joined him with her own radio feature, *Pegeen Prefers*, and in 1939 handled some WOR assignments during the World's Fair. She is credited with developing the concept of the breakfast table banter that established a new, albeit sparsely populated, breed of radio performers.

FITZMAURICE, MICHAEL T. b. April 28, 1908, Chicago, Ill.; d. Aug. 31, 1967, New York, N.Y. *Actor, Announcer, Emcee*. **Series:** *The Abe Burrows Show* (1947–1948); *The Adventures of Sherlock Holmes* (local announcer, 1947–1948); *The Adventures of Superman* (actor, 1950–1951); *Adventures of the Red Feather Man* (actor, 1946); *American Cancer Society* (1950); *Brenda Curtis* (actor, ca. 1939–ca. 1940); *California Melodies* (mid 1930s); *CBS is There* (actor, 1947, 1948); *Crisis in War Town* (actor, 1949); *Five Minute Mysteries* (actor, ca. 1945–ca. 1948); *The Heart of America* (1959); *Her Honor, Nancy James* (actor, ca. 1938–ca. 1939); *Highway Patrol* (actor, 1943); *Joyce Jordan, M.D.* (actor, ca. 1940s, 1950s); *The Land of the Lost* (1943–1946, 1947–1948); *Lora Lawton* (actor, 1940s); *Lux Radio Theater* (actor, 1936–1938); *Murder at Midnight* (actor, 1946); *Myrt and Marge* (actor, ca. 1930s–ca. 1942); *Nick Carter, Master Detective* (1943–?; actor, 1948); *The 1957 March of Dimes Galaxy of Stars* (1957); *Pepper Young's Family* (actor, ca. 1930s–1950s); *Quiet Please* (actor, 1948); *Quiz of Two Cities* (master of ceremonies, 1944–1947); *The Right to Happiness* (1940s, ca. early 1950s); *Rosemary* (actor, ca. mid 1940s–mid 1950s); *The Sparrow and the Hawk* (actor, 1945–1946); *Stella Dallas* (actor, ca. 1950s); *Studio One* (actor, 1948); *Suspense* (actor, 1942); *Tales of Fatima* (1949); *This is Our Enemy* (actor, 1942–1943); *This Life is Mine* (actor, 1943–1945); *Voice of the Army* (actor, 1946); *War Town* (actor, 1945); *When a Girl Marries* (ca. 1939–early 1940s); *Words at War* (actor, 1944).

After graduating from the University of Dublin, by the mid 1920s Michael Fitzmaurice was reporting for *The Los Angeles Times*. He followed print journalism as an electronic newsman at Hollywood's KNX Radio (1931–1938). Meanwhile, Fitzmaurice also appeared in a half-dozen B-movie productions: *The Plough and the Stars* and *The House of a Thousand Candles* (released in 1936); *A Girl with Ideas*, *Reported Missing* and *Night Key* (all in 1937); and *Fourteen Hours* (1951).

He left the West Coast in the late 1930s. Moving to New York, he won legions of announcing and acting slots on major national radio series. At the same time Fitzmaurice played in Broadway productions of *The Chocolate Soldier* and *The Merry Widow*. From 1950 to 1967 he was the voice of MGM *News of the Day* and for three years (1964–1967) he provided voiceovers on commercials destined for many radio and television stations. He was in demand for numerous radio spots sponsored by charitable causes like the American Cancer Society, Community Chest and

March of Dimes and for government-backed agencies, especially during the war years. Some of those programs were produced as syndicated series for local consumption. In later years Fitzmaurice was also linked with Charles Kebbe in coaching professional TV acting hopefuls.

FLEETWOOD, HARRY. b. ca. 1917, New Jersey; d. Jan. 18, New York, N.Y. *Announcer, Disc Jockey.* **Series:** *Music through the Night* (disc jockey, 1953–?).

Harry Fleetwood majored in education in his undergraduate days at Temple University before he earned a master's degree in romance languages from the University of Pennsylvania. He served with the U.S. Army in Europe during the Second World War, and stayed behind in France when it was over, enrolling at the Sorbonne in Paris. After returning to America, Fleetwood got into radio, announcing for stations in Philadelphia and Camden, Pa. In addition, he conducted interview features and read poetry over the air.

The zenith of his career occurred between 1953 and 1975, when he was selected over 1,500 applicants to host *Music through the Night*, a five-and-a-half-hour classical music series starting at midnight weeknights on New York's NBC flagship station, WNBC. The program also premiered over the full NBC Radio network on Aug. 31, 1951, where it ran for multiple years. When WNBC no longer had a spot for Fleetwood's brand of music, nearby competitor WNCN snapped it up and he persisted with the overnight format until the late 1980s. A local observer maintained that over a durable broadcast career, Fleetwood was an identifiable "fixture" with still more Gotham outlets including WQXR and WBAI.

Almost until his death Fleetwood was a permanent fixture at the annual fall conventions in Newark of vintage radio collectors and enthusiasts, Friends of Old Time Radio. On occasions during those events, he participated on panel discussions focused on classical music on the ether.

FLEMING, EDWARD J. b. June 27, 1918, Baraboo, Wis. *Newscaster, Announcer.* **Series:** *Ed Fleming and the News* (early, late 1940s); *Front Page Farrell* (1950–1954); *Our Gal Sunday* (1941–1943, 1946–ca. 1956).

The Flemings, Ed and Jim, have provided old time radio historiographers with one of the great mysteries of unverified text until now: Was there only one or were there two people by that surname in broadcasting laboring in similar capacities for the same network, producers and sponsor simultaneously? The answer unequivocally is that there were *two* Flemings and (surprise!) they were related—siblings. Both ultimately went into television, also.

Ed Fleming, the younger, was greatly influenced by his older brother, he conceded in early 2006. In his freshman year at the University of Wisconsin, from which he graduated, he followed in his brother's footsteps by taking a job at Madison's WHA. After college, in 1941 he joined WCBS in New York, the network flagship station, as a newscaster. Almost immediately he was hired by series producer-packager Anne Hummert to announce one of her venerated daytime dramas, *Our Gal Sunday*. Ed Fleming's was the voice that allowed: *Once again, we present Our Gal Sunday, the story of an orphan girl named Sunday from the little mining town of Silver Creek, Colorado, who in young womanhood married England's richest, most handsome lord, Lord Henry Brinthrope. The story that asks the question: Can this girl from the little mining town in the West find happiness as the wife of a wealthy and titled Englishman?*

Fleming returned to the audio narrative following a three-year absence for military service (1943–1946) and added a second daytime serial, *Front Page Farrell*, at the same time. It was also produced by the Hummerts for the same sponsor, American Home Products (Anacin, Bi-So-Dol, Kolynos, Kriptin, et al.). Jim, meanwhile, had worked for the Hummerts and American Home Products on *Mr. Keen, Tracer of Lost Persons*, a mystery drama that Ed occasionally substituted for. Interspersed with these shows, both Ed and Jim were newscasting on the CBS chain, also.

As soon as he returned from the Air Force in 1946, Ed began receiving a myriad of assignments in television with WCBS-TV. While he purportedly was a newscaster there, by the early 1950s he left CBS for WPIX-TV in New York, where he not only delivered the news but handled some of its sportscasting, children's programming and "a little of everything else," he chuckled. A few years later, seeking a change in the direction his broadcasting pursuits were taking him, he casually mentioned his discontent to his Westport, Conn., neighbor, Douglas Edwards. The two men often commuted to their homes following their evening newscasts (Edwards was the anchor at CBS-TV). Edwards referred to an opportunity for a news anchor at the CBS television outlet in Los Angeles—KNXT at that time. Fleming applied, won an audition and spent six years there (1958–1964). He devoted the next three years to a similar capacity at San Francisco's KRON-TV. Subsequently, he left broadcasting altogether to become an investment broker, a career he pursued until he reached retirement.

FLEMING, JAMES F. b. April 23, 1915, Baraboo, Wis.; d. Aug. 10, 1996, Princeton, N.J. *Newscaster, Announcer, Producer.* **Series:** *CBS News* (correspondent, ca. 1938–1949); *Collector's Item* (actor, 1954); *Gold is Where You Find It* (quizmaster, 1941); *The Goldbergs* (1941–?); *John's Other Wife* (1940–1941); *The Light of the World* (ca. 1940–ca. 1943); *Monitor* (executive producer, 1955–ca. late 1950s); *Mr. Keen, Tracer of Lost Persons* (1940–1943); *Sunday/Friday with Dave Garroway* (1954); *Vic and Sade* (1940–?); *Voices and Events* (host, 1949–1950); *World News Today* (1943).

James Fleming attended the University of Wisconsin for two years and the University of Chicago for two years, receiving a bachelor's degree from the latter institution in 1938. At both schools he was active in radio, hired as a sportscaster at Madison's WIBA in 1937. He was also instrumental in directing his younger brother, Ed, into radio announcing and newscasting. After graduation, Jim Fleming worked for Chicago's WGN, where he introduced aircasts of the Chicago Symphony, and then covered news and special events for CBS in New York. Later, as a war correspondent for that chain, Fleming was stationed in Europe, the Middle East and Russia. When the war ended he took a post with the Marshall Plan as head honcho with its radio and film division.

Jim Fleming left CBS for NBC in 1949 and was the original newscaster of the latter's premiering *Today* show on TV in 1952, remaining in that capacity for 14 months. In 1956 he was hired as producer of the competition, *The Morning Show* on CBS-TV. The program lasted to 1957. After several months, in 1961 he was replaced as the host of CBS-TV's *Accent* documentary. Furthermore, he produced a myriad of specials and documentaries for television networks in the late 1950s and throughout the decade of the 1960s.

Perhaps his crowning achievement, indisputably, was to be picked by NBC president Pat Weaver as the inaugural executive producer of Weaver's ingenious 40-hour weekend radio service, *Monitor*. It began in June 1955. Fleming had the support of his superior in implementing an innovative programming design in broadcast entertainment and information. While he was there only a couple of years, he was literally on the cutting edge of fresh concepts that persisted in radio for two decades, far beyond the proverbial end of the medium's golden age.

FORBES, DONALD TELFER. b. June 9, 1912, Camrose, Alberta, Canada; d. Nov. 28, 1995, West Hollywood, Calif. *Newscaster, Announcer.* **Series:** *The Richfield Reporter* (newscaster, 1940–1941); *Ten-Two-Four Ranch* (1941–1945).

Don Forbes launched a radio career in 1930, migrating to Los Angeles and establishing himself in newscasting. Diversifying into film, he narrated an Oscar-winning documentary, *The Sea Around Us*, in 1952. Between 1940 and 1960 he also appeared in a dozen B-movies, almost always in uncredited roles, frequently as an announcer. Forbes' filmography includes: *The Man Who Wouldn't Talk* (1940); *Yesterday's Heroes* (1940); *Secret Agent of Japan* (1942); *A Guy, a Gal and a Pal* (1945); *In This Corner* (1948); *The Damned Don't Cry* (1950); and *The Left Hand of God* (1955). He was an occasional television actor, turning up in episodes of *The Millionaire* (1955) and *Lost in Space* (1965) and a single installment of *MacGyver* (1989). In the early 1960s Forbes joined Bowles Advertising and produced a handful of popular TV series—*The Andy Griffith Show*; *Cheyenne*; *The Dick Van Dyke Show*; and *Perry Mason*.

FORMAN, BILL. *Announcer, Actor, Producer.* **Series:** *Father Knows Best* (ca. late 1940s–early 1950s); *The Fitch Bandwagon*

(1946–1948); *Frontier Town* (1952–1953); *The Hermit's Cave* (producer, 1940–1944); *Kay Kyser's Kollege of Musical Knowledge* (1940s); *The Phil Harris and Alice Faye Show* (1948–1954); *The Rexall Summer Show* (1948); *Richard Diamond, Private Detective* (ca. early 1950s); *The Tony Martin Show* (ca. 1947–ca. 1948); *The Whistler* (narrator-actor, 1942–1955); *The Zane Grey Show* (1947–1948).

Bill Forman produced *The Hermit's Cave* over KMPC, Los Angeles, in syndication from 1940 to 1944, which proved a veritable training ground for budding actors. Forman was billed on *Kay Kyser's Kollege of Musical Knowledge* as "Dean Forman—39 throats behind a single collar button." When in November 1951 Forman was revealed by name to the audience as playing *The Whistler* for nearly a decade, a pundit scribbled: "His was the perfect voice for a murder show that contained little on-mike violence. What there was was 'velvet violence,' murder by implication." Forman also provided the voice for the unseen character on a syndicated televersion of *The Whistler* in 1954.

FORSTER, ROGER (born Roger Von Roth). b. June 12, 1915, New York, N.Y.; d. Nov. 15, 2003, Charlotte, N.C. *Announcer.* **Series:** *The CBS Radio Workshop* (1956); *The Couple Next Door* (1957–1958); *Gangbusters* (co-announcer, 1949–1950); *The Guiding Light* (1950s); *Linda's First Love* (1940s); *Mark Sabre* (1951–1954); *Mystery Theater* (1952); *Philip Morris Night with Horace Heidt*, aka *Youth Opportunity Program* (1948); *Twenty-First Precinct* (ca. 1955–ca. 1956).

Roger Forster was one of a trio of announcers of the enduring CBS-TV run of the popular panel show *To Tell the Truth*, seen in network daytime and primetime incarnations from 1956 to 1968. He was with the nighttime version in 1960 only, however.

FOSS, JOSEPH. b. April 17, 1915, Sioux Falls, S.D.; d. Jan. 1, 2003. *Sportscaster, Announcer.* **Series:** *Just Entertainment* (1956).

Joe Foss spent his broadcast career largely as a sportscaster. He was a regular on *Tops in Sports*, a syndicated recruiting series produced by the U.S. Air Force.

FOSTER, CEDRIC W. b. Aug. 31, 1900, Hartford, Conn.; d. March 6, 1975, Denver, Colo. *Commentator, Newscaster.* **Series:** *Cedric Foster News and Commentary* (newscaster-commentator, 1940–1967); *Mutual News* (newscaster, 1940–1967).

Cedric Foster attended Dartmouth College for a year, quitting to discover America on a journey across it. He came home and joined *The Hartford Times*, reporting on the police beat and then becoming financial editor. He was hired to manage local radio station WTHT in 1935. There he learned the news announcing trade. Foster developed a weeknight commentary on international affairs. By the end of the decade it was being aired on the region's Yankee network. Meanwhile, he went on MBS on Jan. 6, 1940, and soon landed a weekday matinee quarter-hour timeslot. During the early days of his national web experience, Foster was also heard locally in Boston over WAAB (1941) and WNAC (1945). He made 50 transatlantic crossings, mostly during the Second World War, including a trio of global excursions and yet another to the Philippines. His eyewitness accounts helped Americans develop a feel for what was happening far from their borders.

While Foster maintained one of the most enduring commentaries on the national ether—extending for more than a quarter-of-a-century without interruption—he could never be considered a major player among audio news analysts. (Irving Fang gave him but a 16-word single-sentence mention in his volume of biographies of radio commentators, for instance.) Foster was heard almost altogether in a nondescript early afternoon time zone (and claimed to be the first matinee commentator heard coast-to-coast) rather than in primetime; as a consequence, his name didn't resonate as a household word like those of some colleagues (in the tradition of Morgan Beatty, H.V. Kaltenborn, Edward R. Murrow, Lowell Thomas, Robert Trout, Walter Winchell and a few more). That in no way diminishes a credible job performance he turned in but is an explanation of why his moniker is not well remembered today.

After his weekday commentary was history in 1967, Foster retired from MBS. Still seeking a new challenge, he left New York to relocate in Denver, Colo., becoming an air personality on KFML, KTLN and KVOD. He affiliated with the Intermountain Radio Network, too, which beamed his features throughout the region. At last, in 1970 he quit broadcasting altogether and went into public relations.

FOY, FRED. b. March 27, 1921, Detroit, Mich. *Announcer.* **Series:** *The Challenge of the Yukon,* aka *Sergeant Preston of the Yukon* (1954–1955); *The Green Hornet* (1952); *The Lone Ranger* (1948–1954 and syndicated repeats 1954–1956); *Theater Five* (1964–1965). **Aphorism:** *Return with us now to those thrilling days of yesteryear!*

Fred Foy launched a radio career in 1940 over Detroit's WMBC. In 1942 he shifted to the legendary WXYZ in Motown. He was assigned to the Special Services Unit of Armed Forces Radio during World War II and, based in Cairo, he worked with Jack Benny, Nelson Eddy and some other major headliner entertainers. After his return to WXYZ, Foy hosted the DJ series *Sunrise Serenade* in 1947. He made his most indelible impression on listeners, nevertheless, as the stentorian-voiced narrator of *The Lone Ranger* beginning in 1948 (*Return with us now to those thrilling days of yesteryear ...*) and several other dramas that originated at WXYZ that were broadcast nationally. He carried the role of interlocutor for *The Lone Ranger* to ABC-TV from 1949 to 1957.

Foy capped his network career in 1969 by introducing the ABC-TV game show *The Generation Gap* and—between 1969 and 1972—*The Dick Cavett Show,* too, a late night entry on the same web. Furthermore, he narrated dozens of documentaries and has been a commercial spokesman for scores of national advertisers. After 24 years he retired from ABC in 1985. Foy penned the book *From XYZ to ABC,* released the CD *Meanwhile, Back at the Ranch* and—in 2000—was inducted into the Radio Hall of Fame. Five years later he continued to make regular appearances at vintage radio conventions held annually across the nation. On some of those occasions he was asked to introduce some dramatic re-creations of the shows that initially made him famous.

FRANK, CARL. b. Feb. 27, 1909, Weehawkin, N.J.; d. Sept. 23, 1972, St. John, U.S. Virgin Islands. *Actor, Announcer.* **Series:** *Aunt Jenny's Real Life Stories* (actor, late 1930s, 1940s); *Betty and Bob* (actor, ca. late 1930s, 1940); *Buck Rogers in the 25th Century* (actor, ca. 1939–1940); *By Kathleen Norris* (actor, 1939–1941); *The Campbell Playhouse* (actor, 1938–1940); *Columbia Presents Corwin* (actor, 1944); *The Columbia Workshop* (actor, ca. late 1930s, 1940s); *The Court of Missing Heirs* (actor, 1937–1938, 1939–1942, ca. 1946, ca. 1947); *Gangbusters* (actor, ca. late 1930s, 1940s); *The Goodwill Hour* (cast, ca. late 1930s, early 1940s); *Her Honor, Nancy James* (actor, 1938–1939); *Hobby Lobby* (cast, late 1930s, 1940s); *The March of Time* (ca. 1930s, 1940s); *Mercury Theater* (actor, late 1930s); *Murder at Midnight* (actor, 1946–1947); *The Royal Gelatin Hour,* aka *The Rudy Vallee Show* (actor, 1937–ca. 1939); *The Shadow* (actor, late 1930s, 1940s); *This is Your FBI* (1945–1946); *Vox Pop; What's My Name?* (co-host, 1948, 1949); *Whispering Streets* (actor, ca. 1952–ca. 1960); *Young Doctor Malone* (actor, early 1940s); *Your Family and Mine* (actor, 1938–1940).

Between 1949 and 1957 Carl Frank portrayed Uncle Gunnar Gunnerson in the popular CBS-TV live drama *Mama.* He also debuted in 1959 as the original Bill Marceau, chief of police in Monticello, on CBS-TV's daytime serial *The Edge of Night.* But he was quickly replaced by a possibly more memorable ex-radio thespian, Mandel Kramer, for a distinguished 20-year run. Frank performed in *Naked City, Studio One* and other live television dramas, too. He was in the cast of one of radio's most celebrated hours, *The War of the Worlds* production on *Mercury Theater* on Oct. 30, 1938.

In between radio and television commitments, Frank appeared on Broadway in *Paths of Glory; Boy Meets Girl; A Sound of Hunting;* and *The Shrike.* He turned up on the silver screen as the district attorney in *Lady from Shanghai* (1948). A graduate of the American Academy of Dramatic Arts where he was later on the faculty, Frank broadcast from overseas during World War II for the Office of War Information. He appeared in Army and Navy training films, too. In 1961 Frank moved from New York to the Virgin Islands where he organized Holiday Homes, a real estate insurance concern.

FRASER, JOHN GORDON (JACK). b. Feb. 4, 1908, Lawrence, Mass.; d. Jan. 1, 2000, Winter Park, Fla. *Newscaster, Announcer,*

Producer. **Series:** *John Gordon Fraser and the News* (newscaster, 1944–1945, 1947–1948); *Monitor* (producer, editor, writer, 1955–1974); *Your Gospel Singer* (1946).

When he entered the University of Maine and later Brown University, John Gordon (Jack) Fraser had nothing specific in mind except acquiring a liberal arts education. As he liked English and music, he majored in both. In time he became the director, pianist and tenor soloist of a varsity quartet. Solo and quartet concerts led him to some appearances on a local Providence, R.I., radio station. A direct consequence was that Fraser was offered a permanent job at the station in 1930. He accepted. Subsequently, he joined the announcing staff of New York's WMCA, then left it to become a freelance announcer for a year and ultimately signed with New York's WOR. In March 1936 Fraser joined NBC in New York and announced and eventually won his own newscasting and music shows. Additionally, he covered sports for the network.

In between network engagements, during the 1940s Fraser also delivered the news to listeners of New York's WJZ, his third major station connection in Gotham. He was given the distinction of announcing a historic demonstration of television during the 1939 World's Fair in New York featuring President Franklin D. Roosevelt. Fraser covered World War II for the NBC Blue network. He was instrumental in helping launch NBC's innovative weekend radio service *Monitor* in 1955 and persisted with the show for 19 years. He moved to Florida in 1974 and from 1978 to 1990 was employed by the Rollins College radio station.

FRAZER, JOHN. b. March 15, 1915, Los Angeles, Calif.; d. May 11, 1945, Pacific Ocean. *Announcer.* **Series:** *The Bob Hope Show* (ca. late 1930s, early 1940s); *Brenthouse* (1939–1940); *Candid Woman* (1938–1939); *The Chase & Sanborn Hour* (1930s, early 1940s); *The Circle* (1939); *Do You Want to Be an Actor?* (1937–1938); *The Fitch Bandwagon* (1938–ca. 1944); *Interesting Neighbors* (1938–1939); *Life Can Be Beautiful* (ca. 1938–ca. 1941); *Noah Webster Says* (1942–ca. 1943); *Personal Column of the Air* (1937); *The Raleigh and Kool Program*, aka *Tommy Dorsey's Orchestra* (ca. 1937–1940); *The Signal Carnival* (1939–1941).

In mid 1937, while enrolled in law school near his home, John Frazer accepted an announcing position with Hollywood's KEHE. He was so enamored with its possibilities that he decided to abandon his intentions of a legal career and remain with radio. As the mid 1940s approached, he was stationed as a lieutenant with the U.S. Navy in the Pacific theater near the end of the Second World War. At age 30 he was killed in action, leaving behind a wife and infant daughter and cutting short a promising future in broadcasting.

FREDERICK, PAULINE. b. Feb. 13, 1908, Gallitzin, Pa.; d. May 9, 1990, Lake Forest, Ill. *Newscaster, Commentator.* **Series:** *At the U.N.* (news analyst, 1954–1955); *Biography in Sound* (hostess, 1955); *Meet the Press* (interviewee, 1956, 1961, 1967); *Pauline Frederick and the News*, aka *News of Tomorrow* (newscaster, 1946–1975, sometimes under network identifications); *Second Sunday* (correspondent, 1968).

In their early documentaries of vintage radio, Frank Buxton and Bill Owen identified Pauline Frederick as "one of the few successful female commentators." Only two more were named (Lisa Sergio, Dorothy Thompson). Luther F. Sies opined: "From radio's earliest days there was an anti-female bias that made it difficult for them to work as announcers, newscasters or commentators. Fredericks [*sic*] found it necessary to lower the pitch of her voice in order to broadcast." NBC News producer Beryl Pfizer exclaimed, "She was the first full-fledged woman correspondent and opened doors for women's acceptance in television and radio journalism."

During her high school days Frederick was a society reporter for multiple journals in the environs of Harrisburg, Pa. Her intent was to become an attorney, as she later enrolled at American University in Washington, D.C. Ultimately, nonetheless, she settled on journalism as a better method of applying her undergraduate and master's degrees. She began by contributing unsolicited articles to *The Washington Star* and the North American Newspaper Alliance and became a correspondent for *U.S. News and World Report*. This led to a part time job copywriting for ABC Radio correspondent H.R. Baukhage, who cautioned her to "stay away from radio—it doesn't like women." That may have been all the impetus that a determined Frederick required.

She had six years of Washington print journalism in her background and reported on World War II from 19 nations as a part timer for ABC when the network hired her in September 1946 as a full time news correspondent. She was soon airing six morning radio shows and three telecasts weekly. After gaining a barrage of lighter tasks, she was dispatched to a gathering of foreign ministers. "It was the best thing that ever happened to her," penned one wag. Frederick began taking on more assignments and was soon sent to cover the United Nations—for 28 years!—the first seven while at ABC and the rest at NBC. She later admitted: "Since I was a little kid, I was always interested in international relations, and I chose the United Nations because this was the center of international activity. This seemed to be the one place toward which I gravitated all the time." In 1975 she departed network TV, capping off a venerable career with National Public Radio as a news analyst. She had married Charles Robbins, managing editor of *The Wall Street Journal*, in 1969.

In 1949 the newswoman presided over *Pauline Frederick's Guestbook*, a weekly quarter-hour primetime interview series on ABC-TV. She was subsequently one of four anchors of that chain's *All Star News* in 1952–1953 that proffered 4.5 hours of national reportage spread over Sunday, Monday, Wednesday, Thursday and Friday nights. In late 1958 she appeared with 12 men of notable news stature (David Brinkley, Cecil Brown, Welles Hangen, Joseph C. Harsch, Herb Kaplow, Irving R. Levine, Robert McCormick, Frank McGee, Edwin Newman, John Rich, Ray Scherer, Charles Van Doren) on an hour-long NBC-TV special, *Kaleidoscope*, predicting world events in 1959. That exposure signified just how far the feminine journalist had come, as she crashed through any perceived glass ceilings that might have forbidden her hobnobbing with the boys. Similar opportunities abounded, highlighting her increased status.

In 1954 Frederick became the first of her gender to win a George Foster Peabody Award for distinguished reporting. She was the first woman, in 1976, to moderate a presidential debate. Four years later she received the Paul White Radio-TV News Directors Association Award. Furthermore, she was the first feminine president of the U.N. Correspondents Association, among numerous analogous honors she won. She served on the boards of American University and Save the Children Foundation, was named to several halls of fame and was awarded 23 collegiate honorary degrees. Frederick authored *Ten First Ladies of the World* (Meredith, 1968).

FREDERICKS, DIRK. b. July 13, 1919, Brooklyn, N.Y.; d. Dec. 31, 1976. *Emcee, Announcer*. **Series:** *Music Tent* (host, 1955).

Dirk Fredericks was employed by ABC from 1950 until his death in 1976. One of his early assignments was as one of four roving announcers (the others, George Ansbro, Art Fleming and Ed Michael) on ABC-TV's version of the radio quiz show *Dr. I.Q.* (1953–1954, 1958–1959). The quartet of interlocutors navigated the studio audience seeking contestants who could deliver answers to questions proffered by an emcee; the announcers doled out silver dollars in exchange for correct responses.

FREDERICKS, DON. *Announcer, Producer*. **Series:** *Gentleman Adventurer*, aka *Special Agent* (1948); *Married for Life* (1946–1947); *This is Jazz*, aka *For Your Approval* (producer-announcer, 1947); *The Vic Damone Show* (1947).

FREEMAN, FLORENCE. b. July 29, 1911, New York, N.Y.; d. April 25, 2000, Illinois. *Actress, Newscaster*. **Series:** *Abie's Irish Rose* (actress, 1942–1944); *Alias Jimmy Valentine* (actress, 1938–1939); *Aunt Jenny's Real Life Stories* (actress, ca. 1937–ca. 1955, ca. 1956); *Dot and Will* (actress, 1935–1937); *Jane Arden* (actress, 1938–1939); *John's Other Wife* (actress, 1936–1942); *Madame Sylvia of Hollywood* (actress, 1933–1935); *Mr. Keen, Tracer of Lost Persons* (actress, 1947–1948, 1951–1953, 1955); *The Open Door* (actress, 1943–1944); *The Paul Whiteman Show* (actress, 1930s); *Pepper Young's Family* (actress, ca. 1930s–ca. 1950s); *Show Boat* (actress, ca. 1933–ca. 1937); *Valiant Lady* (actress, 1951–1952); *Wendy Warren and the News* (actress-newscaster, 1947–1958); *Young Widder Brown* (actress, 1938–1954).

A soap opera queen who played an imaginary journalist, for 11 years Florence Freeman delivered "news reports from the women's world" every weekday in the hybrid newscast-serial *Wendy Warren and the News.* Her bulletins directly followed respected CBS newsman Douglas Edwards, who dispatched headlines in a three-minute news bulletin board. For an additional 60 seconds Freeman (as Warren) offered current events items of selective interest to milady before the feature's initial commercial for Maxwell House coffee. Following that interlude, Wendy went on with her life in the make-believe storyline in which she was not only an electronic journalist but a reporter for the mythical *Manhattan Gazette* also. It was a unique insertion in the schedule and there was nothing like it elsewhere. Millions of men tuned in to hear the news reports; some stayed with the dramatic intrigue that followed, its narrative proffering an underlying theme about subversives from overseas undermining the U.S. federal government. If it was aired today, it could be considered an intrusion by international terrorists but indeed, it was six decades ago.

Freeman earned a bachelor's degree at Wells College of the State University of New York and a master's degree at Columbia University. She taught high school English for a couple of years before entering radio at New York's WMCA in 1933. For $50 weekly she was on call for performances every day but thought she was "very fortunate" in the depths of the Depression to have work when so many didn't. The wife of a Jewish rabbi serving a Jersey City, N.J., temple, she devoted many hours to temple concerns and charity endeavors. For several years she relinquished some lucrative evening broadcasts to be at home with her family. Every weekday for many years she was the heroine of not one but two durable washboard weepers, *Warren* and the domestic saga *Young Widder Brown* (as tearoom proprietor Ellen Brown of fictional Simpsonville). She was also the feminine lead of a couple of other drainboard dramas, *Dot and Will* and *Valiant Lady.*

In the years she appeared as Wendy and Ellen, Freeman's schedule called for her to leave home at about 9:30 A.M. each day, traveling by commuter train. That put her at the CBS studios in time for *Warren* rehearsals, which started at 10:30. After this broadcast ended at 12:15 P.M., unless she had luncheon appointments with writers, directors or publicity agents, her time was her own for leisurely dining and shopping. At 3:45 P.M. she reported to NBC for rehearsals for *Brown,* which went on the air at 4:45 during most of its run. It moved to 4:30 in 1951.

FUNT, ALLEN. b. Sept. 16, 1914, Brooklyn, N.Y.; d. Sept. 5, 1999, Monterey, Calif. *Emcee, Writer.* **Series:** *Candid Microphone* (master of ceremonies, 1947–1948, 1950). **Aphorism:** *Remember ... sometime ... somewhere ... when you least expect it ... someone will step up to you and say ... 'Smile, you're on Candid Camera'!*

Allen Funt got his start in radio as a writer and gimmick inventor. He scripted Eleanor Roosevelt's 1940–1941 dialogue show and subsequently thought up stunts for *Truth or Consequences* during the following decade. With the inception of his inspired *Candid Microphone* Funt became "the nerviest man in radio," according to a critic. He would "ask anybody to do anything, in a deadpan way that made the victims believe he was absolutely serious." It was a dress rehearsal for even greater things. From 1948 to 1990 Funt presided over an enormously popular video *Candid Camera,* originally on ABC followed by NBC, CBS and since then in syndication and on PAX. He was a regular in the cast of *The Garry Moore Show* on CBS-TV in 1959–1960. Funt also produced CBS-TV's *Tell It to the Camera* in 1963–1964. Commoners registered their opinions and gripes there.

When the mastermind's health curtailed his professional activities, Funt's son, Peter, and others took over anchoring the laugh-filled exhibition of unknowing subjects reacting to oddball situations. It became, in fact, a forerunner of contemporary reality TV. For decades *Remember ... sometime ... somewhere ... when you least expect it ... someone will step up to you and say ... 'Smile, you're on Candid Camera'!* was the show's parting delicacy. The concept was simple, yet genius; it started in an aural venue with people who didn't realize their responses were being tape-recorded. Most of those subjects subsequently gladly gave their permission to have their voices played back on the air as America eavesdropped on the fun.

GALBRAITH, JOHN. *Announcer, Actor.* **Series:** *Are These Our Children?* (1946–1948); *Bill Clifford and His Orchestra* (1941); *The Jack Webb Show* (announcer-actor, 1946); *Pat Novak for Hire* (actor, 1946–1947); *Stan Kenton and His Orchestra* (1941).

GALLOP, FRANK. b. June 30, 1900, Boston, Mass.; d. May 17, 1988, Palm Beach, Fla. *Announcer, Actor, Emcee.* **Series:** *The Adventures of the Abbotts* (1955); *Amanda of Honeymoon Hill* (early 1940s); *The Cresta Blanca Carnival of Music* (host, 1943–1944); *The Doctor Fights* (1944); *An Evening with Romberg* (host-announcer, 1945–1948); *Gangbusters* (1940s); *The Helen Hayes Theater* (1945–1946); *Her Honor, Nancy James* (1938–1939); *Hilltop House* (ca. late 1930s, early 1940s); *The Hour of Charm* (ca. late 1930s, 1940s); *The Jack Pearl Show*; *Kaltenborn Edits the News* (late 1930s, early 1940s); *The Milton Berle Show* (1947–1948); *Monitor* (co-communicator, 1955–1960); *The New York Philharmonic Orchestra* (host-musicologist-announcer); *The Prudential Family Hour* (1941–1948); *Quick as a Flash* (1944–ca. 1949); *Romance* (1943–1944); *So This is Radio* (cast, 1939); *Stella Dallas* (early 1950s); *The Summer Family Hour*; *Texaco Star Theater* (ca. 1940s); *Twenty-Six by Corwin* (actor, 1941); *When a Girl Marries* (1939–1941); *A Woman of America* (mid 1940s).

In 1934 Boston stockbroker Frank Gallop prevailed in a bet with a friend by auditioning for a part time radio announcer's post, winning it and going on the air. Gallop subsequently encountered some interesting reactions to his on-air deliveries. He was often mistaken for an Englishman by virtue of his princely inflections. Commenting on his epigraph to the *Romance* anthology narratives, a pundit observed that Gallop was "a sober-voiced announcer at best, ... an undeniable talent with comedy; he gave this an almost teary presence." On those occasions, Gallop volunteered that he was "your guide through the pages of all the great stories of all time—tender love stories of today, the memorable love stories of the past." As he introduced the soap opera *Amanda of Honeymoon Hill*, his usual restrained deportment collapsed while he aroused listeners with: "*Amanda of Honeymoon Hill*, the story of a young girl laid against a tapestry of the deep South." Years later, between 1955 and 1963 on NBC-TV, he welcomed viewers to *The Perry Como Show*, and—during a brief lull in its progression—invariably offered the bass voice that exploded out of nowhere, resounding like it came from an echo chamber, to the star: "Oh, Mr. C...."

Gallop appeared in several more places on television screens. He hosted a thriller and suspenseful dramatic anthology, *Lights Out*, on NBC-TV from 1950 to 1952. He was in a large company of regulars on NBC's talk-variety series *Broadway Open House* in 1951, airing three mornings a week for an hour. He turned up as a panelist on one of TV's shortest game shows, *What Happened*, in August 1952 on ABC. Moderator Ben Grauer and his panel of regulars must have wondered what really did happen, for the plug was pulled after only three weeks. A review labeled it a "shabby imitation" of CBS's highly acclaimed *I've Got a Secret*. During the 1952–1953 television season Gallop was the ringmaster for the NBC primetime entry *The Buick Circus Hour*. In the summer of 1961 he hosted the *Kraft Mystery Theater*, an hour-long NBC dramatic anthology. That same season he presided over *Great Ghost Tales*, a separate 30-minute NBC anthology, which TV historian Alex McNeil identified as "the last live dramatic series on commercial television." For six months in 1963 Gallop narrated ABC's *Cartoonies*, a Saturday morning animated feature for the small fry.

Ray Poindexter recalled a poignantly amusing memory from the radio era: "Frank Gallop walked into the 17th story CBS studio one day in September [1939] ten minutes prior to time for him to introduce H.V. Kaltenborn on the program *Kaltenborn Edits the News*. Sitting down at the mike, Gallop made a hand gesture of greeting to the engineer in the adjacent control room. Thinking that Gallop wanted to interrupt the current program for a war bulletin, he cut the *Alibi Club* and turned on Gallop's mike. The announcer, not knowing he was on the air, was clowning with the introduction: "Kaltenborn edits the news!" The commentator was listening in his office. Thinking he was late, he grabbed his notes and dashed for the studio. Then Gallop began saying Kaltenborn's name to the beat of 'Old McDonald Had a Farm': 'Aich Ve-ee Kal-ten-born, E-yi, E-yi-O!'"

GARAGIOLA, JOSEPH HENRY. b. Feb. 12, 1926, St. Louis, Mo. *Sportscaster.* **Series:** *Monitor* (sports commentator-interviewer, ca. early 1960s–1975; segment host, 1969–1970).

Sportscaster Joe Garagiola arrived on the broadcasting scene just after television replaced radio as the chief entertainment medium in most American households. An affable and talented Garagiola, however, proved adept at doing all kinds of things in the visual medium, some far apart from his lifelong passion for baseball. In 1991 he received the Ford Frick Award for outstanding broadcasting accomplishments from the Baseball Hall of Fame.

An outstanding athlete in his youth, at 16 Garagiola was signed by the St. Louis Cardinals, and made his major league debut at 20. In nine seasons he played ball with four clubs: the Cardinals, Pittsburgh Pirates, Chicago Cubs and New York Giants. He subsequently penned a volume of humorous anecdotes that he and others experienced in his sport, *Baseball is a Funny Game* (Lippincott, 1960). Garagiola followed that up with *It's Anybody's Ballgame* (Contemporary Books, 1988). By 1955 he was into broadcasting, airing games over the Cardinals' flagship station, KMOX. Six years later he launched an NBC career covering major league baseball matches. From 1965 to 1968 he called games of the New York Yankees, returning to NBC games exclusively from 1975 to 1988. After the 1988 World Series, Garagiola resigned from NBC Sports and briefly was a TV commentator for the California Angels. In recent years he has been an outspoken opponent of the use of chewing tobacco. His son, Joe Jr., became general manager of the Arizona Diamondbacks while Joe Sr. contracted to provide on-air coverage of Diamondbacks' games.

In 1961–1964 and 1975–1988 Joe Sr. and multiple cohorts called NBC-TV's *Baseball Game of the Week*. Between 1963 and 1965 he contributed sports reports and commentary on NBC-TV's hour-long news and information show, *Sunday*. He did the same on the web's early morning *Today* from 1967 to 1975 and again from 1991 to 1992. Garagiola hosted the syndicated game show *He Said, She Said* in 1969. He presided over a contestant-driven *Joe Garagiola's Memory Game*, a weekday half-hour on NBC-TV in 1971. From 1971 to 1973 he performed similar duties on NBC's weekday game show *Sale of the Century*. In the summers of 1972–1975 he hosted *The Baseball World of Joe Garagiola*, a quarter-hour commentary feature that preceded NBC's major league baseball game of the week. The broadcaster won an Emmy for that one in 1973, incidentally. In 1977–1978 Garagiola moderated a syndicated version of the popular panel show *To Tell the Truth*. During the 1980–1981 season he turned up as a guest interviewee on NBC's primetime sports feature *Games People Play*. And in the 1986–1987 season he was master of ceremonies for a syndicated quiz show that borrowed an earlier TV title, *Strike It Rich*, but was little match for its predecessor "institution" as competing couples tried their luck in answering multiple-choice questions.

Despite all of the television exposure, Garagiola seemed particularly cheerless on the final broadcast of NBC Radio's *Monitor* on Jan. 16, 1975, as he expressed his farewell. He noted that he had performed there "around 2,500 times aside from my segment host duties" over the course of the show's dual decades' weekend-long run and, "for me, today is the saddest." A self-effacing Garagiola pointed not to his own accomplishments in his pithy summation but "the voices you never heard" on the air—unsung heroes like the producers, directors, writers, engineers and a myriad of other nameless contributors who stayed in the background. He claimed to be departing "with pride" as he signed off with "for the *very last time* ... 'This is Joe Garagiola for *Monitor* Sports.'"

GARDINER, DONALD. b. Jan. 10, 1916, New York, N.Y.; d. March 27, 1977, Quoque, Long Island, N.Y. *Announcer, Newscaster.* **Series:** *David Harding, Counterspy* (ca. late 1940s, 1950s); *Dick Tracy* (narrator, ca. 1943–1948); *Gangbusters* (ca. late 1940s, early 1950s); *Monday Morning Headlines* (newscaster, 1944–1958); *Tomorrow's Headlines* (newscaster, 1948–1949); *When a Girl Marries* (ca. mid 1940s).

After serving as a page at NBC, Don Gardiner began announcing with Winston-Salem's WAIR and Washington's WRC. During the latter stint, in 1941 he covered the third inaugural of President Franklin Delano

Roosevelt. He joined the Blue network (soon to be ABC) two years later in New York. He was still with ABC at the time of his death 34 years later.

GARY, ARTHUR. b. 1914, New York, N.Y.; d. Oct. 31, 2005. *Announcer.* **Series:** *The Amazing Mr. Malone* (ca. late 1940s, ca. early 1950s); *The Colgate Sports Newsreel,* aka *Bill Stern Sports* and various other monikers (ca. 1937–ca. 1956); *The Eternal Light* (1946); *For the Record* (1944); *Living 1948* (1948); *News of the World* (1968).

Arthur Gary's career in broadcasting extended from 1936 to 1984.

GIBBONS, RAPHAEL FLOYD PHILLIPS. b. July 16, 1887, Washington, D.C.; d. Sept. 24, 1939, Saylorsburg, Pa. *Commentator, Announcer, Emcee.* **Series:** *The Elgin Adventurer's Club* (host, 1932); *Floyd Gibbons* (commentator, 1933); *Floyd Gibbons and the News* (newscaster, 1930–1931); *The General Electric Program,* aka *Adventures in Science* (host, 1929–1931); *The Headline Hunter* (commentator, 1929–1933); *Nash Program,* aka *Speed Show* (1936–1937); *World Adventures* (1930–1931).

Floyd Gibbons entered Washington's Georgetown University for formal preparation for his life's work. Before he was expelled for childish pranks, he flunked English, Latin and Greek—and still had a good time. The future "swashbuckling war correspondent," according to a biographer, launched a professional journalism career as a police reporter for *The Minneapolis Daily News* at $7 weekly. A succession of newspapers followed: *The Milwaukee Free Press*; *The Minneapolis Tribune*; *The Chicago World*; *The Chicago Tribune*. Only five weeks before the U.S. entered the First World War, Gibbons was aboard the *Laconia* en route to London to dispatch reports for *The Chicago Tribune* when a German submarine sunk the liner. He was spared but was wounded later while covering the U.S. Marines in combat at Belleau Wood, France. In that skirmish he lost his left eye and consequently wore a signature white patch in its place for the rest of his life.

Returning to America, in the 1920s Gibbons was characterized by a pundit as "a rollocking, free-wheeling" reporter for his paper. The *Trib* also owned Chicago's WGN. On Christmas Eve in 1925, Gibbons was pressed into a broadcast in which he recounted some of his overseas experiences. (In the course of his brief lifespan he covered battlefronts in Russia, Morocco, China, Ethiopia and Spain.) He was so terrified of the mike for that airdate, however, that the station manager tried to distract him by hiding it from his view. His apprehensions notwithstanding, the print journalist was an instant hit with listeners, paving the way for lots more to follow.

The veteran newspaperman's first real opportunity to permanently move into electronic journalism resulted from an NBC audition in the spring of 1929. Gibbons averaged speaking 3.6 words per second or 217 words per minute that resulted in his being hired for a Wednesday night spot, *The Headline Hunter,* on which he recalled many of his unusual personal encounters. He spoke "a mile a minute," according to one critic. He was also assigned the task of overseeing NBC's remote broadcasts. By early 1930 he was on the air with the first daily network newscast.

While still employed by NBC, in 1931 Gibbons also joined International News Service and Universal News Service and—in November—sailed across the Pacific to cover the Japanese-Chinese War. He broadcast over NBC in January 1932 from Manchuria, his base of operations until his return to the states that year in time for the summer political conventions. A frenetic lifestyle in work and word brought on a heart attack at age 46; a second one at 52 killed him, just at the outbreak of the Second World War—the "big one" he most wanted to cover.

In a span of a dozen years Gibbons penned a quartet of gripping volumes detailing his eyewitness accounts of far-flung adventures: *How the Laconia Sank and The Militia Mobilization on the Mexican Border: Two Masterpieces of Reporting* (Daughaday, 1917); *And They Thought We Wouldn't Fight* (Doran, 1918); *The Red Knight of Germany: The Story of Baron von Richthofen, Germany's Great War Bird* (Doubleday, 1927); and *The Red Napoleon* (Cape & Smith, 1929). He was the subject of two biographies: *Floyd Gibbons, Knight of the Air* by Gilbert Douglas (McBride, 1930) and *Floyd Gibbons, Your Headline Hunter* by Edward Gibbons (Exposition Press, 1953).

A chronicler characterized him as "a restless, unorthodox roving reporter" who "brought high excitement, courage, and ingenuity into his foreign and war correspondence to earn his reputation as the premier war correspondent of his generation." The reviewer continued: "A man of physical and moral courage who went for the story against any odds, Gibbons was noted for ... clarity and empathy.... His keen sense of humor and other personal qualities endeared him to both his readers and his listeners. He was not awed by greatness nor impressed by his own achievements. He always saw the dignity of the common man and sought to convey that dignity in his ... reporting."

GIBNEY, HAROLD T. b. Aug. 26, 1911, Woodland, Calif.; d. June 1973, Fillmore, Calif. *Announcer.* **Series:** *Charlie Lung*; *Dr. I.Q.*; *Dragnet* (co-announcer, 1949–1957); *From Hollywood Today* (1939–1940); *Front and Center* (1947); *Hawthorne House* (ca. 1935–?); *Hello Mom* (ca. 1942–1943); *House of Melody*; *Irene Rich Dramas* (ca. 1930s, 1940s); *Jimmy Fidler*; *Let's Laugh and Get Acquainted* (1946); *The Magic Key of RCA* (ca. 1935–1939); *Muted Rhythm*; *Names of Tomorrow* (master of ceremonies); *The NBC University Theatre* (1950); *Roosty of the AAF* (1944–1945); *The Sealtest Variety Theater* (1948–1949); *The Six Shooter* (1953–ca. 1954); *Soldiers with Wings* (ca. 1942, ca. 1943, ca. 1944, ca. 1945); *The Standard Symphony* (ca. late 1930s); *Tales of the Texas Rangers* (1950–1952); *Walter Winchell*; *Winning in the West*.

Hal Gibney launched his broadcast career in 1931 by announcing for KSFO and KTAB in San Francisco. His next stop was Portland's KGW; by 1936 he was at NBC in Hollywood where he introduced a profusion of continuing aural series over the next couple of decades.

Gibney's best-recalled lines from his most memorable series, *Dragnet*, were: "Ladies and gentlemen ... the story you are about to hear is true. Only the names have been changed to protect the innocent." He introduced that show on NBC-TV, too, from 1951 to 1959. Gibney also had another unique line on the ether. Presenting *Tales of the Texas Rangers* for more than two years, he characterized the immense breadth of that story: "Texas! More than 260,000 square miles! And 50 men who make up the most famous and oldest law enforcement body in North America!"

GILMORE, ART. b. March 18, 1912, Tacoma, Wash. *Announcer, Actor.* **Series:** *The Adventures of Frank Race* (1949–1950, ca. 1951–1952); *Amos 'n' Andy* (ca. 1950s); *Dr. Christian* (ca. 1937–ca. 1938, 1942–1954); *Golden Days of Radio*; *Jonathan Trimble, Esquire* (1946); *Lux Radio Theater* (actor, 1940s, 1950s); *Meet Me at Parky's* (1945–1947); *Miss Pinkerton, Inc.* (1941); *Murder and Mr. Malone*, aka *The Amazing Mr. Malone* (ca. 1947–ca. 1950, ca. 1951); *O'Hara* (1956); *The Pacific Story* (actor, 1943–1947); *Point Sublime* (1940s); *Red Ryder* (ca. 1940s); *Rhapsody in Rhythm* (1946, 1947); *The Sears Radio Theater*, aka *The Mutual Radio Theater* (1979–1981); *Stars Over Hollywood* (mid 1940s–1954).

"The day I heard the voice of Ted Husing [on the radio] I thought, *That's* what I want to do! I'll work for nothing," exclaimed Art Gilmore. He found a job at a Tacoma radio station that paid him *almost* nothing nevertheless—$15 per month for a five-day-a-week duty. Sensing he needed more credentials, young Gilmore trotted off to Washington State University for added training. There he not only acquired the same speech professor as future legend Edward R. Murrow, in 1934 he supplemented the staff of campus station KWSC, Pullman, Wash., as an announcer.

The following year Gilmore joined Seattle's KOL, consequently moving to Hollywood's KFWB and in 1936 to KNX, Los Angeles, where he landed CBS's *Dr. Christian* for 17 years. Other network series followed. He became a freelance announcer in 1941 and was also acting on an occasional show now and then. That led him into television, where the tall, imposing, handsome man with tresses of white hair may have made his most indelible contributions.

On one memorable occasion while announcing *Dr. Christian*, Gilmore was visited by an old hindrance of hiccups shortly before the live broadcast took to the air. Drawing on an announcer's time-honored cure, he swallowed a teaspoon of vinegar. The hiccups dissipated. Summarizing his career years later, he acknowledged: "The announcer's life is a pretty lonely job. You're sort of the Lone Ranger—you do your job and you go home. The announcer isn't part of the show." He confessed that on most shows he usually went out with the crew afterward and not the cast. Leonard Maltin recited a tale suggesting that announcers were "the bedrock of radio," however, and could be counted upon to come to "the rescue of a broadcast," to wit:

"Art Gilmore was drifting into the doldrums during a broadcast of *Dr. Christian* one day when I heard this snapping of fingers, and I looked over. Jean Hersholt [who played Dr. Christian] was at a table ... and he snapped his fingers. I thought, What the heck is going on? I went over; he had left the last seven pages of his script in the dressing room upstairs. Now, we're on live, coast to coast. Well, talk about luck; normally I'd read my commercial and then I'd turn to the back page and sit there. And fight sleep. Five-thirty in the afternoon is a dull time; you're kind of ready for dinner and you need a little pep. That one particular night, I was following along with him and when I heard the snapping I was able to give him my script.'"

Gilmore was the regular announcer on several prominent TV series: *The Red Skelton Show* (1951–1971, NBC, CBS); *Captain Midnight* (1954–1956, CBS); *The George Gobel Show* (1954–1960, NBC, CBS); *Climax!* (1954–1958, CBS); *Highway Patrol* (1955–1959, syndication); *Men of Annapolis* (1957, syndication); *The Woody Woodpecker Show* (1957–1958, ABC); and *The Fred Astaire Theater*, aka *Alcoa Premiere* (1961–1963, ABC). On *Highway Patrol*, his was the familiar voice affirming in all 156 episodes: "Whenever the laws of any state are broken, a duly authorized organization swings into action—the Highway Patrol." He claimed he read the copy for each of those installments without seeing the footage until it came on TV. Gilmore further hosted *The Comedy Spot*, a summertime filler for CBS's comic Red Skelton in 1960, 1961 and 1962. On NBC's *Dragnet* (1967–1970) he portrayed an L.A. police captain. He also turned up in the dramatic (and sometimes comedic) casts of isolated episodes of *Adam-12*; *Emergency!*; *The Mary Tyler Moore Show*; and *The Waltons*.

Gilmore reportedly voiced some 10,000 movie trailers and scores of newsreels across three decades. Between 1942 and 1964 he narrated 77 movies and shorts. Forty-five were instructional/advice/self-help films with titles that began either "So You Want to ..." or "So You Think You're ..." or "So You're Going to ..." and were completed with phrases like "Give Up Smoking," "Need Glasses," "Allergic," "Play the Horses," "Keep Your Hair," "A Nervous Wreck," "Be a Father," "Be in Pictures," "Be a Salesman," "Hold Your Wife," "Be a Gambler," "Build a House," "Be a Detective," "Be in Politics," "Be on the Radio," "Not Guilty," "Having in–Law Trouble," "Get Rich Quick," "Be an Actor," "Hold Your Husband," "Have an Operation," "Be a Handyman," "Be a Cowboy," "Buy a Used Car," "Be a Bachelor," "Enjoy Life," "Wear the Pants," "Love Your Dog," "Be on a Jury," "Be Pretty."

He narrated 11 more celluloid shorts whose titles started with "This World of Ours" and ended with a specific geographic region—Ceylon, Singapore, Germany, Japan, Hong Kong, Formosa, Ireland, Thailand, the Caribbean, Turkey and Venezuela. Finally, from 1941 to 2001 Gilmore played in 25 additional motion pictures, frequently as a broadcaster, sometimes unseen. A sampling of his credits in that arena: *Yankee Doodle Dandy* (1942); *The Man Who Dared* (1946); *Backlash* (1947); *King of the Rocket Men* (1949); *Tea for Two* (1950); *When Worlds Collide* (1951); *The Story of Will Rogers* (1952); *It Should Happen to You* (1954); *Rear Window* (1954); *Dragnet* (1954); *Francis in the Navy* (1955); *Suicide Battalion* (1958); and *Moonbeams* (2001). He was the voice of a newsreel announcer in the 1977 made-for-TV flick *The Amazing Howard Hughes*.

Gilmore interrupted his radio career during the Second World War to serve with the U.S. Navy. Afterward, at the University of Southern California, he taught returning GIs and other aspirants to become radio announcers. Gilmore headed both the Los Angeles branch and the national troops of the American Federation of Television and Radio Artists (AFTRA) and was the inaugural president of the Pacific Pioneer Broadcasters (PPB). He was honored by the Society to Preserve and Encourage Radio Drama, Variety and Comedy (SPERDVAC) in 1999 for his lifetime achievements and personal contributions to the industry. He and Glenn Y. Middleton co-authored *Television and Radio Announcing* (Hollywood Radio Publishers, 1946). "The very foundation of radio speech is naturalness," the pair insisted.

GLADE, EARL J., JR. b. July 17, 1911, Utah; d. May 14, 2001, Utah. *Announcer, Producer.* **Series:** *Music and the Spoken Word from the Crossroads of the West*, aka *The Mormon Tabernacle Choir* (producer-announcer, 1929–ca. 1940s).

After his livelihood-producing ties with the Mormons ended, Earl Glade was still a young man—then in his thirties. He relocated to Idaho and ultimately purchased KBOI Radio, a key station broadcasting the athletic competitions during the 1950s that involved the University of Idaho.

GODDARD, DON. b. July 5, 1904, Binghamton, N.Y.; d. March 20, 1994, Arizona. *Newscaster, Announcer.* **Series:** *Don Goddard and the News* (newscaster, 1940–1941, 1944–1945); *Pancho and His Orchestra* [one of manifold band remotes] (1944).

Don Goddard grew up on a farm in upstate New York and performed the typical farm boy chores. It came as little surprise, therefore, that—following his college graduation—he wanted to run a newspaper to improve farming conditions. Being realistic, nevertheless, Goddard initially signed with *The New York World* as a reporter to gain experience. For a half-dozen years beyond—which he later acknowledged were the six hardest years of his life—Goddard lived out his dream.

Simultaneously, as he witnessed the development of radio, he realized that the new medium was having a strong impact on farmers. His interest grew. When an ex-newspaper colleague offered a position in the News and Special Events Department at NBC, he accepted it. Goddard eventually supplemented his network newscasting stints with similar feats at various New York local radio outlets: WEAF (1942), WMCA (1946), WINS (1947–1948). In the mid 1940s he presented *News at Noon* weekdays to a WEAF audience. Goddard also appeared on many one-time-only network exhibitions that commemorated D-Day (June 6, 1944), V-E Day (May 7, 1945) and False V-J Day (Aug. 10, 1945).

In the summer of 1950 he presided over a Sunday afternoon NBC-TV series for youngsters, *Watch the World*, primarily comprised of film features. Within a short while Goddard transferred to ABC Television. From 1955 to 1957 he hosted a half-hour documentary series, *Medical Horizons*, focused on medical technology and health care. In 1958 he was tapped as the chain's early news anchor (at 7:15 P.M. Eastern Time) in a short-lived weeknight experiment (to December 1960) that shifted John Daly from that customary slot to 10:30 P.M. Goddard appeared with a group of the web's correspondents in December 1958 assessing the top stories of the year on *Prologue 1959*, a public affairs special on ABC-TV.

In the summer of 1963 Goddard moderated a weekly primetime documentary, *Focus on America*, including film footage previously produced and shown by local ABC affiliates.

GODFREY, ARTHUR MORTON. b. Aug. 31, 1903, New York, N.Y.; d. March 16, 1983, New York, N.Y. *Master of Ceremonies, Announcer.* **Series:** *The Arthur Godfrey Digest* (master of ceremonies, 1950–1955); *Arthur Godfrey Time* (master of ceremonies, 1945–1972); *Arthur Godfrey's Talent Scouts* (master of ceremonies, 1946–1956); *The Fred Allen Show* (1943); *Manhattan Parade*; *Professor Quiz* (early 1940s); *Singin' Sam*.

Time considered Arthur Godfrey "the greatest salesman who ever stood before a microphone" while a pundit labeled him "radio's most trusted pitchman." Following a near-fatal vehicular crash in 1931, Godfrey laid in a hospital bed for months, suspended in traction. Having nothing else to do, he tuned to radio stations and was astounded by the formal drivel he heard from announcers selling goods and services. It was the watershed experience of his life. Returning to the airwaves later—he was an announcer and disc jockey at Washington, D.C.'s WRC—he began to personalize his commercial deliveries, speaking to the listener as if *that listener* was his *sole audience*. It was a radical departure from longstanding practice and became a hallmark of his career, eventually having a powerful effect on the methods employed in communicating broadcast advertising elsewhere in the industry.

Godfrey, who responded in 1926 to a dare by some beer-drinking buddies that put him up to plunking his banjo in a talent contest on station WFBR in Baltimore, gained three quarter-hour shows weekly as a result at $5 per broadcast. After his successive stint at WRC, he moved to WMAL and WJSV in the nation's capital. He aired his early morning *Sundial* wake-up show for 105 minutes over WJSV, followed by 90 added minutes over WABC in New York, the flagship affiliate of CBS. He was soon introducing several network features, although he lasted only six weeks with Fred Allen due to personality differences. Two weeks before going on the air with his own epic morning series over CBS, which persisted for 27 years, Godfrey offered an emotional commentary on the passing of the funeral cortège of President Franklin D. Roosevelt.

The emcee became a legendary entertainer in four shows bearing his name (*Arthur Godfrey and His Friends* was exclusively on CBS-TV; the others were on radio and *Arthur Godfrey's Talent Scouts* was simulcast on both radio and television). He was the consummate radio broadcaster. He corralled some of the most talented—yet until then, obscure—singers and musicians available; they performed before a live audience for 90 minutes on weekdays and in other shows each week. By 1953 he was responsible for deriving 12 percent of CBS's annual revenues, including $27 million for the web and another million-plus for himself. On the air he often claimed that he paid the chain's expenses for the day before CBS chairman William S. Paley awoke every morning.

Godfrey possessed a mean streak, however, one that an adoring public was unaware of until he fired popular vocalist Julius La Rosa while on the air on Oct. 19, 1953. The autocratic leader of the "all the little Godfreys" inadvertently made a serious miscalculation of the public's reaction; their widespread admiration quickly diminished and in some circles evaporated completely. Instead of learning from his error, however, Godfrey went the other way, firing more favorite cast members the fans had put on pedestals and with whom he became disenchanted. It was the beginning of the end as he started a slow downhill slide from the pinnacle of near-idol worship to a disregarded entertainer. By the late 1950s, most of an appealing staff was gone. His daily program was reduced to a half-hour and the other programs were history. He continued for another 15 years with an announcer and a recurring singer or two. But his show business command was eclipsed, nevermore to return.

In the twilight of his career, Godfrey appeared in three motion pictures: *Four for Texas* (1963); *The Glass Bottom Boat* (1966); and *Where Angels Go ... Trouble Follows* (1968). He co-hosted *Candid Camera* on CBS-TV with creator Allen Funt but the two men's personalities—just as with Fred Allen on radio—conflicted and the arrangement quickly dissolved. Godfrey worked tenaciously at returning to the TV limelight permanently but was never able to bring it off, having to settle for an occasional guest spot. How far the mighty had fallen!

GODWIN, EARL. b. ca. 1881, Washington, D.C.; d. Sept. 23, 1956, Rehoboth Beach, Del. *Newscaster, Commentator.* **Series:** *Collector's Item* (cast, 1954); *Earl Godwin and the News* (newscaster, 1935–1941, 1944–1949); *Watch the World Go By* (news analyst, 1942–1944). **Aphorism:** *God bless you, one and all.*

Earl Godwin was a print journalist extraordinaire when he got into radio as a daily NBC commentator in 1935. His dad was city editor and managing editor of *The Washington Evening Star*. Earl, meanwhile, gained his first serious journalism experience as a member of the Washington staff of *The Baltimore Sun* in 1931. He later covered Congress for *The Washington Star*, serving through much of the first Woodrow Wilson administration. During that stretch he was also Washington correspondent for several foreign newspapers, including *The Montreal Star*. He covered the House for *The New York World* and provided special dispatches to *The New York Times*. By the late 1930s he was White House correspondent for *The Washington Times-Herald*. During the Second World War, he enlisted in the U.S. Army and—following the war—he became associate editor of *The Washington Times*. Altogether, his career as a print journalist spanned in excess of three decades. Godwin gained the distinction of covering all of the national political campaigns from Wilson to Franklin D. Roosevelt.

FDR christened him "the Earl of Godwin" and appointed a chair for him near the presidential desk at White House press conferences during his administration. Godwin was so traumatized by Roosevelt's demise in April 1945 that colleague H.R. Baukhage was ushered in to replace him on his broadcast. Godwin routinely concluded his newscasts with *God bless you, one and all.* In addition to his national newscasting stints, he augmented his income with news reporting for a couple of Washington radio outlets—WMAL (1938, 1945–1948) and WRC (1938–1939). Godwin was also commentator for NBC-TV's *Meet the Veep* in 1953.

GOLDER, HARRY. b. July 10, 1908, Detroit, Mich.; d. Oct. 16, 1968, Los Angeles, Calif. Announcer. **Series:** *The Lone Ranger* (ca. 1930s, 1940s).

In addition to performing his duties for *The Lone Ranger*, Harry Golder tripled as a newscaster (1937–1941) and sportscaster (1940) at the epic drama's originating station, Detroit's WXYZ.

GOODWIN, WILLIAM NETTLES. b. July 28, 1910, San Francisco, Calif.; d. May 9, 1958, Palm Springs, Calif. *Announcer, Actor, Emcee.* **Series:** *The Adventures of Gracie* (1934–1935); *The Al Pearce Show*, aka *Al Pearce and His Gang* (1939–1940s); *Atlantic Spotlight* (actor, mid 1940s); *The Bill Goodwin Show*, aka *Leave It to Bill* (actor, 1947, 1957); *Billy Swift, Boy Detective* (ca. 1938–1939); *Blondie* (1939–1942); *The Burns and Allen Show*, aka *The Swan Soap Show*, aka *Maxwell House Coffee Time*, aka *The Ammident Show* (1941–1944); *California Melodies* (1934–ca. 1936); *A Date with Judy* (1940s); *Dollar a Minute* (master of ceremonies, 1950–1951); *The Edgar Bergen and Charlie McCarthy Show*; *Frank Sinatra in Person*, aka *Songs by Sinatra* (1944–?); *The Gracie Fields Show*, aka *The Gracie Fields Victory Show* (1942–1945, ca. 1952–ca. 1953); *Hollywood Showcase* (1938); *Jack Oakie's College*, aka *The Camel Caravan* (1936–1938); *The Joe Penner Show* (1933–1935); *Johnny Fletcher*, aka *A Johnny Fletcher Mystery* (actor, 1948); *The Louella Parsons Show* (ca. 1940s); *The Park Avenue Penners* (ca. 1936–ca. 1939); *Paul Whiteman Presents* (1943); *The Pepsodent Show Starring Bob Hope* (1939–1941); *Philco Hall of Fame*, aka *The Philco Radio Hall of Fame* (cast, ca. 1943–ca. 1946); *Skippy Hollywood Theater* (actor, 1940s); *Three Ring Time* (1941–1942); *Tommy Riggs and Betty Lou* (1942).

Bill Goodwin was studying pre-law at the University of California when he decided to channel his career into show business. In 1929 he appeared in *Broken Wing*, a professional stage play production, and then performed with the Henry Duffy Players in Portland, Ore. For a while he was on the air at KFVK in Sacramento but not long afterward he shifted to KFRC in nearby San Francisco, his hometown. Affiliating with the Don Lee West Coast chain, in 1932 Goodwin moved south to KHJ, Los Angeles. He got a shot at announcing a network show within two years with *California Melodies*. CBS summoned him to New York that same year (1934).

In 1944 Goodwin was making $1,000 weekly announcing *The Burns and Allen Show* but coveted becoming a comedian. He decided to put some humor into his performance, singing the show's sign-off one week in a high-pitched whine ending with a hysterical giggle: "This is CBS, the Columbia Broadcasting System." The following week he concluded with an agonizing "ouch" and another week simply with "ugh!" He consequently found comical work on Frank Sinatra's program with Sinatra playing Goodwin's straight man while also paying him $1,000 per broadcast.

During its inaugural season on CBS-TV in 1950–1951, Goodwin appeared as himself while announcing *The George Burns and Gracie Allen Show*. He left to preside over his own Tuesday and Thursday afternoon 30-minute variety series on NBC-TV, *The Bill Goodwin Show*, which persisted six months in 1951–1952. He was master of ceremonies on ABC-TV's game entry *Penny to a Million* in 1955. Concurrently, that same year he had similar duties on NBC-TV's *It Pays to Be Married* game show. From 1956 to 1958 Goodwin provided voiceovers of the lead character on CBS's animated cartoon series *The Boing Boing Show*.

Goodwin's broadcasting career was augmented with 30 motion picture appearances between 1941 and 1958. Among his credits were *Blondie in Society* (1941); *Wake Island* (1942); *Henry Aldrich Gets Glamour* (1943); *So Proudly We Hail!* (1943); *The Stork Club* (1945); *House of Horrors* (1946); *The Jolson Story* (1946); *Heaven Only Knows* (1947); *The Life of Riley* (1949); *Jolson Sings Again* (1949); *Tea for Two* (1950); *The Opposite Sex* (1956); *Going Steady* (1958); and *The Big Beat* (1958).

In 1956 Goodwin purchased Palm Springs' Nooks Hotel. Until his death at 47 in 1958 sustained from a heart attack while driving his automobile, he was on a constant shuttle between his Palm Springs home and Hollywood to meet his radio, TV and movie obligations. Goodwin's final video assignment was as host of *Colgate Theatre* telecast on Los Angeles' KTTV.

GORDON, DON. b. Nov. 23, 1926, Los Angeles, Calif. *Announcer, Actor.* **Series:** *Bachelor's Children* (1940s); *Captain Midnight* (1940); *Curtain Time* (1940s); *Ladies Fair* (announcer–emcee's assistant, early 1950s); *Surprise Serenade* (1949); *Tom Mix Ralston Straight Shooters*, aka *Curley Bradley, The Singing Marshal* (1940s, ca. early 1950s); *Wings of Destiny* (actor, ca. 1940–ca. 1942).

In 1934 Don Gordon left WTMJ, Milwaukee, for KMOX, St. Louis. Eight months later he was back in Milwaukee at WTMJ. In 1940 he joined WBBM in Chicago. After his radio series bit the dust, Gordon turned to television acting. He played a recurring role in 1960's syndicated *The Blue Angels*; he was an ongoing figure on ABC-TV's *Lucan* in 1977–1978; and he capped off his career before the cameras in 1980 as yet another continuing character in CBS-TV's *The Contender*.

GOSS, FRANK B. b. Nov. 20, 1910, Washington, D.C.; d. May 7, 1962, Hollywood, Calif. *Announcer.* **Series:** *The City* (1947); *Escape* (ca. late 1940s); *Hallmark Playhouse*, aka *The Hallmark Hall of Fame* (1948–1955); *Hollywood Showcase* (1941–1942); *Irene Rich Dramas* (ca. 1940s); *Somebody Knows* (1950); *Stars Over Hollywood* (early 1940s).

In 1937 Frank Goss, who had been toiling part time for a while, was hired full time as an announcer and publicity director for KFOX, Long Beach, Calif. The following year he joined KFWB in Hollywood. On the staff of Los Angeles' KNX-CBS Radio from late 1940 to 1962, veteran newscaster Goss maintained local daily morning and evening programs in addition to a handful of network commitments. He interrupted his civilian service in 1943 when the U.S. Army called him in as a first lieutenant. In 1957 the Associated Press honored Goss with its Best Radio Award while the following year the Southern California Radio-TV News Club gave him its Golden Mike Award.

GRAHAM, FRANK. b. Nov. 22, 1911, Detroit, Mich.; d. Sept. 2, 1950, Hollywood, Calif. *Actor, Announcer, Emcee.* **Series:** *Armchair Adventures* (actor); *The Adventures of Bill Lance* (actor, 1944–1945); *Cavalcade of America* (actor, ca. 1940s); *Crook's Cruise* (actor, 1948); *Darts for Dough* (mid 1940s); *Dealer in Dreams*; *The Electric Hour* (1944–1946); *Encore Theater* (1946); *Fray and Braggiotti*; *The Ginny Simms Show*, aka *Purple Heart* (1942–1945); *Jeff Regan, Investigator* (actor, 1949–1950); *The Jim Backus Show* (ca. 1942, ca. 1947–1948); *The Judy Canova Show* (ca. 1940s); *Lum and Abner* (actor, late 1930s, 1940s); The Man Called X (actor, ca. 1940s, early 1950s); *Night Cap Yarns* (actor, 1938–1943); *The People's Vote* (1938–1939); *The Rudy Vallee Show* (ca. 1940s); *Romance* (host, 1944–1946); *Romance of the Ranchos* (storyteller, early 1940s); *The Rudy Vallee Show* (ca. 1930s); *Satan's Waitin'* (host, 1950); *Tommy Riggs and Betty Lou* (1942–1943); *White Fires of Inspiration* (1938).

Frank Graham could smell the greasepaint at two years of age when he went backstage at theaters across the Midwest where his opera soprano mom, Ethel Briggs Graham, performed. Young Graham exhibited a determined interest in dramatics from the time he entered school as the family transferred from Washington State to Michigan, Oregon, California, and again to Washington, where Frank completed high school studies in Seattle. He briefly attended the University of California in Berkeley but soon dispensed with it to launch his show business career. After a fleeting stint with the Los Angeles Theatre Guild, Graham joined the Seattle Repertory Theatre and worked his way up to leading man.

A Seattle radio station hired him and

gave him visibility beyond the local confines. Consequently, in August 1937 CBS hired Graham for its network owned-and-operated affiliate KNX in Hollywood. That gave him exposure on programs nationwide. He eventually earned a billing as "the man with a thousand voices." In addition to radio, Graham appeared in the 1945 Walt Disney flick *The Three Caballeros.*

GRAHAM, SHEILAH (born Lily Shiel). b. Sept. 15, 1904, Leeds, England; d. Nov. 17, 1988. *Commentator.* **Series:** *Heinz Magazine of the Air* (recurring guest, 1936–ca. 1938); *Sheilah Graham* (gossip commentator, 1949–1950); *Three City Byline* (commentator, 1953–1954); *Vanity Fair* (film reviewer, 1937); *Yours for a Song,* aka *Conti Castille Show* (gossip commentator, 1948–1949).

Syndicated newspaper columnist Sheilah Graham is misidentified by some radio scholars as the replacement for the long-running Hollywood gossip commentator Jimmy Fidler on MBS. While it's true Fidler left the network air on July 3, 1949, he returned briefly on May 21, 1951, then continued in syndication for what appears to have set a record among the breed—at least into the 1970s and possibly as late as 1983, according to one media scholar. Nevertheless, Graham established herself as a Hollywood insider in the 1930s through print and broadcast media, although she never gained the stature of contemporaries Fidler, Hedda Hopper and Louella Parsons. Nor was she seemingly despised by as many enemies as Fidler collected over his enduring professional life, considered by a source as "radio's most threatening menace to movies and movie people."

Jewish by birth, Sheilah Graham seldom publicly acknowledged the fact. She was reared at Jews Hospital and Orphan Asylum in the Norwood section of London between the ages of six and 14. After her "graduation" from the orphanage, she became a chorus girl (the equivalent of Ziegfeld Follies) and a freelance writer. In 1933 she emigrated to the U.S.A. where her livelihood consisted of ferreting out Hollywood gossip and publicizing it. She was divorced young and left with two children; she raised them as Episcopalians.

Graham built a reputation in broadcasting, meanwhile, through a gossip column that was circulated to 178 newspapers during its peak, and in books—at least one of which recalled a multiple-year romantic entanglement with an eminent author. An observer disclosed: "Graham became most famous as the mistress of writer F. Scott Fitzgerald, who spent his last years as a Hollywood scriptwriter. While Graham helped Fitzgerald negotiate Hollywood, he helped her complete her education through a reading program, which she described in her book, *College of One* [Viking, 1967]." Fitzgerald died in her living room of a heart attack a few days before Christmas 1940. "I won't be remembered for my writing," Graham allowed. "I'll be remembered as Scott's mistress."

Graham's first book, *Beloved Infidel: The Education of a Woman* (Holt, 1958), shared its title with a poem Fitzgerald penned for her. A movie (*Beloved Infidel*) based on that volume was released in 1959 starring Gregory Peck (as Fitzgerald) and Deborah Kerr (as Graham). A review of the film revealed: "When writers are depicted in Hollywood movies, you can bet they'll be accompanied by alcohol—served on the rocks. *Beloved Infidel* follows the last years of real-life novelist F. Scott Fitzgerald ... when he worked in Hollywood to support his asylum-bound wife and began a relationship with British-born gossip columnist Sheilah Graham."

For six months in 1951 the columnist presided over *The Sheilah Graham Show*, aka *Sheilah Graham in Hollywood,* on NBC-TV. The quarter-hour feature had been airing on local television in Los Angeles for several months when NBC decided to make a kinescope of the live Tuesday evening series and fly it to New York each week for replay on the network at 11 P.M. Saturdays. The program consisted of movie news, gossip, fashion tips and exchanges with visiting luminaries.

Subsequently, in the winter, spring and summer of 1955, Graham and a guest celebrity co-hosted *Hollywood Today* on NBC-TV on weekdays. Later retitled *Hollywood Backstage*, it presented themes similar to her radio series and column. Initially the entry was seen in quarter-hour installments but as summer arrived it expanded into a half-hour. Graham herself was a guest celebrity on the syndicated TV series *Girl Talk* (1963–1970) which a critic appraised despairingly: "If any TV show of the 1960s deserved to be called a 'bitch session,' *Girl Talk* was it." On one episode, actress Natalie Schafer allegedly told Graham, "I'm so glad to meet you—you were the cause of my divorce." Graham once said, "No one has a closest friend in Hollywood." Her line of work simply wasn't known for spawning lots of durable alliances.

Graham's daughter, Wendy Fairey, authored a memoir of growing up in Hollywood as the offspring of Sheilah Graham and discovering the identity of her true father (not Fitzgerald) in *One of the Family* (W.W. Norton, 1992).

GRANDIN, THOMAS B. b. July 19, 1907, Cleveland, Ohio; d. October 1977. *Correspondent*. **Series:** *ABC News* (correspondent, 1944–1945); *CBS News of Europe* (correspondent, 1939–1940); *World News Today* (correspondent, 1940).

Thomas Grandin was one of the infamous Murrow Boys, a cluster of hand-picked colleagues that CBS overseas news chief Edward R. Murrow selected to cover the Second World War and Europe's preparations for it. Appointed to Paris in the spring of 1939, Grandin was in the group only briefly, although Stanley Cloud and Lynne Olson, Murrow Boys biographers, stated, "Historical accuracy demanded our inclusion of Grandin." They depicted him thus: "Grandin ... not only had a terrible voice, he had no journalistic experience at all. The thirty-year-old Grandin was a slim, bespectacled Ivy League intellectual." He had attended Yale, then studied in Berlin and Paris and was a resident scholar for the Geneva Research Center, a derivative of the Rockefeller Foundation. Multilingual, he spoke French fluently and was an authority on French politics.

Still, noted Cloud and Olson, "He had a pedantic manner—he used words like *expatiate* and *prognosticate* in his broadcasts—and a soft, high-pitched voice that [CBS news director Paul] White considered unmanly." In fact, White never quit trying to persuade Murrow to fire him. Grandin's intellect and appreciation of France far outweighed anything negative from Murrow's perspective in a time that storm clouds were gathering over Europe. He was satisfied to have him on the team.

Before long Murrow hired his first "true disciple," Eric Sevareid, to run the operations of the Paris bureau with Grandin becoming his associate. Sevareid, 26, was married, broke and holding down two jobs paying him a combined $50 weekly: reporter and editor of *The Paris Herald* in the day and copy editor for United Press at night. While he was terrified of the microphone and did a miserable job with his live audition, Murrow still saw tremendous potential in him (he was, after all, a trained journalist) and he effectively put him in charge of Paris reporting.

Grandin developed and was given several assignments away from Paris. Meanwhile, he fell in love with a Rumanian state radio broadcaster who spoke no English, Natalia Parligras, and married her in February 1940. As war seemed imminent, Sevareid and Grandin determined to get their wives and Sevareid's newly born twins out of the country and bound for America. For his part, Grandin planned to take Natalia, who was pregnant by then, to Bordeaux and place her aboard the S.S. *Washington* for the U.S.

He did so in June 1940, telling Sevareid he would return once she was aboard ship. When he discovered that she—without benefit of American passport—would be denied entry into the U.S. without an accompanying spouse, he phoned Sevareid to tell him he was going, too. Several people, including Janet Murrow (Ed's spouse), Murrow Boy William L. Shirer and Paul White, indicated they thought Grandin took the easy way out of a difficult situation. "Murrow didn't agree," said Cloud and Olson. His departure seemed "entirely justifiable under the circumstances," Murrow allowed. He later nominated Grandin for the post of assistant editor of the FCC's foreign-broadcast monitoring service in Washington in 1941, a job he won. "I cannot find words to express my deep appreciation of your kind and straightforward words in my behalf," Grandin wrote Murrow.

Grandin was subsequently placed in charge of confidential government missions to Algeria, Egypt, England, India, Italy, Tunisia and Turkey. The newly formed American Broadcasting Co. (ABC) hired him in 1944. On D-Day, June 6, he reported from Omaha Beach. He left ABC when the war ended to become a sales executive and eventually an Arizona rancher. In 1948, meanwhile, Murrow—back in New York—received a telegram from Grandin: "Your broadcasts are so extremely valuable I cannot resist again telling you I think so."

GRANT, PETER (born Melvin Maginn). Series: *Avalon Time* (1939); *Famous Jury Trials* (1936–); *Front Page Parade* (1939, 1946–1947).

Peter Grant earned a law degree in 1932 and readily ditched the courtroom for the studio, preferring to be a full time announcer at Cincinnati's WLW, after arriving from St. Louis. He rose to chief announcer in 1937, interrupting his support in 1942 when Uncle Sam called him into the Army. Grant had been presiding for several years over the popular late-night WLW feature *Moon River*. Interspersed with that duty were newscasts and other feature assignments as well as announcements between programs. By 1955 Grant was a regular contributor to WLW's popular news feature *World Now*.

In 1938 Grant experienced an unusual predicament resulting from inflections in his voice. Some listeners believed his intonation paralleled that of President Franklin D. Roosevelt. Although Grant assured critics he wasn't deliberately attempting to mimic the chief executive, station officials nevertheless decided to remove him from a network feature. One of Grant's defenders was an unlikely source—comic Red Skelton, whose *Avalon Time* NBC show Grant worked as announcer, broadcasting from the WLW studios weekly. The comedian admonished: "You can't take a man's livelihood away from him just because he sounds like the President." Grant modified his delivery and continued on the series.

For the record, in 1939 it was determined that—while a typical announcer could read 2,200 words per quarter-hour—Peter Grant, on Mutual's *Front Page Parade*, was spouting out 2,600 words in the same time frame!

GRANT, TAYLOR (born Grant T. Cushmore). b. Feb. 8, 1913, Philadelphia, Pa.; d. Feb. 24, 1998, Glenside, Pa. *Newscaster*. Series: *Headline Edition* (newscaster, 1945–1955).

Taylor Grant was a newscaster and sometimes sportscaster at Philadelphia's WCAU (1938–1945) before going on ABC with a weeknight quarter-hour newscast. He was also heard Sunday nights on the network during part of that era (1952–1954). Meanwhile, ABC-TV evening news had been spotty since originating in 1948 as it attempted to lure affiliates to carry it and viewers to watch it with a myriad of formats and monikers. In the fall of 1953, a renewed effort began with a Monday-through-Friday quarter-hour anchored four nights weekly by John Daly and on Tuesdays by Taylor Grant. The experiment lasted through the 1953–1954 TV season, after which Daly—then vice president for news, special events and public affairs for the chain—persisted alone at the anchor desk for the duration of the 1950s.

With Grant's passing, his son-in-law acknowledged: "From the 1940s to the early 1970s, he worked in sports announcing, television, and radio broadcasting.... Taylor was a champion of civil rights and a die-hard liberal. My kind of man."

GRAUER, BENNETT. b. June 2, 1908, Staten Island, N.Y.; d. May 31, 1977, New York, N.Y. *Announcer, Newscaster, Emcee*. Series: *America's Town Meeting of the Air* (ca. 1940s); *American Portraits* (1951); *Atlantic Spotlight* (host, 1944–1946); *The Baker's Broadcast* (ca. 1935–1937); *The Battle of the Sexes* (1938–1944); *Behind the Mike* (host, ca. 1941–1942); *Believe It or Not* (1937–ca. 1938); *Blackstone Plantation*, aka *The Frank Crummit and Julia Sanderson Show* (1931–1933); *The Boston Pops Orchestra* (1949–1951, 1954–1957); *The Chesterfield Supper Club* (1947–1948); *Circus Days* (1933–1934); *Columbia Presents Corwin* (actor, 1940s); *Eleanor Roosevelt* (1940); *Grand Central Station* (ca. 1937–1938, ca. 1940–1942); *The Henry Morgan Show* (1949–1950); *Home is What You Make It* (host, 1945–1948); *Information Please* (1943–1946); *Kay Kyser's Kollege of Musical Knowledge* (ca. 1940s); *Living 1948, 1949, 1950, 1951* (host, 1948–1951); *Love Notes* (1945); *The Magic Key* (1935–1939); *Meet the Press* (ca. mid to late 1940s); *The Metropolitan Opera Auditions on the Air*; *Mr. and Mrs. North* (early 1940s); *Mr. District Attorney* (ca. 1940s); *Mr. Keen, Tracer of Lost Persons* (1937–1940); *Monitor* (co-communicator, 1955, 1957–1960); *Name the Place* (master of ceremonies, 1939); *NBC News* (newscaster, 1940–1948); *The NBC Symphony Orchestra* (1942–1954); *Pot o' Gold* (master of ceremonies, 1939–ca. 1940); *Richfield Country Club* (1933); *Salute to Youth* (1943–1944); *Senor Ben* (disc jockey, 1954); *The Sealtest Sunday Night Party*; *Service with a Smile*, aka *Army Camp Program*, aka *The Army Show* (1941–1942); *Sleep No More* (1952–1957); *The Studebaker Champions* (ca. late 1930s); *True Story Time* (1939); *Twenty Thousand Years in Sing Sing*, aka *Behind Prison Bars*, aka *Criminal Case Histories* (late 1930s); *Vacation Serenade* (1943, 1944); *Vox Pop* (ca. 1935–ca. late 1930s or early 1940s); *Walter Winchell's Journal*, aka *The Jergens Journal* (1932–1939); *What Would You Have Done?* (master of ceremonies, 1940); *Your Hit Parade* (1935–1937); *Yvette Sings* (1940).

Ben Grauer's professional career began at age eight after a motion picture agent invited dancing school pupils to take part in a movie production. For several years, in fact, he worked as a film extra before going into broadcasting, appearing as a youngster in five motion pictures: *The Mad Woman* (1919); *His Woman* (1919); *The Idol Dancer* (1920); *Annabel Lee* (1921); and *My Friend the Devil* (1922). Following high school Grauer attended New York's City College where he was dramatic critic of the school newspaper and editor-in-chief of the literary magazine. On the stage he played juvenile roles in *Betty at Bay, Maytime, Processional* and revivals of *Floradora* and *The Blue Bird*.

In a 1930 competition with some 200 entrants, Grauer won the Sandham Prize for Extemporaneous Speaking. And after performing in some dramatic programs for NBC, he signed with the chimes chain in October 1930 as a staff announcer. According to a pundit, due to the cosmic proliferation of aural features on which he appeared, Grauer "became as much an aural identification mark for NBC as the roar of Leo the Lion for MGM." The documentation above, for instance, places him in no fewer than 46 ongoing radio series, surely a near record volume.

In a short while Grauer—who devoted several years to announcing journalist Walter Winchell's newscasts—planted the idea that Winchell should sign off his weekly visits that were sponsored by Jergens body creams "with lotions of love." Grauer was one of a quartet of NBC announcers dispatched to the 1936 political conventions to provide live coverage for his web. He broadcast an eyewitness account of the maiden flight of the dirigible *Akron*, called horse races from Aquaduct Park, reported from the initial United Nations Conference gathering in San Francisco and surveyed a New Year's Eve celebration in teeming Times Square.

He was also present when television was ushered in during the 1939 World's Fair in New York City. By 1944 he was certified by the National Academy of Vocal Arts as possessing "the most authoritative [voice] in the world." The group labeled him NBC's "best announcer" at the time.

Returning to the silver screen at the pinnacle of his radio career, Grauer was a narrator for a trio of celluloid features: *Gaslight Follies* (1945); *Fight of the Wild Stallions* (1947); and *Kon-Tiki* (1950).

Moving to NBC Television, Grauer hosted the documentary series *Eye Witness* in 1947–1948; moderated the history-oriented panel show *Americana* in 1948–1949; announced *Kay Kyser's Kollege of Musical Knowledge*, a carryover from radio, in 1949–1950; was master of ceremonies for the game show *Say It with Acting* in 1949–1950 and 1951–1952 (the latter season on ABC-TV); interviewed authors on *The Ben Grauer Show* in 1950, which a critic branded as "nothing more than an extended commercial for its sponsor" (book publisher Doubleday); announced the *Lewisohn Stadium Concert* featuring the New York Philharmonic Symphony from a Manhattan venue in weekly summer outings in 1950; presided over the daytime panel show *It's a Problem*, aka *What's Your Problem?* in 1951–1952; moderated the fleeting game show *What Happened* in the summer of 1952; and narrated the *Big Story* drama anthology from 1955 to 1957. Grauer also reported for ABC-TV's *The March of Medicine* documentary during four weeks in the summer of 1958. In 1960 he narrated a TV mini series, *The Sacco-Vanzetti Story*.

Retiring from Radio City in 1974, Grauer continued on radio's *Voice of America* and persisted a while longer elsewhere by providing voiceovers for radio and television commercials.

GRAY, BARRY (born Bernard Yaroslaw).

b. July 2, 1916, Red Lion, N.J.; d. Dec. 21, 1996, Manhattan, New York, N.Y. *Emcee, Announcer.* **Series:** *Author Meets the Critics* (moderator, 1946–1947); *Barry Gray on Broadway* (moderator, 1945–ca. 1947); *Scout about Town* (host, 1947); *Uncle Don* (ca. 1940s).

In the late 1930s—when he was in his early twenties—Barry Gray served in the Depression-era Civilian Concentration Corps (CCC). Afterward, on the West Coast, he entered radio, hosting live remote broadcasts from supermarket openings. His career was placed on hold for a while as he served in the U.S. Army during the Second World War. Radio historiographer Luther Sies picks up Gray's adventures following his return from combat:

"When Gray first came to New York [WOR, 1945–1947], he conducted a late night DJ show at WOR but he soon turned it into a 'talk' show. After going to Florida and working for a few years at Miami Beach's WKAT [1947–1950], he returned to WMCA [New York City, 1951] to broadcast a talk show from Chandler's Restaurant in Manhattan. At Chandler's, he interviewed the stars including Grace Kelly, Kay Armen, Phil Foster, Irving Berlin, Milton Berle and Danny Thomas. While there he became embroiled in a feud with [print and electronic journalist] Walter Winchell as the result of Winchell's alleged bad treatment of Josephine Baker at the Stork Club. As a result of the argument with Winchell, Gray maintained that he lost many of the stars who had previously come by to talk with him on his program from Chandler's. After Chandler's, he broadcast for WMCA from such clubs and restaurants as Bob Olin's, the Town and Country Club and the Seville Hotel in Miami Beach. Gray's long broadcasting career, primarily on New York local radio, extended until shortly before his death in 1996. His quick mind, resonant voice and interviewing skills made him a skillful pioneer in talk radio programming. Only Long John Nebel did more to develop talk radio."

A critic said Gray "turned his program [at WOR] into radio's first talk show," a statement that could be challenged, although it appears Gray was a pioneer in the field. Later in his career he hosted the game show *Winner Take All* on CBS-TV and was a panelist on *Songs for Sale* on the same network, both shows airing in 1952.

GREENE, LORNE. b. Feb. 12, 1915, Ottawa, Ontario, Canada; d. Sept. 11, 1987, Santa Monica, Calif. *Narrator.* **Series:** *The Sears Radio Theater,* aka *The Mutual Radio Theater* (host, 1979–1981).

Lorne Greene, one of early television's most acclaimed thespians—remembered as the three-time widower Ben Cartwright in NBC's durable frontier drama *Bonanza* (1959–1973)—was also one of radio's last dramatic series hosts. During an attempt to return drama to the aural airwaves at the end of the 1970s, a quintet of entertainment legends introduced an anthology of narratives offered by CBS Radio as *The Sears Radio Theater.* A year beyond, those plays were reprised under the moniker *The Mutual Radio Theater.*

Joining Greene—Monday's narrator on western night—were Andy Griffith on comedy night (Tuesday), Vincent Price on mystery night (Wednesday), Cicely Tyson on drama night (Thursday) and Richard Widmark on adventure night (Friday). The attempt to revive radio as a form of mainstream amusement ultimately failed; it made little difference to listeners that—in addition to such revered hosts—the programs included writing, direction and production by stalwarts like Norman Corwin and Arch Oboler. About all the endeavor accomplished, according to a critic, was "proving the sad fact that radio's day in the sun was over."

While Greene enrolled at Queens University, Kingston, Ontario, to study chemical engineering, a romance with the theater overtook him. He tested those waters when a French teacher assigned him a part in a high school play and he was smitten with it for the rest of his life. Greene produced, acted and directed productions of his college's Drama Guild (1932–1937). Subsequently, he won a fellowship to the Neighborhood Playhouse School of the Theater in New York City. Returning home in 1939, he was hired by the Canadian Broadcasting Corp. and eventually branded "The Voice of Canada" after reading the news on the air every weeknight. (His broadcasts were even aired in movie theaters, similar to *Amos 'n' Andy's* early experiences in *this* country!) Greene also appeared in many radio plays.

Following service in the Royal Canadian Air Force during the Second World War, he went home to launch an Academy of Radio Arts in Toronto. After a few years he assisted in creating and marketing to radio announcers a stopwatch that ran backwards. It helped them gauge the time still available to them. While on a promotional trip to New York City in 1953, he was cast in a live CBS-TV *Studio One* adaptation of George Orwell's *1984*. The focus of Greene's professional life was set in a new direction thereafter. Over a longstanding career he appeared in 87 films screened in theaters and on television. In addition to his durable performance as "Hoss" Cartwright on *Bonanza*, Greene turned up in another 64 television guest appearances in continuing dramatic features, including several miniseries.

GRIFFIS, WILLIAM. b. ca. 1916; d. April 13, 1998, Chapel Hill, N.C. *Actor, Announcer.* **Series:** *Adventure Theater* (actor, 1977–1978); *The Adventures of Father Brown* (actor, 1945); *Archie Andrews* (actor, 1943–1953); *Believe It or Not* (1947–1948); *Chick Carter, Boy Detective* (actor, 1943–1945); *The CBS Radio Mystery Theater* (actor, ca. 1974–ca. 1982); *Crime and Peter Chambers* (actor, 1954); *Dimension X* (actor, 1950–1951); *Dr. Sixgun* (actor, 1954–1955); *Fantasies from Lights Out* (actor, 1945); *The Marriage* (actor, 1953–1954); *Road of Life* (actor, ca. 1940s, 1950s); *Roger Kilgore, Public Defender* (actor, 1948); *X-Minus One* (actor, 1955–1958).

Bill Griffis was the clerk in the CBS-TV courtroom anthology *The Witness*, screened for four months in primetime during the 1960–1961 season. From 1977 to 1981 and again in 1983 Griffis appeared as Harlan Tucker in the ABC-TV daytime serial *All My Children*. Although only three episodes of ABC-TV's *Once a Hero* aired in the fall of 1987, Griffis was cast as Gent in the ill-fated drama.

GRIFFITH, ANDREW SAMUEL. b. June 1, 1926, Mount Airy, N.C. *Narrator.* **Series:** *The Sears Radio Theater*, aka *The Mutual Radio Theater* (host, 1979–1981).

Andy Griffith was one of radio's final dramatic series hosts, presiding on Tuesday comedy nights on CBS's attempt to return narrative fiction to the air via *The Sears Radio Theater*. Alongside Griffith was a quartet of luminaries who introduced specific themes on other nights each week: Lorne Greene, Monday, western; Vincent Price, Wednesday, mystery; Cicely Tyson, Thursday, drama; Richard Widmark, Friday, adventure. It was an interesting experiment but regrettably never attracted the numbers required to make it a prevailing success. The dramas persisted in a second and partial third season under the banner *The Mutual Radio Theater*.

Griffith is best known for headlining a couple of popular television series: *The Andy Griffith Show* (1960–1968, CBS) in which he played mythical Mayberry, N.C. sheriff Andy Taylor, and *Matlock* (1986–1992, NBC; 1992–1995, ABC) in which he played Atlanta criminal defense attorney Ben Matlock. Griffith acknowledged that the latter role was his personal favorite. Both series continue in reruns on cablevision somewhere in the world virtually every day. Griffith was also executive producer of—but did not appear in—*Mayberry, R.F.D.*, a subsequent CBS-TV series (1968–1971). He formed his own movie and television production company in 1972.

He began his life in entertainment as a good ol' down-home boy, appearing before audiences as a standup comedian, becoming famous through recordings of his humorous conversational-style presentations. Griffith's topics (in the early 1950s) included *What It Was Was Football, Make Yourself Comfortable* and *Romeo and Juliet*. He acquired a music degree from the University of North Carolina and, in 1950, became a recurring artist on a couple of premier CBS-TV variety series, *The Steve Allen Show* and *Toast of the Town*, aka *The Ed Sullivan Show*. In recent years he recorded several albums of hymns and spiritual tunes.

GRIFFITH, LESTER LEE. b. March 1, 1906, Illinois; d. Nov. 20, 1991, New York, N.Y. *Announcer.* **Series:** *Candid Microphone* (ca. 1947–1948, ca. 1950); *Cavalcade of Music* (1951, 1952); *Champion Roll Call* (1947); *Cliché Club* (1950); *Crossword Quiz* (1947); *Dan Harding's Wife* (1936–ca. 1938); *Gangbusters* (ca. 1935, 1940s); *Girl Alone* (ca. 1935–ca. 1941); *Grandma Travels* (1944); *Hannibal Cobb* (1950–1951); *Melody Promenade*, aka *Ralph*

Norman and His Orchestra (ca. 1949–1950); *The Story of Mary Marlin* (ca. late 1930s, early 1940s); *There Was a Woman* (1937–1938); *The Tom Mix Ralston Straight Shooters* (ca. 1930s, 1940s); *Young Hickory* (1936–1937).

In 1935 Les Griffith made the big leap from WOOD, Grand Rapids, Mich., to NBC at Radio City in New York. In 1943 he joined ABC, his employer for three decades, lasting to 1973.

GRIMES, TAMMY. b. Jan. 30, 1934, Lynn, Mass. *Narrator.* **Series:** *The CBS Radio Mystery Theater* (hostess, 1982).

Tammy Grimes took over the hosting role on CBS's—and commercial network radio's—final major dramatic anthology, *The CBS Radio Mystery Theater*, after the debuting voice, E.G. Marshall, departed just before the long-running series ran out of gas. Grimes studied acting at New York City's esteemed Neighborhood Playhouse and bowed on the New York stage in *Jonah and the Whale* (May 1955). The following year she not only performed in an off-Broadway production of *The Littlest Revue* but also wed Canadian thespian Christopher Plummer (destined to become the male lead opposite Julie Andrews in *The Sound of Music* a few years later, although by then he and Grimes were divorced). They are parents of prolific film actress Amanda Plummer.

Grimes appeared in 27 films in theaters and on television and—for four weeks in 1966—starred in the ABC-TV sitcom *The Tammy Grimes Show*. Furthermore, she made 40 guest appearances in various television dramatic and variety series and performed in still more Broadway productions.

GUNN, GEORGE. *Announcer.* **Series:** *America's Town Meeting of the Air* (late 1940s); *Dick Tracy* (mid to late 1940s); *Ladies Be Seated* (ca. late 1940s–1950); *Starring Boris Karloff*, aka *Presenting Boris Karloff* (1949); *Wake Up America* (1942–ca. 1943).

In 1939–1940 George Gunn was a sportscaster for a couple of Washington, D.C., stations—WMAL and WRC. In 1942 he transferred from those outlets to the NBC Blue chain in New York.

GUNTHER, JOHN JOSEPH. b. Aug. 30, 1901, Chicago, Ill.; d. May 29, 1970, New York, N.Y. *Correspondent, Commentator.* **Series:** *John Gunther Comments* (commentator, 1941, 1943–1944); *NBC News* (correspondent, 1939–1945).

John Gunther showed promise when, at 12, he prepared a compendium for children in the form of an encyclopedia. It was the first of many works in print. When he grew up he reported for *The Chicago Daily News*, including a stint in Vienna in 1930. He left print journalism later in that decade and joined NBC Radio, assigned to London in the summer of 1939, where he covered preparations for war and the outbreak of the hostilities. Gunther was a NBC war correspondent until 1941, in fact. From 1942 to 1944, he was a correspondent for the U.S. War Department.

He turned up often as a guest on the *Information Please* panel show from the late 1930s through the 1940s. An oft-told tale from the program recalls when Gunther correctly identified the Shah of Iran as Reza Pahlavi. "Are you shah?" moderator Clifton Fadiman quipped. "Sultanly," retorted Gunther.

From 1959 to 1960 he presided over ABC-TV's weekly primetime half-hour travelogue *John Gunther's High Road*. Yet he is probably best recalled for writing a series of *Inside* volumes from the 1930s to the 1960s published by Harper & Brothers (*Inside Africa, Asia, Australia and New Zealand, Europe, Latin America, Russia, Twelve Cities* and *the United States of America*, each a separate title). In total, Gunter produced several dozen fiction and non-fiction works, many of them travelogues, character studies and political commentaries, making him one of the most frequently published of the ex-radio newsmen.

Included among his works were these (not a complete list): *The Red Pavilion* (Harper, 1926); *D-Day* (Avon, 1944); *The Troubled Midnight* (1945, Harper); *Behind the Curtain* (Harper, 1949); *Roosevelt in Retrospect: A Profile in History* (Harper, 1950); *The Riddle of MacArthur: Japan, Korea and the Far East* (Harper, 1951); *Eisenhower: The Man and the Symbol* (Harper, 1952); *Alexander the Great* (Random House, 1953); *Julius Caesar* (Random House, 1953, coauthored with Joseph Cellini); *Days to Remember: America 1945–1955* (Harper, 1956, coauthored with

Bernard Quint); *Meet North Africa* (Harper, 1957, with Sam and Beryl Epstein); *Meet South Africa* (Harper, 1958); *The Golden Fleece* (Harper, 1959); *Meet the Congo and Its Neighbors* (Harper, 1959); *Taken at the Flood: The Story of Albert D. Lasker* (Harper, 1960); *A Fragment of Autobiography: The Fun of Writing the Inside Books* (Harper, 1962); *Death Be Not Proud: A Memoir* (Pyramid, 1964; re-released by HarperCollins, 1998); *The Lost City, a Novel* (Harper, 1964); *Meet Soviet Russia: Leaders, Politics, Problems* (Harper, 1964); *Procession: Dominant Personalities of Four Decades as Seen by the Author of the Inside Books* (Harper, 1965); *Chicago Revisited* (University of Chicago Press, 1967); *The Indian Sign, a Novel* (Harper, 1970); *Quatrain, a Novel* (Hamilton, 1970); *Paul: Messenger and Exile, a Study in the Chronology of His Life and Letters* (Judson, 1972); *St. Paul's Opponents and Their Background: A Study of Apocalyptic and Jewish Sectarian Teachings* (Brill, 1973).

GWINN, BILL. Series: *What's the Name of That Song?* (quizmaster, 1948).

Bill Gwinn was master of ceremonies of an ABC-TV audience participation series that underwent three name changes in its short life (1951–1952), with titles in this order: *It Could Be You*; *This Could Be You*; *The Bill Gwinn Show*; *This Is My Song*. Briefly, in 1959 Gwinn was the presiding judge on the ABC-TV primetime series *Accused*. For a short while he found similar work as a "regular" in the cast of the ABC-TV daytime dramatic anthology *Day in Court*, aka *Morning Court* (1960–1961).

HALE, ARTHUR. b. Aug. 21, 1916, Connecticut; d. November 1978, Hartford, Conn. *Announcer, Commentator, Newscaster.* **Series:** *Calling America*, aka *Listen, America* (1939–1940); *Confidentially Yours* (commentator, 1939–1947); *Uncle Don* (ca. 1930s); *Your Richfield Reporter* (newscaster, 1945–?).

By the early 1930s, Arthur Hale was associated with the announcing staff of New York's WOR, one of the founding stones of the soon-to-be-established MBS chain. Hale was also a newscaster for the station. For nearly a decade some of his news and analysis features were aired nationally. Before going to New York, Hale was affiliated with WICC in Bridgeport, Conn.

HALL, RADCLIFFE. b. Sept. 2, 1914, New York, N.Y.; d. March 11, 1997, Nyack, N.Y. *Announcer, Newscaster.* **Series:** *Dough Re Mi* (1942); *Hildegarde* (ca. 1944–ca. 1945); *NBC News* (newscaster, 1945–?).

Radcliffe Hall emanated to NBC in New York from Schenectady's WGY where he was a sportscaster in 1939.

HAMILTON, GENE. b. Dec. 12, 1910, Toledo, Ohio; d. Nov. 22, 2000, Nassau, N.Y. *Announcer, Emcee.* **Series:** *The Armour Hour* (ca. 1931); *The Art of Living*, aka *Dr. Norman Vincent Peale* (1955); *Biography in Sound* (narrator, 1955); *The Boston Pops Orchestra* (1947); *Carnegie Hall* (1948–1950); *The Chamber Music Society of Lower Basin Street* (host, 1940–1942, 1950); *Clara, Lu and Em* (ca. early to mid 1930s); *Classical Music for People Who Hate Classical Music* (host, 1957–1958); *Concert Time* (ca. late 1940s); *Dr. Gino's Musicale* (host, 1951–1952, 1953–1954); *The First Nighter* (ca. 1930–ca. late 1930s); *The First Piano Quartet* (1941–1942, 1944–1945, 1946, 1947–1948, 1950–1953); *General Motors Concert* (1935–1937); *The Guiding Light* (public service announcement spokesman, 1944); *Kaltenborn Edits the News* (1940–1955); *Lum and Abner* (ca. mid to late 1930s); *Monitor* (segment co-host, 1955); *Morning News Roundup* (ca. 1941); *The Music Appreciation Hour* (1930s–ca. 1942); *NBC Summer Symphony* (1953); *NBC Symphony Orchestra* (late 1930s, early 1940s); *News of the World* (1968–1969); *Paul Whiteman Orchestra* (1930s); *Professor Quiz* (ca. 1946–1948); *Promenade Concerts*; *The Radio Hall of Fame* (interviewer, 1945); *The Sammy Kaye Show* (1938–1940, 1941–1943, 1944–1952, 1953–1956); *String Symphony* (ca. mid 1930s–ca. 1941); *The Voice of Firestone* (1938–1942); *What's the Score?* (1952).

The son of a concert baritone, Gene Hamilton acquired an early interest in music naturally. He toured the country extensively as a dancer and guitar-strumming member of a vaudeville flash act. For a little while, until 1929, he was a vocalist and guitarist at WAIU, Columbus, Ohio. That year he moved to Cleveland's WTAM, joining NBC there as an announcer and master of ceremonies. By 1931 he was working on several network features out of Chicago's Merchandise Mart. He moved to Radio City in New York in 1933.

Meanwhile, Hamilton studied voice and seriously debated the merits of dual careers—as a radio announcer and a vocalist. He won an audition as a basso for the Fred Waring Glee Club but ultimately decided to concentrate on announcing altogether. A pact negotiated by the American Federation of Television and Radio Artists assured him and a few other professionals of lifetime employment at NBC. After 46 years with the chain, Hamilton retired in 1975.

HANCOCK, DON. b. Oct. 10, 1910, Illinois; d. May 6, 1980, Anderson, Ind. *Announcer, Newscaster.* **Series:** *The Adventures of Ellery Queen* (1945–1947); *Believe It or Not* (1940s); *CBS News* (newscaster, ca. early to mid 1940s); *The Children's Hour* (1930s, ca. 1940s); *Front Page Farrell*; *The Goldbergs* (1940–?); *The Golden Theater Group* (1939); *The Gracie Fields Show* (ca. 1940s); *Grand Central Station* (ca. 1940s); *The Harvest of Stars* (1948–1949); *A Helping Hand* (1941–1942); *The Jack Smith Show* (ca. 1945–ca. 1952); *Just Entertainment* (1938, ca. 1945); *Lawyer Tucker* (1947); *Life Can Be Beautiful* (1940s, ca. early 1950s); *Major Bowes and His Original Amateur Hour* (ca. late 1940s, early 1950s); *Music Box Theater* (1936); *Poetic Melodies* (1936–1938); *The Romance of Helen Trent* (1933–?); *The Shadow* (1944–1947); *Stepmother* (1938–1940); *Stop the Music!* (1948–1952).

In 1949 Don Hancock announced a daytime Monday-through-Friday local feature over New York's WJZ, *Old Gold Party Time.* It was a variety quarter-hour hosted by Bert Parks and proffered the music of the Buddy Weed Trio and vocalist Kay Armen.

As radio began to slide, Hancock became one of daytime television's early commercial spokesmen, pitching a line of healthcare and household commodities for American Home Products on two commanding early TV soap operas—*Love of Life* (beginning in 1951 and for several years afterward) and *The Secret Storm* (beginning in 1954 and for a few years more). These plugs, often two or three in a single quarter-hour, were all performed live. Late in his career Hancock provided voiceovers for other TV commercials. He was a CBS staff announcer until he retired in the late 1970s. Hancock was subsequently the announcer for summer concerts of the Indiana Symphony in 1977, 1978 and 1979.

HANLON, THOMAS, JR. b. Nov. 7, 1907, Fort Scott City, Kan.; d. Sept. 29, 1970, Hollywood, Calif. *Announcer, Newscaster.* **Series:** *Beulah* (ca. 1946); *CBS News* (newscaster-correspondent, ca. early to mid 1940s); *Escape* (1947–1954); *The Ford Show* (1946–1947); *Gene Autry's Melody Ranch* (1940–ca. 1943); *The Gulf Headliner,* aka *The Phil Baker Show* (1938); *Hallmark Playhouse* (1948–?); *The Hollywood Barn Dance* (1946); *Jane Endicott, Reporter* (1942); *Lux Radio Theater* (commercial spokesman, 1944); *Melodies Organistic* (1947); *Paducah Plantation,* aka *Plantation Party* (ca. 1936–1937); *Red Barber Sports* (1946–?); *The Sweeney and March Show* (1946–ca. 1948); *That's My Pop* (1945); *Theater of Romance* (ca. 1946); *We, the People* (ca. 1944–ca. late 1940s).

When Ken Carpenter left Los Angeles' KFI in 1936 to freelance on Bing Crosby's *Kraft Music Hall,* he was replaced as chief announcer at KFI by Tom Hanlon. Beginning in 1939, Hanlon was to wear many hats at Los Angeles' CBS owned-and-operated station KNX, including those of announcer, disc jockey, newscaster and sportscaster—between his shifts on a handful of locally originated series for the web. After being night manager of KNX, Hanlon's talents were channeled into athletics. He covered major league games in multiple sports for his station and chain.

Hanlon furthermore enjoyed an extensive run in motion picture productions. Between 1926 and 1954 he appeared in 64 mostly B-films, 55 times as an announcer of some persuasion (radio, sports, news, auction, transportation, etc.). Titles among his theatrical appearances included *The Collegians* (1926); *Maybe It's Love* (1930); *Night Alarm* (1934); *The Big Broadcast of 1936* (1935); *Kentucky Moonshine* (1938); *St. Louis Blues* (1939); *Broadway Serenade* (1939); *The Lady's from Kentucky* (1939); *It's a Wonderful World* (1939); *The Heckler* (1940); *Where Did You Get That Girl?* (1941); *Babes on Broadway* (1941); *Pardon My Stripes* (1942); *Follow the Boys* (1944); *The Woman in the Window* (1945); *The Blonde from Brooklyn* (1945); *The Undercover Man* (1949); *It Happens Every Spring* (1949); *Kill the Umpire* (1950); *I'll Get*

By (1950); *Three Husbands* (1951); *The Harlem Globetrotters* (1951); *The Pride of St. Louis* (1952); *White Lightning* (1953); and *The Bob Mathias Story* (1954).

HANNES, ART. b. July 28, 1920, Kentucky; d. March 30, 1992, Los Angeles, Calif. *Announcer.* **Series:** *The CBS Radio Workshop* (1956–ca. 1957); *The Couple Next Door* (ca. 1957–ca. 1960); *Funny Side Up* (ca. 1959); *Gangbusters* (ca. mid 1950s); *Hearthstone of the Death Squad* (1951–1952); *The Show Goes On,* aka *The Robert Q. Lewis Show* (1950); *Sing it Again* (ca. 1948–ca. 1951); *Twenty-First Precinct* (1953–1956); *Whispering Streets* (ca. 1940s, 1950s); *Yours Truly, Johnny Dollar* (ca. 1960–1962).

In 1940 Art Hannes was a newscaster at WHDL, Olean, N.Y. He would later introduce one of early television's most prestigious hour-long dramatic anthologies, CBS's *Studio One,* which aired live from New York each week between 1948 and 1958. He was employed by CBS for two decades, 1947–1967.

HARKNESS, RICHARD C. b. Sept. 29, 1907, Artesian, S.D.; d. Feb. 16, 1977. *Newscaster, Correspondent.* **Series:** *Harkness of Washington* (political analyst, 1949–?); *Monitor* (newscaster, 1955–1972); *NBC News on the Hour* (newscaster, ca. mid 1950s–1972); *NBC News Roundup* (correspondent, 1945–?); *Richard Harkness and the News* (newscaster, 1944–1945, 1947–1953).

Richard C. Harkness was educated at the University of Kansas before accepting reporting assignments for the wire service United Press in Kansas City, Mo. He began chasing fire engines in 1928. Still honing his skills as a journalist a dozen years later, by then he was traipsing the country covering Franklin D. Roosevelt and Wendell Willkie in their respective bids for the presidency. After spending eight years based in UP offices at Oklahoma City, Dallas and Jefferson City, Mo., Harkness was appointed UP's White House correspondent. He left that employer the following year, in 1937, to affiliate with the Washington bureau of *The Philadelphia Inquirer.*

Joining NBC's news staff in Washington in 1942, he launched a news program which aired over both WNBC in New York and WRC in Washington, D.C. For several years in the 1940s, in fact, he provided news series for those two NBC stations that were separate and apart from his ongoing network features. From 1948 to 1953 his NBC evening newscasts—aired twice weekly from 1948 to 1951 and every weeknight thereafter—were underwritten by the Pure Oil Co., whose memorable motto *Be sure ... with Pure!* became integrated into the vernacular of large numbers of habitual listeners.

When Harkness arrived at NBC, a publicist for the network wrote: "His decade reporting and observing the Washington scene has earned for Harkness the reputation of being one of the keenest and most incisive minds among the Capital's younger news veterans." He was to remain with the chain for three decades.

Harkness was given several opportunities in developing television news and public affairs. For a year from early January 1948 to early January 1949 on NBC-TV's *The Richard Harkness Show,* the newsman interviewed important figures in current events. The quarter-hour public affairs entry aired weekly. On seven Sunday afternoons in the summer of 1951 he narrated a half-hour informational series on NBC-TV, *Survival.* Presented by the Federal Civil Defense Administration, it utilized films, graphs and live guest interviews to demonstrate how the public could prepare for and react to an atomic attack. For two months in early 1952—prior to the premier of the *Today* show on NBC-TV—Harkness anchored the web's initial news program to air before five o'clock Eastern Time weekdays. *Richard Harkness News Review* was telecast at 11:45 A.M. for a quarter-hour Monday through Friday in that period. He surfaced sporadically on NBC-TV's successive news series, contributing especially during political campaigns and elections.

Following his retirement from the network in 1972, Harkness became the press representative of a drug abuse venture inaugurated by President Gerald R. Ford (1974–1977).

HARPER, TROMAN. *Commentator.* **Series:** *Troman Harper, Rumor Detective* (1942–1943).

News commentator Troman Harper became MBS's response to CBS's Rex Stout and the popular *Our Secret Weapon* series. In their respective ways, both men exposed enemy-induced lies not only to educate but entertain Americans during the midst of World War II. For his part, Harper emphatically stated that duplicity offered by Axis propaganda machines (tales intercepted by shortwave radio) were "Malarky" and "Horse-feathers." Addressing a vast audience of listeners every Sunday night, he cautioned: "If you believe rumors, you're a sucker; if you repeat rumors, you're one of Hitler's best soldiers. The truth is a banner; with it, you can jab and slice a rumor to ribbons."

HARRICE, CY. b. March 1, 1915, Chicago, Ill. *Announcer.* **Series:** *The Adventures of the Abbotts* (1955); *The Adventures of Sherlock Holmes* (ca. mid 1950s); *The Adventures of the Thin Man* (ca. 1940s, 1950); *The Big Story* (1947–1955); *A Brighter Tomorrow*, aka *The Gabriel Heatter Show*, aka *Behind the Front Page*, aka *Gabriel Heatter Comments* (1946–1948); *Cavalcade of America* (1950–1953); *Crime Cases of Warden Lawes* (1946–1947); *Ethel and Albert* (ca. late 1940s); *Grand Central Station* (ca. 1940s, early 1950s); *The Kaiser Traveler*, aka *The Burl Ives Show* (1949); *National Barn Dance* (commercial spokesman, 1936–ca. 1942); *Quick as a Flash* (ca. late 1940s, early 1950s); *The RCA Victor Show* (1945–1946); *Uncle Ezra* (commercial spokesman, 1936–1939); *Walter Winchell's Journal* (ca. 1950s); *What Makes You Tick?* (1948). **Aphorism:** *And ... they are mild!*

While enrolled at his hometown's Northwestern University in 1936, Cy Harrice became a commercial spokesman for Miles Laboratories and its Alka-Seltzer distress reliever on a couple of WLS-originated network features: the *National Barn Dance* on Saturday nights and *Uncle Ezra* on weeknights. Harrice affiliated full time with WLS in 1940, branching into copywriting, newscasting and programming. Gaining that valuable experience, in 1942 he transferred his loyalty to rival station WGN, becoming the latter's chief on-air newsman. Three years later he departed the Windy City for New York City to become a freelance announcer.

With only a brief time to prepare, he was once pressed into acting opposite Ginger Rogers for a 1950s *Cavalcade of America* broadcast. Harrice later confessed: "Acting wasn't my bent. My specialty was selling over the air." He was the second voice the listeners heard on signature Pall Mall cigarette commercials during radio's heyday, beginning in 1946 and extending into television with a total 24-year run. The first voice—usually belonging to announcer Ernest Chappell—finished the recurring sales pitch with: *Outstanding!* Cy Harris added a rich, resonant baritone, immediately following Chappell with: *And ... they are mild!* Harrice was identified with several other major broadcasting underwriters for lengthy periods, too, including E.I. Dupont, General Motors and Procter & Gamble. After radio's golden age passed, Harrice syndicated a half-minute series to local stations titled *What's the Good Word?*

HARSCH, JOSEPH CLOSE. b. May 25, 1905, Toledo, Ohio; d. June 3, 1998, Jamestown, R.I. *Commentator, Correspondent, Newscaster.* **Series:** *CBS World News Roundup* (ca. 1940–1941); *Joseph C. Harsch Commentary* (news analyst, 1943–?, 1955–1956, 1967–1971); *The Meaning of the News* (commentator, 1947–1949); *Nightline* (commentator, 1957–ca. 1959).

Joseph C. Harsch was well educated, having earned bachelor's degrees from Williams College in 1927 and Corpus Christi College at Cambridge University in 1929, plus a master's degree from the former institution still later. He was a *Christian Science Monitor* reporter from 1929 to 1943 who continued to file stories for that paper from wherever he was throughout a lengthy professional career in broadcasting. Harsch (who applied his middle initial on the air) substituted for his colleague and friend, CBS's William L. Shirer, in Germany around 1940–1941. By early 1943 he had so awed CBS's news chief, Paul White, that he was given a five-minute weeknight commentary. An extensively traveled newsman, Harsch was appraised by a critic as offering "consistently intelligent commentary during and after World War II." He aired over CBS's network owned-and-operated affiliate in the nation's capital, WTOP, in the mid 1940s.

Later in that decade Harsch filled weekly CBS network timeslots. By 1950 he and Marquis Childs originated the *Washington Report* in the District of Columbia, a news commentary aired over the Labor-Liberal FM web. Harsch went to NBC for twice-a-week appearances in the mid 1950s. That segued into his being appointed one of a handful of continuing news analysts for NBC's 90-minute sustained weeknight marathon *Nightline* hosted by Walter O'Keefe. His tenure with NBC continued from 1953 to 1967, after which he became an ABC commentator for four years. Harsch returned to *The Christian Science Monitor* from 1971 to 1974 as its chief editorial writer.

Irving Fang recalled a choice morsel drawn from Harsch's journalism career. "He happened to be vacationing in Honolulu on December 7, 1941, the only full-time foreign correspondent in the Hawaiian Islands. Alas, his credentials did him no good: 'By the time I woke up to the fact that there was a war on, they had clamped down on cable and wireless services, and I had to sit there for four days awaiting their release. By that time, there were a hundred or more correspondents there.' To add to Harsch's agony, a local stringer watched the attack from his house overlooking Pearl Harbor and telephoned the news to San Francisco as it was happening."

The print and electronic journalist penned several volumes, including *Pattern of Conquest* (Doubleday, 1941); *The Curtain Isn't Iron* (Doubleday, 1950); and *At the Hinge of History: A Reporter's Story* (University of Georgia Press, 1993).

HARTZELL, CLARENCE L. b. Oct. 26, 1910, Huntington, W. Va.; d. March 5, 1988, Bella Vista, Ark. *Actor, Announcer.* **Series:** *Author's Playhouse* (actor, 1941–1945); *Doc, Duke and the Colonel* (actor, 1945); *In Care of Aggie Horn* (actor, 1941–1942); *Li'l Abner* (actor, 1939–1940); *Lum and Abner* (actor, 1946–1950); *One Man's Family* (actor, ca. 1940s, 1950s); *The Road to Danger* (actor, 1942–1945); *Secret City* (1941–1942); *The Silver Eagle,* aka *Silver Eagle, Mountie* (actor, 1951–1955); *Those Websters* (actor, 1945–1948); *Today's Children* (actor, ca. 1930s, 1940s); *Uncle Ezra* (actor, 1930s, ca. 1940–1941); *Vic and Sade* (actor, ca. 1930s–1946); *Waterloo Junction* (actor, 1939).

Clarence Hartzell's sole appearance as a radio announcer occurred on the single-season Blue network crime drama *Secret City* with Bill Idelson playing private detective Ben Clark. A few years later, from 1949 to 1951, Hartzell was *Cactus Jim* in the weekday juvenile series by that name on NBC-TV. He played in the NBC-TV sitcom *Those Endearing Young Charms* in 1951–1952. Following his broadcast exposure, Hartzell and his spouse moved to Arkansas where they operated an antique sales emporium.

HARVEY, PAUL (born Paul Harvey Aurandt). b. Sept. 4, 1918, Tulsa, Okla. *Newscaster, Commentator.* **Series:** *Paul Harvey News and Comments* (commentator, 1950–present); *The Rest of the Story* (narrator, ca. 1970s–present).

At 14 Paul Harvey became a jack-of-all-trades at hometown station KVOO in Tulsa. He was cited early for his linguistic capacity, recognized as a brilliant orator in high school. He was permitted to regularly step out onto the ether at KVOO, making announcements and delivering news reports. "When he gave the local station break after each network show," a pundit remarked, "he imitated the announcer he had just heard." While enrolled at the University of Tulsa, Harvey became a staff announcer at the station. His career advanced to other outlets at Salina, Kan., Abilene, Texas, Oklahoma City and St. Louis, where he increasingly gained more and more responsibility. At varying times he was a newscaster, special events director and station manager. While serving as program director at WKZO, Kalamazoo, Mich. (1941–1943), Harvey went into the U.S. Army. His civilian career resumed the next year (1944) at Chicago's WENR where his twice-daily quarter-hour news commentaries reached the pinnacle of local ratings. By 1948 he also presided over a weekday evening quarter-hour at WGN, *Speak Your Mind*, on which listeners voiced their opinions—a precursor to contemporary talk radio.

Harvey eventually beamed his news programs to 600 radio stations and 18 million listeners via the ABC chain. A media critic observed: "He delivered a provocative and entertaining tabloid newspaper of the air in a style of homespun eloquence." Said another: "Paul Harvey is corny but fascinating, especially in small doses." Ultimately adding a third program to his weekday mix, Harvey stretched his good fortune and resulting notoriety into books, magazine articles, public speaking circuits, a tri-weekly newspaper column, recordings and television. In 1952–1953 ABC-TV carried a quarter-hour *Paul Harvey News* every Sunday night.

Assessing Harvey's enduring tenure, a radio historiographer pontificated: "Despite his stylized delivery, he never achieved the dramatic impact produced by the timing of Edward R. Murrow. Harvey is best known for his bland humor, human interest stories and brief commentaries with a conservative bent." Another historian pointed out the "unmistakable touches of [sportscaster] Bill Stern" that are obvious in Harvey's style: long pauses, repetition and hyped emphasis—"to lift ordinary events out of the ordinary." Although he is frequently supplanted by visiting commentators, in autumn 2006— more than 55 years after he began addressing a nationwide audience—Harvey was still at it, an unprecedented record for any national radio newscaster and one not likely to be repeated.

HASKELL, JACK. b. ca. 1920, Akron, Ohio; d. Sept. 26, 1998, Englewood, N.J. *Vocalist, Announcer.* **Series:** *Bits of Hits* (vocalist, 1940s); *The Dave Garroway Show*, aka *Reserved for Garroway*, aka *Dial Dave Garroway*, aka *Next, Dave Garroway* (vocalist, 1947, 1949–1951); *Design for Listening* (vocalist, 1949); *Fitch Bandwagon* (commercial spokesman, 1940s); *Jack Haskell* (host-vocalist, 1950, 1951); *The Jim Backus Show* (vocalist, 1957–1958); *Les Brown Orchestra* (vocalist, 1940s); *Music from the Heart of America* (vocalist, 1948); *NBC Bandstand* (vocalist, 1957); *Pastels in Rhythm* (vocalist, 1940s); *The Peter Lind Hayes Show* (1954); *Stop the Music!* (vocalist, 1954–1955); *Terkel Time* (vocalist, 1950).

Raised in Cleveland, Ohio, baritone Jack Haskell was a music major at Chicago's Northwestern University and sang on WBBM and WGN and with various bands during his collegiate years. Simultaneously, on Sunday nights he was the shampoo sponsor's advertising envoy on NBC's *Fitch Bandwagon*. Following graduation, he became a vocalist with Doris Day and the Les Brown Orchestra. He interrupted his pursuits in the mid 1940s when called up to be a U.S. Naval flight instructor in the South Pacific, returning to his old stand in 1946. For several years Haskell was closely identified with entertainer Dave Garroway and when the latter left Chicago for New York and expanding television roles, Haskell wasn't far behind. In Gotham he made recordings, appeared in summer stock and in 1962 performed on Broadway in the Irving Berlin musical *Mr. President*. He won parts in Broadway musicals on a recurring basis, in fact.

From 1949 to 1951 Haskell sang on *Garroway at Large* aired live from Chicago on NBC-TV. Haskell was a vocalist on *The Dave Garroway Show* on NBC-TV from New York in 1953–1954 and on *The Jack Paar Show* on CBS-TV weekday afternoons in 1955–1956. In the summer of 1956 he sang on the fleeting daily *Of All Things* variety series on CBS-TV hosted by Faye Emerson. In the summer of 1962 he was a recurring performer on NBC-TV's *The Tonight Show*.

HATOS, STEFAN. b. Aug. 20, 1920, Aurora, Ill.; d. March 2, 1999, Toluca Lake, Calif. *Producer, Writer, Announcer.* **Series:** *Beulah* (producer-director, 1953–1954); *The Curt Massey Show* (producer-director, 1956); *David Harding, Counterspy* (writer, 1941–1942); *David Harum* (writer, 1941–1942); *The Green Hornet* (writer, ca. 1940–1941); *The Hermit's Cave* (writer, ca. 1940–1941); *It Pays to Be Married* (producer-director, 1953–1956); *Ladies Be Seated* (producer-director, ca. 1947–ca. early 1950s); *The Lone Ranger* (1940); *The March of Time* (producer-director-writer, ca. 1940–1941); *Meet Corliss Archer* (producer-director, 1954); NBC staff announcer, WXYZ (ca. 1939–1941); *Nick Carter, Master Detective* (writer, 1941–1942); *Radio Reader's Digest* (producer-director, ca. 1946–1948); *Treasury Agent* (writer, 1941–1942); *The Wayne King Show* (producer-director, 1946–1947); *Welcome Travelers* (producer-director, 1948–1951); *Your Hit Parade* (director, 1947–?).

A first generation American with Hungarian parentage, the multitalented, versatile Stefan Hatos was a well-educated broadcasting pioneer. After graduating from East Aurora (Ill.) High School, he attended Wayne University, the University of Michigan, law school at the latter institution and the U.S. Naval Reserve Midshipman Academy at Columbia University. While in training on music and basketball scholarships, Hatos played oboe and English horn with the Detroit Civic Symphony. He covered the rest of his college expenses playing tenor and bass saxophone at dance band gigs. Majoring at Michigan in creative writing, music, history and philosophy, at 19 he became a $35-a-week announcer at Detroit's WJLB. Three months beyond he joined Motown's WXYZ, an affiliate of the Blue chain, as a staff announcer with network duties.

Throughout an extensive career Hatos was much more quickly drawn to writing and production than performing. While at WXYZ, he was also penning episodes for network epics like *The Lone Ranger* and *The Green Hornet*—both WXYZ originations—and *The Hermit's Cave*, a widely syndicated feature produced by Detroit's WJR. While based in the Motor City, Hatos became a regional stringer producer-director-writer for *The March of Time*, too. He relocated in New York subsequently and briefly—until the U.S. Navy commissioned him for service in the Mediterranean and Pacific Theater (1942–1945)—wrote scripts for several hit dramatic series. In addition, he was a CBS producer-director-writer before and after the war, soon joining Foote, Cone & Belding advertising agency as a radio producer-director. His assignments in the late 1940s covered a handful of popular aural fare.

Hatos was—even then—convinced that television was still two decades away from overtaking radio as America's chief entertainment and information source. The ad agency, however, saw things differently and forced him to direct TV programming starting in 1948. A whole new avenue opened to him in video; he was quickly occupied in creating, producing or directing a plethora of diverse features for the small screen. Included in his vast repertoire were: *The Adventures of Uncle Mistletoe*; *Al Pearce and His Gang*; *The Bob Hope Show*; *Chain Letter*; *Fun for the Money*; *It Could Be You*; *It Pays to Be Ignorant*; *It Pays to Be Married*; *It's Anybody's Guess*; *Let's Make a Deal*; *Masquerade Party*; *Mind Readers*; *Panhandle Pete and Jennifer*; *Split Second*; *There's One in Every Family*; *The Tony Martin Show*; *Three for the Money*; *World Quiz Show*; and *Your First Impression*. Beginning in 1963, an enduring association with Monty Hall, master of ceremonies for *Let's Make a Deal*, led Hatos-Hall to co-create no fewer than nine of the audience-participation shows just named.

HAVRILLA, ALOIS. b. June 7, 1891, Pressov, Czechoslovakia; d. Dec. 7, 1952, Englewood, N.J. *Announcer, Emcee.* **Series:** *The Campbell Soup Orchestra* (1930–1932); *The Chevrolet Program*, aka *The Jack Benny Program* (1933–1934); *The Colgate House Party* (1934–1935); *Double or Nothing* (1940–ca. 1947); *Jack Frost Melody Moments* (1931–ca. 1934); *The Palmolive Hour* (1927–?); *Strange as It Seems* (host, 1939–1940).

At age six, Alois Havrilla and his family immigrated to the United States and settled in a Slovakian commune at Bridgeport, Conn. Within a year the lad's musical aptitude was beginning to be witnessed by others. His alto voice possessed a range of three octaves. John Baker, a vocal coach, tutored him in voice and English, the latter subject in the curriculum of the school in which he was enrolled. As a youth Havrilla took solo parts in church music productions and studied music at New York University. Becoming a professional vocalist, he appeared at many venues, including Carnegie Hall with Percy Grainger in 1923.

According to legend, NBC announcer Graham McNamee was once in the Carnegie Hall audience when Havrilla performed there. So impressed was he with Havrilla's voice clarity that he urged him to audition for radio as an announcer. The rest is history. Others recognized similar qualities in Havrilla. In November 1935 he won the prestigious diction medal given annually by the American Academy of Arts and Letters to "the best radio announcer from the standpoint of pronunciation, articulation, tonal quality, accent and general cultural effect." This—to someone who couldn't speak any English for several of his formative years!

Between 1924 and 1946 Havrilla was on the staffs of a quartet of New York radio stations—WEAF, WJZ, WABC, WOR—as announcer, narrator and commentator. He joined NBC in the year of its formation, 1926, as a baritone soloist and announcer. Between 1928 and 1946 he narrated Pathe newsreels plus a trio of mini-movies—*This is America* (1933), *Paramount Paragraphics: Bits of Life* (1939), *Wings of Courage* (1946)—and a dozen film shorts in a sequential series titled *Stranger Than Fiction*. Havrilla joined WPAT, Paterson, N.J., in 1946 and transferred to Newark's WNJR in 1949, his employer at the time of his death.

On one of his early network features, *Jack Frost Melody Moments*, the ad agency decided that the sales pitches would be downplayed by referring the listeners elsewhere. Therefore, on a typical occasion, Havrilla observed: "Because we feel that we are your hosts, we are not going to talk shop. You will be more interested in the advertising story of Jack Frost packaged sugar as it appears regularly in the newspapers or as your grocer will gladly tell you than if we told it at length here." It was a marketing strategy not readily embraced by other sponsors.

Havrilla's eating and drinking habits were baffling to George Ansbro, his chum and colleague at NBC. Ansbro recalled an amusing anecdote in his memoir: "He [Havrilla] kept a bottle of Scotch in his locker at all times for that moment when he just plain felt like a nip, which I witnessed many times. He was not one who frequented bars or cocktail lounges. To my knowledge he was never seen in Hurley's, the Down Under, or the English Grill, the busiest watering holes in the building, where the NBC crowd congregated. Where he ate lunch or dinner nobody ever knew, and no one ever caught him eating out of a paper bag in our lounge."

HAWLEY, ADELAIDE CUMMING (born Dieta Adelaide Fish). b. March 6, 1905; d. Dec. 21, 1998, Bremerton, Wash. *Consultant (women's issues)*. **Series:** *Adelaide Hawley Show* (consultant, 1939–1946).

Adelaide Hawley offered tips and topics of interest to women during her radio series, but she was destined to become a lot more when television emerged. From 1949 to 1964 she became the embodiment of "Betty Crocker," the corporate advertising mascot which General Mills Inc. applied in personalizing its baking goods. The moniker had been selected in 1921 by a previous manufacturer and another woman initially gave expression to it in 1924 over the *Betty Crocker Cooking School of the Air* on local radio. After Hawley was selected a quarter-of-a-century later, her image appeared not only on television but on billboards, in magazines, newspapers and product literature, on commodity packaging and wherever "Betty Crocker" turned up in visual form.

When General Mills ultimately dropped Hawley for an updated, more sophisticated icon, she proceeded to return to school. In 1967 at the age of 62, she graduated from New York University with a doctorate in speech communication. She had earned a degree in 1926 in piano and voice from the Eastman School at the University of Rochester. Afterward—before getting into radio—she performed with a touring vaudeville trio. She and her first spouse, Mark Hawley, a CBS announcer who was also known as the voice of Pathe newsreels, were charter members of the American Federation of Radio Artists (AFRA), an organization that eventually became the AFTRA after television was recognized by its membership.

In the 1950s General Mills publicists affirmed that Hawley was the nation's "second most recognizable woman, next to Eleanor Roosevelt," following her designation as the infamous Betty Crocker. A television critic, meanwhile, labeled her "the most famous woman created through advertising in the 20th century." Hawley (as Crocker) presided over her own half-hour CBS-TV series, *The Betty Crocker Show* (1950–1951) followed by *The Betty Crocker Star Matinee* on ABC-TV (1951–1952). Neither show was a ratings success. She also regularly appeared in commercial plugs on *Bride and Groom, The George Burns and Gracie Allen Show* and others, where she exhibited a proclivity in the kitchen as she hawked her wares. Hawley considered herself a feminist and took an active leadership role in pursuing issues of interest to and on behalf of her gender. During her later years—until only a few days before her death at 93, in fact—she was teaching English to international students.

HAWLEY, MARK HIRAM. b. Feb. 17, 1910, New York, N.Y.; d. Sept. 5, 1986, San Jacinto, Calif. *Announcer, Newscaster*. **Series:** *CBS News* (newscaster, 1941–1943); *Death Valley Days* (ca. 1930s, 1940s); *Famous Fortunes* (narrator, 1938); *The Fred Allen Show*, under varied monikers (ca. 1930s); *Mr. District Attorney* (ca. 1939–early 1940s).

After working at Buffalo's WMAK, in 1929 Mark Hawley was invited by CBS president William S. Paley to move to New York

City. Hawley announced Guy Lombardo's inaugural New Year's Eve broadcast from the Roosevelt Hotel that year. The announcer segued into radio news reporting in the 1930s while introducing a handful of network features in the same era. From 1935 to the early 1940s he was a newscaster at New York's WOR, a flagship outlet of the newly created Mutual Radio chain.

While serving in the U.S. Navy during the Second World War, Hawley established and directed the Fleet Motion Picture Office in Honolulu under Admiral Chester Nimitz. Producing and directing training films was a derivative of that assignment. Following the war he produced spoken recordings, including some with the revered actor Orson Welles. NBC-TV employed Hawley from 1947 to 1950. In 1955 he became manager of Reno's KOLO Radio. During his last professional career post he was an industrial management consultant.

A charter member of the American Federation of Radio Artists, Hawley was dubbed "The Voice of Pathe News" for copious Pathe newsreels screened in cinema houses which he narrated in the 1930s and 1940s. In the meantime, his spouse, Adelaide Hawley, was the original Betty Crocker commercial spokeswoman in the television era to be hired by General Mills, Inc. She fulfilled that challenging opportunity from 1949 to 1964.

HAY, BILL. b. April 18, 1887, Dumfries, Scotland; d. Oct. 12, 1978, Santa Monica, Calif. **Announcer. Series:** *Amos 'n' Andy* (1928–1943); *The Goldbergs* (1934–?). **Aphorism:** *Heah they ah.*

After Bill Hay arrived in the United States in 1909, he studied violin, took vocal lessons and sang in churches. Radio historiographer Ray Poindexter recalls a few anecdotes:

> Westinghouse began using short wave stations to boost KDKA's coverage. In Pittsburgh, 8XS was built and broadcast KDKA's programs several hours each evening. On March 4, 1923, short wave repeater station KDPM was established in Cleveland. On November 22, KFKX was placed into service at Hastings, Nebraska, near the geographical center of the country. Millions of listeners were able to hear KDKA programming. Lloyd Creighton Thomas was secretary-manager of the Hastings Chamber of Commerce. He soon convinced Westinghouse officials that some broadcasts should originate at KFKX. The studio was located in a room above a music and furniture company. Thomas knew a young man who sold pianos, musical instruments, and sheet music for the store and also directed the Methodist Church choir. He was twenty-six-year-old William G. 'Bill' Hay, a Scotchman. Thomas arranged for Hay to be the announcer and program director. He took the job on the condition that he would be permitted to mention the name of the piano used on the programs. He traveled great distances in search of talent. As a result, KFKX became one of the nation's most popular stations, and Hay earned quite a reputation as an announcer. His brogue-style station break itself was a good show: "KFKX, Haastings, Neebrrawska." [Poindexter's assertion that Hay was 26 appears to be in error. According to several reliable sources he would have been 36 in 1923.]

Within a year a drought in Nebraska so severely hampered local living conditions that the piano concern was in deep financial distress. When a relative extended an invitation to Hay to join a commercial concern in Chicago, he accepted and in late 1924 left Hastings far behind. Because of KFKX's far-reaching signal, however, Hay's reputation as a radio entertainer preceded him. After several months in the Windy City he was persuaded to join WGN full time. There he met a couple of staff vocalists, Freeman Gosden and Charles Correll. By early 1926 the three were on the air together—Gosden and Correll as *Sam 'n' Henry*, the precursor to their forthcoming *Amos 'n' Andy* hit series, with Hay as their announcer. It was a slot he would fill from 1926 to 1942.

The trio shifted from WGN to rival station WMAQ in 1928 for the *Amos 'n' Andy* launch. Correll and Gosden vowed that Hay *must* be included in their WMAQ pact, part of a $25,000 financial transaction compensating their services for a year. The show went on NBC's coast-to-coast hookup in 1929 with the two principals earning a guaranteed $50,000 in their first year. It wasn't a bad way to make a living during the first year of the Great Depression! Following a dentifrice commercial, Hay would bring the dual stars on with a mere *Heah they ah*.

Hay's contributions to the show were little short of monumental nevertheless, according to Gosden and Correll biographer Elizabeth McLeod, who claimed: "The constant repetition of the slogan 'Use Pepsodent Toothpaste twice a day—see your dentist at least twice a year' by *Amos 'n' Andy* announcer Bill Hay is credited with creating the American habit of twice-yearly dental examinations." By 1937 Hay, organist Gaylord Carter, a commercial pitchman and the show's director were physically located in another studio apart from Gosden and Correll—on separate floors from the duo, in fact—to diminish the possibility that those wits might be diverted from their characterizations. Hay additionally became WMAQ's sales manager, meanwhile. In that capacity he transferred his allegiance to Chicago's WMAZ in 1934. By then he was also introducing the daily visits of *The Goldbergs* to aural audiences. Ernest Chappell replaced him on *Amos 'n' Andy* temporarily in 1940 when the durable announcer suffered a heart attack.

In 1943 a purely business decision was made to end the long-running serialized version of *Amos 'n' Andy* and reorder it as a weekly half-hour situation comedy, complete with scriptwriters, orchestra, chorus, enlarged cast and a live studio audience. According to radio historiographer John Dunning, "The toughest choice was that of announcer.... His [Hay's] delivery was of the old school, low-key and simple.... Bill Hay was out, heartbroken." Del Sharbutt took the show for a few months and was soon replaced by Harlow Wilcox, Carlton KaDell and Art Gilmore, well-known names among radio listeners, each bearing impressive credentials on a myriad of series.

HAY, GEORGE DEWEY. b. Nov. 9, 1895, Attica, Ind.; d. May 9, 1968, Virginia Beach, Va. *Emcee, Director, Announcer.* **Series:** *Grand Ole Opry*, aka *WSM Barn Dance* (creator-director-master of ceremonies, 1925–1951). **Aphorism** (after a steamboat whistle): *All right, let'er go, boys!*

George D. Hay, "The Solemn Old Judge," was aptly branded "the father of country music." It was his influence and persistence more than of any other single individual that launched not one but *two* major aural hillbilly hoedowns—Chicago's *WLS Barn Dance* in 1924, which became the venerated *National Barn Dance* in 1933, and Nashville's *WSM Barn Dance* in 1925, which became the legendary *Grand Ole Opry* in 1927. Both series would ultimately realize extensive coast-to-coast runs on NBC.

Hay was tagged as "The Solemn Old Judge" from an experience in childhood when "Judge" became a stand-in for "George." Hay fell in love with Southerners while training at Camp Gordon, Ga. during World War I. Following his tour of duty, he became a police beat reporter for *The Commercial Appeal* in Memphis, covering 137 murders in one year. Subsequently given his own column ("Howdy Judge"), Hay was tapped as the paper's radio editor after the owners initiated station WMC in 1923. One of his newly acquired obligations was to recall his newspaper experiences to an aural audience for an hour every weeknight. He loved it and so did the listeners.

During that same epoch, he made a trip on muleback to the Ozark Mountains of northern Arkansas near Mammoth Spring. That 1919 visit was to have profound implications for the rest of Hay's life and on the entertainment that billions of people around the globe came to like for generations. He encountered homesteaders living unadorned existences as they observed customs dating from the American Revolution. The primitive mountain sounds those people enjoyed at dances and socials were particularly beguiling to Hay. Following a folk dance in a log cabin lit by coal oil lamps, he remarked, "No one has ever had more fun than those Ozark mountaineers had that night."

Hay never let the experience drift far from his mind. Invited to join WLS in 1924, he carried the landmark backwater encounter with him and applied it when he had the chance. He solicited pickers, pluckers, strummers, yodelers and singers from across the Midwest and gave them a platform on which to amuse with gusto at the debuting Saturday night barn dance in the Windy City. The response from listeners and aspiring, often untrained artists was overwhelmingly favorable. Within a short while readers of the fanzine *Radio Digest* picked Hay as the nation's "most popular announcer." At about the same time, meanwhile, officials at Nashville's National Life and Accident Insurance Co. were planning to put their own powerful voice on the ether. Hay's widespread recognition didn't escape their notice and he was invited to WSM's inaugural.

On that occasion station executives explored the possibility with him of developing a similar shindig for WSM. They perceived Hay as the instigator, leader and master of ceremonies of such a show. The WLS host was still passionate about his love for the South. When an offer was extended, he readily accepted. On Nov. 28, 1925, the hills and hollows of middle Tennessee, southern Kentucky and northern Alabama started emptying out on Saturday nights as a new wave of hillbillies began trekking toward a new Mecca. The town—and the industry that ultimately grew up around it—would never quite be the same, thanks to the pervasive influence of George D. Hay.

One night a couple of years later—following a performance of NBC's *Music Appreciation Hour* carried by WSM and directed by eminent composer-conductor Walter Damrosch—Hay offered an unplanned observation on the air: "For the past hour, we have been listening to music taken largely from Grand Opera. But from now on, we will present the Grand Ole Opry." The label stuck. Before the rustic sounds began on Saturday nights, he opened the show with a long blast on a steamboat whistle and then cried: *All right, let'er go, boys!* The picking and sawing began.

In late 1947 the inspired originator of the *Grand Ole Opry* suffered an emotional collapse. Although he remained with WSM to 1956, his duties were severely curtailed, limited primarily to hosting a trio of segments on the Saturday night show and a quarter-hour Saturday morning feature called *Strictly Personal* on which he discussed *Opry* stars. One of his Saturday night chores was to sign-off the marathon multi-hour hoedown. It was a classic routine.

> *That's all for now friends,*
> *Because the tall pines pine,*
> *And the pawpaws pause,*
> *And the bumblebees bumble all around....*
> *The grasshoppers hop,*
> *And the eavesdroppers drop,*
> *While, gently, the ole cow slips away...*
> *George D. Hay saying so long for now.*

In 1966 Hay was elected to the Country Music Hall of Fame, one of numerous byproducts of the multibillion-dollar commerce stimulated by the prospering show. Today the George D. Hay Foundation at Mammoth Spring, Ark., perpetuates his legacy. A museum honoring the patron saint of country music exists and since 2004 local bands have played regularly on Saturday nights in the George D. Hay Music Hall of Fame Theater.

HAYWORTH, VINTON J. b. June 4, 1906, Washington, D.C.; d. May 21, 1970, Van Nuys, Calif. *Actor, Announcer.* **Series:** *The Adventures of Father Brown* (actor, 1945); *The Adventures of Michael Shayne* (actor, 1952–1953); *Archie Andrews* (actor, ca. early 1940s); *Betty and Bob* (actor, 1930s); *Chaplain Jim* (1940s); *The Chase* (actor, 1952–1953); *The First Nighter* (host); *It's Higgins, Sir* (actor, 1951); *Life Can Be Beautiful* (actor, ca. 1940s); *Lights Out* (actor, 1945); *Lone Journey* (actor, ca. 1940s, early 1950s); *Meet Me in St. Louis* (actor, 1950); *Mr. Keen, Tracer of Lost Persons* (actor, 1946–1948); *Myrt and Marge* (actor, ca. 1937–1942, 1946); *The Redhead* (1952); *Second Husband* (actor, ca. early to mid 1940s); *The Strange Romance of Evelyn Winters* (actor, 1940s).

Vinton Hayworth launched a stage career in 1926 in Washington, D.C. According to *Variety*, he directed the first live TV show in Chicago in 1930. He was a founder of the American Federation of Radio Artists (AFRA). Hayworth returned to television after a concentrated career in radio and film. From 1957 to 1959 he played Magistrate Galindo in the ABC-TV western *Zorro*. He appeared sporadically in supporting roles on NBC-TV's *Dragnet* between 1967 and 1969. During the final season of NBC-TV's sitcom *I Dream of Jeannie* (1969–1970), he was cast as Gen. Winfield Schaeffer.

Hayworth appeared in many theatrical releases spanning his professional lifetime, often under a couple of pseudonyms. Assuming the alias of Jack Arnold, he premiered on the silver screen in 1934's *Enlighten Thy Daughter* as Stanley Jordan. Between 1937 and 1942 he turned up in 17 B-movies under the acting moniker—of all names!—Stanley Jordan. Among those features were *Blind Alibi* (1938); *Tarnished Angel* (1938); *The Day the Bookies Wept* (1939); *Oh Johnny, How You Can Love* (1940); *Tillie the Toiler* (1941); and *Juke Box Jenny* (1942). Hayworth concluded his lengthy film career by appearing in 49 more under his own name between 1936 and 1966. Included in his largely B-movie repertoire continuance were *Night Waitress* (1936); *You Can't Buy Luck* (1937); *Crime Ring* (1938); *Fugitives for a Night* (1938); *Lucky Devils* (1941); *Tight Shoes* (1941); *The Stork Pays Off* (1941); *Two-Faced Woman* (1941); *Playmates* (1941); *You're Telling Me* (1942); *Mexican Spitfire's Elephant* (1942); *It Ain't Hay* (1943); *The Girl He Left Behind* (1956); *Spartacus* (1960); *The Police Dog Story* (1961); and *Chamber of Horrors* (1966).

HEATTER, GABRIEL. b. Sept. 17, 1890, New York, N.Y.; d. March 30, 1972, Miami, Fla. *Newscaster, Commentator, Emcee.* **Series:** *America Today* (host, 1935–?); *Behind the Front Page*, aka *A Brighter Tomorrow* (host-narrator, 1946–1948); *Borden's Home News* (newscaster, ca. 1937–1938); *The Cavalcade of America* (1938–1939); *Gabriel Heatter News and Comment* (newscaster-commentator, 1935–1965); *NBC Bandstand* (1957); *Of All Things* (1956); *We, the People* (moderator, 1937–1941). **Aphorism:** *Ah, there's good news tonight!*

Gabriel Heatter was born into a family of Jewish immigrants from the Austro-Hungarian Empire and raised in tenements on Manhattan's lower east side. Despite an intense love for reading, he wasn't a scholar. Mathematics was his albatross—he couldn't pass a math test and failed to receive a high school diploma as a result. Newspaper magnate William Randolph Hearst, running for governor in 1906, employed him at age 16 and he was soon labeled "the boy orator." Warming up street corner crowds for the candidate's speeches, Heatter received a barrage of eggs and tomatoes at campaign appearances. The youthful spokesman also took an occasional punch in the nose after expounding on the political attributes of his superior.

During this period he accepted a part time job as a reporter for a rival-owned newspaper, *The New York Record*, where he learned economy of expression, something of special consequence for journalists. He became a full time reporter for *The Brooklyn Times* at 19 and, in addition, added an assignment as Brooklyn correspondent of Hearst's paper, *The New York Journal*. In his early twenties he was a political correspondent at the Albany state house. Shortly after starting a family, Heatter was overwhelmed by some lifelong insecurities that constantly plagued him, including depression, resulting in a nervous breakdown. He was virtually unable to function for a couple of years in the late teens. Afterward Heatter held a temporary publicity job in the Warren Harding campaign; then he penned articles for *Forest and Stream* magazine. In 1932 he submitted a piece to *The Nation*, which was published.

When he was approached that year about debating perennial Socialist candidate Norman Thomas over New York's WMCA, Heatter accepted. Thomas was a no-show—called out of town—but Heatter filled the airtime by discussing the article in *The Nation* that placed him there. The station liked it and invited him back the following week for another topic. That resulted in an offer to become a seven-night-a-week quarter-hour news commentator at $40 weekly. He took it and within a year moved to WOR, a bigger station, where a beer sponsor underwrote his nightly performances to the lucrative tune of $75 per quarter-hour. Those humble beginnings eventually led the new electronic journalist to earn $400,000 annually in his peak years when 196 MBS stations carried him six nights weekly.

On his way there, in 1936 Heatter leaped into widespread notoriety by reporting—mostly ad-libbing—at the execution of Bruno Richard Hauptmann, who kidnapped and murdered the Lindbergh baby. A radio historian branded it Heatter's *tour de théâtre*. An unanticipated error left him filling 45 minutes of unexpected airtime. "He went through this ordeal by verbiage without dropping a syllable or sounding an unprofessional 'er' or 'uh.' Nothing like it had been witnessed since Lillian Leitzel did 102 consecutive one-arm somersaults over her own shoulder on a trapeze in Ringling Brothers-Barnum and Bailey Circus," observed the reviewer. Heatter was already a daily presence on the MBS chain and that single broadcast netted him in excess of 50,000 letters.

He was one of two Mutual eyewitnesses at that summer's political conventions and was soon asked to sub for the vacationing host of CBS's *We, the People*. Before long he was named permanent master of ceremonies of that highly rated human-interest feature.

On his news programs, meanwhile, he read all of the commercial messages himself and was in the habit of blending them into his commentary without pause or change in emphasis, a significant departure from the norm.

Although a leading propagandist and anti–Nazi campaigner, Heatter contributed substantially to civilian morale during the Second World War. He was adept at presenting something to cheer even during the battle's darkest days, hence his greeting *Ah, there's good news tonight!* made him a popular figure among wartime broadcasters. His autobiography, *There's Good News Tonight*, was released in 1960. In mid 1945, shortly before the war's conclusion, Heatter offered this petition for the American troops:

> Merciful God, watch over these men. They march in a crusade for humanity and freedom. These are not men of hate or vengeance. These are humble men. Men whose hearts will never forget pity and mercy. They fight to give all the children of men peace on earth. They fight to banish tyranny and fear. Merciful God, our homes are empty; our hearts are torn with this desperate vigil. Into your care we give our prayers ... our lives ... our sons ... all that we are and can ever hope to be on this earth. Send these men back to us, home to us, for they are part of man's spirit, of man's dream of a world which is free and where kindness lives. Watch over these men, who are meek and humble. We whose faith is strong ask this. Send these men back to our hearts and our homes—this is our prayer.

Heatter was saddled with several labels over his broadcast career including "The Old Crier," "The Unhappy Warrior" and "The Voice of Doom," despite the note of optimism he injected into the launch of each commentary. At mid century, he turned up in a couple of full length motion pictures: *Champagne for Caesar* (1950) and *The Day the Earth Stood Still* (1951).

He moved to Miami Beach in 1951 and continued his nightly commentaries over MBS. He penned a column for *The Miami Beach Sun*, appeared regularly on WIOD Radio and briefly tried television. In the meantime his son, Basil Heatter, took up where his pop left off, joining WOR as a newscaster in 1954. In 1965, three decades after Gabriel Heatter began network broadcasting, illness forced his retirement, although he persisted in writing the newspaper column for a while.

HEMINGWAY, FRANK. *Announcer.* **Series:** *Breakfast at Sardi's*, aka *Breakfast with Breneman*, aka *Breakfast in Hollywood*, aka *Welcome to Hollywood* (ca. late 1940s, early 1950s); *Deadline Mystery* (1947); *One for the Book* (1945); *The Roy Rogers Show* (actor, ca. 1951); *Voice of the Nation* (1945).

In 1942 Frank Hemingway was newscasting over Portland, Oregon's KGW and KEX. In 1945 he shifted to Los Angeles' KMPC, where he was fortunate to pick up a few network and syndicated series.

HERLIHY, ED. b. Aug. 14, 1909, Dorchester, Mass.; d. Jan. 30, 1999, Manhattan, N.Y. *Announcer, Emcee, Newscaster.* **Series:** *The Adventures of the Thin Man* (1941–1942); *America's Town Meeting of the Air* (1935–?); *The Army Hour* (host, 1944–1945); *The Big Show* (1950–1952); *Brave Tomorrow* (1943–1944); *Dick Tracy* (ca. later 1930s); *Ed Herlihy and the News* (newscaster, 1945–1947); *The Falcon* (1945–?); *Grand Central Station* (ca. 1937–1938, ca. 1940–1942); *Hearts in Harmony* (1941–?); *The Henry Morgan Show* (ca. 1947–1948); *Honeymoon in New York* (host, 1947); *The Horn and Hardart Children's Hour* (host, 1940s); *Information Please* (1940s); *Inner Sanctum Mysteries* (1941–1943); *Irene Rich Dramas* (ca. 1930s, 1940s); *It's the Tops* (1949–1950); *The Jane Pickens Show*, aka *Pickens Party* (ca. late 1940s, 1950s); *Just Plain Bill* (ca. late 1930s, early 1940s); *Kraft Music Hall* (1946–1947); *Life Can Be Beautiful* (ca. 1940–?); *The Martin and Lewis Show* (ca. early 1950s); *Melody Puzzles* (1937–1938); *Mr. District Attorney* (ca. 1939–1940s); *NBC News* (newscaster, 1947–1948); *The O'Neills* (ca. 1936–1943); *People Are Funny* (ca. 1940s, 1950s); *The Pet Milk Show* (ca. 1948–1950); *Rosemary* (ca. 1944–1945); *Thanks for Tomorrow* (1949); *That's a Good One* (1943); *This Small Town* (1940–1941); *Truth or Consequences* (early 1940s–1956); *Vacation with Music* (cast member, 1946); *Vic and Sade* (1935–1944); *Weekend* (host, 1953–1955); *Your Radio Reporter* (newscaster, 1943–1945).

Ed Herlihy hailed from a Massachusetts family that was rife with show business kin. His uncle was comedian Fred Allen; his sibling, Walter, followed that duo into broadcasting, becoming a lesser-known but still quite active ABC Radio and Television announcer. Ed, meanwhile, launched a prolific, enduring ethereal career during his years at Boston College where he also acted in stage productions. For $10 a week he got on the air in 1932 at Boston's WLOE. Then he accepted an announcing post at Beantown's WHDH. He transferred to WEEI in the same city in 1933 and—two years beyond that—made the gargantuan leap to NBC's Radio City in New York.

There he became, as a radio historian aptly clarified it, "A studio workhorse with the versatility to handle a broad spectrum of general utility chores at the NBC microphone, day and night." Another pundit affirmed: "No radio orator is more closely associated with the golden age than Ed Herlihy, who for sixty-three years on NBC read commercials, hosted shows, and introduced soap operas, game shows, detective classics, kids' programs, political forums, and, basically, announced whatever needed announcing. Herlihy's friendly yet authoritative voice was, if not the unofficial Voice of Radio, the official Voice of Kraft Foods." For 42 years Herlihy maintained a commercial relationship with the Kraft Foods Co. as its chief spokesman on a variety of broadcast ventures in dual mediums. He was simultaneously the voice of Universal-International newsreels for a quarter-of-a-century.

Presiding every Sunday morning for 15 years over the *Horn and Hardart Children's Hour* aired by NBC's flagship outlet in New York City, Herlihy advanced with the series into local television, where it ran for an additional decade. That prepared him to transition from other aural-only features into the demands of burgeoning video opportunities, all of them on NBC-TV. From 1947 to 1955 he was the announcer on the hour-long live dramatic anthology *Kraft Television Theatre*. Herlihy introduced *Your Show of Shows* from 1950 to 1954. He announced *The Perry Como Show* between 1959 and 1963. He presented the *Tonight* show during a fleeting spell in the late summer of 1962. "Herlihy was a (non-buffoon) equivalent of Ed McMahon on 'The Tonight Show' before Johnny Carson came along in 1962, bringing McMahon with him," affirmed one source. He was the announcer for the *Kraft Music Hall* variety series between 1967 and 1971.

Among his big screen credits, Herlihy performed in these motion pictures: *Pee-wee's Big Adventure* (1985); *Police Academy 2: Their First Assignment* (1985); *A Fine Mess* (1986); *Who Framed Roger Rabbit* (1988); and *Malcolm X* (1992). His voice was heard in a quartet of made-for-TV movies, too: *Don't Drink the Water* (1994); *Sports on the Silver Screen* (1997); *Howard Hughes: His Women and His Movies* (2000); and *Poitier: One Bright Light* (2000).

HERLIHY, WALTER F. b. ca. 1914, Massachusetts; d. Oct. 6, 1956, Forest Hills, N.Y. *Announcer.* **Series:** *The Best Bands in the Land* (1947); *Dorothy Kilgallen's Diary* (1945); *Police Woman* (ca. 1946–1947); *Powers Charm School* (1946–1947).

Walter Herlihy, brother of the better-known Ed Herlihy and nephew of comic Fred Allen, was notably the first announcer at ABC Radio assigned to television. In that capacity, he appeared on a variety of pioneering series, among them shows headlined by entertainers Gloria DeHaven and Lisa Ferraday as well as *Blind Date* (1949–1951); *Dr. I.Q.* (1953–1954); and *Kraft Television Theatre* (1953–1955).

HERMAN, GEORGE. b. Jan. 14, 1920, New York, N.Y.; d. Feb. 8, 2005, Washington, D.C. *Correspondent, Newscaster, Writer.* **Series:** *CBS News* (newscaster, ca. 1950s–1980s); *CBS World News Roundup* (correspondent, ca. 1950s–1980s).

A 1941 graduate of Dartmouth College, George Herman earned a master's degree in journalism at Columbia University before launching an enduring career at CBS in 1944. Never as prominent as his radio news contemporaries, Herman was a news writer in his initial assignment with the web. In that capacity he rubbed elbows with the greats (Ed Murrow, Eric Sevareid, Lowell Thomas, Charles Collingwood, et al.). He gained the prestigious duty as the network's White House correspondent in the 1950s and early 1960s. For a few years into the early 1970s he covered the Supreme Court. Herman is best remembered, nevertheless, as the moderator of CBS-TV's public affairs series *Face the Nation*. He presided there between 1969 and 1983—longer than five others in that post—at least, until Bob Schieffer assumed the helm in 1991. Herman remained with the network for 43 years, to 1987.

On *Face the Nation*, Herman and print journalist Jack Anderson contributed heavily to altering the Democratic ticket in 1972. Their pointed questions to Missouri Sen. Thomas Eagleton—then the party's candidate for vice president—on one occasion concerning his past bouts with depression left him observably uncomfortable. Shortly after the July 30, 1972 inquisition, Eagleton was history. *Variety* recalled, "He left the impression of a man clinging to a life raft in very stormy waters."

Herman experienced many "firsts" at CBS. He made his first TV appearance during the network's first televised political conventions in 1948, getting in on video's ground floor. He went to Asia as a stringer with a 16mm camera and audio recorder in 1949 to provide CBS with its first sound and film reports from overseas. In 1972 he delivered the first broadcast report of a break-in at Democratic Party headquarters in the Watergate office building.

HICKS, GEORGE FRANCIS. b. Aug. 26, 1905, Tacoma, Wash.; d. March 17, 1965, Jackson Heights, Queens, N.Y. *Announcer, Newscaster.* **Series:** *Countess Olga Medlolago Albani* (1930); *Death Valley Days* (1932–1941); *George Hicks and the News*, aka *News by Hicks* (newscaster, 1944–1945, 1947–1951, 1953–1955); *The Jack Benny Program*, aka *The Canada Dry Ginger Ale Program* and other monikers (ca. 1932–ca. 1933); *Larry Clinton's Musical Conversations*, aka *Sensation and Swing* (1939–1940); *Metropolitan Echoes* (1930); *Seth Parker* (1938–1939); *The Theater Guild on the Air*, aka *Theater Guild Dramas*, aka *U.S. Steel Hour* (commercial spokesman, 1945–1953); *Tremendous Trifles* (host-narrator, 1955–1956); *V.D.* (Venereal Disease) *Radio Project* (1948).

While studying for a year at the University of Washington followed by a year at Puget Sound College, an industrious George Hicks interspersed his training with money-making chances at logging camps, sawmills, shipyards, door and pickle factories, a hardware store and trucking firms. He also auditioned for a job at a hometown radio station; while he didn't get it, he discovered that he had a "good speaking voice." Afterward, he sought jobs on ships, having cultivated a wanderlust to see the world. On one such adventure he visited relatives in Washington, D.C., and decided to seek an announcing job in the nation's capital. When WRC advertised for one, 100 candidates applied. Hicks won the post outright and went to work in September 1928. He completed his collegiate studies at George Washington University.

In November 1929 he joined NBC as a staff announcer at WEAF in New York. From his inception there he hosted a local show, *New Business World*. Before Pearl Harbor, he invested a decade in developing light features for NBC. He and a trio of colleagues (Ben Grauer, Tom Manning and Graham McNamee) covered the political conventions and campaigns for the White House in 1936 for their web. After the war began, Hicks persuaded the Blue chain to add a daily series about men at war that the critics applauded as riveting human-interest narrative.

In 1942, he again swayed his superiors to let him be the new distinctly Blue network's first and only foreign correspondent—in London—at a time when the fledgling operation hardly had enough cash to support domestic coverage, let alone overseas reporters. Once Hicks got an assistant in London he was off to the battlefront. A 10-minute recording made on D-Day, June 6, 1944, that caught a German bombing mission on tape turned into a classic segment of unfolding wartime drama for radio audiences. It significantly elevated Hicks' stature as a redoubtable newsman and won for him a National Headliners Club award. In the postwar era, his daily quarter-hour newscasts variously aired on ABC and NBC for the better part of a decade.

In 1948, in an unusual syndicated series written by media historian-critic Erik Barnouw and sponsored by the U.S. Public Health Service labeled *V.D. Radio Project*, Hicks was given a blood test while on the air to check for syphilis. He also had the good fortune to be selected by the U.S. Steel Co. as its chief spokesman for a primetime radio series that aired eight years (1945–1953) and persisted as *The U.S. Steel Hour* on television for yet another decade (1953–1955, ABC; 1955–1963, CBS). Furthermore, he presided over the weekly live half-hour public affairs broadcast of *The U.N. in Action* on CBS-TV from 1955 to 1959. And in 1961 he hosted the weekly half-hour ABC-TV religious series

Directions. In later years Hicks was occasionally featured in spot advertising.

HICKS, JOHN. *Announcer, Producer*. **Series:** *Ethel and Albert* (1940s); *Jack's Place* (1953–1954); *Mutual Chamber Music Concert* (producer-announcer); *Nick Carter, Master Detective* (ca. late 1940s, early 1950s); *The Spike Jones Show* (1949); *Strictly from Dixie* (co-host, 1941).

HIESTAND, JOHN (BUD). b. Jan. 16, 1907, Madison, Wis.; d. Feb. 5, 1987, Newport Beach, Calif. *Announcer, Actor*. **Series:** *The Burns and Allen Show* (1940–ca. 1941); *The Cinnamon Bear* (narrator-actor, 1937); *The Edgar Bergen Hour* (1950s); *The Fabulous Dr. Tweedy* (1946–1947); *The Great Gildersleeve* (1950–1957); *The Hormel Program* (1940–1941); *Kay Kyser's Kollege of Musical Knowledge* (ca. 1940s); *Let George Do It* (1946–1954); *Meet Corliss Archer* (ca. 1940s, 1950s); *The Mickey Mouse Theater of the Air* (1938); *Young Love* (actor, 1949–1950).

John (Bud) Heistand was a graduate of Stanford University. In addition to his radiocasting, between 1943 and 1971 he turned up in 10 mostly B-movies, often as an announcer, narrator or newscaster. His silver screen repertoire included *Riding High* (1943); *The Hucksters* (1947); *You're My Everything* (1949); *Good Morning, Miss Dove* (1955); and *The Incredible Shrinking Man* (1957).

After most of his radio and film work played out, Heistand could be heard introducing *Ford Theater*—which aired on CBS-TV, NBC-TV and ABC-TV, in that order, between 1949 and 1957—plus a quintet of weekly sitcoms on the tube: *The Adventures of Hiram Holiday* (1956–1957, NBC); *My Living Doll* (1964–1965, CBS); *Green Acres* (1965–1971, CBS); *Hogan's Heroes* (1965–1971, CBS); and *The Second Hundred Years* (1967–1968, ABC).

HIETT, HELEN. b. Sept. 23, 1913, Tazewell, Ill.; d. Aug. 22, 1961, Chamonix, France. *Correspondent, Newscaster*. **Series:** *Helen Hiett News* (newscaster, 1941–1942); *News Roundup* (correspondent based in Paris, 1940); *Sunday Evening News Roundup* (correspondent based in Madrid, 1941).

In 1934, having earned a four-year political science degree in three years from the University of Chicago, Helen Hiett set out for Europe on a summer scholarship. She remained for a year as an assistant at the League of Nations' Geneva research center. Studying in Rome in 1936, she traveled in Greece and Italy before continuing her academic pursuits at the London School of Economics. For two weeks in 1937 Hiett worked in a German girls' labor camp, then went to Spain to observe the echoing effects of that nation's civil war. In 1939 she traversed the Balkans, lectured in the United States and relocated in Paris, transmitting numerous short-wave broadcasts. Following another speaking tour in the U.S. in 1940, Hiett joined the European staff of NBC, based in Paris.

Notably, for one season Heitt accomplished what most of her gender never did. In 1941 she was given a quarter-hour of radio time to deliver the news over the NBC Blue chain every weekday morning at 10:15 A.M. "As more men got drafted, we would begin to hear more women on the air in nontraditional roles," a source disclosed. Shortly before that—while still an NBC correspondent temporarily stationed in Madrid—Hiett joined an entourage of chorus girls that was slated to entertain British troops stationed at the Rock of Gibraltar. For three days during their performances enemy troops bombed Gibraltar. Hiett revealed who she was and returned to Madrid to deliver an eyewitness account of the bombing mission to her radio listeners. The National Headliners Club subsequently selected her as its first feminine recipient of a coveted journalism award.

Heitt left NBC Blue's employ in the mid 1940s, eventually becoming director of forums for *The New York Herald Tribune*. She wed Theodore Waller, formerly of San Francisco, in March 1948. Waller held an overseas post with the U.S. federal government at the time. Thirteen years later, while climbing in the French Alps, Ms. Waller was fatally injured.

HILL, EDWIN CONGER. b. April 23, 1884, Aurora, Ind.; d. Feb. 12, 1957, St. Petersburg, Fla. *Newscaster, Commentator, Announcer*. **Series:** *The Campbell Playhouse* (premiering narrator, 1938); *Freedom USA* (narrator, 1952); *Hart, Schaffner and Marx*

Trumpeters (newscaster, 1931–1932); *The Human Side of the News*, aka *Edwin C. Hill Commentary*, aka *Your News Parade*, aka *Behind the Headlines* (commentator, 1933–1935, 1936–1945, 1946–1947, 1950, 1951–1952); *Inside Story of Names That Make the News* (interviewer, 1933); *John B. Kennedy–Edwin C. Hill News* (commentator, 1956); *The Mercury Theater on the Air* (1938); *The Realsilk Program* (master of ceremonies, 1936–1937); *This is London* (correspondent, early 1940s).

A graduate of Butler College in Indianapolis, starting in 1901 Edwin C. Hill reported for newspapers in Indianapolis and Cincinnati. He moved to *The New York Sun* in 1904 where he became one of its foremost staff writers. After nearly two decades in print media, he left it in 1923 for a brief sojourn (to 1927) directing Twentieth Century–Fox newsreels and editing scenarios for Fox movies. He returned to print for a while before devoting the remainder of his career to radio. During this epoch he also penned a trilogy of volumes: *The Iron Horse* (1925); *The American Scene* (1933); and *The Human Side of the News* (1934).

Initially appearing in 1931 as a newscaster over New York's WOR, Hill landed his own network slot within a year and persisted on the ether for another couple of decades. He aired as few as one and as many as six quarter-hours weekly over three national chains. A syndicated newspaper column that he penned, *The Human Side of the News*, often bore the common moniker of his ethereal news commentaries. A reviewer labeled him "one of New York's best reporters, with a flair for human interest." His voice was "deep, rich and sonorous" and he grabbed a substantial and loyal listener base. On the air he "could express far better than printer's ink the movement, the color, and the emotion of his words," declared a broadcast colleague. Every year at Thanksgiving and Christmas some of his poignant narratives were recalled for appreciative audiences.

Writing in *Radio Stars* a few weeks after the inception of Franklin D. Roosevelt's "Fireside Chats" with the American people on March 12, 1933, at the summit of the Great Depression, Hill observed: "It was as if a wise and kindly father had sat down to talk empathetically and patiently and affectionally [*sic*] with his worried and anxious children, and had given them straightforward things that they had to do to help him along as the father of the family. That speech of the President's over the air humanized radio in a great governmental, national sense as it had never before been humanized."

Despite the apparent admiration for the nation's chief executive, only a few months following Roosevelt's death—on his broadcast of Sept. 4, 1945—Hill openly rebuked him and his administration for the 1941 debacle at Pearl Harbor. "As the years went by," noted critic Irving Fang, "'The Human Side of the News' grew more political and more politically conservative."

HILLMAN, WILLIAM. b. Sept. 5, 1895, New York, N.Y.; d. May 30, 1962, New York, N.Y. *Newscaster, Correspondent.* **Series:** *News Here and Abroad* (newscaster, 1942–?); *News Roundup* (correspondent, 1940); *Roundup of War Reports* (correspondent, 1940); *Weekly War Journal* (newscaster-analyst, 1942–1944); *William Hillman* (newscaster, 1940, 1947–1948); *William Hillman and Bill Henry* (co-newscaster, 1950).

After graduating from Columbia College in 1917, William Hillman enlisted in the U.S. Army and served in France during World War I, where he was commissioned a second lieutenant. Having prepared himself for a career in journalism, after the war in 1926 he took a newspaper appointment that sent him overseas to Paris, Berlin and London. He was chief of staff of Hearst newspapers' foreign correspondents from 1934 to 1939.

In London he held posts as administrative agent for King Features Syndicate, director of the British News Service, Ltd., European manager of International News Service and finally as European manager of *Collier's Weekly* (1939–1940). He was recognized by industry pundits for several accurate forecasts of world events prior to their occurrence. He appeared on NBC on July 7, 1940 with some of his predictions.

Hillman returned to the United States before the nation entered World War II and launched a news broadcast career in the nation's capital, reporting for local stations and networks. He was on the air over WMAL in 1941. The following year he and Ernest K. Lindley applied their skills to a joint quarter-hour newscast four nights weekly over the NBC Blue/ABC chain. By 1946 Hillman was with WOL in Washington. Later that decade he acquired a solo newscast over MBS.

Meanwhile, between the mid 1940s and 1962 he was also a roving correspondent with the North American Newspaper Alliance. He edited a collection of President Harry S Truman's [sic] letters, diaries and personal papers released in 1952 under the banner *Mr. President*. For another decade, until his death, Hillman assisted Truman in composing his *Memoirs* and in other literary and TV projects focused on the ex-president.

HITE, BOB. b. Feb. 9, 1914, Decatur, Ind.; d. Feb. 18, 2000, West Palm Beach, Fla. *Announcer.* **Series:** *Bob Hite and the News* (newscaster, 1944–1945); *Casey, Crime Photographer* (ca. 1943–1946, ca. 1948–1950, ca. 1954–1955); *The CBS Radio Workshop* (ca. 1956–1957); *The Challenge of the Yukon* (1938–ca. 1945); *Cimarron Tavern* (1945–1946); *The Green Hornet* (ca. late 1940s–ca. 1952); *The Kathy Godfrey Show* (1955–1956); *The Lone Ranger* (1940s); *Ned Jordan, Secret Agent* (1938–1942); *Night Life* (1946).

When the CBS color logo appeared at the beginning of a show on television, it was Bob Hite's voice the viewers heard giving the announcement: "CBS presents this program in color." The identifying letters popped into the center of the screen, followed by the eye (corporate logo) going across the screen, and the letters changing into color: the 'C' was green, 'B' was blue and 'S' was red; the eye was golden. Hite retired from CBS in 1979 and moved to Florida.

HODGES, RUSSELL PATRICK. b. June 18, 1910, Dayton, Tenn.; d. April 19, 1971, San Francisco, Calif. *Sportscaster.* **Series:** *Russ Hodges, Sports* (sportscaster, 1941, 1947); *The White Owl Smoker* (sportscaster, 1947). **Aphorism:** *Bye-bye baby*.

In 1931 Russ Hodges took a post as a rookie announcer at WCKY, Covington, Ky. Its reach easily included nearby Cincinnati. Within two years he was elevated to sportscaster and called baseball games of the Cincinnati Reds on the airwaves. By then he had also earned a law degree from the University of Kentucky. Hodges saw greater potential in broadcasting than in being a barrister. In 1935 he joined WIND, Gary, Ind., on Chicago's extreme southeast side as a sports reporter. There he also aired Cubs baseball games.

In 1939 he traveled to Charlotte's WBT and that autumn he covered Pittsburgh's professional football games over KDKA. Hodges departed WBT in 1941 for Washington, D.C.'s WOL, an MBS affiliate, where he acquired a nationally broadcast feature. He joined Arch McDonald in covering Senators baseball games in 1943. In 1944 Hodges became MBS's chief sportscaster. Two years hence he advanced to New York's WINS and two years after that to WMCA in the same city.

Hodges and Mel Allen collaborated on broadcasting Yankees baseball over WINS in 1946. Subsequently, Hodges handled Columbia University football for the station before moving to WMCA, where he announced New York Giants baseball and football (1949–1954). Possibly the most stunning broadcast of his life was a match between the Giants and Dodgers on Oct. 3, 1951 in which Bobby Thompson's winning home run was branded "the shot heard 'round the world." Hodges exclaimed repeatedly: "The Giants win the pennant!" Describing any Giants home run, incidentally, he immortalized the phrase *Bye-bye baby*, which became a part of the lexicon of baseball fans of many uniforms.

Signifying his achievements, *Russ Hodges' Scoreboard* was a quarter-hour weeknight sportscast carried by Dumont Television in 1948–1949. From 1948 to 1950 and 1951 to 1955 Hodges was ringside announcer on CBS-TV's *International Boxing Club Bouts* (aka *Pabst Blue Ribbon Bouts*) matches originating at St. Nicholas Arena in White Plains, N.Y. He also announced *NCAA Football* games on NBC-TV from 1951 to 1953 and again in 1955.

When the Giants relocated to San Francisco in 1958, Hodges went with them. He continued working for the "new" San Francisco Giants until his retirement in 1970. He suffered a fatal heart attack in 1971; nine years afterward, in 1980, Hodges became the fourth recipient of the Ford C. Frick Award for excellence in baseball broadcasting, presented posthumously. The honor was named for a former baseball commissioner. The Giants, meanwhile, didn't soon forget Hodges' 22 years of service to the team (1948–1970). In 2000 they labeled the press box in their new stadium the Hodges-Simmons Broadcast Center for Hodges and a former partner, Lon Simmons.

HOFFMAN, HOWARD RALPH. b. Nov. 4, 1893, Ohio; d. June 27, 1969, Hollywood, Calif. *Announcer, Actor.* **Series:** *Chandu, the Magician* (actor, 1935–1936); *Magic Rhythm* (1948–1949); *Silver Eagle, Mountie* (actor, 1951–1953, 1954–1955); *Sweet River* (1943–1944).

Howard Hoffman performed on Keith and Orpheum vaudeville circuits early in his show business career and later appeared in Broadway stage productions. He initially landed in radio over Chicago's WEGM. After working extensively for CBS and NBC until most radio drama ended, he migrated to the West Coast where he was cast in parts for the small and large screens. Hoffman was a television actor from the mid 1950s to the mid 1960s as well as a panelist on the 1951 ABC-TV game show *Q.E.D.* He played in a quintet of motion pictures: *The Littlest Hobo* (1958); *Macabre* (1958); *Haunted Hill* (1959); *A Summer Place* (1959); and *Strait-Jacket* (1964). Shortly before his death, Hoffman lectured and interpreted poetic works.

HOGAN, GEORGE. b. Nov. 27, 1909, Kansas City, Mo. *Announcer.* **Series:** *Adventure Parade* (1946–1949); *High Adventure* (ca. 1947–ca. 1949, 1950); *Luncheon at Sardi's* (1954–1955); *The Saturday Night Swing Club* (1936–ca. 1939); *Snow Village Sketches* (1946).

Following his high school graduation in Kansas City, George Hogan attended the University of Missouri and—while he was still a collegian—linked himself with the radio station his brother owned. Although George occasionally pursued formal training at the Kansas City Law School and at nearby advertising and art institutes, he admitted he found radio "more fun than school." As a result, he launched a broadcasting career that was seemingly in reverse of the norm. Beginning as part owner of a station, he subsequently became a sponsor, then a producer, announcer and occasional actor.

Hogan moved on to other stations in St. Louis, Ft. Worth, Chicago, Detroit, Philadelphia and New York, working at assorted tasks like writer, producer, actor, vocalist or announcer. Following a few opportunities to introduce network series, Hogan settled at New York's WOR for a spell. There he announced the popular local matinee feature *Luncheon at Sardi's* (1947–ca. 1958) for 45 minutes six days weekly. The live production emanated from a popular New York bistro where Broadway performers and other celebrities converged. With Bill and Tom Slater as co-hosts, a quarter-hour of the show was also carried over MBS in 1954–1955.

HOLBROOK, JOHN F. b. Aug. 28, 1910, Cameron, Wis.; d. Sept. 20, 1978, Sapphire, N.C. *Announcer, Director.* **Series:** *The Bickersons* (ca. 1946–ca. 1948); *Call for Music,* aka *The Dinah Shore Show* (1948); *Chicago Theater of the Air* (1940–?); *Double or Nothing* (1940s); *The Horace Heidt Show* (ca. 1930s); *Little Known Facts About Well Known People* (1933–1935); *Moon Dreams* (director, 1946–1947); *Newspaper of the Air* (ca. late 1940s–1950s); *The Philip Morris Playhouse* (ca. 1948–ca. 1951); *The Red Skelton Show* (ca. 1940s); *This is Your Life* (1948–ca. 1950).

John Holbrook attended Vida Ravenscroft Sutton's school for network announcers (she was a NBC personality starting in 1929). As a result of that training, he won the American Academy of Arts and Letters' annual radio diction award in 1931. An earlier recipient was Milton J. Cross (1929); a later one was Jimmy Wallington (1933). Holbrook was associated with Chicago's WGN early in his professional career and with Hollywood's KHJ late in his career.

HOLCOMBE, HARRY JOHN. b. Nov. 11, 1906, Malta, Ohio; d. Sept. 8, 1987, Valencia, Calif. *Director, Announcer.* **Series:** *The Benny Goodman Show,* under several monikers (late 1930s); *The Camel Caravan* (1938–1940); *Curtain Time* (director, 1945–1948); *The Dixieland Song Shop,* aka *The Bob Crosby Show* (1939); *Dr. I.Q., the Mental Banker* (director, 1940s, ca. 1950); *The Joe Penner Show,* under various sponsor monikers (cast member, 1930s); *Judy and Jane* (director, 1932–1934, 1935, ca. 1941–1942); *The Lux Radio Theater* (director, ca. 1939–ca. 1940); *Tena and Tim* (director, 1944–1946).

A minister's son, Harry Holcombe (who is referenced by some scholars with a surname spelling of Holcomb) was schooled in the Ohio burgs where his dad served parishes. During his third year at Ohio Wesleyan College, the youth made a trip East with the school glee club. He decided then that he wanted to study drama at New York's American Laboratory Theater, which he did. He followed that by performing with the Stuart Walker Stock Co. in places like Cincinnati, Indianapolis and Huntington, W. Va. In 1930 Holcombe went on the air over WLW, Cincinnati, in a dramatic role on a local serial, *Judge Perkins*. He soon expanded his repertoire to include programming, writing, producing and announcing in addition to acting. He was one of numerous hosts of the revered local late-night show *Moon River* that originated in the 1930s and 1940s over WLW. He moved to New York City next and began taking network announcing and directing appointments.

From the late 1950s to the late 1960s, Holcombe turned up in several video roles as a character actor. He portrayed the namesake part in 1953's *The Wonderful John Acton* on NBC-TV, Malcolm Overton on CBS-TV's daytime serial *Road of Life* (1954–1955), Frank Gardner on CBS-TV's daytime serial *Search for Tomorrow* (1957), Doc Barton on NBC-TV's *Bonanza* from 1968 to 1973 and Arthur Kendricks on *Barefoot in the Park* on ABC-TV (1970–1971). Holcombe was the kindly grandfather figure in Country Time lemonade commercials throughout the 1970s and 1980s. He appeared in at least two motion pictures, also, *The Purple V* (1943) and *Matilda* (1978).

HOLLENBECK, DON. b. March 30, 1905, Lincoln, Neb.; d. June 22, 1954, New York, N.Y. *Commentator, Newscaster, Announcer.* **Series:** *Candid Microphone* (narrator, 1947–1948, 1950); *CBS Views the Press* (moderator, 1950); *Don Hollenbeck and the News* (1946–1947); *Hear It Now* (commentator, 1950–1951); *We Take Your Word* (moderator, 1950–1951); *You Are There* (reporter, 1947–1950).

In 1943 Don Hollenbeck—formerly with the U.S. Office of War Information in London—joined NBC's London office. Returning to America, in 1945 he joined New York's WJZ, flagship outlet of the ABC (formerly NBC Blue) network, as a newscaster. One morning in 1946 he began his early morning stint—which immediately followed a singing commercial—by announcing: "The atrocity you have just heard is not a part of this program." He learned quickly how much influence a sponsor wields. By noon he was history with that station.

Hollenbeck was subsequently hired by CBS and given his own slot on the web. He lost yet another broadcast gig a few years afterward when he condemned Sen. Joseph McCarthy, then on a rigorous crusade to expose Communist sympathizers among the highest levels of power and influence. Meanwhile, in the summer of 1950, Hollenbeck anchored *The Saturday News Special* on CBS-TV for a quarter-hour. It was his only ongoing network television assignment, although he conducted a nightly newscast over New York's WCBS-TV at the time of his death. In 1954, ill, hounded and depressed by McCarthy partisans—in particular, a few well placed newspapers that bombarded him with doubts about his patriotism—Hollenbeck was driven to suicide, one of very few electronic journalists to exit in that manner. His wife and daughter survived.

HOPPER, HEDDA (born Elda Furry). b. June 2, 1890, Hollidaysburg, Pa.; d. Feb. 1, 1966, Hollywood, Calif. *Commentator, Actress, Emcee.* **Series:** *Brenthouse* (actress, 1939–1940); *The Campbell Playhouse* (actress, 1938–ca. 1939); *The Hedda Hopper Show* (mistress of ceremonies, 1950–1951); *Hedda Hopper's Hollywood* (gossip commentator, 1939–1942, 1944–1946); *Hollywood Showcase* (mistress of ceremonies, ca. 1942); *Leave it to the Girls* (panelist, 1945–1949); *The Royal Gelatin Hour*, aka *The Rudy Vallee Show* (guest celebrity, late 1930s); *This is Hollywood* (gossip commentator, 1946–1947); *This is My Story* (judge, 1944–1945).

Hedda Hopper's careers before radio included being a chorus girl, a stage and silent screen and "talkies" actress and a real estate saleslady. Wed to comedian DeWolf Hopper, she altered her moniker to Hedda and—when she got into radio—was frequently mistaken for a beauty tip advisor of those early audio days, Edna Wallace Hopper (1931–1932). Hedda Hopper performed in 149 motion pictures, where she gained a myriad of contacts in multiple sectors of the movie-making industry. (Specific references to her film work appear at the conclusion of this entry.) She was also identified professionally by her given name and surname at birth (Elda Furry) plus a handful of pseudonyms: Elda Curry, Elda Millar, Ella Furry as well as Mrs. DeWolf Hopper (whom she divorced in 1922 after nine years of marriage—she never remarried).

With a quarter-century affiliation with the Hollywood community, at the age of 46 Hopper hired a manager, West Coast entertainment hobnob Dema Harshbarger, in an attempt to conquer territory held by the reigning queen of broadcast gossip, Louella Parsons. But as some historians have noted, Hopper wasn't easy to secure. Appearances on Rudy Vallee's variety hour and a brief local aural series plus some NBC fashion commentaries from distant venues led her to the heroine's role in the daytime serial *Brenthouse* on NBC Blue. She also turned up in pithy celebrity gigs on a plethora of audience participation shows like *Double or Nothing*; *People Are Funny*; and *Welcome Travelers*. That ephemeral broadcast track record seems to be about all she had to her credit as Harshbarger valiantly attempted to peddle her client. After three years of trying, CBS and a sponsor, Sunkist Farms, were persuaded to sign her for a three-a-week quarter-hour effective Nov. 6, 1939. Her national run was extended to three years. Hopper had finally become a major player among the Hollywood tattletale dispensers.

Unlike some others of the breed who developed a newspaper column that transported them into radio, Hopper worked the arrangement in reverse. According to one wag, her broadcasting success led to a syndicated column distributed by *The Chicago Tribune–Daily News* and achieved for her "near-equal status" with Parsons. At her peak her column was available to 30 million readers. Appalling, oversized millinery and an arresting vocabulary became her professional trademarks in an overpopulated genre. She also characteristically treated the stars and studios with respect, or did so most of the time. As the 1940s evolved, nevertheless, gossip fell out of favor with the masses of population. As a consequence, Hopper turned her series into a variety format at the dawn of the 1950s; she prattled, presented music and introduced movie narrative scenes, the latter played out by real actors. Hopper's chitchat reflected her spirited conservative bent almost every time out. She wound up as a "right-wing Red baiter like [Walter] Winchell," surmised one critic.

In regard to her competitors, she maintained a pronounced disdain for archrival Parsons and the feeling was unmistakably mutual. They battled in and out of the public eye for years. Parsons lost some turf to Hopper when the latter infiltrated the territory; it was not until her Sunday night Jergens show (1944–1951) that Parsons successfully regained the ground she had relinquished to the enemy. Between the pair, Hopper appeared to be better received by the public in most popularity polls. Just as importantly, *Life* magazine observed Hopper was "infinitely more liked by the movie colony than her ruthless rival." (CBS-TV offered its viewers *Malice in Wonderland* on May 12, 1985. It starred Elizabeth Taylor and Jane Alexander as the feuding Parsons and Hopper.) Meanwhile, Jimmy Fidler, who operated somewhat in the shadows of Hopper and Parsons, was more feared by some studios and stars than either of those femmes fatales. Yet another gossip columnist-broadcaster, Sheilah Graham, was an "also ran" by comparison, arriving after the others had long-established monopolies in the strain.

Hopper appeared as herself in the March 14, 1955 installment of CBS-TV's *I Love Lucy*. Shortly after her death, ABC-TV screened an animated rendition of *Alice in Wonderland, or What's a Nice Girl Like You Doing in a Place Like This?* on March 30, 1966, with Hopper in a prime voiceover part. The gossipmonger's son, William Hopper, played the role of private detective Paul Drake in the long-running CBS courtroom drama *Perry Mason* (1957–1966). Earlier, Doubleday published her memoir, in 1952. It was titled *From Under My Hat: The Fun and Fury of a Stage, Screen and Column Career.*

Between 1916 and 1966, a half-century, Hopper performed in bit parts in 149 full-length films. She appeared as herself in cameo roles in several of those, including a half-dozen numbered films released in 1941–1942 under the umbrella banner *Hedda*

Hopper's Hollywood, plus *Breakfast in Hollywood* (1946); *Sunset Boulevard* (1950); *The Patsy* (1964); and *The Oscar* (1966). Most of Hopper's celluloid productions were of the B-movie variety. Some were *Virtuous Wives* (1918); *Sherlock Holmes* (1922); *Women Men Marry* (1922); *Why Men Leave Home* (1924); *Her Market Value* (1925); *Pleasures of the Rich* (1926); *Children of Divorce* (1927); *Undressed* (1928); *Such Men are Dangerous* (1930); *Murder Will Out* (1930); *Our Blushing Brides* (1930); *A Tailor Made Man* (1931); *The Man Who Played God* (1932); *As You Desire Me* (1932); *Downstairs* (1932); *Little Man, What Now?* (1934); *I Live My Life* (1935); *Doughnuts and Society* (1936); *Topper* (1937); *Tarzan's Revenge* (1938); *Maid's Night Out* (1938); *Laugh It Off* (1939); and *Reap the Wild Wind* (1942).

HOTTELET, RICHARD C. b. Sept. 22, 1917, New York, N.Y. *Correspondent, Newscaster, Commentator.* **Series:** *CBS Morning News Roundup* (correspondent, mid 1940s–?); *CBS World News Roundup*, aka *The World Tonight* (correspondent, ca. 1944–ca. 1985); *Crisco Radio Newspaper* (correspondent, mid 1940s); *Richard C. Hottelet* (news analyst, 1944–1948); *The World is Our Beat* (correspondent, 1949); *You Are There* (reporter, 1947–1950).

Richard C. Hottelet, a first generation American of German parentage, gained a distinction that none of his journalism contemporaries did and one he would just as soon have missed. He became a prisoner of war, held in a German concentration camp, the only U.S. reporter singled out by the Gestapo for prolonged detainment. He earned a bachelor's degree in philosophy at Brooklyn College in 1937. A year later, while a graduate student at the University of Berlin, he quit school—which he discovered was promoting propaganda rather than education—to become a correspondent in Berlin for United Press International. From a very strategic vantage point, he was an eyewitness to Adolf Hitler's preparations for global conflict. Hottelet reported his observations candidly. The Nazis arrested him in 1941 for suspected spying activity against the Third Reich, however, and he was held in solitary confinement. After four months at Alexanderplatz and Moabit prisons, to his utter relief he and another American newsman were exchanged for a couple of German journalists held prisoner by the Allies.

Hottelet subsequently worked in London for the U.S. Office of War Information, although he reportedly found government work disappointing. Hired by Edward R. Murrow—the last of the contingent of infamous journalist "Murrow Boys"—Hottelet joined CBS News in London in January 1944. He would also, coincidentally, remain with CBS longer than any of the others in that special entourage. On D-Day, June 6, 1944, he provided American radio listeners with vivid word pictures of the plethora of ships situated at Normandy as he flew above them with the Ninth Air Force. Hottelet continued to be a major continental correspondent for CBS after the war ended, reporting from London, Moscow, Berlin, Bonn and other strategic locales.

In 1956 the network sent him to cover the United Nations in New York. From 1957 to 1961 he also presided over two daily *CBS News* programs on television, a quarter-hour early in the day (*CBS Morning News*) and five minutes on weekday afternoons. Following more than four decades at CBS, Hottelet retired in 1985 and worked for a while as the spokesman for the U.S. ambassador to the United Nations. Finally, in 1993, he ended his professional life by working for National Public Radio, moderating the broadcast series *America and the World*. He was the last of the Murrow Boys to cast his voice broadly over the nation.

HOUSTON, MARK. b. Oct. 3, 1913, Ohio; d. May 1971. *Announcer.* **Series:** *Queen for a Day* (ca. 1945–ca. 1950s).

HOWE, QUINCY. b. Aug. 17, 1900, Boston, Mass.; d. Feb. 19, 1977, New York, N.Y. *Commentator, Newscaster.* **Series:** *Invitation to Learning* (panelist, 1940–ca. 1964); *Quincy Howe and the News*, aka *Quincy Howe Comments* (commentator, 1938, 1943–1946, 1953–1957); *The World Today* (analyst, 1940–1946).

Quincy Howe was assessed as "an isolationist whose humor and intellect made him a formidable debater." He was also described as "a caustic-tongued Yankee." Having already been an editor, the Harvard grad turned up on New York's WQXR from 1939 to 1942 and captured his own news commentary slots on MBS, CBS and ABC. They included up to six nights a week on CBS in 1945 and five nights a week on ABC in later seasons. "Howe helped to make analysis an accepted part of news reporting," a source inferred. He also wrote more about the nature of radio commentary itself than any of his peers did. He expressed himself on it in *The News and How to Understand It* (Simon and Schuster, 1940) and in multiple periodical contributions.

When a sponsor became unhappy with his comments in 1947, Howe was removed from the CBS Radio airwaves. For a while, he left radio altogether to be a journalism professor. By 1953, nonetheless, he was back at the microphone, this time at ABC. There was some speculation, incidentally, that CBS's action in removing him likely prompted "more independence for the news division." At least one record suggests that Howe's ABC news commentary persisted to 1966 while another insists it lasted to 1968. Several others state that it ended in 1957. In between his radio network stints, meanwhile, he narrated important local series like *Frontiers of Science* in 1947 over New York's WCBS, the CBS flagship station.

His television stints were extensive while fleeting. He was one of two joint moderators for the CBS-TV Sunday evening documentary *U.N. Casebook* in 1948–1949. He moderated the CBS-TV primetime public affairs discussion *People's Platform* from 1948 to 1950. His next two continuing engagements, both in 1949–1950, were over CBS-TV where he interviewed subjects on the quarter-hour *In the First Person* and hosted the *Overseas Press Club*, a Sunday afternoon public affairs forum. Howe was also a panelist on the audience participation game show *It's News to Me* in 1951–1952 on CBS-TV. All of his later ongoing television work was at ABC. In 1953 he presided over a Sunday public service series, *Both Sides*. He was the debuting czar of the 1955 documentary *Medical Horizons*. Howe conducted a travelogue, *Outside the U.S.A.*, from 1955 to 1956. He anchored the weekly summertime *Campaign Roundup* in 1956. In 1961 he was a regular contributor for several months on the public affairs presentation *Eichmann on Trial*.

Radio historian Luther Sies contributed this appraisal of the commentator-newsman:

One of the most intellectually gifted and objectively honest news broadcasters, Howe wrote several significant books in addition to delivering his uniformly excellent analytic news broadcasts. His radio career began when moonlighting from his editor's job at Simon and Schuster.... He left both WQXR and Simon and Schuster to join CBS radio in 1939....

Howe was a keen observer of the American scene and a perceptive historian. His insights into the broadcasting news business were also particularly penetrating.... [In 1975] Howe commented: "For thirty years I was broadcasting news commentaries, mostly by radio, sometimes by TV, but the day of the all-purpose news analyst has long since vanished. It filled its purpose at the time but has gone the way of the wheelbarrow."

HOWELL, WAYNE (born Wayne Chappelle). b. ca. 1921; d. July 8, 1993, Pompano Beach, Fla. *Announcer, Newscaster, Emcee.* **Series:** *Honeymoon in New York* (1948); *The Jane Pickens Show*, aka *Pickens Party* (ca. 1948–ca. 1957); *The Martin and Lewis Show* (1949–?); *Monitor* (segment host, 1961); *Name That Tune* (1952–1953); *The NBC Radio Theater*, aka *The RCA Radio Theater* (1959–1960); *The $64,000 Question* (1955); *Wayne Howell and the News* (newscaster, 1949–1950, 1951); *The Wayne Howell Show* (host–disc jockey, 1950).

Wayne Howell was a sportscaster in 1940 with WTMA, Charleston, S.C. A decade later he was a disc jockey at NBC in New York and the same year announced network television's first regularly scheduled late night feature, *Broadway Open House* (1950–1951), on NBC-TV. He followed it in the fall of 1951 on New York's WNBT television, presiding over a half-hour daytime variety series, *The Leftover Revue*. It lasted just nine weeks. He introduced *The Jonathan Winters Show* (1957); *Concentration* (1958–1961); and the *Miss America Beauty Pageant* (1966–1985), all on NBC-TV. After 39 years with NBC's radio and television chains, Howell retired from active service in 1985.

HUDSON, TOM. *Announcer.* **Series:** *I Sustain the Wings* (ca. 1943–1945); *The Rudy Vallee Show*, aka *Vallee Varieties*, aka *Sealtest Village Store* (ca. 1940–ca. 1943); *Teentimers Club*, aka *Teentimers Canteen* (1945–1947, 1948).

HULL, WARREN. b. Jan. 17, 1903, Gasport, N.Y.; d. Sept. 14, 1974, Waterbury, Conn. *Announcer, Actor, Emcee.* **Series:** *The Gibson Family* (actor, 1934–1935); *Good News of 1938/1939/1940* (1938/1939/1940); *The Jack Haley Show* (1938–1939); *Log Cabin Jamboree* (actor, 1937–1938); *The Maxwell House Show Boat* (1937–?); *Melody and Madness* (host, 1939); *Mother Knows Best* (host, 1947–1948); *Spin to Win* (emcee, 1949); *Strike It Rich* (emcee, 1949–1957); *The Vicks Open House* (host, 1934–1938); *Vox Pop* (co-host, 1942–1948); *Your Hit Parade* (1935–?).

Long before he became the decade-long star of a radio and television series that made him publicly recognizable and famous for life, Warren Hull was plying his craft as an entertainer at other venues. After a semester at the University of Rochester's Eastman School of Music, he transferred to New York University. Musical comedies and operettas introduced him to the stage. He appeared in productions of *Follow Through*; *The Love Song*; *My Maryland*; *Rain or Shine*; and *The Student Prince* in a single season, 1924–1925. After that, he built a reputation by performing in B-movies, the second features that filled out twin bills at cinema houses. Signed by Warner Brothers, Hull surfaced in countless *Spider* and *Green Hornet* serials while playing in excess of 35 less-than-memorable films, among them: *Bengal Tiger*; *Bowery Blitzkrieg*; *Freshman Love*; *Her Husband's Secretary*; *The Lone Wolf Meets a Lady*; *Miss Pacific Fleet*; *Night Key*; *Paradise Isle*; *Personal Maid's Secret*; *Remedy for Riches*; *Star Reporter*; and *Wagons Westward*.

In the 1930s he looked toward broadcasting as a sideline venture which ultimately turned his career into a totally new dimension. Although continuing to appear in celluloid, he found the emergence of radio as an enchanting diversion. Hull gained opportunities as a vocalist, writer and producer in the new medium. He was so well entrenched by 1937 that he was elected one of the inaugural officers of the newly formed American Federation of Radio Artists (AFRA), which later incorporated television into its body and became AFTRA. Within a decade Hull was turning up in *that* new medium, too. He was master of ceremonies of *Radio City Matinee*, a local hour-long show three days a week beginning in May 1946 over WNBT, the New York video outlet of NBC. His TV credits were extended in 1948–1949 when he hosted a variety series, *Ladies Day*, subsequently renamed *The Warren Hull Sh*ow. Simultaneously, he presided over *This is the Missus* on television, an extension of *The Missus Goes a-Shopping* game show that had appeared earlier on radio.

Unquestionably, however, Hull's most notable claim to prominence was "the show with a heart," *Strike It Rich*, a series that sought to help people who were down on their luck. While it appeared on CBS or NBC Radio continuously for 10-and-a-half years (1947–1957), it reached its zenith when CBS took it to television on May 7, 1951, where it appealed to millions who had only heard it— or heard about it. The feature was CBS's initial attempt to offer sustained daytime entertainment programming prior to noon. A couple of months later, NBC-TV added a weekly primetime telecast of the live show, exposing it to vast numbers of added watchers (July 4, 1951–Jan. 12, 1955). Meanwhile, the weekday series persisted on CBS-TV through Jan. 3, 1958. It later returned in three brief reincarnations, albeit with different hosts: Bert Parks, 1973; Tom Kelly, 1978; and Joe Garagiola, 1986.

On *Strike It Rich*, Hull (the 23rd great grandson of English King Henry II) was a visibly demonstrative reactionary to the lamentable situations presented. His eyes frequently moistened, tears stained his cheeks and sometimes his lips quivered at the stories told by some of *Strike It Rich*'s contestants. He was so deeply touched by the personal plights of those appearing before him that, on rare occasions, producer Walt Framer sent in announcer Ralph Paul to take over the show while Hull composed himself. Hull's strong emotions may have stemmed from personal convictions originating in the Quaker environment in which he was raised. His behavior often evidenced tender, benevolent, supportive traits, seemingly characteristics of "the show with a heart."

HUNTLEY, CHET. b. Dec. 10, 1911, Cardwell, Mont.; d. March 20, 1974, Big Sky, Mont. *Newscaster, Announcer.* **Series:** *Chet Huntley and the News* (newscaster, 1956); *I Was There* (narrator, ca. late 1930s–ca. early 1940s); *Richfield Reporter* (newscaster, ca. early 1950s).

Chet Huntley belonged to a minuscule handful of network reporters from radio that experienced the good fortune of landing in permanent anchor chairs before network TV cameras during that medium's embryonic days. (Others include ABC's John Daly and CBS's Douglas Edwards.) Huntley, who was to be paired with David Brinkley for NBC's *Huntley-Brinkley Report* (1956–1970), began his network training at CBS, as did competitors Daly and Edwards. Daly's program, aired on fewer affiliates and with a far smaller budget, was an also-ran in the ratings. Not until the NBC show made inroads into CBS's lead, however, did the latter chain think seriously about replacing Edwards, which occurred in 1962. By then Huntley and Brinkley owned first place.

Born and raised on a cattle-and-sheep ranch in Montana, Huntley later enrolled at the University of Washington as a premed student. But in his senior year, while working odd jobs at a small Seattle radio station, he got hooked on the concept of a radio career. He subsequently launched that pilgrimage in 1934 at Spokane's KHQ, relocating to KGW, Portland, Ore., in a couple of years. The following season (1937) he landed at KFI in Los Angeles. By 1939 he transitioned across town to Hollywood's KNX. From then until the early 1950s, his voice was carried by the CBS West Coast hookup, where he was a member of the special events staff.

In 1943 Huntley inaugurated a 10-minute news analysis entry for the Pacific coast chain. During that epoch he seized several opportunities to deliver some innovative programming, a portion of which might be considered divisive in its day. In 1944, for instance, he developed an imposing feature, *These Are Americans*, focused on the plight of Negroes in society. The entry won critical acclaim for KNX. Between 1951 and 1955 Huntley was affiliated with ABC in Los Angeles. Afterward, he moved east, joining NBC in New York in 1955.

Gary Paul Gates, who chronicled the history of CBS News, assessed: "During his years as a top newscaster in Los Angeles, Huntley acquired a reputation as a fearless commentator who took strong stands on McCarthyism and other controversial issues. In 1955, when NBC hired him and brought him to New York, there was talk that he would become that network's answer to [CBS's premiere reigning journalist] Ed Murrow. The political climate of the time was such that some NBC executives were a little nervous about that prospect. But they had nothing to fear. As it turned out, NBC would have it both ways with Huntley: he would become a star of Murrovian magnitude but in a way that was seldom divisive or troublesome. Indeed, in the years that followed, it was Brinkley, far more than Huntley, who made waves with his political commentary."

NBC-TV's coverage of the 1952 political conventions was fairly disastrous. To avoid a repeat of it in 1956, the brass decided to try what hadn't been done before by placing two professionals in anchor chairs before the cameras. Huntley and Brinkley got the nod and—while their web remained squarely in second place behind CBS at the conventions—they significantly improved the net's ratings. Better still, the critics were elated, including Jack Gould's *New York Times* column which suggested they "interjected the much-needed note of humor in commentary." They were, from then on, an "item" and weren't about to slip from NBC's limelight.

The Huntley-Brinkley Report debuted in October 1956, yet it steadily lost audience to *Douglas Edwards with the News* at rival CBS throughout its first year. It took until autumn 1958, in fact, for Huntley and Brinkley to pull even with Edwards. (One factor making a difference was that the Texas Co. and its Texaco products and services had purchased the entire NBC show that spring, infusing it with guaranteed revenue and more of it, increasing the program's ability to do more things and to do them better.) The two news shows continued neck-and-neck until the team performed a rout of CBS's traditional reporting techniques at the 1960 political conventions. Huntley-Brinkley's huge victory derived enough momentum to give them a commanding lead over Edwards on weeknights, a trophy they maintained for seven years.

The show's concluding words every night became quite familiar to millions of Americans, turning into a snicker with some. Brinkley said: "Goodnight, Chet." To which his opposite replied: "Goodnight, David. And goodnight for NBC News." Reuven Frank, the show's commencing producer, derived the epigraph. Years later, after his trademark signature resonated with the audience, Frank gleefully boasted: "I wrote something that got into the language."

Huntley gathered many other NBC Television credits for his portfolio beyond the nightly news: 1956–1962, host of *Outlook*, aka *Chet Huntley Reporting*, aka *Time: Present—Chet Huntley Reporting*, a weekly half-hour analysis of offbeat and non-publicized news events; 1960, co-host with Frank McGee of *World Wide 60*, a primetime hour-long current events documentary; 1961, narrator of the premiering hour-long *Dupont Show of the Week*; and 1962–1968, periodic narrator of *Actuality Specials*, a collection of hour-long documentaries on a variety of themes.

In 1970 at age 58 Huntley retired from broadcasting, returning to Montana to establish Big Sky, a recreational complex. NBC-TV floundered following his departure while Cronkite and CBS reaped the spoils of it for years.

HUSING, EDWARD BRITT (TED). b. Nov. 27, 1901, Bronx, N.Y.; d. Aug. 10, 1962, Pasadena, Calif. *Announcer, Sportscaster.* **Series:** *The Campbell's Tomato Juice Program*, aka *The Burns and Allen Show* (ca. 1935–ca. 1937); *Caravan* (1934–1935); *The Jane Froman Show*, aka *The Pontiac Show* (1938); *Joe Palooka* (1932); *The Linit Bath Club Revue*, aka *The Fred Allen Show* (1932–1933); *Saturday Night Swing Club* (ca. 1938–1939); *Here's Morgan*, aka *The Henry Morgan Show* (ca. early 1940s); *The March of Time* (narrator, 1931); *The Oldsmobile Program* (sportscaster, 1933); *The Old Gold Hour*, aka *The Paul Whiteman Show* (1929); *Philco Radio Hour*, aka *Philco Concert Orchestra* (ca. 1929–ca. 1931); *Rhythm at Eight* (1935); *Seven Star Revue* (1933–1934); *The Studebaker Champions* (sportscaster, 1930s); *Ted Husing* (1936); *Ted Husing's Sportslants* (ca. 1928–ca. 1930); *Tonight on Broadway* (1946); *The True Story Hour with Mary and Bob* (1932); *The Variety Show* (interviewer, 1946).

"Ted Husing," claimed a media source, "is ... in a class by himself and is regarded by many fans as the greatest of all sportscasters." Entertainer Ralph Edwards conceded, "Marconi invented radio, but Ted Husing knew what to do with it."

Another radio historiographer, John Dunning, offered a perceptive characterization of Husing in his second chronicle of the medium:

Husing (... as [Red] Barber saw it) spent his announcing career "possessed by the greatness of [Graham] McNamee." Although the *New York Herald-Tribune* lauded him in 1927 as "consistently better than the more famous Graham McNamee and Phillips Carlin," Barber maintained that "Ted was to spend his entire life trying to outdo Graham." Husing was "devious," wrote Barber; "he schemed" and was difficult to like. He arrived at WJZ in 1924 and quickly became man-of-all-work at the microphone. He opened the station at 9 A.M. and closed it at midnight: he announced most of the morning shows as well as the band remotes more than 12 hours later....

In 1925 he became assistant to Maj. J. Andrew White and began to cover sports.... In 1927 he moved to the fledgling network that was about to become CBS. Maj. White had helped organize it, and Husing came in as his assistant.... In 1928, when White was ill and could not travel to Chicago for a football commitment, Husing was sent in his place. His announcing was poised and supremely self-assured..., and from then until 1946 he was the network's top man.

He covered his first World Series in 1929 and his first Kentucky Derby the same year.... He suffered a setback in 1935, when he was barred from baseball coverage by Commissioner K.M. Landis.... The commissioner had found Husing's criticisms of umpires annoying.

Husing moved on to other sports. He began his Orange Bowl coverage in 1936, covered the America's Cup race from a Coast Guard cutter in 1937, and was regarded by a *Radio Guide* writer as "one of the ablest golf reporters working in radio or any other medium."

Husing, then a payroll clerk at a hosiery mill, had gotten to WJZ originally when he answered a newspaper ad for a radio announcer, reportedly beating out 600 contenders for the $45-a-week job. In a dispute over money, he left WJZ in 1927 to work for Boston's WBET. He returned to New York later that year, to WHN, prior to the formation of the Columbia Phonograph Broadcasting System (as it was then called) on Sept. 18. Husing joined CBS on Dec. 25. One of his more memorable assignments was to cover the presidential inauguration of Herbert Hoover in March 1929 for his web. He was comfortable meeting dignitaries of many persuasions in his work as the years flew by.

Meanwhile, at the suggestion of his CBS

superiors, Husing acquired more sonorous sounds when—under the supervision of a physician—his nose was purposely shattered by a small mallet and reset, widening his antrums (or sinuses) to alter the resonance of his tone. That wasn't an uncommon practice at the time. Indeed, some announcers went to extreme lengths to protect their earning capabilities and to make them even more valuable to their employers! "My voice sounded better, and my nose didn't lose its sensitivity," Husing allowed.

Nearly two decades hence—after departing CBS in the mid 1940s—he rejoined WHN as a $250,000-a-year disc jockey and presided over *Ted Husing's Bandstand* (1947). He ultimately conducted a similar program under the very same banner at New York's WMGM (1948–1954) while offering that station's listeners *Ted Husing Sports* (1951–1952) as a bonus. In 1954 he was sidelined by a brain tumor. Husing made a brief stab at returning to the air in 1957 with CBS, where he was paid $150 weekly for a few appearances on Los Angeles' KFI. He was virtually blind by then, however, and an invalid. His broadcasting days were over and after a few months of trying to prove otherwise, he focused on writing his second autobiography. *My Eyes Are in My Heart*, released in 1959, supplanted *Ten Years Before the Mike*, a memoir published in 1935.

IRISH, JACK. *Announcer.* **Series:** *The Adventures of Father Brown* (1945); *Official Detective* (1947–?); *Take a Number* (1948–1952, ca. 1953–ca. 1955); *Twenty Questions* (ca. 1946–?).

IRVING, CHARLES (born Irving Zipperman). b. July 30, 1912, Minnesota; d. Feb. 15, 1981, Minneapolis, Minn. *Director, Actor, Announcer.* **Series:** *Bobby Benson and the B-Bar-B Riders* (actor, 1949–1951); *The Breakfast Club* (1943–1944); *Coronet Quick Quiz* (host, 1944–1945); *A Crime Letter from Dan Dodge* (director, 1952–1953); *Exploring the Unknown* (narrator, 1945–1948); *The Fat Man* (1946–ca. 1950); *Here's Morgan*, aka *The Henry Morgan Show* (ca. early to mid 1940s); *Heritage* (narrator, 1952–1953); *The Joe Dimaggio Show* (actor, 1949–1950); *The Morey Amsterdam Show* (1948–1949); *Tales of Willie Piper* (actor, 1946–1948); *The Texaco Star Theater*, aka *The Milton Berle Show* (actor, 1948–1949); *This is Nora Drake* (director, ca. early 1950s); *Those Websters* (1945–1948); *Vic and Sade* (ca. 1940s); *Young Doctor Malone* (actor, mid 1940s–1947).

Charles Irving was on the air at Chicago's WGN in 1942 as a newscaster. It was the first of many hats he would wear across a diversified broadcasting career that lasted a quarter-of-a-century. The multifaceted Irving produced ABC-TV's short-lived musical comedy *That Wonderful Guy* in 1950 and was the original producer-director of CBS-TV's daytime serial *Search for Tomorrow* (1951–1957). At the inception of that venerable soap opera that set standards for much of what followed in video daytime fare for a decade, Irving was connected with 60 radio shows weekly as an actor, announcer or director. Simultaneously he was also producing *The Sammy Kaye Show* on CBS-TV, a live 30-minute performance every Saturday night (1951–1952). In her memoir, Mary Stuart, the actress who played the heroine in *Search for Tomorrow*, surmised that Irving, a workaholic, "was the busiest man on Madison Avenue and about to run himself to death."

He was fired from his duties with the daytime serial in 1957 (where he had been that pioneering cast's empathetic conduit to management over numerous issues for years) after a new advertising agency took over the show. Irving relocated on the West Coast to be with his wife Holly, an actress with a small part in a short-lived NBC-TV sitcom *Blondie*. Irving found work there, too, winning a role in the 1957 Warner Bros. movie *A Face in the Crowd*, the first and most important of a half-dozen celluloid productions he appeared in over the next decade. He also directed or acted in TV series like *Bewitched* and *The Andy Griffith Show*. For a year (1965–1966) Irving portrayed Admiral Vincent Beckett on the NBC-TV hour-long drama *The Wackiest Ship in the Army*.

JACKSON, ALLAN HARRY. b. Dec. 4, 1915, Hot Springs, Ark.; d. April 26, 1976, New York, N.Y. *Newscaster, Announcer.* **Series:** *Allan Jackson and the News* (newscaster, 1950–1956); *CBS Morning News Roundup* (news anchor, mid 1940s–?); *CBS News* (newscaster, 1940s–mid 1970s); *Chevrolet Spotlights the News* (newscaster, mid 1950s);

Crisco Radio Newspaper (newscaster, mid 1940s); *The New York Philharmonic Symphony Orchestra* (1950); *News of the World* (newscaster, 1943–1944); *The World Tonight* (newscaster, 1940s–mid 1970s).

Who's Who in TV & Radio stated: "Allan Jackson's crisp, cosmopolitan delivery belies his deep South origin." Harry Jackson (the moniker he used at the time) left Arkansas to attend the University of Illinois at Champaign-Urbana. While enrolled there, he did some part time radio announcing at Urbana's WILL. Returning home for the summer to the Land of Opportunity, he added to his preparation for a career in network radio by presiding over local dance band remotes aired by Hot Springs' KTHS.

Jackson became a full time announcer at Kalamazoo's WKZO about 1936 and returned to his roots at KTHS in 1937 after a physician advised him to seek a warmer climate. Other announcing opportunities arrived in quick succession at Cincinnati's WLW, Louisville's WHAS and—by 1939—with the Texas State Network. By then he was becoming widely known as Allan Jackson. He signed on at Memphis' WMC not long afterward and left it in 1943 to go to New York as a member of the elite CBS news staff. He remained in that coveted spot 32 years.

Aside from his 15-minute weeknight presentation for Metropolitan Life Insurance Co. for a half-dozen years, Jackson was one of the most reliable and authoritative news voices Americans heard on their dials in the final decade of radio's golden age, often on weekends, always on CBS. He gained the pivotal 6 o'clock nightly quarter-hour when in March 1950 Mel Life cancelled a four-year contract to underwrite a newscast at that hour with Eric Sevareid.

The latter newsman, one of the original "Murrow Boys," was by then a highly controversial staffer who took caustic potshots at Sen. Joseph McCarthy and his ilk for branding many public figures as communists, often by innuendo. As a consequence, McCarthy's cohorts labeled Sevareid "Eric the Red." Sevareid won a Peabody Award for his nightly news show in 1949; nonetheless, he was being hammered by the mail, and was quietly transferred to an unsponsored 11 P.M. slot, losing a $1,200 weekly fee in the bargain. Jackson, meanwhile, was considered a "newscaster who could be relied upon not to make many waves," according to one source, and Met Life resumed sponsorship of the early evening series.

During the 1953–1954 television season, Jackson was given the additional assignment of moderating a CBS-TV public affairs discussion series, *Youth Takes a Stand*. Each week different young people confronted a well-known newscaster (e.g., Charles Collingwood, Douglas Edwards, et al.), exchanging their perspectives on current events transpiring in the nation and the world.

In the 1940s and 1950s Jackson appeared on numerous one-of-a-kind CBS Radio features including D-Day Coverage (June 6–7, 1944); Junction of Russian-American Forces (April 27, 1945); V-E Day Coverage (May 8, 1945); Prelude to Moscow (March 9, 1947); Berlin Air Supply (July 20, 1948); As Europe Sees the Marshall Plan (Sept. 11, 1948); Atomic City U.S.A. (Feb. 25, 1950); The [Douglas] MacArthur Story (April 11, 1951); The *Andrea Doria* Sinking (July 26, 1956); The Best of [Jack] Benny (March 31, 1957); and The Big News of 1957 (Dec. 29, 1957). Jackson was the first network reporter to inform a radio audience of President John F. Kennedy's death on Nov. 22, 1963. Using their own resources, competing networks confirmed the story about 15 minutes after Jackson announced it on CBS.

JACKSON, JAY. b. Nov. 4, 1918, Stockdale, Ohio; d. Aug. 16, 2005, Jupiter, Fla. *Announcer, Actor, Emcee.* **Series:** *The Beatrice Kay Show* (1946); *The Bickersons* (commercial spokesman, 1951); *Broadway Talks Back* (1946–1947); *David Harding, Counterspy* (ca. 1950–ca. 1952); *The Falcon* (1950); *Gangbusters* (ca. 1948–1949); *Information Please* (ca. 1940s); *The Philip Morris Playhouse on Broadway* (actor, 1951); *The Radio Reader's Digest* (ca. 1946–1948); *The Sammy Kaye Show* (1948–1949); *Twenty Questions* (quizmaster, ca. early 1950s).

Jay Jackson was educated at a couple of universities in his native Buckeye state, Miami and Ohio State. In 1937, new to radio, he joined WCOL in Columbus. He relocated to WBNS in the same city five years later.

Jackson readily adapted to television

when it came along. His radio show, *Twenty Questions*, made the leap to the tube and Jackson was one of its quizmasters, appearing on Dumont Television in 1953–1954 and ABC-TV in 1954–1955. He presided over the primetime version of *Tic Tac Dough* in 1957–1958 on NBC-TV. In the 1950s he also announced *Father Knows Best*, *Masquerade Party* and *The Perry Como Show* for the small screen audiences. He narrated a trio of Laurel and Hardy video retrospectives in the 1960s, too.

According to David Schwartz of the Game Show Network, Jackson hosted what would arguably become one of TV's most memorable imaginary portrayals of a real game series. On Jan. 28, 1956 Jackson played Herb Norris, fictional quizmaster of *The $99,000 Answer* during a classic installment of Jackie Gleason's CBS-TV sitcom *The Honeymooners*. Spoofing *The $64,000 Question*, bus driver Ralph Kramden (Gleason) competed in the category of popular songs. An arrogant Kramden—who kept his apartment house neighbors awake all week while cramming with pianist Ed Norton (Art Carney)—blew the first question upon returning to the quiz show for a second appearance.

JACOBS, JOHNNY. b. June 22, 1916, Milwaukee, Wis.; d. Feb. 8, 1982, Los Angeles, Calif. *Announcer, Instrumentalist*. **Series:** *The Beulah Show* (1953–1954); *December Bride* (1952–1953); *The Doris Day Show* (ca. 1952–ca. 1953); *Dreamboat* (1951); *Earn Your Vacation* (1949–1950); *Frontier Gentleman* (1958); *I Love Lucy* (1952); *The Jo Stafford Show* (ca. 1953); *The Johnny Mercer Show* (1953–1954); *Juke Box Jury* (1954–1956); *Junior Miss* (ca. early 1950s); *Make-Believe Town, Hollywood* (1949–1950, 1951); *The Martin and Lewis Show* (ca. early 1950s); *My Friend Irma* (ca. late 1940s, early 1950s); *Our Miss Brooks* (ca. 1940s, 1950s); *The Rosemary Clooney Show* (1953, 1954–1955); *Stars in the Air* (1951–1952); *The Steve Allen Show* (early 1950s); *Tell It Again* (percussionist, 1948–1949); *Your Tropical Trip* (1951).

As his radio fortunes faded, television lit up for Johnny Jacobs. He was the primetime announcer for *The Betty White Show* in 1958 on ABC-TV. During the 1962–1963 season he introduced not just one or two but *three* (count 'em!) sitcoms simultaneously: *Fair Exchange* (CBS); *I'm Dickens, He's Fenster* (ABC); and *Mr. Smith Goes to Washington* (ABC). Subsequently, Jacobs became the interlocutor for the year-long beauty competition *Dream Girl of '67* carried by ABC-TV in 1966–1967. He moved into the audience participation arena as he welcomed a handful of popular shows beginning with *The Newlywed Game* (1966–ca. 1974, ABC) emceed by Bob Eubanks and *The Joker's Wild* (1972–1975, CBS) hosted by Jack Barry. In the latter year (1975), Jacobs welcomed three short-run features: *Blank Check* (NBC), with Art James presiding; *Spin-Off* and *Give-N-Take*, both CBS properties with Jim Lange as host.

JAMES, DENNIS. b. Aug. 24, 1917, Jersey City, N.J.; d. June 3, 1997, Palm Springs, Calif. *Announcer, Emcee*. **Series:** *Lawyer Q* (master of ceremonies, 1947); *The Peter Donald Show* (1947); *Ted Mack's Original Amateur Hour* (1948–1951).

Dennis James was educated at St. Peter's College and Carnegie Hall's Theatre School of Dramatic Arts. He was a local radio announcer and actor when—in 1938—Dumont Television hired him as an announcer for its embryonic New York–based operation. In his new capacity he initiated a number of firsts for the 300 TV set owners at the time in and around Gotham. Media historian Ray Poindexter enumerated them: master of ceremonies of a variety show and of a daytime show; host of a sports show and of a commercial show; narrator of the Easter Parade; live eyewitness news commentator; actor in a dramatic program; and commercial, wrestling and kinescope announcer. He would later preside over Dumont's *Prime Time Boxing* (1948–1950). In the meantime, James left Jersey City's WATT in 1940 for the more promising challenges proffered by New York's WNEW.

It was in television, however, that James made a name for himself, particularly as a game show host extraordinaire. His credits included associations with all of the following: *Cash and Carry* (1946–1947, Dumont); *Ted Mack's Original Amateur Hour* (1948–1949, Dumont; 1949–1954, 1957–1958, NBC; 1955–1957, 1960, ABC; 1959, 1960–1970, CBS); *Okay Mother* (1948–1951, Dumont); *Stop the Music!* (occasional host, 1949–1952, 1954–1956, ABC); *The Dennis James Show* (1951–1952, ABC); *Chance of a*

Lifetime (1952–1953, 1955–1956, ABC; 1953–1955, Dumont); *Turn to a Friend* (1953, ABC); *Judge for Yourself* (1954, NBC); *The Name's the Same* (1954–1955, ABC); *On Your Account* (1954–1956, CBS); *Two for the Money* (ca. 1954–1956, CBS); *High Finance* (1956, CBS); *Club 60* (1957–1958, NBC); *Haggis Baggis* (1958–1959, NBC); *Your First Impression* (1962–1964, NBC); *People Will Talk* (1963, NBC); *P.D.Q.* (1965–ca. 1966, syndication); *Can You Top This?* (1969–1970, syndication); *The Price is Right* (1972–1974, syndication); *Name That Tune* (1974–1980, NBC).

JAMES, HUGH (born Hugh McIlrevey). b. Oct. 13, 1915, Bronxville, N.Y.; d. June 17, 2001, Madison, Conn. *Announcer.* **Series:** *Call the Police* (1948–1949); *Famous Jury Trials* (ca. late 1930s, 1940s); *House in the Country* (1941–1942); *Lowell Thomas and the News* (1937–?); *The Parker Family* (1939–ca. early 1940s); *The Right to Happiness* (mid 1950s); *The Second Mrs. Burton* (ca. 1946–ca. early 1950s); *Star for a Night* (1943–1944); *Three Star Extra* (1947–1949); *True Detective Mysteries* (ca. 1944–ca. late 1940s or early 1950s); *The Voice of Firestone* (ca. late 1930s–1957); *Walter Winchell's Journal*, aka *The Jergens Journal*; *Wendy Warren and the News* (1947–1958, adopting the pseudonym Bill Flood); *When a Girl Marries* (1940s–ca. 1951); *Youth vs. Age* (1939–1940).

While in high school in the early 1930s, Hugh James decided to devote the rest of his life to radio. He had already performed on stage and screen in high school. A determined James was hired as a page at NBC during his teenage years. Progressively he advanced to tour guide (conducting the first group of sightseers through the newly completed Radio City studios) and subsequently delivering on-air station breaks. At age 20 he was appointed to a local outlet's announcing staff in Philadelphia. Within a few months he was transferred to NBC's Washington, D.C., deputation. James assisted with the web's coverage of President Franklin D. Roosevelt's second inaugural in early 1937. He was summoned to New York in August that year to introduce the weeknight radio commentaries of Lowell Thomas. James was later appropriated to the Blue network as it began operating independently of the NBC Red.

After becoming a freelance announcer in the 1940s, the narrator shifted back and forth between webs throughout a typical workday. For 15 years he presided over four daily network series. Although his deep bass voice could be instantly recognized on various soap operas carried by competing chains for rival soap and foodstuffs manufacturers—for 11 years he was "Bill Flood" on *Wendy Warren and the News* to avoid a conflict between sponsors—if there was a single *voice* of Firestone, it was Hugh James. Attired in tux, tails, white shirt and bow tie, he was the epitome of the traditions espoused by the sponsoring Firestone family and the commercial manufacturing concern they represented. For many years James introduced that venerable, widely admired series of semi-classical music, initially on radio and then simulcast in most of its later years by NBC Radio and Television (1949–1954) and by ABC Radio and Television (1954–1957). James once observed, "Sincerity is the most important quality an announcer can possess."

JAMES, OWEN. *Announcer.* **Series:** *The Adventures of Bill Lance* (substitute announcer, 1944–1945; regular announcer, 1947–1948); *The First Hundred Years* (1949); *Hawthorne's Adventures* (1948); *A Johnny Fletcher Mystery* (1948); *Mirth and Melody* (1948); *The Vera Vague Show* (1949); *The Whistler* (whistler).

JEWETT, EDWARD K. (TED). b. Yokohama, Japan. *Announcer, Actor.* **Series:** *Cavalcade of America* (actor, ca. 1935–ca. 1939, ca. 1940–ca. 1953); *The Chicago Theater of the Air* (ca. 1930s, 1940s); *Ellen Randolph* (actor, ca. 1940–ca. 1941); *G.E. Circle*, aka *Home Circle* (1931–1933); *The March of Time* (actor, 1930s–mid 1940s).

Ted Jewett's dad was a businessman in the silk trade and also the Danish consul in Japan at the time of his son's birth. In 1910 the family resettled at Plainfield, N.J., and the youngster attended local private schools before enrolling at Princeton University. After leaving Princeton in 1926, young Jewett joined his father in the silk industry. But he was restless, having studied public speaking and even having considered becoming an actor or statesman. He soon focused his attention on radio. Jewett was frustrated when he was passed over more than once for radio opportunities but he was rewarded at last in June 1930 with an announcing slot at NBC.

JOHNSON, EDWARD. Emcee. **Series:** *The Metropolitan Opera Auditions of the Air* (host, 1935–1945, 1948–ca. 1958).

Edward Johnson was managing director of the Metropolitan Opera Co. between 1935–1950.

JOHNSTONE, JACK. b. May 7, 1906, New York, N.Y.; d. Nov. 16, 1991. *Director, Writer, Announcer.* **Series:** *The Adventures of Superman* (writer, ca. 1940s); *Buck Rogers in the 25th Century* (writer-producer-director-announcer, 1930s); *The CBS Radio Workshop* (director, ca. 1956–ca. 1957); *Crime Doctor* (director, 1940s); *Hollywood Star Playhouse* (director, 1950–1953); *Hollywood Startime* (director, 1946–1947); *Jack Johnstone's Dramas* (director, 1938–ca. 1939); *Johnny Presents* (director, 1937–1941); *The Man Called X* (director, ca. 1945–ca. 1948); *Orson Welles' Radio Almanac* (director, 1944); *Philip Morris Playhouse* (director, ca. 1948–1949); *The Prudential Family Hour of Stars* (director, 1948–1950); *Richard Diamond, Private Detective* (director, ca. 1949–ca. 1953); *The Six Shooter* (director, 1953–1954); *Somebody Knows* (narrator-director, 1950); *The Whistler* (director, ca. 1940s, 1950s); *Who Knows?* (producer-announcer, 1940–1941); *Yours Truly, Johnny Dollar* (writer-producer-director, 1955–1956; writer-director, 1956–1960; writer, 1960–ca. 1962).

While Jack Johnstone worked for an ad agency at $32 weekly, a cohort was given the task of writing *Buck Rogers in the 25th Century* for radio. Johnstone's pal asked if he would like to pen a few episodes; the upshot was a continuing writing collaboration. On one occasion—at the request of the show's director, Carlo D'Angelo—Johnstone pinch-hit for him in his absence during a rehearsal. Not long afterward, D'Angelo suggested Johnstone as his replacement as director. He got the job and in time Johnstone took over all the show's writing as well as directing it. His take-home pay had increased from $32 to $300 weekly! And after he filled in for a missing announcer one day, he was asked to perform that duty permanently as well. Years later, looking back on the professional demands of his calendar in the 1930s and 1940s, Johnstone recalled that he was so busy, "I left the house right after breakfast, got home between midnight and one o'clock."

JORDAN, MAX. b. April 21, 1895, San Remo, Italy; d. Nov. 28, 1977. *Correspondent, Commentator.* **Series:** *NBC News* (news analyst, 1936–?, 1946–?); overseas correspondent, 1939–?).

Max Jordan joined NBC News in 1931 as a European representative. Before the end of that decade he had been named the chain's European staff director. That was the easy part. Getting there was a demanding pilgrimage. He lived in Italy, Germany and Switzerland during adolescence, learning Italian, French and German while growing up. He studied at the universities of Frankfort, Jena and Berlin, earning a doctorate at Jena.

Although he worked as a newspaperman as far back as high school, Jordan decided to seek a chair on a university faculty teaching religious philosophy. That didn't happen and he ruled it out in 1920. Instead, he accepted a post with a newspaper consortium in Berlin that year, focusing on international affairs. He joined the overseas staff of the Hearst newspaper syndicate in 1922 and was soon sent to New York and then reassigned to Washington, D.C. In between freelance magazine articles and other work, Jordan traveled extensively in this hemisphere, from Alaska, Canada and the U.S. through Central America, the Caribbean and South America. His preparatory years of training for his future at NBC might have qualified him better than for anyone else going into a similar capacity in that period.

JOY, DICK. b. Dec. 28, 1915, Putnam, Conn.; d. Oct. 31, 1991, Medford, Ore. *Announcer.* **Series:** *The Adventures of Bill Lance* (1944–1945); *The Adventures of Sam Spade, Detective* (1946–1951); *The Baby Snooks Show* (ca. late 1940s, early 1950s); *Blue Ribbon Town* (1943–1944); *The Danny Kaye Show* (1945–1946); *Dr. Kildare* (1950–1951); *Forever Ernest* (1946); *My Secret Ambition* (1937–1938); *The Nelson Eddy Show* (1942–1943); *The New Old Gold Show* (1942–?); *The Sad Sack* (1946); *The Saint* (1945); *Silver Theater* (1940); *The Spike Jones Show,* aka *Spotlight Review* (1949); *The Telephone Hour* (1945–ca.

1946); *Those We Love* (1942–1945); *Vox Pop* (1939–1943, 1945–1946).

While he was a student at the National School of Broadcasting in Los Angeles, Dick Joy handled the sound effects for a religious program that aired over Long Beach's KFOX. Moving to the University of Southern California afterward, he was the radio reporter for the collegiate newspaper. Instead of spending his life in print journalism as he had intended, Joy was persuaded to pursue electronic media instead. He gained a slot on the campus station in March 1935 and never looked back, performing on "hundreds" of USC programs, a source affirmed. Some of those were picked up by Hollywood's KNX, a 50,000-watt powerhouse. Joy's career progressed with a staff announcing job at nearby KEHE while he was still in college. He later switched to KHJ. By 1937 he was airing KNX-originated series broadcast from Los Angeles over CBS.

Nine years afterward he and some more investors purchased KCMJ at Palm Springs, reportedly the city's initial radio station. Joy lived there for a couple of years, commuting back and forth between home and his network assignments in L.A. Selling his interest in KCMJ in 1951, he bought into KTTV television. For 17 years he was also news director and lead newscaster at KFAC Radio. On network television, Joy introduced the CBS domestic sitcom *December Bride* (1954–1959) starring Spring Byington and the NBC private eye drama *Meet McGraw* (1957–1958) featuring Frank Lovejoy.

KADELL, CARLTON. b. Aug. 21, 1907, Danville, Ill.; d. March 14, 1975, Chicago, Ill. *Actor, Announcer, Emcee.* **Series:** *Amos 'n' Andy* (1936, 1945–1947); *Armstrong of the SBI* (actor, ca. 1950–1951); *Backstage Wife* (actor, ca. 1940s, 1950s); *Big Town* (1937–1942); *The Cases of Mr. Ace* (1945); *The Dorothy Lamour Show*, aka *Front and Center*, aka *Sealtest Variety Theater* (1947, 1948–1949); *The Edgar Bergen and Charlie McCarthy Show*, aka *The Chase and Sanborn Hour* (1937–?); *The Goldbergs* (1940); *The Jack Carson Show* (ca. 1940s); *Kay Fairchild, Stepmother* (ca. 1938–?); *Kitty Keene, Incorporated* (actor, ca. 1937–1941); *A Life in Your Hands*, aka *Jonathan Kegg* (actor, 1950, 1952); *Masquerade* (actor, 1946–1947); *Mayor of the Town* (1940s); *Music from Hollywood*, aka *Hal Kemp and His Orchestra*, aka *Chesterfield Time* (1937); *Red Ryder* (actor, ca. 1943–1945); *The Right to Happiness* (actor, ca. 1940s, 1950s); *Road of Life* (actor, ca. 1940s, 1950); *The Romance of Helen Trent* (actor, 1939–ca. 1940); *The Saint* (ca. 1940s); *Sky King* (actor, 1954); *Strange as it Seems* (1939–1940); *Tarzan* (actor, 1934–1936); *Treasury Star Parade* (host, 1942–1944); *Wings of Destiny* (actor, ca. 1940–ca. 1941).

At 16, Carlton KaDell captured second prize ($5) when he warbled "Little Mother of Mine" during a Norfolk, Neb., amateur talent competition. Despite the fact he hailed from a tribe of musicians (his dad performed with a circus band), the youth turned to dramatics for his livelihood. After graduating from Norfolk High School, he enrolled in an Omaha institute for aspiring thespians. For a couple of years afterward he performed on a Chautauqua circuit with a troupe representing his alma mater. During a trio of subsequent seasons, KaDell played in stock theater, ending the run with a road tour of *Ladies of the Jury* starring Minnie Maddern Fiske.

When he was only 23, in 1931 a small Chicago radio station, WJJD, hired him and there he performed as an actor, announcer, vocalist and continuity writer. Six months later he signed with NBC as a dramatic artist. Six months beyond that he was on the West Coast as a freelance actor and announcer. KaDell appeared with a myriad of big name radio series emanating from Hollywood between July 1932 and August 1939. Then he returned to Chicago for a part in *The Romance of Helen Trent*, eventually making his way to the West Coast again.

Nonetheless, he came back to the Windy City in the early 1950s and permanently put down roots. In 1953 he appeared in an acting role on NBC-TV's daytime serial *Hawkins Falls* originating in Chicago. During the latter part of his professional career KaDell aired over the city's KEFM Radio. Throughout his life he collected books and phonograph recordings, loved sports of many types, enjoyed cooking and played the piano for his own amusement.

KALISCHER, PETER. b. Dec. 25, 1914, New York, N.Y.; d. July 7, 1991, New Orleans, La. *Correspondent, Writer.* **Series:**

Cavalcade of America (writer, 1952); *CBS News* (correspondent, 1957–ca. 1980s); *CBS World News Roundup* (correspondent, 1957–?); *Edward R. Murrow and the News* (correspondent, 1957–1959); *The World Tonight* (correspondent, 1957–ca. 1980s).

By the time Peter Kalischer's name became at least somewhat familiar to American listeners, video was replacing audio-only as the major source of many people's electronic news. He was credited by a media historiographer as decidedly useful to Dan Rather in educating that newly installed CBS-TV anchor at the start of the 1980s. An early overseas tour of foreign CBS correspondents proved "an enriching experience" for Rather, in which he observed and profited from the lessons shared by "some of the top veterans of the [legendary Edward R.] Murrow Era." Included were Charles Collingwood, Alexander Kendrick, Winston Burdett and Kalischer.

Despite the innovation and accompanying patterns resulting from the tube, Kalischer persisted in posting intelligence for both radio and television audiences, keeping them informed about an area of the globe he well knew. For more than two decades he applied his journalistic craft in the Far East. His initial foray into Japan came in 1945 as an officer in the Counter Intelligence Corps attached to the headquarters of Gen. Douglas MacArthur. After the war Kalischer stayed behind in Tokyo, reporting at the outset until 1952 for United Press International, followed by *Collier's* magazine, and subsequently for CBS.

From his earliest days with the network beginning in 1957, Kalischer traversed much of the Orient, bringing to American ears and eyes accounts of disputes involving the islands of Matsu and Quemoy and the collapse of the Syngman Rhee regime in South Korea. That changed by the 1960s, however, when he found himself based almost exclusively in Saigon, Vietnam, dispatching details of America's involvement in conflict there. He became weary of the repetitious nature of that reportage after a while to be sure and was transferred to Paris in 1966. There he became the web's chief correspondent for Western Europe, Poland, the Middle East, Greece and Turkey. Yet even in that distant locale he was still caught up in the fallout of the Vietnam War, assigned in 1968 to cover the stalled peace talks in its aftermath. They continued for more than a quadrennial, in fact.

In the meantime, Kalischer had been awarded a citation for best reporting for TV spot news in 1963 from the Overseas Press Club of America. He remained in Paris until he left CBS News in 1978. By then he had been with the chain more than two decades and lived overseas for about three-and-a-half decades. At that juncture he returned to the U.S. where he joined the faculty of New Orleans' Loyola University as associate professor of communications, and persisted in the post until he retired in 1982.

KALTENBORN, HANS VON. b. July 9, 1878, Milwaukee, Wis.; d. June 14, 1965, New York, N.Y. *Commentator, Correspondent, Newscaster.* **Series:** *H.V. Kaltenborn Comments,* aka *Current Events,* aka *Kaltenborn Edits the News* (commentator, 1927–1928, 1929–1930, 1931–1939, 1940–1955); *Headlines and Bylines* (correspondent, 1937–1938); *The Mercury Theater on the Air* (narrator for single episode, 1938); *Who Said That?* (panelist, 1948, 1949, 1950).

"The dean of American commentators," H.V. Kaltenborn was so labeled because he got on the air with the first radio commentary, his career was the most enduring of the breed and "his combination of talents was the most remarkable," radio historiographer John Dunning allowed. He was the son of a German immigrant, a Hessian nobleman who eked out an American living as a building materials salesman and repairman. At 14 the younger Kaltenborn (dubbed by chums "Spiderlegs" because he was an avid bicyclist) earned $5 weekly reporting for *The Merrill Advocate*, the paper in the small sawmill municipality in north central Wisconsin where he lived from age 13. The editor took him under his wing, in fact, teaching him the news trade while inspiring him to read books. Until then, at least, Kaltenborn had been little more than a mediocre school student, geography being one of his poorest subjects. Considering the life of travel that lay ahead of him—early in his career he made it a practice to devote three months to touring the world every year—it seems incongruous now.

At 19 he left home to join the Army during the Spanish-American War. From an Alabama infantry camp he dispatched eyewitness reports of Wisconsin boys to a trio of home state journals. Yet by the time he was trained for action, a truce had been signed. On returning home, Kaltenborn was promoted to city editor of the *Advocate* but he was restless and took several other jobs in succession. He soon made his way to New York City and boarded a livestock barge that was Europe-bound. There he debuted as a foreign correspondent for $1 per submission to the *Advocate* as he attended the 1900 Paris World's Fair. Afterward, he remained on the continent for a while as a freelance journalist while picking up other enterprising merchandising opportunities.

At last coming back to the United States, in 1902 Kaltenborn became a reporter for *The Brooklyn Eagle*, then a prominent newssheet. During that same period he enrolled at Harvard University as a special student. Yet when wanderlust overtook him again in 1907, he left for Berlin as secretary of the Harvard Professional Exchange. He later resumed his studies on Harvard's campus and was elected to Phi Beta Kappa while claiming the Boylston Prize for public speaking and the Coolidge Prize for debating. In 1909 Kaltenborn graduated cum laude. The following year he rejoined the staff of *The Brooklyn Eagle*. He climbed up the ranks through a succession of increasing challenges until, in 1921, he was appointed the paper's associate editor.

That same year, on April 21, he also participated in a broadcast demonstration proffered by Newark's WJZ. Ray Poindexter recalled it vividly: "Members of the Brooklyn Chamber of Commerce wanted to be better informed about the thing called radio. They arranged for a receiving set to be installed for one of their meetings. A forty-three-year-old public-minded citizen [Kaltenborn] volunteered to go to Newark and talk over an experimental station so that they could hear him.... He was interested in the new medium; in fact, he owned a crystal set himself."

The following year (1922) Kaltenborn appeared on WVP, a government-supported local station, in which he offered his first expressions of opinion on current events. On Oct. 23, 1923, despite a severe case of mike jitters, he premiered on a regular series underwritten by his newspaper that was aired over New York's WEAF. The exposure on a prestigious station was brief, however, as he displeased WEAF officials and politicos with his dogmatic observations. His newspaper stood behind him, nevertheless, and he remained on the air until his contract expired in 1925 (at least one account claims it was only 1924). At that juncture he shifted to nearby WAHG, Richmond Hill, on Long Island. The latter outlet received 30,000 letters affirming his reportage. Incidentally, while still at WEAF, Kaltenborn noted that censorship of broadcast ideas and individuals was a confirmable reality. Doubtlessly, there could hardly have been any way that WEAF could have retained him after that on-air admission!

Kaltenborn soon transferred again, the next time to the more esteemed, influential and powerful WOR. By 1927 he was being heard far beyond the confines of Manhattan and its surrounding boroughs. At age 52 (in 1930) he joined CBS at $100 weekly, quitting *The Brooklyn Eagle* to do so. It was a life-changing commitment, and included many subsequent voyages he would make to Europe during the 1930s. Kaltenborn was fluent in German, Italian and French and "could chat easily with world leaders without cumbersome translators," noted Dunning. He sought and gained interviews with principals on the world's stage including Hitler (in 1932), Mussolini, Gandhi and Chiang Kai-shek.

Kaltenborn was once captured by Chinese bandits and held for ransom. In 1936 while hiding in a haystack in Spain with sounds of gunfire providing the din in the background, he gave CBS listeners their first bystander account of an actual battle—in this case, the Spanish Civil War. For nine hours he transmitted via telephone to New York, even after his cable was twice shot to smithereens! In September 1938 he aired 102 broadcasts from New York over an 18-day run during the Munich crisis as Hitler and Chamberlain determined the course of Czechoslovakia's short-term future. For the newsman, it gained him a sponsor, increased recognition and a confirming sense of destiny.

In 1939 Kaltenborn gave up his daily

broadcasts from New York (replaced by Elmer Davis) to go to London to augment Edward R. Murrow and other CBS staffers. Murrow, however, considered Kaltenborn pompous and demanding and more of an intrusion than a reinforcement. Not long afterward, in early 1940 Kaltenborn left CBS for NBC. He had experienced many run-ins with CBS news honcho Paul White on matters of objectivity and finally decided it wasn't worth it any longer. Kaltenborn discovered similar restrictions at his new broadcast address, possibly to his surprise. More than two decades later he appeared as the interviewee of CBS newsman Charles Collingwood (one of Murrow's legendary "Boys") on the 1963 CBS-TV primetime series *Portrait* in which his long-term fabled career was the focus of a half-hour discussion.

During the war years Kaltenborn's average Hooper rating (15.9) was exceeded only by Walter Winchell's among all radio commentators, indicating the depth of his following among the listeners. Kaltenborn was instrumental in founding the Association of Radio News Analysts in 1942 and was the panel's first president. Among the organization's charter members were 31 New York commentators, including distinguished voices like those of Elmer Davis, Quincy Howe, William Shirer, Raymond Gram Swing, Lowell Thomas and John Vandercook.

Kaltenborn authored multiple volumes including a memoir, *Fifty Fabulous Years, 1900–1950: A Personal Review* (G.P. Putnam's Sons, 1950). His other titles included: *We Look at the World* (Rae D. Henkle, 1930); *Kaltenborn Edits the News* (Modern Age Books, 1937); *I Broadcast the Crisis* (Random House, 1938); *Kaltenborn Edits the War News* (Dutton, 1942); *Europe Now: A First Hand Report* (Didier, 1945); and *It Seems Like Yesterday* (G.P. Putnam's Sons, 1956). In 1953 he narrated old newsreels on a syndicated TV documentary series also titled *It Seems Like Yesterday*. The following year (1954) Kaltenborn became a panelist for a fleeting video incarnation of a radio show he had appeared on a few years earlier, *Who Said That?*, over NBC-TV.

Dunning proffered this assessment: "He was the only newscaster in radio who could strap on a pair of shortwave earphones, listen without translation to speeches by Hitler, Mussolini, or Daladier, go on the air immediately with only his cryptic notes as a script, and deliver a polished analysis. He was a rapid-fire commentator but spoke in simple sentences packed with one-syllable words and was easy to understand. He could read a one-line news bulletin and immediately give a quarter-hour explanation of its significance and probable consequences."

Radio historian Luther Sies judged: "Kaltenborn was known for his rapid, staccato speech delivery that varied from 150 to 175 words per minute with occasional bursts of up to 200 words per minute. In addition, his integrity and authoritativeness was recognized. When CBS declared in 1939 that all news analysts should be neutral and objective, Kaltenborn responded honestly by saying that no commentator could meet that standard. The selecting or omitting of news items, the shading or emphasis given the events selected for description and every editorial judgment of the commentator, Kaltenborn noted, was an expression of opinion."

Harry S Truman parodied Kaltenborn's clipped speech following the commentator's inaccurate forecast of a Thomas E. Dewey victory in the 1948 presidential election. With newspaper headlines blaring "Dewey Wins!" the misnomer made a humorous sound byte and fascinating footage that has been replayed endless times across ensuing decades.

KAUFMAN, IRVING. b. Feb. 8, 1890, Syracuse, N.Y.; d. Jan. 3, 1976, Indio, Calif. *Emcee, Vocalist.* **Series:** *Come On, Let's Sing*, aka *The Palmolive Community Sing* (occasional host, 1936–1937); *Happy Jim Parsons* (1940, 1941–1943); *The Happy Rambler* (host, 1932); *The Piano Troubadours* (musician, mid 1920s); *Lazy Dan, the Minstrel Man* (soloist, 1933–1936); *Radio Revels* (cast member, 1935).

KEATING, LARRY. b. April 13, 1899, St. Paul, Minn.; d. Aug. 26, 1963, Hollywood, Calif. *Announcer, Emcee.* **Series:** *The Bob Hope Show* (ca. late 1940s); *County Fair* (assistant, ca. mid to late 1940s); *The First Nighter* (1940s); *The Fitch Bandwagon* (1945–1946); *Furlough Fun* (ca. 1943–ca. 1944); *The Hoagy Carmichael Show*, aka *Tonight at*

Hoagy's (1944–1945); *Hollywood Startime* (host-interviewer, 1944); *Murder Will Out* (1945–1946); *Professor Puzzlewit* (quizmaster, 1937–1939); *Scramby Amby* (1943, 1944–1945, 1946–1947); *A Song is Born* (1944); *This is Your FBI* (1948–1953).

Larry Keating jump-started his radio announcing career at San Francisco's KPO before shifting to the local NBC affiliate, KGO. A few years later—for *This is Your FBI*—he posted one of radio's more familiar billboards, instantly identifying that series to listeners tuning in across a five-year run: "To your FBI you look for national security, and to your Equitable Society for financial security. These two great institutions are dedicated to the protection of you, your home, and your country!"

For two decades between 1945 and 1964 the infamous network radio narrator plied his talents in a separate arena—as a celluloid actor—showing up in 40 Hollywood films. Some of Keating's best-recalled movies include *Dancing in the Dark* (1949); *Ma and Pa Kettle Go to Town* (1950); *Stella* (1950); *My Blue Heaven* (1950); *The Mating Season* (1951); *Follow the Sun* (1951); *Francis Goes to the Races* (1951); *When Worlds Collide* (1951); *Come Fill the Cup* (1951); *Inferno* (1953); *Daddy Long Legs* (1955); *The Eddy Duchin Story* (1956); *The Best Things in Life Are Free* (1956); *The Buster Keaton Story* (1957); and *Boys' Night Out* (1962).

As his radio work began to dry up, Keating became a regular in the cast of the program that introduced the laugh track to television, *The Hank McCune Show*, in the final months of 1950 on NBC-TV. Subsequently he performed on the boob tube on *The George Burns and Gracie Allen Show* on CBS-TV (1953–1958) and again on *The George Burns Show* on the same network (1958–1959). He portrayed Burns neighbor Harry Morton ("Dad always said ..." was his weekly recurring interjection to wife Blanche Morton played by Bea Benaderet). Between 1961 and his death from leukemia in 1963, Keating appeared as neighbor Roger Addison on CBS-TV's equine-oriented sitcom *Mister Ed*.

KEECH, KELVIN KIRKWOOD. b. June 28, 1895, Punahou, Hawaii; d. May 1977, Jackson Heights, N.Y. *Announcer, Vocalist, Instrumentalist.* **Series:** *Billy and Betty* (1935–1937, 1938, 1939–1940); *The Eveready Hour* (1926–1930); *Heartthrobs of the Hills* (1939); *Popeye the Sailor* (1935–1936); *Terry and the Pirates* (soloist and ukulele player, 1937–1943); *Twenty Thousand Years in Sing Sing* (1933–1939).

Although Kelvin Keech graduated in engineering from Franklin and Marshall College in 1914 and was a radio operator with the U.S. Signal Corps in France, he nevertheless focused on music for a while. Keech had learned ukulele at a young age in his native Hawaii and spent a year strumming and singing in vaudeville before going overseas. He organized a European jazz combo called White Lyres, moving to London and playing his music over 2LO, a BBC outlet. Keech turned up in America for several radio performances beginning in 1928 and joined NBC as an announcer the following year. He left NBC in 1935 to freelance but returned to the security of that fold two years hence.

KELLY, PATRICK J. b. 1892, Australia; d. unknown. *Announcer.* **Series:** *Halsey Stuart Program* (1931–1932).

The primetime financial services series *Halsey Stuart Program* for Halsey, Stuart & Co. originated regionally on Chicago radio in 1928 and went to the full NBC Red web in 1931.

Before spending several years as a sailor, Patrick J. Kelly attended school in Sydney. During this epoch he studied music and when he left nautical work, he went to New York for further vocal training. The San Carlo Opera Co. offered him various roles. He joined NBC's New York announcing staff in 1929, soon becoming supervisor of the chain's 21 announcers. Matching personnel to programs became one of his major challenges, he allowed. He remained in that post until his retirement in 1954.

Michael Shoshani, who created a website devoted to the famous identifying NBC chimes, elucidates on the strategic functions of the announcers at NBC: "Through the use of a control console known as 'The Announcer's Delight' the Network Announcer joined his studio to the local NBC-owned station and/or to either the Red or Blue networks. The Network Announcer also threw the actual 'You're On the Air' cue to the program announcers and talent. Once the program was finished, the Network Announcer gave the National Broadcasting Company system outcue, rang the chimes, disconnected his studio from the network, and gave the local station ID before removing his studio from the local station.... This may give some idea of how important the job of Network Announcer was—the Announcer really was more than just a mellifluous voice."

KENDRICK, ALEXANDER. b. July 6, 1910; d. May 17, 1991. *Correspondent.* **Series:** *CBS News* (correspondent, late 1940s–?); *CBS World News Roundup* (correspondent, late 1940s–?); *Edward R. Murrow and the News* (correspondent, 1947–1959); *The World Tonight* (correspondent, late 1940s–?).

When broadcast historians Stanley Cloud and Lynne Olson compiled names of journalists for their "Murrow Boys" list—those impeccable reporters who were heavily influenced by veteran CBS newsman Edward R. Murrow during the Second World War—they omitted postwar correspondents David Schoenbrun, George Polk, Daniel Schorr, Alexander Kendrick and others of their ilk because "they did not have the same war-derived status as the Murrow Boys." Nevertheless, Cloud and Olson still classified this "non" crowd as "outstanding journalists in their own right." Kendrick felt close enough and inspired by the illustrious Murrow to pen a biography about his superior anyway: *Prime Time—The Life of Edward R. Murrow* (Little, Brown, 1969). He affirmed that working with Murrow was "the fullest and most satisfying professional expression that any news staff has ever had."

Alexander was a sharp Eastern European specialist and distinguished correspondent for *The Chicago Sun* when Murrow hired him in the late 1940s to staff CBS's newly created outpost in Vienna, Austria. Cloud and Olson depicted Kendrick as a man of "steel-wool voice, Coke-bottle glasses, twisted ties, and rumpled suits." His appearance, they suggested, validated "there was life yet in the iconoclastic Murrow hiring tradition" despite the fact Kendrick arrived too late to be one of the original "Boys."

Alexander and other foreign correspondents "fought" to get on Murrow's weeknight quarter-hour news commentary, often at the expense of other CBS news features. The sponsor paid them $75 per appearance on Murrow's program in addition to the exposure they harvested before legions of faithful listeners. Murrow treated them as the "experts"; he pitched unexpected questions to them while proffering himself as a rank novice, then sat back to listen while they demonstrated extensive capacities. Kendrick and his colleagues relished such treatment and privately gushed with joy and gratitude for their mentor.

KENNEDY, JOHN B. b. Jan. 16, 1895, Quebec, Canada; d. July 22, 1961, Toronto, Canada. *Commentator, Newscaster, Emcee.* **Series:** *The Collier Hour* (narrator—as magazine "editor" Uncle Henry); *Conoco Presents* (1934); *General Motors Concert* (narrator—scientific narratives, 1937); *John B. Kennedy News,* aka *Looking Over the Week* (newscaster-analyst, 1933–1935, 1936–1937, 1939–1940, 1942–1943, 1944–1946, 1948–1951*); John B. Kennedy—Edwin C. Hill News* (newscaster, 1956); *The Magic Key* (commentator, 1935–1939); *The Packard Hour* (1934–ca. 1937); *The People's Rally* (discussion moderator, 1938–1939); *Radio City Party* (master of ceremonies, 1934–1935).

Educated in England, Canada and the United States (in the U.S. at St. Louis University), John B. Kennedy loved journalism and shifted from newspaper to newspaper acquiring greater responsibilities with every move. He ultimately left daily print deadlines for the less frequent ones of magazine publishing. Kennedy became editor of the Knights of Columbus periodical *Columbia* while managing that organization during the First World War era. His next stop was at *Collier's* magazine for a decade, where he was both associate and managing editor.

In 1926 he became an announcer and newscaster at New York's WJZ but considered it a sideline to his regular work. While at *Collier's* he was given responsibility for overseeing *The Collier Hour,* an NBC feature beginning in 1927. It offered narratives that were adapted from the slick's human-interest pages. Kennedy had planned to shift his attention from print journalism for only a little while, but the radio bug bit him and he revised his career to accommodate it. Already on the air by 1933, he joined NBC full time as an announcer the following year.

In addition to his network programming assignments, from April 1941 to January 1944 he was a local newscaster on New York's WNEW Radio, heard weeknights at 7:30 for a quarter-hour. Later in the decade he was also a news commentator over New York's WOR. In 1943 he joined the news staff of the Blue network, considered fully separate from the Red web by then. By 1948 he was conducting *Eye-Witness News* over Philadelphia's WFIL in addition. He became an ABC news commentator in 1950.

KENNEDY, JOHN MILTON. b. June 23, 1912, Farrell, Pa. *Announcer.* **Series:** *Lux Radio Theater* (early 1940s–late 1940s).

In the summer of 1949 John Milton Kennedy played Mr. Crime Interrogator on CBS-TV's *Armchair Detective*, his only documented network television exposure.

KENNEDY, WILLARD A. b. June 27, 1912, Cleveland, Ohio; d. Jan. 27, 1997, Palm Beach, Fla. *Announcer.* **Series:** *Nobody's Children* (1939–1941).

Bill Kennedy was a jack of several trades, including entertainment. Before finding his niche, from 1932 to 1933 he worked in the brokerage business and beginning in 1934 he drove a truck. From 1936 to 1942 he was a radio announcer and newscaster. Kennedy left broadcasting for a while in favor of motion pictures, although he appeared in only one film, *Winning Your Wings* (1942). He subsequently returned to the air as a Detroit television newscaster.

By 1952, however, he had convinced others as well as himself that—if he couldn't star on the screen—he could at least tell others about Hollywood happenings. Kennedy launched a pattern of local TV gigs that year which he hosted, beginning with *Bill Kennedy at the Movies* and *Your Hollywood Host*. From 1956 to 1959 he presided over *Bill Kennedy's Showtime* on Windsor, Ontario's CKLW-TV. Returning to the United States later, he joined Detroit's WKBD-TV as the emcee of *Bill Kennedy at the Movies*, starting in 1969.

KENT, ALAN BRADLEY. b. Aug. 4, 1909, Chicago, Ill.; d. Dec. 4, 1993. *Announcer, Writer, Emcee.* **Series:** *Blackstone, the Magic Detective* (1948–1949); *The Career of Alice Blair* (1939–1940); *Cosmo Tune Time* (host, 1945); *Duffy's Tavern* (writer, ca. 1940s); *Frank Crummit and Julia Sanderson*, aka *Blackstone Plantation* (ca. 1930s); *Hobby Lobby* (ca. late 1930s, 1940s); *Jane Arden* (1938–1939); *The Old Gold Hour*, aka *The Paul Whiteman Orchestra* (1930s); *Pepper Young's Family* (ca. mid 1940s–1950s); *Perry Mason* (ca. 1943–mid 1940s).

Alan Kent's dad was convinced that exposure to widespread travel would provide more of a positive and enlightening impact on his children than public education could. Hence the Kent family was a nomadic tribe that routinely traversed the nation, putting down temporary roots in many places. Young Alan picked up whatever formal schooling he was to get in places like Chicago, Detroit, Cleveland and Orlando. By the start of the Great Depression the family had situated in New York. Just out of his teens, Alan had never earned a dollar and had no skills for anything, but he found a job clerking in a sporting goods store.

Radio was on the increase then and he was intrigued by it. His inexperience worked against him, however, as he applied at several New York stations. In the summer of 1931 at last a small outlet, WOV, put him on the air announcing on weekends without pay. To sustain himself he kept the salesman's job he already had. Later that year, nevertheless, Kent—then 22—accepted a full time announcing gig at NBC at half his selling wages "for the experience." In affiliating with NBC he was also linked to WEAF (Red) and WJZ (Blue), the dual chain's flagship New York outlets. He departed the web in 1938 to join New York's WNEW but returned to the network in 1940.

The following year a demonstrably talented and versatile Kent penned the lyrics of one of the nation's earliest singing commercials for the Newell-Emmett advertising agency. The product was Pepsi-Cola ("Pepsi-Cola hits the spot, twelve full ounces, that's a lot..."). His lexis was adapted to a tune composed by Austin Herbert Croom-Johnson from an old English hunting song, "D'ye Ken John Peel?" The Tune Twisters performed the jingle on radio initially; they were a vocal trio comprised of Gene Lanham, Andy Love and Bob Walker.

Kent's laid-back delivery on the air, embracing a conversational tone as he pitched the salient points of Camay—"the mild beauty soap for a smoother, softer complexion" and the indentured sponsor of the durable daytime serial he introduced for so many years, *Pepper Young's Family*—obviously resonated with listeners as the commodity's market share soared. Kent routinely addressed his audience in one-on-one style: "You'll see a real improvement in your complexion if you'll change from incorrect skin care to regular, mild Camay care," he'd allow in the most soothing timbre imaginable. "Follow the Camay mild soap diet. Directions are on the wrapper. And I promise ... with your very first cake of Camay ... you'll have a lovelier-looking skin ... yes, a softer, a smoother complexion." It was just what the housewives wanted to make them feel better about themselves. And it sold billions of soap bars in the process.

KIERNAN, WALTER. b. Jan. 24, 1902, New Haven, Conn.; d. Jan. 8, 1978, Daytona Beach, Fla. *Emcee, Commentator.* **Series:** *Cliché Club* (moderator, 1950); *Kiernan's Corner* (interviewer, 1945–1948); *Monitor* (co-communicator, 1955–1960); *Mystery File* (master of ceremonies, 1950–1951); *One Man's Opinion* (commentator, 1949–1951); *Sparring Partners* (co-host, 1953); *Stroke of Fate* (host-narrator, 1953); *Weekday* (segment co-host, 1955–1956); *Weekend* (host, 1953–1955).

Walter Kiernan launched a journalism career in his hometown of New Haven in 1920. He left the Associated Press and a newspaper he self-published (1930–1935) to affiliate with the International News Service, becoming INS' bureau chief in Hartford in 1935. A column he penned, *One Man's Opinion*, was distributed by INS and became the moniker for a daily radio commentary later. (From 1958 to 1969 he applied the same title to local New York broadcast features; WOR Radio and TV employed him then, his final full time address before retiring.) In 1943 Kiernan launched a news show over New York's WJZ, a key station originating Blue web programming. The move signified a permanent transition from print to electronic media that was to typify his professional pursuits for the remainder of his life.

Kiernan traversed the television threshold via sundry opportunities. His popular radio human-interest interview series *Kiernan's Corner* was extended for another season on ABC-TV (1948–1949). He hosted a humorous talk show, *That Reminds Me*, in 1948 on the same network. Although it lasted only five weeks, the newsman-turned-quizmaster was master of ceremonies for the 1949 ABC-TV entry *Sparring Partners with Walter Kiernan*. It was a show that pitted teams of opposing genders against each other. From 1951 to 1953 he was master of ceremonies for the Dumont TV game show *What's the Story?* He was a regular panelist in 1952 on CBS-TV's *I've Got a Secret*. From 1951 to 1954 he moderated the panel of NBC-TV's *Who Said That?* Kiernan held the same post on the ABC-TV game show *Who's the Boss?* in 1954. He presided over *The Greatest Moments in Sports* on NBC-TV from 1954 to 1955.

KILGALLEN, DOROTHY MAY. b. July 13, 1913, Chicago, Ill.; d. Nov. 8, 1965, New York, N.Y. *Commentator, Emcee.* **Series:** *Chandu, the Magician* (actress, ca. 1950); *Leave it to the Girls* (intermittent guest panelist, 1945–1948); *Star Time with Dorothy Kilgallen* (reporter-hostess, 1947–1948); *The Voice of Broadway* (reporter-hostess, 1941–1942, 1944); *What's My Line?* (panelist, 1952–1953).

Dorothy Kilgallen moved to New York City when her dad, reporter Jim Kilgallen, took a job with International News Service. After graduating from Brooklyn's Erasmus Hall High School, she enrolled at New Rochelle College. In 1931, during the summer vacation of her freshman year, she became a cub reporter for *The New York Evening Journal*. Ink had long run in her veins, thanks to her father, and she found she liked journalism so well she withdrew from school. She preferred pursuing politics, police beats and courtroom trials instead. At 20 she had her own byline and at 26—as her paper's representative in a round-the-world commercial air competition—she came in second in a three-way race after a 24-day journey. Her memoir of that exhibition, *Girl Around the World*, was published in 1936 and inspired the movie *Fly Away Baby* the following year, for which she wrote the screenplay. The newspaper, in the meantime, by then renamed *The New York Journal American*, gave her a gossip column of her own in November 1937, *Hollywood*

Scene. The next year she inaugurated *The Voice of Broadway.* She was soon widely known for ferreting out the secrets of celebrities of a myriad of persuasions and telling them to readers far and wide.

"The juicy stories always went to Dorothy," observed TV executive producer Gil Fates. "The Lindbergh kidnapping, the coronation of Queen Elizabeth II, the Dr. Sam Sheppard trial, the wedding of Princess Margaret, and the Finch/Tregoff murders in California, were all on her beat and she made almost as much stir on the scene as the principals. She was among the first to pronounce Fidel Castro a Communist and a threat to America and the Western Hemisphere."

Kilgallen appeared in a couple of motion pictures, as reporter Jane Mills in *Sinner Take All* (1936), and as an uncredited role in *Pajama Party* (1964). Her long-running syndicated *Voice of Broadway* newspaper column reached an estimated 20 million readership in 1950. That same year she began appearing every Sunday night on the panel of CBS-TV's *What's My Line?* (1950–1965). At midcentury, she turned up acting in two or three episodes of radio's *Chandu, the Magician,* too. As a newspaper reporter chum of the series hero, she was presented under the not-so-coincidental moniker of Dorothy Kilgallen.

In addition, the upper crust, erudite, cosmopolitan Kilgallen became widely known to 20 million radio listeners in and around New York for her durable *Breakfast with Dorothy and Dick* program over WOR (1945–1963). The columnist and her spouse, veteran radio actor-producer Richard Kollmar (*Boston Blackie, Gangbusters, Grand Central Station,* et al.), whom she married in 1940, "inherited" a 45-minute timeslot six mornings weekly. The pair succeeded pioneering predecessors of the subgenre Ed and Pegeen Fitzgerald (1942–1945) who left WOR for WJZ. For $75,000 annually the Kollmars' toast-and-bacon chatter emanated from their colossal 16-room Park Avenue apartment at 66th Street. (*Tex and Jinx,* featuring Tex McCray and spouse Jinx Falkenburg, soon followed in that same vein elsewhere in Gotham radio, 1946–1959.)

Notwithstanding, Kilgallen's immense contacts with the entertainment world ran deep. She and hubby reported on opening nights on Broadway, revealed gossip from the many parties they attended and carried fans on insider visits to venues like the Stork Club and the Waldorf Astoria. Offspring Jill, Dickie and Kerry Kollmar turned up sporadically on the ether along with a singing canary. "The Kollmars preened amidst the birdseed," assessed one reviewer. And few knew that their program was prerecorded the afternoon prior to its airing during much of its enduring run.

Over her lengthy exposure, the newspaper column sometimes got Kilgallen into trouble. She became the object of barbs tossed by TV entertainers Arthur Godfrey, Jack Paar and others for her printed annotations. Kilgallen's death was unexpected and was widely reported to be under "suspicious circumstances," although the official cause listed was "undetermined." She had a history of anemia and substance abuse and had taken an overdose of alcohol and decanal which could have resulted in heart failure. Suicide, accident and murder (the third, to silence her reporting further on the alleged John F. Kennedy conspiracy) were theorized; an autopsy didn't substantiate homicide as a conclusive option, however. Her obituary in *The New York Journal American,* complete with photographs, ran seven pages.

KINARD, SPENCER. *Announcer, Producer, Director.* **Series:** *Music and the Spoken Word from the Crossroads of the West,* aka *The Mormon Tabernacle Choir,* aka *The Salt Lake City Tabernacle Choir* (producer-director-spokesman, 1971–1990).

KING, DELMER RANDOLPH. b. May 18, 1908, Kansas City, Mo.; d. Aug. 22, 1964. *Announcer.* **Series:** *Avalon Time* (1938–1939); *The Red Skelton Show* (1939).

A baritone, Del King's intent was to become a concert vocalist. His first professional engagement was a solo in which he sang *The Road to Mandalay* as the prologue to the movie of the same name starring Lon Chaney. King joined the Kansas City Opera Company, studied voice and made an initial foray into radio in 1926 as a vocalist on hometown station KMBC. The following year he was bitten by the announcing bug and spent the next nine years freelancing in Chicago. He subsequently joined the staff of Cincinnati's WLW, where he announced a national series for NBC and briefly intersected with rising comic Red Skelton. King moved with the show in May 1939, returning to Chicago. At that point he acquired an added duty, becoming assistant radio director for the advertising agency that packaged the series he announced.

KING, DENNIS. b. Nov. 2, 1897, Coventry, Warwickshire, United Kingdom; d. May 21, 1971, New York, N.Y. *Vocalist, Actor, Announcer.* **Series:** *Dennis King* (vocalist, 1934); *The Paramount-Publix Hour,* aka *The Paramount-Publix Radio Hour,* aka *The Paramount Hour,* aka *Paramount Playhouse* (intermittent vocalist, 1930–1931); *Somerset Maugham Theater* (actor, 1951–1952); *Swift Garden Party* (vocalist, 1932, 1933, 1934, 1935); *When a Girl Marries* (ca. early 1940s).

Former British stage actor Dennis King turned up in thespian roles on the syndicated dramatic anthology *The Play of the Week* (1959–1961) on American TV.

KING, EDWARD. b. 1912, Portland, Ore. *Announcer, Actor.* **Series:** *The Eddie Albert Show* (actor, ca. 1949–ca. 1950); *Four Star Playhouse* (1949); *It's a Man's World (ca. late 1940s); The Sixty-Four Dollar Question* (1950–1951); *The Judy Canova Show* (ca. late 1940s, ca. 1951–ca. 1953); *Richard Diamond, Private Detective* (1949–1950); *Rocky Fortune* (1953–1954).

It should be noted that there were two Edward Kings operating in vintage radio within the same era. The one most of the old time radio historians have documented was a director of New York–originated shows (*Best Plays, The Chase, David Harum, Dimension X, Just Plain Bill,* et al.). The individual ignored by most sources was a West Coast announcer, humorist and musician and the subject of this entry.

Eddy King got his start in radio playing piano and announcing at a 100-watt outlet in his native Portland, Ore. He covered boxing matches, ice hockey ("of which I knew nothing," he later admitted) and baseball. In the latter case, seated alongside a Western Union operator in a radio studio, King offered a "vocal pictorial" of games played at Vaughn Street Park. Those were primitive days in which live on-site coverage had not yet materialized in many places. Three years hence King transferred to a 5000-watt Portland station where he was given a half-hour piano and vocal show. He joined forces on the air with a childhood buddy, Mel Blanc, while there.

A couple of months into that he was hired by KGW, the Portland NBC outlet, and confirmed: "Now I was really a full fledged announcer." At KGW King was part of an entourage that included future network staffers Larry Keating, Chet Huntley and Archie Presby. Mel Blanc was added and in time he and King were paired with a local show called *Cobwebs and Nuts* in which the duo created many diverse voices. It was a watershed transition for Blanc throughout a durable and distinguished career.

In 1937 King won an audition with NBC Radio in San Francisco. Joining him there were Keating and Presby. Huntley, meanwhile—a future pioneering NBC-TV newscaster—was hired by CBS. *The Eddy King Show,* a local comedy entry, was one of the newcomer's earliest assignments. Sherman (Scatman) Crothers joined with him as a series regular. King interrupted his tenure in the early 1940s to spend three years during the war in Guadalcanal, New Guinea and the Philippines aligned with Armed Forces Radio.

Returning to San Francisco thereafter, he launched a new local show, *Barbasol Hall,* a music series in which he frequently interviewed celebrated vocalists. In the late 1940s King won an audition to fill an announcing slot in Hollywood at the NBC studios at Sunset and Vine. He was soon heard nationwide on multiple continuing aural features. Frequently presiding over remote aircasts, he introduced the bands playing the Cocoanut Grove at Los Angeles' Ambassador Hotel and at other popular venues, including the orchestras of Eddie Bergman, Henry Busse, Stan Kenton, Freddy Martin, Joe Reichman and more.

As his audio-only opportunities began to wane, King secured slots in video. He introduced a couple of major NBC-TV primetime series: *The Jimmy Durante Show* (1954–1956) and *The Joey Bishop Show* (1961–1964).

KING, JEAN PAUL. b. Dec. 1, 1904, North Bend, Neb.; d. Aug. 21, 1965, Los Angeles,

Calif. *Announcer, Actor, Newscaster.* **Series:** *Clara, Lu and Em* (ca. 1931–ca. 1936); *Death Valley Days* (actor, ca. 1930s); *Famous Jury Trials* (actor, ca. 1930s, 1940s); *The Goldbergs* (ca. 1936–ca. 1938); *Good News*, aka *Baby Snooks* (1937–1938); *Great Moments in History* (actor, 1927); *Hecker's Information Service* (newscaster, 1937–1938); *The Lanny Ross Show* (ca. 1930s, 1940s); *Minute Mysteries* (1930s); *Myra Kingsley, Astrologer* (1937–1938); *Myrt and Marge* (1937–1938); *National Players* (actor, 1927); *The Palmolive Beauty Box Theater* (1937); *Singing Cinderella* (mid 1930s); *Terminex Show* (announcer-emcee, 1934).

Jean Paul King attended public schools in Tacoma, Wash., before going to Miami University and graduating from the University of Washington. As a member of a harmony duo in college, he appeared on radio. He performed in vaudeville and devoted four seasons to stock company acting as a juvenile with the Henry Duffy Players. King also worked in silent pictures, the newspaper business, musical comedy and light opera. After attaining a degree, he joined NBC in San Francisco as a staff announcer but soon returned to the stage with the San Francisco Theater Guild. For a while he alternated venues between broadcasting and theatrical performances until he moved to Cincinnati in the late 1920s. There he was appointed production manager at radio stations WLW and WSAI.

In 1934 King joined NBC in Chicago as a staff announcer, relocating in New York the following year. The industry publication *Variety* reported in its June 8, 1938 edition—without stating a reason—that King was banished the previous week by Colgate-Palmolive Co. from all of its programs. He had been appearing on several series that the personal and household goods manufacturer underwrote.

For a couple of years King provided voiceovers for *News of the Day* newsreels augmented by responsibilities as a local radio announcer, narrator and news commentator. Furthermore, he made commercial pictures, recordings and slide films and was the instructor for a course in broadcasting technique at Provincetown (Mass.) Wharf Theatre. His vocational pursuits were put on hold temporarily in 1942 when the U.S. Navy requested his services. Aside from the diverse responsibilities that have already been mentioned, King was a disc jockey at multiple radio outlets, signing with New York's WABC (1942), Las Vegas' KENO (1952) and Hollywood's KABC (1955).

KING, JOHN REED. b. Oct. 25, 1914, Wilmington, Del.; d. July 8, 1979, Woodstown, N.J. *Announcer, Emcee, Actor.* **Series:** *Adventures in Science* (ca. late 1930s, early 1940s); *The American School of the Air* (ca. 1930s); *Americans at Work*; *Bobby Benson and the B-Bar-B Riders* (and assorted monikers); *Break the Bank* (intermittent master of ceremonies, 1945–1946); *Carol Kennedy's Romance* (1937–1938); *Chance of a Lifetime* (master of ceremonies, 1949–1952); *The Chrysler Air Show* (1936); *The Columbia Workshop* (ca. 1936–?); *Death Valley Days*; *Double or Nothing* (quizmaster, 1943–1945); *Duffy's Tavern* (ca. early 1940s); *The Gay Nineties Revue* (1939–1944); *Give and Take* (quizmaster, 1945–1953); *Go for the House* (quizmaster, 1948–1949); *Grand Central Station* (narrator, ca. late 1930s, 1940s); *The Great Day* (master of ceremonies, 1952–1953); *The Heinz Magazine of the Air* (ca. 1936–1937); *The Missus Goes a-Shopping* (master of ceremonies, 1941–1951); *Our Gal Sunday* (ca. 1937–?); *The Sheriff* (1944–ca. 1945); *Sky King* (actor, ca. late 1940s–1950); *So You Think You Know Music* (ca. 1939–1940s); *The Stu Erwin Show* (1945); *The Texaco Star Theater* (ca. 1943, 1944–1946); *Torme Time*, aka *The Mel Torme Show* (1947); *Three's a Crowd* (quizmaster, 1948); *The Victor Borge Show* (ca. 1940s); *What's My Name?* (master of ceremonies, 1941); *The Woman* (1946); *Ziegfeld Follies of the Air* (1932, ca. 1936).

John Reed King parlayed a broadcasting career that began as a virtual unknown radio announcer into one of the most widely recognized names among masters of ceremonies and quizmasters in dual mediums on the ether. "King ran game shows in wholesale lots in the 1940s," declared one pundit. Ultimately the versatile entertainer presided over no fewer than nine network aural game features and several more locally in New York, making him one of the busiest audience participation show honchos in the audio medium's halcyon days.

Princeton-educated, King broke into

radio during his collegiate era by reading news reports and announcing big band remotes originating from Atlantic City, the town he had lived in from his teens. During World War II he introduced listeners to CBS newsmen Edward R. Murrow and Robert Trout while also supplying a weekly newscast in French that was transmitted to occupied France. After a terrific run on network radio, where he is best recalled as a game show host, by the 1950s King carried his widespread following into similar features in video. There he emceed *Missus Goes a-Shopping* (1947–1948, CBS); *Chance of a Lifetime* (1950–1952, ABC); *Battle of the Ages* (1952, Dumont and CBS); *Give and Take* (1952, CBS); *There's One in Every Family* (1952–1953, CBS); *Tootsie Hippodrome* (1952–ca. 1953, ABC); *Where Was I?* (1952–1953, Dumont); *Why?* (1952–1953, ABC); *What's Your Bid?* (1953, ABC); *On Your Way* (1954, ABC); and *Let's See* (1955, ABC).

After his network broadcast opportunities faded, King became a news anchorman for radio stations in Pittsburgh, Pa., and Fresno, Calif. At his death he was director of public relations for the First Federal Savings Association of Fresno. He was stricken by a heart attack and died while visiting a brother back East.

KING, JOSEPH. b. ca. 1882; d. April 11, 1951. *Announcer.* **Series:** *CBS D-Day Coverage* (1944); *The Eileen Barton Show* (1954); *Here's to Veterans* (1948); *Mr. and Mrs. North* (1953–ca. 1954); *The Philip Morris Playhouse on Broadway* (ca. 1951–ca. 1953); *A Report to the Nation* (1942); *Songs by Morton Downey* (ca. 1948–ca. 1951); *Spotlight Revue* (ca. 1947–1948); *The Toni Arden Show* (1954).

KING, WALTER WOOLF. b. Nov. 2, 1896, San Francisco, Calif.; d. Oct. 24, 1984, Beverly Hills, Calif. *Announcer, Emcee.* **Series:** *The Eddie Cantor Show*, aka *The Chase and Sanborn Hour*, aka *The Eddie Cantor Pabst Blue Ribbon Show*, aka *The Eddie Cantor Camel Caravan*, aka *Time to Smile* (ca. 1930s, 1940s); *The Fleischmann Yeast Hour* (actor, 1935); *The Flying Red Horse Tavern* (master of ceremonies, 1936); *Lux Radio Theater* (actor, 1952); *Paul Whiteman's Musical Varieties* (guest performer, 1936).

Using his legitimate stage name, Walter Woolf, King broke into show business as a vaudeville performer with pianist Charles LeMaire. In Chicago he was hired by Walter Dunbar to appear in Gilbert & Sullivan operettas before accompanying Dunbar to New York where he was cast in *Passing Show of 1921.* Throughout the 1920s he sang in Broadway musicals like *Countess Maritza*; *Dream Girl*; *Floradora Girl*; *Lady in Ermine*; *The Last Waltz*; and *The Red Rogue.* He returned to the New York stage later in his career in George White's *Melody* and the operetta *May Wine* and on the West Coast in *Music in the Air.*

King debuted in films in 1930 with *Golden Dawn*, by then appearing under the moniker Walter King. He followed that with more than two dozen other cinematic features, among them: *Girl Without a Room*; *Experience Unnecessary*; *Ladies All*; *Lottery Lover*; *One More Spring*; *Spring Tonic*; *Ginger*; *A Night at the Opera*; *Go West*; *Walking Down Broadway*; *Big Town Czar*; *Melody for Three*; *The Helen Morgan Story*; and *Rosie*.

KIRBY, DURWARD. b. Aug. 24, 1911, Covington, Ky.; d. March 15, 2000, Fort Myers, Fla. *Announcer, Newscaster, Emcee.* **Series:** *Alka-Seltzer Time*, aka *Herb Shriner Time* (1948–1949); *Break the Bank*; *The Breakfast Club* (1941–1942); *Club Matinee* (1939–1943); *Crime Fighters* (1949, 1950–1952, ca. 1953, ca. 1954–ca. 1956); *Crisco Radio Newspaper* (newscaster, mid 1940s); *The Fred Waring Show*; *The Garry Moore Show* (1950, 1959–1961); *Hap Hazard* (1941); *Here's Morgan*, aka *The Henry Morgan Show* (cast member, ca. 1940s); *Here's to Romance* (1947); *Hilltop House* (late 1940s); *Honeymoon in New York* (master of ceremonies, 1945–1947); *Li'l Abner* (1939–1940); *Lone Journey* (early 1940s); *Meet Your Navy* (1943–1944); *Press Radio News* (newscaster, 1937); *The Quiz Kids* (1940s); *Sunday Dinner at Aunt Fanny's* (1938–1939); *Two for the Money* (ca. 1952–1956).

Durward Kirby launched his durable broadcasting career in 1934 with a 30-minute daily remote pickup from the 1934 Indiana State Fair on Indianapolis' WFBM. By the time the week ended, the neophyte ad-libber had been hired as a permanent announcer and disc jockey. The following year he graduated from the station to an announcing post with Cincinnati's WLW just across the Ohio River from his Kentucky birthplace. He departed from WLW in 1937 for NBC in Chicago. Working on the staffs of WENR and WMAQ in the Windy City, in 1941 Kirby became the first national recipient of the H.P. Davis Announcer Award, named for the pioneer broadcasting developer of the Westinghouse Corp. A medal and a prize of $300 accompanied the signal honor.

For about three decades Kirby was a sidekick to comic entertainer Garry Moore. The 6'4" blond announcer contrasted radically with the diminutive, flat-topped Moore, but the duo made a favorable impression with audiences, initially on radio and subsequently on *The Garry Moore Show* on CBS-TV (weekdays, 1950–1958, and in primetime weekly, 1958–1964 and 1966–1967). In addition to introducing their series in dual mediums, Kirby was cast in the humorous routines and narratives performed there, often appearing in outlandish costumes prompted by the scripts.

Moore said: "Meeting up with Durward in 1940 in Chicago was the luckiest thing that ever happened to me in my professional life! Here is a man who can not only read a comedy line ... he can read it funnier than it was written.... When you hired Durward, you got not only one man—you got an entire stock company! On top of that he can mimic almost anyone. He was the best co-star in comedy that Carol Burnett ever had." At Kirby's death, an obit writer confirmed: "Kirby could be sketch actor, singer, dancer and with ease switch from slapstick to suave sales pitches for a sponsor's product. He became so well-known to TV viewers that the Rocky and Bullwinkle cartoons had a plotline about the search for 'Kirward Derby,' which could make its wearer the smartest man in the world."

With originator Allen Funt, Kirby co-hosted CBS-TV's *Candid Camera* from 1961 to 1966, occasionally taking part in the pranks involving unsuspecting and secretly filmed citizens in amusing predicaments. He penned a trio of volumes including an autobiography, *My Life ... Those Wonderful Years!* (Tabby House, 1992).

KIRBY, GENE. b. July 21, 1909; d. March 1985. *Sportscaster, Announcer, Director.* **Series:** *The Adele Clark Show* (1945–1946); *America's Town Meeting of the Air* (ca. mid 1950s); *Big Moments in Sports* (director, 1955); *Claude Thornhill and His Orchestra* (1948); *The Clock* (1946–1948); *The Fat Man* (1946); *Game of the Day* (sportscaster, 1951–?); *Greatest Sports Thrills* (director, 1956–1958); *The Joe Mooney Quartette* (1946); *Johnny Olsen's Rumpus Room* (1946); *Tops in Sports* (contributor, 1961).

Gene Kirby attended Ohio State University before getting into radio. He served on the staffs of a trio of national hookups—ABC, NBC and MBS—and then joined New York's WINS as a sportscaster.

KIRBY, GROVER C. (KLEVE). b. Sept. 6, 1915; d. March 5, 1949, Wauconda, Ill. *Announcer, Actor.* **Series:** *The Sheaffer Parade* (1947–1948); *Stories of Escape* (1943–1944); *Today's Children* (actor, 1943–1949).

Kleve Kirby was a newscaster at New Orleans' WWL in 1938–1939. In the 1940s, he became a staff announcer at Chicago's WMAQ. He died from injuries sustained in an automobile accident that also seriously injured another WMAQ announcer, George Stone (George Steingoetter).

KNIGHT, FRANK. b. May 10, 1894, St. John's, Newfoundland, Canada; d. Oct. 18, 1973, New York, N.Y. *Announcer, Actor.* **Series:** *The Adventures of Superman* (ca. late 1930s, early 1940s); *Arabesque* (actor, 1937–1940); *Author, Author,* aka *Author's Quiz* (1939–1940); *The Chesterfield Quarter Hour* (ca, 1932–ca. 1933); *The Choraliers* (1949, 1953–1955); *Collier's Radio Review,* aka *The Collier Hour* (actor, ca. 1928–1932); *The First National Hour* (actor, ca. late 1920s, early 1930s); *Literary Digest,* aka *Lowell Thomas and the News* (1930–1931); *The Longines Symphonette* (ca. 1943–1957); *The New York Philharmonic Symphony Orchestra* (1930–?); *Murder Clinic* (1942–1943); *The Robert Burns Panatella Show,* aka *The Burns and Allen Show,* aka *The White Owl Program* (1932–1934); *Uncle Don* (ca. 1930s, 1940s).

Although born outside the United States, by the time he was 26 Frank Knight had adopted this country as his homeland. In addition to a pervasive radio-broadcasting schedule, the velvet-toned interlocutor moderated a late evening discussion series on world affairs, *Chronoscope,* on CBS-TV from

1951 to 1955. Launching his career on the ether in 1928 at New York's WABC, meanwhile—a station soon purchased by Columbia as its flagship outlet—Knight persisted after all of his early CBS colleagues had departed from the fold. His voice "bordered on the pompous with an almost cathedral formality," claimed one wag. Yet during the 1930s, the American Academy of Arts and Letters presented Knight with its Diction Award, a prestigious honor in elocution. He was also among the founding fathers of the American Guild of Radio Announcers and Producers, a union of CBS staff announcers whose membership extended to hundreds of individuals.

Of all of his broadcast series, Knight was likely associated in most listeners' memories as the interlocutor on *The Longines Symphonette*. Seldom at a loss for words, he passionately touted the sponsor's product, qualifying both the program and the commodity as matchless. While the instrumentalists played the program's theme, Beethoven's *Moonlight Sonata*, Knight shamelessly introduced the weekly performances with an inveterate boast: "This is the world's most honored music program presented as a salute to Longines, the world's most honored watch. The Longines Symphonette, a group of the world's finest musicians under the distinguished leadership of Mishel Piastro, plays the world's most honored music. These beautiful melodies and Longines watches have this in common: throughout the world, where there is an appreciation of things fine and beautiful, *both* are held in the highest esteem."

In the 1960s The Longines Symphonette Society of Larchmont, N.Y., released a couple of multiple long-playing hi-fidelity recordings that reminisced over radio's golden age and included a multitude of top-drawer excerpts from actual broadcasts. Comedian Jack Benny and Frank Knight narrated the first of those collections labeled *Golden Memories of Radio*. For the subsequent issue, titled *I Remember Radio*, Knight was the sole raconteur. The dual Longines sets prompted a wave of nostalgia-driven recordings and reel-to-reel tapes that centered on old-time radio in the pre-cassette, pre–CD, pre–MP3 epoch.

KOLLMAR, RICHARD. b. Dec, 31, 1910, Ridgewood, N.J.; d. Jan. 7, 1971, New York, N.Y. *Actor, Announcer, Vocalist.* **Series:** *The Adventures of Superman* (actor, ca. 1930s, 1940s); *The Adventures of Topper* (1945); *Armstrong Theater of Today*, aka *Theater of Today* (actor, ca. 1941–ca. 1954); *Big Sister* (actor, ca. 1940s); *Boston Blackie* (actor, 1945–1950); *Bright Horizon* (actor, 1941–?); *Claudia and David* (actor, 1941); *Gangbusters* (actor, ca. 1930s–ca. 1950s); *Grand Central Station* (actor, ca. 1930s–ca. 1950s); *Heartthrobs of the Hills*, aka *Hillbilly Heartthrobs*, aka *Dreams of Long Ago* (vocalist, ca. 1935–ca. 1938, ca. 1939); *John's Other Wife* (actor, ca. 1941–1942); *Life Can Be Beautiful* (actor, ca. 1940s); *The Life of Mary Sothern* (actor, 1935–1938); *The Palmolive Beauty Box Theater* (narrator-actor, 1934–1936, 1937); *Pretty Kitty Kelly* (actor, ca. 1937–ca. 1940); *Radio Reader's Digest* (narrator, 1946–1947); *The March of Time* (actor, 1930s, 1940s); *When a Girl Marries* (actor, 1940s).

Richard Kollmar was a dramatics scholar at Yale University before premiering on radio as master of ceremonies at a 1935 fashion show. During the 1940 run of George Abbott's musical *Too Many Girls*, in which he performed on Broadway, Kollmar wed Dorothy Kilgallen, newspaper reporter and *Voice of Broadway* columnist for *The New York Journal-American*. (See references to their popular daily New York radio series *Breakfast with Dorothy and Dick* under her listing.)

In addition to extensive radio work primarily in acting roles, he hosted the fleeting NBC-TV 1949 variety series *Show Business, Inc.* (subsequently re-titled *Broadway Scrapbook* and *Broadway Spotlight*). He was master of ceremonies of the pithy Dumont Television game show *Guess What?* in 1952; became a permanent panelist on the 1954 ABC-TV series *Who's the Boss?*; and turned up as an occasional guest panelist on CBS-TV's *What's My Line?* during its long run (1950–1968). Wife Dorothy Kilgallen was a permanent member of the latter panel.

Kollmar produced several plays: *Are You with It?*; *The Body Beautiful*; *By Jupiter*; *Plain and Fancy* among them. He also appeared in a single movie portraying Martin Beaumont in 1948's *Close-Up*.

KRAMER, HARRY. b. Feb. 9, 1911, Philadelphia, Pa.; d. Jan. 23, 1996, Sarasota, Fla. *Announcer.* **Series:** *The Alfredo Antonini*

Orchestra (1939); *Hits and Misses* (ca. 1946–ca. 1951); *Mike and Buff's Mail Bag* (1954); *Mr. Keen, Tracer of Lost Persons* (1952–1955); *Our Gal Sunday* (ca. 1950s).

A graduate of New York University, in the mid 1930s a perceptibly erudite Harry Kramer launched a nearly four-decades-long broadcasting career in New York. One of his earliest assignments was to preside over an all-night opera feature that put his fluency in Italian to good use. He was equally articulate in German and Spanish. During the 1930s and 1940s, he was master of ceremonies for the *Dance Barn* aired by WNEW. In 1937 he was also a news analyst for WNEW's *New York Lighting Electric Stores News*. He was the final announcer on broadcasting's most durable detective series, *Mr. Keen, Tracer of Lost Persons*, a crime drama that persisted for 18 years (1937–1955). At about the same time he introduced a couple of early CBS-TV daytime features, the fleetingly innocuous game show *Winner Take All* in 1951 and *The Mel Torme Show* in 1951–1952.

From 1952 to 1954 he introduced *The Red Buttons Show* on CBS-TV. Kramer's baritone was the voice of CBS News for many years, announcing legions of special reports and documentaries, including those dealing with political conventions and elections, space flights, assassinations and numerous other momentous events. From 1962 to 1971 Kramer's memorable tones addressed millions of Americans every weekday evening as he delivered a familiar missive to TV viewers: "Direct from our CBS newsroom in New York ... this is ... *The CBS Evening News* ... with Walter Cronkite." At that juncture, he'd add whatever was appropriate for a particular night's agenda: "*and* ... Hughes Rudd in Dallas ... Morley Safer in Amsterdam ... Eric Sevareid at the United Nations ... Winston Burdett in Rome ... Dan Rather at the White House ... Harry Reasoner at the Pentagon ... and Bob Schieffer in London." In that epoch he introduced some of the nation's most watched programs and his voice became widely recognized by his countrymen, even though his face was never seen. Simultaneously, Kramer was announcing the *CBS Weekend News* and *60 Minutes*.

Two hours before he went on *The CBS Evening News* weekday evenings, he invited yet another CBS audience to follow the exploits of an afternoon crime tale. In ominous tones—delivered immediately after 10 stinging piano chords that riveted the viewers all by themselves—Kramer proclaimed: "*Theeeeee Edggggeeee of Night!*" The opening act launched a half-hour of suspenseful action that was intermittently stalled by Kramer's posts at appropriate intervals over background din. Heard daily, Kramer's cutaways reminded the fans who was making it possible and informed them what they could anticipate next: "This portion of *The Edge of Night* is brought to you by Kellogg's," he'd allow after the opening act on days that firm sponsored the narrative: "The best to you each morning ... with Kellogg's Frosted Flakes." (Or a similar plug.) In other spots he'd acknowledge: "We return you now to our story," a throwback to the radio serials of an earlier day. At the end of the half-hour he'd allow: "This is Harry Kramer inviting you to join us every weekday afternoon for "*Theeeeee Edggggeeee of Night!*" His voice wavered suitably. He persisted on the show from 1958 to 1972, when he retired from CBS with a sendoff party from the cast and crew.

KRUPP, ROGER THURSTON. b. July 31, 1909, Minnesota; d. May 25, 1987, Ely, Minn. *Announcer, Newscaster, Actor*. **Series:** *The Adventures of Ellery Queen* (1939–?); *The American Album of Familiar Music* (ca. 1950–1951); *Arnold Grimm's Daughter* (ca. 1937–?); *Backstage Wife* (ca. 1950s); *The Bing Crosby Show* (ca. early 1930s); *David Harding, Counterspy* (1942–?); *Dunninger, the Mentalist* (ca. 1943–ca. 1944); *Emil Vandis and His Orchestra* (1945); *Famous Jury Trials* (ca. 1940s); *Jungle Jim* (ca. 1940s); *Just Plain Bill* (ca. late 1940s, early 1950s); *Kay Fairchild, Stepmother* (1938–1942); *Kelly's Courthouse* (actor, 1944); *The Kemtone Hour* (announcer-newscaster, 1944); *Kraft Music Hall* (1934–1936); *Lowell Thomas and the News* (1944–?); *Lum and Abner* (ca. 1930s, 1940s); *Manhattan Merry-Go-Round*; *Mr. Chameleon* (ca. late 1940s); *Modern Cinderella* (1936–1937); *The Quiz Kids* (ca. 1940s–early 1950s); *Scattergood Baines* (ca. late 1930s, 1940s); *Silver Theater* (1940s); *Stella Dallas* (ca. early to mid 1950s); *Vic and Sade* (ca. early to mid 1940s); *Vox Pop* (ca. mid to late 1940s).

Reacting to what was essentially a dare, Roger Krupp pursued the proposal of some

Minnesota cronies who urged him to apply for a radio job. Auditioning in 1930 at Minneapolis' WRHM, he was hired on the spot. Before long he was picked up by KSTP in nearby St. Paul. By 1932 he found himself on the staff of Oakland's KTAB and simultaneously among the announcing entourage at NBC, San Francisco. That same year Krupp purportedly became the first radio announcer to perform as an announcer in a theatrical film, MGM's *Are You Listening*.

A year later (1933) he advanced to Los Angeles' KFI. That didn't last long: in succession Krupp rapidly took assignments with the Post Broadcasting System in Hawaii, as assistant art director at New York's J. Walter Thompson advertising agency and—in 1934—returning to radio, on the staff of Gotham's WNEW. Not long after he moved westward again, to Chicago's WBBM, and—in 1939—to Hollywood's KMTR. In the early 1940s Krupp migrated east again, thence to New York's WHN. In most of his local station affiliations he maintained a freelance announcing status that allowed him to supplement his regular income by appearing on a plethora of network programming.

KURALT, CHARLES BISHOP. b. Sept. 10, 1934, Wilmington, N.C.; d. July 4, 1997, New York, N.Y. *Correspondent, Commentator.* **Series:** *CBS News* (correspondent, ca. 1958–1967); *On the Road with Charles Kuralt* (commentator, ca. 1967–ca. 1978).

Charles Kuralt became a disciple of small-town ex-reporter Norman Corwin, whose magnificent CBS series of patriotic and poetic broadcasts on *The Columbia Workshop* (1936–1947) and *Columbia Presents Corwin* (1944, 1945) inspired millions of Americans of that generation. "They had a book of Corwin's plays in the school library in North Carolina," he recalled. "I read it at thirteen and knew what I wanted to do with my life." Kuralt, himself, would be recalled by legions for his reports from the small towns and back roads of America, endearing him to the nation.

By the time he was 14, Kuralt was delivering sports scores on the ABC affiliate in Charlotte, WAYS. Before graduating from high school, he won an American Legion essay contest and a trip to the nation's capital to meet President Harry S Truman. Following in his journalistic mentor's footsteps, Kuralt studied the subject at the University of North Carolina, editing the student newspaper there. Graduating in 1955, he became a reporter for *The Charlotte News* in the state's largest newspaper market. The following year he won the Ernie Pyle Memorial Award for his offbeat human interest columns. Along the way he gave radio another try at Charlotte's 50,000-watt CBS affiliate, WBT. It didn't take long for the network to find him. In 1957 he was hired to rewrite news copy at CBS in New York but he quickly developed into an on-the-air correspondent. He covered the presidential campaign three years hence and then became head of the web's newly created Latin America bureau. By 1963 he was chief West Coast correspondent. Ultimately be became a roving correspondent and was labeled by one of his superiors "the next Ed Murrow," a comparison Kuralt found "ridiculous," even though both men were natives of the Tar Heel state.

After four tours in Vietnam covering the war, in 1967 he decided he wanted out of hard news. "I was always worried that some NBC man was sneaking behind my back getting better stories," he acknowledged. Accompanied by a three-man crew, he launched a three-month trial of *On the Road* in 1967. It immediately struck a nerve with American radio listeners and TV watchers. Kuralt ultimately logged more than a million miles before taking over as anchor of *Sunday Morning*, a CBS-TV newsmagazine, described by one pundit as "a crown jewel of the CBS News division." Kuralt presided from the show's inception on Jan. 28, 1979, to April 3, 1994, when he did the unthinkable at age 60 and retired. At the time he was the longest tenured air personality in CBS's news division.

Over his 37-year career Kuralt won three Peabody awards and 10 Emmys. In 1981 he received the George Polk Memorial award for national television reporting and was named Broadcaster of the Year in 1985 by the International Radio-Television Society. He also wrote several books: *To the Top of the World: The First Plaisted Polar Expedition* (Holt, Rinehart, and Winston, 1968); *Dateline America* (Harcourt, Brace, Jovanovich, 1979); *On the Road with Charles Kuralt* (Putnam,

1985); *Southerners: Portrait of a People* (Oxmoor House, 1986); *North Carolina is My Home* (East Woods Press, 1986); and *A Life on the Road* (Putnam, 1990).

Frank Sesno, chief of CNN's Washington bureau, assessed: "The chronicle of the country and the nation that he [Kuralt] brought was among the most beautiful and vivid journalism that I've ever heard in broadcast.... His voice, his inflection, his delivery. Everything about him was just pure art."

Complications from lupus took Kuralt's life only three years beyond his retirement. He was interred on the grounds of the University of North Carolina at Chapel Hill. That institution still exhibits many of his awards and has recreated his office in its journalism school. Putnam released a commemorative volume in 1995 following the newsman's death, *Charles Kuralt's America*.

LA FRANO, ANTHONY J. b. May 10, 1911, New York, N.Y.; d. Sept. 12, 1961, Los Angeles, Calif. *Announcer, Producer*. **Series:** *Adventures in Rhythm* (1946); *California Melodies* (mid 1940s); *Elsa Maxwell's Party Line* (producer, 1943–1947); *Family Theater* (1947–1962); *Johnny Modero, Pier 23* (1947); *Music Depreciation* (1944–1945); *The Tommy Dorsey Playshop* (1946).

A graduate of Syracuse University, at the time of his death from a heart attack Tony La Frano was vice president of RKO–General Corp. and executive director of operations for its West Coast broadcasting interests, including KHJ radio and television in Hollywood and KFRC in San Francisco. His long association with KHJ and eventually KHJ-TV began in 1939. Earlier he was a program executive in Santa Barbara, Calif. Until it dissolved in 1948, La Frano was vice president and program director of the Don Lee regional network.

LAIR, JOHN. b. July 1, 1894, Livingston, Ky.; d. Nov. 13, 1985, Lexington, Ky. *Emcee, Announcer, Director*. **Series:** *National Barn Dance* (director, 1927–1937); *Renfro Valley Barn Dance* (host, 1938–1951); *Renfro Valley Sunday Mornin' Gatherin'* (host, 1940s, 1950s).

Created by John Lair in 1937, the *Renfro Valley Barn Dance* was situated in a replica of a 19th century Kentucky hamlet. Lair was born nearby and went north in 1927 to be program director and music librarian at Chicago's WLS. In that capacity he influenced folk musicians to appear on the *National Barn Dance* and other WLS programming. He also organized the Cumberland Ridge Runners in 1932, a country music act that performed on multiple Chicago area stations (WLS, WIND, WJJD) between the mid 1930s and mid 1940s, plus the *National Barn Dance* beamed nationwide by NBC. Country vocalist Red Foley—who, in the 1940s, presided over the NBC portion of Nashville's venerable *Grand Ole Opry*—was a member of the entourage Lair inspired.

Moving to Cincinnati in 1937, Lair along with Foley and country humorist Benjamin "Whitey" Ford purchased some real estate at Renfro Valley, Ky., on which they built a music barn. Lair instigated the *Renfro Valley Barn Dance* radio show transmitted by Cincinnati's powerful WLW. Three years hence the roadside Saturday night barn dance that was spearheaded by Lair had swelled enormously, sometimes topping 10,000 patrons annually, netting 200 or more paid admissions weekly. Between 1938 and 1951, the show was carried live on all four major networks at separate times. It continued in syndication for several years beyond that.

An enterprising Lair soon saw a way to extend his operations by instituting a country-folk music series with a religious-oriented theme, airing early on the Christian Sabbath. In the 1940s he debuted *The Renfro Valley Sunday Mornin' Gatherin'* carried by CBS for 45 minutes weekly and sponsored by General Foods Corp. Lair penned the series' theme song, *Take Me Back to Renfro Valley*. The feature consisted primarily of hymns and gospel songs accompanied by an organ and sung by members of the audience, many of whom were weekend visitors that attended the *Barn Dance* broadcast the night before. As a result, for several years before and after the mid 20th century an entrepreneurial Lair netted dual nationwide audiences 52 weeks a year.

On Feb. 28, 2002, Lair was welcomed posthumously into a newly created Kentucky Music Hall of Fame and Museum at Renfro Valley. Other inductees on the original list included The Everly Brothers, Red Foley, Tom T. Hall, Grandpa Jones, Loretta Lynn, Bill Monroe, The Osborne Brothers, Jean Ritchie and Merle Travis.

LANGLEY, RALPH. *Announcer.* **Series:** *A Date with Judy* (ca. 1941–1949); *El Lobo Rides Again* (1949).

Morning Watch with Ralph Langley was the billing given Langley's DJ show over Los Angeles' KECA starting in 1947.

LATHAM, JOHN JACKSON. b. Dec. 27, 1914, Washington (state); d. Jan. 1, 1987, Riverside, Calif. **Series:** *The Man Called X* (ca. 1940s–early 1950s); *Wake Up, America* (1943).

In 1944–1945 Jack Latham was a newscaster with Los Angeles' KFI.

LATTING, ROBERT. b. Dec. 29, 1921, Michigan; d. Sept. 29, 1983, Santa Clara, Calif. *Actor, Announcer.* **Series:** *The Casebook of Gregory Hood* (actor, 1946–?); *Cavalcade of America* (actor, 1944); *Constance Bennett Calls on You* (1945–1946); *The Story of Sandra Martin* (actor, 1945); *Woman in White* (actor, ca. 1946–1948).

LAWRENCE, JERRY. b. 1912, Rochester, N.Y.; d. Sept. 24, 2005, Los Angeles, Calif. *Announcer.* **Series:** *The Frank Sinatra Show* (1944); *The Spade Cooley Show* (1946, 1951); *Truth or Consequences* (ca. early to mid 1950s).

While born in the East, Jerry Lawrence grew up in the West at Long Beach, Calif. Yet he cultivated a radio career in the 1930s at New York City stations WOR, WNEW and the CBS chain. During the war he presided over a popular local overnight disc jockey series beamed to troop ships and war industry workers, *Moonlight Savings Time*, aired from 2:30 to 5 o'clock weekday mornings.

Returning to the Los Angeles area in 1945, Lawrence worked in radio and early TV at KTLA, KCOP and KFWB. He announced NBC-TV's *Truth or Consequences* in 1954–1955. He also made guest appearances on *The Donna Reed Show*, *Dragnet* and other video comedies and dramas. Lawrence appeared in bit parts in a couple of theatrical productions, too: *The Hitch-Hiker* (1953) and *X-15* (1961).

LAWRENCE, MORTON. b. Dec. 4, 1914, Philadelphia, Pa.; d. Aug. 27, 1967, New York, N.Y. *Announcer, Actor.* **Series:** *Baseball Round Table* (1956); *The Future of Cancer Research* (1956); *High Adventure* (actor, 1950); *Special Agent* (actor, 1948); *The Mysterious Traveler* (actor, 1947); *Quiet, Please* (actor, 1948); *Walk a Mile* (ca. 1952, ca. 1953).

In 1937 Mort Lawrence was on the announcing staff at Philadelphia's WCAU. Not long afterward he became a freelancer before joining the same city's WFIL in 1940, moving in rapid succession to WIP, where he became one of the nation's first all-night disc jockeys. Lawrence departed the City of Brotherly Love in 1942 to affiliate with New York's WHN, projecting him to the big time for an ephemeral moment in time. He was one of multiple masters of ceremonies for *The Big Payoff*, a game show airing in the daytime on both NBC-TV (1951–1953) and CBS-TV (1953–1959). The series appeared on NBC-TV in primetime during the summers of 1952 and 1953.

Lawrence was also doing lots of local TV in the same epoch. He hosted the *Starlight Film Theater* on Philadelphia's WFIL-TV in 1950, *TV Shoppers Revue* on New York's WOR-TV in 1951 and the *Night Owl Theater* on WPIX-TV, also in Gotham, subsequently.

LEMOND, ROBERT W. b. April 1911, Texas. *Announcer.* **Series:** *The Bob Hawk Show* (1949–early 1950s); *Crime Classics* (1953–ca. 1954); *Granby's Green Acres* (1950); *The Hoagy Carmichael Show* (1946–1948); *Hollywood Showcase* (1948); *Honest Harold*, aka *The Harold Peary Show* (1950–1951); *How To* (1951); *Joan Davis Time* (ca. 1946–1947); *Life with Luigi* (1948–?); *Lights Out* (1942); *Meet Millie* (1951–1954); *My Favorite Husband* (1948–1951); *My Friend Irma* (ca. early 1950s); *Our Miss Brooks* (ca. late 1940s, early 1950s); *Rogers of the Gazette* (sporadic announcer, 1953–1954); *Romance of the Ranchos* (1941–ca. 1942); *The Spade Cooley Show* (1951); *Sweeney and March* (1946–1948); *T-Man* (1950); *The Whistler* (1940s).

Bob Lemond was affiliated with Los Angeles' KEHE before leaving it for what turned out to be a pithy rendezvous with San Francisco's KYA. He returned to KEHE in

1938. The following year he departed from the station once again, this time relocating at nearby KNX. Lemond was just getting his feet wet in network radio when, in 1942, he was summoned to the U.S. Army Air Corps. As a special services officer he was linked with Armed Forces Radio. He became an established presence on multiple comedy and dramatic radio features shortly after his return from the service.

During the 1950s and 1960s Lemond routinely introduced a quintet of sitcoms airing on a trio of national video chains: *Life with Father* (1953–1955, CBS); *The Ann Sothern Show* (1958–1961, CBS); *Fibber McGee and Molly* (1959–1960, NBC); *Westinghouse Playhouse*, aka *The Nanette Fabray Show* (1961, NBC); and *The Farmer's Daughter* (1963–1966, ABC). In the summer of 1955 he concurrently announced the NBC-TV comedy variety feature *And Here's the Show*.

Lemond's wife, Barbara Brewster, who died on June 21, 2005, was the surviving member of the infamous "Brewster Twins" of the late 1930s. Twentieth Century–Fox identified them as "The Most Beautiful Twins in America." The Lemonds met when Barbara was performing with the USO in the South Pacific. They were married 58 years.

LESCOULIE, JACK. b. Nov. 17, 1911, Sacramento, Calif.; d. July 22, 1987, Memphis, Tenn. *Announcer, Emcee.* **Series:** *The Grouch Club* (master of ceremonies–grouchmaster, 1938–1940); *Meet the Champions* (1956–1957).

Dubbing the well groomed, blonde-haired, twinkle-eyed, engaging Jack Lescoulie as "grouchmaster" for a broadcast series seems an anathema. The man who grinned into the cameras in the 1950s while introducing *The Jackie Gleason Show* on CBS-TV hardly seems to exhibit grumbling qualities. But on his early West Coast CBS Radio series—one he invented and originated in San Francisco—Lescoulie was so designated. Commoners who had a complaint dispatched their written gripes, arguing against public policy, professional life and even their spouses, offspring, parents, siblings and in-laws! An affable Lescoulie attempted to resolve their issues no matter how acute the qualms. The series was such a hit that it thrust its host across the country, landing him at WMCA in New York late in 1938 where he presided over a similar half-hour show every Tuesday night. His feature, under the same moniker, was quickly picked up by NBC and transmitted nationwide.

Meanwhile, in 1942 Lescoulie moved over to WNEW where he assisted Stan Shaw with the overnight *Milkman's Matinee* disc jockey series. When Shaw moved to WINS later that year, Lescoulie took over the program single-handedly. He wouldn't have long to ply his craft there, however, for Uncle Sam called him in 1943. Another radio "name" followed him on *Milkman's Matinee*, Art Ford, who was grooming himself as a recognized record-meister for several successive decades.

Returning from wartime service as a U.S. Air Force combat reporter, Lescoulie joined New York's WOR, where he and Gene Rayburn formed a popular on-air early morning alliance, *The Jack & Gene Show*. By 1947 Lescoulie was back into an accustomed groove, on the air all night as a WOR disc jockey. He did the same thing 15 years earlier for a dollar a night at Los Angeles' KGFJ. The combination platter and patter spinner was in town attending Los Angeles City College and concurrently picked up tips in dramatics at Pasadena Playhouse. He later affiliated with KFAC, Los Angeles, before abandoning it in 1935 to perform with a stock company based in New York. Lescoulie returned to the coast not long afterward, situating in San Francisco, near his native Sacramento.

Before the middle of the 20th century, the adaptable announcer leaped into television where—within a few years—his name was to become a household word in millions of American homes. On Jan. 6, 1949, Lescoulie was the master of ceremonies of ABC-TV's *Fun and Fortune* game show, a program that never made a repeat appearance. While it was an inauspicious prologue to the new medium, things improved for him fairly rapidly. On June 16, 1949, Lescoulie was a one-time thespian in the initial dramatic play shown on NBC-TV's live anthology *Volume One*. In 1952 and for a few consecutive years thereafter—and again from 1962 to 1963—on weekday mornings he posted sports scores and presented features on NBC-TV's *Today*. For the same network Lescoulie delivered commercials on *The Milton Berle Show* (1954–1955); interviewed sports figures on *Meet the Champions* (1956–1957, a simulcast entry heard on NBC Radio); co-hosted the game series *Brains and Brawn* (1958) as well as the juvenile educational series *1, 2, 3—Go!* (1961–1962). For a few months in 1957 he loosely coordinated the chain's *Tonight! America After Dark*, presenting correspondents Bob Considine, Hy Gardner, Earl Wilson and others of that ilk scattered about the country. Lescoulie appeared with comedian Jackie Gleason on Saturday nights between 1952 and 1959 over CBS-TV.

LESTER, JACK (born Jack Swineford). b. Aug. 10, 1915, Oklahoma; d. Sept. 18, 2004, North Hills, Calif. *Actor, Emcee, Announcer.* **Series:** *The Bobby Doyle Show* (1947); *Dreamboat* (cast regular, 1951); *Jack Armstrong, the All-American Boy* (ca. 1940s); *Junior Junction* (host, 1946–1952); *Masquerade* (actor, 1946–1947); *The New Junior Junction* (host, 1950); *Silver Eagle, Mountie* (actor, 1951–1955); *The Skip Farrell Show* (1947); *Sky King* (actor, 1947–1949); *Those Sensational Years* (1947); *The World's Great Novels* (actor, 1944–1945).

Jack Lester's training for "net" work included stints as a sportscaster at New Orleans' WNOE in 1946 and as a disc jockey (*The Jack Lester Show*) at Chicago's WENR in 1949. Meanwhile, in 1949–1950 he announced the primetime game show *Majority Rules* on ABC-TV. He played Blaney Cobb in the daytime sudser *The Bennetts* on NBC-TV for six months in 1953–1954. During five later months in 1954 he was protagonist Carl Sherman on the NBC-TV daytime washboard weeper *A Time to Live*. Lester returned to broadcasting more than two decades after that as the voice of *McDuff, the Talking Dog*, a animated NBC-TV series about the ghost of a 100-year-old English sheepdog. It persisted for only a couple of months in late 1976.

For a half-century Lester also sustained work in 15 motion pictures, starting with an uncredited role in *Love on Skis* (1933) and ending with voiceovers in *The Last Unicorn* (1982). Other B-movie films in his repertoire included *Non-Stop New York* (1937); *Crackerjack* (1938); *Rose of Tralee* (1938); *No Orchids for Miss Blandish* (1948); *Port of Escape* (1956); *Across the Bridge* (1957); *The Sheriff of Fractured Jaw* (1958); *The Two Little Bears* (1961); *Deadwood '76* (1965); *Rat Fink* (1965); *The Road Hustlers* (1968); *Jennie: Wife/Child* (1968); and *The Incredible 2-Headed Transplant* (1971).

LESUEUR, LAWRENCE EDWARD. b. June 10, 1909, New York, N.Y.; d. Feb. 5, 2003, Washington, D.C. *Correspondent, Newscaster, Announcer.* **Series:** *An American in Russia* (narrator, 1943); *CBS World News Roundup* (correspondent, 1942–ca. 1950s); *Chevrolet Spotlights the News* (mid 1950s); *Larry Lesueur and the News* (newscaster, 1946–1958, not continuous); *This is London* (correspondent, early 1940s); *We, the People* (writer-actor, 1938–1939); *The World Tonight* (correspondent, ca. 1950s–ca. 1963).

Born in New York City, for a while in his younger days Larry Lesueur lived in Chicago. He often spent summers on a family farm at Greencastle, Ind., where he fished, hunted and wandered wherever the paths took him. The boy loved the outdoors and only reluctantly left it to return to city life's confines during school years in Chicago and New York. The Lesueurs, meanwhile, had printer's ink in their blood. Larry's grandpa published the town journal in the hamlet of Tama, Iowa. Larry's dad was a foreign correspondent for *The New York Sun* and *The New York Tribune*.

Temporarily breaking with tradition, following high school the youth accepted a discomfiting post as an office boy in Macy's advertising department. After graduating in 1932 from New York University and following months of job searching, he signed on in Depression-ensconced New York as assistant to a private investigator. It was a loathsome task, he admitted, and he soon returned to Macy's as a floorwalker. That, too, was less than fulfilling for somebody with a grand journalistic heritage. When he learned of a reportorial spot at *Women's Wear Daily* in 1935, he went for it.

Less than a year into that the United Press wire service recruited him at $37.50 per week for a workweek that often extended beyond 60 hours. In the meantime, after submitting some usable scripts to CBS's *We, the*

People and portraying a few on-air voices, things got even better for him in 1939. The broadcast chain added Lesueur to its London staff to cover human-interest angles of the British involvement in what was ultimately to be global conflagration. (It was *after* he joined CBS, incidentally, that he began capitalizing the "s" in his surname, as *LeSueur*, the first in his family to do so.) Hired by celebrated newsman Edward R. Murrow—thereby becoming one in the elite journalistic circle known as the "Murrow Boys"—Lesueur augmented CBS's daily transmissions from London during the Blitz. In early 1940 he was dispatched to British Royal Air Force headquarters in France. And after the fall of France, he returned to London.

In autumn 1941 Lesueur was sent to Moscow. Before going, however, he acquired a working familiarity with no less than 400 terms in the Russian vocabulary. There, in a couple of miserably desolate winters, he covered the war's Eastern front. To perform the job adequately, he traversed vast expanses of countryside, seeing what was transpiring from many far-flung vantage points as Nazi forces invaded the once proud empire. Lesueur's eyewitness accounts were some of the war's most pragmatic. He toured "factories, schools, hospitals, collective farms, Red Army encampments, camps for prisoners, theaters, public gatherings and ordinary Russian homes," *Current Biography* reported. His verbal treatises were short-waved to England for broadcast over the BBC and transmitted to CBS in New York. Lesueur later summarized his observations in *Twelve Months That Changed the World* (Knopf, 1943).

Following his sojourn in Russia ending in December 1942, Lesueur went home to New York. After requesting another overseas assignment, nevertheless, he was sent to London in June 1943 where he again labored alongside Murrow, lasting to the Normandy invasion in 1945 that he also covered. A pundit noted that Lesueur seemed to get himself into every hotspot in Europe the war had to offer. Returning to America thereafter, in 1946 he launched a CBS Radio news commentary that persisted erratically to 1958. He is cited as the first newsman to air regular news reports on CBS's flagship television station, WCBS-TV in New York, predating Douglas Edwards in that capacity. Edwards' subsequent weekend network anchor news show, instigated in 1947, in due course developed into what for decades has been known as *The CBS Evening News.*

During the same era, Lesueur succeeded Charles Collingwood in a protracted run as the web's United Nations correspondent that won for Lesueur a prestigious George Foster Peabody Award for his reportorial efforts. He moderated a late night CBS-TV world issues feature, *Chronoscope*, from 1953 to 1955. Between 1955 and 1960 Lesueur presided over an intermittent Sunday morning CBS-TV public affairs series, *The U.N. in Action*, highlighting that body's mission.

Seeking a new challenge, in the early 1960s he transferred from CBS's New York bureau to the one in Washington, D.C. Yet by the mid 1960s—in an epoch in which his longtime pal and beloved mentor Ed Murrow languished with cancer and died (1965)—Lesueur departed CBS (in 1963) and signed on as a news analyst with the United States Information Agency's Voice of America. Subsequently he became that body's White House correspondent before retiring in 1983. Biographer Stanley Cloud, who collaborated with Lynne Olson to produce *The Murrow Boys: Pioneers on the Front Lines of Broadcast Journalism* (Houghton Mifflin, 1996), considered Lesueur "the best and bravest of the 20th century's war reporters." They also dubbed him CBS News's "forgotten man," ranking his reporting during the war with that of Sevareid, Collingwood and Murrow, and citing his D-Day coverage as enough to "have earned him a permanent place in the network's pantheon." Sadly, they observed: "Whenever CBS staged one of its commemorative extravaganzas extolling Murrow and the Boys, the people in charge always neglected to include Larry LeSueur."

LEWIS, FULTON, JR. b. April 30, 1903, Washington, D.C.; d. Aug. 21, 1966, Washington, D.C. **Commentator. Series:** *Top of the News from Washington* (commentator, 1937–ca. 1957).

Radio historiographer John Dunning noted that the 1954 autobiography of Fulton Lewis Jr., *Praised and Damned*, wasn't a misnomer: "Lewis was loved and hated with equal intensity." In an epoch in which the nation was growing increasingly liberal, Lewis was a controversial conservative commentator. Before the outbreak of the Second World War, he urged America to devote its resources to itself, building up its own defenses instead of inserting forces into European disagreements.

"Lewis was known for his complete lack of objectivity," insisted Eric Boehlert, a contemporary scribe. "An erstwhile Rush Limbaugh, Lewis was the master of partisan smear who rarely strayed from GOP talking points." John Crosby, radio columnist of *The New York Herald Tribune*, advocated in 1948 that Lewis "be recognized as a campaigner, not as a commentator, and his national air time be paid for and so listed by the Republican National Committee." The following year *The New Republic* observed that Lewis's "wild charges" were part of a campaign he instigated "to smear in every way possible the New Deal ... and everybody not in accord with the most reactionary political beliefs." Two decades following his death *The Washington Post* remembered him as "one of the most unprincipled journalists ever to practice the trade."

Born into a family of privilege "with a golden spoon in his mouth," Lewis attended the University of Virginia for three years before quitting. He enrolled at George Washington University's School of Law but quit there, too. In 1925 he realized what he really wanted to do after landing a job as a reporter for *The Washington Herald*. By 1927 he was also reading news bulletins every night on the paper's station, WMAL, his baptism into electronic journalism. Lewis became the journal's assistant city editor but left his post in 1928 to accept an opportunity with the conservative Hearst papers' Universal News Service. In time he rose to Washington bureau chief in that organization. Meanwhile, in 1929 when he married the daughter of the chairman of the Republican National Committee, the president's spouse—Mrs. Hoover—as well as Vice President Curtis, flanked by Supreme Court justices, senators and other dignitaries, attended the nuptials! It was likely the most high-ranking knot-tying ceremony ever witnessed among mere journalists.

From 1933–1936 Lewis penned a syndicated newspaper column, *The Washington Sideshow*, appearing in 60 papers. It helped propel him into radio permanently: when he volunteered to substitute for a vacationing newsman, he filled the spot with significantly increased reportage from outside the studio. So inspired with his ingenuity was local Mutual affiliate WOL, it put him on the air in October 1937 for several news commentaries. Within a couple of months, Lewis was airing nationally. He would do so for a couple of decades, in fact. At his peak 10 million listeners tuned to 500 MBS outlets carrying his program every weeknight. Biographer Irving Fang labeled him "Washington's best known radio commentator." A resourceful but independent Lewis who, nevertheless, moved to the beat of his own drum, subscribed to no wire services; he preferred to handle the newsgathering himself. He also pursued local sponsors to underwrite his broadcasts on every station, a departure from the then-prevailing formula.

"As the medium of radio waned during the rise of television in the late forties and early fifties," declared *Radio Days*, "Lewis' appearance on the small screen was simply not good television. He appeared too much out of place and so he continued on radio. It was in the fifties that Lewis' star began to wane. He was a strong supporter of Joe McCarthy, the Wisconsin Senator who presided over the committee investigating communists in the government. Even as McCarthy's committee turned into a witch hunt, Lewis continued to support him. As McCarthy fell, so too did Lewis. He continued broadcasting, but his audience had dwindled." The support of McCarthy, by the way, opened deep apertures between Lewis and his colleague commentators and reporters.

Radio Days continued: "Despite his political stances, Lewis was a keen reporter who helped add respect of radio journalists among the Washington-establishment. It was Fulton Lewis Jr. who finally convinced Congress to allow radio coverage of Congressional activities. [As such, he founded the Radio Correspondents' Association that accredited the press for inclusion in the policy-making galleries.] His broadcasting style was somewhat folksy making the listener feel Lewis was speaking directly to him. And he spoke in a voice that intoned knowledge and authority."

LINDLAHR, VICTOR HUGO. b. Feb. 14, 1897, Montana; d. Jan. 26, 1969, Miami Beach, Fla. *Commentator.* **Series:** *Journal of Living* (commentator, 1937–1938); *Victor Lindlahr* (commentator, 1938–1953).

Nutritionist and author of *You Are What You Eat* (National Nutrition Society, 1942), Victor Lindlahr devoted his mostly quarter-hour visits with Americans to the topics of nutrition, health and diet, one of the earliest radio commentators to stress those themes. Between 1944 and 1953 he was commercially linked to underwriter Serutan ("Remember, Serutan is Natures spelled backwards"), a health supplement in pill form, on radio and later on television. Lindlahr became so inseparably identified with that product in fact, it wasn't altogether clear whether he or the commodity was possibly being exploited.

Lindlahr was a 1918 graduate of the Chicago College of Osteopathy. He plugged a 600-calorie, seven-day reducing diet that caught the imagination of hordes of listeners, a concept that many hadn't given much attention to before his discerning revelations. His numerous published titles include *Calorie Countdown—The Easy Way to Reduce*; *Eat and Reduce*; *The Lindlahr Vitamin Cookbook*; *The Natural Way to Health*; and *201 Tasty Dishes for Reducers*. The innovative Chicago health practitioner introduced "catabolic foods" which, he claimed, sustained "reverse calories." His ideas have, in modern times, evolved into popular plans known as the Cabbage Soup Diet and the Negative Calorie Diet.

LINDSLEY, CHARLES FREDERICK. b. April 2, 1919, Minnesota; d. Sept. 2, 1990, Orange, Calif. *Announcer, Emcee.* **Series:** *Calling All Cars* (narrator, 1933–1939); *Noah Webster Says* (quiz arbiter, 1942–1943, 1945–1951).

Charles Frederick Lindsley taught on the faculty of Occidental College.

LOWE, DONALD HERBERT. b. Jan. 10, 1911, Hartford, Conn.; d. June 1, 1991. *Announcer, Emcee.* **Series:** *Betty Clarke Sings* (1949–1950); *David Harding, Counterspy* (mid 1940s–?); *DeRose and Breen* (1927–?); *Dunninger, the Mentalist* (ca. 1945, 1946); *Ethel and Albert*, aka *The Private Lives of Ethel and Albert* (ca. late 1940s); *The Fat Man* (ca. late 1940s, early 1950s); *The Fishing and Hunting Club of the Air* (ca. late 1940s); *Lorenzo Jones* (ca. 1940s); *The Metropolitan Opera Auditions of the Air* (host, 1953–1958); *Mr. President* (mid 1940s–?); *The Moylan Sisters* (ca. 1939–ca. 1944); *The Nellie Revell Show*, aka *Neighbor Nell*, aka *Meet the Songwriters*, aka *Strolling Songsters* (cast member, mid 1930s–?); *Piano Playhouse* (mid 1940s–?).

Orphaned at an early age, Don Lowe grew up on a New England farm milking cows, chopping kindling, hoeing and plowing. He was an outstanding high school student, loved dramatics and played leading roles in amateur theatrical productions. Until his voice turned bass he sang soprano in a boys' choir at Hartford's Christ Church Cathedral. Later he vocalized for pay before clubs and other groups and found sideline employment at a settlement house, as a store clerk and in landscape gardening. For a year he was a professional actor performing with a Waterbury stock company. He followed that by moving to Boston, where he became a relief announcer at WBZ and played bit parts in aural dramatic productions.

Several New England radio stations subsequently hired him. During this pilgrimage Lowe landed at one in Worcester, Mass., where he was given the title of assistant manager. His duties included writing continuity copy, acting, singing and publicity. Ultimately, he moved to New York, joining a small station as an announcer and broadcasting at nightclub venues from Greenwich Village to Harlem. NBC added him in 1933 and he was soon dispatched to its owned-and-operated outlet, WRC, in Washington, D.C. A year later the chain recalled him to New York and Lowe's voice expanded to millions of listeners across the nation.

LOWTHER, GEORGE. b. April 9, 1913, New York, N.Y.; d. April 28, 1975, Westport, Conn. *Writer, Director, Narrator.* **Series:** *The Adventures of Dick Tracy* (writer, 1930s); *The Adventures of Superman* (writer-director-narrator, early 1940s); *The CBS Radio Mystery Theater* (writer, 1974–1975); *The Shadow* (writer); *The Tom Mix Ralston Straightshooters* (writer); *Terry and the Pirates* (writer, 1930s).

At 14, George Lowther withdrew from school after he was hired as NBC's first page.

At that juncture the fledgling network was just a year old and the teenager grew up with the soon-to-be broadcasting giant. Initially joining the web's station relations department, he eventually shifted to the continuity department. In seven years there he scripted the juvenile adventure serials *The Adventures of Dick Tracy* and *Terry and the Pirates*.

It prepared him to pen the dialogue and action for *The Adventures of Superman*, a show he also narrated. In 1942, when Jack Johnstone departed as director of that pivotal quarter-hour adolescent escapism aired weekday afternoons on MBS, Lowther was tapped to replace him. In 1943 Jackson Beck was appointed narrator of the serial while Lowther continued directing it.

LUND, JOHN. b. Feb. 6, 1911, Rochester, N.Y.; d. May 10, 1992, Coldwater Canyon, Calif. *Actor, Announcer.* **Series:** *Academy Award Theater* (actor, 1946); *The Bob Crosby Show* (ca. 1943–ca. 1944); *Chaplain Jim* (actor, 1942–?); *NBC Star Playhouse* (actor, 1953–1954); *Screen Director's Playhouse*, aka *Screen Director's Guild* (actor, 1949–1951); *Suspense* (actor, ca. early 1950s); *Yours Truly, Johnny Dollar* (actor, 1952–1954).

John Lund was employed by a New York advertising firm when he was assigned to appear in an industrial show during the 1939 New York World's Fair. That event was pivotal, for it prompted him to refocus his life's direction, concentrating on acting as his future. He debuted on Broadway in a 1941 production of *As You Like It*. For Broadway's *New Faces of 1943*, Lund penned the lyrics and wrote the book on which the play was based. He also went into radio, appearing most often as a thespian in occasional and continuing dramatic roles.

Nevertheless, Lund is more widely recalled for his performances on the silver screen. Between 1946 and 1978 he turned up in 29 theatrical productions, including such films as *The Night Has a Thousand Eyes* (1948); *My Friend Irma* (1949); *My Friend Irma Goes West* (1950); *The Mating Season* (1951); *The Battle at Apache Pass* (1952); *Five Guns West* (1955); *High Society* (1956); *Battle Stations* (1956); *The Wackiest Ship in the Army* (1960); and *If a Man Answers* (1962). With the exception of a single uncredited movie role in 1978, Lund left acting in the early 1960s to concentrate on private business.

LUTHER, FRANK (born Frank Luther Crow). b. Aug. 4, 1899, Kansas City, Mo.; d. Nov. 16, 1980, New York, N.Y. *Vocalist, Emcee, Announcer.* **Series:** *Ethel Park Richardson* (recurring cast member, mid 1930s); *Five Star Theater* (vocalist, 1932–1933); *The Frank Luther Show* (vocalist, 1935, 1947–1948); *Friendship Town* (vocalist, 1932); *Happy Wonder Bakers Trio* (vocalist, 1928–1931); *Hillbilly Heartthrobs*, aka *Dreams of Long Ago*, aka *Heartthrobs of the Hills* (vocalist, 1933–1938); *Hollywood Nights* (vocalist, 1931–1932); *I'll Never Forget* (vocalist, 1940); *The Life and Love of Dr. Susan* (1939); *Luncheon at the Waldorf* (vocalist, 1940–1941); *Luther-Layman Singers* (vocalist, 1939–1941); *Manhattan Merry-Go-Round* (1932–1933); *Your Lover* (host-vocalist, 1934).

Frank Luther, who was also billed as Bud Billings in some professional listings, pursued courses in vocal music and piano at Kansas State Normal College. The tenor toured with multiple ensembles and was a music evangelist for three years. He penned a myriad of tunes for adolescents (dubbed "Bing Crosby of the sandpile set"), lectured on many aspects of music and authored *Americans and Their Songs* (Harper & Brothers, 1942). A pundit surmised that Luther brought "more stories in song to children than anyone else on radio and records." His was a familiar voice to the little tykes as he dispensed nursery rhymes and melodic bromides especially tied to manners, math, diet and fitness.

Luther's foremost notoriety appeared to stem from the music hall favorite *Barnacle Bill, the Sailor*, which he co-wrote with Carson J. Robison. Reared in Bakersfield, Calif., Luther sang and played piano with gospel quartets before relocating in New York City in the late 1920s. Subsequently, when Robison split with his partner Vernon Dalhart in 1928, he (Robison) joined forces with the Luther Brothers—including Frank and sibling Phil Crow—and the threesome was billed as the Carson Robison Trio. After Phil Crow left them to go solo, the duo appeared as Bud and Joe Billings. Together they cut records for Conqueror, Decca and RCA Victor.

From 1933 to 1935, Luther was a recurring guest on Ethel Park Richardson's radio folk culture dramatizations (on New York's WOR and on NBC). After devoting some time to a couple of country music movies—he performed in 1934's *The Girl from Paradise* and 1937's *High Hat* (and contributed the lyrics and compositions for the latter film's music)—he re-focused himself on children's recordings. They consisted of stories, ballads and cowboy songs, most often for Decca. Luther then recorded with his wife, vocalist Zora Layman, and with singing cowboy Ray Whitley. He composed "Down in the Valley," a song featured in the 1944 film *Moonlight and Cactus*. In the 1950s Luther transitioned to a music industry executive for the remainder of his professional career.

LUTHER, PAUL. *Announcer, Actor, Writer.* **Series:** *The Adventures of Dick Cole* (1942); *Backstage Wife* (actor, ca. late 1930s, early 1940s); *Bright Horizon* (early to mid 1940s); *Broadway is My Beat* (actor, 1949); *The Cavalcade of America* (1951); *Don Winslow of the Navy* (ca. 1937–ca. 1942); *The Man Behind the Gun* (actor, 1942–1944); *Our Secret Weapon* (writer-actor, 1942–1943); *Suspense* (actor, 1942); *Vic and Sade* (early 1940s).

LYON, CHARLES ALBERT. b. March 1, 1903, Detroit, Mich.; d. May 11, 1985, Los Angeles, Calif. *Announcer.* **Series:** *The Bob Hawk Show* (early 1950s); *The Curt Massey-Martha Tilton Show* (1949–1954); *Family Skeleton* (1953–1954); *The Frigidaire Frolics* (1936); *Gene Autry's Melody Ranch* (ca. late 1940s–ca. 1956); *Girl Alone* (ca. 1938–1941); *Lassie* (1947–1950); *Life with Luigi* (ca. 1948–ca. 1953, ca. 1954); *Lum and Abner* (1930s); *The Passing Parade* (ca. late 1930s, 1940s); *Plantation Jubilee*, aka *Plantation Party*, aka *The Curt Massey Show* (1938–1943, 1949); *Those Websters* (ca. mid 1940s); *Truth or Consequences* (ca. 1950s); *Uncle Walter's Doghouse* (1939–1941); *Vic and Sade* (ca. 1940s); *Wild Bill Hickok* (1951–1954, 1955–1956); *The Woman in My House* (1951–ca. 1959); *Yours Truly, Johnny Dollar*.

Charlie Lyon was able to attain but a year of formal training at the University of Michigan before joining the workforce. Initially he was a seaman plying the waters of the Great Lakes. Later he was hired aboard a ship sailing to Europe. Lyon scrubbed decks to earn his passage home; then he took off for Hollywood to pursue a longtime dream as an actor. For a winter season he played youthful roles in *Cameo Comedies*. Other parts followed on stage, including an occasional diversion on Broadway. Lyon also auditioned at Cleveland's WTAM but after he won an announcing slot he turned it down for another acting gig. Following a 16-week run in Dayton, he settled on the WTAM opening that was still available.

A short time afterward NBC purchased WTAM and by April 1931 Lyon shifted to the chain's Chicago announcing staff. There he gained many chances to widen his grasp by appearing on a myriad of network broadcasts. Very soon he assisted the web in its coverage of the 1932 political conventions. In between assignments he was a newscaster at NBC's Chicago outlet, WMAQ. He spent a few weeks in 1937 in Hollywood but soon returned to NBC in the Windy City. By the late 1940s Lyons' name was commonplace to many radio listeners, as he aired from Hollywood on a plethora of durable aural series.

MACCORMACK, FRANKLYN. b. March 8, 1906, Waterloo, Iowa; d. June 12, 1971, Chicago, Ill. *Announcer.* **Series:** *Bouquet for You* (1946–1947); *Caroline's Golden Store* (1939–1940); *The Curley Bradley Show* (1949); *Easy Aces* (1935); *Hymns of All Churches* (ca. 1936–ca. 1938); *Jack Armstrong, the All-American Boy* (early 1940s); *Myrt and Marge* (1932); *Poetic Melodies* (host-reader, 1932–1933, 1935–1938); *The Story of Joan and Kermit* (1938); *The Wayne King Show* (ca. 1930s, 1940s); *Woman in White* (1938–1942, 1944–1948).

Following high school, Franklyn MacCormack joined a stock company in Joliet, Ill. But when his opportunities on the stage, including a Broadway production of *Seventh Heaven*, started to vanish and the stock outfit paying his salary folded at the close of the 1920s—the beginning of the Great Depression—MacCormack looked to radio for a livelihood. With a poetry-reading feature, he launched an ethereal career at South Bend, Ind. Not long afterward, in 1930 he moved to St. Louis' WIL, where a similar engagement drew 40,000 requests for photos. By 1933 MacCormack transferred to Chicago's WBBM and found work as an actor, announcer and producer. His new aural address (a CBS affiliate) led him to several assignments that were followed by listeners across the nation. MacCormack settled in at a geographic location where he was to drop anchor forever.

Among a myriad of programming concepts, he presided over the Windy City version of the celebrated *Make Believe Ballroom* DJ show that was making the rounds of the major radio markets in the 1930s and 1940s. In the late 1940s, MacCormack reprised his fêted radio-programming concept that appealed to nationwide fans more than a decade earlier, exclusively for Chicagoland listeners. On a series labeled *Poetic Melodies*, which appeared to copy a popular late night program (*Moon River*) already running on Cincinnati's WLW, he read rhymes backed by orchestral accompaniment. *Poetic Melodies* was so successful, in fact, that it progressed to three major chains during the 1930s. His recorded recitation "Why Do I Love You?" to Wayne King's instrumental backdrop sold four million copies.

In 1947 MacCormack diversified that formula as he read aloud anonymous romantic notes on *Love Letters*, beamed over the Windy City's WENR for a quarter-hour three nights a week at 11:15. Starting in 1948, for an hour each weeknight at nine o'clock, MacCormack read inspirational prose and romantic poetry over Chicago's WCFL on *Great Day for Music*. The melody was, by then, prerecorded. But the interlude during the dark hours was a fond throwback to some of radio's earliest nights. He followed this feature, from 1959 until his death while on the air in 1971, with *All Night Showcase* over WGN. MacCormack died of a heart attack conducting that pleasant nocturnal reverie, perhaps doing what he did best and loved most. An obituary writer branded his durable career-ending series a "quiet blend of soft music, nostalgic poetry and tranquil patter ... for the city's night people."

MACK, FLOYD (born Floyd MacLaughlin). b. Oct. 23, 1912, Ava, Ohio; d. Jan. 3, 1983, Newark, Ohio. *Emcee, Commentator, Newscaster*. **Series:** *The Bell Telephone Hour* (host-commentator, 1940–1958); *Encores from the Bell Telephone Hour* (host-commentator, 1968–1969); *Floyd Mack and the News* (newscaster, 1942–ca. 1944).

Floyd Mack handled hosting duties not only for the long-running radio version of *The Bell Telephone Hour* but also for the show in video form, carried by NBC-TV from 1959 to 1968. Throughout those years while linked with that durable program he operated his own recording business. When the series left the air, Mack moved to Newark, Ohio. There he was a special projects coordinator for funding and grants while inaugurating a service that provided local transportation for older citizens known as the Senior Sedan Program.

MACVANE, JOHN F. b. April 29, 1912, Portland, Maine; d. Jan. 28, 1984, Brunswick, Maine. **Series:** *Correspondent, Newscaster*. *ABC News* (correspondent, ca. 1954–1977); *Associated Press—One Hundred Years of News* (correspondent, 1948); *The Breakfast Club* (correspondent, 1941); *Early Morning Roundup* (correspondent, 1940–?); *John MacVane and the News* (newscaster, 1945–1948, 1953–1956); *NBC News Roundup* (correspondent, 1940–?, 1942–?); *The NBC War Telescope* (correspondent, 1945); *News of the World* (correspondent, 1942); *Rhythmic Melodies* (correspondent, 1941); *Sunday Evening News Roundup* (correspondent, 1940–?); *Weekly War Journal* (correspondent, 1942–?).

John MacVane attended the public schools of Portland, Maine, and Phillips Exeter Academy. He earned a bachelor's degree from Williams College and a bachelor of literature from Oxford University. In 1935 he became a reporter and ship news editor for *The Brooklyn Daily Eagle*. In 1936 he joined *The New York Sun* as a reporter and rewrite editor. Surprisingly, an eight-week European summer hiatus in 1938 turned into a seven-year stay. MacVane became sub-editor of *The London Daily Express* that year. He also met and married his American wife in England. For two years he worked in the Paris bureaus of the *Daily Express* and International News Service.

MacVane was based in Paris as the Germans invaded the French capital. Joining NBC in London in 1940, his and others' eyewitness accounts of the start of the Blitz—including daily bombings of the British capital—was riveting to American listeners at home. For 57 consecutive days beginning Sept. 7, 1940, the Germans bombed London.

After that, the siege persisted intermittently to May 11, 1941, when Hitler withdrew his planes to focus them on Russia.

Beginning in autumn 1940, MacVane was dispatched to other African and European hot spots as the war continued. According to his own account, *On the Air in World War II* (William Morrow, 1979), MacVane was the first radio newsman ashore on D-Day at Omaha Beach and—in August 1944—was the first American journalist to enter Paris with Allied liberating forces. While Berlin was still flaming in 1945, he was among a quartet of correspondents journeying there. On-air competition was keen, nonetheless, and co-authors Stanley Cloud and Lynne Olson revealed in *The Murrow Boys: Pioneers on the Front Lines of Broadcast Journalism* (Houghton Mifflin, 1996) that on at least two strategic newsworthy occasions—the 1942 assassination of French Adm. Jean Darlan in North Africa, when CBS's Charles Collingwood outfoxed MacVane, and the liberation of Paris, when MacVane was scooped by CBS's Larry Lesueur—he lost out to his rivals.

After the war ended in 1945, MacVane became a United Nations press rep for NBC. By the end of the decade he transferred to ABC and continued holding the same post until he retired in 1977. Meanwhile, for 16 months in 1951–1952, MacVane hosted a weekly primetime half-hour forum, *United or Not?*, on ABC-TV that focused on the United Nations. He presided over a weekly quarter-hour syndicated video series, *U.N. Review* from 1958 to 1961. Between 1961 and 1963 MacVane delivered the news at the start of telecasts of the ABC Sunday afternoon public affairs series *Adlai Stevenson Reports*.

MALLIE, THEODORE A. b. June 3, 1924, Brooklyn, N.Y.; d. Jan. 25, 1999, Jamaica, N.Y. *Announcer.* **Series:** *I Love a Mystery* (ca. 1949–1952); *The Jean Shepherd Show* (1955–?); *John Steele, Adventurer* (1949–1952, ca. 1953, ca. 1954–ca. 1956); *The Shadow* (1953–1954); *The Sylvan Levin Opera Concert* (1949); *There's Always a Woman* (1948); *Wild Bill Hickok* (ca. 1951–ca. 1954, ca. 1955–ca. 1956).

After his web-based radio opportunities faded, Ted Mallie spent his days and nights as a newscaster and announcer at WOR, New York, one of the cornerstone originators of Mutual Broadcasting System programming. Mallie was a continuing participant in a local edition of *The Jean Shepherd Show* via that outlet in the 1960s.

MANLOVE, DUDLEY D. b. June 11, 1914, Oakland, Calif.; d. April 17, 1996, San Bernardino, Calif. *Announcer.* **Series:** *Candy Matson* (1949–1951).

In 1939 Dudley Manlove was a newscaster for San Francisco's KSAN Radio.

MANNING, CHARLES KNOX. b. Jan. 17, 1904, Worcester, Mass.; d. Aug. 26, 1980, Woodland Hills, Calif. *Announcer, Emcee.* **Series:** *The Adventures of Sherlock Holmes* (1939–1943); *The AFRS Story* (1953); *Behind the Scenes* (host); *Feature Page* (narrator, 1947); *Forecast* (1940, ca. 1941); *Get That Story* (host, 1946); *Headlines on Parade* (1937–1939); *Hollywood Preview* (host, 1945–1946); *I Was There* (ca. 1935–ca. 1940); *Just Between Us* (host); *Melody and Madness* (1939); *The Miracle of America* (host, 1950); *Show Stoppers* (host, 1946); *So the Story Goes* (host-narrator, 1945–1946); *Stars Over Hollywood* (ca. mid 1940s); *This is the Story* (narrator); *Your Voice of America* (host, 1951).

Although a Boston radio station hired him as an actor in 1930, the duties of Knox Manning quickly broadened to include announcing, commentary and narration. He subsequently worked many series carried by the Yankee and Don Lee networks, the latter after he relocated on the West Coast, where he captured small movie roles and became a motion picture narrator. He was also heard twice daily over Los Angeles' KNX Radio. The American Federation of Radio Artists (AFRA) elected him their president in 1952 just as the group expanded to include television professionals (becoming the AFTRA).

In addition to his broadcasting credits, Manning was even more prevalent in theatrical productions. Between 1939 and 1953 he narrated 52 movies and appeared in 20 more, most often as a radio announcer. Manning was spokesman for these films and others: *Mandrake the Magician* (1939); *The Tanks Are Coming* (1941); *Divide and Conquer* (1942); *The Batman* (1943); *Spade Cooley, King of Western Swing* (1945); *Brenda Starr, Reporter* (1945); *Chick Carter, Detective* (1946); *Buck*

Privates Come Home (1947); *Jack Armstrong* (1947); *The Babe Ruth Story* (1948); *Tex Granger, Midnight Rider of the Plains* (1948); *The Lawton Story* (1949); *Atom Man vs. Superman* (1950 serial); *Cody of the Pony Express* (1950); *Captain Video, Master of the Stratosphere* (1951); *Son of Geronimo, Apache Avenger* (1952); *Blackhawk, Fearless Champion of Freedom* (1952); and *The Great Adventures of Captain Kidd* (1953). In the meantime, Manning also performed in *Meet John Doe* (1941); *Wings for the Eagle* (1942); *Remember Pearl Harbor* (1942); *Hit Parade of 1947* (1947); *Destination Moon* (1950); *Invasion USA* (1952); and many more.

Many of Manning's radio credits were earned while hosting or narrating series paid for by organizations like the United Textile Manufacturers, Voice of America, U.S. Air Force and other federally funded agencies and private corporations.

MARBLE, HARRY W. b. June 11, 1905, Brownville, Maine; d. Aug. 1, 1982, Damariscotta, Maine. *Announcer, Newscaster, Emcee.* **Series:** *Columbia Presents Corwin* (cast member appearing as himself, 1944); *First Anniversary of the United Nations* (1946); *Harry Marble and the News* (newscaster, 1939–1944); *In Town Today* (1952); *March of Dimes Victory Program* (1954); *Margaret Arlen* (1943–1952); *Matinee Theater* (1944–1945); *Mid-Century Broadcast* (1950); *News of the World*, aka *CBS World News Roundup* (newscaster, early 1940s); *Radio Reader's Digest* (1940s); *The United Nations Today* (host, 1951); *Up for Parole* (narrator, 1950); *World News Tonight* (newscaster, early 1940s); *You Are There*, aka *CBS is There* (host, 1947–?).

Harry Marble was a newscaster at Philadelphia's WCAU in 1938, the year before he shifted to CBS in New York in a similar capacity.

MARSHALL, E.G. (born Everett Eugene Grunz). b. June 18, 1914, Owatonna, Minn.; d. Aug. 24, 1998, Bedford, N.Y. *Emcee.* **Series:** *The CBS Radio Mystery Theater* (host, 1974–1981).

E.G. Marshall presided over network radio's most ambitious comeback when CBS instituted a series of live-on-tape mystery dramas seven nights a week in 1974. Most chain radio offerings had been absent long enough for its reappearance to intrigue, even enthrall, legions, including the many who were hearing web-based radio again. For eight years a somber-voiced Marshall introduced the grim dramas of the macabre and corralled a loyal following eager to hear the squeaking door slam shut again; it was a prop that producer-director Himan Brown had borrowed from *Inner Sanctum Mysteries* two decades earlier. The resurgence was exciting and, for as long as it lasted, held a core segment of listeners at rapt attention.

Marshall, an alumnus of the University of Minnesota, was an inexhaustible stage, film and television actor. He performed in no fewer than 92 films on TV and in cinema houses (1945–1998) while making 138 guest appearances in televised dramatic series (1949–1995). His first continuing role was in the CBS-TV courtroom drama *The Defenders* (1961–1965) in which he played a defense attorney. He returned to recurring acting as a physician in NBC's *The Bold Ones* (1969–1973).

MARTIN, H. GILBERT. *Announcer.* **Series:** *Behind the Mike*, aka *This is the Truth*, aka *Nothing But the Truth* (1940–1942); *Gangbusters* (ca. 1940s).

When the Blue network began operating independently of the NBC Red chain in 1942, H. Gilbert Martin was one of 16 individuals named permanent staff announcers for the web. All had been previously employed under the National Broadcasting Co. umbrella. The following year the Blue net would be officially divorced from NBC and by 1945 would emerge as the American Broadcasting Co. (ABC).

MARTIN, JEFF FRANK, JR. b. May 10, 1914, Oklahoma; d. Dec. 22, 1994, Solvang, Calif. *Announcer, Actor.* **Series:** *Alias Jane Doe* (1951); *The Dick Haymes Show* (mid 1940s); *Dimension X* (commercial spokesman, 1950); *Everything for the Boys* (1944–1945); *Hashknife Hartley* (actor, 1950–1951); *His Honor, the Barber* (1945–1946); *Lights Out* (ca. 1940s); *Mayor of the Town* (1940s); *Meet Corliss Archer* (actor, 1943); *The Merry Life of Mary Christmas* (actor, 1945); *The Penny Singleton Show* (1950); *Sara's Private Caper* (1950); *Suspense* (ca. 1947); *Tales of the Texas Rangers* (actor, 1950–1952); *Your Lucky Strike* (1948–1949).

MARVIN, ANTHONY. b. Oct. 5, 1912, New York, N.Y.; d. Oct. 10, 1998, Boynton Beach, Fla. *Announcer, Emcee, Newscaster.* **Series:** *The Arthur Godfrey Digest*, aka *The Arthur Godfrey Roundtable* (1950–1955); *Arthur Godfrey Time* (1945–ca. 1957); *Casey, Crime Photographer* (1946–1948); *The Charlie Ruggles Show* (1943–1945); *Cinderella Incorporated* (1946–1947); *The Columbia Workshop* (ca. 1940s); *Could Be* (master of ceremonies, 1939); *Major Bowes' Original Amateur Hour* (1941–?); *The Sparrow and the Hawk* (1945–1946); *This Life is Mine* (1943–1945); *Tony Marvin and the News* (newscaster, 1942–ca. mid 1940s; 1959–?). **Aphorism:** *Here's that man himself.*

Following graduation from St. John's University, Tony Marvin enrolled at Long Island College of Medicine. But a career in medicine was not to be. The Great Depression forced him to drop out after two years and pursue odd jobs wherever he could find work, including as an auto mechanic. As fate would have it, one day while he was working on a patron's vehicle, he sang to himself. The vehicle's owner overheard him and was so impressed by his ability that he offered to underwrite vocal lessons for him. For a year Marvin was tutored by an MGM voice coach and then performed regularly with the New York Operatic Guild, winning leading roles on stage in comedy productions.

He got into radio by announcing at New York's WNYC. By 1937 he was chief announcer at the station and two years later was designated the "official voice" of the New York's World Fair. That same year he departed from WNYC and joined CBS Radio as an announcer-newscaster, introducing reports of respected newsmen like Robert Trout, Edward R. Murrow and William L. Shirer, who often spoke from Europe. He would be with CBS for the next two decades.

While in 1958 he inaugurated *The Tony Marvin Show*, a two-hour DJ feature over New York's WABC Radio every afternoon except Sundays at 2 o'clock, it was as sidekick to entertainer Arthur Godfrey that established Marvin in legions of Americans' minds. For a decade-and-a-half he was the deep-voiced, reliably affable and erudite foil for emcee-humorist-vocalist Godfrey and his lighthearted repartee. Marvin's input contributed emphatically to Godfrey's multiple broadcast features in dual mediums. When Godfrey was absent, Marvin played second banana to substitute Robert Q. Lewis, never overstepping his boundaries. He introduced the 90-minute *Arthur Godfrey Time* on weekday mornings (*And now, here's that man himself* he bellowed as anticipation built at the top of each quarter hour after 30-second breaks for station identification); *The Arthur Godfrey Digest* on Sunday afternoons (a recorded recap of snippets from the morning series); and he filled in on *Arthur Godfrey's Talent Scouts* Monday nights on rare occasions when regular announcer George Bryan was away.

Partnered with Godfrey "and all the little Godfreys" at the inception of television, Marvin presented the Old Redhead several times a week on the tube. He was on hand as the morning series joined CBS Television from 1952 to 1957 as a simulcast Monday through Thursday mornings (Godfrey took Fridays off, replaced by Garry Moore and announcer Durward Kirby). Marvin also introduced *Arthur Godfrey and His Friends* for an hour on Wednesday evenings over CBS-TV (1949–1959), a show that featured singers from the morning program (Archie Bleyer and His Orchestra, Pat Boone, The Chordettes quartet, Janette Davis, Haleloke, The Mariners quartet, Marion Marlowe, The McGuire Sisters, Frank Parker, Lu Ann Simms, Carmel Quinn and several more—until Godfrey went on a rampage and fired most of them). Marvin, in fact, was the only one of the old gang that remained with Godfrey in a final TV season that was reduced to a half-hour in 1958–1959, hardly a gathering of "friends" as the show's title intimated.

In the 1950s, Marvin became the original voice of Tony the Tiger on the Kellogg's cereal commercials. He returned to newscasting in 1959, departing from CBS to proffer his services at MBS. An era had surely come to an end.

MASTERSON, PAUL C. b. Nov. 11, 1917, Montana; d. May 10, 1996, Orange, Calif. *Announcer.* **Series:** *The Adventures of Ellery Queen* (1947–1948); *Tommy Riggs and Betty Lou* (ca. 1940s).

In 1940 Paul Masterson was a newscaster at KOY, Phoenix, Ariz.

MATHER, JOHN E. (JACK). b. Sept. 21, 1907, California; d. Aug. 15, 1966, Wauconda, Ill. *Actor, Announcer.* **Series:** *Cavalcade of America* (actor, 1942); *The Cisco Kid* (actor, 1946, 1947–1956); *Command Performance* (actor, 1942); *Doctor Christian* (actor, 1940); *The Edgar Bergen–Charlie McCarthy Show* (actor, 1946); *Family Theater* (actor, 1947); *Fibber McGee and Molly* (actor, 1953); *Gene Autry's Melody Ranch* (actor, 1940–1943, 1945–1956); *The Jell-O Program Starring Jack Benny* (actor, 1942); *Jonathan Trimble, Esquire* (actor, 1946); *Let George Do It* (actor, 1949); *The Lux Radio Theater* (actor, 1943); *The Phil Harris–Alice Faye Show* (actor, 1949); *Plays for Americans* (actor, 1942); *Radio Almanac* (1944); *Rocky Fortune* (actor, 1953–1954); *Speed Gibson of the International Secret Police* (actor, 1937–1938); *This is My Story* (actor, 1943); *Tommy Riggs and Betty Lou* (ca. 1940s); *Wild Bill Hickok* (actor, 1953).

Jack Mather was typecast in roles linked with juvenile western adventure series (*The Cisco Kid*, *Gene Autry's Melody Ranch*, *Wild Bill Hickok*) on radio. He found time to appear in a trio of motion pictures, too: *Dream Boat* (1952); *River of No Return* (1954); and *This Earth is Mine* (1959). Mather's death a few years later resulted from a heart attack.

MAXWELL, ELSA. b. May 24, 1883, Keokuk, Iowa; d. Nov. 1, 1963, New York, N.Y. *Commentator.* **Series:** *Elsa Maxwell's Party Line* (commentator, 1938–1939, 1942, 1943–1946).

Affectionately dubbed "The Hostess with the Mostest" by publicists, Elsa Maxwell summarized her celebrity-studded life, allowing: "Not bad for a short, fat, homely piano player from Keokuk, Iowa, with no money or background, [who] decided to become a legend and did just that." Despite her own assessment, a source observed that "her fans regard as ... campy quality ... her endless name-dropping and snobbery." Nevertheless, she became an American socialite, lyricist, radio host and gossip columnist who gave lavish, animated parties, feting the high-society and entertainment legends of her day.

Born in Iowa and growing up in California, she left school at 14, yet later claimed she resumed her education at the University of California and the Sorbonne. Despite a lack of formal musical training, in her early teens she was earning a living playing piano at a theater. At 22 she joined a Shakespearean company doing odd jobs, subsequently working her way onto the vaudeville stage and in music halls in South Africa. She was composing songs by 24 and saw at least four score of them published.

It wasn't long afterward that Maxwell began meeting socially with prominent people, turning up at soirées in America and Europe, working her way up the social ladder and into the international leagues. By 1919 she was throwing parties for royalty and high society throughout the European continent. Her events were not only characterized by the elite celebrities she invited but also by the novel amusements she included. For instance, she is credited with having created the scavenger hunt, a popular party game during the 1930s. On several occasions her chic guests were asked to arrive dressed as transvestites. (A widely held rumor, apparently never proved or disproved, was that the spinster-hostess was a lesbian.) Returning to New York City early in the early 1930s, by 1938 she was living in Hollywood, acting in no fewer than three unpromising films (the first two were shorts): *Elsa Maxwell's Hotel for Women* (1939), *The Lady and the Lug* (1940) and *Stage Door Canteen* (1943).

In the same era she went into radio (initially on NBC, later on NBC Blue and finally on MBS) where she delivered gossip about venerated personalities and interviewed some as guests. She also initiated a syndicated newspaper gossip column while continuing to organize parties for prominent social figures. *Harper's Bazaar* published her serialized *I Live By My Wits* in 1936; *Cosmopolitan* followed with her serialized *Life of Barbara Hutton* in 1938. Maxwell wrote a quartet of widely read tomes: *Elsa Maxwell's Etiquette Book* (Bartholomew House, 1951); a memoir, *R.S.V.P.* (Little Brown & Co., 1954); *How to Do It: The Lively Art of Entertaining* (Little Brown & Co., 1957); and *The Celebrity Circus* (Appleton-Century, 1963). More than a quarter-century after her subject's demise, Rosemary Kent penned a biography, *Party Girl: The Elsa Maxwell Story* (Donald I. Fine, 1989).

Maxwell departed Hollywood in the 1950s, returning to New York permanently to take up residence in a suite at the Waldorf-Astoria Hotel. In the epoch in which Jack Paar presided over NBC-TV's *Tonight* show (1957–1962), she was a weekly guest and dispatched risqué hearsay. During a party she threw for opera virtuoso Maria Callas in 1957, meanwhile, Maxwell introduced the honoree to Aristotle Onassis. Giovanni Battista Meneghini, Callas's spouse, cited the hostess as "the ugliest woman I have ever seen."

MCBRIDE, MARY MARGARET. b. Nov. 16, 1899, Paris, Mo.; d. April 7, 1976, West Shokan, N.Y. *Commentator.* **Series:** *Mary Margaret McBride* (hostess-interviewer, 1937–1954).

A biographer dubbed Mary Margaret McBride "the Oprah Winfrey of the pre–TV generation" and characterized her as "a soothing, trustworthy media maven who commanded a legion of loyal, predominantly female followers." Six million of them, in fact, tuned in daily to "the first lady of radio" at the peak of a lengthy career, picking up cooking tips and perceptive insights on a variety of topics while captivated by interviews with "colorful plumbers" and public figures like Eleanor Roosevelt and Harry S Truman—in excess of 1,200 across two decades. (*Time* labeled her interviewing skills "brilliant" and a critic branded her "the premier interviewer of her day.")

A source certified McBride as "the female Arthur Godfrey" while *Life* thought her voice "girlish, hesitant, often bewildered." (Actually, radio historian Gerald Nachman denigrated Godfrey as "the second most successful salesperson on the air, after hostess and interviewer Mary Margaret McBride.") Nevertheless, just like the chatty songstress Kate Smith whose midday show emanated from *her* home, McBride often broadcast from her Manhattan apartment—as a pundit proclaimed—"swaddled in her silk pajamas and Asian housecoat."

A farmer's daughter, she enrolled at a private boarding school in the Show Me State in 1906, Williams Woods College, in reality a preparatory school. In 1916 she entered the University of Missouri, where she pursued an abiding interest in journalism. To pay her way there she found work with the local newspaper as a part-time reporter. Following commencement in 1919, McBride became a reporter with *The Cleveland Press*. The following year she moved to the Interchurch World Movement headquartered in New York City as assistant to the publicity director. Also that same year (1920) she became a feature writer with *The New York Evening Mail*. In 1924, after a quadrennial with that organ, she resigned to become a freelance writer, an occupation she pursued for a decade.

McBride achieved liberal success in selling a plethora of articles to assorted periodicals (*Cosmopolitan, Good Housekeeping, The Saturday Evening Post* and others of their ilk). She also penned self-help and travel volumes and for a while it was altogether financially lucrative. She was a co-author on several of those tomes including *Jazz* (with Paul Whiteman, 1926); *Charm* (with Alexander Williams, 1927); and a quartet of texts with Helen Josephy: *Paris is a Woman's Town* (1929); *London is a Man's Town* (1930); *New York is Everybody's Town* (1931); and *Beer and Skittles, A Friendly Modern Guide to Germany* (1932).

But by 1934, with the country in the throes of severe economic depression, some of her markets began to evaporate as magazines that previously were accepting freelance material suddenly relied on their own staffs to produce most of their copy in a belt-tightening stance. While working for the Newspaper Enterprise Association, McBride looked beyond writing for sustenance. She learned that New York's WOR Radio was holding tryouts for a hostess slot on a women's broadcast series that it was about to premier. What did she have to lose? She got the job and reported later, "I was the only one of fifty applicants who made no salary demands." At $25 weekly, she went on the air on May 3, 1934.

At the program's inception, WOR identified her as "Martha Deane," a "quintessentially perfect grandmother with superhuman homemaking skills." While an instant hit, McBride—in whom deeply held Southern Baptist beliefs and practices had been imbued at an early age—knew she was a fake. On May 26, 1934, after being "Martha Deane" just three weeks, she "broke character and confessed to her audience that she not only wasn't a grandmother, she wasn't even married." By then she had already built a following and it pledged allegiance to her, forgiving her for the ruse in which she had participated.

When she joined CBS in 1937 McBride dispensed with the "Martha Deane" alias altogether and applied her own moniker, although she continued using it on her separate daily matinee talk series on WOR. That station assigned her a news commentary slot starting in 1937 in addition to her homemaking feature. (Parenthetically, others assumed the Deane pseudonym when she left WOR in 1940. Not long afterward she went over to WEAF, the flagship affiliate of NBC, and launched yet another local show also under her own moniker.) Meanwhile, her popularity steadily increased: "The Mary Margaret McBride phenomenon foreshadowed the talk-show tornado that would sweep through radio and television," a chronicler affirmed. Her income from radio reached $100,000 annually. And for the record—the "ultimate homemaker" never married and never had children.

When NBC-TV added her to its television lineup on Sept. 21, 1948, however, she failed to connect. "Photogenic and animated she was not," her biographer claimed. The series persisted in video just three months, from Sept. 21 to Dec. 14, 1948. While the timeslot she was given (Tuesdays, 9–9:30 P.M.) could be partially blamed for her quick exit, *The New York Times* cited her as the first casualty among radio stars trying to leap to the small screen. She continued for several more years on radio. After her various New York–based series folded, McBride syndicated one aural show and broadcast another from WGHO in upstate Kingston, N.Y., near her home in the Catskills. Her broadcast legacy there spanned more than two decades, from 1954 until the spinster's demise in 1976.

She penned a syndicated newspaper column distributed by the Associated Press from 1953 to 1956. Across her lifetime, she authored or co-authored a dozen volumes that included a couple of books for girls, *Tune in for Elizabeth* (Dodd Meade, 1945) and *The Growing Up of Mary Elizabeth* (Dodd Meade, 1966); a couple of autobiographies, *A Long Way from Missouri* (G.P. Putnam's Sons, 1959) and *Out of the Air* (Doubleday, 1960); and a plethora of cookbooks. In 2005 New York University Press released a new volume about the "practically forgotten" broadcast luminary written by Susan Ware—*It's One O'Clock and Here is Mary Margaret McBride: A Radio Biography*. Says Ware: "Mary Margaret McBride was one of the first to exploit the cultural and political importance of talk radio, pioneering the magazine-style format that many talk shows still use." The book recreates the world of daytime radio from the 1930s through the 1950s, underscoring the colossal impact of radio on everyday life, especially for women, while confirming McBride's strategic contributions in establishing that impact.

McBride acknowledged:
> I believe that in every life there is one miracle and that radio, my third career in New York, was my miracle. I was middle-aged or nearing it ... when it happened to me, and I needed a miracle desperately. I had been jobless and broke for nearly four years.... Radio was too good to be true—that I should have this job year after year, that sponsors should wait in line to get on the program, that I should actually be paid for a chance to perform for the public that ordinarily wouldn't have been drawn to a person with my lack of histrionic ability and training.... I wanted to be a great writer and now I never shall be. The trouble was, I suppose, that I wanted to be a writer but I didn't especially want to write, and anyway, I had nothing of consequence to say. So I was far better off as a day-to-day talker than as a would-be creative writer.... I touched a good many lives in the years, and I hope I alleviated some loneliness and awakened a few to the horrors of cruelty and injustice. If so, I am reasonably content.

Among the hordes of celebrities interviewed by McBride was Vice President Alben Barkley, Jack Benny, Gen. Omar Bradley, Adm. Richard Byrd, Eddie Cantor, Bette Davis, the Dionne quintuplets, Jimmy Durante, Amelia Earhart, Jinx Falkenburg, Bob Hope, Fannie Hurst, Danny Kaye, Mary Martin, Groucho Marx, Tex McCrary, George Montgomery, Dinah Shore, Elizabeth Taylor, James Thurber, Carl Van Doren, Fred Waring and scores of other icons.

MCCALL, DON. *Announcer, Director.* **Series:** *Behind the Story* (director, ca. 1949–ca. 1957); *Hashknife Hartley* (1950–1951); *The Johnson Family* (ca. 1940s–1950).

In 1940 Don McCall was a newscaster at WEBC in Duluth, Minn.

MCCARTHY, CHARLES F. b. June 3, 1919; d. July 4, 1988, New Bern, N.C. *Newscaster, Announcer.* **Series:** *Charles F. McCarthy and the News* (newscaster, 1946–1948); *The NBC Story Shop* (1947–1948); *The Sunday News Desk* (newscaster, 1952).

Before he joined NBC in New York in the 1940s, Charles F. McCarthy was a newscaster at WRAL, Raleigh, N.C. in 1939.

MCCARTHY, CLEM. b. Sept. 9, 1882, East Bloomfield, N.Y.; d. June 4, 1962, New York, N.Y. *Sportscaster.* **Series:** *All Sports Program* (sportscaster, late 1930s); *The Clem McCarthy Sports Show* (host, 1947–1949); *The Eddie Bracken Show* (sportscaster, 1945); *Krueger Sports Reel* (sportscaster, 1940); *Racing Scratches* (1940); *Sports* (sportscaster, 1936).

While covering many athletic events, often from a ringside seat at a decisive boxing title match, sportscaster Clem McCarthy was more notably associated with equestrian competitions than any other sport, including posting from the sidelines at the Kentucky Derby and other major parks. The son of a horse trader and auctioneer, he was radio's pioneering eyewitness in reporting the most revered horse races. Although much of his professional career was underwritten by NBC, the gravelly-voiced, quick-spoken (at 224 words a minute) McCarthy simultaneously drew paychecks from New York's WINS and WMCA in the 1930s and WHN in the 1940s for local sportscasts. (He succeeded Ford Frick in 1934 as sportscaster at WINS, for instance, when Frick became secretary of the National Baseball League, an initial springboard that ultimately led to his election as the nation's baseball commissioner. McCarthy covered boxing bouts for WMCA beginning in 1936. By 1944 he was at WHN.)

In the 1920s, meanwhile, he was a successful handicapper and reporter for a San Diego newspaper before transferring his abilities to a couple of daily racing sheets, *The Morning Telegraph* and *The Daily Racing Form*. By then he had finally abandoned a longtime dream of becoming a jockey himself. (Ted Sloan convinced him he wasn't "sufficiently streamlined" for it.) In 1925 McCarthy made it possible for the fans at Bowie Racetrack to be informed of the progressive action on the track by convincing its owners to mount a public address system, conspicuously absent until then.

Two years hence he accomplished the same outcome at Chicago's Arlington Park. There they made him the track's first "announcer." That thrust McCarthy into the purview of KYW and then NBC, which was just organizing in November 1927. The web hired him and shipped him off the following May to Louisville, where he broadcast the very first network airing of the Kentucky Derby. Beginning in 1896 he attended every Derby, by the way. For 23 seasons (1928–1950) he called "the fastest two minutes in sports." If he couldn't ride the ponies, at least he could announce the winners' names to the millions tuning in. Few jockey wanabees could ever do that.

It didn't work out that way on at least one occasion, nevertheless. NBC and rival CBS both covered the Derby in the earliest days of those web transmissions. During the 55th Run for the Roses in 1929, Ted Husing represented CBS by himself while McCarthy headed a 14-member contingent from NBC. With the big race remaining close to the finish, both Husing and McCarthy reported different winners in that nose to nose climax. For McCarthy and NBC, regrettably, Husing happened to call the outcome correctly.

McCarthy was one of several NBC sportscasters jointly hosting *NBC Takes You to the Races*, a live summertime series airing between 1949 and 1951 from New York's Roosevelt Racetrack. He was also one of multiple commentators on NBC-TV's *Gillette Summer Sports Reel* on Friday nights in 1953.

MCCARTHY, JACK. b. ca. 1915; d. May 24, 1996. *Actor, Announcer, Writer.* **Series:** *American Agent* (actor, 1950–1951); *The Chamber Music Society of Lower Basin Street* (writer, ca. 1950, ca. 1952); *Connee Boswell Presents* (1944); *Fish Pond* (1944); *The Green Hornet* (actor, 1946–1952); *Ned Jordan, Secret Agent* (actor, 1939–1942); *Willie Piper* (ca. 1946–ca. 1948).

In 1940 Jack McCarthy was a newscaster at Detroit's WXYZ.

MCCARTHY, JOHN. b. Aug. 23, 1914, New York, N.Y. *NBC staff announcer.*

John McCarthy joined NBC in New York as a staff announcer March 13, 1936.

MCCORMICK, ROBERT K. b. Aug. 9, 1911, Danville, Ky.; d. Sept. 4, 1984. **Series:** *Robert McCormick and the News* (newscaster, 1947–1949).

For a couple of years in the late 1940s, Robert McCormick delivered a quarter-hour matinee newscast to radio listeners five days a week. He regularly signed off the air each day with "Robert McCormick ... NBC News ... Washington." He is not to be confused with yet another Robert McCormick, the publisher of *The Chicago Tribune*, and the newspaper that owned and operated WGN in that era.

The radio newscaster presided over one of television's earliest news commentaries, *Current Opinion*, screened by NBC on Wednesday nights during the month of November 1947. Perspectives based on facts were the series' focus. McCormick later hosted a documentary spotlighting U.S. involvement in the Korean conflict, *Battle Report*. It aired weekly in primetime for 30 minutes on NBC-TV between August 1950 and August 1951. The feature persisted on Sunday afternoons from September 1951 through April 1952.

MCCOY, JACK E. b. Nov. 10, 1918, Akron, Ohio; d. March 18, 1991. *Emcee, Announcer*. **Series:** *Breakfast at Sardi's*, aka *Breakfast in Hollywood* (master of ceremonies, 1952–1954); *Escape* (late 1940s and/or early 1950s); *The Hardy Family* (1952); *It's a Great Life* (1948); *Kay Kyser's Kollege of Musical Knowledge* (1948–1949); *Live Like a Millionaire* (master of ceremonies, 1950–1953); *Maisie* (ca. 1945–ca. 1947, 1949–1953); *My Mother's Husband* (1950).

Briefly in 1951 Jack McCoy was master of ceremonies of a CBS-TV version of *Live Like a Millionaire*, the same feature he was hosting right then on NBC Radio. John Nelson soon supplanted him in the video incarnation, however. In 1953–1954 McCoy was executive producer and host of NBC-TV's daytime makeover competition *Glamour Girl*. He was also in the cast of that chain's *Pinky Lee Show* on Saturday mornings in 1955–1956.

MCCULLOUGH, DAN. *Announcer, Disc Jockey*. **Series:** *The Adventures of Superman* (ca. 1940s); *Life Begins at Eighty* (1948–1949, 1952–1953); *Musical Matinee* (disc jockey, 1955–1956).

By 1960 Dan McCullough was plying his talents as a DJ over New York's WOR.

MCDONNELL, CRAIG. *Actor, Announcer*. **Series:** *The Adventures of Dick Tracy* (actor, ca. 1930s, 1940s); *Bobby Benson and the B-Bar-B Riders*, aka *Bobby Benson's Adventures* (actor, 1932–1936, 1949–1955); *Bringing Up Father* (actor, 1941); *Daddy and Rollo* (actor, 1942–1943); *David Harum* (actor, ca. 1947–ca. 1950); *Destiny's Trails* (actor, 1945); *Ed Wynn, the Fire Chief*, aka *Happy Island* (actor, 1944–1945); *Gramps* (actor, 1947); *Jack and Cliff* (actor, 1948); *The Jerry Wayne Show* (actor, ca. 1942, ca. 1945); *The NBC Story Shop* (narrator, 1947, 1948); *Official Detective* (actor, 1947–1957); *The O'Neills* (ca. late 1930s, early 1940s); *The Second Mrs. Burton* (actor, ca. late 1940s, 1950s); *Under Arrest* (actor, 1946, 1947, 1948); *Valiant Lady* (actor, 1940s).

MCELHONE, ELOISE. d. July 1, 1974. *Emcee, Panelist*. **Series:** *Leave it to the Girls* (panelist, 1945–1949); *Modern Romances* (hostess-narrator, ca. 1949–1950s); *S.R.O.* (panelist, 1953); *Think Fast* (panelist, 1949–1950).

Eloise McElhone was dubbed "The Mouth" by the pundits. A couple of her radio series transferred to the tube with McElhone as a permanent panelist: *Think Fast* (1949–1950, ABC-TV) and *Leave it to the Girls* (1949–1954, NBC-TV).

MCELROY, JACK. b. Oct. 21, 1913, Kansas; d. March 2, 1959, Santa Monica, Calif. *Emcee, Announcer*. **Series:** *Breakfast at Sardi's*, aka *Breakfast in Hollywood* (master of ceremonies, 1949–1950, 1952–1954); *Bride and Groom* (1945–1950).

MCGEEHAN, PATRICK JOSEPH. b. March 4, 1907, Pennsylvania; d. Jan. 3, 1988, Los Angeles, Calif. *Actor, Announcer, Emcee*. **Series:** *The Abbott and Costello Show* (actor, 1940, 1942–1949); *Adventure Incorporated* (host-narrator, 1948); *The Adventures of Bill Lance* (actor, 1945); *The Adventures of Maisie* (actor, 1945–1947, 1949–1951, 1952); *Aunt Mary* (actor, ca. 1942–1951); *The Cavalcade of America* (actor, 1941); *The CBS Radio Mystery Theater* (actor, 1974–1982); *Ceiling Unlimited* (narrator, 1942–1943; announcer, 1943–1944); *Command Performance* (actor, 1946); *The Diary of Fate* (actor, 1948); *The Eddie Cantor Pabst Blue Ribbon Show* (guest star, 1948); *Family Theater* (actor, 1948–?); *The Gallant Heart* (actor, 1944); *Guest Star* (1948); *Gunsmoke* (actor, 1950s); *Hollywood Preview* (actor, 1945); *The Hour of St. Francis* (actor, 1949); *Jeff Regan, Investigator* (actor, 1948); *Let George Do It* (actor, 1950); *Meet Mr. McNutley* (actor, 1954); *Purple Heart Theater* (1946); *The Raleigh Cigarette Program Starring Red Skelton*, aka *The Red Skelton Show* (ca. 1944–ca. 1953); *Red Feather Roundup* (actor, 1948); *Romance of the Ranchos* (actor, 1941–ca. 1942); *The Roy Rogers Show* (actor, 1951–ca. 1953); *Screen Director's Playhouse* (actor, 1949); *Stars Over Hollywood* (actor, ca. 1941–ca. 1954); *Strange as it Seems* (narrator, ca. 1939–ca. 1940); *Suspense* (actor, 1944); *Symphonies Under the Stars* (master of ceremonies, 1948); *They Burned the Books* (actor, 1942); *The Unexpected* (actor, 1948); *The Whistler* (actor, 1949).

Pat McGeehan—whose radio acting talents were often, though not always, channeled into single-episode narratives instead of continuing roles—supplied voiceovers for NBC-TV's 1950–1951 weekday afternoon animated cartoon series *NBC Comics*.

MCGOVERN, JOHN. b. April 26, 1912; d. July 25, 1985. *Actor, Announcer.* **Series:** *The Abbott and Costello Kids' Show* (1947–1949); *The Adventures of Maisie* (actor, 1945–1947, 1949–1951, 1952); *Backstage Wife* (actor, ca. late 1930s–1940s); *California Caravan* (actor, 1947–1952); *The Casebook of Gregory Hood* (actor, 1946–1947, 1948–1949, 1950, 1951); *Columbia Presents Corwin* (actor, 1944, 1945); *A Date with Judy* (actor, 1941, 1942, 1943, 1944–1950); *Dimension X* (actor, 1950–1951); *Doorway to Life* (actor, 1947–1948); *East of Cairo*, aka *Echoes of Cairo* (actor, 1930); *Ellen Randolph*, aka *The Story of Ellen Randolph* (actor, 1939–1941); *The Gibson Family*, aka *The Gibsons* (actor, 1934–1935); *Gunsmoke* (actor, 1952–1961); *The Halls of Ivy* (actor, 1950–1952); *Highway Patrol* (actor, 1930s); *Mysteries in Paris* (actor, 1932–1933); *NBC Presents: Short Story* (actor, 1951–1952); *The O'Neills* (actor, 1934–1943); *On Stage* (actor, 1953–1954); *One Foot in Heaven* (actor, 1945); *The Orange Lantern* (actor, 1932–1933); *Our Gal Sunday* (actor, ca. late 1930s–1940s); *Pages of Romance* (actor, 1932–1933); *Red Ryder* (actor, 1947–1950); *Sam Pilgrim's Progress* (actor, ca. 1949); *Tennessee Jed* (actor, 1945–1947).

For six months in 1958 John (Johnny) McGovern—who sometimes applied the pseudonym John Wilder in professional entertainment—portrayed Peter Hall in the NBC-TV daily matinee serial *Today is Ours*.

MCINTIRE, JOHN HERRICK. b. June 27, 1907, Spokane, Wash.; d. Jan. 30, 1991, Pasadena, Calif. *Actor, Announcer, Emcee.* **Series:** *The Adventures of Bill Lance* (actor, 1944–1945); *The Adventures of Mr. Meek*, aka *Meet Mr. Meek* (actor, 1940–1942); *The Adventures of Sam Spade, Detective* (actor, 1946–1951); *Cavalcade of America* (actor, 1940–1941); *Crime Doctor* (actor, 1940–1942); *Dragnet* (actor, ca. 1940s, 1950s); *Ellen Randolph*, aka *The Story of Ellen Randolph* (actor, 1939–1941); *Glamour Manor* (actor, 1944); *Gunsmoke* (actor, 1952–1961); *The Hour of Charm* (host, 1930s); *I Love a Mystery* (actor, ca. 1943–ca. 1944); *I Love Adventure* (actor, 1948); *The Jack Pearl Show* (actor, 1936–1937); *Lincoln Highway* (1940–1942); *The Lineup* (actor, 1950–1953); *The Man Called X* (1944); *The March of Time* (actor, ca. 1931–1939, 1941–1945); *Meet Mr. Meek* (actor, 1940–1942); *The Mercury Theater on the Air* (actor, 1938); *News of the Week in Industry* (industrial news editor, 1941); *On Stage* (actor, 1953–1954); *One Man's Family* (actor, 1946–1947); *Philip Morris Playhouse* (actor, 1951–1953); *Raymond Gram Swing and the News* (ca. early 1940s); *The Sears Radio Theater* (actor, 1979–1981); *Suspense* (actor, ca. 1940s, 1950s); *Tarzan* (1934–1936); *This is My Best* (1944–1945); *We, the Abbotts* (actor, 1940–1942); *The Whistler* (actor, 1942–1955); *Wings Over America* (host, 1940–1941).

John McIntire spent part of his Montana youth as a bronco-busting and riding champion. In the latter 1920s while an undergrad at the University of Southern California, he got a start in radio as a part-time announcer at Beverly Hills' KEJK. Not long after—when a local gas supplier bought the outlet—that firm's initials were incorporated into the station's call letters. As the total broadcasting "staff" harvesting a huge Depression-era salary of $25 weekly for his efforts, McIntire gained the distinction of originally stating into a microphone: "This is KMPC, the Macmillan Petroleum Company station, Beverly Hills, California." He also exhibited an entrepreneurial spirit early when he created a sideline venue as a result of his radio ties. Leonard Maltin recalled it like this:

> The station's greatest success came with the formation of the Beverly Hillbillies. Long before the TV comedy of the same name, McIntire and his crony Glen Rice thought of this appellation for a group of cornpone entertainers. It wasn't just their music that attracted listeners: it was the mythology that these were genuine backwoods people who lived up in Beverly Glen, behind Benedict Canyon, and just happened to wander down to the station to perform. The five-piece group was such a hit that they started making personal appearances, with McIntire as their interlocutor, Mr. Fancypants. Soon the personal appearances were such a hit ... that McIntire had to cut back on his announcing duties at the station.

Nevertheless, in 1934 McIntire departed KMPC to try his wings as a freelance announcer, soon picking up legions of network programming opportunities, becoming a noteworthy radio thespian in addition to his announcing gigs. Recalling the inception of transmissions from the West Coast, McIntire allowed: "There was an awful lot of wonderment about whether it was going to work, and the difference in time [between East and West Coast origination]. It was a very momentous thing when they had the hookups [national chains]." In 1935 McIntire wed prolific radio actress Jeanette Nolan and the two appeared together in scores of audio dramatic series. "They were among the cream of the crop," according to Maltin. McIntire's career was interrupted for a couple of years during the Second World War while he served on a cargo ship as a seaman.

When radio waned, he found dramatic acting openings on such TV series as ABC's *Naked City* (1958–1959); NBC's and ABC's *Wagon Train* (1961–1965); NBC's *The Adventures of Gallegher* (1965–1968); NBC's *The Virginian,* aka *The Men from Shiloh* (1967–1970); NBC's *The Innocent and the Damned* (1979); NBC's *Shirley* (1979–1980); and ABC's *American Dream* (1981). But greater than anything McIntire had previously done, he developed an extensive film acting career. Between 1947 and 1989 he performed in 70 theatrical releases and between 1968 and 1989 he was in 16 additional made-for-TV movies.

The cinematic productions included *The Hucksters* (1947); *Call Northside 777* (1948); *The Asphalt Jungle* (1950); *Winchester 73* (1950); *Walk Softly, Stranger* (1950); *Westward the Women* (1951); *You're in the Navy Now* (1951); *Horizons West* (1952); *The Mississippi Gambler* (1953); *Apache* (1954); *The Kentuckian* (1955); *Psycho* (1960); *Elmer Gantry* (1960); *Seven Ways from Sundown* (1960); *Herbie Rides Again* (1974); *The Fox and the Hound* (1981); *Cloak & Dagger* (1984); *Turner & Hooch* (1989); and many more. Among McIntire's numerous television features were *The New Daughters of Joshua Cabe* (1976); *Lassie, A New Beginning* (1978); *American Dream* (1981); *The Cowboy and the Ballerina* (1984); and *As Summers Die* (1986).

MCKEE, ROBERT. *Announcer, Writer.* **Series:** *The Breakfast Club* (commercial spokesman, 1941–1942); *Doctors Today* (narrator, 1948); *The First Nighter* (ca. 1930s, ca. 1940s, ca. early 1950s); *Jack Armstrong, the All-American Boy* (ca. late 1940s–ca. 1951); *A Life in Your Hands* (writer, ca. 1949, 1950, 1951, 1952); *The World's Great Novels* (narrator, ca. 1944–1948).

In the 1950s and into the 1960s Bob McKee was a nightly newscaster for Pittsburgh's KQV Radio.

MCNAMEE, GRAHAM. b. July 10, 1888, Washington, D.C.; d. May 9, 1942, New York, N.Y. *Announcer, Sportscaster, Emcee.* **Series:** *The Al Trahan Revue* (host, 1934); *The American Radiator Musical Interlude* (1935); *The Atwater-Kent Hour,* aka *Atwater-Kent Auditions* (ca. 1926–1931); *The Atwater-Kent Summer Series* (late 1920s, early 1930s); *Behind the Mike* (master of ceremonies, 1940–ca. 1941); *Believe It or Not* (ca. 1938); *The Cities Service Orchestra* (1927); *The E.R. Squibb Program* (mid 1930s); *Ed Wynn, the Fire Chief,* aka *The Texaco Fire Chief* (straight man, 1932–1935); *Elsa Maxwell's Party Line* (ca. 1938–ca. 1939, ca. 1942); *Fireside Recitals*

(ca. 1934–1938); *Four Star News* (ca. 1930s, early 1940s); *Major Bowes' Original Amateur Hour* (1935–ca. 1936); *Millions for Defense* (1941); *Radio-Keith-Orpheum Hour*, aka *The RKO Theater of the Air* (1930–ca. 1932); *Royal Crown Revue* (1938); *The Rudy Vallee Show*, aka *The Fleischmann Yeast Hour*, aka *The Royal Gelatin Hour* (1929–1939); sportscasts of diverse persuasions (sportscaster, 1926–ca. 1934); *Tim and Irene* (1938); *The Time of Your Life* (master of ceremonies, 1937); *Treasury Hour* (1941–1942); *The Voice of Firestone* (1928); *Vox Pop* (late 1930s).
Aphorism: *Good evening, ladies and gentlemen of the radio audience.*

Graham McNamee's mom had been a vocalist of some standing before his birth and it was her intent to carry on a tradition through her son. Apparently against his wishes, she forced him to take piano as a lad after they relocated in St. Paul, Minn., when he was two. By high school he was, nevertheless, active in baseball, football, basketball, hockey and boxing. He quit piano at 18, taking up singing, which he relished. He was a clerk for the Rock Island Railroad in his first occupation and left it to become a salesman for Armour and Co. By the time he was 19, McNamee's divorced mom insisted that the two of them resettle in New York City to proliferate his opportunities as a professional vocalist.

He became a soloist in church choirs while continuing to pursue voice lessons. Eventually he sang in a Broadway production followed by a role with a grand opera company. He was featured in his own concert at Aeolian Hall. The critics were kind to him. "He performed with apparent justness, care and style," wrote *The New York Sun* of his 1921 stage debut. *The New York Times* lauded him on 150 recitals during his initial year. A concert season took him to several major metropolitan venues across the nation. Yet there weren't many performing opportunities available as summer approached in May 1923. Consequently, McNamee stumbled into radio at age 35.

While serving on jury duty at $3 recompense daily, he passed by WEAF's studios at 195 Broadway one day during the court's noon recess. Saving the 50 cents he would have spent for lunch, he went inside to look over the station's two tiny broadcast studios. The man who arguably became "the first announcer superstar," according to critic Leonard Maltin, launched his trip up "the proverbial ladder to success" that day. McNamee decided to cast his luck with radio for five months, until he could line up some concert bookings for fall, and see how much appeal broadcasting had for him. WEAF hired him as a combination announcer and baritone soloist.

"Within a year McNamee would be the most famous man in radio—without question the most influential and hardest-worked announcer in the medium's first decade," media historian John Dunning insisted. Authors Frank Buxton and Bill Owen affirmed the neophyte as "the most prominent of the early sportscasters" and suggested, "He is properly known as 'the father of sportscasting.'" Radio historiographer Luther Sies validated: "By a happy coincidence when radio needed a touch of drama, excitement, or even romance in its broadcasts, a personality emerged who supplied all of them.... [Graham McNamee] was exactly what radio needed at the time." Colleague Red Barber noted that WEAF and later NBC "scheduled him for everything." In the course of developing circumstances, "He had to announce opera and concert stars, political conventions, prizefights, football and baseball. I don't know how he did it," Barber conjectured.

On Sept. 14, 1923, during what is characteristically cited as "the first great radio fight" featuring prizefighting contenders Firpo and Dempsey, the former knocked the latter through the ropes and outside the ring where Dempsey landed on top of McNamee. The novice broadcaster was assisting veteran Maj. J. Andrew White with coverage. White described the action while McNamee later recalled, "My heart was thumping at my breast until I thought it would rend my ribs." That autumn McNamee shared the microphone with a sports journalist, providing play-by-play descriptions of the third World Series to be beamed across the air, carried over a limited Westinghouse station hookup.

Dunning remembered it this way: "He was in a job with no established procedure. McNamee was the first of his calling, the first complete announcer who could do play-by-play and also handle color. In a sense he was telling a story, with the roar of the crowd his one basic sound effect. The sudden shout of 50,000 people was the guarantee to a million listeners that they could believe what he was telling them, that the base runner was at that moment sliding under the catcher's mitt in a cloud of dust.... The good sports broadcaster needed more than a gift of gab: he needed imagination. He did not fictionalize, but he did embellish—he made the quiet moments vivid and interesting."

By the fourth inning of the third game of that World Series, the sportswriter acquiesced and handed the mike to McNamee, who became the Series broadcaster for the next 12 years. He received 1,700 pieces of mail following that initial Series, the fans liking his enthusiasm and the excitement he generated, which sealed his fate regarding serious thoughts about professional singing. "By the end of 1923 he was famous," acknowledged Dunning. "His opening and closing signatures (*Good evening, ladies and gentlemen of the radio audience* and *This is Graham McNamee saying good night all*) were known throughout the East." Within two years, at World Series time he received 50,000 pieces of mail addressed to him personally. One impressed fan allowed: "I thought I was there with you."

McNamee, who would be recalled for many Rose Bowls and Kentucky Derbies, drew other prestigious assignments away from the sporting arenas. In 1924 he reported from both political conventions, including one that lasted 14 days and 103 ballots to name a Democratic contender. In 1925 he covered the inauguration of President Calvin Coolidge. In 1927 he was on hand for the triumphant return of aviator Charles Lindbergh following a heroic first-time solo flight across the Atlantic. In 1934 he aired the National Football League's first broadcast Thanksgiving scrimmage. He penned a Sunday column, *Graham McNamee Speaking*, providing "interesting gossip of the broadcasting studio" to syndicated newspaper readers across the land. His book, *You're on the Air* (1928), was one of the first tomes published on broadcasting.

But none of McNamee's breaks seemed as momentous as the singular one he was given on Nov. 15, 1926. On that occasion he presided over the four-hour inaugural broadcast of the National Broadcasting Co. Originating from the Grand Ballroom of the Waldorf-Astoria Hotel in New York, the evening spectacular—with Graham hosting—spotlighted guests from a myriad of celebrated circles with a few of them performing on the air. Several years hence George Kent recalled that extraordinary event for readers in the January 1935 issue of *Radio Stars*: "'Good evening, ladies and gentlemen,' said Graham when the white light flashed. Historic words! Thirty-six hundred miles of telephone wire carried his greeting to nineteen stations extending as far west as Kansas City, thence out over the air to 10 million listeners. If you were one of them you must remember your excitement when he introduced Mary Garden, singing from Chicago, and then Will Rogers, doing a monologue from Independence, Missouri. These great swoops of radio, commonplace today, were brand new in 1926. This, you and the rest of us decided, was romance, adventure, a new world."

In the meantime, McNamee's descriptions of sporting events weren't exhibiting the greatest accuracy or demonstrating familiarity with all the rules of the games. He found himself reprimanded by the print media frequently as well as chastised by some of the fans. Pressed by a critic, NBC vice president Merlin H. Aylesworth rushed to McNamee's defense on one occasion. Asked what his star sportscaster really knew about football, he admitted: "Damned little, but he certainly puts on a great show."

That worked for a while, but as the 1930s rolled on and the fans became more sophisticated, expectant and intolerant, and as a gang of youthful but knowledgeable sportscasters arrived, it prevailed only so long. McNamee was acutely disappointed when he was pulled from the 1935 World Series, replaced by Red Barber and Bob Elson. That signified the beginning of a fading career. McNamee devoted most of his final decade on the ether—to his death in 1942 from a cerebral embolism—to being a foil for comic Ed Wynn, the pair tossing witticisms back and forth. McNamee might have been the first interlocutor to be a comedian's straight man, in fact. He was also an announcer for Rudy Vallee and filled many similar in-studio capacities. While still an admitted disciple of McNamee, Barber ultimately suggested, "He'd lived a thousand years."

Writing in a newspaper column following McNamee's passing, Heywood Broun testified: "McNamee justified the whole activity of radio broadcasting.... A thing may be a marvelous invention and still dull as ditch water. It will be that unless it allows the play of personality. A machine amounts to nothing more unless a man can ride. Graham McNamee has been able to take a new medium of expression and through it transmit himself—to give it vividly a sense of movement of feeling. Of such is the kingdom of art."

Announcer George Ansbro, one of many who were heavily influenced by McNamee, penned an eloquently poignant, while still cheerless commentary on that mentor's death:

> I was saddened when Graham McNamee passed away.... For a man of his professional stature, he couldn't have been kinder to me when I was starting out as the first junior announcer [at NBC], so I wanted to pay my respects to him in death. He was reposing at Campbell's Funeral Home, a well-known mortuary on Madison Avenue. When I arrived at about 8 o'clock, I noticed the scarcity of people in the lobby.... I expected the lobby of a funeral establishment to be filling up with mourners going to different wakes. Not so here. Inquiring where Mr. McNamee was laid out, I was directed to take the elevator to the proper suite upstairs. Upon entering it I found it hard to believe that I was the only living person there. I was alone in the room with the remains of one of the most famous personages in America. Not even an attendant. Even when the deceased is a nobody, an employee/attendant is customarily close by. I knelt by the casket, studied his countenance, reflected on his remarkable life and prayed for him, all the while expecting to be joined by someone, anyone. For the best part of an hour I stayed, completely alone. An indescribable sadness came over me.... Still unable to understand it, I smiled for the last time at Graham McNamee and said good-bye. That night I tossed and turned an awful lot, wondering what exactly fame was all about.

MCCRARY, JOHN REAGAN (TEX). b. Oct. 13, 1910, Calvert, Texas; d. July 29, 2003, New York, N.Y. *Commentator.* **Series:** *Meet Tex and Jinx* (1947, 1948).

Yale-educated Tex McCrary was a journalist with *The New York Daily Mirror* when he drew the assignment in 1941 of interviewing stunning model-actress Jinx Falkenburg (born Eugenia Lincoln Falkenburg). That propitious occasion turned out providential; both single, they fell for one another. Following a courtship abroad as guests of the U.S. armed services—he joined the Army Air Force and became a colonel while she entertained the servicemen with the USO—the duo was hitched on June 10, 1945. Ten months later, on April 22, 1946, they became the third renowned wedded pair in New York radio to premier a breakfast talk show. *Tex and Jinx* on WEAF (later renamed WNBC) followed the trail blazed by Ed and Pegeen Fitzgerald (as *The Fitzgeralds* on WJZ) and Dorothy Kilgallen and Richard Kollmar (*Breakfast with Dorothy and Dick* on WOR). The McCrary feature ran in the morning hours to 1954; as radio began changing with the rise of television, they shifted to afternoon and then evening before leaving the air in 1958.

Assessing the trio of infamous breakfast patter shows in Gotham, a radio historiographer allowed: "Of the three, *Tex and Jinx* clearly took the high road: they didn't even pretend to eat while talking world affairs with the rich and famous. McCrary, who ran the show, resisted the prattling stream-of-insipidity that often characterized the others.... While the Fitzgeralds bickered about Pegeen's weight on WJZ and the Kollmars preened amidst the birdseed on WOR, the McCrarys were interviewing Bernard Baruch, Margaret Truman, or Ethel Waters.... McCrary built the show on the assumption that the early morning audience was not stupid, as programmers generally assumed; that people in general had fresher minds and were more open to serious topics at the beginning of the day." Another source distinguished the feature thusly from the others: "The Falkenburg-McCrary show focused on guest personalities and issues like the UN and the atomic bomb."

McCrary and Falkenburg's radio series was also easily adaptable to the new medium of television. In early 1947 NBC-TV experimented with formats by offering them as part of a Sunday evening quarter-hour labeled *Bristol-Myers Tele-Varieties*. A reviewer confirmed, "The McCrarys were naturals for TV, ... with their combination of friendly chatter, interviews, and features." That summer the network awarded the couple an exclusive Sunday night half-hour under the moniker *At Home with Tex and Jinx*. They moved to CBS-TV in 1949 for 30 minutes on Monday nights for six months under the title *Preview with Tex and Jinx*. The pair collaborated on *The Tex and Jinx Show* (initially *Closeup*) for a year in 1957–1958 on NBC-TV's daytime lineup. "Tex McCrary's Southern drawl, gentlemanly manners, and manly good looks, coupled with Jinx's beauty, charm, and intelligence, made the couple especially appealing to TV viewers and their TV show became as successful as their radio program," wrote another journalist. McCrary was later grilled by a couple of newsmen on the 1952 ABC-TV weekly interview series *The Hot Seat*.

McCrary's first job out of Yale in 1932 was as a copy boy and cub reporter with *The New York World-Telegram*. He was *Literary Digest* editor in between newspaper gigs, joining the *Daily Mirror* in 1936. McCrary coauthored *The First of Many*, a volume of personal recollections released in 1944 about the 8th Air Force in England. When hepatitis sidelined Falkenburg from their broadcasting commitments in 1958, McCrary continued their radio show solo for a couple of additional years. In the 1980s, the couple separated, although they remained on genial terms. While he was eight years her senior, she died just 29 days following his demise.

MCVEY, TYLER. b. Feb. 14, 1912, Bay City, Mich.; d. July 4, 2003, Rancho Mirage, Calif. *Actor, Announcer.* **Series:** *Dr. Christian* (actor, ca. 1940s, 1950s); *Dragnet* (actor, 1949–1957); *Fibber McGee and Molly* (actor, ca. 1940s, 1950s); *Gene Autry's Melody Ranch* (actor, ca. 1940s, 1950s); *The George Burns and Gracie Allen Show* (actor, ca. 1940s); *Glamour Manor* (actor, 1944–1946); *The Great Gildersleeve* (actor, ca. 1940s, 1950s); *Heartbeat Theater* (actor, 1956–); *The Hermit's Cave* (actor, 1942–1944); *The Jack Benny Program* (actor, ca. 1940s, 1950s); *Jerry of the Circus* (actor, 1937); *Lux Radio Theater* (actor, 1939–ca. 1955); *Omar, the Mystic* (actor, 1953–1954); *One Man's Family* (actor, ca. 1940s, 1950s); *The Red Skelton Show* (actor, ca. 1940s, 1950s); *The Sears Radio Theater* (actor, 1979–1981); *The Smiths of Hollywood* (1947); *Today's Children* (actor, 1947–1950); *Wild Bill Hickok* (actor, 1951–1954, 1955–1956).

Tyler McVey launched his professional career playing in amateur theatricals in his Michigan hometown. At 21 he joined an outfit staging shows throughout upper New York state and New England. He invested heavily in a highly unprofitable venture, *The Trial of the Century, or Who is Nellie Bly*, a show he not only acted in but directed and produced. He wasn't deterred, however. Within two years he was on the West Coast seeking work. He found it in a less-than-noteworthy radio series, *Jerry of the Circus*. Two years later he was on *Lux Radio Theater* and his career took off, eventually surpassing—according to his own estimate—1,000 broadcasts. In 1994 McVey recalled: "Live radio was the greatest way in the world to make a living. There were probably 150 of us in Hollywood that worked quite steadily on the many shows that emanated from there."

When radio ebbed, McVey moved to television, appearing in dramatic series like *Bonanza*; *Climax!*; *Lassie*; *Men Into Space*; *My Friend Irma*; and many more. For a quarter-of-a-century (1951–1975) he performed in 42 motion pictures. Among them: *The Day the Earth Stood Still* (1951); *Washington Story* (1952); *One Minute to Zero* (1952); *Horizons West* (1952); *From Here to Eternity* (1953); *All the Brothers Were Valiant* (1953); *The Caine Mutiny* (1954); *Francis Joins the WACS* (1954); *Young Jesse James* (1960); *Man's Favorite Sport?* (1964); *Seven Days in May* (1964); *Never a Dull Moment* (1968); *Hello, Dolly!* (1969); and *The Strongest Man in the World* (1975).

Until shortly before his death, McVey attended multiple annual vintage radio conventions in Cincinnati, Los Angeles, Newark and Seattle where he performed in re-creations of some of the shows on which he originally appeared. His wife, Esther Geddes, a former radio organist, accompanied him to those events and participated in the reenactments. He joined the American Federation of Radio Artists in 1938 and was later elected president for five years of the Los Angeles local of the successor body, American Federation of Television and Radio Artists (AFTRA). Subsequently, he was elected that group's national president. McVey was also active in Pacific Pioneer Broadcasters for many years.

METZ, STUART BLIM. b. March 20, 1908, Buffalo, N.Y.; d. Jan. 5, 1994, Pine Island, Minn. *Announcer.* **Series:** *The Frankie Laine Show* (1951); *Grand Central Station* (narrator); *The Light of the World* (1940s); *Mr. Keen, Tracer of Lost Persons* (1954); *Pepper Young's Family*; *Suspense* (ca. 1950s, early 1960s); *You Are There* (late 1940s).

Stuart Metz favored mathematics while attending the public schools of Williamsville, N.Y. It was his intent to become an electrical engineer. A bank hired him as a teller following graduation, yet he spent his free time studying technical radio engineering. Young Metz constructed his own radio transmitter and receiver, acquired an amateur license and put station W8AGI on the air. By then he was hooked and eventually joined the engineering staff of Buffalo Broadcasting Corp.

For 18 months he manipulated the controls and announced at its local outlet. Then he transferred to the outfit's program department where he created, announced and produced several shows. For seven years he was assistant program director and chief announcer. After making a recording of one of his own program creations, he was summoned to NBC in New York for an audition. Metz was hired as a staff announcer and his career took off in a direction he hadn't begun to envision in high school.

MEYERS, EDWARD THEODORE. b. Dec. 31, 1913; d. Nov. 25, 1996. *Announcer.* **Series:** *The Bullock's Show* (ca. 1944, 1945); *Calling All Cars* (1933–1939); *The Lady Esther Screen Guild Theater* (ca. 1942–ca. 1947); *People Are Funny* (ca. 1950s–ca. 1960); *Star Performance* (1944); *Stop or Go* (1943–1945); *Suspense* (commercial spokesman, 1945); *Tarzan* (ca. 1932–1934, 1936, ca. 1951–1952); *Yarns for Yanks* (1942–1944).

Some sources spell Ted's surname *Myers*.

MICHAEL, ED. *Announcer.* **Series:** *At Home with Music* (1952); *News of Tomorrow* (ca. 1948–ca. 1950); *Quiet, Please* (1947–1949); *Saga* (1955); *Second Honeymoon* (1948–1950).

Ed Michael was employed by ABC from 1948 to 1961.

MICHAEL, JAY. *Announcer, Actor.* **Series:** *American Agent* (1950–1951); *Challenge of the Yukon*, aka *Sergeant Preston of the Yukon* (ca. 1945–?); *The Lone Ranger* (actor, ca. 1940s).

After leaving network radio in Detroit, Jay Michael joined WCAE, Pittsburgh, Pa., where he was a disc jockey from 1952 to 1957.

MILLER, MARVIN (born Marvin Mueller). b. July 18, 1913, St. Louis, Mo.; d. Feb. 8, 1985, Santa Monica, Calif. *Announcer, Actor, Newscaster.* **Series:** *The Adventures of Maisie* (actor, 1949–1953); *The Affairs of Anthony* (actor, 1939–1940); *The Andrews Sisters Eight-to-the-Bar Ranch* (1944–1945); *Armchair Adventures* (actor, 1952); *Aunt Jemima* (1943–ca. 1945); *Aunt Mary* (ca. 1940s); *Author's Playhouse* (actor, 1941–1945); *Backstage Wife* (actor, ca. mid to late 1930s, early 1940s); *Beat the Band* (1940); *Beulah* (1947–1953); *The Bickersons* (ca. mid to late 1940s); *The Billie Burke Show* (1943–mid 1940s); *Bold Venture* (1951–1952); *Captain Midnight* (1940–?); *The Chicago Theater of the Air* (actor, 1941–?); *The Cisco Kid* (ca. 1940s, 1950s); *Confession* (1953); *Coronet Storyteller* (1944–1945); *Cousin Willie* (actor, 1953); *The Danny Thomas Show* (1948); *A Date with Judy* (1940s); *Dear Mom* (1941); *The Don Ameche Show* (1949); *Dragnet* (ca. late 1940s, 1950s); *The Dreft Star Playhouse* (ca. 1943–ca. 1944); *Duffy's Tavern* (1945–1946, 1948–1949); *Family Skeleton* (actor, 1953–1954); *The Family Theater* (ca. 1947–?); *Father Knows Best* (1949–?); *The First Nighter* (actor, ca. 1930s, early 1940s); *The Frank Sinatra Show*, aka *Songs by Sinatra* (1945–1947); *The Gay Mrs. Featherstone* (1945); *The George Burns and Gracie Allen Show* (actor, ca. 1942–ca. 1950); *Great Gunns* (1941); *The Guiding Light* (actor, ca. late 1930s, early 1940s); *Harold Teen* (1941–1942); *Heartbeat Theater* (1956–?); *The Hotpoint Holiday Hour*; *Irene Rich Dramas*, aka *Woman from Nowhere* (1944); *Jack Armstrong, the All-American Boy* (ca. 1933–ca. 1942); *Jeff Regan, Investigator* (1948, 1949–1950); *The Jo Stafford Show* (ca. 1948–ca. 1949, ca. 1953); *Judy and Jane* (actor, ca. 1932–ca. 1935, ca. 1941–ca. 1942); *Kay Fairchild, Stepmother* (actor, ca. 1938–ca. 1942); *Knickerbocker Playhouse* (1939, 1940–1942); *Lassie* (ca. 1947–ca. 1950); *Lonely Women* (1942–1943); *Louella Parsons* (ca. 1940s, ca, 1952–ca. 1954); *Ma Perkins* (ca. 1930s, early 1940s, under pseudonym Charlie

Warren); *Madison Square Garden Boxing* (1941–ca. 1942); *The Martin and Lewis Show* (ca. 1949–ca. 1950, ca. 1951–ca. 1953); *Marvin Miller and the News* (newscaster, 1944); *Marvin Miller, Storyteller* (host-storyteller, 1948–1949, 1958); *Me and Janie* (actor, 1949); *Midstream* (actor, 1939–1940, 1941); *Moon Dreams* (host-reader, 1946–1947); *Name the Movie* (1949); *The NBC University Theater* (actor, 1948–1951); *The Old Gold Show* (ca. late 1940s); *One Man's Family* (ca. mid 1940s, 1950s, portraying 20 different roles); *Peter Quill* (actor, 1940–1941); *Play Broadcast* (1940–1941); *Press Club* (actor, 1939–1940); *The Railroad Hour* (1948–1954); *The Red Skelton Show*; *The Right to Happiness* (actor, ca. 1939–ca. 1941); *Road of Life* (actor, ca. 1937–early 1940s); *The Romance of Helen Trent* (actor, 1939–1942); *The Roy Rogers Show* (ca. 1940s, 1950s); *The Rudy Vallee Show*; *Scattergood Baines* (actor, ca. 1937–ca. 1942); *The Sears Radio Theater* (actor, 1979–1981); *Smilin' Ed and His Buster Brown Gang* (actor, 1948–1951); *Space Patrol* (early 1950s); *Stars Over Hollywood* (1940s, 1950s); *Stop That Villain* (co-host, 1944); *Strange Wills*, aka *I Devise and Bequeath* (1946); *Tell It Again* (narrator, 1949); *That Brewster Boy* (1941–1945); *The Theater of Famous Radio Players* (actor, 1945–1946); *This is Life* (1941–1942); *Today's Children* (actor, 1933–1937); *Treet Time* (1941–1942); *Uncle Walter's Doghouse* (ca. 1939–ca. 1942); *The Whistler* (announcer-actor, 1942–1945); *Wings of Destiny* (1940–1942); *Woman in White* (actor, ca. 1938–ca. 1942).

Few individuals would appear on as many continuing radio series as Marvin Miller, dubbed radio's "man of a thousand voices." Over his lifetime Miller's dulcet tones resonated on no fewer than 88 network or syndicated audio shows and perhaps more. His resume included ongoing roles in at least 20 soap operas—ostensibly a record for males—eclipsed only by actress Ethel Owen with 22 of those serials to her credit.

Miller's infatuation with broadcasting began while he was enrolled at Washington University in his hometown of St. Louis. His earliest days in radio were with KWK and WIL before going over to local CBS affiliate KMOX. Until he was 30 he was a freelance announcer in Chicago, appearing on 40 network shows weekly. By the early 1940s he left the Windy City for the West Coast, where he invested the rest of his life in scads of broadcast features and motion pictures.

Miller played Michael Anthony in *The Millionaire* (1955–1960) on CBS-TV where he delivered million-dollar cashier's checks weekly to unsuspecting recipients from mythical benefactor John Beresford Tipton. It may have been his best-remembered role. Additionally, Miller provided voiceovers for ABC-TV's *The F.B.I.* (1965–1974) and seven cartoons: *The Famous Adventures of Mr. Magoo* (1964–1965, NBC-TV); *Aquaman* (1968–1969, CBS-TV); *Fantastic Voyage* (1968–1970, ABC-TV); *Here Comes the Grump* (1969–1971, NBC-TV); *The Pink Panther Show* (1969–1979, NBC-TV/ABC-TV); *Land of the Lost* (1974–1976, NBC-TV); and *The Pink Panther and Sons* (1984–1985, NBC-TV/ABC-TV). He also narrated the hour-long NBC-TV adventure series *Maya* in 1967–1968 and the same season he reprised a role he held on radio two decades earlier—introducing *The Danny Thomas Hour* on NBC-TV.

Miller appeared in legions of supplementary TV shows, often playing oriental figures. He is recalled in that arena as the infamous sleuthing Dr. Yat Fu on ABC-TV's *Mysteries of Chinatown* (1949–1950). On the other hand, Miller was the evil Mr. Proteus on the same web's *Space Patrol* (1951–1952). He performed in a quintet of made-for-TV movies, too: *Our Mr. Sun* (1956); *Hemo the Magnificent* (1957); *Brinks: The Great Robbery* (1976); *The Call of the Wild* (1976); and *Evita Peron* (1981). When he was 71, the seasoned announcer-actor taped a five-minute series, *Almanac*, which was syndicated to local stations as a lead-in to regional weathercasts.

During the four decades between 1945 and 1985 Miller and/or his voice turned up in 76 theatrical motion pictures. Frequently he narrated those films, although he did some voiceover work in addition to serious acting. Nearly all of them were of the B-movie variety. Among the titles: *Blood on the Sun* (1945); *Johnny Angel* (1945); *Deadline at Dawn* (1946); *A Night in Paradise* (1946); *The Corpse Came C.O.D.* (1947); *The Fat Man* (1951); *The Prince Who Was a Thief* (1951); *Red Planet Mars* (1952); *Forbidden Planet* (1956); *Sleeping Beauty* (1959); *The Phantom*

Planet (1961); *The Agony and the Ecstasy* (1965); *Transylvania Mania* (1968); *Blood of the Iron Maiden* (1970); *How to Seduce a Woman* (1974); *I Wonder Who's Killing Her Now* (1975); *Empire of the Ants* (1977); *Kiss Daddy Goodbye* (1981); and *Hell Squad* (1985).

MILLET, W. ARTHUR. b. ca. 1909; d. 1943, New York, N.Y. Announcer. **Series:** *Adopted Daughter* (1939–1941); *The American Album of Familiar Music* (ca. late 1930s–ca. 1943); *Bobby Benson and the B-Bar-B Riders*, aka *Bobby Benson's Adventures*, aka *H-Bar-O Rangers* (ca. early-mid 1930s); *Famous Jury Trials* (ca. late 1930s–ca. 1943); *The Goldbergs* (ca. 1938–ca. 1943); *Leith Stevens Harmonies* (ca. 1934–1935); *Maudie's Diary* (1941–1942); *Our Gal Sunday* (ca. 1937–ca. 1943); *Rich Man's Darling* (1936–1937); *Valiant Lady* (ca. 1938–ca. 1943).

Art Millet was on the air at WRR, Dallas, and WGN, Chicago, before joining the CBS announcing staff in New York in the mid 1930s. A few years later he left CBS to become a freelance announcer, appearing on various series of competing webs.

MITCHELL, ALBERT. b. May 31, 1893, Elsberry, Mo.; d. Oct. 4, 1954, Paris, France. Emcee, Commentator. **Series:** *The Answer Man* (host, 1937–1950).

Albert Mitchell, a lyricist and vaudeville impresario, served in Uncle Sam's Army during the First World War. Following his discharge in 1919, he joined Paul Whiteman's entourage and—until 1926—penned arrangements and directed one of Whiteman's instrumental units. Mitchell's initial appearance on radio occurred during that period; in 1923 he not only conducted a band but announced for Whiteman, then one of the most formidable names among popular musicians. (Mitchell's daughter, Dolly, was a blues singer with Whiteman's orchestra in the 1940s.) Mitchell subsequently managed a touring faction of *Major Bowes' Original Amateur Hour* talent champs.

Yet the obviously multifaceted Mitchell reached his show business zenith in the decades following when he became—as one radio historian put it—"a factoid wizard" and "a supreme know-it-all." *The Answer Man* audio series was depicted as "a hard-core fact-fest that eliminated the middleman, the studio contestant." Mitchell co-created the unusual feature with Bruce Chapman, who continued as producer. There was enough "exotic information," according to another pundit, to keep it running for a quarter-hour on weeknights "almost 20 years." That was without Mitchell, of course. Regional clones of the program, relying on local Answer Men, surfaced in such far flung places as Germany, Greece, Holland, Luxembourg, Los Angeles, Poland and a myriad of other sites.

The show carried customer service to uncanny and unthinkable summits. With as many as 2,500 questions arriving every day at the executive offices in New York, Chapman and a coterie of 40 assistants answered nearly a million pieces of mail annually. Each inquiry received a response by mail, including the handful of about 200 questions that made their way onto the air every week in a total of five installments. "They never gave legal advice except to read exactly what the law said, though they did settle thousands of bets and provided help on such household problems as getting rid of ants or removing stubborn stains," remembered a reviewer.

While branded "personable" by a critic, Mitchell didn't beat around the bush; he took a somewhat brusque, matter-of-fact, don't-mess-with-me stance. As soon as the announcer introduced the show by naming whatever sponsor was underwriting it at the time (including Colgate toothpaste, Frommer beer, Post Grape Nuts Flakes cereal or Rayve shampoo), he'd acknowledge: "... presents Albert Mitchell's program *The Answer Man*. And here he is, the Answer Man." Mitchell routinely beckoned: "Good evening, ladies and gentlemen. Now, if you're ready, the first question is...."

When the show reached the end of a lengthy run over New York's WOR and in syndication to other stations, Mitchell joined the European staff of the Marshall Plan, moving to Paris for the brief remainder of his life. (The series he inspired, meanwhile, continued in regional manifestations for a few years beyond his death.) The Marshall Plan, named for U.S. Secretary of State George C. Marshall, was an American-backed unification and assistance package aiding devastated European economies following World War II.

MOORE, TOM. b. Aug. 18, 1912; d. April 1986, San Antonio, Texas. *Emcee, Announcer, Vocalist.* **Series**: *Captain Midnight* (1940s); *Dear Mom* (1941); *Florida Calling* (host-vocalist, 1955); *Ladies Be Seated* (master of ceremonies, 1949–1950); *Ladies Fair* (master of ceremonies, 1950, 1951–1954); *Let's Be Lazy* (co-host, 1940); *Meet Your Match* (master of ceremonies, ca. 1949–ca. 1950); *The Quiz Kids* (1940s); *Smoke Dreams* (host, 1945–1946).

Who's Who in TV and Radio offered these glimpses into Tom Moore's nurturing in 1951: "Tom Moore ... lays claim to being born in a trunk August, 1912, the son of vaudeville parents. Throughout his nomadic childhood, he himself trod the boards of vaudeville as a boy soprano with Field's Minstrels, a showboat star and a medicine show spieler. His wandering family finally settled in Mattoon, Illinois, and Tom attended the University of Illinois and spent two years at the U.S. Naval Academy. During his school days, he supported himself by singing with bands. In 1939, he turned to radio in Chicago and modestly considers his luck in this medium phenomenal."

Moore was tutored for his ultimate role as a daytime emcee by understudying with WBBM's Tommy Bartlett on a couple of Windy City audience participation features beginning in 1940 and for a few years afterward. In those days, the show business veteran Moore occasionally substituted for Bartlett on *Meet the Missus* and *The Missus Goes to Market*. Bartlett, of course, was to later become a major daytime series personality, hosting *Welcome Travelers* from Chicago initially on ABC and then on NBC in the late 1940s and early 1950s.

For a couple of months in the spring of 1949, in the meantime, Moore co-hosted *Ladies Be Seated*—his initial TV exposure, albeit a brief one—during the primetime hours on ABC. It was a show he was concurrently hosting every day in an aural matinee format. In addition, for a few weeks in 1950 Moore was master of ceremonies for the ABC-TV primetime panel quiz *Majority Rules*. Possibly because he remained in Chicago instead of migrating to New York City, where many more chances prevailed for audience participation hosts, Moore was mostly absent from the game show arena. He didn't become one of the "heavy-hitters" like contemporaries Bud Collyer, Bill Cullen, Johnny Olsen, Bert Parks, John Reed King and a handful of peers who settled in Gotham by the 1940s, presiding over infinite numbers of ethereal contests in radio and television.

MORGAN, EDWARD P. b. June 23, 1910, Walla Walla, Wash.; d. Jan. 27, 1993, McLean, Va. *Newscaster.* **Series**: *Edward P. Morgan and the News* (1955–1967).

Following his formal training at Whitman College and the University of Washington, in the 1930s Edward P. Morgan was hired by a Seattle newspaper as a reporter. That was followed with a turn as a United Press International correspondent, during which he saw lots of action with U.S. troops in Italy and with Haganah fighters during the British mandate in Palestine. While working for UPI, Morgan made a few preliminary forays into radio. His most notable broadcast was an account of the murder of ex–Russian revolutionary Leon Trotsky, who was stabbed by a Joseph Stalin sympathizer in Mexico City on Aug. 20, 1940.

Morgan left UPI following the war to serve on the editorial staff of *Collier's* magazine. In 1951 he joined CBS where newscast listeners began to recognize his moniker. He appeared sporadically, for instance, as a correspondent on the popular weeknight summary *Edward R. Murrow and the News*. By the latter part of 1954, Morgan nevertheless decided to cast his fortune with rival chain ABC, which permanently situated him in Washington, D.C., apparently to his liking. He stayed put, in fact, for the remainder of a lengthy professional career, including almost two decades with ABC and some features aired by public broadcasting. Morgan's unperturbed delivery style was cited by critics as a refreshing departure from the machine gun reporting of most other audio journalists. His commentaries, in the meantime, were markedly liberal leaning, contrasting sharply with those of a handful of earlier broadcast analysts. "Fifteen million Americans bring you *Edward P. Morgan and the News*," announced Frank Harden when presenting Morgan's nightly spot underwritten by the AFL-CIO unions.

Morgan's tenure was marked by several striking reports—including his coverage of the assassination of President John F. Kennedy in Dallas on Nov. 22, 1963, and the sinking of the passenger liner *Andrea Doria* in the north Atlantic on July 25, 1956, after it collided with the *Stockholm*. His observations in the latter instance were particularly heartrending to audiences and possibly the most poignant of his long career. Morgan's own daughter, an only child—whom he believed had perished in the tragic mishap—actually survived the disaster. Morgan received a Peabody Award that year for his distinguished radio reportage of the event. Three years later he was the recipient of the Sidney Hillman Foundation Award given for radio news analysis. A year afterward he won the Alfred I. DuPont Award for "best broadcast" commentary.

In October 1951 Morgan delivered the headlines on CBS-TV's pithy Saturday night quarter-hour newscast *Up to the Minute*. In 1953 he moderated the fleeting *Chronoscope*, a CBS-TV late night discussion series on world affairs. From 1967 to 1969 he presided over National Educational Television's two-hour Sunday evening magazine, biweekly in the first season, weekly in the second. It was titled *PBL,* standing for Public Broadcasting Laboratory, largely funded by the Ford Foundation. Morgan was also prominent in a number of ABC-TV news and documentary specials. Typical among them were *Prologue 1959*, a round-up of the top news stories of the year, in December 1959; *Year Out, Year In*, a similar year-end focus on Dec. 26, 1965; and *We Are Not Alone*, an examination on Oct. 21, 1966, of the possibility of life on other planets.

MORGAN, HENRY (born Henry Lerner von Ost Jr.). b. March 31, 1915, New York, N.Y.; d. May 19, 1994, New York, N.Y. *Emcee, Announcer, Actor.* **Series:** *Bulldog Drummond* (ca. early to mid 1940s); *The Columbia Workshop* (narrator, 1941); *The Dorothy Gordon Show* (late 1930s); *Here's Morgan*, aka *The Henry Morgan Show* (host, 1940–1943, 1946–1948, 1949–1950); *Laugh and Swing Club*, aka *Laugh Doctors* (comedian, 1939–1941); *Lone Journey* (ca. early to mid 1940s); *Monitor* (segment host, 1966–1969); *Music and Manners* (comedian, 1949–1950); *The Other Generation* (narrator, 1969); *Sears Radio Theater* (writer-actor, 1979); *Take a Note* (comic, 1939); *Uncle Don* (ca. late 1930s, 1940s); *Who Said That?* (intermittent panelist, 1948, 1949, 1950). **Aphorism:** *Hello, anybody. Here's Morgan.*

The pundits' candid portrayals of entertainer Henry Morgan were forthright and similarly consensual. Frank Buxton and Bill Owen termed him "one of radio's 'angry young men'" and boasted that his "acerbic satires left very little untouched." Vincent Terrace considered Morgan "the bad boy of radio" while Tom DeLong affirmed it, labeling him "radio's sharp-tongued 'bad boy' of the 1940s." Still, the latter critic went further: "He built a reputation for insubordination, especially to sponsors and broadcast executives." Classifying him "an intelligent man's wit," John Dunning nevertheless characterized Morgan as "the most notorious sponsor-drubber of the day." Their assessments were typical of others, indicating that radio's "bad boy" was unlike most of his contemporaries airing in the 1940s and 1950s. "Henry Morgan was a victim of bad timing, a transition figure in radio who was simply too acerbic for the generally amiable postwar era," wrote Gerald Nachman.

Morgan never seemed to mind the consequences of his actions. Instead, he built a powerfully loyal following that remained steadfast while he clearly bucked trends of "normalcy" in audio programming, whatever "normalcy" was. He got away with things others wouldn't try. And as time elapsed and his superiors realized the intimidating effect of his anti-establishment tricks, he was too popular to cancel and literally beyond their control.

"He was way ahead of his time," said announcer Ed Herlihy, who briefly worked alongside Morgan in Boston. "He was also hurt by his own disposition. He was very difficult. He was so brilliant that he'd get exasperated and he'd sulk. He was a great mind who never achieved the success he should have." Comic Arnold Stang, who appeared on Morgan's radio series, confirmed: "He was a masochist, a neurotic man. When things were going well for him, he would do something to destroy himself. He just couldn't deal with success. He'd had an unhappy childhood that warped him a little and gave him a sour outlook on life. He had no close friends."

Soon scrubbing the accouterments of his formal moniker (Henry Lerner von Ost Jr.), in 1931 Morgan, an affluent banker's offspring, was hired as a page by New York's WMCA. Within two years, at 18, he had nudged himself in front of a microphone and the industry locals christened him "the youngest announcer in radio." It's possible he was just that in Gotham but there were younger U.S. teens (some cited in this text) performing the same feat elsewhere. Morgan was physically situated in the city room of *The New York Daily Mirror* in 1933 between two o'clock in the afternoon and midnight each weekday. Part of his responsibility was to observe current events as they transpired. During sustaining WMCA programming, he went on the air with bulletins that signified the station's newsgathering efforts as sensitive to immediacy and responsiveness.

During the next seven years the young man on the cusp of radio's rise to prominence (as his own fame prospered) progressed to a handful of other stations where he filled brief announcing stints before moving on. They included WCAU in Philadelphia; WEBC in Duluth, Minn.; WNAC in Boston; and WOR in New York. In the same timeframe he educated himself in other dialects, gaining a working acquaintance of British English as well as French, German and Russian vernacular. Out of those efforts he created a litany of zany dialogue, thereby making himself even more enticing to the listeners.

Morgan felt his talent was underused at WOR. Pressing management for his own show, at last by mid 1940 he was given a quarter-hour in an out-of-the-way spot on Saturday at 6:45 A.M. for *Meet Mr. Morgan*. The entry was soon deemed worthy enough to shift to 6:45 P.M. and expanded to thrice weekly. By summer's end, WOR had cleared that quarter-hour for him five evenings weekly. He was on his way. Even then, Morgan was already exhibiting the prohibitions that often got him into trouble. If his jokes fell flat, for instance, he urged listeners to tune in to the competition, mentioning Lowell Thomas by name, then on WEAF at the same hour, "to see if he is any funnier."

By late October 1940 Morgan acquired national exposure on MBS. *Here's Morgan* left the ether in 1943 as its star anticipated military duty. He resigned from WOR and joined the U.S. Army Air Corps Reserve. His call-up was delayed to 1944, however, and as a bored Morgan hung in limbo, he was snapped up by New York independent WHN in the interim. Returning home from active service, he was hired by WJZ, flagship outlet of the recently designated ABC chain. He was on the air locally with a quarter-hour six days weekly when—a short time hence—he was again heard nationally. After *The Henry Morgan Show* departed ABC in 1948, the headliner shifted to NBC and carried forward for another year. On these programs Morgan played wacky turntable recordings from his personal collection while presenting a recurring cast in comedic vignettes that took exception to seemingly everything and everyone, an extension of the master's wit and personality. Despite that, a modern intellect noted, "In the late 1940s, Henry Morgan was especially incisive in his parodies of great occurrences in history, current events, social conventions, and American perceptions of foreigners."

He was probably the most notorious when he lampooned sponsors. He actually relished biting the hand that fed him. Dunning surveyed the situation: "Morgan clobbered his clients with such unprecedented candor that some of them fired him and one threatened to sue. This was delightful to listeners who scorned the radio commercial as an odious interruption of an otherwise enjoyable half-hour. It made Morgan the darling of his generation's rebels and thinkers, the grand guru of a hard core of intellectuals...." He was so offbeat and obnoxious, in fact, his 1994 death notice in *The New York Times* observed: "His mordant humor did not sit well with certain people, and some of them concluded that he must be either a Communist or friendly to Communists." Morgan's "scorched-earth policy burned him up," assessed another critic.

As Morgan's popularity rose, he was in demand for others' radio shows in addition to his own. Occasionally he appeared as a "slick-talking male" on *Leave it to the Girls*, a weekly half-hour MBS panel entry between 1945 and 1949. The show turned up on NBC-TV with Morgan in tow from 1949 to 1951 and ABC-TV from 1953 to 1954. There he dutifully represented his gender, defending it against a variety of arguments proffered by a rotating coterie of "girls" that included the likes of Lucille Ball, Constance Bennett, Ilka Chase, Jinx Falkenburg, Dorothy Kilgallen and several distaff celebs of lesser-known quantity. Morgan played an unaccustomedly serious role in "Dream Song" on CBS Radio's *Suspense* on Nov. 6, 1947, and made seven guest appearances during that decade on *The Fred Allen Show*, headlined by another of radio's irreverent comics. In 1947 Morgan was featured on *Guest Star*, a syndicated aural series circulated by the U.S. Treasury Department. He was still demonstrating his talent three decades hence when he wrote and acted in a single performance of "Here's Morgan," a production for CBS's *Sears Radio Theater* on April 24, 1979.

After his national radio series ended, the funnyman advanced to yet another New York station, WMGM, where he reigned as a humorous disc jockey beginning in 1952. He starred in the 1946 motion picture *So This is New York*; he appeared in the 1960 film *Murder, Inc.*; and he narrated 1968's *The Great Stone Face*. Barricade published his memoir, *Here's Morgan*, in 1994, the year of his demise. There are also nine comedy albums featuring the inscrutable performer. He persisted in show business until retiring in the early 1980s.

Morgan's age allowed him to move seamlessly from radio to television as the latter medium began to overtake the former for the audience's affection. On his initial video outing he performed for five Sunday nights on ABC-TV's *On the Corner* in the spring of 1948. He returned to the small screen in spring 1949 where *The Henry Morgan Show* continued on NBC-TV for six weeks. That chain gave him another shot with *Henry Morgan's Great Talent Hunt* in 1951; it lasted less than five months. For eight weeks in the spring of 1952 Morgan was master of ceremonies on the CBS-TV game show *Draw to Win*. TV historian Alex McNeil concluded, "The principal reason that all of Morgan's series were short-lived was his apparently incurable habit of ridiculing his sponsors." Old behaviors died hard. Life Savers, one of Morgan's clients, dropped him after one week when he accused the firm of cheating the public by drilling holes in its confections. He teasingly informed the fans he would market Morgan's Mint Middles to replace the holes.

Unquestionably, the entertainer's most durable run on the tube—the broadcast series for which he is still recalled—was as a panelist on the Garry Moore–and Steve Allen-hosted game show *I've Got a Secret* on CBS-TV (1952–1967) and in syndication (1976). Although portrayed by a critic as "dour-faced" on that program, Morgan made invaluable contributions to the guessing game and was a sterling addition to a celebrity deputation composed much of the time by Bill Cullen, Jayne Meadows and either Bess Meyerson or Betsy Palmer. Morgan reported for several other television projects, too. He was a regular on the NBC-TV satirical comedy *That Was the Week That Was* from 1964 to 1965. Occasionally in 1969–1970 he put in an appearance as Phil Jensen in the whimsical NBC-TV sitcom *My World and Welcome to It*.

MORGAN, RAYMOND. b. Dec. 15, 1917, Utah; d. Jan. 18, 1975, Los Angeles, Calif. *Announcer, Actor, Producer.* **Series:** *Chandu, the Magician* (producer, ca. 1948–1950); *The Greatest Story Ever Told* (actor, 1947–1949); *Murder at Midnight* (narrator, 1946–1947); *The National Air Travel Club* (1947); *The Radio Edition of the Bible* (1945); *Refreshment Time*, aka *Coke Club* (1950–1951); *The World's Most Honored Flights* (1946).

In addition to his network assignments, Ray Morgan was a newscaster or sportscaster on the staffs of radio stations in a handful of markets: WPG, Atlantic City, N.J., 1939, news; WCOP, Boston, Mass., 1940, news; WBAB, Atlantic City, N.J., 1940, sports; and WWDC, Washington, D.C., 1946, sports, continuing at the latter post in the 1950s. On *I'd Like to See* Morgan introduced film shorts on topics requested by home viewers on the NBC-TV Tuesday night half-hour series from late 1948 to early 1949, his initial network television exposure. He hosted a documentary on the United States, *American Inventory*, on Sunday afternoons in 1951–1952 via NBC-TV. Several of his radio series, meanwhile, did not appear on major networks but were instead prominently distributed through syndication.

MORRISON, BRET. b. May 5, 1912, Chicago, Ill.; d. Sept. 25, 1978, Hollywood,

Calif. *Actor, Announcer, Emcee.* **Series:** *Arnold Grimm's Daughter* (actor, (1938–1942); *Attorney at Law* (actor, 1938); *Best Sellers* (host-narrator, 1945); *Beyond Tomorrow* (actor, 1950); *Carnation Contented Hour* (narrator, 1940s); *The CBS Radio Mystery Theater* (actor, ca. 1974–ca. 1978); *The Chicago Theater of the Air* (actor, ca. early 1940s); *Clara, Lu 'n' Em* (1942); *The First Nighter* (actor, 1937–1941); *Great Gunns* (actor, 1941); *The Guiding Light* (ca. 1940s); *Heartbeat Theater* (1956–1978); *The Light of the World* (narrator, 1940s); *Listening Post* (host, mid 1940s); *Musical Bouquet* (host-narrator, 1945); *The Mysterious Traveler* (actor, ca. 1943–ca. 1952); *Parties at Pickfair* (actor, 1936); *Road of Life* (actor, ca. late 1930s–early 1940s); *Road to Danger* (actor, 1942–1944); *Quick as a Flash* (actor, ca. mid 1940s–early 1950s); *The Romance of Helen Trent* (actor, ca. late 1930s–early 1940s); *The Shadow* (actor, 1943–1944, 1945–1954); *Somerset Maugham Theater* (actor, 1951–1952); *Song of the Stranger* (actor, 1947–1948); *The Story of Mary Marlin* (actor, ca. late 1930s–early 1940s); *Superman* (ca. early 1940s); *Vanity Fair* (actor, 1937); *Win Your Lady* (actor, 1938); *Woman in White* (actor, ca. late 1930s–early 1940s).

After leaving Chicago's Senn High School, Bret Morrison attended Northwestern University and studied further at the Chicago Art Institute, becoming a commercial artist upon graduation. For a while he was an instructor in stage makeup. He also mastered 14 dialects, making him invaluable for stage productions. He collaborated in founding the Players Guild at Evanston, Ill., and for two seasons toured with the Chicago Art Theater Company. Morrison performed in a trio of motion pictures: as narrator for 1952's *Magia Verde*; as a radio voice in 1971's *Guess What We Learned in School Today?*; and as Majors in 1974's *Black Eye*. As a sideline occupation, he supplied upscale automobiles to movie production houses.

Morrison premiered on the radio in a promotional adaptation of the film *Dracula*. He hoped for extensive work in Hollywood movies that simply didn't materialize, but he dubbed voices for foreign films in the 1960s and 1970s. After a lengthy, distinguished radio career, he supplied the voice of the hero in a 1956 syndicated television series for juveniles—*Bobo the Hobo*—starring a repertory company of puppets. Morrison turned up in the CBS-TV daytime soap opera *The Edge of Night* in 1957–1958 as district attorney Bruce Thompson. In 1978, at 66, having just completed recording a *Heartbeat Theater* installment for future airing on radio, he left the studio and collapsed along famed Vine Street in Hollywood, suffering a fatal heart attack.

MORROW, DON. b. Jan. 29, 1927, Stanford, Conn. *Announcer.* **Series:** *The Dizzy Dean Show* (early 1950s), *The Adventures of Rin Tin Tin* (1955).

Don Morrow arrived in broadcasting almost too late for radio but just in time for television, gaining his greatest opportunities on the cathode ray tube. He delivered the live tobacco commercials on NBC-TV's *Martin Kane, Private Eye* in 1954. He was master of ceremonies for the ABC-TV weekday game show *Camouflage* in 1961–1962. On *Science All-Stars*, a 1964 and 1965 ABC-TV feature, Morrow introduced adolescents who showed off their science projects as qualified scholars in that field reacted to their creations. Morrow presided over the daytime game show *Let's Play Post Office* on NBC-TV in 1965–1966. Following a long dry spell, he hosted yet another daytime audience participation entry, *Sale of the Century*, in 1988–1989 on NBC-TV.

Morrow introduced a plethora of additional TV programming: *Arthur Murray Party*; *Broken Arrow*; *The Edge of Night*; *General Electric Theater*; *The Loretta Young Show*; *Lux Video Theater*; *Rin Tin Tin*; *This is Your Life*; *Warner Bros. Presents*; and *Wide Wide World*.

MOSS, ARNOLD. b. Jan. 28, 1910, Brooklyn, N.Y.; d. Dec. 15, 1989, New York, N.Y. *Announcer, Actor, Writer.* **Series:** *Against the Storm* (actor, 1939–1940); *The Archibald MacLeish Program* (actor); *Barrie Craig, Confidential Investigator* (actor, 1954–1955); *Big Sister* (actor, ca. mid 1930s–early 1940s); *Cabin B-13* (actor, 1948–1949); *Café Istanbul* (actor, 1952); *The CBS Radio Mystery Theater* (writer-actor, ca. 1974–ca. 1982); *The Chase* (actor, 1952–1953); *Columbia Presents Corwin* (actor, 1944, 1945); *The Columbia Workshop* (actor, ca. mid 1940s, 1956–1957); *Dimension X* (actor, 1950–1951); *Ford Theater* (actor, 1947–1948); *Grand Central*

Station (actor, ca. early 1940s); *Great Novels* (actor); *Great Plays* (actor, ca. 1938–1942); *The Guiding Light* (actor, late 1940s, early 1950s); *Inner Sanctum Mysteries* (actor, ca. early 1940s); *Jane Arden* (actor, 1938–1939); *The Light of the World* (narrator, 1947); *The Man I Married* (actor, ca. 1939–ca. 1942); *Manhattan Mother* (actor, 1939–1940); *The March of Time* (actor, ca. 1940s); *The Mighty Show* (actor, 1938–1939); *Mrs. Miniver* (narrator, 1944); *Molle Mystery Theater* (actor, 1940s); *The New York Philharmonic Symphony Orchestra* (ca. 1940s); *The Open Door* (narrator, 1943–1944); *So This is Radio* (actor, 1939); *Spoon River Anthology* (actor); *Stella Dallas* (actor, ca. early 1940s); *The Story of Mary Marlin* (actor, 1942–1943); *This is Our Enemy* (actor, 1942–1943); *Thomas Jefferson* (actor); *Valiant Lady* (actor, ca. 1938–1940s).

An erudite Arnold Moss held an earned doctor of philosophy degree in theater and from that standpoint he differed from the typical radio announcer and actor. Before getting into broadcasting, he served an apprenticeship for a couple of years at New York's Civic Repertory Theatre. He also taught drama and speech at Brooklyn College while performing on Broadway. He became noted, in fact, as a Shakespearean thespian, playing such roles as Prospero in a 1945 production of *The Tempest*. Moss was still a teen when he made his stage debut as an Indian in a production of *Peter Pan* at Eva La Gallienne's Civic Repertory Theatre in New York in 1929. By 1981 he acquired 30 additional stage roles. An active member of New York City's Phoenix Theater in the 1950s and 1960s, Moss performed in regional stage shows, too.

He played in a couple of made-for-TV movies, 1971's *Gideon* and voiceovers for 1974's animated *Yes, Virginia, There is a Santa Claus*. Across two decades (1946–1967) he played in 18 Hollywood theatrical motion pictures, among them: *Temptation* (1946); *Kim* (1950); *My Favorite Spy* (1951); *Salome* (1953); *Bengal Brigade* (1954); *Gambit* (1966); and *The Caper of the Golden Bulls* (1967).

In 1966 Moss portrayed a villainous Shakespearean actor (King Lear) in a memorable episode of NBC-TV's science fiction drama *Star Trek*. He was also a character actor in *Alfred Hitchcock Presents* on CBS-TV (1958) and NBC-TV (1962); *The Time Tunnel* on ABC-TV (1966); and *The Monkees* on NBC-TV (1967). Moss turned up in many other single or occasional roles on dramatic video series and specials, too, among them: ABC—*Amos Burke, Secret Agent* (1965), *Fantasy Island* (1978), *The Kraft Television Theatre* (1953), *The Rifleman* (1960), *Tales of Tomorrow* (1952, 1953); CBS—*Climax!* (1956), *General Electric Theatre* (1962), *Motorola Television Hour* (1954), *Route 66* (1964), *Somerset Maugham Theatre* (1950), *Studio One* (1953), *Suspense* (1949, 1950, 1952—three episodes), *Theatre Guild on the Air*, *The U.S. Steel Hour* (1956), *You Are There*; NBC—*Bonanza* (1968), *Campbell Playhouse* (1953), *Daniel Boone* (1967), *Hallmark Hall of Fame* (1971), *Lights Out* (1950—two episodes, 1951); and *The Man from U.N.C.L.E.* (1965).

Moss broke into radio in the late 1930s as an actor in a variety of species including soap operas, mysteries and dramas. In the late 1950s he established the Shakespeare Festival Players repertory company. The outfit performed on a 1959 tour before 50 American collegiate audiences. Moss was multitalented, also becoming a noted writer. His volume *The Cross and the Arrow* was adapted for NBC's battle era radio series *Words at War* (1943–1945). For the *Molle Mystery Theater* he wrote and acted in *To the End of the World*. In the 1970s and 1980s, he penned more than 60 installments of *The CBS Radio Mystery Theater*. He narrated numerous talking books at the American Foundation for the Blind in New York City and also created crossword puzzles that frequently appeared in *The New York Times*. During his later years, he verbalized the catchphrase for Hebrew National meat product commercials, *We answer to a higher authority*.

MUELLER, MERRILL F. b. Jan. 27, 1916, New York, N.Y.; d. Nov. 30, 1980, Los Angeles, Calif. *Correspondent, Newscaster, Commentator.* **Series:** *ABC News* (ca. 1970–ca. 1980); *Merrill Mueller News Commentary* (news analyst, 1945–1946); *Monitor* (newscaster, 1955–ca. 1970); *NBC News* (correspondent, ca. early 1940s–ca. 1970).

Merrill Mueller (dubbed "Red" by colleagues for sporting a head of flaming hair) was one of NBC's key overseas correspondents during the Second World War. On D-Day, June 6, 1944, he enthralled Americans with word pictures from the outpost Allied headquarters of Gen. Dwight D. Eisenhower. In fact, Mueller provided "pool coverage" for all the radio networks, an assignment that lasted for several months, possibly his most significant news contribution. By 1945 he was posting eyewitness reports from the Pacific theater while awaiting an anticipated invasion of Japan that never occurred.

Following the war, Mueller returned to his homeland to become a fleeting NBC news commentator and analyst of some stature. He continued dispatching news for that web, being one of the chain's workhorses and most respected journalists. Mueller was on hand for political campaign coverage and other newsworthy events from the 1940s through the 1960s. From the mid 1950s he was a regular newscaster on weekends at Radio Central for NBC's marathon programming service *Monitor*, often appearing on half-hour news specials in that connection.

While he persisted most heavily in radio, Mueller was one of a handful of journalists turning up on NBC-TV's coverage on the afternoon of Nov. 22, 1963, following the assassination of President John F. Kennedy. Mueller and Jay Barbree co-anchored multiple space launches for NBC Radio during the 1960s. By April 1970, nonetheless, Mueller left his employer of three decades to work for rival ABC Radio. He anchored most of the Apollo 13 crisis coverage for an aural audience while there.

MURPHY, ROBERT LEO. b. May 6, 1917, Bismarck, N.D.; d. Oct. 25, 1959, Wilmette, Ill. *Announcer.* **Series:** *The Breakfast Club* (ca. 1940s).

Bob Murphy was connected with KSTP, St. Paul, Minn., before he joined Don McNeil and his gang in Chicago. Initially a sportscaster at KSTP in 1937, from 1940 to 1942 he was a newscaster. In the summer of 1949, Murphy was master of ceremonies on NBC-TV's *R.F.D. America* originating in Chicago, a how-to Thursday night half-hour focused on plants and animals.

MURROW, EDWARD R. (born Egbert Roscoe Murrow). b. April 25, 1908, Pole Cat Creek, N.C.; d. April 27, 1965, Pawling, N.Y. *Newscaster, Commentator, Correspondent.* **Series:** *An American in England* (co-producer, 1942); *The American School of the Air* (contributor, 1938); *CBS Morning News* (correspondent, 1940s, 1950s); *CBS World News Roundup* (correspondent, 1938–ca. late 1940s); *Edward R. Murrow and the News* (commentator, 1942–1944, 1947–1959); *Hear It Now* (host, 1950–1951); *This I Believe* (pundit, 1951–1955); *This is London* (correspondent, late 1930s, early 1940s); *The World Today* (correspondent, 1940–1946); *Years of Crisis* (facilitator, 1950–1960). **Aphorism:** *Good night ... and good luck.*

Edward R. Murrow was a reportorial giant—"the godhead of radio and TV network news," according to one critic; his carefully measured metaphors were laced with an echo of doom, "a coppery baritone charged with authority," *The Saturday Evening Post* opined. He was responsible for dispatching world news at critical instants in America's pilgrimage, particularly during the gruesome battles of World War II. An independent, incisive London-based newsman, he colorfully depicted the air raids and incendiary fires there and provided firsthand accounts of air missions over enemy targets.

In 1913, when he was only five, the Murrow family left their farm at Pole Cat Creek, N.C. (near Greensboro) and rode a train to Blanchard, Wash., on Puget Sound. For a while they lived in a tent alongside the home of relatives. The senior Murrow took a job as an engineer for a private rail line operated by a logging enterprise. Egbert (as he was then known) would eventually find work as a lumberjack. He also changed his name to Edward when his logger peers ribbed him over his given name. In the meanwhile, he became a champion debater in school and was elected president of his senior class.

Entering Washington State College in 1926, he earned some of his expenses as a sorority house dishwasher during his freshman year. As a sophomore, he became a waiter. Although Murrow majored in speech and acted in college dramatic productions, he signed up for the school's only course in radio broadcasting. The class was purportedly the first academic offering like it at an institution of higher learning. His school was a pioneer in the field; its campus radio station,

KWSC, went on the air in 1922. Murrow's voice was initially beamed across a little bit of ether when he became a sportscaster.

Graduating from Washington State, in June 1930 he journeyed to New York City and was hired at $25 weekly as president of the National Student Federation of America. His duties included coordinating collegiate European excursions. In that capacity Murrow made an overseas trip, too, acquiring an initial taste of continental living where he would soon invest almost a decade of his own life. Returning to his homeland, he spoke on university campuses, soliciting funds for varied educational efforts.

Sometimes he had opportunities to address radio listeners, markedly expanding his outreach. He assisted CBS in lining up guests for its early *University of the Air* series. Other European trips followed with Murrow addressing diverse groups. In 1932, he was appointed to assist the director of the Institute of International Education, helping facilitate international student exchange programs. Coincidentally, three years later—on learning that he wouldn't be on the air—journalist Raymond Gram Swing rebuffed CBS's offer to be its director of talks while Murrow applied for the post. The latter, without any professional journalism in his background, was hired.

While attending sessions of the National Education Association in New Orleans in 1937, Murrow took a telephone call from New York inquiring if he would go to Europe. "It was the most important decision of my life," he acknowledged years later. "It gave me a front-row seat for some of the greatest news events in history." Consequently, Ray Poindexter offered a stirring account of the launch of an authoritative *CBS World News Roundup* series that premiered on March 13, 1938, and persisted to June 26, 1992 (under the eventual appellation *World News Tonight*). It involved Murrow from its inception:

> It was 8:00 o'clock Sunday night, New York time, when Bob Trout in Studio 9 introduced the feature, not knowing for certain whether it would work. First heard was William Shirer in London, where it was 1:00 A.M. Englishwoman Ellen Wilkinson, a member of Parliament, followed him. Next were Edgar Ansel Mowrer from Paris, Pierre Huss from Berlin, and Frank Gervasi from Rome. Ed Murrow concluded the experimental half-hour roundup from Vienna. It was his first significant news report. Both Murrow and Shirer received silver plaques from the Atlantic City Headliners Club. Radio news had just begun to prove that it could get the job done.

There were other CBS news reports from Europe, although sporadic ones, throughout the spring and summer of 1938. By Sept. 22, however, Murrow was on the air regularly from London with eyewitness accounts of history-in-the-making, transmitted by shortwave to listeners thousands of miles across the Atlantic. He went on the air that night with a phrase that was to become his trademark commence for eight years. "This is London," he acknowledged. His speech teacher at Washington State, in the meantime—who had also tutored West Coast network announcer Art Gilmore—tuned in to Murrow's newscasts and forwarded some ideas for enhancing his programs. In a letter she cautioned Murrow that the opening was too hurried and should be "more deliberate and meditative." He accepted her suggestions and altered the introduction to the distinctly more memorable "This ... is London," adding accent with a two-second pause after the initial word. It worked. Contemporary critic Luther Sies, later assessing the career of newscaster Paul Harvey, observed, "Despite his stylized delivery, he never achieved the dramatic impact produced by the timing of Edward R. Murrow."

On instructions from CBS in New York, Murrow began hiring a squad of foreign correspondents and placing them at strategic locations around the continent as war clouds gathered overhead, manifested demonstrably in air raids over the British Isles. That entourage came to be commonly tagged as the "Murrow Boys." They would become some of the most conspicuous and legendary reporters in the brief history of electronic news. Stanley Cloud and Lynne Olson identified 11 individuals who qualified as that acclaimed collect: Mary Marvin Breckinridge, Cecil Brown, Winston Burdett, Charles Collingwood, William Downs, Thomas Grandin, Richard C. Hottelet, Larry Lesueur, Eric Sevareid, William L. Shirer and Howard K. Smith. According to those authors, Murrow hired a half-dozen of their number himself: Collingwood, Downs, Hottelet, Lesueur, Sevareid and Shirer. Those six became Murrow's special pals and confidantes—cherished contacts, not only during the war years but also for the remainder of his life a quarter-of-a-century hence.

Ultimately, their pride and sense of being a breed apart would lure a salient new peer group of correspondents to CBS. "When CBS was really riding high in news, it wasn't because of ratings," claimed newsman Robert Pierpont, who wasn't part of that acclaimed inner circle. "It was because of the Murrow Boys, because of the Murrow legacy." Colleague Daniel Schoenbrun added: "For a few brief years, the Murrow team was nonpareil. There was CBS and then the others.... While it lasted, it was dazzling."

Astute radio historiographer J. Fred MacDonald candidly noted: "In the twenty-seven months between the outbreak of World War II and the American entry into it, network radio struggled to remain as neutral as possible. This was especially difficult for foreign correspondents like Edward R. Murrow and William L. Shirer. Strongly anti-fascist and, by nature, Anglophiles, it was no easy task for them to report an unbiased description of Rotterdam being leveled by Nazi bombs, or to stand in a London studio of the British Broadcasting Corporation and report on the Blitzkrieg that was being unleashed on the British capital." A perceptive Murrow informed his listeners: "This is a war for the conquest of men's minds." Once the U.S. was an active participant, nevertheless, the foreign correspondents boosted the nation's morale with depictions of the stubbornly heroic resistance of the British. Murrow in particular could be credited with energizing the national confidence. "With his innate flair for theatrics, and given the European theater of war as his stage, he transcribed—in effect, televised—dramatic images to listeners in their homes," wrote reviewer Gerald Nachman.

Against better judgment, Murrow found an important post awaiting him at CBS following the war when Chairman William S. Paley insisted that he take the job of vice president for public affairs. Murrow wasn't happy as a corporate administrator, however, preferring to be in the trenches (e.g., on the air). He negotiated a transition back to the microphone, acquiring a loyal following in an influential quarter-hour commentary weeknights at 7:45 P.M. Eastern Time. He refused to allow his sponsor to interrupt with a middle commercial, situating the selling near the end of his time. He held the audience with the promise of a pithy "Word for Today" reflection afterward. Nightly he left the air with *Good night ... and good luck* (making effective use once again of that important pause).

Ernest Chappell introduced Murrow for a while. When the interlocutor departed from that responsibility, Murrow took a few moments to honor the members of the announcing fraternity:

I would like to talk about radio announcers, particularly those who announce news programs. Maybe many of you think they just announce commercials supplied by advertising agencies, but this is not the case. Often the announcer is the only tangible audience the commentator has, for he is the man across the mike, the only one you can see. You walk into the studio when the big red hand is sweeping the face of the clock for the last time. A good announcer is likely to say: "What have you got tonight?" and you reply: "It's a turkey, there is no news, and what there is has been written badly and the end result will probably be merely a contribution to confusion." And the announcer says: "It can't be that bad. Sit down and give it a reading," and while you read he listens and seems interested.

When you fluff a line or get a backlash on a sentence and it begins to strangle you, he grins and shrugs his shoulders and says with his eyes: "Go on, let it alone. If you go back for a second try, it would be worse anyway and it wasn't as bad as you think." And occasionally, not too often, this good announcer, when the big hand has gone around the clock fifteen times and the program is off the air will turn to you and say: "You had a couple of minutes of good stuff in that show tonight." With a good announcer you always feel that if your throat closes up or you go crazy, you can throw him the copy and penciled notes and he will carry on and get you off on time. That's the kind of announcer Ernest Chappell is. After tonight, he will not be announcing this news broadcast and I wanted to take a minute of your time to say my thanks to him. Thanks, Chappie, carry on.

For 45 minutes on Jan. 1, 1950, a handful of CBS news correspondents engaged in a freewheeling, scholarly exchange on the precarious state of global affairs at mid century. Although Murrow fielded the questions and summarized it all at the program's conclusion, he turned the spotlight on his colleagues, allowing them to bask in the glow that he might have reserved for himself. It bespoke volumes on why they had long admired their mentor. The program itself was so well received that the web decided to air a similar year-end roundup dialogue for more than a decade, titling it *Years of Crisis*. The infamous Murrow Boys gathered one afternoon between Christmas and New Year's Day each of year for that exchange, assessing where America stood in light of the previous year's events. "The conversation was absolutely brilliant," one source attested.

In the postwar period, Murrow, radio's highest paid newscaster, earned $112,000 a year. His salary jumped to nearly $250,000 when he became the only major radio news figure to make a completely successful move to television. His 1951–1958 series *See It Now* was ranked as the best documentary on TV, and his 1953–1959 *Person to Person* at-home celebrity interviews attracted large audiences. The former evolved out of a 1950–1951 CBS Radio documentary, *Hear It Now*. The aural series had its origins in a trio of Columbia longplaying recordings issued in 1948, *I Can Hear It Now*, produced by Fred W. Friendly and Murrow.

The vinyl discs had been popular and Friendly was fascinated with the idea of video documentaries. But Murrow's counsel prevailed; he "distrusted a medium that depended more on pictures than words." The newsman openly loathed TV for most of his life, lambasting it as "slumming" and rejecting it for him and his revered radio protégés. "If television and radio are to be used for the entertainment of all the people all of the time," he demurred, "we have come perilously close to discovering the real opiate of the people." In the meantime, the magazine-type feature *Hear It Now* exhibited film of current events of the previous week and was cited by industry insiders as "the biggest adventure in news gathering ever attempted." Murrow biographer Joseph E. Persico disclosed that *Hear It Now* was akin to "building the best gas lamp at the turn of the century, when most people were wiring their homes for electricity." Murrow reluctantly gave in and carried the show to the small screen under the moniker *See It Now*.

Murrow ultimately placed a strong stamp on both media, duly recognized with the George Foster Peabody Award for excellence in 1943, 1949, 1951 and 1954. Given by the celebrated School of Journalism at the University of Georgia, those prestigious citations were considered marks of distinction by broadcasters. Subsequently, on June 16, 1959, Murrow signed off his radio and television series and temporarily left the air. (*Person to Person* continued for two more years on CBS-TV with "Murrow Boy" Charles Collingwood hosting it.) Murrow took what turned into a year-long sabbatical. His 25-year association with the network ended permanently in 1961 when President John F. Kennedy appointed him director of the U.S. Information Agency. His duties there included managing the Voice of America. He strongly emphasized voice clarity and communication, a Murrow hallmark, while it was under his control.

Undoubtedly one of the most noteworthy ventures of his career—beyond the war years for certain—was a public debacle in which he virtually dismantled a respected lawmaker, the tenacious, determined Sen. Joseph R. McCarthy (R-Wis.). At mid 20th century McCarthy appeared to find communists behind every tree. The fanatical, out-of-control legislator stood before microphones claiming he possessed the names of hundreds of communist sympathizers who had infiltrated the U.S. government. As part of his massive cleansing operation, he saw scores of entertainers and celebrities blacklisted, prevented from earning a livelihood due to mere innuendo as well as their perceived fraternization with alleged conspirators.

While several key broadcasters took offense to McCarthy's charges (there were a few outspoken supporters as well), the most incisive journalistic enemy that McCarthy created was Murrow. In early 1954, according to Fred MacDonald, he "became the first powerful media figure to risk his career by attacking McCarthy and his crusade.... Murrow's argument with the Wisconsin senator was not with anti–Communism or the exposure of traitors. Instead, he opposed the unconstitutional method by which, without seeing any evidence, without being permitted to face their accusers, and without due process of law, Americans were being accused of crimes against society. On March 9, 1954, on the regular telecast of *See It Now*, Murrow openly criticized McCarthy.... Murrow accused McCarthy of lies, half-truths, and exploitation of his senatorial immunity...."

Going for the jugular and using the senator's own words to expose him, the newsman offered a masterful challenge of the intimidation McCarthy employed against his victims. It took the famed Army-McCarthy hearings a few weeks later to ultimately bring down the senator, but Murrow had plainly been a key in shifting the public tide from its near blanket endorsement of the senator. "The age of television news was born on the evening Senator McCarthy was exposed," one pundit assured.

By the end of 1954, McCarthy was finished. The U.S. Senate publicly humiliated him, censuring the lawmaker in a 67–22 vote for bringing "dishonor and disrepute through ... displays of contemptuous and insulting behavior" upon that body as well as "obstructing ... constitutional process." Historians heavily credited Murrow with initiating the process that realized and thwarted the demagoguery that prevailed, although Murrow himself never believed that he had been responsible for such a transformation. Despite that, he never doubted that broadcast journalism had a duty to offer informed and reasoned analysis, especially at times when a conspiracy of silence existed among social institutions.

A postscript is in order. In October 2005, a full-length feature film, *Good Night, and Good Luck*, documenting that historic episode between Murrow and McCarthy, was released to movie theaters, gaining widespread acclaim among audiences and critics.

In the 1950s Murrow penned several published articles and later contributed to a text edited by Edward Bliss Jr., *In Search of Light* (Knopf, 1967). Across his lifetime he wrote three books, all published by Simon and Schuster, and all named for some of his broadcast series: *This is London* (1941); *This I Believe* (1952–1954); and *See It Now* (1955). A chain smoker for much of his life, Murrow developed cancer by 1963 that resulted in his death a couple of years later. Family, friends and colleagues mourned his passing. Newsman Eric Sevareid eulogized him: "There are some of us here, and I am one, who owe their professional life to this man. There are many working here and in other networks and stations who owe to Ed Murrow their love of their work, their standards and sense of responsibility. He was a shooting star and we will live in his afterglow a very long time."

NAGEL, CONRAD. b. March 16, 1897, Keokuk, Iowa; d. Feb. 24, 1970, New York, N.Y. *Actor, Announcer, Emcee.* **Series:** *Alec Templeton Time* (1939); *The Conrad Nagel Show* (disc jockey, 1952–?); *First Love* (director, 1937); *Lux Radio Theater* (guest actor, ca. mid to late 1930s); *The Passing Parade* (host, 1938–1939); *Proudly We Hail* (host-actor, 1941, ca. 1948–ca. 1957); *Radio Reader's Digest* (narrator, 1942–1945); *Screen Guild Players* (guest actor, ca. 1930s); *Seventy-Six Revue with Conrad Nagel* (host, 1938); *Silver Theater* (director-host-narrator-infrequent actor, 1937–ca. 1939); *Treasury Star Parade*, aka *Treasury Star Salute* (guest actor, ca. 1942–ca. 1944).

Conrad Nagel enrolled at Des Moines' Highland Park College at 15; two years thereafter he had earned a bachelor of arts degree there. Nevertheless, while speeding through his collegiate career, he found time to run the 100-yard dash in 10 seconds, play summer stock in a Chautauqua and—to train his voice—work in his spare time as a hotel telephone operator. The day following his graduation, he joined the Princess Stock Co. at $5 weekly, touring with an entourage and eventually landing on Broadway in productions of *The Natural Law* and *Forever After*. Enlisting in the U.S. Navy as a seaman in 1917, young Nagel was on an admiral's staff as the armistice was signed. In 1918 he debuted on the silver screen in *Little Women*. It was the first of 112 B-movies in which he was to appear over a 42-year career. He remained in Hollywood from 1923 to 1939.

Nagel's celluloid repertoire included some provocative and unusual titles like *The Redhead* (1919); *What Every Woman Knows* (1921); *Profane Love* (1921); *Saturday Night* (1922); *Hate* (1922); *Nice People* (1922); *Grumpy* (1923); *Lawful Larceny* (1923); *Three Weeks* (1924); *Married Flirts* (1924); *So This* is Marriage? (1924); *Cheaper to Marry* (1925); *Sun-Up* (1925); *The Waning Sex* (1926); *Slightly Used* (1927); *If I Were Single* (1927); *The Fog* (1928); *Red Wine* (1928); *The Idle Rich* (1929); *Redemption* (1930); *The Divorcee* (1930); *One Romantic Night* (1930); *Numbered Men* (1930); *A Lady Surrenders* (1930); *Free Love* (1930); *The Bad Sister* (1931); *Three Who Loved* (1931); *The Pagan Lady* (1931); *The Man Called Back* (1932); *The Constant Woman* (1933); *One Hour Late* (1935); *Bank Alarm* (1937); *I Want a Divorce* (1940); *All That Heaven Allows* (1955); and *The Man Who Understood Women* (1959).

On a lark, Nagel faced a microphone for the first time in 1925. It was a new diversion that would lead him to be on the cutting edge of dual broadcast mediums. Meanwhile, in 1933 he was elected president of the Academy of Motion Picture Arts and Sciences and was actively involved in the Motion Picture Relief Fund. In 1939 Nagel moved to New York City where he performed on the Broadway stage and in radio and television.

A pundit recalled an amusing incident involving a balding Nagel, although that fact had been a well-kept secret kept from his admirers. During the period he hosted his first show with a live audience, *Silver Theater*, one day he was standing with announcer Dick Joy in the atrium of CBS's Columbia Square. As the two men conversed, they encountered some feminine fans. Without thinking, Nagel instinctively tipped his hat. The look of shock on their faces snapped him back into consciousness—he had stashed his toupee in the briefcase in his hand.

As some of Nagel's professional opportunities began to wane, he prevailed in radio as a disc jockey. Capitalizing on his name as a draw, NBC served him up for a half-hour on weekday afternoons in 1952 while the screen idol interspersed theatrical chitchat between tunes.

Nagel also developed a fleeting career in television. For a few months in 1948–1949 he moderated a celebrity panel on the weekly CBS-TV primetime game show *Riddle Me This*. From 1949 to 1950 he moderated the subsequent *Celebrity Time*, aka *Celebrity Quiz* on ABC-TV and CBS-TV. Also in 1949–1950 the latter web reprised a dramatic anthology that Nagel introduced to radio listeners a decade earlier, *The Silver Theater*, with him again as interlocutor. The show offered mostly live dramas featuring actors like Geraldine Brooks, Glenda Farrell, Paul Lucas, Burgess Meredith and more.

In 1953–1954 Nagel presided over the Dumont Television primetime news-talk series *Broadway to Hollywood Headline Clues*. He also hosted a couple of half-hour syndicated video series in 1955. One was *The Conrad Nagel Theater*, a dramatic anthology. The other, *Hollywood Preview*, ran clips of recently released screen flicks. None of Nagel's small screen ventures were rip-roaring successes, nevertheless, even in a day when there wasn't much competition for viewers.

NARZ, JACK. b. Nov. 13, 1922, Louisville, Ky. *Announcer.* **Series:** *Curt Massey Time* (ca. late 1940s); *Meet Corliss Archer* (ca. late 1940s, ca. early 1950s); *Space Patrol* (1950–ca. 1955); *The Tennessee Ernie Ford Show* (1954–1955).

In 1947 Jack Narz was a sportscaster at Burbank's KWIK. Despite some limited opportunities as a network radio announcer—having arrived too late to be a major radio presence—he left his mark instead on television as a seemingly inexhaustible audience participation show host. Narz began his ascendancy there announcing the ABC televersion of *Space Patrol* (1950–1955). He introduced the syndicated comedy *Life with Elizabeth* starring Betty White on the tube from 1953 to 1955. From 1953 to 1957 Narz was a regular on CBS-TV's daily *Bob Crosby Show*. In the summer of 1954 he welcomed viewers to *Kay Kyser's Kollege of Musical Knowledge* on NBC-TV. He was also in the recurring cast and interlocutor for *The Giselle Mackenzie Show* on that chain in 1957–1958.

Things changed for Narz beginning in 1958 when he presided over the infamous *Dotto* game show that debuted in daytime on CBS-TV and moved to primetime on NBC-TV that summer. It may have been the only series Narz wished he had never heard of. Among those programs implicated in the notorious quiz show scandals of the late 1950s, *Dotto* was in a pivotal spot in the industry-altering controversy: a game show investigation by the New York district attorney's office resulted when a *Dotto* standby contestant, Edward Hilgemeier Jr., accidentally discovered some notes given to a previous contestant.

The annotations provided answers to questions asked that day. The subsequent inquiry triggered the cancellation of multiple game shows including *Dotto* on Aug. 19, 1958. (Others and their dates of departure: *The $64,000 Challenge*, Sept. 7, 1958; *Twenty-One*, Oct. 16, 1958; and *The $64,000 Question*, Nov. 2, 1958. Nearly two decades elapsed before a syndicated revival of the original big-money quiz that doubled players' winnings surfaced—*The $128,000 Question* appeared in 1976 with Mike Darrow and later Alex Trebek as host. It lasted just two years. A 1950s national fascination with big-money payoffs obviously had evaporated.)

Narz wasn't scathed in the resulting melee. In fact, a polygraph test proved that he never knew *Dotto* was tainted at all, removing him from the machinations that had transpired in the background. An executive producer admitted the rigging during a meeting that brought officials of CBS and sponsor Colgate-Palmolive-Peet together. By 1959, meanwhile, Narz was back on the air conducting another CBS-TV daytime game show, *Top Dollar*. The next year he returned to primetime television as host of a competitive couples' entry on CBS, *Video Village*. He followed it by emceeing the ABC daytime game show *Seven Keys* (1961–1964). Next came the 1965 NBC daytime game show *I'll Bet* that lasted nearly six months.

Parenthetically, Narz' younger brother, Tom Kennedy (James Narz), followed in his sibling's footsteps as a recurring quiz show host, possibly becoming the consummate game show guru (*Big Game*; *Body Language*; *Break the $250,000 Bank*; *Dr. I.Q.*; *50 Grand Slam*; *Name That Tune*; *Password*; *The Price is Right*; *Split Second*; *To Say the Least*; *Whew!*; *Wordplay*; and *You Don't Say*). Kennedy was among several of the breed presiding over the early 1970s syndicated *It's Your Bet*, a direct descendant of *I'll Bet*. If Tom Kennedy wasn't the consummate game show host, yet another family member probably was: Bill Cullen, who presided over nearly a score of broadcast game series, was Jack Narz' brother-in-law.

Narz, meanwhile, was master of ceremonies of a syndicated *Beat the Clock* in 1969, extending into the early 1970s. By 1973 he performed the same duty on yet another syndicated game show revival, *Concentration*.

Narz returned to network television hosting *Now You See It* on CBS weekdays in 1974–1975. After that he was frequently seen in celebrity golf tournaments, raising funds for myriad charities.

NEAL, FLOYD. b. Aug. 20, 1906, Iowa; d. Dec. 22, 1985, Los Angeles, Calif. *Announcer.* **Series:** *Uncle Don* (ca. 1930s, 1940s); *Viennese Nights* (1933).

On July 15, 1937, Floyd Neal announced an MBS *Tribute to George Gershwin*.

NEAL, HAROLD (HAL). b. March 25, 1924, Michigan; d. Feb. 27, 1980, Darien, Conn. *Announcer.* **Series:** *The Challenge of the Yukon* (1940s); *The Green Hornet* (1940s).

NEELY, HENRY MILTON. b. Nov. 5, 1877, Philadelphia, Pa.; d. May 1, 1963, Elmhurst, N.Y. *Actor, Announcer, Emcee.* **Series:** *As the Twig is Bent*, aka *We Love and Learn* (actor, 1941–1942); *Down Lover's Lane* (1935); *Eversharp Penman* (1929–1930); *Everybody's Music* (host-narrator, 1936–1937, 1938); *The Fitch Bandwagon* (master of ceremonies, ca. 1938–ca. 1946); *Garden of Tomorrow* (1935); *General Motors Concert* (1929–1930s); *The Greatest Story Ever Told* (actor, 1947–1949); *Green Valley, U.S.A.* (narrator, 1942, 1943); *Hilltop House* (actor, 1937–1941); *Home on the Range* (1930s); *Just Plain Bill* (actor, ca. 1933–?); *Keeping Up with Rosemary* (actor, 1942); *The Philco Hour of Theater Memories* (narrator, 1927–1930); *Philco Radio Hour* (ca. 1931); *The Rollickers* (host-announcer, 1932); *Show Boat* (writer, ca. 1932–ca. 1937); *This Life is Mine* (actor, 1943–1945); *Orphans of Divorce* (actor, 1939–1942); *Stella Dallas* (actor, ca. 1930s, 1940s); *Two Seats in the Balcony* (host, 1934–1935).

Henry M. Neely (whose name appears in some documentaries spelled *Neeley*) had a colorful, multifaceted background prior to his contributions as a radio thespian. He was a film and theater critic for *The Philadelphia Evening Ledger*; edited and published one of the aural medium's original fanzines, *Radio in the Home*; inaugurated the syndicated newspaper daily radio column; founded the Philadelphia Opera Society and became its premiering secretary; and in 1921 was appointed director of radio station WIP in the City of Brotherly Love.

Leaving radio in 1946, Neely lectured and wrote on astronomy, primarily at the Hayden Planetarium, speaking as often as a dozen times weekly. Astronomy buffs dubbed Neely "the dean of New York stargazers." Following his death in 1963, a couple of elementary texts he penned in that field were published: *A Primer for Star-Gazers* (Harper & Row, 1970) and *The Stars by Clock and Fist* (Viking, 1972). He also authored multiple short stories and novels.

NELSON, FRANK. b. May 6, 1911, Denver, Colo.; d. Sept. 12, 1986, Hollywood, Calif. *Actor, Announcer.* **Series:** *The Abbott and Costello Show* (actor, ca. 1940, ca. 1942–ca. 1949); *The Adventures of Maisie* (actor, 1945–1947, 1949–1953); *The Baby Snooks Show* (actor, ca. 1937–ca. 1948, ca. 1949–ca. 1951); *Birds Eye Open House*, aka *The Dinah Shore Show* (actor, 1943–1946); *Blondie* (actor, ca. 1945–ca. late 1940s); *The Burns and Allen Show* (actor, ca. 1930s, 1940s); *The Cinnamon Bear* (actor, 1937); *Cousin Willie* (actor, 1953); *The Danny Kaye Show* (commercial spokesman, 1945–1946); *A Day in the Life of Dennis Day* (actor, 1949–1951); *The Eddie Cantor Show* (actor, 1946–1949); *Fibber McGee and Molly* (ca. 1939–?); *Flywheel, Shyster & Flywheel* (actor, 1932–1933); *Four-Star Playhouse* (actor, 1949); *The Frank Morgan Show* (actor, 1944–1945); *Heartbeat Theater* (actor, 1956–?); *Honor the Law* (actor, 1938); *It's a Great Life* (actor, 1948); *The Jack Benny Program* (actor, 1934–1955, 1956–1958); *The Jack Paar Show* (1947); *Jeff Regan, Investigator* (actor, 1949–1950); *The Life of Riley* (actor, 1946); *Lux Radio Theater* (actor, ca. 1936–ca. 1955); *Makers of History* (actor); *Meet Me at Parky's* (actor, 1945–1947); *On Stage* (actor, 1953–1954); *The Phil Harris and Alice Faye Show* (actor, 1946–1954); *The Roy Rogers Show* (actor, 1944–1945, 1946–1947, 1948–1953, 1954–1955); *Sara's Private Caper* (actor, 1950); *The Sears Radio Theater*, aka *The Mutual Radio Theater* (actor, 1979–1981); *Tarzan* (actor, 1932–1934); *That's Rich* (actor, 1954); *The Three Musketeers* (actor); *Today at the Duncans* (actor, 1942–1943); *Vendetta* (actor). **Aphorism:** *Yeeeeeessss?*

Frank Nelson premiered on radio in 1926 over Denver's KOA. By 1929 he affiliated with local stations on the West Coast where he began to routinely appear in dramatic roles. In 1932 announcer-actor Nelson shifted his allegiance from KFAC to KMTR, both in Los Angeles. His brief apprenticeship in local and regional aircasting catapulted him into legions of network series, firmly establishing him as one of the area's premier and prolific supporting audio thespians.

Nelson eventually discovered his niche: almost every week he portrayed caustic, abrasive, nameless figures on *The Jack Benny Program*. One week he played an irritating mailman, the next week he was a bumbling waiter, a third week he could be a nauseating cab driver, etc. Years hence he remembered his "calling" as "the guy whose sole purpose in life was to annoy the hell out of Jack Benny." A critic certified him as "the greatest heckler of all, the bile-dipped Frank Nelson."

Said radio historian John Dunning:

> One of Benny's busiest utility actors was Frank Nelson, who first appeared June 1, 1934. But the character Nelson created in the 1930s was not fully realized until the mid-1940s, when he became one of the funniest voices on the air. One week he'd be a psychiatrist, the next week a floorwalker; he was a doorman at a posh hotel, a lawyer, a ticket clerk at the train depot. No matter what he was, Nelson's voice and manner were always the same. 'There's the floorwalker,' Benny would say in a department store skit: 'Oh, mister! ... Mister!' On this cue, Nelson would whirl into the microphone and scream, *Yeeeeeessss?* For the next few minutes, Benny was abused, insulted, and berated for even the simplest requests. 'You really do hate me, don't you?' Benny would ask, and Nelson's reply—a screaming, 'Ooooooooooh, *do* I!'—never failed to draw huge laughs from the audience.

Chronicler Gerald Nachman put it this way: "On the Benny show, the nuts ran the asylum while Benny, as their helpless administrator, tried to retain control. He was unable to get from one end of the show to the other without being humiliated by his underlings—not to mention Frank Nelson's gallery of snide clerks, waiters, and floorwalkers (Benny: 'Excuse me, are you the ticket agent?' Nelson: 'Well, what do you *think* I am in this cage—a *canary*?').... Only a secure performer would let lesser comics get all the laughs." From 1934 to 1942 Benny's show was officially named *The Jell-O Program Starring*

Jack Benny for its widely admired dessert sponsor. In a medical skit in 1951, Frank Nelson portrayed a physician who X-rayed the contents of Benny's stomach, only to reveal: "Strawberry, raspberry, cherry, orange, lemon and lime—haven't you eaten since then?"

Dunning remembered:

Perhaps the best Frank Nelson story involved a fluff.... On Jan. 8, 1950, Nelson was to appear as a doorman in a restaurant. Early in the show, [announcer] Don Wilson bobbled a line referring to Drew Pearson, the famous columnist, making it "Drear Pooson," and Benny joined the audience in helpless laughter. Immediately the writers summoned Nelson into the booth and, without Benny's knowledge or permission, changed his coming lines. Nelson was leery ("Nobody ad-libbed with Jack," he recalled years later) but agreed to do it if the writers would take responsibility. The scene arrived. "Oh mister! Mister!" Benny called. "Are you the doorman?" At his absolute surliest, Nelson snarled, "Well, who do you think I am in this uniform, Dreeeeeaaaarrr Poooooosson?" Benny was instantly convulsed. "He began to laugh," Nelson recalled; "he slid down the mike to the floor, pounded on the floor, got up, staggered clear across the stage to the far wall, turned around into the curtains, slid down the curtains, pounded the floor some more, got up, staggered back to the mike, and we're on live and laughter is going on through this whole thing." Nelson thought this laugh exceeded even that of Benny's most famous gag, when a robber demanded, "Your money or your life!" and the hilarity kept building while Benny thought it over.

For one season, 1942–1943, Nelson co-starred with his first wife, actress Mary Lansing, as John and Mary Duncan on the CBS Radio sitcom *Today at the Duncans*. It originally aired for a quarter-hour three nights weekly but was ultimately reduced to once a week only. In 1970 he married actress Veola Vonn. Nelson was elected local and national president of the American Federation of Television and Radio Artists (AFTRA). While he was in office from 1954 to 1957 the panel created a pension and welfare relief program for its membership.

After radio ebbed, Nelson was a prolific commercial voiceover artist and was also heard as animated characters on a quartet of video film specials projected at the small fry: *The Mouse and His Child* (1977); *Puff, the Magic Dragon* (1978); *Thanksgiving in the Land of Oz* (1980); and *The Little Rascals' Christmas Special* (1982). He also gave voice to figures in the 1986 made-for-TV movie *Garfield in Paradise*. During the same era he was heard in another sextet of continuing cartoon series on TV: *The Jetsons* (1962–1963, ABC); *The Oddball Couple* (1975–1977, ABC); *Baggy Pants and the Nitwits* (1977–1978, NBC); *The All-New Popeye Hour* (1978–1982, 1983, CBS); *Monchichis* (1983–1984, ABC); and *The Snorks* (1984–1986, NBC). Additional television credits included regular appearances on *The Hank McCune Show* (1950, NBC); *The Jack Benny Program* (1950–1965, CBS, NBC); and *The Betty White Show* (1958, ABC). He was in a guest shot on CBS-TV's *I Love Lucy* in 1957.

At one point Nelson feigned disinterest in motion pictures. "You were running from [radio] show to show; you had sometimes five, six, seven shows in a day," he recalled. "You had to take a long hard look as to whether or not it was in your best interest to take a picture and go away for three weeks or six weeks and maybe lose a lot of these shows that you were on.... I decided I was pretty much going to stay with radio. It would've taken a real good part to pull me away. So with the exception of a couple of things I did that were fairly good, I simply gave up the attempt to get into pictures."

His protestations to the contrary, nevertheless he was associated with 26 films between 1936 and 1985, frequently providing his voice only—not actually appearing—in animated films in the 1970s and 1980s when he was doing similar work on TV. His silver screen repertoire included *Fugitive in the Sky* (1936); *Gang Bullets* (1938); *Down Memory Lane* (1949); *When You're Smiling* (1950); *Fourteen Hours* (1951); *You Never Can Tell* (1951); *Bonzo Goes to College* (1952); *Here Come the Nelsons* (1952); *It Should Happen to You* (1954); *It's Always Fair Weather* (1955); *Kiss Them for Me* (1957); *The Mouse and His Child* (1977); *Oz* (1980); *The Looney, Looney, Looney Bugs Bunny Movie* (1981); *The Malibu Bikini Shop* (1985); and more.

NELSON, JOHN. b. March 3, 1915, Spokane, Wash.; d. Nov. 3, 1976, Palm Springs, Calif. *Emcee, Announcer, Producer.* **Series:** *Add a Line* (master of ceremonies, 1949); *Breakfast at Sardi's*, aka *Breakfast in Hollywood* (host, ca. 1948–ca. 1949); *Bride* *and Groom* (master of ceremonies, 1945–1950); *Eleanor and Anna Roosevelt* (co-producer and announcer, ca. 1950–1951); *Ellery Queen* (actor, 1948); *Know Your NBCs* (quizmaster, 1953–1954); *Live Like a Millionaire* (1950–1953); *Rebuttal* (co-producer, 1950).

John Nelson received formal preparation for a life in broadcasting at Gonzaga University, among whose infamous alumni earlier included a budding young vocalist, Harry Lillis (Bing) Crosby. Following a three-year stint in the U.S. Navy, Nelson produced shows for the U.S. Air Force. The 1953 edition of *TV-Radio Annual* credited Nelson, John Masterson and John Reddy—dubbed "TV's Three Musketeers" and all Gonzaga alumni—with originating the giveaway program, carrying it to its peak. After his years of service on the airwaves, nevertheless, Nelson became an NBC programming executive. Beyond that post he managed KPLM in Palm Springs.

Live Like a Millionaire—which Nelson introduced every day on radio—was reincarnated in primetime TV on CBS (1951–1952) and on ABC-TV (1952–1953). Nelson followed radio host Jack McCoy as that series' master of ceremonies. Concurrently, Nelson also presided over the extended televersion of yet another of his daytime radio features, CBS-TV's *Bride and Groom* (1951–1953) which was subsequently carried on NBC-TV (1953–1954). Also in 1951 he produced *Your Pet Parade*, a 30-minute Sunday afternoon entry on ABC-TV about pets and animal care.

NELSON, WAYNE. b. May 19, 1910; d. February 1984. *Announcer.* **Series:** *The Camel Caravan* (early 1950s); *The New York Philharmonic Symphony Orchestra* (mid 1940s); *The Ted Lewis Show* (ca. 1946, 1947–1948).

In 1929 Wayne Nelson was announcer and director of WNRC, Greensboro, N.C.

NESBITT, JOHN BOOTH. b. Aug. 23, 1910, Victoria, British Columbia, Canada; d. Aug. 10, 1960, Carmel, Calif. *Announcer, Actor, Commentator.* **Series:** *Family Theater* (actor, 1947); *Fibber McGee and Molly* (actor, 1942); *John Charles Thomas*, aka *The Westinghouse Program*, aka *The Westinghouse Sunday Concert* (narrator-storyteller, 1943–1946); *John Nesbitt and the News* (commentator, 1937); *The Passing Parade*, aka *The Meredith Willson-John Nesbitt Show* (host-storyteller, 1937, 1938–1939, 1940–1941, 1943–1945, 1948–1949, 1950–1951); *Radio Reader's Digest* (actor, 1947); *So the Story Goes* (host-narrator, 1945–1946); *The Treasury Hour* (1941); *Treasury Star Parade* (narrator, 1942–1944).

At age five John Nesbitt, grandson of Edwin Booth, whom some theatergoers considered "the foremost American actor of the 19th century," wandered onto a Boston stage. A dress rehearsal for a play was in progress at that moment. Young Nesbitt was on a visit to the theater where his dad was currently transacting some business. His movements were so natural that the director was absolutely awestruck by the lad and prevailed on the boy's father to allow him to remain in the cast. A part was written especially for him and the young professional was paid $8 for eight performances.

His early appearance before the footlights affected Nesbitt for a long time: years later, while attending St. Mary's University in California, he organized a Little Theater. Following graduation, Nesbitt joined a stock company in Vancouver and toured in multiple productions throughout the Northwest. He later managed shows on the road for a similar New York–based outfit. Following a brief fling at newspaper reporting in Seattle and Spokane, Nesbitt traded his typewriter for a microphone. He was hired by a Spokane radio station and soon became one of the city's most popular announcers.

By 1933 he was in San Francisco, where he joined NBC. There he developed a unique style for broadcasting human-interest news that he labeled *Headlines of the Past*. As a result of that single feature, within three years Nesbitt's popularity placed him among the highest echelon of West Coast commentators. The local show evolved into *The Passing Parade* and was offered by three nationwide chains at differing times. His concept became so accepted, in fact, that MGM signed him to produce a number of movie shorts under the same title and premise, for which Nesbitt won triple Academy Awards. On the screen a gifted Hollywood dramatic cast—plus tenor soloist Al Garr and Oscar Bradley's orchestra—performed in those productions.

NILES, KENNETH L. b. Dec. 9, 1906, Livingston, Mont.; d. Oct. 31, 1988, Los Angeles, Calif. *Announcer, Producer, Actor.* **Series:** *The Abbott and Costello Show* (announcer-actor, 1940, 1942–1949); *The Adventures of Maisie* (ca. 1945–ca. 1947); *The Affairs of Ann Scotland* (1946–1947); *The Amazing Mr. Smith* (1946–1947); *The Amazing Mrs. Danbury* (1946); *Beulah*, aka *The Marlin Hurt and Beulah Show* (1945–1946); *Big Town* (ca. mid 1950s); *Blue Ribbon Town* (1943–1944); *The Burns and Allen Show* (1934–1937); *Calamity Jane* (1946); *The Camel Caravan*, aka *The Camel Comedy Caravan* (1942–1943); *Campbell's Tomato Juice Program* (ca. 1936–1937); *The Danny Kaye Show* (1945); *A Date with Judy* (1947–1949); *Gateway to Hollywood* (1939); *Hollywood Hotel* (co-producer and announcer, 1934–1938); *The Judy Canova Show* (ca. 1943–ca. 1944); *Kay Kyser's Kollege of Musical Knowledge* (ca. 1938–ca. early 1940s); *King for a Night*; *The King's Men* (1949); *Lady Esther Serenade* (ca. 1932–?); *Leave it to Joan* (1949–1950); *The Life of Riley* (ca. 1944); *Parties at Pickfair*, aka *Mary Pickford Dramas* (1934–1936); *Phone Again Finnegan* (1946–1947); *The Rudy Vallee Show* (1946–1947); *Southern Cruise* (producer-announcer, 1941); *Suspense* (1947); *Take It or Leave It* (1947–1948).

Entering radio in the late 1920s at Seattle's KJR, Ken Niles introduced West Coast audiences to one of the very first programs offering original dramas, *Theatre of the Mind*. Niles' brother, Wendell Niles, was also eminently recognized for similar pursuits, coincidentally. Meanwhile, in 1930 Ken Niles added some duties as a drama coach at Los Angeles' KHJ. Three years hence the outlet promoted him to the rank of chief announcer. From 1961 to 1962, he narrated *Top Cat*, a primetime animated series on ABC-TV. As his professional career moved along, he became a busy voiceover speaker before he retired from active service in the early 1980s.

Network announcer Dick Joy affirmed that—for warming up a studio audience for a live radio show—he took his cues from Ken Niles, whose style was "the best I ever saw." In the mid 1940s, Niles offered some sage counsel to wannabe announcers: "Voice quality is important, technique is a must, but above all, be natural, sincere and friendly."

Between 1937 and 1951 he performed in 14 motion pictures, by then so widely recognized that he played himself in a trio of those flicks: *Hollywood Hotel* (1937); *Harmon of Michigan* (1941); and *Screen Snapshots No. 6* (1947). His other films included: *Men Are Such Fools* (1938); *Sweepstakes Winner* (1939); *Hit Parade of 1943* (1943); *Shantytown* (1943); *Swingin' on a Rainbow* (1945); *The Inner Circle* (1946); *Magic Town* (1947); *Out of the Past* (1947); *You Were Meant for Me* (1948); *My Friend Irma* (1949); and *The Fat Man* (1951). In the majority of those movies, Niles portrayed a radio announcer.

NILES, WENDELL EDWARD, SR. b. Dec. 29, 1904, Twin Valley, Minn.; d. March 28, 1994, Toluca Lake, Calif. *Announcer.* **Series:** *The Adventures of Philip Marlowe* (1947); *The Bob Hope Show* (1943–1948); *The Burns and Allen Show* (1937–ca. late 1930s); *The Charlotte Greenwood Show* (1944–1946); *The Edgar Bergen and Charlie McCarthy Show*, aka *The Chase and Sanborn Hour* (1937–1939); *The Don Ameche Variety Show* (1940); *The Fitch Bandwagon* (ca. early 1940s–1945); *Gene Autry's Melody Ranch*; *Hedda Hopper*, aka *Hedda Hopper's Hollywood*, aka *This is Hollywood* (1930s, 1940s); *Here Comes Elmer*, aka *The Al Pearce Show*, aka *Al Pearce and His Gang* (1940–ca. 1942, 1944–1945); *Hollywood Star Playhouse* (1952–1953); *Hollywood Startime* (1946–1947); *Johnny Mercer's Music Shop* (1944); *Lum and Abner* (1948–1950); *The Man Called X* (1947–1948); *Mr. and Mrs. Blandings* (1951); *My Friend Irma* (ca. late 1940s–early 1950s); *Niles and Prindle*, aka *Ice Box Follies* (actor, 1945); *The Tommy Dorsey Show* (1946); *When a Girl Marries* (1939–1941).

Wendell Niles was educated at the University of Montana and New York University. For a while he earned his livelihood by developing some rather unique talents, especially for one who would rely on the spoken word for most of his professional success as he addressed vast unseen audiences. At one point he was Montana's lightweight boxing champion. At another time he coached aeronautical students at a Boeing Field ground school in Seattle. He formed his own orchestra and played the vaudeville circuits for a while. It was in the latter capacity that he initially appeared on radio, beginning in 1923 in

Seattle after becoming a popular master of ceremonies for a floorshow at the Olympic Hotel. Out of that experience behind the microphone, he drifted into radio announcing permanently, a domain he would dominate across much of the medium's golden age.

Niles took his family to Hollywood in 1936 and was soon introducing George Burns and Gracie Allen on the air. Niles was the slightly older brother of another firmly entrenched radio interlocutor and actor, Ken Niles. Following a trail his sibling had blazed to Burns and Allen when he performed for them (1934–1937), Wendell Niles temporarily adopted the pseudonym Ronnie Drake to avoid the obvious confusion in identities. Not long afterward, Wendell Niles was privileged to gain similar capacities for many of the other key entertainers on the ether. In a subsequent episode, according to pundit Leonard Maltin, he "was ready to sacrifice a portion of his lucrative announcing career to star in the adventure serial *The Adventures of the Scarlet Cloak* in 1950, but an audition episode never yielded a sponsor." Show business continued in the family: his eldest son, Wendell E. Niles Jr., grew up to produce Johnny Carson's *Tonight Show* on NBC-TV.

When television came along, Wendell Sr. readily adapted to it, too. He not only announced but occasionally assisted host Bill Leyden on the NBC-TV game show *It Could Be You*, appearing daily between 1956 and 1961 and in a primetime version during the 1958 and 1961 summer seasons. In 1957–1958 Niles announced the stunt show *Truth or Consequences* on NBC-TV. For six months in the 1963–1964 season he appeared with invincible stunt show host Monty Hall on NBC-TV's daytime *Let's Make a Deal*. Finally, for a few months in 1966 he introduced host Jan Murray on the NBC-TV game show *Chain Letter*.

As a profitable diversion, Niles narrated many film shorts and "coming attraction" movie trailers for several major motion picture studios. He was a newscaster in the 1966 made-for-TV movie *Sakima and the Masked Marvel*. But long before that, for a quarter-of-a-century between 1932 and 1957, he performed in 35 Hollywood movies, frequently as a radio announcer. Some of those celluloid titles included *The Crowd Roars* (1932); *Ever Since Eve* (1937); *Broadway Musketeers* (1938); *The Roaring Twenties* (1939); *Three Faces West* (1940); *Harmon of Michigan* (1941); *Swingin' on a Rainbow* (1945); *My Friend Irma Goes West* (1950); *The Caddy* (1953); *Beyond a Reasonable Doubt* (1956); and *Jet Pilot* (1957).

NOBLES, CHARLES A. b. Oct. 22, 1908, Holyoke, Mass. *Wake Up America* (1940–1943).

Graduating with honors from Cornell University, Charles A. Nobles attempted several occupations (as a saxophone player and band leader while in college, a soda jerk, mechanic, dance and dramatics instructor) but—dissatisfied with them all—he joined the U.S. Army Air Corps. Faulty eyesight prevented him from becoming a pilot so he was an airplane mechanic. In 1935 he determined to invest his career in radio, starting at a Springfield, Mass., station. He was subsequently hired by Boston's WBZ where, among other features, he introduced *Kellogg's Melody Time* in 1937 over Boston-Springfield's WBZ and WBZA, a weekly Wednesday evening quarter-hour musicale.

Nobles joined NBC's Radio City staff in September 1937. In 1942, when the NBC Blue network began operating independently of the Red chain, Nobles was one of 16 men forming the Blue chain's inaugural staff announcing coterie. By late 1943 that web was divorced entirely from NBC and was soon renamed ABC.

NOEL, DICK. b. May 30, 1927, Brooklyn, New York, N.Y. *Vocalist, Announcer.* **Series:** *The Breakfast Club* (vocalist-announcer, ca. late 1950s–1961); *The CBS Radio Workshop* (1956–1957); *Count Basie and His Orchestra* (1957); *The FBI in Peace and War* (ca. 1950s); *The Glenn Miller Orchestra* (1958); *Guest Star* (vocalist, 1962); *Indictment* (1956–1959); *Ray Anthony and His Orchestra* (vocalist); *The Tennessee Ernie Ford Show* (1950s).

Dick Noel sang regularly on two daytime television series: *Ruth Lyons 50 Club* (1951–1952, NBC) and *The Tennessee Ernie Ford Show* (1962–ca. 1963, ABC). Also, one night a week in the summer of 1953 Noel presided over the Dumont Television travelogue *It's a Small World*. In addition he announced *That Was the Week That Was* on NBC-TV in 1964.

NORDINE, KEN. b. Aug. 14, 1911, Cherokee, Iowa; d. Sept. 15, 1993, Jamestown, N.Y. *Actor, Announcer, Emcee.* **Series:** *The Adventurer's Club* (host, 1947–1948); *American Novels* (actor, 1947); *Biography in Sound* (1955–ca. 1958); *The Breakfast Club* (1947–1948); *Armstrong of the SBI* (1950–ca. 1951); *Faces in the Window* (reader, 1953); *Incredible but True* (narrator, 1950–1951); *A Life in Your Hands* (early 1950s); *Night Life* (host, 1955); *Ralph Morrison and His Orchestra* (1944); *The Silver Eagle*, aka *Silver Eagle, Mountie* (early 1950s); *Sky King* (actor, ca. 1946–ca. 1954); *Welcome Travelers* (1949); *The World of Nordine* (host, 1955); *The World's Great Novels* (actor, 1944–1945, 1947–1948).

For one season, 1951–1952, Ken Nordine introduced the *Chicago Symphony Chamber Orchestra* to ABC-TV viewers in primetime each Tuesday evening. He is also cited by a website for the Grateful Dead: "Word Jazz is the name Ken [Nordine] gave to the unique art form he invented as a creative diversion from his day job. Falling into the cracks somewhere between Beat poetry, shaggy-dog storytelling and standup comedy (delivered sitting down), Word Jazz earned Nordine an avid cult following, with the release of a string of albums on various labels in the late 1950s and early '60s, and a National Public Radio series in the '80s. Among Ken's earliest and most rabid fans was a loose collection of Northern California seekers of fun, truth and music that eventually mutated into the Grateful Dead."

NORRIS, KATHLEEN. b. June 1, 1919, Newark Ohio; d. June 15, 2005, London, England. *Writer, Announcer, Emcee.* **Series:** *Bright Horizon* (writer, 1945); *By Kathleen Norris* (writer, 1939–1941); *Escape with Me* (hostess-narrator, 1952); *Modern Romances* (hostess-narrator, 1949–ca. early 1950s).

In the 1940s Kathi Norris was an advertising executive at W.R. Grace Co. in Chicago and later a director of the Better Business Bureau of New York. She married advertising executive Richard L. Guiterman, who was with Grant Advertising from 1940 to 1945, a newspaper columnist in 1945–1946 and who later appeared with her on ABC Radio's *Escape with Me* (1952). She wouldn't forget her advertising roots, nevertheless, becoming a General Electric spokesperson on the three largest TV networks from 1954 to 1956 and for Purina from 1962 to 1964.

On *By Kathleen Norris* prolific dramatic producer Phillips H. Lord borrowed an idea from his legendary cops-and-robbers epic *Gangbusters*: fiction author Norris narrated each weekly tale "by proxy." Actress Ethel Everett substituted for her (in a show she, Norris, penned) and the narratives often were light romantic fare but frequently tinged with mystery and suspense, a couple of Lord hallmarks.

Norris was poised to jump from one medium to another when television began coming on strong. Initially on the small screen she dispensed shopping hints for housewives on Dumont Television's *TV Shopper* (1948–1950). During the same era she became one of several masters of ceremonies on the pithy Dumont quiz show *Spin the Picture* (1949–1950). She was soon presiding over the daytime talk series that took her name, *The Kathi Norris Show*, from 1950 to 1951 on NBC-TV. In 1953 she hosted a segment of that network's *Today* show, "The Woman's View of the News," while Dave Garroway was anchor. She also developed many TV series pilots.

Between 1957 and 1961 Norris was the hostess-narrator of NBC-TV's live midday Saturday dramatic anthology, *True Story*. As a unique feature there, she faced the camera as if she was interviewing figures in the individual stories being presented. Charles Grodin, Jean Stapleton and Ruth Warrick were among the thespians performing in those narratives that stemmed from *True Story* magazine. The periodical had also prompted *My True Story* on radio (1943–1962).

O'BRIEN, JOE. b. July 16, 1915, Yonkers, N.Y.; d. July 24, 2005, Pittsfield, Mass. *Announcer.* **Series:** *Jack and Cliff* (cast member, 1948); *Rosemary* (ca. 1940s).

In 1940 Joe O'Brien, a staff announcer at New York's WMCA, introduced *Dr. Wynne's Food Forum* each Tuesday evening to a metropolitan audience for a half-hour of lively conversation. This early emphasis on fitness and nutrition spotlighted the city's former health commissioner, Dr. Shirley Wynne, in a dialogue with home economist Ella Mason. Simultaneously, O'Brien hosted a weekly half-hour variety series on WMCA, *Sally's Movieland Review* (sponsored by Sally's Furriers). It featured vocalists Bob Carroll and Winnie Shaw and the Broadway and Hollywood gossip of Jack Eigen.

Within a year O'Brien was sportscasting for WMCA (1941–1947) and afterwards he conducted an airshift at the record turntables at that station (1954–1968). He joined WNBC in New York in 1968, retired from full time broadcasting in 1986 and continued to perform weekend specials until 2000 over WHUD, Peekskill, N.Y. Just after his 90th birthday, O'Brien was a victim in a fatal automobile mishap at Lenox, Mass.

O'CONNOR, BOB. *Actor, Announcer.* **Series:** *Lux Radio Theater* (actor, 1954); *Results, Incorporated* (1944); *Richard Diamond, Private Detective* (actor, 1951); *Romance* (actor, 1952).

Before moving into radio, Bob O'Connor was enjoying a career playing bit parts in movies. He appeared in 28 B-films between 1927 and 1948, including *The Second 100 Years* (1927); *Babes in Toyland* (1934); *The Bohemian Girl* (1936); *Our Relations* (1936); *Swiss Miss* (1938); *Ragtime Cowboy Joe* (1940); *The Masked Rider* (1941); *Once upon a Honeymoon* (1942); *The Falcon in Mexico* (1944); *Genius at Work* (1946); and *Vengeance is Mine* (1948).

O'CONNOR, CHARLES PETER. b. June 10, 1910, Cambridge, Mass.; d. March 17, 1942. *Announcer, Correspondent.* **Series:** *Breezing Along*, aka *Jingo* (1939–1940); *The Court of Human Relations* (1934–1935); *Crime Doctor* (1940–1942); *Major Bowes' Original Amateur Hour* (ca. mid to late 1930s); *Name the Place* (1939); *NBC News* (correspondent, 1931–1942); *Philip Morris Presents* (1939–1940).

At five years of age, Charles O'Connor gave a recitation in public in his hometown of Cambridge, Mass. in a precursor to his life's work. Following a year at Boston College where he played football, he dropped out of school to tour with a stock company throughout the East. Later, Boston's WBZ, an NBC affiliate, employed him as an announcer in January 1931. That same year O'Connor was one of 10 spielers to audition for—and win—an announcing spot at NBC's Radio City in New York. Reportedly, 2,500 aspirants sought those coveted posts during 1930 and 1931, shortly after the stock market crash of 1929 prompted nationwide economic collapse. WBZ, incidentally, had already sent five announcers to Radio City prior to O'Connor's arrival in Gotham, an unusually convincing track record.

O'Connor soon assisted in providing NBC listeners with radio's most ambitious on-the-spot news coverage to that time. On March 1, 1932 he and a few colleagues launched truck-mounted mobile transmitting stations to report from Hopewell, N.J. on the kidnapping of the Lindbergh baby. Competitors at CBS did the same, ushering in a nascent dimension in radio newscasting. On June 1, 1936 O'Connor, Nelson Case, Howard Claney and Fred Bate covered a festive gala for NBC, the arrival of the *Queen Mary*'s maiden voyage into New York harbor.

O'Connor was assigned to handle numerous football scrimmages and other special events during his brief career. His death at age 31 removed one of the youngest and most promising national radio announcers and newscasters of the epoch.

O'CONNOR, ROD. b. Jan. 18, 1914; d. June 5, 1964, Los Angeles, Calif. *Announcer, Actor.* **Series:** *The Cascade of Stars* (host, 1952); *Command Performance* (ca. mid to late 1940s); *The Count of Monte Cristo* (1944–1945); *Crime is My Pastime*, aka *Time for Crime* (actor, 1945); *The David Rose Show* (1950); *Duffy's Tavern* (late 1940s, ca. early 1950s); *Family Theater* (narrator, 1953); *Glamour Manor* (1945–1946); *Guest Star* (ca. mid to late 1940s); *In Your Name* (1947–1948); *Murder is My Hobby* (1945–1946); *People Are Funny* (ca. 1940s, 1950s); *The Raleigh Cigarette Program Starring Red Skelton*, aka *The Red Skelton Show* (mid 1940s to early 1950s); *You Were There* (1945).

A nomadic Rod O'Conner (similar to many others in his profession) announced for a plethora of radio stations in the Midwest and far West before being summoned to introduce a handful of national series on the ether. His colorful trek from the middle of the country to its far western shores, returning to the Midwest and once again to the West Coast, began in the 1930s at Minneapolis'

WTCN. Stops along his route included, in sequence, WVEC, San Luis Obispo, Calif.; KID, Idaho Falls, Idaho; KLO, Ogden, Utah; KUTA, Salt Lake City; KSL, Salt Lake City (1940); WCCO, Minneapolis (1941); WGN, Chicago (1942); and KHJ, Los Angeles (1944).

In its Jan. 3, 1942 issue, *Billboard* reported a humorous connection to the war coverage that inundated radio listeners in the previous month. It specifically mentioned announcer O'Conner, who was then at WCCO in Minneapolis: "In the first 48 hours after the attack on Pearl Harbor, O'Connor had broken into so much regular programming with war updates that finally, to relieve the tension, he announced on the air, 'We interrupt the news flashes to bring you a regularly scheduled program.'"

Permanently settling on the West Coast allowed O'Connor to appear in uncredited roles in a couple of motion pictures released in 1948: *The Fuller Brush Man* and *A Southern Yankee*. Furthermore, he turned up in a single episode of *Fury* on NBC-TV on Dec. 24, 1955.

OLSEN, JOHNNY (aka Johnny Olson). b. May 22, 1910, Windom, Minn.; d. Oct. 12, 1985, Santa Monica, Calif. *Emcee, Announcer.* **Series:** *Beat the Clock* (1949); *Break the Bank* (alternating master of ceremonies, 1945–1946); *Get Rich Quick* (quizmaster, 1948); *Get Together* (1940s); *The Johnny Olsen Show*, aka *Johnny Olsen's Rumpus Room*, aka *Johnny Olsen's Get-Together*, aka *Johnny Olsen's Luncheon Club* (master of ceremonies, 1946, 1949, 1950–1951, 1954–1957); *Ladies Be Seated* (co-master of ceremonies, 1944–1949); *On Stage Everybody* (1945); *Prince Charming* (1940s); *Swingshift Frolics* (1944); *True or False* (ca. mid 1940s–mid 1950s); *Whiz Quiz* (quizmaster, 1948). **Aphorism:** *Come on down!*

Johnny Olsen's initial on-air duty was as the Buttermilk Kid on a Madison, Wis. station. He transferred to KGDA in Mitchell, S.D., where he not only managed but also sold, announced, sang and preached, too, on a daily devotional series. Next, Olsen was elevated to chief announcer at Milwaukee's WTMJ and then went off to Hollywood for a year. Returning to Milwaukee, he hosted an audience participation show that quickly became something of a trademark for him, *Johnny Olsen's Rumpus Room*.

In 1944 he left Milwaukee forever to join ABC in New York City as a staff announcer. Over the years he warmed up audiences prior to introducing lots of studio-originated series with live onlookers, ultimately becoming a master of ceremonies for several game shows himself. The affable, bespectacled, balding toastmaster with an elfin grin and a smile in his voice briefly revived one of his previous local series appellations, *Johnny Olsen's Rumpus Room*, during an extensive ABC daytime run (through 1951) and on MBS (1954–1957). From 1949–1952 the feature—which his spouse, Penny Olsen, cohosted—was extended on Dumont Television after a successful five-year stretch on ABC Radio. Earlier, in 1945, the couple had supplied a five-week trial exhibition of televising their other audience participation show, *Ladies Be Seated*, on Dumont. It was one of the earliest examples of videocasting similar features and helped lay the groundwork for successors to do it regularly as the techniques and technologies continued to advance.

In 1949 Olsen presided over ABC-TV's *Fun for the Money* game show that pitted the genders against each other. From 1951 to 1953 he was a principal in the cast of *Kids and Company*, a Saturday morning adolescent-focused feature on Dumont TV.

One of Olsen's most noteworthy roles after Jack Lescoulie left comic Jackie Gleason at the end of the 1950s was to introduce *You're in the Picture*, aka *The Jackie Gleason Show* (1961) and *Jackie Gleason and His American Scene Magazine* (1962–1966) on CBS-TV every Saturday night live from New York. Subsequently, the veteran announcer did the same for *The Jackie Gleason Show* on CBS every Saturday night live from Miami Beach (1966–1970). During the same era, meanwhile, Olsen was turning up as interlocutor for a coterie of imposing daytime and primetime game shows airing from New York—among them *Snap Judgment* (1967–1969, NBC), *To Tell the Truth* (1960s, CBS) and *What's My Line?* (1960s, CBS)—plus sundry variety series and specials. To handle the calendar after Gleason moved his entourage to the Sunshine State in the mid 1960s, Olsen flew to Miami every weekend for a quadrennial. In so doing he maintained a lucrative commitment to The Great One while keeping all of his Gotham-based affiliations. His resiliency spoke volumes about the value Olsen placed on the singular opportunity of introducing Gleason's comedy hour every week.

But without any doubt, Olsen's most distinctly notorious role—the one for which he is *still* recalled by millions, even a couple of decades following his demise—was as the infamous interlocutor who originated the national catchphrase *Come on down!* Olsen (by then *Olson*, as he had altered the spelling of his surname in the 1970s) shouted that idiom to aspiring contestants several times an hour: the show, of course, was CBS-TV's daytime guessing gala *The Price is Right* and he was there from its CBS inception on Sept. 4, 1972, until his death on Oct. 12, 1985.

O'RILEY, JACK. *Announcer.* **Series:** *I Packed My Trunk* (1947); *Lombardoland, U.S.A.* (ca. 1948–ca. 1957); *Official Detective* (1947–1950s); *One Night Stand* (late 1940s); *The Song Writing Machine* (1948); *The Voice of Vic Damone* (1947); *The Wheel of Fortune* (host, 1955).

ORTEGA, SANTOS. b. June 1899, New York, N.Y.; d. April 10, 1976, Ft. Lauderdale, Fla. *Actor, Announcer.* **Series:** *The Adventures of Ellery Queen* (actor, 1939–1940, 1942–1944, 1945–1947); *The Adventures of Nero Wolfe* (actor, 1943–1944); *The Affairs of Peter Salem* (actor, 1949–1953); *The Amazing Mr. Smith* (actor, 1941); *Arch Oboler's Plays* (actor, 1939–1940); *Barrie Craig—Confidential Investigator* (actor, 1951–1954); *Big Sister* (actor, ca. 1936–ca. 1940s); *Blackstone Plantation* (cast member, ca. 1929–1934); *Boston Blackie* (actor, ca. 1944, ca. 1945–ca. 1950); *Bright Horizon* (actor, ca. 1941–ca. 1945); *Broadway Matinee* (1943); *Bulldog Drummond* (actor, ca. 1943–?); *By Kathleen Norris* (actor, 1939–1941); *Casey—Crime Photographer* (actor, ca. 1940s, early to mid 1950s); *The CBS Radio Mystery Theater* (actor, 1974–1982); *Charlie Chan* (actor, ca. 1947–1948); *City Hospital* (actor, 1950s); *Criminal Casebook* (actor, 1948); *Crooked Square*, aka *Mysteries of the Crooked Square* (actor, 1945); *Dimension X* (actor, 1950–1951); *Don Ameche's Real Life Stories* (actor, 1949); *The Ethel Merman Show* (actor, 1949); *The Ford Theater* (actor, 1947–1948); *Gangbusters* (1935, 1936–ca. mid 1950s); *Grand Central Station* (actor, 1940s, 1950s); *Green Valley U.S.A.* (narrator, 1944); *Hannibal Cobb* (actor, 1950–1951); *Joyce Jordan, M.D.* (actor, ca. 1938–ca. 1940s); *The Light of the World* (actor, 1941–1942); *The Man I Married* (actor, 1939–1942); *Mr. and Mrs. North* (actor, 1942–1943); *Myrt and Marge* (actor, 1939–1942); *The Mysterious Traveler* (actor, 1943–1952); *Mystery Theater* (actor, 1940s); *The Newlyweds* (actor, 1930); *The O'Neills* (actor, ca. 1934–ca. 1943); *Our Gal Sunday* (actor); *Perry Mason* (actor, 1943–mid 1940s); *Portia Faces Life* (actor, ca. 1940s); *Quick as a Flash* (guest actor, 1940s); *Radio Hall of Fame*, aka *Philco Summer Hour* (actor, 1943–1946); *The Robert Burns Panatela Show* (ca. 1932–ca. 1933); *Roger Kilgore—Public Defender* (actor, 1948); *Romance* (actor, 1943–1944); *The Scorpion* (actor, 1932); *The Shadow* (actor, ca. 1938–ca. 1954); *Special Investigator* (actor, 1946–1947); *Stroke of Fate* (actor, 1953); *The Third Man*, aka *The Lives of Harry Lime* (1952); *This Day is Ours* (actor, 1938–1940); *This is Your FBI* (actor, 1945–1947); *Treasury Agent* (actor, ca. 1947, ca. 1948); *Valiant Lady* (actor, 1938–?); *Who Dun It?*, *Words at War* (actor, 1943–1945); *X-Minus One* (actor, 1955–1958); and *Yours Truly—Johnny Dollar* (actor, 1960–1962).

At the age of 17 Santos Ortega launched a show business career by singing at the Hippodrome Theater in his native New York City. He played a myriad of detective roles on network radio series and industry insiders considered him one of the most capable actors in voicing characters with diverse dialects. Ortega was in demand for guest shots, support roles and leads in a variety of features and sustained many recurring roles in soap operas. While he appeared as an actor or occasional announcer in no fewer than 57 aural series, it was as a thespian in a single televised daytime drama for which legions of fans would always remember Ortega.

Three days after her first half-hour soap opera, *As the World Turns*, premiered on CBS-TV in April 1956, the drama's creator and head writer—Irna Phillips—fired actor William Lee, who had debuted in the part of Grandpa Hughes, a cast principal. She replaced him instantly with radio serial veteran

Santos Ortega. That turned out to be a prudent move for Ortega was a critical figure in that show until he died in the spring of 1976, two decades later. He was never replaced in that key role.

OSGOOD, CHARLES (born Charles Osgood Wood III). b. Jan. 8, 1933, New York, N.Y. *Commentator, Correspondent, Emcee.* **Series:** *ABC News* (correspondent, 1963–1967); *Newsmark* (host, ca. 1980s); *The Osgood File* (commentator, 1971–). **Aphorism:** *See you on the radio.*

Christened "one of the last great broadcast writers" by Charles Kuralt, his predecessor-host on CBS-TV's weekly *Sunday Morning*, Charles Osgood is revered by the Radio Hall of Fame's website as "the voice of CBS News" and is dubbed by people both inside and outside the industry as CBS Radio's "Poet-in-Residence." Indeed, his soothing radio commentaries are frequently delivered in verse, following a pithy introduction for background.

For many years Charles Osgood signed off both his radio and television series with the saying *See you on the radio*. He explained to his aural audience—and in a book by that title (G.P. Putnam's Sons, 1999)—that in the Theater of the Mind one can *see* greater images than anything video mediums could ever hope to provide. For that alone, he became a patron saint of vintage radio to its legions of hobbyists nationwide. The raconteur has four additional tomes to his credit: *Nothing Could Be Finer Than a Crisis That is Minor in the Morning* (Holt, Rinehart & Winston, 1979); *There's Nothing I Wouldn't Do if You Would Be My POSSLQ (Persons of Opposite Sex Sharing Living Quarters)* (Holt, Rinehart & Winston, 1981); *Osgood on Speaking: How to Think on Your Feet without Falling on Your Face* (William Morrow, 1988); and *The Osgood Files* (G.P. Putnam's Sons, 1991).

The Fordham-educated Osgood, who earned a degree in economics in 1954, didn't take over *Sunday Morning* until 40 years later, when Kuralt retired. In the meantime, he presided over a late televised *CBS Sunday Night News* in the early to mid 1970s and co-anchored the *CBS Early Morning News* on the small screen from 1987 to 1992. In between times he was—and still is, as of early 2006—a regular on CBS's New York flagship station, WCBS. He has penned and produced his daily radio feature for 35 years (since 1971), a record in longevity for a non-news radio commentary. Before joining CBS News in September 1971 Osgood was program director and manager of Washington's WGMS Radio; general manager of the nation's original pay television outlet, WHCT, Hartford, Conn.; general assignment reporter for ABC News (1963–1967); and anchor-reporter for WCBS, New York (1967–1971). He also authors a biweekly syndicated newspaper column.

The recipient of no fewer than 10 honorary doctorates from various institutions of higher learning, Osgood holds at least two additional honorary degrees, is a trustee of three educational institutions and an overseer of still another. He plays piano and banjo as a sideline and has performed with the Mormon Tabernacle Choir, the New York Pops and the Boston Pops orchestras. His first broadcasting gig, in fact, was on a Philadelphia station where he played organ for a radio drama. The National Father's Day Committee picked him as Father of the Year in 1985 (he has five offspring).

Inducted into the Radio Hall of Fame in 1990, Osgood received an award in 1999 for significant broadcast achievement given by the International Radio and Television Society. He is the recipient of three George Foster Peabody Awards (two for CBS Radio's public affairs series *Newsmark* in 1985 and 1986 and one for *Sunday Morning* in 1997). He holds many other honors, including five coveted Best in Business Awards presented by *The Washington Journalism Review*. Osgood appears in public and on television wearing a bow tie, another trademark in addition to his rhyming radio commentaries.

O'SULLIVAN, TERRY. b. July 7, 1915, Kansas City, Mo. d. Sept. 14, 2006, St. Paul, Minn. *Announcer, Actor.* **Series:** *Anchors Aweigh* (1941–1943); *Dreft Star Playhouse* (ca. 1944–1945); *The General Mills Hour* (interlocutor for *The Guiding Light, Woman in White* and *Today's Children*, 1940s); *Glamour Manor* (commercial spokesman, 1944–ca. 1947); *Make-Believe Town, Hollywood* (actor, 1949–1950, 1951).

Beginning in 1952, newly widowed heroine Jo Ann Barron (actress Mary Stuart) of

CBS-TV's *Search for Tomorrow*—a poignant, compelling daytime drama that enjoyed an air-life of 35 years (1951–1986)—fell head over heels for her superior at Henderson Hospital, business manager Arthur Tate. A tall, dark and handsome Terry O'Sullivan portrayed Tate. Allowing for a brief time-out in 1955–56 during which O'Sullivan turned up as Elliott Norris in CBS-TV's washboard weeper *Valiant Lady*, the actor persisted as Tate until his character succumbed to a fatal heart attack in 1968, a lengthy run for a serial thespian.

He became one of several ill-fated spouses of the beleaguered Barron as the tale slowly unfolded, dispensing misery and conflict for its principals across the decades. And during his latter days of playing Arthur Tate, O'Sullivan concurrently appeared as Richard Hunter in NBC-TV's *Days of Our Lives* (1966–68). After leaving the casts of both dramas, he arrived on CBS-TV's *The Secret Storm* where he portrayed Judge Sam Stevens (1968–69). Counting the simultaneous course of *Search for Tomorrow* and *Days of Our Lives*, O'Sullivan packed a couple of decades' worth of serialized narrative into his career as a daytime video actor, unquestionably exceeding most others of that era in his final profession.

O'Sullivan, who also introduced a couple of series during the 1953–1954 television season on competing networks—Dumont's *Dollar a Second* game show and ABC's feminine panel feature *Leave it to the Girls*—got his show business start as a thespian in Midwestern tent shows. For a while he was wedded to one of radio's most prolific dramatic actresses, the late Jan Miner, whose infinite professional credits included the heroines of a couple of daytime serials, *Hilltop House* and *Lora Lawton*. He was married six times.

PARDO, DONALD GEORGE. b. Feb. 22, 1918, Westfield, Mass. *Announcer, Newscaster.* **Series:** *Barrie Craig, Confidential Investigator* (1951–ca. 1955); *Dimension X* (ca. 1950–1951); *Escape with Me* (1952); *The Eve Young Show* (1951); *Friday is a Big Day* (1950); *George Olsen and His Orchestra* (newscaster, 1948); *Jane Ace, Disc Jockey* (1951–1952); *Johnny Long and His Orchestra* (1948); *Just Plain Bill* (1955); *Let's Go Nightclubbing* (ca. 1943–1946); *The Magnificent Montague* (1950–1951); *The Mindy Carson Show* (1949–1950); *Monitor* (interviewer, ca. 1950s, 1960s); *Musicana* (announcer-newscaster, 1948); *NBC News* (newscaster, 1944, 1948); *Will Osborne and His Orchestra* (1948); *X Minus One* (ca. mid 1950s).

Although he launched his broadcasting career in radio, NBC stalwart Don Pardo is still recalled by far more Americans of multiple generations for his work in television. In the summer of 1954 he announced the celebrity game feature *Droodles*. He introduced the weekly quarter-hour *Jonathan Winters Show* in 1956–1957. Pardo enjoyed even longer runs as he presented a couple of daytime game shows—*The Price is Right* hosted by Bill Cullen from 1956–1963 (Pardo filled in for Cullen a couple of times when the emcee couldn't make it) and *Jeopardy* hosted by Art Fleming from 1964 to 1975 and 1978 to 1979. But without question, his most memorable contribution occurred on the weekends since.

When NBC-TV's *Saturday Night Live* premiered in 1975, producer Lorne Michaels made the unusual choice of NBC veteran Pardo to introduce the show. "His old-fashioned, hard-sell approach was in sharp contrast to the hip, young feel of the comedy program, yet it seemed to work for the show," observed critic Leonard Maltin. Pardo "functioned exactly as radio announcers would in the old days: ... rarely if ever appeared on camera, yet ... voice and delivery set the tone for ... shows, and became indelibly identified with them." Pardo was there for every season except 1981–1982 to the early 2000s, in fact. Although he officially retired from NBC at the close of 2004, he continued to leave his Tucson, Ariz. home weekly to announce *Saturday Night Live* on countless weekends thereafter. A little known fact of trivia: Pardo is one of only two individuals to whom NBC offered lifetime contracts. The other was Bob Hope.

PARKER, ROLLON. b. 1908. *Actor, Announcer.* **Series:** *The Green Hornet* (actor, 1938–ca. 1940s); *The Green Valley Line* (actor, 1934); *The Hermit's Cave* (actor, ca. 1935–mid 1940s); *The Lone Ranger* (actor, 1930s–ca. 1940s); *Ned Jordan, Secret Agent* (ca. late 1930s, early 1940s).

By the early 1940s Rollon Parker acted

in episodes of *Challenge of the Yukon* beamed to a regional audience by Detroit's WXYZ. That important juvenile series didn't go on the ABC network until 1947, after Parker had fled the scene. Parker was subsequently a member of the Chicago Mummers.

PARKS, BERT. b. Dec. 30, 1914, Atlanta, Ga.; d. Feb. 2, 1992, La Jolla, Calif. *Emcee, Announcer, Producer.* **Series:** *The Abbott and Costello Show* (mid 1940s); *The Adventures of Ellery Queen* (1940); *The Benny Goodman Show* (ca. 1930s); *Break the Bank* (master of ceremonies, 1945–1950); *Camel Caravan* (master of ceremonies, 1939–1940); *The Columbia Workshop* (late 1930s, ca. 1940s); *Cugat Rhumba Revue, The Xavier Cugat Show* (1941–ca. 1942); *The Eddie Cantor Show* (1938–1939); *Forty-Five Minutes in Hollywood* (1934); *Funny Side Up* (master of ceremonies, 1959); *Harry James and His Orchestra* (1942–ca. 1944); *Here's to Veterans* (ca. 1946–1947); *How'm I Doin?* (1942); *Judy, Jill and Johnny* (1946–1947); *The Kate Smith Show* (ca. 1930s, 1940s); *Luncheon at the Waldorf* (1940–ca. 1941); *Matinee at Meadowbrook* (host, 1941); *McGarry and His Mouse* (1946, 1947); *Monitor* (co-communicator, 1960; host, 1967; interviewee, 1968); *NBC Bandstand* (host, 1956–1958); *Renfrew of the Mounted* (1936–ca. 1937); *Reunion* (producer, 1947); *Second Honeymoon* (master of ceremonies, 1948–1950); *Stars for Defense* (host, ca. 1957–1962); *Stop the Music!* (master of ceremonies, 1948–1952); *Summer Stars* (1937); *Take a Break* (1947); *Treasury Salute* (1945); *Voice of the Army* (1949).

Bert Parks' extensive professional life in show business was jump started at age 16 when he went on the air regularly over WGST in his hometown of Atlanta. Hired as a combination announcer and vocalist, the youth performed proficiently enough to be noticed by CBS officials in New York. Two years hence, in 1933, he moved up to the big time where he was compensated at $50 weekly for providing the system cues between network series and whatever other assignments were given him. Parks' extroverted demeanor soon brought the attention of entertainer Eddie Cantor, who put him on his show as announcer, singer and as foil to himself. Before long the genial Parks was also emceeing the programs of bandleaders Xavier Cugat and Benny Goodman. With that, his career was set for a while—and Parks was introducing a handful of New York-originated features of varied breeds.

Summoned by Uncle Sam during the early 1940s like so many of his counterparts, he interrupted a budding career to serve a grateful nation. Returning to radio following the hostilities, he picked up new program assignments. By then he could hardly be contained as a mere behind-the-mike interlocutor, too. Bursting upon the scene as a rotating emcee—a fresh shot of adrenaline to *Break the Bank's* audience—Parks unveiled his manifold talents to public scrutiny and quickly developed a big following. He was never to be comfortable in the shadows again, once attesting immodestly, "I created a whole era. I started the pattern."

It was *Break the Bank* that initially thrust Parks before an adoring American public and in due time led him to successively greater ventures. Only 33 when he signed on with the series, he possessed unflagging dynamism that didn't escape the notice of Edwin Wolfe, *Bank's* producer. Characterized as "young, hungry, hyperkinetic ... the most excitable man on radio," the handsome, virile, supercharged Parks possessing a contagious smile under arching eyebrows liked people and wanted them to like him. He was everything *Bank* required, and he would be its matchless star throughout its years of primetime broadcasting.

A couple of years after *Bank's* premier he was instrumental in launching another audience participation show on a local New Jersey station. *Second Honeymoon* aired weekdays in 1947 over WAAT as a remote from Bamberger's department store in Newark. It was a human-interest series of the *Queen for a Day* model. Housewives selected to appear on the show fathomed why they merited subsequent wedding trips. A panel of judges picked winners, showering them with merchandise prizes and dispatching them on dream vacations. As its master of ceremonies, Parks moved with the program to the ABC network in 1948. A year later the series transferred to MBS for a final ephemeral run.

The year 1948 was, incidentally, an extraordinarily exceptional one for Parks. He was selected to host yet a *third* concurrent ABC audience participation show: *Stop the*

Music! (Parenthetically, it was the show that brought to an end the long-running radio career of NBC comedian Fred Allen; "Radio actually died when *Stop the Music!* got higher ratings than Fred Allen," a couple of historiographers posited.) Nevertheless, the series was surely Parks' crowning achievement in the aural medium. By then he was widely respected as one of its top five or six game-show emcees. Beyond that, radio projected him onto the Broadway stage where he played the title role in *The Music Man* and in a myriad of other tune-filled productions.

By the 1950s he also gained lots of television exposure. A half-hour of his daily two-hour radio series, *NBC Bandstand*, was picked up for simulcast by NBC-TV in 1956. In the meantime, he had already hosted a triweekly daytime variety entry on the tube, *The Bert Parks Show* (1950–1952), first on NBC, then CBS. Reprising his radio successes in Videoland as a game and variety show host, Parks presided over *Double or Nothing* (1952–1954 on CBS in the daytime and 1953 on NBC in primetime); *County Fair* (1958–1959 on NBC in daytime); *The Big Payoff* (1959 on CBS in daytime); and *Yours for a Song* (1961–1962 in primetime and 1961–1963 in daytime, both on ABC).

In spite of all of this, Parks is better remembered by nearly everybody in the country who was alive at the time as the singer with the leaping eyebrows who bellowed *There She Is! Miss America!* From 1954 to 1979 he presided over the nationally televised Miss America Pageant, requesting the envelope from the judges that contained the name of the winner while she, the runner-ups and seemingly the whole country waited with bated breath. Withdrawing the moniker of the lucky lady who was to be crowned, he read her state's name aloud, and then crooned to her as she traipsed down the runway ensconced in a long formal gown. It was a tradition not easily forgotten—although contemporary alterations in the pageant may make it seem like it occurred in another life! Parks was eventually replaced by younger personalities in that coveted role. None possessed the vigorous voice or leaping eyebrows, however.

Long after his Miss America reign had passed, Parks turned up playing a singer in the band in the Hollywood theatrical production *The Freshman*, released in 1990. For a guy who had been so astonishingly the rage in other venues for so many years, it seemed peculiar that his silver screen exposure was limited to just one flick. Possibly there would have been more had he not died only a couple of years later.

PARSONS, LOUELLA (born Louella Rose Oettinger). b. Aug. 6, 1880, Freeport, Ill.; d. Dec. 9, 1972, Santa Monica, Calif. *Commentator, Emcee*. **Series:** *Hollywood Hotel* (hostess, 1934–1938); *Hollywood Premiere* (hostess, 1941); *Louella Parsons* (commentator, 1934, 1944–1951, 1952–1954).

Some luminaries in the public eye with seemingly interesting lives penned a memoir recalling their fascinating encounters. Some who lived long enough wrote more than one autobiography. Louella Parsons was in that category, releasing *The Gay Illiterate* (Doubleday, Doran & Co., 1944) at age 64 and *Tell It to Louella* (Putnam, 1961) at 81, the latter 11 years before her demise. Had she not expired, who could say there wouldn't have been a third volume? (A limited few did that very thing.) There can be little question, nonetheless, that she led an enchanting existence: she was remembered with not one but *two* stars on the Hollywood Walk of Fame—one for motion pictures and one for radio. This prima donna of the gossipmongers may be aptly considered *The First Lady of Hollywood*, the title of a contemporary biography authored by Samantha Barbas (University of California Press, 2005).

Parsons was also a fighter, scrapping relentlessly with others of her trade (*Life* branded her a "ruthless rival") as she sought to defend her territorial rights, particularly when realizing that some of the sacred ground she occupied was in danger of being captured by peers. Interestingly, Parsons and a trio of other tattletales who made most of their livelihoods by divulging personal secrets of the celebrated in print and broadcast mediums—Hedda Hopper, Parsons' chief rival as Hollywood queen; Walter Winchell, who tenaciously worked at scooping Parsons; and Sheilah Graham, perhaps the most successful "successor" of the genre that those early birds set in motion—were all born of Jewish descent, yet some disavowed it. (Parsons herself converted to Catholicism.) The only leading contender of the ilk without that common heritage, Jimmy Fidler, was despised by a large and unforgiving segment of the Tinseltown community, although he seemed to revel in it. Thus, at any given time, the rumormongers were warring factions, capable of carving up their rivals when it appeared that one of them might be getting ahead of a competitor.

Louella Rose Oettinger was raised at Dixon, Ill., where she gained her first paid assignment in journalism as drama editor of *The Dixon Morning Star* while still in high school. After her marriage to John Parsons, Louella settled into small town family life at Burlington, Iowa, a condition she detested. After their marriage started to fall apart, she uprooted and took her only child, Harriet, to Chicago. Louella became a scriptwriter for Essanay Studios, a movie production house. Harriet, meanwhile, who grew up to become a film producer herself, appeared in celluloid several times, billed as "Baby Parsons." Her mom authored one of those films, *The Magic Wand* (released in 1912) and in the same period finished an instructional volume for would-be screen scribes: *How to Write for the "Movies"* (A.C. McClurg, 1915). She also wrote the film *Chains* (1912) and *His New Job* (1915). She later authored the screenplay for the Columbia motion picture *Isle of Forgotten Women* (1927).

It was in 1914 that she launched the nation's very first movie gossip column, appearing regularly in *The Chicago Record-Herald*. Four years beyond, the legendary journal magnate William Randolph Hearst purchased the paper and she was dismissed. Having discovered a niche that she knew quite a bit about by then, and having developed contacts that could offer still more, Parsons wasn't about to let the idea drop. She shifted her operations to Gotham and inaugurated a similar piece in *The New York Morning Telegraph*. Four years afterward, in 1922 Hearst was convinced that movie news was mainstream and came knocking on Parsons' door. Shrewd bargaining by both parties resulted in her signing with a major Hearst paper, *The New York American*. She would remain his employee for the rest of her professional life, and—according to her biographer—use the privileges at her disposal to blackmail in the service of Hearst's political and personal agendas.

She married and divorced her second husband by the mid 1920s when she contracted tuberculosis and was advised that she only had six months to live. Parsons moved to Arizona for better weather and soon relocated to Los Angeles. At about the same time, in 1926 she married for a third time, to a surgeon, and never remarried after his death in 1964. In the interim, with her disease in remission, she returned to work as a syndicated columnist for Hearst. That column, originated for *The Los Angeles Examiner*, was eventually reprinted in more than 600 newspapers around the globe, perhaps second in number only to Winchell's, who purportedly reached 2,000 newspapers in his heyday. At her peak, meanwhile, Parsons was said to be followed by more than 40 million readers. She was especially recognized for an "uncanny ability to scoop her competitors with the juiciest stories and for knowing all the secrets of everyone in screendom."

Sunkist Growers put her under contract in 1928 for local radio interviews of celebrities, principally of the silver screen variety. Her promotion there, in addition to the newspaper exposure the residents were seeing, allowed for a second local venture in 1931 underwritten by Charis foundation garments. Three years later CBS put her on a sustained matinee quarter-hour tell-all on Wednesdays. By then she was cited as "the country's top purveyor of gossip," a trophy she would not easily nor quickly surrender—and certainly not without a fight. Campbell Soup Co. was her next sponsor, bringing *Hollywood Hotel* to CBS on Oct. 5, 1934, fostering a variety series with a nasal-toned Parsons as hostess and Dick Powell as master of ceremonies during most of its run.

There were increased costs then in originating shows from the West Coast as opposed to New York or Chicago. Parsons offset those by swaying local luminaries to appear for free. "Parsons was then the most feared and powerful newspaper columnist in Hollywood," affirmed a pundit. "Her column ... was widely seen as a maker or breaker of films and careers." As a consequence she had the ability to corral movie screen idols that would normally earn $1,000 for one radio appearance; every show featured five or six of them, without expense to Campbell's beyond a case of soup. Ultimately more than $2 million worth of movie talent appeared gratis. She was truly sitting in the catbird seat.

Hollywood Hotel evolved into the most enchanting series of the era (predating the legacy that would be established by the *Lux Radio Theater* a short time hence) and became a basis for major antipathy within filmdom. Some found it demeaning to work without pay and refused to appear; as a general rule, the careers of those who did perform prospered handsomely, infused by the "free" publicity and public relations acquired by donating an evening's time. "Parsons was known for ruthlessness and a long memory," attested a radio historiographer. Those who refused to cooperate were sometimes paid back by being snubbed in her column and on the air. (While not necessarily in connection with this show, she fostered turbulent relationships for lengthy spells with people like Joan Crawford, Louis B. Mayer, Ronald Reagan, Frank Sinatra, Orson Welles and some others.)

Not until the Radio Guild openly revolted against the practice of free broadcasts in 1938 did it all come to a halt and Campbell had to start paying celebrities what they were accustomed to receiving elsewhere. By then Dick Powell was gone as emcee—replaced in brief stints by five other Hollywood leading men—and Parsons, too, was off the show. "If she had done nothing else," observed a critic, "Parsons had opened the West to radio." *Lux Radio Theater*, *Kraft Music Hall* with Bing Crosby, *Shell Chateau* with Al Jolson and other noteworthy series left the Eastern shore to relocate in the West. By the 1940s, Los Angeles was originating much of the audience participation entertainment aired in American homes. Parsons was at the forefront of that conversion.

Parsons attempted a reprise of the earlier *Hollywood Hotel* in 1941 with a low-budget imitation, *Hollywood Premiere,* also on CBS, this time for Lever Brothers. Showing some kind of resiliency or possibly stupidity, she still convinced yet another sponsor she could attract big names on her name. But it didn't work that time: the icons were accustomed and determined to be paid for their services and after three months of it, Parsons reneged on her promise to deliver them gratis. The American Federation of Radio Artists and the Screen Actors Guild came down on the show—and her. For five months, guests were paid their just due and then the show quietly left the air, leaving Parsons somewhat sullied.

In that epoch Parsons saw her popularity as the reigning queen of Hollywood gossip threatened by Hedda Hopper, an upstart who came through the ranks of silent and sound pictures, acquired some minor radio acting roles and was—by then—on the air for Sunkist Growers (1939–1942), a latent Parsons underwriter. Hopper also had launched her own newspaper gossip column. The two women would seldom if ever see eye-to-eye, and Parsons would recapture what she had lost at all costs. She did that very thing by signing with Andrew Jergens in 1944 for a quarter-hour on Sunday nights immediately following her old nemesis Walter Winchell, who aired for the same sponsor. That in itself was cutthroat competition for he moved heaven and earth to ferret out morsels of Hollywood gossip that she intended to divulge when she came on the air just after he signed off. "Her hatchet was unsheathed," observed one reviewer. Parsons was trying to keep Winchell at bay while fending off assaults in print and on the air from Hopper. It was a precarious spot, yet she gradually regained her tarnished status as the queen of the Hollywood gossipmongers. That radio series lasted to 1951.

Parsons turned up in a few movies, too: *Show People* (1928); *Hollywood Hotel* (1937); *Screen Snapshots 25th Anniversary* (1945); *Without Reservations* (1946); *Screen Snapshots No. 5* (1947); *Screen Snapshots—Jimmy McHugh's Song Party* (1951); *Hollywood Glamour on Ice* (1957); and in a cameo in *Starlift* (1951).

Parsons maintained her influence into the 1960s. She wrote her last column in December 1965. An assistant, Dorothy Manners, acquired the column; she had reportedly been writing it for more than a year. Parsons' longstanding feud with Hedda Hopper was highlighted in *Malice in Wonderland,* a CBS-TV movie on May 12, 1985 starring Elizabeth Taylor as Parsons and Jane Alexander as Hopper.

A source summarized Parsons' career-long contributions: "Parsons established herself as the social and moral arbiter of Hollywood. Her judgments were considered the final word in most cases, and her disfavor was feared more than that of movie critics. Her column was followed religiously and thus afforded her a unique type and degree of power."

PAUL, RALPH. b. Oct. 11, 1920, Denver, Colo.; d. November 1987, Amityville, N.Y. *Announcer.* **Series:** *The Aldrich Family* (ca, 1952–1953); *The Mighty Casey* (1947); *Mother Knows Best* (1949–1950); *Scout About Town* (1946); *Seven Front Street* (1947); *Strike It Rich* (1947–1957); *True Detective Mysteries* (ca. late 1940s–ca. early 1950s); *Walk a Mile* (1952–?).

In 1941 Ralph Paul—who was to build a show business reputation by introducing a few continuing features in a couple of mediums in the 1940s and 1950s—accompanied coloratura soprano Margaret King on piano and solovox for a quarter-hour each week on the *Monday Musicale* over WBRE, Wilkes-Barre, Pa., where he was a staff announcer. His best-remembered assignment, however, was as emcee Warren Hull's durable sidekick on the radio and television charity audience participation feature *Strike It Rich.* The live show aired weekly on CBS Radio from 1947 to 1950 (in its final months there as a weekday entry) and continued daily on NBC Radio from 1950 to 1957. A daytime video incarnation also aired on CBS-TV from 1951 to 1958 (extending beyond the radio broadcasts), plus a weekly primetime presentation on NBC-TV from 1951 to 1955.

For most of those lengthy runs a gregarious Warren Hull presided and the genial Ralph Paul was pitching sponsor Colgate-Palmolive-Peet's "mar-*vel*-ous" Vel dishwashing powder and "*fab*-u-lous" Fab laundry detergent while introducing the contestants with hard-luck stories. (Paul also announced for Hull on the fleeting variety program *Mother Knows Best.*) Speaking of Hull's role on *Strike It Rich,* however, he once exclaimed: "Those bedroom eyes of his added to the intensity he brought to the show."

Hull was demonstrably involved with the victims of misfortune appearing before him, so much so that he became immersed in their sad situations and emotional in responding to it. *Strike It Rich* producer Walt Framer observed all of this early in Hull's status with the show and even set up a defense mechanism to deal with it. At such times, tears dimming his eyes, his voice lost in a well of emotion, Hull simply wasn't in any condition to continue until he regained his composure. Sensing that he was breaking down, Framer would signal Ralph Paul to stand by. "On occasion, he [Paul] has had to walk right onto the stage and take over," Framer confided to a magazine reporter. In Paul's case, at least, the "star" (as well as the show) was even more dependent upon its announcer to occasionally carry the program than most other broadcast series expected.

PEARSON, ANDREW RUSSELL (DREW). b. Dec. 13, 1897, Evanston, Ill.; d. Sept. 1, 1969, Maryland. *Commentator, Emcee, Newscaster.* **Series:** *Drew Pearson* (commentator, 1941–1942); *Drew Pearson Comments* (commentator, 1942–1953); *Listen America,* aka *Calling America* (commentator, 1939–1940); *Sunday Evening News of the World* (newscaster, 1940–1941); *Washington Merry-Go-Round* (co-host, 1935–1936, 1940).

Journalist Drew Pearson had the ability to make the headlines as readily as he reported them. Not all of his shenanigans endeared him to the hearts of public figures who were frequently his subjects, however. For instance, President Franklin D. Roosevelt branded him "a chronic liar" and FDR's successor in office—Harry S Truman—declared that "S.O.B. is as simple as ABC" in reference to the newsman. Sen. Walter George (D-Ga.) went further, characterizing Pearson as "an ordinary, congenital, deliberate and malicious liar." Sen. Kenneth McKellar (D-Tenn.) was more emphatic, labeling Pearson "an ignorant liar, a pusillanimous liar, a peewee liar ... a natural born liar, a liar during his manhood, a liar by profession, a liar for a living, a liar in the daytime, a congenital liar, a liar in the nighttime. It is remarkable how he can lie.... This human skunk cannot change his smell." Sen. Theodore Bilbo (D-Miss.) pontificated: "He gathers slime, mud and slander from all parts of the earth and lets them ooze out through his radio broadcasts and ... a few newspapers."

Pearson was capable of offending members of both political parties equally. Sen. Joseph R. McCarthy (R-Wis.) tagged him "a journalistic fake and prostitute ... degenerate liar ... twisted, perverted mentality." To Sen.

William Jenner (R-Ind.) Pearson was merely a "filthy brainchild conceived in ruthlessness" while to Rep. Phillip Bennett (R-Mo.) he was a "dishonest, unreliable, vicious character assassin." One of Pearson's contemporary broadcaster-columnists, Walter Winchell, allowed: "This S.O.B. makes a racket, a business, a mint of money writing fiction in the guise of news reporting." Still another, newspaper columnist Westbrook Pegler, viewed him as "a slippery, devious fellow, absolutely insensitive to the inhibitions of truth and ethics." And they are only *samples* of the feathers Pearson ruffled over a protracted career in print and electronic journalism! Luther Sies, contemporary radio historiographer, mused pontifically: "Drew Pearson must have been a valuable commentator if he could attract such a widely diverse set of enemies."

Pearson was born into a family of moderate financial means. His dad had been a Methodist minister but left his faith to teach elocution and English at Swathmore College, a Pennsylvania Quaker school. The family quickly embraced that religion, which was to have significant impact on their lives. Dr. Paul Pearson (Drew's father), a Democrat, was later appointed by President Herbert Hoover, a Republican, as governor of the U.S. Virgin Islands. Drew, meanwhile, earned a scholarship to Phillips Exeter Academy, and acquired a developing interest in foreign affairs, intending to pursue diplomatic service. He graduated from Swathmore in 1919 and joined a Quaker unit working among refugees of the First World War in what is presently Serbia and Montenegro. For a couple of years he devoted himself to helping those people—mostly farmers by trade—restore their lives to normalcy.

Returning to America, Pearson taught geography for a little while at the University of Pennsylvania. Exhibiting a wanderlust that remained with him for years, he was soon off on a round-the-world journey that took a year-and-a-half to complete. He had pre-sold freelance articles on his adventures to several newspapers and made good on his pledge. The environment laid the groundwork for a syndicated column he would proffer throughout the remainder of his life. There were several additional trips overseas from which he would return to write and recall on the lecture circuits.

Finally settling down for a while, in his mid twenties he became a geography instructor at Columbia University. Then he was hired as the foreign editor of the *United States Daily*, precursor newsmagazine of the *U.S. News & World Report*. Concurrently, he accepted a position as diplomatic correspondent of *The Baltimore Sun*. While performing those dual duties, Pearson took a third—prohibited—job as the western hemisphere director of the Irish Sweepstakes. That secret assignment compensated him with $30,000 annually and provided a chauffeured Lincoln Continental as one of its perks. In his responsibility he oversaw ticket smuggling and sales efforts while generating publicity for the enterprise. Astonishingly, for whatever the reason, his scandalous involvement in a totally illicit activity was never publicly revealed. Had they known of his shady and illegal dealings, legions of Pearson's adversaries would have used it to great personal advantage.

In the meantime, Pearson found in world affairs writer Robert S. Allen, the Washington bureau chief of *The Christian Science Monitor*, common interests and an enduring friendship. The pair collaborated on a book published anonymously under the title *Washington Merry-Go-Round* (Horace Liveright, 1931). It was a collection of gossip-ridden news items surrounding key figures in public service. When the authorship was ultimately identified some time later, Allen was promptly fired by his newspaper. He was later hired by International News Service and then fired a second time due to pressure from a disgruntled victim of his exposé. Not until the duo issued a sequel, *More Merry-Go-Round* in 1932, however, was Pearson terminated by both publications employing him. In one sense he should have quit while he was ahead; on the other hand, it paved the way for a lifetime of journalistic notoriety.

United Features Syndicate subsequently accepted a daily newspaper column titled "Washington Merry-Go-Round" from Pearson and Allen. Launched with six subscribers, it eventually grew to 620 papers. The column put the screws to those in the seats of power and in proper Washington society, too, making unflattering disclosures a practice. Historian Sies acknowledged: "His [Pearson's] attacks against perceived wrongs, probably was never more valuable than when he led the charge against Joseph McCarthy." The foibles of public servitude revealed in that column—plus what transpired with the messenger—makes absorbing reading in Oliver R. Pilat's meticulous report *Drew Pearson: An Unauthorized Biography* (Harper, 1973).

In addition to the newspaper column, which Pearson penned solo after Allen departed for wartime service (1941–1945)—the two men severing their partnership after Allen's return—Pearson himself published 10 volumes. Prominent among them were *The American Diplomatic Game* (Doubleday, 1935); *U.S.A.—Second Class Power?* (Simon and Schuster, 1958); *The Case Against Congress: A Compelling Indictment of Corruption on Capitol Hill* (Simon and Schuster, 1968); and *Drew Pearson: Diaries, 1949–1959* (Holt, Rinehart & Winston, 1974), plus a newsletter, *Personal from Pearson*.

Before their split, nonetheless, Pearson and Allen's notoriety put them before a microphone where they gave listeners an engaging audible version of the sometimes shocking tidbits appearing in their column. Pearson continued alone on the air after 1940. That year he set off a tumult when—as a guest on the NBC public affairs series *The University of Chicago Roundtable*—he advanced the notion that promoters of Herbert Hoover were stumping Dixie in an effort to purchase delegates to the Republican National Convention. University VP Fred C. Woodward unleashed another hullabaloo on the following week's program by denouncing Pearson's assertions as patently false while expressing contrition for his (Pearson's) remarks to Hoover. An irate Pearson warned of a possible lawsuit. If little else was accomplished, it clearly demonstrated his mettle.

An announcer introduced him on each installment with "And now, Drew Pearson, whose predictions have proved to be eighty-four per cent accurate!" That left no less than a 16 percent margin for error. He may have met his quota. One such occasion occurred in July 1940 when Pearson prophesied that Germany would defeat Great Britain. To a nation highly sensitive to the issue and exhibiting a robust compassion for the Anglo-French stance, the remark drew extensive unfavorable reaction. His reputation was sullied further when he took unswerving liberal positions during the Cold War epoch of the late 1940s and early 1950s. A groundswell of anti–Communist fanaticism was sweeping the industry then, inviting scrupulous prying by government agencies into the particular leanings of those with power to influence. Unlike some of his peers, Pearson kept his job on that occasion but some of his verbiage was suspect just the same.

Always one to appreciate a good fight, Pearson was involved in righting perceived racial inequities long before it was popular to do so. He adopted a strong position against the Ku Klux Klan. Not only that, he came down hard on the white supremacist ex-governor of Georgia, Eugene Talmadge. In a rainstorm in July 1946 he set up his microphone outside the Peach State's capitol in Atlanta and flaunted his tirade against the establishment while airing his ABC program live. In 1947 he revealed that Rep. Robert F. Jones (R-Ohio), who had been nominated (and was subsequently elected) to the Federal Communications Commission by President Truman, was identified a dozen years earlier with the infamous secret racist and revolutionary society Black Legion. Indeed, when Pearson saw something he disagreed with, somebody would hear about it. He may have fought for righteous causes but many of those created remorseless enemies for him.

Pearson was among a cadre of ABC-TV reporters providing on-the-spot coverage of the 1952 political conventions. For about eight months in 1952–1953 the Washington political columnist presided over the *Washington Merry-Go-Round*, a half-hour commentary initially aired by ABC-TV and later by Dumont Television. It bore the same moniker as Pearson's widely read syndicated newspaper column. In addition to his news analysis there, he continued to offer his "Predictions of Things to Come," having done so on radio earlier. Between 1954 and 1957 the feature was reduced to a quarter-hour and syndicated to local television stations.

Following his death, a tax-exempt charitable trust that Pearson created was renamed the Pearson Foundation; it awarded citations annually for investigative journalism brilliance. Citing the trio that was recognized in 1972—*Washington Post* reporters Carl Bernstein, Robert Woodward and Barry Sussman, who uncovered the Watergate mess—biographer

Irving Fang concluded: "No doubt Drew Pearson, the S.O.B., would have been pleased."

PEARSON, FORT. b. May 3, 1909; d. Feb. 19, 1989. *Announcer.* **Series:** *Beat the Band* (ca. 1944); *Comedy of Errors* (1949–1952); *The Guiding Light* (1937–?); *Hoosier Hot Shots* (1950–1951); *Lonely Women* (ca. 1942–ca. 1943); *Queen for a Day* (ca. late 1940s, 1950s); *The Quiz Kids* (1940–ca. late 1940s); *Terry Regan, Attorney at Law* (1938).

Fort Pearson's broadcasting career began at Shreveport, La. and successively carried him in the 1930s to Port Arthur and Houston, Tex. (to KPRC in the latter city) before landing him in the big time in Chicago. In between network gigs, at varying times from the mid 1930s to the mid 1940s Pearson served on the staffs of a couple of major Windy City outlets, WENR and WMAQ. Rotating back-and-forth between them, he carried responsibilities on the air as an announcer, newscaster and sportscaster. He was also a sportscaster for NBC, operating out of Chicago. Pearson's ethereal responsibilities were interrupted temporarily in the early 1940s when he served as a lieutenant in the U.S. Navy.

PEARSON, TED. b. Nov. 3, 1902, Arlington, Neb.; d. Oct. 5, 1961, California. *Announcer.* **Series:** *The Adventures of the Thin Man* (ca. late 1940s, early 1950s); *The Armour Hour* (1927–1931); *The Cavalcade of America* (1947–1948); *The CBS Radio Workshop* (1956–1957); *Conoco Tourist Adventures* (1930–1932); *The Empire Builders* (1929–1931); *Florsheim Frolics* (1930–1933); *Good News of 1938* (1937–1938); *The Halsey, Stuart Program* (1928–1932); *The King Cole Trio* (1946–1948); *Maytag Minstrel Show* (1929); *The Paul Whiteman Painters* (1931–1932); *The Studebaker Champions* (1929–1931); *We, the Abbotts* (1940–1942); *Young Doctor Malone* (ca. 1939–early 1940s).

After graduating from high school in Arlington, Neb., Ted Pearson's ambition to become a professional vocalist carried him to Minneapolis where—following six months of working with a paving gang and modeling for art classes—he enrolled at MacPhail School of Music. Afterward he enrolled at the American Conservatory of Music in Chicago. On a visit home to Arlington, Pearson met a radio executive who offered him a post at a small Gary, Ind. station, WJKS. There he spent 12 hours daily announcing, digging up talent and filling airtime singing and reading monologues.

An NBC talent scout was responsible for Pearson's return to Chicago where he began introducing early morning programs. Within a couple of years he was announcing feature series from Chicago, New York and Hollywood. Pearson was among the pioneering interlocutors that broke ground for NBC-based series emanating from the Midwest. Some of the shows he introduced on the Red and Blue chains were previously heard in trial runs on local outlets and regional hookups.

Pearson also enjoyed a brief acquaintance with theatrical productions, appearing in bit parts in seven films: *Navy Blue and Gold* (1937); *You're Only Young Once* (1937); *Test Pilot* (1938); *Dick Tracy's G-Men* (1939); *Boy Friend* (1939); *The Day the Earth Stood Still* (1951); and *Mr. Belvedere Rings the Bell* (1951).

PELLETIER, VINCENT J. b. March 21, 1908, Minneapolis, Minn.; d. Feb. 25, 1994, Los Angeles, Calif. *Announcer.* **Series:** *Aunt Mary* (ca. early 1950s); *Calling All Detectives* (narrator, 1945); *The Carnation Contented Hour* (1942–1945); *Father Knows Best* (actor, 1949–1954); *The First Nighter* (1952–1953); *Grand Hotel* (ca. early to mid 1940s); *Hollywood Bowl Concert* (1952); *Hollywood Searchlight* (1953); *Hymns of All Churches* (1938–1946); *Masquerade* (ca. 1946–1947); *The Railroad Hour* (actor, 1949–154); *Speak Up, America* (1940); *This is Life* (host-reader, 1941–1942); *Today's Children* (ca. 1943–?); *Vic and Sade* (ca. 1940–ca. 1942).

Vincent Pelletier—the son of concert artist Mabel Pelletier—first went on the air at 15 as an amateur vocalist. (Some authorities spell the surname Peletier.) The year was 1923. After graduating from high school, he attended the University of Minnesota for two-and-a-half years. Anxious to earn enough to complete college, Pelletier gained an audition at a local radio station that netted him a spot as an announcer. As so often happens, his success prevented him from returning to school. In addition to his interlocutory skills, Pelletier also appeared with a quartet, at times as a baritone vocalist or as a piano accompanist. Later, he was studio manager of yet another Minneapolis station.

He persisted there until 1937 when he joined NBC's Chicago announcing staff. Subsequently, Pelletier developed longstanding links with the Carnation Co. and General Mills, Inc. (the latter firm headquartered in his native city) and was one of their prime commercial spokesmen for many years. On NBC-TV he introduced *The Nat King Cole Show* (1956–1957), a weekly pop music series starring the namesake vocalist and pianist.

PERRIN, VICTOR HERBERT. b. April 26, 1916, Menomonee Falls, Wis.; d. July 4, 1989, Los Angeles, Calif. *Actor, Announcer.* **Series:** *The Adventures of Nero Wolfe* (actor, ca. 1943, 1944, 1946, 1950–1951, 1952); *The Adventures of Philip Marlowe* (actor, 1947, 1948–1950, 1951); *The CBS Radio Workshop* (actor, 1956–1957); *The Clyde Beatty Show* (actor, 1950–1952); *Coronet Storyteller* (1944–1945); *Crime Classics* (actor, 1953–1954); *Dr. Paul* (actor, 1951–1953); *Dragnet* (actor, 1949–1957); *Escape* (actor, 1947–1954); *Fort Laramie* (actor, 1956); *Frontier Gentleman* (actor, 1958); *Gunsmoke* (actor, 1952–1961); *Have Gun, Will Travel* (1958–1960); *Heartbeat Theater* (actor, 1956–?); *Luke Slaughter of Tombstone* (actor, 1958); *One Man's Family* (actor, ca. 1950s); *Pete Kelly's Blues* (actor, 1951); *Rogers of the Gazette* (actor, 1953–1954); *The Roy Rogers Show*, aka *Happy Trails* (actor, ca. 1944–1945, 1946–1947, 1948–1953, 1954–1955); *The Sears Radio Theater*, aka *The Mutual Radio Theater* (actor, 1971–1981); *The Story of Holly Sloan* (actor, 1947–1948); *Suspense* (actor, ca. 1940s–ca. 1962); *Yours Truly, Johnny Dollar* (actor, ca. 1949–ca. 1962); *The Zane Grey Show*, aka *The Zane Grey Theater* (actor, 1947–1948).

A junior staff announcer at NBC in Hollywood in the early 1940s, Vic Perrin soon advanced to chief announcer for the Blue Network. He was cast in copious roles of the so-called "adult" westerns that arrived on radio en masse in the 1950s. Perrin, whom media historian John Dunning classified as one of *Gunsmoke's* "steadiest" character actors, recalled years later: "Doing *Gunsmoke* was more fun than attending the Academy Awards." He penned at least one script for the venerable aural series "with a good part for himself," noted critic Leonard Maltin. From 1963 to 1965 he contributed the infamous voiceovers for the introduction and conclusion of the ABC-TV science fiction anthology thriller *The Outer Limits*: "There is nothing wrong with your television set...."

PETRIE, HOWARD. b. Nov. 22, 1906, Beverly, Mass.; d. March 24, 1968, Keene, N.H. *Announcer.* **Series:** *Abie's Irish Rose* (1942–1944); *Big Sister* (ca. 1940s); *Blondie* (1940s); *The Edgar Bergen and Charlie McCarthy Show*; *The Garry Moore Show*, aka *The Show Without a Name*, aka *Everything Goes* (1942–1943, 1949–1950); *The Jack Carson Show* (ca. 1955–1956); *The Jimmy Durante Show* (1947–1950); *The Jimmy Durante–Garry Moore Show* (1943–1945); *The Judy Canova Show* (1947–1951); *The Man I Married* (1939–1942); *The O'Neills* (ca. early 1940s); *The Ray Bolger Show* (1945); *The Rexall Summer Theater* (1945, 1947); *Sweeney and March* (ca. 1948).

In the first few years of his life, Howard Petrie's family resided in multiple New England coastal hamlets, finally putting down permanent roots at Sommerville, Mass. in 1915. Between then and the time he was 14 the adolescent went to Boston on Sundays where he sang in the choir at the Cathedral Church of St. Paul. Meanwhile, he joined his high school drama group, debate team and glee club and played violin with assorted instrumental ensembles. Following graduation in 1924, Petrie pursued a developing interest in music, enrolling at the New England Conservatory of Music. He was a private voice pupil of Ivan Moawski in Boston and a violin student of John C. Mullaly, an ex–Boston Symphony artist. In his spare time, Petrie devoted himself to choir work for a myriad of congregations and was bass soloist at Dorchester's historic Meeting House First Parish Church.

In August 1929, perhaps providentially—two months before the worst economic collapse in the nation's history—he stopped by the studios of Boston-Springfield's WBZ-WBZA to try out for an announcing vacancy. Petrie was hired on the spot as a junior interlocutor. After less than a year's understudy he signed with NBC in New York on June 16, 1930. Actually, he was one of 10 making the final cut out of 2,500 applicants in 1930–1931.

After almost all of his network radio series left the air, Petrie enjoyed something of a show business revival from 1947 to 1957 in another medium, film. During that decade he turned up in 31 motion pictures. Among the titles: *The Hal Roach Comedy Carnival* (1947); *Fancy Pants* (1950); *Walk Softly, Stranger* (1950); *The Racket* (1951); *Bend in the River* (1952); *The Wild North* (1952); *Red Ball Express* (1952); *Carbine Williams* (1952); *Trouble Along the Way* (1953); *Seven Brides for Seven Brothers* (1954); *The Bob Mathias Story* (1954); *The Return of Jack Slade* (1955); *The Maverick Queen* (1956); *A Kiss Before Dying* (1956); *Johnny Concho* (1956); and *The Tin Star* (1957).

Petrie acquired yet another "career" in television where he appeared as a character actor on numerous series between the mid 1950s and early 1960s. He is found in occasional episodes of at least 26 video series: *Alcoa Theatre*; *Appointment with Destiny*; *Bat Masterson*; *Bonanza*; *Broken Arrow*; *Bronco*; *The Californians*; *Casey Jones*; *Cheyenne*; *Colt .45*; *Crossroads*; *Death Valley Days*; *Frontier Justice*; *Gunsmoke*; *Have Gun, Will Travel*; *Johnny Ringo*; *Lawman*; *Letter to Loretta*; *The Life and Legend of Wyatt Earp*; *M Squad*; *Maverick*; *National Velvet*; *Perry Mason*; *Rawhide*; *Wanted—Dead or Alive*; and *The Zane Grey Theater*. In addition, from 1964 to 1965 Petrie played Otto Zimmerman in the CBS-TV daytime serial *The Edge of Night*.

PETRUZZI, JACK. *Actor, Announcer.* **Series:** *The Count of Monte Cristo* (actor, 1946–1947, 1948, 1949–1952); *The Green Hornet* (actor, 1938–ca. early 1940s); *Jeff Regan, Investigator*, aka *The Lion's Eye* (actor, 1948, 1949–1950); *The Lone Ranger* (actor, ca. 1930s–ca. early 1940s); *Ma Perkins* (actor, ca. early-mid 1940s); *Masquerade* (actor, 1946–1947); *Ned Jordan, Secret Agent* (ca. late 1930s, early 1940s); *Road of Life* (actor, ca. early–mid 1940s).

PFEIFFER, ROBERT O. b. June 12, 1926, Iowa; d. April 22, 2003, Council Bluffs, Iowa. *Announcer.* **Series:** *Answer Please* (1958); *The Bickersons* (commercial spokesman, 1951); *Ma Perkins* (late 1950s–1960).

In 1947 Bob Pfeiffer was a newscaster at WMT, Cedar Rapids, Iowa. In 1948 and 1949 he hosted *Operation Success* on the Dumont Television network. It was a public service series in which Pfeiffer interviewed disabled vets, asking the audience to respond with job offers. The show claimed 100 percent placement. A few years later, beginning Nov. 2, 1953, he introduced a stunt show for adolescents, *Choose up Sides*, on WCBS-TV in New York with Dean Miller as emcee. By 1956 the show went national on NBC-TV with Don Pardo announcing and Gene Rayburn hosting.

On Nov. 25, 1960—soap opera's final day on network radio—Pfeiffer uttered syllables that have been immortalized by vintage radio fans during the years since. Presenting actress Virginia Payne, who had unceasingly given expression to possibly the medium's most beloved heroine, he concluded the last of those quarter-hour visits by lamenting: "And so, after more than 7,000 broadcasts—27 years—we say 'good-by' to *Ma Perkins*. This is Bob Pfeiffer speaking." It was a somber moment and—captured on tape—generally has been a quintessential reminder signifying a most unpleasant day for legions of daytime serial partisans.

PIERCE, CARL WEBSTER. b. June 30, 1898, Quincy, Mass.; d. Aug. 16, 1962, Los Angeles, Calif. *Announcer.* **Series:** *Breakfast at Sardi's*, aka *Breakfast with Breneman*, aka *Breakfast in Hollywood* (1942–ca. 1948).

POST, EMILY (born Emily Price). b. Oct. 27, 1873, Baltimore, Md.; d. Sept. 25, 1960, New York, N.Y. *Consultant (etiquette).* **Series:** *Emily Post* (consultant, 1930–1933, 1934); *How to Get the Most Out of Life* (consultant, 1937–1938); *The Right Thing to Do* (consultant, 1938–1939).

According to one source, Emily Post "became the nation's most famous authority on how to behave graciously in society and business." Left to raise two children following her divorce in 1905, she turned to writing for financial subsistence. She penned newspaper articles on a couple of special interests, architecture and interior decoration, as well as society columns, travelogues, features and serialized narratives. She sold these to newspapers and sundry mass circulated slick periodicals like *The Century*, *Harper's* and *Scribner's*. Furthermore, she authored several graceful fiction volumes including *The Flight of a Moth* (Dodd, Mead, 1904); *Purple and Fine Linen* (D. Appleton and Co., 1905); *Woven in the Tapestry* (1908), *The Title Market* (1909) and *The Eagle's Feather* (1910). Yet it was a later tome, *Etiquette: The Blue Book of Social Usage* (Funk & Wagnalls, 1922) that defined her career, establishing her as the nation's key advisor in matters of manners, etiquette and social and business graces. The latter book, incidentally, was updated 10 times and was in its 89th printing at the time of her death.

Many other volumes followed: a syndicated column appeared in more than 200 newspapers nationwide; radio series on three of the four major chains (all but MBS); legions of speaking engagements and—in 1946 she founded the Emily Post Institute, where problems of gracious living were scrutinized. The institute persisted following her demise, directed initially by Elizabeth Lindley Post, then by Peggy Grayson Post, the latter a great-granddaughter-in-law. Contemporary versions of Emily Post, according to a web site, include Judith "Miss Manners" Martin and Martha Stewart.

POWELL, KENNETH C. b. ca. 1914; d. March 11, 1976. *Announcer, Newscaster.* **Series:** *Chick Carter, Boy Detective* (1943–1945); *Dr. I.Q., the Mental Banker* (roving announcer, 1940s); *News for Women* (newscaster, 1945); *Nick Carter, Master Detective* (1943–?).

From 1947 to 1949 Ken Powell was the disc jockey in residence at the *1400 Club* over Elmira, New York's WELM.

PRENTISS, ED. b. Sept. 9, 1909, Chicago, Ill.; d. March 18, 1992, Los Angeles, Calif. *Announcer, Actor.* **Series:** *The Air Adventures of Jimmy Allen* (1933–1934, 1935–1936); *Armstrong of the SBI* (ca. 1950–ca. 1951); *Arnold Grimm's Daughter* (actor, 1937–?); *The Bartons* (actor, 1939–early 1940s); *Captain Midnight* (actor, 1938–1949); *Dave Garroway Show,* aka *Dial Dave Garroway,* aka *Sunday/Friday with Dave Garroway* (substitute announcer, 1947, 1949–1953, 1954–1955); *The First Nighter* (host); *The Guiding Light* (actor-narrator, 1937–1946); *Holland Housewife* (cast member, 1941); *Jack Armstrong, the All-American Boy* (ca. 1940s); *Johnny Lujack of Notre Dame* (actor, 1949); *A Life in Your Hands* (actor, 1949, 1950, 1951, 1952); *Painted Dreams* (actor, 1933–1934, 1935–1936, 1940); *The Right to Happiness* (actor, 1940s); *The Romance of Helen Trent* (actor, ca. 1930s–ca. 1950s); *Silver Eagle, Mountie* (early 1950s); *Sweet River* (actor, 1943–1944); *A Tale of Today* (actor, 1936–1939); *This is the Story* (1944); *Today's Children* (narrator, 1944–1946); *Woman in White* (narrator, 1944–1946).

Ed Prentiss was paid the ultimate compliment when a 1944 character in NBC's West Coast serial drama *The Gallant Heart,* portrayed by actor Ken Christy, was named Ed Prentiss for a radio thespian.

When soap opera drama mama Irna Phillips launched several experimental innovations among the daytime serials airing in what was commonly referred to as "The General Mills Hour" in the early 1940s on NBC—all underwritten by the Minneapolis mega foods manufacturer—she elevated Ed Prentiss, who was then appearing as Ned Holden in *The Guiding Light,* to narrator for a trio of Phillips-inspired narratives in that time zone: in addition to *Light, Today's Children* and *Woman in White* were included. Removing the walls that had heretofore separated the three serials, Phillips allowed figures from those programs to interact with residents of the other tales included under that umbrella. Prentiss acted as the "glue" holding the trilogy together.

Prentiss left radio to act in a few television series: he narrated a sitcom lasting three months in 1949, ABC's *That's O'Toole*; he presided over three fleeting ABC entries in the 1949–1950 season—*Action Autographs, Dr. Fix-Um* and *Majority Rules*; he appeared sporadically as a banker on NBC's *Bonanza* (an epic western drama airing from 1959 to 1973); and landed stints in a couple of NBC daytime serials, *Morning Star* (1965–1966) and *Days of Our Lives* (1966).

PRESBY, ARCH. b. March 16, 1906, Canada; d. March 1987. *Announcer, Emcee.* **Series:** *Abbott and Costello Junior Youth Foundation* (1947); *Breakfast in Hollywood* (host, ca. late 1940s–1950); *Bughouse Rhythm* (1936–1937); *The Cass Daley Show* (1950); *Smilin' Ed and His Buster Brown Gang* (1944–1953); *The Truitts* (1950, 1951); *Your Crossword Quiz* (1948).

In the late 1930s Arch Presby left the NBC affiliate in Portland, Ore., KGW, where he had been honing his skills as an announcer, to join NBC's staff in San Francisco.

On *Smilin' Ed and His Buster Brown Gang*, Presby doubled as Froggy the Gremlin whenever he and the host rendered a duet. For the benefit of an energized studio audience filled with little tykes convulsing into raucous laughter, shouting, foot-stomping and hand-clapping—a response that invariably electrified millions of other kids listening at home—Presby appeared in amphibian attire after McConnell instructed: "Come out from behind that curtain, Froggy, and let the kids see what you really look like!" At that, Froggy plunked his magic twanger and materialized on stage to the crowd's delight, harassing the show's erudite guests. Froggy (Presby) repetitiously exclaimed in toad-style basso profundo: "Now I'll sing my song, I will. I will."

Smilin' Ed was such a success on radio that it was reincarnated in the newer format of television in 1950, complete with the original cast of characters heard on radio, including a Presby-inspired Froggy the Gremlin. From its debut in video, the show was filmed in Hollywood, most unusual for a 1950s series beamed at adolescents. For a year it ran on NBC; switched to CBS in 1951; then to ABC in 1953; went off the networks after McConnell's demise on July 24, 1954; and returned to NBC from 1957 to 1958 as *Andy's Gang* hosted by comic actor Andy Devine.

In the summer of 1952, meanwhile, Presby appeared on a half-hour daily NBC-TV series, *The Johnny Dugan Show*, about which a pundit wrote: "This was an unspectacular musical variety show from Hollywood with a studio audience starring little-known vocalist Johnny Dugan, with Arch Presby as his sidekick and Barbara Logan as a singer." Perhaps a magic twanger would have made it spectacular after all.

PRICE, VINCENT LEONARD, JR. b. May 27, 1911, St. Louis, Mo.; d. Oct. 25, 1993, Los Angeles, Calif. *Announcer.* **Series:** *The Series Radio Theater*, aka *The Mutual Radio Theater* (host, 1979–1981).

Vincent Price is best recalled by millions of theater-goers for roles in a plethora of low-budget horror motion pictures in which his distinctive voice and serio-comic demeanor typecast him throughout his working life. "In such films," a source said, "his tall physique and polished urbane manner made him something of an American counterpart to the older Boris Karloff." Yale-educated, Price first appeared on stage in 1935; he made his first movie three years later. Over his career he turned up in 168 theatrical and television films (1938–1995, the last released two years after his death). He was in another 132 guest shots on various televised series and was a recurring panelist on CBS-TV's game show *Pantomime Quiz* (1950–1952).

Price also contributed to bringing radio drama back to the airwaves when CBS presented an anthology five nights weekly in 1979. A different host each weeknight introduced a particular style of narrative. Price offered mysteries on Wednesday nights. Other narrators: Lorne Greene, Monday (western night); Andy Griffith, Tuesday (comedy night); Cicely Tyson, Thursday (drama night); Richard Widmark, Friday (adventure night). The series persisted through 1981 although in those days it was under a new moniker on a different network and virtually in repeats of earlier broadcasts. By then the bloom was definitely off the rose.

PURVIS, MELVIN. b. Oct. 24, 1903, Timmonsville, S.C.; d. Feb. 29, 1960, Florence, S.C. *Announcer.* **Series:** *Top Secrets of the FBI* (narrator, ca. 1930s); *True Adventures of Junior G-Men* (announcer-host, 1936–1938).

Former FBI agent Melvin Purvis opened and closed *Top Secrets of the FBI*, a radio feature celebrating the work of "the most efficient, the most scientific law enforcement organization in the world." Purvis was present at the fatal shooting of John Dillinger—the FBI's "most wanted man"—on July 22, 1934, outside Chicago's Biograph Theater. While Purvis never fired at the notorious bank robber, he embellished his involvement in the episode for years, displaying to audiences the weapon he single-handedly "killed" Dillinger with. It is a legend that has persisted since and has often been repeated in print, yet has been refuted by FBI sources.

PUTNAM, GEORGE ARTHUR (aka George Arthur). b. Jan. 21, 1914, Middletown,

N.Y.; d. April 8, 1975, North Hollywood, Calif. *Announcer, Newscaster.* **Series:** *George Putnam and the News* (newscaster, 1943–1944); *Joe and Mabel,* aka *Women and Children First* (1941, 1942); *Justice Triumphs* (narrator, 1947); *Lorenzo Jones* (ca. 1940s, 1950s); *Lucky U Ranch* (1952–1954); *Portia Faces Life* (1940s–1951); *Short, Short Story* (host-narrator, 1940–1941).

In the 1920s George Putnam's family moved across the country from New York to San Diego. By the mid to late 1930s, he was working for that city's KGB Radio. He left KGB in 1938 to return East, joining the announcing staff that year at CBS. Not long afterward he shifted his allegiance to NBC.

Utter confusion has reigned for many years between *this* George Putnam and the one whose entry follows. Multiple published documentaries have transposed some of the details of one's life, mistakenly linking them with the other individual; various sources certify, for instance, that both men were Minnesota natives when actually only one was. Gasoline has been added to the fire by the fact—not only were both born within six months of each other and chose on-air announcing as their professions—both ultimately migrated to the New York and Los Angeles broadcasting markets. With so many commonalities, it's easy to see how mix-ups occurred, especially by sharing a given moniker and surname. (There is further discord in several sources arising from their dissimilar middle names, incidentally.) Both also arrived at NBC within months of one another.

George Arthur Putnam, who is sometimes professionally identified as George Arthur, was a prolific radio announcer (one scholar hints at as many as 55 series) on network programming originating from New York in the 1940s and 1950s. His voice is perhaps best recalled by an extensive association with a couple of NBC daytime serials, *Lorenzo Jones* and *Portia Faces Life.* After his radio opportunities began to fade on the East Coast, he took up residence a second time on the opposite shore, finding work in due course as an announcer at KNXT, a Los Angeles television outlet. The other George Putnam, meanwhile, had wandered from his Minnesota birthplace to New York. To avoid the obvious confusion between their corresponding appellations, in 1946 the Minnesotan added his then-wife's maiden name, Carson, as his middle name, becoming George Carson Putnam to radio audiences. He subsequently divorced his spouse, moved to Los Angeles (leaving the New York–based programming to George Arthur Putnam), and re-launched his career in L.A. simply as George Putnam. When the other Putnam arrived in town, *he* was the one that time to alter his sobriquet—to George Arthur.

While George Carson Putnam was most prominently identified as a newscaster for much of his career, George Arthur Putnam also conducted a couple of daily 10-minute newscasts on New York's WEAF, flagship outlet of the National Broadcasting Co., during a portion of the time both men were in Gotham, adding to the chaos. Furthermore, he dispatched headlines on an NBC newscast while the other Putnam was away in service during the Second World War.

PUTNAM, GEORGE FREDERICK (aka George Carson Putnam). b. July 14, 1914, Breckenridge, Minn. *Newscaster, Announcer.* **Series:** *The Army Hour* (1942–1945); *Campbell Condensed News* (newscaster, 1939–ca. 1942); *George Putnam and the News* (newscaster, 1946–1950); *Humanizing the News* (newscaster, 1946–1950); *Salute to Saturday* (newscaster, 1939–1944); *Spotlight on America* (narrator, 1946); *Sunday News Highlights* (newscaster, 1939–1944).

In 1937 George Frederick Putnam was a sportscaster at KSTP, St. Paul, Minn. He also claims to have announced for impresario Lawrence Welk and his entourage in North Dakota that same year (1937). In the summer of 1939, Putnam joined NBC at Radio City in New York and was soon conducting a trio of news programs. During the Second World War he was drafted into the U.S. Army and then commissioned as a first lieutenant in the U.S. Marine Corps. There he was assigned to coordinate that branch's participation in the Armed Forces Radio Service (1944–1946). Returning to the air as a newscaster for MBS on July 1, 1946, to avoid confusion with another George Putnam at NBC (see entry above), he adopted the maiden name of his wife, war correspondent Lee Carson, as his middle moniker and was billed on the air as George Carson Putnam.

(Several authorities have misspelled her name—and thereby, *his* name—as *Carlson*, adding still more disorder.)

According to *TV Guide*, George Carson Putnam had, by 1951, self-destructed and fallen from grace, was heavily in debt and embroiled in an "unfortunate" marriage that ended in divorce. He left his troubles behind him and took off for L.A. where, late in 1951, he was hired by television station KTTV as a newscaster. Putnam again became identified simply as George Putnam, being 3,000 miles from the other broadcaster by that name.

Nearly two decades later, Maury Green, writing in *The Los Angeles Times* on May 3, 1970, clarified: "Did you know that there are two George Putnams in Los Angeles TV? ... One is the KTTV newscaster. The other is the KNXT announcer, middle name Arthur. Some years ago George (Arthur) Putnam was well-established in radio in New York. Into town came the other George Putnam. To avoid confusion he called himself George Carson Putnam.... Dissolve to Los Angeles several years later. George (no longer Carson) Putnam is well-established as a TV newscaster. Into town comes George (Arthur) Putnam and he gets a job as a TV newscaster. But now the tables are turned so he appears as George Arthur (no Putnam)."

Journalist Walter Winchell claimed George (Carson) Putnam possessed "the greatest voice in radio" and *Time* magazine christened his delivery "silvery, melodious and super-smooth." In between 1941–1944—the "war years"—Putnam was a Movietone newsreel narrator. During the early days of television, meanwhile, he was editor of NBC's *Television Screen Magazine*, an unpolished potpourri of interviews. From 1949 to 1951 he could be found hosting Dumont's daily game show *Headline Clues*, aka *Broadway to Hollywood*.

Putnam gained stupendous notoriety in local Los Angeles television, becoming an object of affection for multiple stations in that market in the 1950s and early 1960s. Columnist Roger M. Grace observed in *The Metropolitan News-Enterprise* in January 2003, "There has never been a more popular and influential newsman in Los Angeles television than Putnam. He's a legend." Putnam's opinionated stands resonated with a segment of viewers and listeners while strongly offending others. In 1934, former President Richard M. Nixon, speaking on videotape on the occasion of KTTV's 35th anniversary, allowed: "He [Putnam] won the admiration and respect of millions of people in southern California due to the fact that everybody could count on him to say exactly what he believed, whether it was popular or not. Some people didn't like what he said; some people liked what he said. But everybody listened to George Putnam. That is why he has been one of the most influential commentators of our times."

Putnam worked for both KTTV and KTLA, competing television stations, twice each. Beginning in the early 1970s he affiliated with various radio stations in the Los Angeles area: KHJ, KCOP, KIEV (since re-lettered KRLA) and KPLS. A call-in show was one of his most admired formats. A star on the Hollywood Walk of Fame, meanwhile, certifies Putnam's substantial contributions to television.

RAWSON, RONALD W. b. Oct. 28, 1917, Iowa; d. July 18, 1994, Cohasset, Mass. *Announcer.* **Series:** *The Adventures of the Thin Man* (1940s); *The Adventures of Topper* (1945); *The Brighter Day* (1948–ca. 1949); *Can You Top This?* (1947); *Guest Star* (1949); *Happy Island*, aka *The Ed Wynn Show* (actor, 1944–1945); *The Hour of Charm* (ca. late 1930s, early 1940s); *Joyce Jordan, M.D.* (1940s); *Life Can Be Beautiful* (1940s, ca. early 1950s); *Lora Lawton* (1947); *Make Yours Music* (1940s); *Mommie and the Men* (1945); *Mystery of the Week* (ca. 1946–ca. 1947); *Portia Faces Life* (ca. late 1940s, early 1950s); *Radio Reader's Digest* (1946–ca. 1948); *The Right to Happiness* (1940s, early 1950s); *Road of Life* (ca. 1940s); *Speed Gibson of the International Secret Police* (ca. 1937–ca. 1938); *Young Doctor Malone* (1940s, 1950s).

Ron Rawson was one of Procter & Gamble's premier pitchmen, plugging commodities from Crisco shortening to Dreft dishwashing powder, Duz detergent to Spic 'n' Span cleanser for walls, woodwork and linoleum. "Liquid Joy makes dishwashing ... almost nice" he assured *Young Doctor Malone* listeners in the 1950s. On *The Right to Happiness*, conversely, he extolled the virtues of the Ivory bar, purportedly 99 and 44/100ths percent pure: "Your fav'rite soap since baby days; It's got those gentle baby ways."

P&G depended on Rawson in dual mediums, in fact. His recognizable voice to daytime radio listeners could be easily identified behind the illustrations during that underwriter's commercials in early television, including such daily fare as *As the World Turns*; *The Edge of Night*; *The Guiding Light*; *Road of Life*; *Search for Tomorrow*; *The Seeking Heart*; and many more.

REDDY, TOM. b. Sept. 30, 1917; d. August 1961. Announcer. **Series:** *The Chesterfield Supper Club* (ca. mid 1940s–1950); *The Fitch Bandwagon* (host, early to mid 1940s); *Guest Star* (1949); *Theater U.S.A.* (1948–1949).

Tom Reddy introduced a syndicated radio series, *The Naval Air Reserve Show*, featuring Paul Weston and his orchestra and The Starlighters vocal ensemble on behalf of Navy recruiting. Reddy hosted *Journey through Life*, a daily CBS-TV series in 1953–1954 in which married couples conferred over their lives together. In the spring of 1958 he returned to the CBS cameras as master of ceremonies for the daytime game show *How Do You Rate* which the network programmed Monday–Thursday. (*The Garry Moore Show* filled the timeslot on Fridays.) The series pit a man and woman against one another in intelligence and problem solving matches.

REED, THEODORE ALAN (born Teddy Bergman). b. Aug. 20, 1907, New York, N.Y.; d. June 14, 1977, Los Angeles, Calif. Actor, Announcer. **Series:** *Abie's Irish Rose* (actor, 1942–1944); *The Adventures of Christopher London* (actor, 1950); *The Adventures of Ellery Queen* (actor, 1947–1948); *The Adventures of Philip Marlowe* (actor, 1947, 1948–1950, 1951); *The Adventures of Sam Spade, Detective* (actor, 1946–1951); *Al Pearce and His Gang* (actor, ca. 1934–1936); *The Baby Snooks Show*, aka *The Ziegfeld Follies of the Air*, aka *Good News of 1938/1939/1940*, aka *Maxwell House Coffee Time*, aka *Toasties Time* (1936, 1937–ca. mid 1940s); *The Bert Lahr Show* (actor, 1933); *Big Sister* (actor, ca. late 1930s–mid 1940s); *The Bob Hope Show*; *Box 13* (actor, 1948–1950s); *Breezin' Along*, aka *Jingo* (co-host, 1939–1940); *The Collier Hour* (actor, ca. 1927–1932); *The Damon Runyon Theater* (actor, 1948); *December Bride* (actor, 1952–1953); *Duffy's Tavern* (actor, 1940, 1941–ca. 1944); *The Eddie Cantor Show* (actor-impersonator, ca. 1930s, early 1940s); *Escape* (actor, 1947–1954); *The Eveready Hour* (actor, ca. 1926–1930); *Falstaff's Fables* (co-host, 1950); *Flash Gordon* (actor, 1935–1936); *Ford Theater* (actor, 1947–1949); *The Fred Allen Show* (actor, 1939–1944); *The George O'Hanlon Show* (actor, 1948–1949); *The Halls of Ivy* (actor, 1950–1952); *Harv and Esther* (actor, 1935–1936); *Heartbeat Theater* (actor, 1956–?); *The Jack Pearl Show* (actor, ca. 1932–1934, ca. 1935, ca. 1936–1937); *Joe Palooka* (actor, 1932); *June's My Girl* (actor, 1948); *The Life of Riley* (actor, ca. 1941, ca. 1944–ca. 1951); *Life with Luigi* (actor, 1948–1953); *Manhattan at Midnight* (actor, 1940–1943); *The Mel Blanc Show* (actor, 1946–1947); *Meyer the Buyer* (actor, mid 1930s); *The Modern Adventures of Casanova* (actor, 1952); *My Friend Irma* (actor, 1947–1954); *Myrt and Marge* (ca. 1930s, early 1940s); *Pages of Romance* (actor, 1932–1933); *Philip Morris Playhouse* (actor, 1941–1944); *Pipe Dreams* (host-comic, 1939); *Quixie Doodles* (1939–1941); *The Rudy Vallee Show*, aka *The Flesischmann Hour*, aka *The Sunshine Hour*, aka *The Royal Gelatin Hour*, aka *Vallee Varieties*, aka *Sealtest Village Store* (mid 1930s–ca. early 1940s); *The Shadow* (actor, ca. 1930s); *The Six Shooter* (actor, 1953–1954); *That's Rich* (actor, 1954); *Tim and Irene*, aka *Fun in Swing*, aka *Royal Crown Revue* (actor, 1934–1935, 1936, 1937–1938); *True Detective Mysteries* (actor, 1929–1930); *Valiant Lady* (actor, 1938–ca. 1944).

For several years following high school, Teddy Bergman—who quickly altered his professional moniker to Alan Reed—toured with his cousin, Harry Green, in vaudeville. They were employed by various stock companies. For broadcasting purposes, Bergman reportedly changed his name "to break the trap of his Jewish identity." He claimed that, too frequently, it limited him to roles in which he replicated ethnic brogue. His earliest performances in that medium, incidentally, were on *The Eveready Hour*, an NBC variety show that ran from 1926 to 1930; on the weekly variety-dramatic series *The Collier Hour* over NBC Blue (airing from 1927 to 1932); and on CBS's *True Detective Mysteries* (1929–1930). Without doubt, Bergman (Reed) was present virtually from network radio's inception. He would perform on no fewer than 49 separate aural series during his lifetime.

In 1934 he starred in a weekly Tuesday night quarter-hour comedy program, *Blubber Bergman,* over Chicago's WGN. Three years later he presided over *The Blubber Bergman Revue* beamed locally by New York's WNEW. The latter transcribed show—a Tuesday night quarter-hour penned by Hi Alexander—consisted of comedy sketches featuring Bergman interacting with Ray Collins, Arlene Francis, Katherine Renwick and Paul Stewart.

Meanwhile, like so many other performers of that era (Phil Baker, Milton Berle, Edgar Bergen, Bob Burns, Eddie Cantor, Alice Faye, Bert Gordon, Red Skelton, et al.), Rudy Vallee has frequently been credited with giving all of them—including Bergman (Reed)—their initial nationwide ethereal exposure. While this isn't true in Bergman's case and may not be for some or all of the others, it's nevertheless obvious that the careers of all of them received significant jumpstarts by appearances with the legendary showman on programs that aired under a myriad of appellations.

Reed performed on Broadway with the eminent stars Alfred Lunt and Lynn Fontanne. Yet he may be best remembered by more people for his brief association with radio's Allen's Alley on *The Fred Allen Show.* As one of its original residents, in the early 1940s he exchanged comic repartee with that forum's venerable host while playing the character of Falstaff Openshaw. Following his escapades there, Reed departed New York to settle on the West Coast where he was soon transformed into a motion picture actor.

Included were 34 celluloid productions between 1944 and 1978, among them: *Days of Glory* (1944); *The Postman Always Rings Twice* (1946); *Perfect Strangers* (1950); *The Redhead and the Cowboy* (1951); *Here Comes the Groom* (1951); *I, the Jury* (1953); *The Far Horizons* (1955); *Lady and the Tramp* (1955); *The Desperate Hours* (1955); *The Revolt of Mamie Stover* (1956); *Peyton Place* (1957); *Marjorie Morningstar* (1958); *1001 Arabian Nights* (1959); *Breakfast at Tiffany's* (1961); *Alice in Wonderland or What's a Nice Kid Like You Doing in a Place Like This?* (1966); *The Man Called Flintstone* (1966); *In Name Only* (1969); and *The Seniors* (1978).

In addition to his careers in radio, stage and film, Reed was active as a television actor and voiceover specialist. He played in CBS-TV's *Life with Luigi* in 1952 and the 1954 syndicated *Duffy's Tavern,* both video series in which he had regularly appeared in radio. He also turned up in recurring roles on CBS-TV's *Mr. Adams and Eve* (1957–1958); NBC-TV's *Peter Loves Mary* (1960–1961); and ABC-TV's *Mickey* (1964–1965). From 1951 to 1955 he was the insufferable guest poet Algernon Archibald Percival Shortfellow on NBC-TV's weekly madcap kiddy tease *Smilin' Ed McConnell and His Buster Brown Gang* (which also appeared earlier on radio). In the voiceover department, Reed performed the lead role of Fred Flintstone in *The Flintstones* on ABC-TV from 1960 to 1966, on NBC-TV from 1967 to 1970 and in a 1972–1974 CBS-TV reprise, *The Flintstones Comedy Hour.* He also gave voice to Mad Dog Maloney on CBS-TV's *Where's Huddles?* in 1970.

REED, TOBY. b. ca. 1911; d. March 3, 1988. *Announcer.* **Series:** *The Baby Snooks Show,* aka *Toasties Time* (1944–1945); *Birds Eye Open House,* aka *The Dinah Shore Show* (1943–1944); *Club Good Cheer* (1944); *Don't You Believe It* (host, 1946–1947); *The Drene Show,* aka *The Bickersons* (1946–1947); *The Fitch Bandwagon* (1940s); *The George Burns and Gracie Allen Show,* aka *Maxwell House Coffee Time* (ca. 1945–1949); *The Lifebuoy Show,* aka *The Bob Burns Show* (1944); *Mail Call* (mid 1940s); *The Maxwell House Summer Show* (1947); *Revere All-Star Revue* (1948); *The Star and the Story* (1944).

Toby Reed was the quizmaster of CBS-TV's primetime word game show *Top Dollar* in the spring and summer of 1958.

REIMERS, EDWIN W. b. Oct. 26, 1912, Moline, Ill.; d. Jan. 28, 1986, Nevada City, Calif. *Announcer.* **Series:** *Matinee in Rhythm* (1939–1941); *Milton Cross Opera Album* (1949). **Aphorism:** *You're in good hands ... with Allstate!*

Educated at the University of Iowa, Ed Reimers entered broadcasting at WHO in Des Moines, where he was an announcer, newscaster and actor between 1932 and 1936. From 1936 to 1942 he served Buffalo's WBEN as program director, immediately before going into the U.S. Marine Corps (1943–1946). On his return, Reimers became special events director of the video wing of his previous employer, WBEN-TV, for a year (1946–1947). He relocated in New York from 1948 to 1949, where he announced for ABC Radio and TV. Then he moved to the West Coast, initially employed by Los Angeles' KTTV television station as an announcer and actor.

For many years Ed Reimers was a prime commercial spokesman for Sears, Roebuck & Company's Allstate Insurance subsidiary. It was *his* voice that people remembered which declared: *You're in good hands ... with Allstate!* Reimers pitched the sponsor's policies on programs Allstate underwrote; he was also a longtime spokesman for Procter & Gamble's Crest toothpaste. Furthermore, he introduced *Pantomime Quiz*, aka *Stump the Stars* during a portion of its lengthy network video run (1949–1963 and syndication 1968–1970). Other tube series he announced: *The Crusader* (1955–1956, CBS); *Do You Trust Your Wife?* (1956–1957, CBS); *Kaiser Aluminum Hour* (1956–1957, NBC); *Wire Service* (1956–1957, ABC); *Mr. Adams and Eve* (1957–1958, CBS); and *Maverick* (1957–1962, ABC).

Reimers was also a part time television actor between the mid 1950s and early 1970s. He performed in a quintet of motion pictures, too: *On the Loose* (1951); *Sergeant Deadhead* (1965); *The Loved One* (1965); *The Barefoot Executive* (1971); and *The Million Dollar Duck* (1971).

RICE, GRANTLAND. b. Nov. 1, 1880, Murfreesboro, Tenn.; d. July 13, 1954, New York, N.Y. *Sportscaster, Emcee.* **Series:** *Cities Service Concert* (sportscaster, 1933–?); *Information Please* (recurring guest panelist, ca. 1938–ca. 1951); *Sports Stories* (host, 1943–1944).

Grantland Rice was one of the pioneers in media coverage of athletics. He embarked on a newspaper career with *The Tennessean* in close-to-home Nashville that eventually took him to *The Atlanta Journal and Constitution* and—in 1911—to *The New York Tribune.* For years Rice penned a widely read column, "The Sportlight." On Oct. 5, 1921 he provided play-by-play commentary on baseball's initial World Series broadcast carried by a limited Westinghouse station hookup.

Rice was a veteran behind the mike by 1922, called upon a second time to provide word pictures to sports buffs tuning in to another World Series. When he returned to that duty for yet a third time in 1923, he shared the microphone with Graham McNamee and invested substantially in that neophyte announcer's meteoric rise to fame a short time thereafter. Paradoxically, all three of those series in between 1921 and 1923 pitted the New York Giants against the New York Yankees. The Giants won the first two sequences.

By the early 1930s, Rice was named to deliver capsule commentaries on current football action over the *Cities Service Concert*, a program of arresting music that NBC had been airing since 1927. Announcer Ford Bond was already providing baseball chitchat on the progressive instrumentals-and-vocals series and starting in late summer of 1933 the producers decided a football tête-à-tête would be well received, too.

In addition to acquiring his own 30-minute NBC Radio feature in the 1940s—plus covering an escalating barrage of live sporting events across the nation—Rice appeared in many one-reel sports films. Despite that pastime, his major contributions were in sundry journalistic arenas. Many contemporary sports fans still point to his 1946 epic poem *Alumnus Football*, famous for introducing the cliché: "It doesn't matter whether you win or lose, but how you play the game."

Rice picked All-American football teams and applied "the four horsemen" to Notre Dame's celebrated 1920s backfield, a trademark that stuck. During the same era—through his newspaper column—he elevated an awareness and development of golfing as a sport, particularly so among middle class Americans, as he gave it exposure that seldom had been accorded the game previously.

RICKLES, DONALD NEWTON. b. Oct. 7, 1927, Portland, Ore.; d. Feb. 19, 1985, Los Angeles, Calif. *Announcer.* **Series:** *Nightbeat* (1950, 1951–1952); *The Whisperer* (1951); *The Whistler* (ca. late 1940s, early 1950s).

In 1945 Don Rickles (not to be confused with the contemporary sultan of insult comedy by the same moniker that was born May 8, 1926 in New York City) was a newscaster at KVAN, Vancouver, Wash.

RICO, LIONEL. Announcer. **Series:** *The Adrian Rollini Trio and The Lenny Herman Quintet* (1948); *David Harding, Counterspy* (1940s, early 1950s); *Dimension X* (1950–1951); *It's Higgins, Sir* (1951); *Radio City Playhouse* (1948); *Stroke of Fate* (1953); *Turn Back the Turntables* (1948); *Whitehall 1212* (1951–1952).

The surname of Lionel Rico in at least one documentary is spelled Ricou.

RIGGS, GLENN. b. July 24, 1907, East McKeesport, Pa.; d. Sept. 12, 1975, Malaga, Spain. Announcer. **Series:** *The Adventures of the Thin Man* (1940s); *The Bing Crosby Show*, aka *Kraft Music Hall*, aka *Philco Radio Time* (1935, 1946–1949); *The Dunninger Show*, aka *Dunninger, the Mentalist* (1943–?); *Ethel and Albert*, aka *The Private Lives of Ethel and Albert* (late 1940s); *The Herb Oscar Anderson Show* (1957–1958); *Hop Harrigan* (1942–1948); *Jungle Jim* (ca. 1935–ca. 1940s); *Ladies Be Seated* (ca. mid 1940s); *Lavender and New Lace* (1941–1942); *Mark Trail* (ca. 1950–1951); *Musical Varieties* (1939–1940); *My True Story* (1943–ca. early 1950s); *Olivio Santoro* (1940–1943); *Philco Radio Hall of Fame* (1943–1946); *Rhythm Road*, aka *The Johnny Morgan Show* (1943); *Stairway to the Stars*, aka *The Paul Whiteman Show* (1946); *True or False* (ca. 1938–?); *Vic and Sade* (1940s).

Glenn Riggs might have been an attorney had dramatics not gotten in his way. He was active in high school and college drama and glee clubs. Yet after a year as a pre-legal student at Juniata College during which he won an extemporaneous speaking competition, he quit to pursue his ambitions on the stage. For sustenance, Riggs took a Pittsburgh-based job purchasing mine supplies, one that wouldn't curtail his show business dreams. Within a year he was playing opposite Ann Harding in stock productions at the local Nixon Theater. He went on short road trips with a touring stock company, too. But with the nation thrown into economic chaos in 1929, he quickly found professional acting opportunities drying up. Few citizens had excess cash to pay for frivolous entertainment.

Riggs, then 22, went over to the local Westinghouse factory in search of work. A personnel officer thought his penchant for performing qualified him for something besides making appliances. He pointed the young man towards the company-owned radio station, KDKA. Just as the interview was finishing, someone ran in shouting, "The announcer didn't get here!" At that, Riggs was shoved into a small studio. A dispatch torn from a teletype machine was placed in his hands and he was ordered to "read it." It was an unexpected baptism into a profession that he was to devote the next 43 years of his life to.

Riggs quickly rose to chief announcer at that strategic and historic venue, soon becoming host of *The Musical Clock*, one of the medium's inaugural recorded breakfast-time features. He left KDKA in 1938 to join NBC at Radio City in New York. On his departure from KDKA, his announcing cronies presented him with a gold ring inscribed with each of their initials. A few years later, in 1943, when NBC's Red and Blue chains split, Riggs was assigned to the Blue net and he ultimately retired from it in 1972. In the mid 1940s that web was renamed the American Broadcasting Co. (ABC). He acquired announcing assignments for the television network after most network radio bowed out.

RIGGS, LEE AUBREY (SPEED). b. Feb. 18, 1907, Silverdale, N.C.; d. Feb. 1, 1987, Goldsboro, N.C. Announcer. **Series:** *Information Please* (commercial spokesman, ca. 1940–1944); *The Jack Benny Program* (commercial spokesman, 1944–1955); *Your All-Time Hit Parade* (commercial spokesman, 1943–1944); *Your Hit Parade* (commercial spokesman, ca. late 1930s/early 1940s–1953).

Tobacco auctioneer L.A. "Speed" Riggs of Goldsboro, N.C. was one of two celebrated commercial spokesmen (the other, F.E. Boone) for the American Tobacco Co. and its flagship product, Lucky Strike cigarettes, featured on a handful of memorable shows during radio's golden age. Riggs was engaged by the firm's president, George Washington Hill, a man exhibiting a savvy predilection for applying innovative marketing and sales techniques sufficiently ahead of his contemporaries. Hill set high standards in broadcast advertising and promotion. Doubling Riggs' annual salary as an auctioneer to $25,000, Hill directed him to repetitively chant (a Hill trademark, incidentally) during a couple of 90-second commercials on all the Lucky-sponsored broadcasts. Using a singsong style,

Riggs rolled out a rapid-fire spiel that couldn't be easily deciphered but was spectacular anyway: *Hey TWENTY NINE nine nine nine nine nine nine, roundem roundem roundem roundem roundem, am I right at thirty thirty thirty thirty thirty thirty thirty thirty thirty thirty thirty thirty THIRTY ONE thirty one thirty one one one one one....* Riggs continued until he inevitably arrived at the number 38—all of this reminiscent of *real* tobacco auctions. Habitually, he finished with the cry: *Sol-l-l-d to A-merican!*

Following the sound of a clicking telegraph, announcer Basil Ruysdael or one of his colleagues concluded the inimitable sales pitch: "From men who know tobacco best ... it's Luckies, two to one!" An authoritative voice put in: "LS/MFT ... LS/MFT ... Lucky Strike Means Fine Tobacco!" To increase the commercial's effectiveness, LS/MFT was added to the bottom of every Lucky Strike pack and carton. It quickly became a part of the American vernacular, reinforcing the pains of Riggs and Ruysdael.

Riggs ultimately transitioned from aural-only broadcasting to video, appearing in the same sponsor's missives on the extensions of the shows American Tobacco underwrote in radio (*The Jack Benny Program* and *Your Hit Parade* were foremost). There an auction setting was filmed as a backdrop for the infamous plugs that had been ringing in listeners' ears for years. Riggs and his peers were sometimes credited for ushering in relatively novel methods of broadcast commercials in that day. Not only did they sell cigarettes by the billions, their marketing skills evolved into a noteworthy byproduct that is still cited by students of modern advertising technique.

RIPLEY, JOSEPH S. b. July 18, 1913; d. Feb. 3, 1993. *Announcer.* **Series:** *Armstrong Circle Theater* (host-narrator, 1952–1953); *Dorothy Dix on the Air* (1949–1950); *Walk a Mile* (early 1950s).

Joe Ripley should not be confused with Joseph Ripley who—in the same era—was a radio director, principally recalled for his ties with CBS's and NBC's *Hour of Charm* musical variety feature (1934–1948).

RIZZUTO, PHILIP FRANCIS. b. Sept. 25, 1917, Brooklyn, New York, N.Y. *Sportscaster.* **Series:** *Phil Rizzuto's Sports Caravan* (sportscaster, 1952–ca. 1960s). **Aphorism:** *Holy Cow!*

Phil ("Scooter") Rizzuto overcame his diminutive size (5'6", 150 lbs.) to anchor a New York Yankees dynasty, helping his team win 10 pennants and eight World Series during his 13 seasons as a durable and deft shortstop (1941–1942, 1946–1956, with time out for duty with Uncle Sam). Rizzuto was an All-Star five times, named the American League's Most Valuable Player in 1950 and elected to the Baseball Hall of Fame in 1994.

Upon retiring from baseball playing he became a Yankees play-by-play broadcaster for four decades, principally on local New York television. He debuted on the airwaves, however, on radio where his *Sports Caravan*, introduced in the early 1950s by NBC and later carried by CBS, became a popular feature with true believers. Rizzuto revealed, "I like radio better than television because if you make a mistake on radio, they don't know. You can make up anything on the radio."

Another sportscasting legend, Harry Carey—whose career embraced the St. Louis Cardinals, Oakland Athletics, Chicago White Sox and Chicago Cubs across a half-century—claimed it was he who instituted *Holy Cow!* as an expression of surprised glee long before it was put into play by Rizzuto with his beloved Yankees. That never kept Rizzuto from applying it whenever the situation warranted, nevertheless.

The very first mystery guest, for which the celebrity panel was blindfolded on the premier of CBS-TV's *What's My Line?* was none other than Rizzuto, then on the New York Yankees' active roster. The date was Feb. 2, 1950. He appeared in September of the same year as a guest on the debuting *Joe Dimaggio Show* on NBC-TV, a feature aimed at youngsters. During the 1954–1955 television season, Rizzuto was a panelist on the Dumont primetime quiz *Down You Go* emceed by Bergen Evans.

Late Night TV host David Letterman once told his audience: "I heard the doctors revived a man after being dead for four-and-a-half minutes. When they asked what it was like being dead, he said it was like listening to New York Yankees announcer Phil Rizzuto during a rain delay."

ROBERTS, DAVID KELLEY, JR. b. Feb. 25, 1912, Jacksonville, Fla.; d. Dec. 24, 1996, Sacramento, Calif. *NBC staff announcer.*

David Roberts had a difficult time while he was in school. His father's nomadic occupational pursuits kept the family in constant upheaval as they transferred from place to place, never putting down roots anywhere very long. In the second grade, for example, young David attended seven schools. He graduated at last from his third high school. Although he enrolled with good intentions at Penn State, he soon dropped out to ship around the world "on any boat on which he could get a job" during the early days of the Great Depression. On landing a position with NBC's Guest Relations Department, however, Roberts settled down and subsequently enrolled in the network's announcing school. After his successful completion of the instructional course there, in October 1936 he was added to the chain's permanent announcing staff.

Roberts—who maintained no regular program assignments—was one of several men the web relied upon for other applications. Their speaking skills were channeled into system cues (e.g., "This is the Red network of the National Broadcasting Company"); into introducing celebrated radio journalists who dispatched late-breaking news bulletins; pitching special promotions; making other clarifications deemed important for listeners' ears; delivering commercials and public service announcements; and supplying other non-programming essentials in between and during continuing broadcast series.

ROBERTS, ED. *Announcer.* **Series:** *Manhattan Mother* (1939); *Vic and Sade* (early 1940s).

In 1938 Ed Roberts was on the staff of Chicago's WCBD where he was a local newscaster. By the 1960s he was on the ether at KSO, Des Moines, Iowa.

ROBERTS, KEN. b. Feb. 12, 1910, Bronx, New York, N.Y. *Announcer.* **Series:** *The Adventures of Ellery Queen* (1939–1940); *The Al Pearce Show* (ca. late 1930s, 1940s); *Baby Snooks* (ca. 1949–1951); *Brenda Curtis* (1939–1940); *Bulldog Drummond* (ca. 1940s); *The Campbell Playhouse* (writer, ca. 1938–ca. 1941); *Candid Microphone* (1947–1948, ca. 1950); *Casey, Crime Photographer* (ca. 1940s); *Chance of a Lifetime* (1949–1952); *The Chesterfield Quarter-Hour* (1931–ca. 1932); *The Choice of a Lifetime* (1949); *Crime Doctor* (1940–1947); *Easy Aces*, aka *Mr. Ace and Jane* (actor-announcer, 1948); *Everybody Wins* (1948); *The Fred Allen Show*, aka *The Linit Bath Club Revue* (1932–1933); *The Goldbergs* (ca. late 1930s, early 1940s); *Grand Central Station* (ca. 1940s); *The Great Gildersleeve*; *Hogan's Daughter* (1949); *The Hour of Charm* (1935–ca. early 1940s); *It Pays to Be Ignorant* (1943–?); *The Jan August Show* (1948); *Johnny Presents* (1939–1941, 1942–1946); *Joyce Jordan, Girl Interne*, aka *Joyce Jordan, M.D.* (1938–ca. 1940s); *Let Yourself Go*, aka *The Milton Berle Show* (1944–1945); *Life Begins*, aka *Martha Webster* (1940–1941); *Life Begins at Eighty* (1948–1949, ca. 1952–ca. 1953); *The Life of Mary Sothern* (1935–1938); *Lorenzo Jones*; *The Mercury Summer Theater* (1946); *One Thousand Dollar Reward* (1950); *The Philip Morris Follies of 1946* (1946); *The Philip Morris Playhouse* (ca. 1948–ca. 1949, ca. 1950); *Quick as a Flash* (quizmaster, 1944–1947); *The Shadow* (1931–1932, 1935–1944); *Sing Along*, aka *The Landt Trio* (1942); *Stoopnagle and Budd*, aka *The Gloomchasers*, aka *The Ivory Soap Program* (ca. 1931–1932); *Take It or Leave It* (1940s); *This is Nora Drake* (1951–?); *Tonight on Broadway* (1946); *Truth or Consequences* (ca. early 1940s); *The Variety Show* (1946); *The Victor Borge Show* (mid 1940s); *What's My Name?* (ca. 1940s); *You Are There* (late 1940s).

While his father had aspirations of Ken Roberts becoming a lawyer, the young man harbored ambitions for himself that were centered around journalism and acting. He studied piano for seven years. He attended DeWitt Clinton High School in New York and St. John's Pre-Law School and worked during summer vacations as a law clerk and a boys' camp counselor. He also appeared in amateur theatricals, making his professional debut at 18 in Hoboken, N.J., performing with Christopher Morley. But he soon faced financial realities and his future looked quite bleak.

As the Great Depression got underway Roberts needed a steady income. He decided to approach every New York borough on a separate day of a single week and call on the various radio stations sequestered in those areas. On Monday, for instance, he planned to visit Brooklyn; on Tuesday, the Bronx; and so on until he secured a job. "I went down to Brooklyn and the first station I walked into was WLTH, 'the voice of Brooklyn,'" he recalled. When he told an interviewer that he was an out-of-work actor, he was advised: "You walked in at a lucky moment. My announcer just left—he got a job at CBS—so I guess I'll hire you." Roberts couldn't believe his good fortune. "No audition?" The station official retorted: "No, you don't have to audition." Repeating the incident many years later, Roberts recalled: "I got the job. And that was the end of my searching. It was 1930, and I got $30 a week, which was considered tremendous money at that time. I stayed there for six months, doing many different things in addition to announcing. I answered the telephone, I swept the office, I tried to sell time on the telephone—we had a sales talk which was written out, I arranged the programs, I read poetry, I played the piano. It was great experience. We were only on the air four hours a day, but during those four hours I did an awful lot."

Eventually he was given chances to hone his skills at WPCH and WMCA which prepared him even further. Then he joined CBS's announcing staff. A few years later, together with a handful of peers, on Aug. 16, 1937, Roberts was instrumental in launching the American Federation of Radio Artists (AFRA), the predecessor union of the American Federation of Television and Radio Artists (AFTRA). Both bodies sought to improve the compensation and working conditions of their member performers. Roberts accepted an ongoing role in helping shape those organizations throughout his working life.

On a 1935 CBS vocal talent series Roberts presented a young feminine soloist to listeners. Unknown to him, however, the diva and another girl singer had switched spots in the program's lineup and hadn't notified the veteran interlocutor that they had done so. The young woman he introduced erroneously gave him a sneer and a loud slap across the face which not only dumbfounded him but carried over on the airwaves. Shocked and humiliated, Roberts still remained a gentleman, standing by serenely, yet absolutely bewildered by her actions.

At another point in his career, Roberts was designated as the exclusive commercial spokesman for Ex-Lax laxative. He paid a price for it. As part of his privileged contract he was required to visit the firm's Brooklyn factory on a weekly basis. There the company president handed him some commercial copy to be read on the air before ushering him into a small room with a microphone where Roberts read the copy aloud. The CEO, meanwhile—back in his office—heard the pitch through a loudspeaker. Subsequently, he coached the veteran announcer on what he perceived as proper voice inflection techniques. This persisted for many weeks. The president invariably attended the live presentations at the network studios, too. "He would grab me and say, 'Kenneth, that was *just* the way I wanted it. It was absolutely perfect,'" Roberts remembered. "Thank you, I appreciate that," the announcer responded.

Nonetheless, the next morning Roberts perpetually received a telephone call from the Ex-Lax CEO asking him to come to the office that day. He would dutifully go out and the man always said something like this: "You know, there was one point in the commercial, where, I don't know, it just wasn't...." Roberts allowed those comments to continue for a while. Finally, he had had a bellyful and decided to challenge his accuser. On that occasion, he inquired of the top guy: "Sidney, what is happening here? You tell me how to do the commercial and I do it your way. I get off the air and you say it was wonderful, that it was perfect, exactly as you wanted. The next morning you're finding fault. I can't go on like this." The president acknowledged: "Well, I'll tell you the truth, Kenneth. I liked it very much, but when I get home my mother says, 'You know, Sidney, when you say Ex-Lax I believe you, but when that announcer says it, I don't believe him.'" Suddenly realizing he faced a winless situation—without mincing words or further deliberation—Roberts cut him off and canceled his select Ex-Lax contract on the spot. He figured some things simply weren't worth doing.

By the 1940s Roberts had been asked so many times to tell how a radio show was put together that he decided to take the bull by the horns and satisfy his inquisitioners much better than any of them could anticipate. He paid for 16-millimeter films to be shot of single episodes of each of a trio of daytime serials that he introduced regularly—*The Goldbergs, Life Begins* and *Joyce Jordan, Girl Interne*. Then he screened them freely for the benefit of interested parties, providing a unique perspective on radio's backstage in an epoch occurring several years before televised drama came into vogue.

While Roberts continued to introduce a plethora of national audio series (at least 45 by actual count), in 1952 he was also appealing to local New York listeners as a WMGM disc jockey with his waxworks feature *Tops in Pops*. One of his national radio programs was reincarnated on ABC-TV and in 1950 Roberts found himself announcing *Chance of a Lifetime* in not one but *two* mediums. A year earlier, in 1949, he introduced ABC-TV's *Blind Date*, precursor of *The Dating Game* in the 1960s and 1970s. During that epoch he performed a couple of gigs on Dumont Television: as host of the all-male primetime panel series *Ladies Before Gentlemen* (1951) and emcee of the short-lived quiz show *Where Was I?* (1952). Building upon his aural legacy with daytime serials, Roberts was the interlocutor for two prominent debuting CBS-TV entries: *Love of Life*—he was there for its total run from Sept. 24, 1951 through Feb. 1, 1980; and *The Secret Storm*—he was present at its inception Feb. 1, 1954 and through most of its inaugural year. He further announced a couple of other video series: ABC's pithy game show *Make Me Laugh* in 1958 with Robert Q. Lewis as emcee and the PBS Children's Television Workshop feature *The Electric Company* from 1971 to 1973.

Between 1961 and 2004 Roberts turned up 21 times as an actor in supporting roles on television dramatic series. Aside from that extensive input, from 1985 to 2006 he appeared in yet another 14 made-for-television movies, four mini series shown on TV and 25 more motion pictures screened in cinema houses. Several of those were prepared specifically for Canadian viewers, even in French. Included among Roberts' theatrical film performances were *Radio Days* (1987); *Murder One* (1988); *Lemonade* (2002); and *Alien Incursion* (2006). In addition, he composed the score of the 1985 filmography *Junior* and was storyboard artist for the 1997 movie *The Night Flier*.

Well on his way to the century mark as this is written, Roberts' lifelong passion for show business is seen in other members of his family, who got caught up with it, too. His son, Tony Roberts, is a celebrated Hollywood actor. Ken's daughter, Nancy Roberts, and granddaughter, Nicole Roberts, have been in television films and guest roles on various video series. Who would have dreamed that the audition the senior Roberts never had in 1930 could have resulted in such a powerful impact upon so many phases of American entertainment? Surely not Ken Roberts, who was just performing his many jobs.

ROBERTS, PETER. b. ca. 1922, Quebec, Canada. *Announcer.* **Series:** *The Big Guy* (1950); *The Falcon* (1950); *The Forty Million* (narrator, 1952); *The Magnificent Montague* (1950–1951); *Who Said That?* (1948, 1949).

Peter Roberts' first big break in American radio came with Philadelphia's KYW in the late 1940s. In time he moved over to WPTZ-TV in the City of Brotherly Love. Later he worked with Bob & Ray on New York's WINS and appeared on NBC. In the 1960s and 1970s, Roberts was a prominent air personality with New York's WOR Radio, working as the newsman on that station's popular *Rambling with Gambling* weekday morning series with John A. Gambling hosting. Roberts remained with WOR through late 1980 when he left by mutual agreement. By 1982 he resurfaced in New York radio over WPAT as morning newsman.

ROBINSON, ALVIN. b. Jan. 15, 1913, Apache, Okla. *NBC staff announcer.*

Alvin Robinson dropped out of school at age 16 and covered the United States and Mexico selling magazine subscriptions. After awhile he returned to his hometown hamlet in Oklahoma and soon secured the post of manager of the local cinema house. When the theater was sold a short time later, however, he lost that job.

Relocating in nearby Tulsa, Robinson found work as an announcer at KVOO. In August 1935, he journeyed to New York City. He liked Gotham so well that he went back there three months later with $90 in his pocket. Just before he spent his last nickel, he found work at last as a page at NBC. Six weeks hence he won a competitive audition for announcers with the chain. He became the youngest announcer hired by the network at that time. While he didn't have any specific programs to introduce, in the 1930s and 1940s his unidentified voice could be heard regularly delivering system cues and making other required announcements.

ROEN, LOUIS BERNARD. b. March 13, 1905, Ashland, Wis.; d. Feb. 15, 1993, San Diego, Calif. *Announcer.* **Series:** *The Breakfast Club* (1941); *The Guiding Light* (1942–?); *Today's Children* (ca. 1943–ca. 1950); *We Love and Learn* (ca. 1950–1951).

After attending Wisconsin's Lawrence College for a couple of years, Louis Roen attempted a surfeit of moneymaking prospects: he was a dance band coordinator; a railroad telegrapher; and a street car operator, among them. Performing the latter duty in Milwaukee, he encountered an old chum who was employed by WTMJ Radio as its program director. Roen's pal steered him to a tryout in 1927 for a spot as an announcer and vocalist and he was hired. He signed with CBS subsequently but stayed there only four months. Next he took a job managing WEBO in Marquette, Mich. Finally he relocated in Chicago where he was tapped for Don McNeill's *Breakfast Club* on the NBC Blue network. Perennial daytime serials creator Irna Phillips would soon put him to work on her Windy City–based dramas.

ROGERS, WILL. b. Nov. 4, 1879, Oolagah, Okla.; d. Aug. 15, 1935, Point Barrow, Alaska. *Emcee, Actor.* **Series:** *The Eveready Hour* (actor, ca. 1928); *Gulf Headliners* (host-actor, 1933–1934, 1935); *NBC Inaugural Gala* (humorist, 1926); *The Will Rogers Program* (host-actor, 1930); *The Will Rogers Show* (capsule replays, 1951); *The Ziegfeld Follies of the Air* (actor, 1932).

Will Rogers, the cowboy laureate, was a wealthy rancher's son who joined a Wild West show in 1903 and carried his rope tricks to vaudeville. Adding homespun humor to his performances, he earned top billing in Ziegfeld Follies stage shows while becoming a raconteur-in-demand and gaining acclaim as a silent screen actor. He was labeled "America's court jester." A critic observed that—by 1931—Rogers and radio's *Amos 'n' Andy* were "public gods."

When the talkies arrived, Rogers was a natural for them, too, appearing in 54 Hollywood features between 1918 and 1935, an average of more than three per year, among them: *Almost a Husband* (1919); *The Strange Boarder* (1920); *Guile of Women* (1920); *Boys Will Be Boys* (1921); *Doubling for Romeo* (1921); *The Headless Horseman* (1922); *Uncensored Movies* (1923); *The Cake Eater* (1924); *Going to Congress* (1924); *Don't Park There* (1924); *A Texas Steer* (1927); *Lightnin'* (1930); *A Connecticut Yankee* (1931); *Business and Pleasure* (1932); *Too Busy to Work* (1932); *State Fair* (1933); *David Harum* (1934); *Life Begins at Forty* (1935); *Steamboat Round the Bend* (1935); and *In Old Kentucky* (1935). As an aside, it was the 1934 *Harum* film that provided the inspiration for radio producers Frank and Anne Hummerts' soapy saga of the daytime airwaves *David Harum*, which persisted from 1936 to 1951 and sold millions of cans of Bab-O cleanser in the process.

Rogers' first broadcast was with the Ziegfeld Follies showgirls from *The Pittsburgh Post's* KDKA studios in 1922. (Apart from films, he was already becoming known for his Broadway appearances. He debuted there three years earlier in *The Ziegfeld Follies of 1919.*) He greeted the KDKA audience with: "Hello folks. I've looked at you from the movie screen and stage, but I've never had a chance to talk to you at home before."

He was suspicious of the microphone, nevertheless, having heretofore played to live audiences except in movies. For several years he professed to detest radio, referring to it as "that thing." Appearing on Detroit's WWJ in the same year (1922), he said he wasn't sure that anybody out there could hear him. But automobile manufacturer Henry Ford, who had made his own radio set and was tuned to WWJ at his Dearborn, Mich. estate, wrote Rogers—and so did scores of other listeners—to inform him that he was indeed being heard.

Still, Rogers avoided radio for years, performing only occasionally on variety series like *The Eveready Hour* and refusing to be pinned down to an ongoing show. "Rogers was the sort of personality radio was made for," insisted radio historian Gerald Nachman. "With his relaxed, shambling, cud-chewing style, Rogers endeared himself to listeners as he had on stage and in movies, where he played himself—a sort of country slicker."

It took Rogers' wife, Betty, and William S. Paley, proud new owner of the Columbia Broadcasting System, to convince him to attempt a regular feature. Drug manufacturer E.R. Squibb Co. agreed to underwrite a Rogers series for 12 weeks, paying the star $72,000, which Paley later discovered Rogers gave away to charity. The entertainer used his time to talk randomly to a live studio audience while broadcasting to the larger number tuning in. He did so without benefit of script, although he had carefully rehearsed where he was going with each show, committing it to memory. "He mused aloud, as if extemporaneously, and listening to him was more like eavesdropping," wrote Nachman. "He didn't play to audiences the way most comics do. He was just a natural-born crowd pleaser who adapted without fuss to radio."

Rogers often began with "All I know is what I read in the papers." He continued from there with a mention of some thought-provoking item that had caught his attention. Politics—and especially politicians—were favorite subjects to lampoon and the audience reacted enthusiastically when he stuck a needle to lawmakers. One of his best lines was: "I'm not a member of any organized political party ... I'm a Democrat." He launched his monologues by setting an alarm clock to ring in 10 minutes. When it did, he quit.

The first 10 Squibb-backed shows aired from Los Angeles' KHJ, the CBS outlet there. He was on the road for the last two weeks of his contract, broadcasting from Boston's WNAC and Chicago's WBBM. By then America had fallen in love with his brand of philosophical humor, and his weekly exposure to a nationwide audience had projected him into being a national treasure.

Rogers agreed to a subsequent series of monologues and variety underwritten by the Gulf Oil Corp. on the NBC Blue chain beginning in the spring of 1933. He shifted all of his earnings for that show from his pocket to the Red Cross. He had already made a mint from vaudeville, stage and film and knew he wouldn't miss it. He continued to speak in many locales, too. When he was away from the show, which continued for a second season, others (singers Carol Deis, James Melton and Hallie Stiles, the Pickens Sisters and the Revelers Quartet, and comic Bert Lehr) carried on in his absence.

He vacationed in the summer of 1935 and decided to accompany his pal, aviator Wiley Post, on a trip to Alaska. Post was seeking a satisfactory air route to Russia. After leaving Fairbanks for Barrow, where unfavorable weather conditions prevailed, Post's aircraft crashed in the desolate Arctic wilderness. Both men died. "It seemed like the passing of a president," said Stephen Chodorov in a documentary. A radio historiographer succinctly expressed, "And the nation grieved."

In addition to his movies and radio work, Rogers penned a syndicated column which was faithfully followed by millions of readers in countless newspaper markets. His popularity remained long after he was gone. Recordings of his monologues are still traded and sold today, in fact. ABC Radio aired three-minute capsules of his wit in 1951 drawn from transcriptions of monologues that originally aired two decades before. The light radio drama, *Rogers of the Gazette*, arrived on CBS in the 1953–1954 season. It followed the release of *The Story of Will Rogers*, a 1952 movie eulogizing America's favorite humorist and folk hero. Will Rogers Jr. played his father in celluloid and continued the legacy on the air. "Although there was no serious attempt to tie the series to *the* Will Rogers," a reviewer allowed, "Rogers Jr. played a country role pumped full of homespun wisdom." The radio narrative was billed as "a heartwarming story of a country newspaper and its friendly editor."

Many other American philosophical wits were favorably compared with Rogers. Among their number were humorists Bob Burns of Arkansas, Herb Shriner of Indiana, Cal Tinney of Oklahoma and Tony Wons of Wisconsin.

Rogers was paid $1,000 for adding humor to the more serious returns that Graham McNamee was giving WEAF listeners in New York on election night in 1924; Calvin Coolidge gained the right to remain in the White House that night. On Nov. 15, 1926, Rogers appeared on NBC's inaugural gala (launching the broadcasting network) which originated from New York's Waldorf Astoria Hotel with pickups from around the country. Rogers was at Independence, Mo., at the time and imitated the nation's chief executive during a humorous monologue. The impersonation was so believable to some, in fact, that the White House received numerous communications in response. Coolidge took it for the prank that it was. Also on that occasion Rogers purportedly issued an enduringly memorable remark: "Radio is simply too big a thing to be out of." He had obviously come to terms with it by then.

In the 1927–28 season of *The Eveready Hour* underwritten by National Carbon Co. on NBC, Rogers was paid $1,000 for a single performance on a variety series, an unprecedented fee for its time. The show's budget had soared from $3,850 in 1923–1924 (when it was heard only in New York, Buffalo and Providence) to $400,000 by 1927–1928 when 30 stations carried it.

Rogers was the catalyst that prompted Gene Autry, who sang cowboy songs while he worked at an Oklahoma telegraph office, to pursue a lifetime in entertainment. Overhearing Autry one day as he transacted some business, the performer urged him to get into radio and to make some recordings. By 1930 Autry was billed as "Oklahoma's Yodeling Cowboy" on Tulsa's KVOO, a response to the potential that Rogers saw in the man who would one day be dubbed "America's Favorite Cowboy." Not long after that Autry made a recording of *That Silver-Haired Daddy of Mine* on the Vocalian label and his future was assured.

ROGERS, WILLIAM. b. Nov. 17, 1916, Thompsonville, Mich. *Announcer, Commentator.* **Series:** *Bill Rogers and the News* (news analyst, 1947–1948); *The Brighter Day* (ca. early 1950s); *Charlie Wild, Private Detective* (1950, 1951); *The Columbia Workshop* (early 1940s); *David Harding, Counterspy* (early 1950s); *Hoot'nanny* (1947).

Bill Rogers was hired by the American Cancer Society to introduce a surfeit of syndicated shows in the 1950s promoting the charitable cause. Among the titles were: *Songs for America* (1951); *Can Baseball Be Made an Even Better Game?* (1952); *A Tribute to ...* (1955); *The Cancer Quack* (1956); *Listening to Jazz* (1957); *Music As You Like It* (1959); *Of These We Sing*; *Let Freedom Sing*; *This is Our Music*; *Music America Loves*; and *The Music We Love.*

RONSON, ADELE. b. Oct. 18, 1906, New York, N.Y.; d. Oct. 31, 2000, New York, N.Y. *Actress, Announcer.* **Series:** *As the Twig is Bent* (early 1940s); *Buck Rogers in the 25th Century* (actress, 1932–ca. 1933); *The Collier Radio Hour,* aka *The Collier Hour* (actress, 1931); *The Coty Playgirl* (hostess, 1931); *The Eno Crime Club* (actress, 1931–ca. 1936); *The Gibson Family,* aka *Uncle Charlie's Tent Show* (actress, 1934–1935); *The Goldbergs* (actress, 1930s, 1940s); *Inner Sanctum Mysteries* (actress, 1940s, 1950s); *John's Other Wife* (actress, 1936–?); *The Little Things in Life* (actress, 1975–1976); *The March of Time* (actress, 1930s, ca. 1940s); *Meyer the Buyer* (actress, mid 1930s); *Mr. Keen, Tracer of Lost Persons* (actress, late 1930s–ca. mid 1950s); *My True Story* (actress, 1940s, 1950s); *On Broadway* (actress, 1937–1938); *Perry Mason* (actress, 1940s–ca. mid 1950s); *Show Boat* (actress, 1936); *We Love and Learn* (early 1940s).

Adele Ronson was educated at Columbia University. In the 1920s and 1930s she performed on Broadway and in community theater productions of *The Legend of Leona; The Portrait of Dorian Gray;* and *Road to Rome.* She got into radio acting in 1930 and was still involved in a syndicated series airing as late as 1976.

She also did voiceovers on radio and television commercials. Still at it in the 1990s, she reminisced: "Nowadays, if they're doing a commercial, you get sent by an agent and there may be fifty people [competing] to do that one line on the commercial. And the people that are doing it now don't know the old guys at all, or what we've done, so lots of times you don't get the damn thing. Then you always think of the time when you just picked up a telephone and somebody would say to you, 'I have a commercial for you, every day.' They didn't audition you or anything; they just knew they wanted to use you."

ROOSEVELT, ELEANOR. b. Oct. 11, 1884, New York, N.Y.; d. Nov. 7, 1962, New York, N.Y. *Emcee, Commentator.* **Series:** *America's Town Meeting of the Air* (guest debater, 1935); *Aunt Jenny's Real Life Stories* (guest, ca. 1942–1943); *Bob Elson on Board the Century* (guest interviewee, ca. late 1940s); *Eleanor and Anna Roosevelt* (co-hostess, 1948–1949);

Eleanor and Elliott Roosevelt (1950–1951); *Eleanor Roosevelt* (hostess-commentator, 1934, 1937, 1940); *It's a Woman's World* (hostess, 1935); *Leo Reisman and His Orchestra*, aka *Pond's Program* (issues orator, 1932–1933); *The Magic Key* (guest speaker, 1938); *Over Our Coffee Cups* (hostess, 1941–1942); *Today with Mrs. Roosevelt*, aka *Mrs. Roosevelt Meets the Public* (moderator, 1950–1951); *The University of Chicago Round Table* (guest, ca. 1940s); *Vanity Fair* (hostess-discussion leader, 1933–1934); *We, the People* (guest, ca. 1940s).

Affirmed one historian: "The maturation of radio in 1932 coincided with the election of Franklin D. Roosevelt to the Presidency of the United States." Many people alive today still recall Roosevelt's "Fireside Chats" on the ether in which he candidly telegraphed one-on-one messages of hope to the American people about issues of import like recovery efforts following the nation's disastrous economic collapse in the 1930s and wartime themes in the 1940s. On the other hand, most of the countrymen don't recall that Roosevelt's spouse, Eleanor, capitalized on that embryonic means of instant messaging with masses of individuals, too. She had done so while he was governor of New York prior to his presidency and continued to make frequent use of the public airwaves as a program guest while hosting multiple series of her own.

Thus, she set a new precedent for the nation's first ladies. She was, in fact, branded "the first lady of the American airwaves" by one periodical. Despite that, radio chronicler Gerald Nachman mentioned her in a somewhat derisive assessment of the medium: "Almost anybody who made a splash, no matter how ill-suited, was handed a show—Babe Ruth, Charles Lindbergh, Mrs. Roosevelt, Max Baer, Elsa Maxwell, Dunninger. The nation was up to its ears, so to speak, in ready-made radio celebrities. If you were gifted, all the better, but name recognition was at least as crucial as talent; ways could be found to wrap a format around the most unlikely or unsuitable celebrity."

Nonetheless, an outspoken Roosevelt was not only a favorite of radio hosts but of the American citizenry. A magazine reviewer claimed in 1936: "Her discussions of pertinent problems facing the women of today are helpful, broadminded, courageous and understanding." Readers of the consumer fanzine *Radio Stars* included her among the "Nine Greatest Women in Radio," the results of a poll published in December 1934. Roosevelt and "the first lady of theater" Helen Hayes and songstress Kate Smith were picked as the nation's "three most popular females" in a subsequent survey in 1942. Radio contributed emphatically to their lofty perch.

In the 1932–1933 radio season, on Friday nights over NBC, Eleanor Roosevelt delivered nine-minute discourses within a half-hour while flanked by Leo Reisman and his supreme society band and vocalists William Sholtz and Lee Wiley. A critic contended: "Her early talks were given in a hesitant, nervous voice, leading to widespread mimicry and even cruel ridicule. 'Eleanor' jokes became common at parties and in the workplace."

But the longer she persisted, the more confidence she acquired; her comfort zone behind the microphone emphatically increased. She appeared on various networks in a variety of formats in 1933–1934 including *Vanity Fair* on NBC Friday nights for more than seven months and a six-week quarter-hour Sunday stint in late 1934 on CBS. On the NBC series she discussed the nation's problems, giving particular attention to the concerns and perspectives of women. It went so well that a commercial sponsor, Selby Shoe Co., purchased a Friday night quarter-hour on CBS in 1935 featuring the first lady in *It's a Woman's World*. New ground for White House grand dames had definitely been broken! (She donated the fees these commercial enterprises generated to several charities to avoid questions of impropriety, although sharp criticism was leveled at her anyway.)

On the premier of the public discussion series *America's Town Meeting of the Air* over NBC Blue on May 30, 1935, Roosevelt demonstrated her mettle for adequately handling controversial topics. She debated Mrs. Eugene Meyer on the New Deal in a themed discourse on *Which Way America—Communism, Fascism, Socialism, or Democracy?*

Pond's beauty products became the next firm to sponsor Roosevelt in a 1937 13-week quarter-hour Wednesday evening entry over

NBC Blue. (Pond's had underwritten the music performances headlined by bandleader Leo Reisman in 1932–1933 on which Roosevelt regularly spoke, but by 1937 it was sponsoring *her* as a headliner.) A pundit reported that—despite the fact there was no studio audience for her broadcast feature—Roosevelt invariably showed up wearing an evening dress and a shoulder orchid. She commented on current events, including programs like her husband's Works Project Administration and foreboding war clouds in Europe; she also interviewed international luminaries like playwright Sherwood Anderson, actress Katherine Cornell and novelist Sinclair Lewis.

In 1938 Roosevelt delivered a short address on the topic "This Troubled World" over NBC Blue's hour-long Sunday afternoon musical variety series *The Magic Key*. In 1940 she was hostess of an NBC quarter-hour on Tuesday and Thursday afternoons for Sweetheart soap. That series was introduced by a "name" announcer, Ben Grauer, and there was something else special: a versatile Allen Funt—who created *The Candid Microphone* for radio (1947–1948, 1950) and *Candid Camera* for 1950s television (and decades thereafter)—exhibited his ingenuity by scripting Roosevelt's Sweetheart soap chat series.

The first lady's subsequent gig, for Pan American Coffee Co., was a 15-minute gabfest on Sunday evenings on NBC Blue that extended to more than six months during the 1941–1942 radio season. In the war years Roosevelt turned up one day on the CBS soap opera *Aunt Jenny's Real Life Stories*. Conversing with the heroine in her sunlit kitchen, Roosevelt appealed to homemakers and others tuning in to unite behind the American troops then engaged in overseas battle. She proffered tips in how they could contribute. Such instances netted positive reactions for the military campaign, just as they were designed to do.

Following her husband's death in 1945, Eleanor Roosevelt earned an aura that approached "senior stateswoman" status. In that epoch she was interviewed on MBS's *Bob Elson on Board the Century*, a talk show with a passenger train motif. She appeared with daughter Anna Boettiger on the 15-minute series *Eleanor and Anna Roosevelt* three mornings weekly on ABC for 10 months (1948–1949). John Masterson created and produced the show with John Nelson and John Reddy directing. By then Roosevelt was using her radio series as a whipping post, occasionally chastising those with whom she disagreed, including some in her own political party. She wasn't intimidated in any regard; the gloves came off and all doubt was removed on how she felt about given issues.

Between 1937 and 1949 she was a guest on the CBS human interest feature *We, the People* at fluctuating spots in the schedule across a long run. She also visited the NBC Sunday afternoon public affairs discussion series, *The University of Chicago Round Table*, which aired between 1933 and 1955. One of her most impressive gigs ran for 45 minutes every weekday on NBC in 1950–1951; it lasted 11 months. For that one she shared the microphone with a controversial son who sometimes exhibited a "bad boy" image, Elliott Roosevelt.

Eleanor Roosevelt also became a fairly familiar face on American television in the 1950s. Aside from news interviews, particularly during political campaigns and election assessments, she moderated the panel discussion series *Mrs. Roosevelt Meets the Public* on NBC-TV on Sunday afternoons in 1950–1951. The feature was simulcast by NBC Radio and originated at New York's Park Sheraton Hotel with a set depicting the Roosevelt home at Hyde Park, N.Y., a national shrine today. Son Elliott produced the series. Some of her guests were divisive but others didn't stir anyone's ire. They included Tallulah Bankhead, John Crosby, Albert Einstein, Jose Ferrer and multiple politicians.

On Friday nights between January and September 1965 ABC-TV ran 30-minute installments of a documentary series analyzing the late chief executive's contributions. It was titled simply *F.D.R.* and narrated by Arthur Kennedy. Eleanor Roosevelt was a consultant in its developmental stages and was expected to appear in the telecasts. However, she died before it reached the air. Prior to her death she was filmed telling reminiscences of FDR's early days. The sequences were injected into some of the early episodes.

ROOSEVELT, ELLIOTT. b. 1910; d. 1990. *Emcee, Commentator.* **Series:** *At Home with*

Faye and Elliott (co-host, 1946); *Eleanor and Elliott Roosevelt* (co-host, 1950–1951); *Elliott Roosevelt Commentary* (commentator, 1939); *Information Please* (guest panelist, ca. 1940s).

Elliott Roosevelt was the fourth of six progeny born to Franklin Delano and Anna Eleanor Roosevelt, who became the nation's 32nd president and first lady (1933–1945). According to a source, "Elliott was Eleanor Roosevelt's favorite child and the one for whom she felt the most responsibility.... However, her favoritism and his willingness to exploit the Roosevelt name for his own gain led to tensions among the other Roosevelt children and eventually to her own rupture with Elliott."

Departing from a family custom set by his siblings, he refused to attend Harvard University. Instead Roosevelt embarked on a plethora of tasks, deciding by the early 1930s to favor communications as his life's work. The press ballyhooed the fact that in 1933 he was picked to manage the Hearst radio chain, claiming he capitalized on the Roosevelt moniker to get the appointment. He received in excess of $500,000 less than a year after his father became the nation's chief executive: it was a commission he "earned" for selling 50 military planes to the Soviet government which resulted from ties he maintained to the U.S. Export-Import Bank through his dad.

Despite his good fortune, he aligned himself with some Texas critics of his father's New Deal recovery program. Roosevelt placed even greater distance between himself and his family when he announced his intent to nominate an alternate for vice president during the 1940 Democratic National Convention, not the man his daddy had announced as his personal choice. The son had been named a Texas delegate to the convention; it took his mother's intervention to deter him for "going for it." He repaired the breach with his parents in 1943, a couple of years before his dad's death, while he was a pilot in the U.S. Army Air Force flying World War II missions during the North African campaign.

Elliott Roosevelt was on the national airwaves with several brief features and guest shots, apparently an outgrowth of his personal involvement in communications. For eight months on Tuesday, Thursday and Saturday evenings in 1939 he offered MBS listeners a quarter-hour news analysis underwritten by Emerson, a maker of radios. Reviewing that pithy series, a radio historian assessed, "Roosevelt made news by loudly disagreeing with some of his father's policies: he was known as a 'hell-raiser' on the air and off."

He and one of his five spouses bought a trio of radio stations in the Lone Star State. Ultimately they developed the Texas State Network, a regional combine of 26 outlets. The chain was affiliated with MBS, nevertheless, which fed it much of its programming.

In 1946 he and his third wife, actress Faye Emerson, conducted a syndicated quarter-hour series, *At Home with Faye and Elliott*, aired by 42 stations. The program included celebrity interviews, household tips and other information appealing to women, plus lots of chatter from the hosts. Guests included celebrities like Desi Arnaz, Lucille Ball, Toots Shor, Jan Struthers, Orson Welles and Earl Wilson. Emerson and Roosevelt, who married at the end of 1944, were divorced a little more than five years later. She was the only woman he wed who was quite well known in her own right.

On one occasion when he appeared on the panel of *Information Please*, Roosevelt had no clue that some explicit citations proffered were drawn from the previous week's newspaper column penned by his mom. He shared an NBC microphone with her for 45 minutes on weekdays in 1950–1951, a gig that persisted for 11 months.

Elliott Roosevelt authored numerous volumes. His first, *As He Saw It: The Story of the World Conferences of FDR* (Duell, Sloan & Pearce, 1946), was as controversial as his life. It was based on his experiences as his dad's wartime aide. He later edited four volumes of his father's letters and penned a series of more than a score of tales in which his mother was an amateur detective. Typical titles included: *Murder and the First Lady* (1984); *The Hyde Park Murder* (1985); *The White House Pantry Murder* (1987); *Murder in the Rose Garden* (1989); *Murder in the Oval Office* (1989); *Murder in the Blue Room* (1990); *Murder in the West Wing* (1992); *Murder in the East Room* (1993); *Murder in the Executive Mansion* (1995); and *Murder in the Lincoln Bedroom* (2000). With a colleague, he produced three non-fiction books about the lives of his parents.

In his later years Roosevelt raised Arabian horses in Portugal and was elected mayor of Miami Beach, Fla., serving from 1965 to 1969.

ROPER, ELMO. b. July 31, 1900, Nebraska; d. 1971, Redding, Conn. *Commentator.* **Series:** *Elmo Roper* (commentator, 1948–1950).

Elmo Roper won widespread acclaim as a collector of public opinion. For two years on a weekly-quarter hour aired by CBS, he divulged all manner of fascinating details about the populace. He began his interest in the field in the 1920s when he and a brother operated an Iowa jewelry emporium. Although they were never able to turn it into a thriving concern, the experience helped Elmo Roper see the importance of knowing and meeting the needs of patrons. While subsequently working for the Traub Co. in the early 1930s, Roper performed his first customer surveys to learn why the firm's commodities didn't result in more sales. So intrigued was he with the concepts of public opinion that, in 1933, he co-founded one of the nation's earliest marketing research enterprises, Cherington, Wood, and Roper.

From 1935 to 1950 Roper conducted the *Fortune Survey*, the country's inaugural poll using scientific sampling techniques. His accurate forecast of Franklin D. Roosevelt's 1936 rout of Republican candidate Alf Landon in the general election boosted scientific polling tremendously, underscoring it as a viable commercial venture. The federal government put Roper's work to use in several areas in the 1940s. After the 1948 national election, when the polls' incredible failure to predict Harry S Truman's comeback triumph over Thomas E. Dewey caused the public opinion industry's greatest crisis—including the erroneous Chicago newspaper headline "Dewey Defeats Truman"—Roper led a public and private defense of polling as he endured the scorn of comedians and politicians, calling for a measured examination of what had gone wrong and why. Behind the scenes his reassurance of his commercial clients, and the strength of his reputation, prevented marketing research from being damaged beyond repair by the fiasco. While public confidence didn't return overnight, polling managed to survive in part because of Roper's calls for calm and reason and his frank admission of errors.

The Roper Center for Public Opinion Research at the University of Connecticut—which he founded at Williams College in 1946—is the world's biggest repository of polling data. Its collections span the globe and date to the 1930s.

ROSS, DAVID (born David Rosenthan). b. July 7, 1894, New York, N.Y.; d. Nov. 12, 1975, New York, N.Y. *Announcer, Emcee, Writer.* **Series:** *Arabesque* (1929–1931); *The Big Break* (1947); *Breezin' Along,* aka *Jingo* (host, 1939–1940); *The Chesterfield Dance Show* (1936); *Chesterfield Presents* (1937–1939); *The Coke Club,* aka *Songs by Morton Downey* (1943–1944, 1945–1947, 1948–1951); *The Columbia Workshop* (ca. 1930s); *Evangeline Adams* (1930–1931); *The Fred Waring Show* (1933–1939); *The Henry Morgan Show* (1940s); *Lombardoland U.S.A.* (1948–1956); *The Meal of Your Life* (master of ceremonies, 1946); *Myrt and Marge* (1930s); *The O'Flynn* (1934–1935); *The Old Curiosity Shop* (writer-actor, early 1930s); *Poet's Gold* (narrator, 1932, 1937–1938); *Rendezvous with Ross* (disc jockey, 1948); *The Shadow,* aka *The Blue Coal Radio Revue* (1931–1932); *The Street Singer* (1931–1933, ca. 1935); *The Studebaker Champions* (1929–ca. 1931); *Take It or Leave It* (1940–?); *Time to Shine* (1937); *Tommy Riggs and Betty Lou* (1939–1940); *The True Story Hour with Mary and Bob,* aka *Mary and Bob's True Stories* (actor, ca. 1931–1932); *Words in the Night* (ca. 1930s).

Before he was old enough to attend school, David Ross was selling newspapers on the sidewalks of New York. As he grew older, he became eager for serious literary exposure. Following high school, he entered the City College of New York, plunging himself into poetry, literature and philosophy studies. Nevertheless, he was soon disenchanted with it and determined to concentrate on farming instead. Ross enrolled in Rutgers University's School of Agriculture in courses to prepare him for his newfound career. But when he failed chemistry, he dropped out of Rutgers and took an eclectic mix of odd jobs: mail boy at a dress factory; actor; supervisor in an orphan asylum;

playwright at summer camps; and—finally—secretary-advisor to a Russian baroness. All the while, some poetry he composed was being published in *The New Republic*, *The Nation* and more recognized periodicals, rejuvenating his interest in literature. It obviously had a profound bearing on how he channeled the remainder of his life.

A media chronologist pegged Ross as "one of the great 'golden-voiced' announcers of radio's early days." He entered radio in 1926 in an unplanned, unintended manner. Ross was visiting WABC one day when there was a sudden lapse in programming with no available entertainment on hand. He volunteered to provide a short dramatic reading on the air. As a result, he was offered a post as a full time staff announcer with occasional poetry reading inserted into the station's schedule. In a brief while, of course, WABC was to become the nerve center of the Columbia Phonograph Broadcasting System (to be renamed CBS before long). Ross's voice coach at WABC, in the meantime, was veteran announcer Norman Brokenshire.

Not long afterward, in 1929 the American Academy of Arts and Letters began bestowing citations for what it perceived to be "the best diction on radio." Given to a single recipient annually, the honor was awarded to Ross in its fourth year, 1932. By then he was presiding over several chain-fed series and independently making poetry recordings for sale. He continued as a busy broadcaster throughout network radio's heyday and hosted Dumont Television's Sunday night poetry-reading quarter-hour series in 1950–1951, *Time for Reflection*. Ross turned up later as a permanent panelist on Dumont's *Where Was I*, a primetime game show in the 1952–1953 video season that was initially moderated by Dan Seymour who was followed by John Reed King.

Ross retired as a freelance announcer in 1972 at age 81. Until his death, however, he continued composing verse for published books and literary periodicals.

ROSS, NORMAN. b. May 16, 1886, Portland, Ore.; d. 1953, Chicago, Ill. *Announcer.* **Series:** *Talk with Irene Rich*, aka *Hollywood with Irene Rich*, aka *Behind the Screen Chatter* (1933–1934); *Theater Guild on the Air* (adapter, 1947).

Norman Ross earned his first dollar as a stock boy before finishing prep school, Portland Academy, in his hometown. The enterprising young man paid his way through Stanford University by selling aluminum to California housewives. Upon graduating in 1917, Ross joined the U.S. Army where he became a military flier and an aerial acrobatic instructor, piling up 440 hours in the air. He narrowly escaped death on one occasion when a wing crumpled at 2,000 feet and he spun into a marsh.

Following the war, Ross learned how to swim by reading a book. Out of those self-taught methods, he became an active competitor over the next seven years in national and international swimming events around the globe. He set 72 records, surpassing all of the world's aquatic numbers for exhibitions between 150 yards and one mile. Ross became the water superstar during the 1919 inter-allied games held at Paris and won both the 400- and 1500-meter freestyle events at the 1920 Olympics games at Antwerp. His trophy collection ultimately numbered more than 500 cups and medals, including decorations from the king of Belgium and Brig. Gen. John J. Pershing, the U.S. Army chief of staff.

Ross returned home a hero after his spectacular swimming prowess acquired by reading a book, settling in Chicago. Enrolling as a law student at Northwestern University, he left it after a year when *The Chicago Daily Journal* hired him as a sportswriter. Forming his own publicity firm was next on his agenda. Subsequently, he was engaged in 1931 by radio station WIBO to provide play-by-play coverage of a World Series game. He performed so well, in fact, and found the assignment so appealing that he joined the outlet's staff when an invitation was extended. At WIBO he handled sporting events along with duties as a news commentator and studio announcer. When he was 47, in August 1933, Ross joined the Chicago announcing staff at NBC.

After he died suddenly at 67, Ross left behind a son, Norman Ross Jr., who became a Chicago broadcaster in his own right. He presided over several local features including one tagged *The Norman Ross Show*. Ross Jr. produced, narrated and starred in a plethora of Windy City radio and television series, wrote a newspaper column and joined the First National Bank of Chicago as vice president for public affairs.

ROWAN, ROY A. b. Jan. 25, 1920, Encino, Calif.; d. May 10, 1998, Paw Paw, Mich. *Announcer.* **Series:** *The Adventures of Philip Marlowe* (1947, 1948–1950); *The Amazing Mr. Tutt* (1948); *Columbia Presents Corwin* (mid 1940s); *Crime Classics* (ca. 1953–1954); *The Doris Day Show* (1952); *Escape* (ca. late 1940s); *Gunsmoke* (1952–ca. 1953); *Meet Corliss Archer* (ca. 1944–1945, 1946, 1947–1948, 1949–1953, 1954, 1956); *My Little Margie* (1952–1955); *Our Miss Brooks*; *Rogers of the Gazette* (1953–1954); *Romance* (1954–ca. 1955); *Rusty Draper* (ca. 1957–ca. 1958); *That's Rich* (1954); *T-Man* (1950); *Young Love* (1949–1950); *Yours Truly, Johnny Dollar* (ca. 1950–ca. 1952).

Roy Rowan launched his professional life in broadcasting by announcing on the radio at WKZO, Kalamazoo, Mich. in 1939. From there his pilgrimage successively carried him to Schenectady's WGY, Buffalo's WGR-WKBW and Chicago's WGN (in 1943) before depositing him on the West Coast at Hollywood's KNX in 1944. He was to be a media fixture in that area for the remainder of his life. He quickly acquired a glut of well-loved radio comedy and drama series which he introduced to faithful fans over the next decade.

When television came along, Rowan moved into it seamlessly, gaining a foothold early and maintaining a strategic position for more than two decades. From 1951 to 1957 he was the announcer and warm-up man for the studio audience observing the filming of CBS-TV's *I Love Lucy* (1951–1957). He also announced these subsequent video features: *Earn Your Vacation* (1954, CBS); *Those Whiting Girls* (1955, 1957, CBS); *It's Always Jan* (1955–1956, CBS); *The Lucy-Desi Comedy Hour/The Lucille Ball–Desi Arnaz Show* (1957–1960, CBS); *Angel* (1960–1961, CBS); *The Lucy Show* (1962–1968, CBS); *The Family Game* (1967, ABC); *How's Your Mother-in-Law?* (alternate announcer, 1967–1968, ABC); *Here's Lucy* (1968–1974, CBS); and *The Joker's Wild* (alternate, 1972, CBS).

Toward the end of his show business tenure, Rowan appeared in a single made-for-TV film, *Incident in San Francisco*, screened for the home viewers in 1971. In the meantime, he became an astute businessman in allied fields after his service before the microphones and cameras. Rowan purchased part ownership in radio stations in San Jose and Stockton, Calif. and Las Vegas, Nev. In 1968 he joined the media brokerage firm of Blackburn & Co., managing its Beverly Hills office until 1990. In the next seven years before he retired in 1997, he operated Rowan Media Brokers of Encino, Calif.

ROY, MICHAEL. b. July 18, 1913, North Dakota; d. June 26, 1976, Los Angeles, Calif. *Announcer.* **Series:** *The Abbott and Costello Show* (mid to late 1940s); *The Adventures of Frank Race* (1949–1950); *The Alan Young Show* (mid 1940s); *All-Star Western Theater* (actor, 1948); *The Andy Russell Show* (1945); *The Camel Screen Guild Players*, aka *The Screen Guild Theater* (1947–1950); *Duffy's Tavern* (mid 1940s); *The Garry Moore Variety Show* (1942); *The George O'Hanlon Show* (1948–1949); *The Martin and Lewis Show* (1949–1950); *Mystery in the Air* (1945); *The Spike Jones Show* (ca. mid to late 1940s); *Spotlight Bands*, aka *Victory Parade of Spotlight Bands* (1943–ca. 1948); *Tommy Riggs and Betty Lou* (ca. 1940s); *The Vaughn Monroe Show* (ca. mid to late 1940s).

In addition to his network radio assignments, Michael Roy picked up duties as a disc jockey at KWIK, Burbank, Calif., in 1947. He could be spotted in the 1961 film *The Forgotten Faces* and in an episode of NBC-TV's paramedic drama *Emergency!* on Oct. 25, 1975.

RUFFNER, EDMUND BIRCH (TINY). b. Nov. 8, 1899, Crawfordsville, Ind.; d. Feb. 23, 1983, Mt. Clemens, Mich. *Announcer, Emcee.* **Series:** *The Adventures of Captain Diamond* (cast member, 1932–1934, 1936–1937); *The Al Jolson Show*, aka *The Lifebuoy Program* (1936–1939); *The Better Half* (quizmaster, 1944–1950); *Blind Date* (master of ceremonies, ca. 1943–ca. mid 1940s); *Clara, Lu 'n' Em* (ca. 1930s); *Duffy's Tavern* (ca. 1940s); *Endorsed by Dorsey* (1946); *The Fred Allen Show*, aka *The Hour of Smiles*, aka *Town Hall Tonight* (1933, 1934–1935); *Maxwell House Melodies* (1930); *Mysteries of the Crooked Square* (1945); *The Palmolive Beauty Box Theater* (1934–ca. 1936); *Pick and Pat*

(1944); *Show Boat*, aka *The Maxwell House Show Boat* (1932–ca. 1936); *State Fair Concert* (1935); *Tony and Gus* (1935); *Treasure Hour of Songs* (1942, ca. 1943–ca. 1947); *The Voice of Firestone* (1928–1930); *Your Happy Birthday* (master of ceremonies, 1941).

Edmund "Tiny" Ruffner had an imposing physique, standing six feet, four and three-fourths inches in height, a figure sometimes inflated by media hype types. He was dubbed with the curious nickname while a heavyweight fighter. The son of a journalist, he left his native Indiana at two years of age when the Ruffners relocated in Seattle. Completing high school there in 1917, the youth enrolled at the University of Washington but quit the following year to join the U.S. Army.

Although he hoped to be a tenor concert artist in due course, in 1918 Ruffner left the Army following World War I and took a junior sales position with Standard Oil Co. of California. Meanwhile, he spent large sums of his income on vocal training. When his employer underwrote a 1924 program of popular operettas by Gilbert and Sullivan and Victor Herbert over Los Angeles' KFI, Ruffner was picked as the masculine lead. Subsequently, he toured the nation on a concert gig, appearing in Shubert productions like *Princess Flavia*.

When he decided to drop anchor again, in December 1927 he auditioned for an announcer's slot at New York's WEAF. By virtue of the fact the station was the flagship outlet of the one-month-old NBC Red hookup, he was trying out for the national chain as well. He won a spot. That kicked off a career as a network interlocutor and ethereal showman. Not long afterwards Ruffner joined Benton & Bowles advertising agency as supervisor of its radio department. In that capacity he placed, penned and produced many airtime favorites including several he himself announced (*The Better Half*; *Fred Allen*; *Palmolive Beauty Box Theater*; *Show Boat*, et al.).

He turned up as the narrator for the 1942 motion picture *Double Talk Girl*. On May 19, 1954 Ruffner appeared as himself when Patrick Joseph Kelly was the subject of Ralph Edwards' NBC-TV human interest feature *This is Your Life*.

RUICK, MELVILLE. b. July 8, 1898, Boise, Idaho; d. Dec. 24, 1972, Sherman Oaks, Calif. *Announcer, Actor.* **Series:** *City Hospital* (actor, early 1950s); *Dear John*, aka *Irene Rich Dramas* (1940–ca. 1942); *Lux Radio Theater* (1936–early 1940s).

Melville Ruick's budding future as an entertainer was temporarily sidelined in 1942 when he joined the U.S. Army Air Corps. In 1951 one of his radio dramas (*City Hospital*) was reincarnated as a weekly ABC-TV entry. He portrayed Dr. Barton Crane for the cameras in one of video's initial medical series. It switched to CBS in 1952 and continued into 1953. Also in 1951 Ruick played John Randolph in the NBC-TV Cold War adventure *Doorway to Danger*, aka *The Door with No Name*. From 1952 to 1954 the thespian was Rev. Dr. Paul Keeler in the CBS-TV daytime serial *The Guiding Light*, yet another radio feature that made its way to the small screen.

RUYSDAEL, BASIL. b. July 24, 1888, Jersey City, N.J.; d. Oct. 10, 1960, Hollywood, Calif. *Announcer.* **Series:** *Cavalcade of America* (1939–1940); *Information Please* (ca. early 1940s); *The Jack Benny Program* (ca. late 1940s–early 1950s); *The Jack Paar Show* (1947); *Your Hit Parade* (1935–ca. early 1950s); *Your Hit Parade on Parade* (1949).

While his mom was a pianist and his dad was a baritone vocalist and linguist, Basil Ruysdael earned a degree in electrical engineering from Cornell University. He also played football and sang in the glee club at Cornell. Even with the degree he earned, the apple still didn't fall far from the tree. Early in the 20th century—virtually as a caper rather than with any apparent solemn intent—young Ruysdael joined the cast of George Ade's operetta *The Sultan of Sulu*. That led him to tour with Henry W. Savage performing comic operas and the operettas of Gilbert and Sullivan. In about 1907 he journeyed to Europe for musical training, studying voice with Sabatini in Milan and Emmerich in Berlin. For a couple of seasons, Ruysdael sang in a Bohemian opera house.

Returning to America, from 1910 to 1918 he was engaged as a leading basso with the Metropolitan Opera Company. Enrico Caruso and Geraldine Farrar were among the Met's stars in those days and Ruysdael often appeared with them. He departed the Met in 1918 to enlist in Navy aviation. On his return he transferred his base of operations to California where he taught voice professionally. Among his pupils was baritone Lawrence Tibbett, who was not only destined to become a Metropolitan Opera star but—in 1945—to sing pop tunes on *Your Hit Parade*, an important radio series that Ruysdale would be announcing at the time. Tibbett succeeded another legend there, by the way, crooner Frank Sinatra. While on the West Coast, Ruysdael was also featured in a couple of theatrical films—*Topsy and Eva* where he costarred with the Duncan Sisters; and on both stage and screen in *Cocoanuts* alongside the zany Marx Brothers.

Ruysdael's broadcasting livelihood began in 1929 at Newark's WOR. He was already in his forties then, yet was getting in on the ground floor of a burgeoning industry. He demonstrated an aptitude for many talents as exhibited in his 1932 WOR weekly half-hour feature *Beggar's Bowl*. Ruysdael penned and narrated the series about a British Secret Service agent residing in India who pursued his vocation under the semblance of a hobo. The announcer was quickly dubbed "the voice of WOR" and wrote and acted in a myriad of series for the station in the 1930s, including shows titled *Master of the Bow*; *Red Lacquer and Jade*; and *Weaver of Dreams*.

Without doubt Ruysdael's most infamous aural credits were earned as the announcer and commercial pitchman for Lucky Strike cigarettes on the durable weekly pop music favorite *Your Hit Parade*. There, flanked by either tobacco auctioneer F.E. Boone of Lexington, Ky., or L.A. (Speed) Riggs of Goldsboro, N.C., Ruysadel delivered the sponsor's repetitive cigarette dispatches, touting: "From men who know tobacco best, it's Luckies, two to one!" Those smokes, he insisted again and again, were "So round, so firm, so fully packed ... so free and easy on the draw."

In the autumn of 1942, when the firm's product packaging was altered from dark green to white—purportedly because the military required the use of the jade tinting and Luckies was responding to a humanitarian need while never stating that women were embracing the white wrappers of archrival Chesterfields brand as Luckies sought to penetrate the feminine market—Ruysadel was among the prime spokesmen whose voice, again repetitiously, informed millions of Americans: "Lucky Strike has gone to war!" The same theme was exhibited on American Tobacco's (Luckies) *Information, Please* and *The Jack Benny Program* and several other radio features of that period.

Ruysdael was a television character actor in the 1950s on *The General Electric Theater* (1953); *Science Fiction Theater* (1955); *Black Saddle* (1959); and *Perry Mason* (1959). But it was in film that the multitalented individual used his thespian talents most often. Between 1929 and 1961 he applied his acting skills to 33 principally B-movies, among them: *The Cocoanuts* (1929); *Colorado Territory* (1949); *Task Force* (1949); *Thelma Jordon* (1950); *Broken Arrow* (1950); *High Lonesome* (1950); *Boots Malone* (1952); *The Shanghai Story* (1954); *Davy Crockett, King of the Wild Frontier* (1954); *The Violent Men* (1955); *Blackboard Jungle* (1955); *These Wilder Years* (1956); *The Last Hurrah* (1958); *The Story of Ruth* (1960); and *One Hundred and One Dalmatians* (1961, this one in voiceover—animated—format).

The multitalented Ruysdael also kept busy writing and producing original programs, working newsreels, narrating program pictures and slide films and making transcriptions.

SABIN, ROBERT COOK. b. Jan. 18, 1912, Illinois; d. Jan. 15, 1959, Los Angeles, Calif. *Announcer.* **Series:** *Modern Romances* (1936–1937).

Following his fleeting network gig, in 1942 Bob Sabin was a newscaster at Gary, Indiana's WIND. Four years later he transferred to KDON, Monterey, Calif., as a sportscaster.

SAERCHINGER, CESAR. b. Oct. 23, 1884, Germany; d. October 1971, Washington, D.C. *Commentator, Emcee.* **Series:** *Cesar Saerchinger Interviews* (interviewer, 1930–1937); *The Story Behind the Headlines* (commentator, 1938–1944).

At the age of nine, Cesar Saerchinger emigrated to the United States. Following the First World War he became a foreign correspondent for *The New York Evening Post*. Some time later CBS and NBC sent emissaries to London to cover a five-power naval conference. When the event continued beyond its anticipated termination date, the

CBS newsman was in a pickle, badly needing to be back in America for other commitments. He arranged with Saerchinger to cover the duration of the meeting for CBS.

After that assignment ended, the print journalist told CBS officials he could arrange for specific British luminaries to appear for radio interviews. That sounded so attractive in New York that—with the approval of William S. Paley, new owner of the Columbia Broadcasting System—the network hired Saerchinger in 1930 and a studio at the British Broadcasting Corp. was reserved for CBS interviews. Saerchinger was literally the pioneer and dean of this esoteric profession of foreign radio representatives. Not only was he CBS's first permanent European newsman, he inaugurated transatlantic broadcasting. Period.

Saerchinger's programs aired on Sunday. Poet John Masefield was an early subject. In October 1931 he attracted George Bernard Shaw, whom he considered a "catch." Shaw greeted the listeners like this: "Hello America! Hello all my friends in America! How are all you dear old boobs who have been telling one another for a month that I have gone dotty about Russia?" He enumerated that nation's advantages so much that CBS subsequently allowed an American to respond to the broadcast, having received a quantity of complaints.

Unfortunately, CBS still didn't quite get it, never placing a high value on Saerchinger's pivotal spot while he held it. In 1932, when Adolf Hitler was about to become chancellor of Germany, Saerchinger enticed him to appear for 15 minutes on a broadcast to the United States for the sum of $1,500. CBS cabled: unwant Hitler at any price. Saerchinger was ordered to return to organizing the broadcast of a song festival in Frankfurt. By the time the newsman left his post five years hence, the window of opportunity for attracting a madman with visions of global domination was permanently shuttered.

CBS dispatched H.V. Kaltenborn to London in June 1933 to cover a financial symposium. Kaltenborn and Saerchinger coordinated the assignment, providing U.S. listeners with a daily man-on-the-street broadcast from Piccadilly Circus, giving the common man's reaction to the event. Their interviews were conducted late at night due to the time difference. Scotland Yard was skeptical, however, afraid that someone would cast aspersions on the British by accidentally surfacing with inappropriate comments on the ether. Saerchinger and Kaltenborn made sure it never happened.

When the *Queen Mary* sailed on its maiden voyage to New York on May 27, 1936, Saerchinger and NBC's London correspondent Fred Bate were aboard. They interviewed passengers en-route and some of their New York–based colleagues as well as representatives from MBS met the ship in the New York harbor, providing festive arrival coverage for all the networks.

Saerchinger resigned as the CBS European director in 1937. Edward R. Murrow, who had been hired in New York two years earlier as director of talks, was appointed his successor at an annual salary of $8,000. Murrow sailed for London that April. A pundit observed: "Not even the sharpest network executive could foresee the future significance of that move." History, of course, would record it for posterity.

Saerchinger was promptly picked up by NBC. That web assigned him to its Radio City headquarters in New York. He was given a quarter-hour series as an NBC commentator which initially aired on Fridays, then Sundays and finally on Saturdays. All but the Saturday broadcasts (which were at 5:30 P.M. Eastern Time) were heard between 10:45 P.M. and 11:30 P.M. He was also a critical part of NBC's D-Day coverage on June 6, 1944, while taking assignments for other special events as well as the normal flow of news reporting.

Given the advantage of distance and time it seems evident that even Saerchinger himself did not fully appreciate the groundbreaking strides he made as a pioneering broadcast journalist. He resigned his European post in May 1937 because, according to a radio historian, he believed "there was no future in it." If Saerchinger failed to recognize the possibilities growing out of where he had been, others likely did too. None of that diminishes his extensive accomplishments, of course. Considering the foundation he laid, overseas reporting appeared to have begun where he left off.

ST. GEORGE, DORIAN. b. Sept. 16, 1911; d. March 1, 2004, Cleveland, Ohio. *Announcer.*

Series: *The Adventures of Charlie Chan* (1932–1933, ca. 1936–ca. 1938); *Candid Microphone* (1947–1948); *Fish Pond* (cast member, 1944); *Hollywood Airport* (1954).

ST. JOHN, ROBERT. b. March 9, 1902, Chicago, Ill.; d. Feb. 6, 2003, Waldorf, Md. *Correspondent, Newscaster.* **Series:** *Monitor* (correspondent, 1959–1960); *NBC News* (correspondent, ca. early 1940s–1942; newscaster, 1942–ca. 1947); *News of the World* (substitute anchor, 1943–ca. 1947); *Robert St. John and the News* (newscaster, 1943–1946).

At the age of eight Robert St. John moved to Oak Park, Ill., attending Emerson School and River Forest High School. Lying about his age, at 16 he enlisted in the U.S. Navy, seeing action overseas during the First World War. When it ended, he attended Trinity College and took a job reporting for *The Hartford* (Conn.) *Courant*. His investigations got him into trouble when he tried to expose the college president for censoring a faculty member; he was promptly dismissed from school.

St. John took reporting jobs with other papers in rapid succession: *The Oak Leaves*, Oak Park, Ill. (1922) and *The Chicago American* and *The Chicago Daily News* (1923). At the height of the Chicago mobster and gangland slayings epoch, from 1923–1926 he and his brother co-owned *The Cicero* (Ill.) *Tribune* where Robert St. John became its spirited editor and publisher. He was just 21. His stories often focused on prohibition; some exposed corruption and the shady activities of notorious gangster Al Capone. Capone's brother, Ralph, reportedly beat the crusading journalist senseless and left him for dead and the mob took over the paper's ownership to silence its exposés.

After he recovered from his ordeal, St. John took a succession of newspaper jobs: managing editor of *The Rutland* (Vt.) *Herald* (1927); city editor of the same paper (1928); staffer at *The Camden* (N.J.) *Courier* (1929); and cable editor of *The Philadelphia* (Pa.) *Record* (1929–1931). He was night city editor of the Associated Press in New York City (1931–1933); a freelance author and farmer at Barnstead, N.H. (1933–1939); and finally Balkan correspondent for the Associated Press (1939–1941). His broadcasting career began in 1942 when St. John joined NBC in London as a commentator. He returned to America in October of that year. An NBC publicist, writing in 1944, observed: "Robert St. John is probably the only man in the world with scars on one leg from Chicago's gangster, Capone, and a bullet in the other leg from Germany's gangster, Hitler." The Nazi bullet was a souvenir received during Germany's invasion of Greece, which he covered.

Settling at NBC headquarters in New York, St. John quickly nabbed one of the plum assignments doled out to the second tier among the web's newsmen: his quarter-hour newscast and commentary aired in a mid morning slot five days a week on a major national chain, something his peers probably coveted. Taking nothing from his expertise, talent and ability, St. John might have acquired that spot that lasted about three years because he was "there." A staffing shortage at Radio City existed as many of the "regulars" were still reporting from overseas, leaving vacancies that might have been filled by some with seniority.

He gained an added benefit by being in that niche. The daytime newscast he anchored was the companion of the network's more prominent *News of the World* every weekday evening, both of those quarter-hours being underwritten by Miles Laboratories, Inc. for Alka-Seltzer and a line of supplementary health care commodities. When the evening anchor (John W. Vandercook or, later, Morgan Beatty) was absent, St. John was the primary substitute for that pivotal showpiece. A critic called the evening post "arguably the best—and certainly the most stable in terms of personnel and sponsorship—nightly newscast of the war." Furthermore, St. John covered the Chicago political conventions in 1944 and the launch of the United Nations in San Francisco in 1945.

Writing of his work in connection with D-Day coverage on June 6, 1944, a media historian noted that St. John—in New York gathering reports from Europe—"exhibited great broadcasting endurance." He was actually available for an aggregate 72 hours. When Japan surrendered in August 1945, he remained in the NBC newsroom 117 hours, sleeping only 10 hours from Friday to the following Wednesday, according to author Irving Fang. During that period St. John delivered regular newscasts plus bulletins and specials and made some television appearances. He later claimed that he began yelling "Japan surrenders!" into the microphone when he heard the teletype bells ringing on that occasion—before any text had printed out—becoming the first newsman to announce the end of the battle.

He was cited as "an outspoken liberal commentator" while at the same time was recognized as a "talented author" and "spellbinding lecturer." Following the loss of his daily program and an internal dispute at NBC (with Morgan Beatty succeeding John Vandercook as anchor of *News of the World*), St. John temporarily left the web. Within a couple of years he patched up his differences and returned to NBC Television. Following the death of Robert L. Ripley of *Believe it or Not* fame on May 27, 1949, St. John succeeded Ripley as host of the televersion of that august series as it resumed between July and November 1949. It should be noted that that duty had little or nothing to do with NBC's news division, his previous employer, nevertheless. His days of broadcast reporting and anchoring had passed.

In the meantime, St. John had become a prolific author and was working on his 23rd book as his death approached. His topics often surrounded the history of Israel. On March 17, 2002, less than a year before his demise, he was presented an honorary doctorate by George Washington University to signify his 100th birthday and reflect on his 80 years of journalistic achievements.

SAVAGE, GUY. b. Jan. 22, 1906; d. Aug. 31, 1981, Fort Worth, Texas. *Announcer.* **Series:** *Play Broadcast* (1940–1941).

Guy Savage earned most of his livelihood in local radio. He began at KTRH, Houston, Texas, in 1930 when he was branded The Whispering Tenor as he crooned romantic tunes on the *KTRH Mothers' Program*. Later he was a sportscaster at all of the following: KABC, San Antonio, Texas, 1937; WGN, Chicago, Ill., 1938–1941; KLEE, Houston, 1948; and KXYZ, Houston, 1950–1960. Although he joined WGN as a newscaster, by 1940 Savage transferred to sportscasting for the focus of his remaining tenure there.

SCHOENBRUN, DAVID. b. March 15, 1915. *Correspondent, Commentator.* **Series:** *CBS Morning News* (correspondent, 1947–?); *David Schoenbrun and the News* (commentator, 1947–1948); *Edward R. Murrow and the News* (correspondent, 1947–1959); *The World is Our Beat* (correspondent, end-of-year annually 1950–1961); *World News with Robert Trout* (correspondent, 1946–1947, 1952–1953); *World News Roundup*, aka *World News Tonight* (correspondent, 1947–1963).

For the much-coveted role of CBS's Paris bureau chief following the Second World War, the net's chief overseas correspondent selected David Schoenbrun, 30. Depicting him as "a short (five foot two), dumpy, and mustachioed former army correspondent," Stanley Cloud and Lynne Olson pontificated that Schoenbrun's "arrogance was exceeded only by his knowledge of France and his unparalleled contacts among the nation's top leaders." Cloud and Olson pointed out in their biography of the Murrow Boys that while Schoenbrun and a handful of other postwar picks were outstanding journalists in their own right, "they did not have the same war-derived status as the Murrow Boys, and we have thus excluded them from our list."

While Schoenbrun was close to Murrow, the fact that he could never belong to that inner circle of confidantes who had been with the master since the war's earliest days and for some even longer might have been a bitter pill to swallow. He absolutely reveled in Murrow's presence. "I've never admired a man more in my life," he exuded. "Such an elegant man," said he. He was simply ecstatic over being added to the CBS fold. He had observed most of the Murrow Boys during the war and "admired them enormously." Schoenbrun confided, "I just thought they were the greatest bunch of guys I've ever worked with in my life. They were gay [not the connotation that often comes to mind today], and sophisticated as hell, and profound students and well read." In short, they were everything Schoenbrun wanted to be.

As the A team—the original group hired by Murrow to cover the war—returned to America following the battle's conclusion, people like Schoenbrun (on the B team) filled their places. Over the next 16 years Schoenbrun, who became the network's correspondent in

Paris, was a well-recognized authority on French politics and culture. William S. Paley, CBS owner-chairman, was fond of saying that Schoenbrun "owned Paris." It might have been an exaggeration. Slightly. "His Francophilia was such that even Charles de Gaulle, normally so aloof and mistrustful of Americans, warmed up to him," wrote CBS News biographer Gary Paul Gates.

No one exulted in the credible marks CBS correspondents acquired overseas more than Schoenbrun. "For a few brief years, the Murrow team was nonpareil," he professed. "There was CBS and then the others. Our day did not last more than a decade before the producers, managers, bookkeepers, and lawyers took over. But while it lasted it was dazzling."

Even Murrow himself, the news division's original fair-haired boy, fell out of favor with his own master, Paley. Things changed significantly within the operation and by the early 1960s, Murrow himself left, taking a government communications job. Schoenbrun lamented: "We realized that, in this new era, the act of challenging management, however slightly, had become a cardinal sin that would not be tolerated. The era of Murrow and the Murrow boys, freewheeling, making all the decisions, had definitely come to a close."

"The heady years in Paris spoiled Schoenbrun," Gates observed. Late in 1961 the Paris newsman was selected to replace Howard K. Smith, who had been fired, in the dual role of CBS's top Washington correspondent and bureau chief. With the Kennedys then taking D.C. by storm, "Schoenbrun assumed that the cachet he brought with him from France would give him entrée into the inner circles of Camelot," wrote Gates. It didn't happen, no matter how hard he tried. "That blow to his outsized ego only made him more determined to prove that he was every bit as important as he claimed to be."

He had been a one-man show in Paris. In Washington, he discovered, he had to share the ether with other front-line correspondents, seasoned journalists like George Herman and Robert Pierpoint, plus a youthful, energetic, gifted newcomer, Roger Mudd. That never kept Schoenbrun from trying numerous times "to hog the best assignments for himself," according to Gates. That led to friction among the staff. Gates continued: "Even more that the intra-bureau competition he had to put up with, Schoenbrun resented the prevailing CBS News system under which all decisions regarding what went on the air were made by producers in New York, and he frequently fought with them and with his superiors on the management level. At one point, in a fury of frustration, Schoenbrun called a staff meeting and announced that if New York did not give the bureau (by which he meant primarily himself) more air time, he intended to stop giving New York film feeds of Washington stories. 'We'll go on strike!' he fumed."

For a year, from September 1962 to September 1963, Schoenbrun presided over a Sunday afternoon news analysis series on CBS-TV, *Washington Report*. Roger Mudd replaced Schoenbrun in March 1963 when CBS shipped him back to Europe as its continental news chief. That, plus the fact he was denied another hosting job, led Schoenbrun to resign in June 1963 from the chain he had professed adoration for. *Washington Report* was replaced in September by the returning *Face the Nation* which had begun in 1954 and had been off the air since 1960. That venerable public affairs series has now passed the half-century mark.

A disillusioned Schoenbrun, meanwhile, went over to rival web ABC, applied for a job and got it. He was a correspondent there in the latter years of his professional life.

SCHORR, DANIEL. b. Aug. 31, 1916, New York, N.Y. *Correspondent, Commentator.* **Series:** *CBS Morning News* (correspondent, 1953–?); *Edward R. Murrow and the News* (correspondent, 1953–1959); *Washington Week* (commentator, 1953); *The World Is Our Beat* (correspondent, end-of-year annually ca. mid 1950s–ca. 1961); *World News Roundup,* aka *World News Tonight* (correspondent, 1953–1976).

Daniel Schorr's apprenticeship in print journalism began in high school and college where he worked on student newspapers. He received a bachelor's degree in 1939 from the College of the City of New York. In the decade of the 1930s, he was a stringer for *The Bronx Home News The Jewish Daily Bulletin* and multiple metropolitan dailies. He filled a plethora of journalistic roles following graduation, some of them fleetingly. Schorr was assistant editor of the Jewish Telegraphic Agency (1939); reported for *The New York Journal-American* (1940); edited for the Dutch news agency ANETA (1941–1943 and 1945–1948, a post interrupted during his service with Uncle Sam's Army in Louisiana and Texas); freelance writer (1948–1953); and he joined CBS News in 1953 (hired by the legendary news commentator Edward R. Murrow), an employer-employee association that extended into 1976. Schorr's assignments with CBS included bureaus in Latin America and Europe (1953–1955) and Moscow (1955–1958); roving reporter in the United States and Europe (1958–1960); the bureau for Germany and central Europe (1960–1966); and as a correspondent in the Washington, D.C. bureau (1966–1976). After leaving CBS Schorr taught at the University of California at Berkeley (1977); wrote a column for *The Des Moines Register-Tribune* Syndicate (1977–1980); was senior Washington correspondent for CNN (1980–1985); and was senior analyst for National Public Radio (1985–1998).

Along the way Schorr penned a few books: *Don't Get Sick in America!* (Aurora, 1970); *Clearing the Air* (Houghton Mifflin, 1977); *Within Our Reach*, by Lisbeth Schorr with Daniel Schorr (anchor, 1989); *Forgive Us Our Press Passes: Selected Works by Daniel Schorr (1972-1998)*, edited by Matthew Passmore and Chris Robertson (O'Brien Center for Scholarly Publications, 1998); and *Staying Tuned: A Life in Journalism* (Atria, 2001). Of the latter work, his memoir, critic Judith Viorst expressed: "The stories are delicious, the recall is astounding, the insights are witty and shrewd—and the writing sings."

According to Murrow Boys biographers Stanley Cloud and Lynne Olson, Schorr was among a handful of CBS postwar correspondents (including Alexander Kendrick, George Polk and David Schoenbrun) who could be considered "outstanding journalists in their own right and personally close to Murrow, [but] they did not have the same war-derived status as the Murrow Boys." They were automatically eliminated from that exclusive list of intimates as a result. "Schorr, hardly a shrinking violet and a remarkable journalist and broadcaster in his own right, never felt part of the inner circle," the authors wrote. Schorr saw the war itself as a great dividing line. "The group that went through danger together, went through the war, had some alumni standing in common that wasn't fully shared by the others," he allowed.

The reverence that the Boys carried for Murrow, nevertheless, had immense impact on Schorr. For year-end broadcast reviews of the year's news events, which involved many of the Murrow-hired principals, Schorr observed that their mentor demonstrated his high esteem for each one of those correspondents. Murrow went from one to another, engaging each in conversation. Cloud and Olson surmised, "Perhaps they thought so much of him because he thought so much of *them*." "What conditioned our relationship with him was his way of expressing enormous respect for journalists," said Schorr. "He'd say, 'I'm not a real journalist. I just drifted into this thing. You guys are the real journalists.' He always made you feel that he was addressing you as somebody who was in some way superior or more knowledgeable or more experienced than himself."

Even though he was ultimately added to an impressive corps of professional journalists serving as CBS correspondents in Washington, Schorr didn't make it to the anchorman level. Even so, he didn't suffer from a lack of recognition. He might have been the only staffer who routinely concentrated on subjects instead of institutions like the Supreme Court and Congress. Gary Paul Gates, CBS News historian, wrote: "In the late 1960s and early 1970s, he reported primarily on social issues and environmental concerns, and since Schorr was both thorough and tenacious in his coverage, he usually had a better than even chance of getting his pieces on the air."

He also had the good fortune, in 1972, of becoming CBS's chief Watergate correspondent. His exclusive on-the-scene coverage at the Senate Watergate hearings earned him a trio of Emmys. Unexpectedly, he found himself a part of his own story when the hearings turned up a Nixon "enemies list" with his name on it, including evidence the president ordered that he be investigated by the FBI. The "abuse of a Federal agency" figured as a single count in the Bill of Impeachment on which Nixon would have been tried if he hadn't resigned in August 1974.

That autumn Schorr moved to cover investigations of the CIA and FBI scandals, dubbing them "the son of Watergate." Again the newsman became a part of his own story. In February 1976 the House of Representatives voted to suppress the final report of its intelligence investigating committee. Schorr had an advance copy published which he had acquired. CBS suspended him and an investigation by the House Ethics Committee ensued. Schorr was threatened with jail for contempt of Congress unless he disclosed his source. He refused on First Amendment principles, acknowledging "to betray a source would mean to dry up many future sources for many future reporters.... It would mean betraying myself, my career and my life." The committee voted 6–5 against the contempt citation; CBS asked Schorr to return but he decided to reveal his perspectives on that situation in the volume *Clearing the Air* (Berkeley Publishing Group, 1978) instead.

Not everything ran smoothly for him after that. Following a couple of post–CBS responsibilities, Ted Turner asked Schorr to help him launch the Cable News Network. He did so, serving in D.C. as senior correspondent. That blew up in his face when he refused to accept some restrictions on editorial independence.

Shortly after he arrived at CBS in the early 1950s, Schorr, along with Griffin Bancroft and Paul Niven, analyzed the news from the nation's capital on the CBS Radio series *Washington Week*. A contemporary reincarnation of that program, *Washington Week in Review*, projecting a decidedly liberal bias, was still being telecast on PBS as this book was written. The video feature originated on National Educational Television in 1967. On Feb. 5, 1978 Schorr also hosted the premier documentary feature on PBS's television series *World*. "The Clouded Window" on that evening examined America's TV news industry, something Schorr knew a whole lot about.

SCHWARZKOPF, H. NORMAN, SR. b. Aug. 28, 1895, Newark, N.J.; d. Nov. 25, 1958, West Orange, N.J. **Announcer. Series:** *Gangbusters* (narrator, 1938–1942).

Norman Schwarzkopf graduated from West Point Academy and worked for the New Jersey state police as superintendent (1921–1936). During his tenure he was linked with the infamous Lindbergh infant kidnapping and the subsequent trial of accused conspirator Bruno Richard Hauptman. In 1936 Hauptman was executed. The notoriety Schwarzkopf acquired from it attracted Phillips H. Lord, producer of radio's *Gangbusters*. Initially substituting for the vacationing Lord as the program's host, Schwarzkopf acquired the spot permanently within a short while.

In case reenactments, Schwarzkopf spoke with a law enforcement officer who contributed significantly to a matter under study. "He interviewed officers connected with the case and dramatized and reviewed each script to help iron out the technical details," wrote Martin Grams Jr. in his volume *Gang Busters: The Crime Fighters of American Broadcasting* (Kirby Lithographic, 2004).

> No error of police procedure or incorrect technical terminology got past his desk. Woe to the script writer who carelessly called a State Organization "Motor Police" when it should be "Highway Patrol."

Grams added:

> The Colonel was probably one of the first to realize the value of radio to the police, starting in 1922 to speak regularly over the air, delivering descriptive and educational matter in police work. "My theory had always been," quoted Schwarzkopf, "that if private citizens understood police methods better, their cooperation would be greater and more comprehensive.... Radio is a rapidly advancing science, and it is the job of the police to keep apace with its developments."

In the meantime, in 1936 New Jersey Gov. Harold Hoffman substituted a political crony for Schwarzkopf. The colonel was soon president of Middlesex Transportation Co., the full time position he held during the years he appeared on the radio program. He also served with the 44th Division of the U.S. Army. When his duties there became too demanding to remain on the air, he was impersonated ("by proxy") by radio actor Don MacLaughlin (the protagonist of *Road of Life* and future star of TV's *As the World Turns*). Schwarzkopf nevertheless tuned into *Gangbusters* each week and often roasted those responsible for perceived shortcomings through follow-up telephone calls he made to the studio after each broadcast. Schwarzkopf's son, "Stormin'" Norman Jr., became even better known: in 1990–1991, the younger Schwarzkopf was commander in chief of U.S. forces in Kuwait during Operation Desert Shield/Desert Storm.

SEVAREID, ARNOLD ERIC. b. Nov. 26, 1912, Velva, N.D.; d. July 9, 1992, Washington, D.C. *Correspondent, Newscaster.* **Series:** *Capitol Cloakroom* (panelist, 1950–1957); *CBS World News Roundup* (correspondent, 1942–?); *Eric Sevareid and the News* (newscaster, 1947–1951); *Report to the Nation* (correspondent, 1940–1945); *This is London* (correspondent, early 1940s); *World News Roundup,* aka *World News Tonight* (correspondent, ca. 1939–ca. 1977); *World News with Robert Trout* (correspondent, 1952–1953).

Radio historian Luther Sies minced no words when he assessed: "Sevareid's somber analysis all too often tended to be intelligently boring." Yet, at Sevareid's death, *The New York Times* established: "His writing ability and experience, combined with an ability to project a sense of fairness and sound judgment, brought him the respect of his peers and audiences."

Native North Dakotan Eric Sevareid graduated from high school in Minneapolis, Minn. At 17 he and Walter C. Port, 19, a childhood chum, took a 2,250-mile 14-week odyssey by 18-foot canvas canoe from Minneapolis up the Minnesota River to Hudson Bay. It was their intent to confirm that a water trip through the continent, though vast, remote and at times frightening, was doable. Throughout the summer and fall the two youths narrowly averted tragedy, encountering multiple dangers before finally reaching their destination. More than once they paused to reconsider their decision to persist. A $100 cash advance that *The Minneapolis Star* awarded them for eyewitness accounts of their adventures was exchanged for supplies they bought en route. "I knew instinctively that if I gave up," Sevareid acknowledged years later, "no matter what the justification, it would become easier forever afterwards to justify compromise with any achievement." His first book, *Canoeing with the Cree* (Minnesota Historical Society, 1935), was among the outcomes of that eventful expedition.

On the boys' return to Minneapolis, Sevareid gained a post with *The Minneapolis Journal* (the *other* paper) as a copy boy. Within six weeks he was promoted to reporter, earning $15 weekly. He enrolled in night classes at the University of Minnesota, satisfying a growing love of journalism. When Sevareid was reassigned by the paper to an early morning shift, he took afternoon classes. Yet he still exhibited an adventurous streak. He hitchhiked to California in the summer of 1932 where he gold-mined in the Sierra Mountains, though to little avail. With a total of 80 cents jingling in his pockets for his seasonal efforts, Sevareid caught freight trains back to Minneapolis. Then he got serious about his education and enrolled full time at Minnesota. He paid his bills, meanwhile, working at the campus post office and contributing pieces to *The Minneapolis Star.*

Still a free spirit, he became intensely involved in radical causes and campus politics. Sevareid joined a left wing student organization; worked tenaciously to stamp out fascism; campaigned against compulsory Reserve Officers Training Corps training on campus; and pledged—along with others—"I will not bear arms for flag or country." It seemed ironic later, in light of the fact he was to spend some of his life traveling with the U.S. armed forces and being shielded by them while reporting from the frontlines of global battle. He received a bachelor's degree in political science in 1935 and the next year was again writing for *The Minneapolis Journal.* But his tenure there was short-lived; when the paper downsized in a cost-cutting move in 1937, Sevareid was terminated.

Still demonstrating a penchant for wanderlust, he took off for Europe. He enrolled at the London School of Economics where he studied political science. After that he went to Paris to attend the Alliance Francaise. In 1938 the Paris edition of *The New York Herald Tribune* hired him as a reporter and within a few months he was promoted to the post of city editor. Meanwhile, he was simultaneously employed as night editor at the Paris bureau of United Press. But his life's direction was about to change dramatically.

Edward R. Murrow, CBS's key newsman in Europe, telephoned him from London in August 1939. "I don't know very much about your experience, but I like the way you write and I like your ideas," Murrow petitioned. Proffering a job, he told Sevareid that at CBS he wouldn't be pressured to provide scoops or sensational stories; instead, Murrow would expect straight facts, eliminating "manufactured" news when there wasn't any to report. Sevareid was apprehensive about broadcasting—a tendency he maintained throughout his lifetime—although he consented to what he believed was to be a closed circuit audition to be beamed to CBS officials in New York City. Shortly beforehand, he learned that his "ordeal" would be carried over the whole chain. His hands shook continuously as he read from a prepared script. The network brass wasn't impressed. Murrow intervened in his behalf, nevertheless, and Sevareid was hired as one of the original "Murrow Boys." Decades later Sevareid compared his "audition" to "being on stage in Carnegie Hall with no pants on."

As time went on, he would become one of his mentor's most trusted confidantes, spending the remainder of his working life in the employ of CBS, decades into the television era. He was possibly the most erudite of the Murrow Boys. So convinced was Murrow of Sevareid's ability that—following the war, when Murrow wanted to return home—Sevareid was offered his post as CBS's chief foreign correspondent. It was one Sevareid politely rejected as he preferred to live in America, too. (The London job went to Howard K. Smith.) At Murrow's funeral two decades hence, Sevareid felt led to speak: "There are some of us here, and I am one, who owe their professional life to this man. There are many working here and in other networks and stations who owe to Ed Murrow their love of their work, their standards and sense of responsibility. He was a shooting star and we will live in his afterglow a very long time."

On his initial assignment, working out of Paris, the newcomer initially traveled with French forces throughout France, Belgium, Holland and Luxembourg. On Aug. 12–13, 1939—speaking from London—he provided radio listeners with the most intense eyewitness account to that date of a battle in progress. Sevareid observed more than a hundred British and German aircraft waging a fierce air battle above Great Britain's largest city. It was an awful but realistic depiction of what lay just ahead for the Brits.

Sevareid returned to Paris and was lucky enough to get out with his life when the Nazis captured the city in late spring 1940. One account reported: "He drove south to Tours and Bordeaux, taking with him all the money that CBS had in Paris, an extra can of gasoline, and a bicycle tied to the top of his car." He ultimately migrated to London and assisted Murrow until October 1940 when he was reassigned to the United States. Sevareid took charge of CBS's Washington bureau on his arrival back in the states. In addition, he was also responsible for news coverage emanating from Mexico and Brazil. During much of the time he was in the nation's capital—when not chasing a story or airing reports for the network—he dispatched local news over CBS's D.C. outlet, WTOP. Sevareid left for a spell but returned to WTOP late in the 1940s, still affiliated with the web that owned it.

In July 1943 he accepted a Far East roving reporter mission. He and 19 others aboard an Army aircraft bailed out in parachutes over the Himalayas when they experienced engine trouble. Encountering a tribe of head-hunting savages, they were fortunate enough to get on their good side and talk their way to safety, although it took 26 days to reach civilization where they could notify someone that they were all alive. Sevareid worked in China, Burma and India from summer until November 1943 when he returned home. By 1944 he was in Italy covering military maneuvers. On D-Day, June 6, 1944, he accompanied the first wave of American troops landing in southern France. He traveled with them through France and across the Rhine River into Germany.

A few months after the war's end, on Feb. 17, 1947, Sevareid went on the air with a CBS Radio quarter-hour weeknight newscast. He persisted there until 1950. In 1950–1951 he acquired a quarter-hour Sunday evening newscast.

Meanwhile, the newsman penned a first-person account of the war years, *Not So Wild a Dream* (University of Missouri Press, 1946). Not only was the volume a chronology of wartime events as witnessed through the eyes of a young reporter, it traced the development of journalistic strategies for covering international affairs. In addition to *Canoeing with the Cree* previously mentioned, he penned a plethora of added titles, either alone or in collaboration with others, including: *In One Ear: 107 Snapshots of Men and Events Which Make a Far-Reaching Panorama of the American Situation at Mid-Century* (Knopf, 1952); *Small Sounds in the Night: A Collection of Capsule Commentaries on the American Scene* (Knopf, 1956); *Candidates 1960: Behind the Headlines in the Presidential Race* edited by Sevareid (Basic Books, 1960); *This is Eric Sevareid* (McGraw-Hill, 1964); *Washington: Magnificent Capital* by Arthur Robert Smith, Eric Sevareid and Fred J. Maroon (Doubleday, 1965); *You Can't Kill the Dream: Reflections* by Malcolm Boyd, Bruce Roberts and Eric Sevareid (John Knox, 1968); *Conversations with Eric Sevareid* (Public Affairs Press, 1972); and *Enterprise: The Making of Business in America* (McGraw-Hill, 1983). A critic insisted that Sevareid invariably maintained that he was a writer first and foremost, putting it well ahead of broadcasting from which he earned the bulk of his livelihood. It tended to reconfirm the lifelong skepticism he maintained in his own ability to tolerably cope with the microphone—and later, with the camera.

Perhaps surprising and a little known fact was that none of the Murrow Boys readily embraced TV, and least of all Sevareid. "That damn picture box may ruin us all," he once told Frank Stanton, the number two man running CBS. He described for a newspaperman the anguish he felt about TV: "A lot of people start blooming when that little light goes on. I start to die." It seems paradoxical, for Sevareid spent most of his time in the newer medium. Yet until the mid 1950s he did not even bother to purchase a television receiver. Before he overcame a very real fear of the radio microphone, a couple of Murrow biographers noted, Sevareid was thrust before the video cameras. "It was a miracle that he not only survived in TV news but actually became a figure of some consequence," said they.

In the decade before he retired from active service in 1977, Sevareid became—according to Murrow Boys biographers Stanley Cloud and Lynne Olson—"with his mane of white hair, his pronounced jaw, his deep and ragged voice, a kind of totem of respectable opinion." Notwithstanding, the newsman remained available to the network as a consultant, persisting until shortly before his death in 1992. As one of a handful of "experts" (he had been designated "national correspondent" in late 1964), CBS-TV news anchors Walter Cronkite and Dan Rather regularly turned to him for enlightened perspectives on domestic and global issues. At first he provided three brief commentaries weekly but those were increased to nightly insertions long before he "retired." According to CBS News biographer Gary Paul Gates, from 1964 Sevareid was "the most distinguished commentator in TV journalism."

Additionally, Sevareid maintained a myriad of his own gigs on the video network.

From 1949 to 1950, he was one of a trio of continuing panelists on *Capitol Cloakroom*, a weekly primetime public affairs half-hour initiated on TV but soon simulcast in its earliest months over both radio and television networks. On Feb. 1, 1953 Sevareid initiated a CBS-TV news discussion series, *State of the Nation*, by interviewing secretary of state John Foster Dulles. As the web's chief Washington correspondent (through 1959), Sevareid presided over *The American Week* in 1954–1955, a summary of the preceding week's major newsworthy events. For a year-and-a-half in 1956–1957 he anchored the televised *CBS Sunday News*, a late afternoon roundup. He hosted *The Search*, a Sunday afternoon CBS public affairs program filmed at colleges and universities in the summers of 1957 and 1958. Between December 1957 and December 1958 Sevareid introduced a half-dozen *International Geophysical Year* specials scattered throughout the calendar on CBS-TV on Sunday afternoons. Those specials showcased contemporary scientific breakthroughs. And in an unusual departure, Sevareid went over to ABC-TV in 1958 for a primetime documentary series, *The March of Medicine*, which—in only four airings—exhibited two "borrowed" narrators, NBC's Ben Grauer and CBS's Sevareid.

For several weeks in the autumn of 1958 Sevareid narrated *The Great Game of Politics*, a CBS Sunday afternoon half-hour that examined the landscape of American partisanship in 1958 and mused over where the country might be politically in 1968. Between 1961 and 1964 he hosted a series of CBS News specials sporadically introduced into the schedule and labeled *The Roots of Freedom*.

Sevareid anchored *The CBS Sunday Evening News* in 1962–1963 when Walter Cronkite vacated that spot after being tapped for the net's weeknight newscast. For a fleeting period in winter 1963 Sevareid hosted *The Great Challenge* on CBS, an hour-long public affairs discussion focused on the arts, freedom, economy, science and education. The series grew out of a handful of specials he had presided over in 1959 that Howard K. Smith had handled before and after that. On the hour-long *Conversations with Eric Sevareid* in the summer of 1975, the host interviewed an individual with a compelling perspective on world affairs.

For a man who professed to be forever uncomfortable in broadcasting, in 1978 Sevareid released 16 half-hour documentaries on American diplomacy that focused on the years 1919–1941; they were distributed in televised syndication under the overall banner *Between the Wars*. Just as unusual, he hosted a syndicated 30-minute news and opinion magazine in 1982, *Eric Sevareid's Chronicle*. Finally, for PBS, Sevareid narrated *Enterprise*, a series on American business that ran from 1981–1984. At his death, Richard Salant, a former president of CBS News, eulogized: "The most important lesson that Eric taught us was that, even in television, in the beginning was the word. Eric was the refutation of the mistaken notion that there must always be pictures, and that the cardinal sin is to show nothing but a talking head.... When Eric's talking head appeared on the *CBS Evening News*, that broadcast was dominant not only among the critics but also among the viewers."

SEYMOUR, DAN. b. June 28, 1914, New York, N.Y.; d. August 1982, New York, N.Y. *Announcer, Emcee, Producer.* **Series:** *The Adventures of Dick Tracy* (ca. 1934–?); *The Aldrich Family* (1948–1950); *Aunt Jenny's Real Life Stories,* aka *Aunt Jenny's True Life Stories* (1939–ca. early 1950s); *The Ben Bernie Show,* aka *Musical Mock Trial* (quizmaster, 1938–1940); *Bobby Benson and the B-Bar-B Riders,* aka *The H-Bar-O Rangers* (ca. 1932–?); *Bulldog Drummond* (ca. 1941–?); *The Gordon MacRae Show* (1945–1946); *The Henry Morgan Show* (ca. mid 1940s); *Hildegarde* (1930s); *Imperial Time,* aka *The Mary Small Show* (1941, ca. 1942); *The Jerry Wayne Show,* aka *Songs of Jerry Wayne* (ca. 1942, 1945); *Kelly's Courthouse* (1944); *Major Bowes' Original Amateur Hour* (ca. late 1930s, early 1940s); *Meet Mr. Meek* (1940–1942); *Meet the Dixons* (1939); *The Mercury Theater on the Air* (1938); *The Molle Mystery Theater* (1946–1948); *Musicomedy,* aka *The Silver Summer Revue,* aka *The Raymond Paige Show* (1948); *My Best Girls* (1944–1945); *Now It Can Be Told* (producer, 1945); *Sing It Again* (master of ceremonies, 1948–1951); *Songs by George Bryan* (1946); *Stop Me if You've Heard This One* (1939–1940); *Summer Hotel* (1937); *Tex and Jinx,* aka *Hi Jinx* (1947, 1948); *Tommy Riggs and Betty Lou* (1938–1939); *Tune-Up Time,* aka *The Andre Kostelanetz-Tony Martin Show* (1939–1940); *Uncle Jim's Question Bee* (1936–1939, 1940, 1940–1941); *We, the People* (host, 1943–1951); *The Whisper Men* (1945–1946); *Young Man with a Band* (1939–1940). **Aphorism:** *For all you bake and fry, rely on Spry!*

Dan Seymour attended the public schools of Paterson, N.J., and Montclair Academy where he was drawn into dramatics. At 18 he traveled across Europe with a stock company. The day after his graduation with a bachelor of arts degree from Amherst College in 1935, Seymour entered radio as a staff announcer at the regional Yankee Network's Boston outlet, WNAC. His duties included a little of everything, from interviews on the street to introductions of opera presentations. He left it the following year to join CBS as an announcer in his native city. Possessing an entrepreneurial spirit, before he was 30 Seymour was reportedly earning an annual salary exceeding $100,000. An NBC publicist, writing in the spring of 1940, observed that his "ambition is to write, direct and act in his own programs." His goals altered before he finished, but only after reaching all of the above.

Seymour introduced one of the most memorable radio broadcasts in history, one still remembered in contemporary times. He was the narrator for Orson Welles' production of H.G. Welles' science-fiction narrative "The War of the Worlds" on *The Mercury Theater on the Air* on Oct. 30, 1938. It was the drama that panic-struck much of the nation—so real was its depiction of Martians landing their spaceships at Grovers Mill, N.J., that millions actually believed it was happening while the live broadcast was on the air.

Another of Seymour's durable radio assignments was his daily visit to the sunlit kitchen of the toastmistress of *Aunt Jenny's Real Life Stories*. The culinary paragon of Littleton baked more pies, corn fritters and biscuits with Lever Brothers' Spry shortening than any human could dispatch at a church bazaar—even if an event was held every single day—and even if she could hawk her wares as well as she could cook them! But no one asked what she was going to do with all those goodies, particularly announcer "Danny" Seymour, who just happened by as an apple crumb cake was coming from the oven. She invariably cut him a tempting slice. Notably, nobody ever mentioned his presumably expanding waistline either. In spite of it all, "The dulcet-toned Seymour ... could wax lyrical on a Spry commercial," a pundit affirmed.

For a quarter-hour Monday through Friday over the background din of a boiling tea kettle, frying skillet or whistling canary, Aunt Jenny narrated a chapter of her current week-long narrative. Then she unabashedly furnished cooking hints tied to her sponsor, aided and abetted by Danny, whose most repetitious line across the years remained: *For all you bake and fry, rely on Spry!* He liberally sprinkled every exchange with it before Aunt Jenny signed off with a moral bromide for the listeners.

The part of Aunt Jenny, incidentally, was originated by radio thespian Edith Spencer (1937–1951) and was subsequently played by Agnes Young (1951–1956). Seymour, meanwhile, appeared as himself, an unusual representation for a soap opera interlocutor. The pair's exploits for Lever Brothers weren't lost on competitor Procter & Gamble, meanwhile, which plugged its own "pure, all-purpose shortening," Crisco. On P&G's midday matinee serial, *Young Doctor Malone*, spokeswoman Bess Pringle exhibited similar tactics to those shown by Aunt Jenny. Pringle regularly ensnared her son-in-law, Tom Baugh, in *her* kitchen. Baugh had a habit of dropping by just as Pringle was pulling a freshly-baked fruit cobbler from the oven, or some other delicacy. She would offer him a taste—who could resist? It was a parody of what Danny and Jenny had developed long before, as both women plugged their mouth-watering, prize-winning recipes to satisfy the most insatiable appetites of "their men" for many years.

Seymour eased from radio into television rather simply. Two of the aural series for which he was master of ceremonies were reincarnated into tube formats: *Sing It Again* (which was simulcast in 1950–1951 over CBS) and *We, the People* (1950–1952 on NBC). Even earlier, for a few weeks in 1948, Seymour hosted NBC-TV's *The Gulf Road Show*, a live variety half-hour. Briefly in 1952 he was the emcee of Dumont Television's panel quiz *Where Was I?* At about the same time, for three months in 1952–1953 he hosted *Everywhere I Go*, a Tuesday and Thursday half-hour daytime talk show on CBS. Finally, in the 1955–1956 season, he turned up acting in a major role on ABC's hour-long international intrigue drama *Casablanca* with its tales based on a 1942 film and set in northern Africa.

Seymour reportedly received large amounts of fan mail from women who—hearing him on the radio—claimed he sounded like "the perfect American male." Despite that and somewhat astoundingly, he claimed he never really liked being a performer: "The process of simply reading lines became a bore. I became fascinated with the whole business of mass communication and mass persuasion," he allowed.

In the early 1950s a highly energized Seymour became supervisor of television programming for Young & Rubicam, a leading New York–based advertising agency. He resigned from Y&R in 1955 to align himself with one of its major rivals, J. Walter Thompson Co., where he directed the firm's radio and television development. By 1964, however, Seymour had risen to Thompson's presidency and was chairman of its executive committee. Those responsibilities allowed him to heavily influence not only the advertising but some of the programming that was exhibited on the small screen in that epoch. Starting out as a local radio announcer, Seymour had climbed through the ranks to command one of the most powerful posts in broadcast activity.

SHADEL, WILLARD R. b. July 1908; d. Jan. 29, 2005, Renton, Wash. *Correspondent.*

Series: *CBS World News Roundup* (correspondent, 1944–?); *This is London* (correspondent, early 1940s); *World News Roundup*, aka *World News Tonight* (correspondent, 1944–).

In the epoch before the National Rifle Association became a brazen, bare-knuckled, crusading lobby, Willard Shadel was editor of the organization's publication, *The American Rifleman*. Earlier he had been a reporter for that periodical. During the Second World War he journeyed to Europe to attain an eyewitness perspective of the battlegrounds and report to his readers. While there, in 1943 his path crossed that of CBS's chief foreign correspondent, Edward R. Murrow. It was to alter the direction of Shadel's life. In late 1943 and 1944 Murrow was hiring a few journalists to augment the chain's European staff, as temporary or part-time workers. The add-ons filled vital supporting roles in the net's war coverage, yet weren't considered members of the revered "Murrow Boys." That legendary elitist coterie reported from strategic places throughout most of the war and earned the respect of their mentor, the network brass and CBS listeners.

An invitation was proffered to Shadel to join the new hires; he accepted, and of that small contingent, he alone ultimately became a full-time CBS News staffer. By his own bemused account, however, he wasn't welcomed into the charmed circle of Murrow intimates. He and Murrow gained the dubious distinction of being the first Allied newsmen to reach a German death camp and report the horrors they discovered at Buchenwald on April 12, 1945—the very day that President Franklin D. Roosevelt died. Shortly after the war and a brief stint in New York, Shadel was assigned to Washington, D.C. In 1945–1946, he reported from the network's owned-and-operated television outlet, WTOP-TV, on a local news program anchored by Walter Cronkite. Shadel was back in New York by 1947.

He was "appalled at the politicking and infighting that went on among his colleagues to get on *Edward R. Murrow and the News* [Murrow's weeknight quarter-hour newscast following the war]," noted Murrow Boys biographers Stanley Cloud and Lynne Olson. "Part of Shadel's distaste stemmed from his own inability to play the game—or anyway to play it as well as [Charles] Collingwood, [Eric] Sevareid, [Larry] LeSueur, and some of the others." Cloud and Olson observed: "The evening roundup was the real prize, because the sponsor paid a correspondent fifty dollars every time he appeared on it. Bill Shadel discovered the hard way just how valued the prize was. When he was hired, Murrow urged him to try to get on both the morning and evening roundups [*World News Roundup*] as much as possible so that listeners back home would start recognizing his name and voice. He tried but was rarely able to get on the evening program. Finally Kay Campbell, Murrow's secretary, explained to Shadel that other correspondents often persuaded the boss to bump him from the schedule and put them on instead." Murrow himself once told Shadel, "You're so damn naïve. You're such a nice person."

Shadel was a permanent panelist on CBS-TV's public affairs discussion series *Capitol Cloakroom* in 1949–1950 and moderated the documentary *The Facts We Face* on CBS-TV in the summer of 1950. Some time after helping CBS launch its weekly news interview feature *Face the Nation* in 1954, he left his employer of two decades for ABC. There he anchored the *Campaign Roundup* news series on ABC-TV in 1960–1961. Shadel also anchored that chain's evening newscast in the same period (1960–1962); regularly appeared on the ABC public affairs series *Eichmann on Trial* in 1961; and hosted the documentary *Focus on America* at ABC-TV in 1962.

In January that same year he occupied the anchor chair for a dozen hours during John Glenn's triple-orbit flight. Shadel moderated one of the presidential debates between John F. Kennedy and Richard M. Nixon on Oct. 13, 1960, aired by the three networks. Following his retirement from broadcasting in 1975, the newsman became a professor of communications at the University of Washington.

SHARBUTT, DELBERT EUGENE. b. Feb. 16, 1912, Fort Worth, Texas; d. April 26, 2002, Palm Desert, Calif. *Announcer.* **Series:** *Amos 'n' Andy* (1942–1943); *The Ask-It Basket* (1938–1941); *The Atlantic Family on Tour*, aka *The Bob Hope Show* (1935–1936); *The Campbell Playhouse* (1940–1941); *Club Fifteen*

(1947–1953); *Fun in Swing Time*, aka *Tim and Irene* (1937–1938); *Hobby Lobby* (1937–1938); *It Happened in 1955* (host, 1945) [sic]; *The Jack Benny Program* (1947–1948); *The Jack Carson Show* (1943–ca. 1947); *The Jack Pearl Show* (ca. 1930s); *The Jim Backus Show* (1947–1948); *The Lanny Ross Show* (ca. 1939–1942); *Lavender and Old Lace* (1934–1936); *Life Begins*, aka *Martha Webster* (1940–1941); *Lum and Abner* (ca. mid 1930s); *Ma and Pa* (1936, 1937); *The Man I Married* (1941–1942); *Meet Corliss Archer* (ca. 1946–ca. 1948); *Meet Mr. McNutley* (1953–1954); *Melody and Madness*, aka *The Robert Benchley Show* (1939); *Myrt and Marge*; *The Phil Spitalny Show*, aka *Hour of Charm* (1936); *Request Performance* (host-announcer, 1945–1946); *The Shadow* (1934); *Singin' Sam* (ca. 1939–1942); *The Song Shop* (1938); *Starlight Serenade* (1944, ca. 1945); *Your Hit Parade* (1947); *You're the Expert* (1941). **Aphorism:** *Uuummmm ... uuummmm ... ggoood!*

Del Sharbutt's Methodist minister-father urged him to become an attorney. But the youngster had other ambitions, preferring to prepare for becoming a great instrumentalist, then a renowned tenor vocalist. He attended schools in Georgetown, Texas, and Texas Christian University. He appeared in dramatics presentations, sang in the glee club, spoke on the debate team and edited the yearbook. As an extracurricular activity, he vocalized with various dance bands. He also learned to play the saxophone, clarinet, flute, oboe, piano and pipe organ and composed countless melodies. Winning an Atwater Kent audition, he received a two-year college scholarship.

Starting out professionally in 1928 as a vocalist over Fort Worth's WBAP, Sharbutt left the Southwestern U.S. in 1934 to join CBS in New York. His steadfast intent was to become a radio singer. Although his goal was never realized, he "used his mellifluous speaking voice to become a highly successful announcer," a historiographer confirmed.

Sharbutt was a particular favorite commercial spokesman of the Campbell Soup Co. of Camden, N.J. From the late 1930s to the mid 1950s he delivered the firm's pitches for an extensive line of soups, juices and Franco-American brand pastas and sauces on a surfeit of radio series: *Amos 'n' Andy*; *The Campbell Playhouse*; *Club 15*; *The Jack Carson Show*; *The Lanny Ross Show*; *Life Begins*; *The Man I Married*; *Meet Corliss Archer*; *Request Performance*; and *You're the Expert*. Sharbutt's sparkling metaphors surrounding a hearty steaming bowl of chicken gumbo or piping hot tomato followed by *uuummmm ... uuummmm ... ggoood!* with just the proper modulation and pauses—a sort of stamp of approval from an imposing basso profundo—persuaded even the most indisposed listener to satisfy his next hunger with the most widely recognized broth on the planet.

For a long time Sharbutt waged a battle with the bottle, meanwhile, even abusing it on occasions between a show's initial East Coast performance and the live reprise for the West Coast three hours later. With the aid of a physician, he at last conquered the scourge of beverage alcohol and thereby retained his career and with dignity intact. In the autumn of 1957 Sharbutt introduced the daily ABC-TV game show *Who Do You Trust?* alongside debuting emcee Johnny Carson. Although Carson used his newfound exposure to get to NBC's *Tonight Show* five years later—taking with him one of Sharbutt's successors, Ed McMahon, for a three-decade partnership on the late-night marathon—Sharbutt's own place on *Who Do You Trust?* ended after only seven weeks of occupancy.

While remaining an NBC staff announcer until his retirement in the 1980s, even so he transitioned into what may have been one of his final major network broadcast challenges: each week during the 1957–1958 season, he presented the most popular songs of the week performed by a recurring cast of singers, dancers and instrumentalists on NBC-TV's *Your Hit Parade*. The series enjoyed an illustrious heritage extending all the way back to 1935 on radio, although by then it was definitely in the throes of death, only a mere shell of its former glorious self. Introducing that show was a return engagement for Sharbutt and must have been bittersweet; he had performed the same task for radio listeners a decade earlier in the show's halcyon days.

SHELDON, HERBERT H. b. Dec. 13, 1912, Connecticut; d. Oct. 27, 1964, Los Angeles, Calif. *Announcer.* **Series:** *Atlantic Spotlight* (1944–ca. 1946); *Ethel and Albert*, aka *The Private Lives of Ethel and Albert* (1940s);

Flight with Music (1946); *The Herb Sheldon Show* (host, 1949–1952); *Honeymoon in New York* (1945–1947); *The Jack Kirkwood Show* (actor, 1943–ca. 1946); *Mirth and Madness* (cast member, 1943–1946); *The Robert Q. Lewis Show* (cast member, ca. 1940s, 1950s); *Treasury Salute* (ca. 1945–1946).

For a few weeks in 1950, Herb Sheldon provided commentary from the Kingsbridge Armory in the Bronx on NBC-TV's late-night *Stock Car Derby*.

SHEPARD, ROBERT L. b. Nov. 10, 1915, New York, N.Y.; d. Dec. 19, 1993, Los Angeles, Calif. *Announcer, Emcee.* **Series:** *Break the Bank* (ca. 1954–ca. 1955); *David Harding, Counterspy* (1942–?); *Jack Bundy's Carnival*, aka *Jack Bundy's Album* (1944, 1945–1946); *Mr. District Attorney*; *Pot o' Gold* (1946–1947); *Take a Number* (quizmaster); *You Can't Take it with You* (1944); *Your Home Beautiful* (ca. 1947, 1948, 1949, 1950, 1951, 1952).

SHERRY, BOB. *Announcer, Emcee, Actor.* **Series:** *Archie Andrews* (1943, 1944, 1945–1953); *Author Meets the Critics* (ca. 1946–1948); *Box Score Review* (1947); *Carnival with Bernie West* (1946); *Finders Keepers* (master of ceremonies, 1944–ca. 1945); *Jack and Cliff* (1948); *Mirth and Madness*, aka *The Jack Kirkwood Show* (actor, 1943–ca. 1946); *The Jimmy Edmondson Show* (1946); *Turn Back the Turntables* (master of ceremonies, 1948).

Bob Sherry hosted NBC-TV's live dramatic anthology *Armstrong Circle Theater* in 1953–1954.

SHIELDS, FREDERICK. b. May 18, 1904, Kansas City, Mo.; d. June 30, 1974, North Hollywood, Calif. *Actor, Announcer.* **Series:** *Captain Flagg and Sergeant Quirt* (actor, 1941–1942); *Crime Classics* (actor, 1953–1954); *The Eddie Bracken Show* (actor, 1945, 1946–1947); *Grapevine Rancho* (1943); *Honor the Law* (actor, 1938); *Meet Corliss Archer* (actor, 1943–1956); *Red Ryder* (actor, ca. 1942, ca. 1948–1949); *Tarzan* (actor, 1932–1934; announcer, 1934–ca. 1935).

Fred Shields went into radio at Kansas City, Missouri's WDAF in 1928 as an announcer. One of his radio roles, Harry Archer on *Meet Corliss Archer*, carried over into CBS-TV's reincarnation of the sitcom in 1951–1952.

SHIPLEY, BILL. b. Aug. 1, 1918, Ottawa, Kan. *Announcer.* **Series:** *The Jimmy Dorsey Show* (1950); *Look Your Best* (1947–1948).

In 1945 Bill Shipley was a newscaster at Kansas City, Missouri's WDAF.

SHIRER, WILLIAM L. b. Feb. 23, 1904, Chicago, Ill.; d. Dec. 28, 1993, Boston, Mass. *Correspondent, Commentator, Newscaster.* **Series:** *CBS World News Roundup* (correspondent, 1942–1947); *Columbia Presents Corwin* (actor, 1945); *William L. Shirer* (correspondent, 1938–1939; newscaster, 1947–1949); *William L. Shirer Commentary* (commentator, 1941–1947); *World News Roundup*, aka *World News Tonight* (correspondent, ca. 1939–1947).

Until the age of nine, William L. Shirer lived in Chicago. His dad, the most influential person in his life until then—a scholarly U.S. attorney who imbued his son with a love of music, education and literature—died when the boy was eight. The child was utterly destroyed. As if life couldn't get any worse, his mom moved the family, including three children, to her parents' home at Cedar Rapids, Iowa. That tree-lined hamlet was, in young Shirer's opinion, an exact opposite of Chicago and its promising and burgeoning opportunities for anyone with an eye toward his future. "From the beginning," a source affirmed, "Shirer made clear he would never conform to the mores of the world into which he had been thrust." On reflection, the assessment most likely could be made of his entire life. While he became an intellect like his father, he acquired a voracious ego and harbored a willful recklessness that put him at odds with contemporaries and superiors, also leaving him a dubious risk as a mate in private life.

Shirer enrolled at Coe College in 1921, a local Presbyterian institute where he had a good time "thumbing his nose at everything the college held dear," confirmed a reporter. "He joined a fraternity, learned to drink, and raised so much hell with his fraternity brothers that the Coe chapter was suspended for a year." He edited the school paper and made it his personal forum decrying everything he deemed political or common travesties. He also became engaged at Coe. Yet when he found an avenue to escape his environment following his graduation in 1925, he grabbed it: Shirer agreed to work aboard a British freighter that would ferry him to Europe from Montreal. Telling his betrothed he would return in a couple of months after the $200 he had on him was spent, he departed. In reality, he wouldn't return to America—certainly not to stay—for the next 15 years!

He fell in love with Paris and its women instantly. But in less than a month, with nothing that could generate sustenance and his $200 virtually gone, he became terrified at the prospect of returning to Iowa. At that moment *The Paris Tribune*, a derivative of *The Chicago Tribune*, proffered a $60-a-month copy editor's post. He started work that evening and his American fiancée was history. Two years hence (1927) he was elevated to *The Chicago Tribune's* foreign correspondent staff, transferring to Vienna. Five years afterward, when the foreign staff was cut as a result of America's Depression, Shirer was among the first to be canned. By then he had married a Viennese woman and the couple moved to Spain, getting by as he contributed to various periodicals. In January 1934, he accepted a copyediting spot on *The Paris Herald*, not the paper that hired him before. In August the *Herald* sent him to Berlin where he affiliated with parent firm Hearst's Universal wire service. He found the experience rewarding as he sounded the alarm about an opportunistic Adolf Hitler's fanaticism. But three years to the month after he arrived in Berlin, Universal told him it was closing its operations and he would be shifted to Hearst's International News Service bureau in Berlin. Ten days later, he was fired.

The same day, ironically, he received a cable from CBS's Edward R. Murrow in London requesting a meeting with him in Berlin in less than two weeks. Murrow, who had been hired as director of talks in 1935 and sent to London in 1937 as the network's chief (and thus far, only) foreign correspondent, hired Shirer at $125 weekly, the salary Shirer was paid by INS, to "cover the continent." The immediate task before both newsmen—two years prior to the outbreak of continental war—was to facilitate "the production of CBS educational and entertainment shows." Shirer was the first member of what would ultimately be known as "the Murrow Boys," a staff of seasoned news colleagues serving in the European theater. The deputation of CBS reporters was to significantly impact global data dispatched before, during and following the Second World War, setting high standards for peers who would practice the craft.

Stationed in Prague in 1938, Shirer transmitted a five-minute daily news summary from his vantage point that was carried by shortwave radio and heard across the Atlantic in America. On the air he exhibited what one pundit branded as a "clipped nononsense" delivery while another despaired, classifying his timbre as "thin and reedy" and suggesting that he "droned in the flat cadences." Providing eyewitness reports of Adolf Hitler's buildup to global dominance, on one occasion—as Shirer attempted to cover the Nazi army's invasion of Austria—he was physically expelled by threat of bayonet from the Vienna broadcast center. He traveled to London instead, airing his account there. In September 1939 he returned to Berlin; daily broadcasts launched with the idiom "This is Berlin" (reminiscent of Murrow's "This is London" at the start of *his* news segments from the British Isles) were beamed under permissive control of the Third Reich. Shirer revealed much about the present circumstances, however, by inserting colloquial dialect into his transmissions that his German observers apparently failed to comprehend.

Shirer went home to America in 1940 and was reassigned to the New York headquarters staff of CBS News. In his possession were some meticulously kept notes of his personal observations while in Deutschland. *Berlin Diary: The Journal of a Foreign Correspondent, 1934–1941* (Knopf, 1942, co-authored with Gordon A. Craig; reissued by Johns Hopkins University Press, 2002) was based on Shirer's closely guarded transcripts. The volume became a best seller. In the meantime—while continuing to practice print journalism as his livelihood was determined by electronic communications—Shirer penned many more tomes about his European encounters. Some of his works include *Rise and Fall of the Third Reich: A History of Nazi Germany* (Simon & Schuster, 1960); *The Nightmare Years: 1930–1940* (Little

Brown & Co., 1984); *This Is Berlin: Radio Broadcasts from Nazi Germany* (Overlook Press, date unknown; *The Collapse of the Third Republic: An Inquiry into the Fall of France in 1940* (Simon & Schuster, 1969); and *The Rise and Fall of Adolf Hitler* (Simon & Schuster, 1960). Across his lifetime Shirer released 14 titles.

The books, and the lecture tours that accompanied them, plus a newspaper column and a weekly radio gig for a half-dozen years in the 1940s (earning Shirer more than $1,000 per week per quarter-hour radio commentary) made him a wealthy man. Murrow Boys biographers Stanley Cloud and Lynne Olson hinted that Shirer lined his pockets well *because of* his job with CBS. It was an affront to some of his peers, nevertheless, who didn't do as well in outside arenas. It further galled the man who hired him—Ed Murrow—who donated his earnings from his extensive 1941 lecture tour to charity. "One my age cannot go about ... making profits out of recounting the heroism of others, and then put the money in the bank," Murrow wrote.

Murrow and the other "Boys" also felt slighted by Shirer when he rebuffed requests to return to Europe during the war except for a couple of pithy VIP-type ventures. He refused to relieve his mentor of his London responsibilities when he was requested to do so, too. Still later, in 1946, he declined to heed Murrow's suggestion that he pursue the congressional races that year from some distance outside New York.

In addition, there was an aristocratic arrogance about Shirer documented by biographers that was spurned by all the other "Boys." Even Shirer himself reflected in the years that followed: "It was easy, with the notoriety and the constant publicity that radio brought, to get puffed up about yourself." He and his spouse lived high, moving in elite social circles. His counterparts in the business, in the meantime, made little attempt to hide their growing resentment. It was as if—because he had been chosen first—he considered himself first among them in every way, and perhaps equal to Murrow himself.

Author Irving Fang also philosophized on the newsmen of that day, proclaiming that Shirer was "the most liberal of the CBS commentators," a statement that probably wouldn't be refuted by many. That stance figured in his ultimate downfall at CBS. The J.B. Mennen Co. sponsored his weekly Sunday afternoon commentary and paid big bucks for it. In an era that gave rise to the likes of Sen. Joseph McCarthy (R-Wis.) and cohorts who, by the late 1940s, believed there were communist advocates everywhere—particularly in influential spots like politics and entertainment—the potential existed for a liberal commentator to create an uncomfortable zone for a sponsor. Mennen's advertising agency delivered the news to Shirer that he was being dropped effective March 30, 1947.

Shirer had also crossed CBS chairman William Paley the previous year when chewing gum magnate William J. Wrigley agreed to underwrite an expensive news analysis series featuring Shirer and originating in Chicago, Wrigley's home base. Shirer balked, declaring he would not return to the city of his birth. Paley ordered him to take the assignment and he still refused. Paley blinked but didn't forget. The following year, when Mennen cancelled, Paley instructed Murrow to tell Shirer he was being replaced on the Sunday show. Even though Murrow had plenty of reason to leave it at that, he couldn't bring himself to do so to an old friend. On his own, Murrow devised a compromise to allow the troubled commentator to remain on the air at CBS: he would pry one of his most loyal Boys, Larry Lesueur, from his Saturday night spot and hand it to Shirer. Shirer was pacified. But when the two met with Paley and the arrangement surfaced, it was evident that Paley had had enough of Shirer. "Your usefulness to CBS has ended," Paley instructed.

Biographers Cloud and Olson stated: "At that moment, in William S. Paley's office, the Murrow-Shirer friendship ended." Shirer went over to MBS and continued to air his diatribes for a couple of years, to April 10, 1949, when he signed off forever to concentrate on his first love in journalism, writing. He hit the lecture circuit regularly and persisted as an author almost until his death. When the opportunity arose, long after Murrow's demise in the mid 1960s, he took potshots at his former mentor, blaming him for his fate. Among Shirer's published works were three autobiographical volumes in which he settled old scores with many he felt had wronged him. He was divorced twice in the 1970s and afterward married a third time.

SHIRLEY, TOM. b. Dec. 1, 1899, Chicago, Ill.; d. Jan. 24, 1962, New York, N.Y. *Announcer.* **Series:** *The Adventures of the Thin Man* (1940s); *The Aldrich Family* (actor, ca. 1952–1953); *Armstrong Theater of Today* (ca. early 1950s); *As the Twig is Bent* (ca. 1941–1942); *Beat the Band* (ca. 1943–1944); *Carton of Cheer,* aka *The Henny Youngman Show* (1944–1945); *The Court of Missing Heirs,* aka *Are You a Missing Heir?* (actor, 1939–1942, ca. 1946, ca. 1947); *Doc Barclay's Daughters* (1939–1940); *Grand Central Station* (1937–?); *Jack Armstrong, the All-American Boy* (1930s); *Just Plain Bill* (ca. 1930s); *The Kate Smith Show*; *Milligan and Mulligan* (ca. 1930s); *Myrt and Marge* (ca. 1930s); *The Paula Stone–Phil Brito Show* (1944–1945); *Smilin' Jack* (1939); *The Telephone Hour,* aka *The Bell Telephone Hour* (1940–1942); *The Vaughn Monroe Show* (ca. 1946–ca. 1954).

At seven years of age Tom Shirley appeared in a silent film, *East Lynne*. He played football and basketball at Chicago's Senn High School while winning interscholastic swimming championships. For a year he was an engineering student at Northwestern University but left to join the U.S. Signal Corps at Fort Leavenworth. Discharged in 1919, he labored in the Oklahoma oil fields before going to Hollywood where he found work as a swimming instructor for movie stars. By 1921 he was assistant to filmdom's Cecil B. DeMille. During the next nine years he produced several pictures and worked alongside the famous director on *The Ten Commandments*. With the advent of "talkies," meanwhile, Shirley supplied voiceovers for many prominent actors.

Turning to radio in 1930, he was sequentially heard over stations in Los Angeles, San Francisco, Salt Lake City and—by 1932—back home in Chicago at WBBM. Initially hired as an actor at the Windy City venue, by September 1933 he was announcing several network series for CBS, of which WBBM was its local affiliate. By the 1940s he reestablished himself in New York City with its still greater opportunities in broadcasting.

Shirley appeared in the recurring support cast of one of radio's earliest soap operas, *Chickie*, albeit one that never made it to an audience beyond the area reached by WBBM's transmitter in 1933. *Variety* depicted the daytime serial as "a plausible picture of the younger generation struggling with the impulses of adolescence," complete with "dialog that rings true." The feature "contained a little more sex than was usually found on the air," the published informant advised.

The announcer-actor went to television as quizmaster for *They're Off*, an obscure game show that appeared on Dumont Television in the summer of 1949. When his radio career passed, he moved to the tube entirely. Initially Shirley portrayed the role of Dr. Buck Weaver on the daytime serial *From These Roots* ca. 1958–1959 on NBC. Subsequently he performed in the part of Henry Carlson on the daytime serial *Love of Life* between 1959 and 1961 on CBS.

SIMMS, HAL. b. June 10, 1919, Boston, Mass.; d. July 2, 2002, Brookline, Mass. *Announcer.* **Series:** *Rate Your Mate* (1950–1951); *The Steve Allen Show* (early 1950s); *Stop the Music!* (ca. late 1940s, early 1950s); *Strike It Rich* (1950–?).

At the same time he was involved in network radio, Hal Simms was a disc jockey on the *Midnight Bandwagon* in 1950 over Philadelphia's WIP. In the meantime, in the summer of 1951 he introduced the celebrity stunt show *Go Lucky* on CBS-TV hosted by Jan Murray. In 1955–1956 Simms further announced the daily *Jack Paar Show* on the same video network. He was employed by CBS altogether for 42 years, 1951–1993.

SIMMS, JAY. *Announcer, Newscaster, Commentator.* **Series:** *Ask Me Another* (1946); *Call the Police* (1947–1949); *Danger is My Business* (1941); *Inside News from Hollywood* (gossip reporter, 1952); *Jay Sims and the News* (newscaster, 1941–1943).

In 1937 Jay Simms (some authorities spell his surname Sims) affiliated with CBS in Chicago as an announcer. He subsequently filled slots at several local stations as a newscaster or news analyst, among them New York's WOR and Cincinnati's WLW, both in 1941; and New York's WABC in 1942. The following year he was summoned to the Army, departing the staff of CBS and WABC.

In the mid 1950s, Simms transformed his career from an on-air broadcaster to playwright for film and television. His movies included *The Killer Shrews* (1959); *The Giant Gila Monster* (1959); *The Creation of the Humanoids* (1962); *Panic in Year Zero!* (1962); and *Resurrection of Zachary Wheeler* (1971).

While he announced CBS-TV's *High Finance* in 1956, Simms also penned scripts for occasional episodes of the following video series: *Have Gun, Will Travel* (CBS, 1957–1963); *The Rifleman* (ABC, 1958–1963); *Adventures in Paradise* (ABC, 1959–1962); *Rawhide* (CBS, 1959–1966); *Thriller* (NBC, 1960–1962); *The Man from U.N.C.L.E.* (NBC, 1964–1968); *The Big Valley* (1965–1969); *Honey West* (ABC, 1965–1966); *Laredo* (NBC, 1965–1967); *Felony Squad* (ABC, 1966–1969); *Gunsmoke* (CBS, 1967); *Here Come the Brides* (ABC, 1968–1970); and *The Courtship of Eddie's Father* (ABC, 1969–1972).

SINGISER, FRANK. b. July 16, 1908, Montevideo, Minn.; d. May 28, 1982, Sudbury, Vt. *Announcer, Newscaster.* **Series:** *The A & P Gypsies* (ca. 1929–ca. 1936); *Cavalcade of America* (1935–1938); *G.E. Circle* (1931–1933); *General Motors Concerts* (ca. 1929–1931, ca. 1934–1937); *Mutual News* (newscaster, 1938–1939); *The Sinclair Headliner* (newscaster, 1944–1946).

Frank Singiser was the son of a Baptist minister who carried the boy at three years of age from his native Minnesota to Pennsylvania. When the youngster was five, he was taken to Rangoon, India, where the family patriarch pastored an English-speaking congregation. The child studied in the schools of Rangoon for five years, then returned to America, finished school and enrolled at Brown University. He graduated with a bachelor's degree at 19 in 1928. Singiser subsequently applied for any type of work at Schenectady's General Electric Co. plant. The firm owned and operated the local NBC radio outlet, WGY, and sent him over there for an audition. Hired as an announcer, he expanded his efficacy at WGY by also directing radio features and penning some narratives for the ether.

The young man came to the attention of NBC officials in New York not long afterward. At 20, in May 1929 Singiser was added to the fledgling network's New York City headquarters announcing staff. His voice was soon beamed across the airwaves as he introduced series underwritten by such well-known names as Dupont, The Great Atlantic & Pacific Tea Co. (A&P), General Electric and General Motors.

Eight years hence, in 1937 Singiser signed as a newscaster at New York's WOR, a key originating station in the recently formed MBS chain. A year later he was feeding the news to all of the stations on the hookup. Singiser's service at WOR temporarily halted in 1942 during the Second World War when he joined the U.S. Power Squadron. A couple of years hence, he was back and Sinclair, a major oil producer, sponsored his thrice weekly newscast over MBS, his most durable web news run. Although his regular newscasts ended in 1946—easily his best-recognized airtime commodity—Singiser persisted as an announcer for another quarter-of-a-century, until his 1971 retirement.

SLATTERY, JACK H. b. Feb. 18, 1917, Missouri; d. Oct. 29, 1979, Lancaster, Calif. *Announcer.* **Series:** *Art Linkletter's House Party* (1945–1967); *You Bet Your Life* (1947). **Aphorism:** *Come on in ... it's Art Linkletter's House Party.*

Jack Slattery became Art Linkletter's sidekick on radio and their friendship and business connection continued for a quarter of a century, starting on radio and persisting on television where *House Party* was a daily feature from 1959 to 1970 (on CBS through 1969, then on NBC). Slattery was the soft-spoken fellow who not only ushered in the show with *Come on in ... it's Art Linkletter's House Party* over the din of audience laughter at the start of each installment, he also introduced a group of precocious youngsters and held a miniature model home as contestants played the game "What's in the House?"

When the original *You Bet Your Life* began on radio, meanwhile—after an audition tape with *House Party's* audience was made—the debuting show "borrowed" the services of Slattery as its first announcer. Producer John Guedel (who was responsible for both features) soon conducted an audition for a permanent announcer for *You Bet Your Life.* Forty-two men tried out but

George Fenneman was the instant winner. He was cited by a radio historiographer as the "eternal straight man" and became the "ideal foil" for the caustic comedian Groucho Marx, master of ceremonies.

SMITH, ED. Series: *We Are Four* (1935–1937).

Ed Smith was a newscaster at WHP, Harrisburg, Pa., from 1937 to 1941.

SMITH, HOWARD KINGSBURY, JR. b. May 12, 1914, Ferriday, La.; d. Feb. 15, 2002, Bethesda, Md. *Correspondent, Commentator.* Series: *CBS World News Roundup* (correspondent, 1941–?); *Howard K. Smith News and Comment* (commentator, 1945–1946, 1950–1952, 1953–1954, 1955); *World News Roundup*, aka *World News Tonight* (correspondent, 1941–1961).

Howard K. Smith was one of only a few "Murrow Boys" (the reader may recall William L. Shirer) whose ability knew few limits, yet who—after making a stunning impact on his environment—shot himself in the foot. Smith and Shirer reduced sterling early careers to little more than a flash in the pan as they exhibited powerfully unwavering and egocentric streaks, keeping them from exceeding their own inhibitions. As a consequence, both departed their longtime employer sorrowing, and each man devoted some of the remainder of his life to licking his wounds, embittered, yet a victim of his own undoing.

Smith lived in Ferriday, Monroe and New Orleans, La., in his younger years. A rebellious youth, he was headstrong and "against just about everything," one account affirmed. Coming to his senses in his junior high school year in the Depression era, he drastically altered the life's direction when he realized he could turn out just like his ne'er-do-well pa, whom he disdained for years. It was a total turn-about: his sullenness faded, as did his poor grades, and he became president of his high school class, a track star and school valedictorian. Smith claimed a scholarship to Tulane University, where he was elected captain of the track team. He set a high-hurdles record that stood for 40 years at Tulane and was student body president. Graduating with the school's highest honors in 1936, he was soon working his way across the Atlantic as a deckhand aboard a freighter. The German government awarded him a summer scholarship to Heidelberg University ("Smith had Adolf Hitler to thank for the opportunity," a source validated, "part of an international propaganda campaign" to sway American students). Smith had already learned German and French with that very prospect in mind. He intended to prepare himself to become a foreign correspondent but was disappointed when he found that most of his formal training that summer was of lectures to stimulate one's submission to Nazi precepts.

When it was over he went back to New Orleans fully intending to return to Europe for another close-up view of the gathering clouds of doom. Given a Rhodes scholarship in 1937, he went back to Germany for a few months before settling at Oxford University where his old tendencies overtook him. Smith became a visibly vocal rabble-rouser, calling for the ouster of British politicians and working ceaselessly in student revolutionary organizations. Coincidentally, the day war broke out, he landed a $25-a-week job at United Press International's London bureau; within three months he transferred to the Berlin bureau. The year was 1940.

Smith was a working associate of Richard C. Hottelet at UPI in Berlin in early 1941 when Hottelet was arrested by the Nazis on suspicion of involvement in espionage activities. The detainee became a prisoner of war, held in a German concentration camp, the only U.S. reporter singled out by the Gestapo for prolonged confinement lasting four months. Hottelet ultimately joined CBS News in London at the start of 1944; but Smith preceded him, hired by CBS foreign news chief Edward R. Murrow as the subordinate member of a two-man Berlin staff in spring 1941. That appointment automatically branded him as one of the revered "Murrow Boys," a contingent of overseas reporters engaged by Murrow to cover the Second World War for CBS throughout the continent.

An expressive critique of Smith, 26 at the time he joined CBS in 1941, read like this: "At first glance the former Rhodes Scholar seemed the archetype of a courtly southern gentleman, with his tall, slim good looks, Louisiana drawl, and soft-spoken manner. But in fact he had been a hotheaded leftist rebel in school, and his experiences in Berlin under Hitler and the Nazis had not mellowed him.... He got into some serious wrangles ... with the Nazis, yelling at officials, insulting the government's chief spokesman to his face."

When it became evident that Harry W. Flannery—sent to Berlin as bureau chief a few months earlier by CBS news director Paul White in New York—simply wasn't panning out, he was recalled to the U.S. in September 1941. Smith ran the German outpost single-handedly from that point. In the meantime, dealings with the Nazis continued to decline. By December, Smith realized his hands were tied; he was figuratively but effectively muzzled. He applied for an exit visa and crossed the border into Switzerland on Dec. 7, 1941. His subsequent best selling eyewitness account, *Last Train from Berlin* (Knopf, 1943), recalled what it was like living in the German capital in the final days before the U.S. entered the war. Some time after his arrival in Bern, the correspondent learned that the Japanese had attacked Pearl Harbor that very day. Subsequently, he discovered that all of the American journalists he had said his farewells to before departing Germany on what was literally the last train out of town were at that moment confined by the Gestapo.

Smith worked out of Switzerland for two years, essentially covering the French underground and miscellaneous guerrilla tactics. Following D-Day on June 6, 1944, and the battle's clear turnaround, he trailed the American advance across Europe and was one of the first U.S. newsmen to arrive in the conquered city of Berlin. It stood in utter rubble, hardly bearing a likeness to the boastful capital he had departed in 1941. Parenthetically, it wasn't until 1944 that Smith and Murrow met face-to-face during a fleeting encounter in Paris, some time following D-Day. Even though Murrow hadn't known Smith when he hired him for wartime coverage, the young reporter had proved worthy of the faith Murrow placed in him. It was borne out again as the war subsided and Murrow prepared to return to America: he offered the strategic London-based chief foreign correspondent's post to Eric Sevaried. But Sevareid wanted to go home, too, and Smith accepted the job as Murrow's second choice. It proved a good decision; Smith remained for a dozen years, distinguishing himself further on copious matters (the Nuremberg war crimes trials in 1946 and the Suez crisis a decade hence were examples), primarily for CBS Radio.

In 1957 he requested a transfer home. His request was granted and Smith was appointed chief Washington correspondent for CBS. Not long afterward, he began building a reputation as a television analyst, appearing sporadically on the evening newscast with anchor Douglas Edwards. After the televised documentary series *CBS Reports* was inaugurated in 1959 anchored by Murrow, Smith supplied that chair on numerous occasions when Murrow was absent. By 1961 Smith was named Washington bureau chief, allowing him some managerial authority in addition to his reportorial work. Early that year Murrow departed CBS to accept an appointment as director of the U.S. Information Agency which was tendered by President John F. Kennedy. It appeared Smith was ideally situated to become CBS's foremost correspondent.

Just then, however, Smith was inviting trouble, creating some difficulties for himself, in particular with his TV commentaries. Like Shirer and a handful of other prominent radio newscasters whose lessons he unfortunately missed, Smith was outspoken on controversial affairs with many viewers protesting vigorously. "CBS News executives were reluctant to terminate them [his commentaries] because they also believed that when Smith wasn't raising hell about something, he was capable of thoughtful and concise analysis; in fact, in their view, he was the best analyst in all of TV journalism," stated Gary Paul Gates, a CBS News biographer. Gates continued:

> If his superiors had a high opinion of Smith, it was nothing compared to Smith's opinion of himself. He had become, by this time, extremely arrogant and intractable. At one point, in early 1961, when a high-level CBS News executive urged him to tone down his more assertive commentaries, Smith said he couldn't do that because the country had just gone through eight years of weak leadership under Eisenhower, and now the President was Kennedy, whom Smith regarded as shallow and as inept as Ike. The country, he proclaimed, was desperately in need of leadership, the clear implication being that he, Howard K. Smith, was the one to provide that leadership, via the CBS television network. A man who could carry self-esteem to such lengths was no doubt destined for trouble.

Smith's situation came to a head over a controversial *CBS Reports* segment on racially-tense Birmingham, Ala. He was exceedingly displeased over a single line of narration that CBS executives deleted from the production. So incensed was he, in fact, that he called for a face-to-face showdown with CBS chairman William S. Paley. (Some others had had such meetings before him and most had left wanting.) It turned into a fiasco. Paley was seething already before their encounter. After Smith and other CBS correspondents covered the civil rights imbroglio, some of the network's affiliates had jumped to ABC and NBC. Others threatened to follow. Smith's reporting had netted a $1 million lawsuit against CBS by the city of Birmingham. To say that his popularity in the front office had eroded was an understatement.

Smith and Paley met in the CBS executive dining room on Oct. 29, 1961. A trio of subordinate network executives was also present. Partially quoting others, authors Stanley Cloud and Lynne Olson deduced: "Smith was 'extremely offensive' to Paley during the lunch: 'He was absolutely rigid on his right to do commentary.' He said in effect, 'Murrow could do it, why can't I?' He just bore down on it, and Paley got angrier and angrier and said, 'Are you saying I can't determine the editorial policy of this enterprise?' Smith said something like, 'Not with me around.'" Cloud and Olson continued: "Midway through the lunch, Paley took Smith's long memo from his inside coat pocket and hurled it across the table. 'If you want to report like this,' he shouted, 'then go somewhere else.' Smith got up and, without another word, strode from the room. In that instant, less than a year after Murrow's departure, Smith's twenty-year career with CBS came to an end."

Unfortunately for Smith, his haste to rid himself of all things CBS went a bit too far: he informed the web they could tear up his five-year contract. It was a request CBS gleefully honored; Smith had released them from any further financial considerations beyond a small pension. After reality set in, Smith realized his wife was right when she said, "We had complete security for the rest of our lives. Now we have nothing." Needing a job to cover some heavy real estate obligations, he negotiated one with NBC that was withdrawn at its final stage—Smith forever felt Paley influenced his old nemesis, David Sarnoff, the chairman of the Radio Corporation of America, NBC's parent firm. Nevertheless, Smith garnered an opportunity at the remaining chain, premiering over ABC-TV on Feb. 14, 1962 with *Howard K. Smith News and Comment*. Despite the fact "he has displeased nearly everyone" reported *Newsweek* in assessing Smith's recent journalism history, the periodical affirmed that "he is now producing the most stimulating news show on television."

Nevertheless, it wasn't long until he was in hot water again, allegedly over his vividly controversial opinions. A few months after his sponsor abandoned him, Smith's promising series left the air. He was left with few duties and effectively vanished in 1966. Later, an ex–CBS colleague, Av Westin—who revered the Murrow Boys legacy—arrived at ABC as executive producer of its struggling evening news. Summoning Smith from mothballs, he paired him and Frank Reynolds as co-anchors of a revamped effort starting in March 1969. The ratings improved steadily; by early 1974 ABC was within a point of second-place NBC. Reynolds departed and was replaced by ex–CBS correspondent Harry Reasoner. Although the public seemed to like the change, both men were egocentric and didn't appreciate having a co-anchor.

In 1975, Reasoner lobbied network officials for single occupancy with Smith limited to commentaries. He won. But the ratings went south and in spring 1976 Barbara Walters arrived as Reasoner's new co-anchor at a much ballyhooed $1 million annually. Reasoner was floored and returned to CBS in June 1978. Walters was dropped, too; Frank Reynolds, Peter Jennings and Max Robinson took over and Smith's commentaries were deleted. Realizing ABC had nothing else for him to do, on April 20, 1979, Smith posted his resignation letter on the bulletin board and left his Washington office.

"More than thirty years after he stormed out of CBS, Smith remained bitter about the way he had been treated—all the more so as he saw himself systematically written out of the network's official history," Cloud and Olson summarized. "The end of his subsequent career at ABC hadn't been much better, and he and Bennie [his spouse] were bitter about that, too. 'We've never been invited to anything at those two networks, which Howard was with for forty years of his professional life,' Bennie said. 'It's astonishing.'"

SMITH, VERNE. b. Nov. 25, 1909, New York, N.Y.; d. March 4, 1978, Seattle, Wash. *Announcer, Actor.* **Series:** *The Adventures of Ozzie and Harriet* (1944–1954); *The Arkansas Traveler*, aka *The Bob Burns Show* (ca. 1941–ca. 1943); *Arnold Grimm's Daughter* (actor, 1937–1942); *Cavalcade of America* (1945); *A Day in the Life of Dennis Day* (ca. 1946–?); *Furlough Fun* (early 1940s); *Jubilee* (1942–ca. 1945); *G.I. Journal* (1943–?); *The Great Gildersleeve* (commercial spokesman, 1941–ca. 1945); *The Judy Canova Show* (mid 1940s); *Kay Kyser's Kollege of Musical Knowledge* (1938–ca. 1945); *The Lifebuoy Show* (1943); *The Louella Parsons Show* (ca. 1940s, ca. 1950s); *Our Miss Brooks*; *The Roy Rogers Show* (ca. 1944–1945, ca. 1946–1947, ca. 1948–ca. 1955); *Showtime* (ca. 1944); *A Tale of Today* (1936–1939); *This is My Best* (1944–1946); *Truth or Consequences*; *Your Dream Has Come True* (1940–1941).

Verne Smith interrupted his broadcasting career in 1943 to report for duty with the U.S. Army.

SPARGROVE, WILLIAM. b. Dec. 10, 1908, Belle Plaine, Iowa; d. September 1984. *Announcer.* **Series:** *Hollywood Byline* (1949–1950).

When he turned 17, having completed high school, Bill Spargrove decided to see the world. Initially he hired out to the Canadian government, helping to harvest the wheat crop that season. But he quit to prospect for gold, though his search proved futile. Returning to the states, he took a position as a salesman, earning enough to enroll at Ohio State University as a pre-med student. Yet with his funds rapidly depleting by 1929 and the nation's citizens facing their greatest economic upheaval in the country's history, he was forced to drop out of school.

Having operated an amateur radio station earlier, Spargrove—just 20 by then—decided to apply at some commercial outlets. He was hired by several Midwestern stations at different times and got some practical experience under his belt. In February 1938 he left his regional roots behind him and took off for New York, joining the NBC announcing staff at Radio City. In the embryonic days of television news—between March and May 1940—Spargrove was the anchor ("reporter" at that time) of the weekly *Esso Television Reporter* seen over the NBC-TV outlet in New York. In that primitive, experimental era—while Spargrove read the news—photos, maps and graphic diagrams were shown as a backdrop. As another enhancement, an organ supplied music while all of this was presented. It was definitely a pioneering venture.

In 1942 Spargrove, by then employed by the Blue network (which would be totally separated from NBC not long afterward), interrupted his on-air presence to answer the call of Uncle Sam, serving in the U.S. Army. On his return to work, he found the Blue chain had been renamed the American Broadcasting Co. (ABC). Spargrove's duties continued on radio essentially as they had been previously.

SPIVAK, LAWRENCE E. b. June 11, 1900, Brooklyn, New York, N.Y.; d. March 9, 1994, Washington, D.C. *Emcee, Producer.* **Series:** *Meet the Press* (panelist-moderator-producer, 1945–1950, 1952–1975).

Lawrence Spivak, editor of the *American Weekly* magazine, was linked to a singular series on both radio and television for nearly three decades. His impact was profound, however. Seeking to raise the profile (e.g., circulation and advertisers) of his publication, he was impressed by a fledgling aural series created by ex-radio writer Martha Rountree. She would moderate and he agreed to accept the role of permanent panelist. Newsmakers would visit weekly and be confronted by a jury of Spivak and a trio of respected journalists who plied the guest with in-your-face questions, hoping to put them on the record about current issues. In doing so, the interviewees were often placed on the spot. It was something entirely new to radio audiences in the mid 1940s.

For his part Spivak's contributions to *Meet the Press* set precedents by which contemporary interviews with celebrated figures are still measured. The show originated over MBS on Oct. 5, 1945 and persisted on Friday nights through Aug. 18, 1950. In the meantime, it had also surfaced on NBC-TV on Nov. 6, 1947, and—as this is written—continues, showing no sign of running out of steam any time soon. It is the most enduring program in television history, in fact. NBC Radio picked up the audio portion of the series on the tube on May 11, 1952 and aired it continuously through July 27, 1986, giving the feature about 39 years of airtime on radio in addition to the TV run.

Spivak purchased Rountree's interest in the show in 1953; Ned Brooks replaced her as moderator; and by 1965 Spivak succeeded him as moderator. He retired from it on the video incarnation's 28th anniversary, Nov. 9, 1975, interviewing a sitting U.S. president (Gerald R. Ford) for the first time in the show's lengthy tenure, on Spivak's final telecast. His successors in the moderator's chair have been Bill Monroe (1975–1984); Marvin Kalb (1984–1987); Chris Wallace (1987–1988); Garrick Utley (1988–1991); and Tim Russert (since December 1991). "Unfortunately," wrote one radio historiographer, "not all the television hosts who succeeded him were as consistently unbiased and as fearlessly willing to ask the 'hard' question as was Spivak." Yet another source depicted him as possessing "terrier-like tenacity"; "objectivity stood in contrast to interviewers who sometimes expressed their own opinions," the documentarian affirmed.

Among the luminaries Spivak pressed for responses were Fidel Castro; Whittaker Chambers; Thomas E. Dewey; James Farley; Herbert Hoover; Hubert H. Humphrey; Joseph McCarthy; Robert McNamara; Pierre Mendès-France; Robert Oppenheimer; Eleanor Roosevelt; Dean Rusk; Harold E. Stassen; Adlai E. Stevenson; Harry S Truman; Earl Warren; and legions more. Virtually from its start *Meet the Press* earned headlines itself, soon covered as a "news event" by major wire services. Spivak maintained an inviolable canon: "Never take anyone who will withhold information." He believed it was the key to the show's ability to generate front-page news. Both he and Rountree were considered "news anticipators" and attempted to book as many personalities as they could who were "ripe for headlines." A radio historiographer explained, "It became simply a matter of asking provocative questions."

Their concept was rewarded again and again: then, and subsequently, the pattern of asking stimulating questions of guests in whom the public is enamored has been repeated ever since on countless network and cable news interview shows. Nevertheless, *TV Guide* cautioned that *Meet the Press* "continues to be a prime forum for newsmakers (domestic and foreign) wanting to make announcements or test political waters." Despite that warning, television critic Jacob Hay of *The Baltimore News-American* summarized: "I find Mr. Spivak a thoroughly objectionable, offensive, intrusive, abrasive, tactless, and generally insufferable newsman. He has a monumental impertinence. In short, Mr. Spivak is the kind of newsman most of us out here would like to be."

STANLEY, DON. b. Aug. 5, 1917; d. Jan. 20, 2003. *Announcer.* **Series:** *Let's Laugh and Get Acquainted* (1946); *Mr. and Mrs. Blandings* (1951); *NBC Presents: Short Story* (1951–ca. 1952); *The NBC University Theater* (1948–1951); *The New Adventures of Nero Wolfe* (1950–1951); *Out of the Deep* (1945–1946); *Presenting Charles Boyer* (1950); *Richard Diamond, Private Detective* (ca. late 1940s, early 1950s); *The Saint* (1950–1951); *The Silent Men* (1951–1952); *Your Radio Theater* (1955–1956).

Don Stanley was an employee of NBC in Los Angeles for 46 years, 1944–1990.

STANLEY, JOHN. *Announcer, Emcee.* **Series:** *The Adventures of Father Brown* (1945); *The Adventures of Sherlock Holmes* (actor); *Mr. Keen, Tracer of Lost Persons* (1951–1955); *Scotland Yard's Inspector Burke* (actor, 1947); *Thanks to America* (master of ceremonies, 1943).

STANTON, ROBERT S. b. April 14, 1905, Minneapolis, Minn. *NBC Staff Announcer, Sportscaster.* **Series:** *Bob Stanton Sports* (1942–?).

Bob Stanton maintained an unusual pilgrimage in radio that included music, announcing, administration and sports, with television added in. He made several amateur appearances with the University of Miami (Fla.) glee club and then took to the air as a member of a college trio, singing over Miami's WIOD. At the same time, he performed with the Melody Boys at the local Olympia Theater. While the trio was supposed to be a straight vocal act, stage fright and goofs turned it into a comedy performance, possibly broadening Stanton's horizons. He joined WIOD as an announcer in 1929 but became a singer by 1932 with the Henry King Orchestra.

Stanton left the Sunshine State later in the decade when he joined New York's WMCA as an announcer. But a year afterward, he accepted the post of program director at WDNC, Durham, N.C. Yet he returned to Gotham in 1939 to become a staff announcer at NBC's Radio City. While there, he was a sportscaster for New York's WEAF at the same time he was performing similar duties for the NBC network—the local outlet was the network's flagship affiliate. He was still performing the same duties when WEAF's call letters were altered to WNBC in the mid 1940s.

During network television's earliest days, Stanton broke new ground for NBC-TV in several dimensions. His initial outing, aimed at teens, *Campus Hoopla* (1946–1947), combined sports and variety elements into a weekly primetime feature. Among other things, Stanton offered current sports scores and narrated films of recent games. He was allegedly also the first to introduce two different sports to network television audiences: in 1946, he interpreted live boxing action on Monday nights from St. Nicholas Arena in Manhattan and on Friday nights from Madison Square Garden; and in the 1948–1949 season he announced games of the semipro New York Gothams, the earliest appearance of basketball on network TV. His Friday night boxing gig, incidentally, resulted in the *Gillette Cavalcade of Sports*, a weekly event carried by NBC for 14 consecutive years, the most durable of any boxing matches. Stanton remained with the boxing exhibitions until he was assigned to the Gothams' games in 1948.

In the meantime, he was an occasional host of NBC-TV's 1948 weekly half-hour potpourri, *Television Screen Magazine*. From 1949 to 1951 Stanton was the announcer of the NBC-TV quarter-hour music series shown multiple nights each week, *Mohawk Showroom*, featuring singer Morton Downey, vocal ensembles and instrumentalists. For seven Saturday nights in early 1950 Stanton also announced *Around the Town* on NBC-TV.

By the mid 1950s, however, it all seemed to have ended for him in New York. Stanton moved to the City of Brotherly Love in 1955 where he became a sportscaster at WPTZ, the local NBC radio and television stations in Philadelphia.

STARK, CHARLES. b. Sept. 11, 1912, Reading, Pa.; d. March 22, 1992. *Announcer, Newscaster, Commentator.* **Series:** *The Bob Hawk Show* (1942–?); *Can You Top This?* (1942–1951, 1953–1954); *Claudia and David* (1941); *Gangbusters* (1935); *Mr. and Mrs. North* (ca. 1940s); *Morning Almanac* (newscaster, 1939–1940); *Mother o' Mine* (1940–1941); *My Son and I* (1939–1941); *Odd Side of the News* (commentator, 1938–1939); *Our Gal Sunday* (ca. 1940s); *The Rudy Vallee Show*, aka *Kraft Music Hall* (1955); *Scattergood Baines* (ca. 1940s); *Strange as it Seems* (1939–1940); *Sunday Evening Party* (1945–1947); *When a Girl Marries* (1941–).

Charles Stark's broadcast career began in his teens in 1927 at WEEU, Reading, Pa. He attended the University of Pennsylvania and moved to Philadelphia where he was hired variously by KYW, WCAU and WIP. At the latter station, his assignments in the mid 1930s included introducing a weekly *Wednesday Matinee* variety half-hour. Stark left the City of Brotherly Love, however, after New York's WMCA tapped him for an announcing vacancy in April 1936. Following a couple of decades in radio, much of it on web-originated programming, his ethereal performances seemed on the decline as he presided over the *Charlie Stark Music Shop*, a New York DJ series in 1948–1952 on local outlet WINS.

In her memoir, daytime serial heroine Mary Jane Higby recalled how she and actor John Raby bubbled over with young love and faith in the future during the early days of *When a Girl Marries*. But that was followed by announcer Frank Gallop's dispatch of "large doses of gloom." Engaging in Hamlet-like soliloquies, Gallop wondered aloud what would happen to the happy family if the wage-earner was suddenly snatched from their midst. "Thankfully," Higby observed, "the doomsayer stayed with CBS when the program transferred to NBC. There Charles Stark brightened the commercial messages as he raved about Baker's chocolate on behalf of General Foods." Possibly few interlocutors were as genuinely well received as Stark was by that seemingly rescued cast!

For six months in 1949, Stark was master of ceremonies on the weekly ABC-TV primetime half-hour, *The Jacques Fray Music Room*, depicted by a critic as "a longhair vaudeville-talent show." Stark returned to the ABC cameras briefly in January 1955 as announcer of the *Kraft Television Theater*, a live dramatic anthology. Nevertheless, he had some active years subsequently in television as a spot and promotions announcer before retiring in the mid 1980s.

STARK, RICHARD S. b. Nov. 7, 1911, Grand Rapids, Mich.; d. Dec. 12, 1986, Stogrande, Spain. *Announcer.* **Series:** *Against the Storm* (ca. 1939–1942); *Hit the Jackpot*; *The Hour of Charm* (ca. 1946–1948); *It Pays to be Ignorant*; *Lone Journey* (1940s); *Mystery of the Week* (ca. 1946–ca. 1947); *Pepper Young's Family*; *The Perry Como Show* (1954–1955); *Perry Mason* (1940s, 1950s); *Walter Winchell's Journal* (1954–1955); *When a Girl Marries*.

Richard (Dick) Stark possessed one of the most riveting voices in Radioland. Particularly was it alluring as the compellingly basal-pitched interlocutor of the daily matinee mischief dispensed on a serialized *Perry Mason*. Enhanced by sharp organ stings at a precise moment, the treatises of an articulate Stark—dispatched before the action ensued, between the drama's scenes and in summaries at the end—kept listeners on edge waiting for the next shoe to drop. Following his final sales plug of the day for Tide detergent, Stark's gripping abstract—punctuated by startling cadences—struck fear in the hearts of the home audience, adding to the intrigue that was sure to cause them to "Join us ... tomorrow ... won't you?" It was all a part of a quarter-hour package inspired by the inimitable scripting of Irving Vendig with assists by a gifted combination organist and pianist, William Meeder.

In the summer of 1949 Stark announced one of his radio carryovers on CBS-TV, *It Pays to be Ignorant*. From 1950 to 1955 he was the on-camera host and commercial pitchman for a live suspenseful dramatic anthology, *Danger*, on CBS-TV. There a soft-spoken Stark sat in front of a solid black background puffing on a cigarette as he welcomed viewers. "The aura of suspense even permeated the commercial breaks," affirmed a pundit, "as announcer Richard Stark habitually appeared visibly shaken by the drama when he delivered the commercials." *Danger* was one of the first narrative series to make effective use of background music, supplied by guitarist Tony Mottola, whose compositions were recorded for sale later, purportedly TV's first soundtrack album. In addition, Stark was the announcer for *The Perry Como Show* (1951–1955), a quarter-hour seen Monday, Wednesday and Friday nights on CBS-TV. By the mid 1950s he was also plugging razors for Remington in live commercials on CBS-TV's popular Sunday night panel entry *What's My Line?*

STEPHENSON, ROBERT ROBINSON. b. Feb. 7, 1901, Washington state; d. Sept. 5, 1970, Los Angeles, Calif. *Announcer, Producer, Director.* **Series:** *The Bob Hope Show* (director, 1940s); *Jeff Regan, Investigator*, aka *The Lion's Eye* (ca. 1949–1950); *The Pepsodent Show* (producer-director, 1947); *Romance* (1950); *Yours Truly, Johnny Dollar*.

STERLING, LEONARD G. b. Sept. 4, 1914; d. Sept. 18, 1992, Reno, Nev. *Announcer, Actor, Vocalist.* **Series:** *Boake Carter* (1941); *The Brighter Day* (commercial spokesman, 1948–?); *Cavalcade of America* (vocalist, 1948; actor, 1951); *The Eternal Light* (actor, 1944, 1945); *The FBI in Peace and War*; *Joyce Jordan, M.D.*, aka *Joyce Jordan, Girl Interne*; *Life Can Be Beautiful* (commercial spokesman, 1947); *Keep it Dark* (1941); *Pot o' Gold* (1946–1947); *The Search That Never Ends* (actor, 1954); *Sportsmen's Club* (1944); *Treasury Salute* (1945–ca. 1946); *Voice of the Army* (1946); *We Are Always Young* (1941).

STERN, HENRY WILLIAM. b. July 1, 1907, Rochester, N.Y.; d. Nov. 19, 1971, Rye, N.Y. *Sportscaster, Commentator.* **Series:** *The Army Hour* (interviewer, ca. 1942–ca. 1945); *Boxing Bouts* (sportscaster, ca. late 1930s); *The Colgate Sports Newsreel*, aka *The Bill Stern Sports Review*, aka *Bill Stern Sports*, aka *Sports Today* (host-narrator-storyteller, 1937–1956); *Four Star News* (sportscaster); *Goodrich

Sports Review (1938–1939); *Sports Scraps* (1940–1941).

Bill Stern attended Hackley School, Tarrytown, N.Y.; Cascadilla School, Ithaca, N.Y.; and Penn Military College, Chester, Pa., where he made three letters. Playing football all four years at Penn—three as varsity quarterback—he was active in basketball, boxing, crew and tennis, too, while leading the college orchestra in vaudeville productions. Receiving his bachelor's degree in 1930, Stern aspired to become a movie actor but settled for being a theater usher for a while. After working for a Rochester stock company, he had trouble getting past the front gates at the Hollywood motion picture studios and finally took a $5-a-day job digging cement post holes on the RKO lot.

Returning home to Rochester, at 18 he broadcast football games over Rochester's WHAM. He gained subsequent opportunities to do the same over stations in Austin, Birmingham, Cincinnati, New Orleans and other metropolitan centers. A few years hence, Stern was hired as assistant stage manager at New York's Roxy Theater and was elevated to stage manager the next year. In 1932, with the opening of the Music Hall and Center Theater at Radio City, he was hired as stage director, a job he held for more than a quadrennial.

After making a virtual nuisance of himself, in the fall of 1934 an eager Stern prompted NBC officials to allow him to cover a couple of minutes of a football game which Graham McNamee was to air. The young man performed well enough to be permitted to assist McNamee with a couple of later games. He was then scheduled to broadcast an Army-Illinois game by himself. As fate would have it, however, the overly ambitious Stern messed up: getting the big head over his coup d'état, he urged his family and friends to dispatch telegrams to NBC lauding his handling of the game. The trouble erupted when the telegrams began arriving a couple of days *before* the broadcast! Stern was promptly fired without ever doing the game for which he had been so lauded.

The following year (1935) he landed a commitment to cover some football games for Centenary College of Shreveport, La. Following a gridiron match with the University of Texas at Austin, Stern lost a leg when he was involved in an automobile mishap. He referred to the episode across the years as his "big break." John F. Royal, an NBC vice president, departed from his previous stance and allowed Stern to rejoin the chain. He broadcast some football games for NBC in the fall of 1936 and by April 1937 went to work as a full time network sportscaster. Things were definitely looking up for him. Just four years later, in 1941, he was named director of NBC sports. Not only that, in the same year Columbia Pictures picked him to narrate a dozen short features under the banner *World of Sports*, screened in the nation's movie theaters.

In the meantime, Stern had been describing Friday night boxing matches to listeners tuned in to the NBC Blue chain practically since his return to the network. Suddenly he moved rapidly to the forefront of radio sportscasters, instantly developing a rapport with the average guy. That allowed him to extend his outreach to cinema houses as the interlocutor of MGM's *News of the Day* newsreels starting in 1938. He used his radio series, in fact, to heavily underscore his theater links. While he dabbled in multiple show business formats, nevertheless, he undoubtedly derived his highest acclaim from those ethereal commentaries which persisted for nearly two decades under assorted appellations. "It isn't a sports show," he corrected those who got it wrong. "It's entertainment for the same kind of people who listen to Jack Benny."

Radio historiographer John Dunning tells it like it was: "True to the old newsman's adage, Bill Stern never let the facts get in the way of a good story. On his *Colgate Sports Newsreel*, he was known to tell the same story twice, a year or so apart, using conflicting facts and passing both versions as truth. Stern covered his tracks, reminding listeners that his stories were 'some true, some hearsay, but all so interesting we'd like to pass them along to you.' It was his manner that suggested gospel. Stern could put more pent-up emotion into his voice than anyone else outside a soap opera. This style helped make his shows some of the most entertaining quarter-hours ever aired."

In a later entry, Dunning was pretty blunt in his observations:

Probably the most controversial sports broadcaster in the radio years was Bill Stern.... He had a well-honed sense of drama, and it was often said that a fan sitting beside Stern at a game would not recognize the event he was watching from hearing Stern's play-by-play. [Sportscaster-columnist Red] Barber's verdict was blunt: "Stern didn't care what he said on the air if he thought it was provocative or controversial. He never admitted he made a mistake." But his flamboyant style took him to the top of NBC sports and to lucrative stints in newsreels. He was openly disdained by many peers. His semi-fictionalizing was perhaps excusable on his *Sports Newsreel*.... But to do this on a straight news broadcast was to other sports reporters unforgivable.

Sports columnist and early sportscaster Grantland Rice, for one, wrote in his column about sitting in the press box observing a baseball game and hearing Stern air the game. Rice opined: "There were two entirely different games played here today—one on the field and another on NBC radio."

Some other media historians viewed Stern similarly. Frank Buxton and Bill Owen labeled him "the most controversial sportscaster of radio's Golden Age." They nailed him, too, insisting: "His emotionally charged, piercing delivery made him ideally suited for play-by-play action, but he had a tendency toward exaggeration and over-dramatization.... His vivid imagination carried over to his highly rated *Sports Newsreel* program, where he elevated Dwight Eisenhower to the All-American roster, revealed that Pope Pius XII had been a baseball player in his youth, made super sports stars of countless prominent politicians, actors, and other celebrities who had, in fact, only dabbled in athletics, and on one occasion related the story of a baseball player who suffered a fatal heart attack between third base and home and was dead when he scored the winning run!"

Nonetheless, Buxton and Owen affirmed: "Despite such flagrant fictionalization, Stern created tremendous interest in sports, particularly college football. He was clearly the most listened-to sportscaster of his day. Those who criticized his lack of concern for veracity admitted to his great talent as an entertainer, and few questioned his knowledge of sports, his energy, sense of timing, and announcing skill."

In a depiction of radio journalist Paul Harvey, a critic allowed that his "success was based more on personality than news.... The unmistakable touches of Bill Stern are evident in his style," a remark hinting at the flamboyancy in verbiage cited already.

Stern had a penchant for corralling some of the major figures in a variety of diverse species for his radio show and usually attempted to tie some specific sports activity to them. Among the luminaries gracing his microphone over the years were Lucille Ball; Albin W. Barkley; Brace Beemer; Jack Benny; Milton Berle; Vivian Blaine; Cab Calloway; Eddie Cantor; Joe DiMaggio; Tommy Dorsey; Morton Downey; Leo Durocher; Judy Garland; Rocky Graziano; Spike Jones; Sammy Kaye; Guy Lombardo; Roddy MacDowell; Elsa Maxwell; Ronald Reagan; Mickey Rooney; Babe Ruth; Dinah Shore; Frank Sinatra; Ezra Stone; Margaret Truman; Rudy Vallee; Orson Welles; and many more.

In addition to his colorful commentaries, Stern is also remembered for his coverage of legions of sporting events. His eyewitness reporting embraced baseball (though never covering a World Series); basketball; bowling; boxing (including most of Joe Louis's title fights); crew; fishing; football bowl games and National Football League championships; golf; hockey; horse racing; rodeo; skiing; tennis; and track and field (including the 1936 Olympics at Berlin and the 1948 Olympics at London).

By 1953 Stern had left NBC behind to join ABC, which evolved from the former NBC Blue chain a decade earlier. In the 1960s, he transferred his loyalty yet again, that time to MBS. He is also celebrated for airing what is believed to be the first televised sporting event, a 1939 baseball contest featuring Columbia and Princeton universities.

Stern had multiple shots on television. In 1949 he and Clem McCarthy announced spirited horse races from the Jamaica, N.Y., racetrack every Saturday afternoon on *NBC Takes You to the Races*, a live video production. Between contests on NBC's *Trotting Races* in 1950 shown from New York's Roosevelt Raceway, Stern conducted a quiz with racing fans drawn from the spectator galleries. He also hosted an interview and discussion series featuring celebs from the sports world, *Spotlight on Sports*, one weekend evening (Saturday or Sunday) each week in the summer of 1950. For a half-hour on Tuesday and Thursday afternoons in 1950–1951, Stern presided over *Remember This Date* on NBC-TV. It was a quiz show on which he dispensed hints to a quartet of players about events or people in the past linked with the specific date of the telecast.

Stern and Candy Jones co-hosted a half-hour audience participation-variety series in 1951, *Star Night*, on NBC. In 1951 (for NBC) and in 1954 (for ABC) Stern announced televised coverage of *NCAA Football* on Saturday afternoons. For three weeks in the summer of 1952 he emceed the NBC-TV game show *Are You Positive* that tested the memories of a panel of sports addicts. He inaugurated *The Saturday Night Fights* in January 1953 over ABC-TV, handling those weekly boxing matches into that year's autumn season. Finally, in 1953–1954, Stern was one of a handful of celebrity panelists on the ABC-TV guessing game *The Name's the Same*.

STEVENS, LEE (born Adolph C. Weinert). b. April 5, 1924, Baltimore, Md. *Announcer*. **Series:** *Big Sister* (ca. 1940s).

Adolph (Ad) Weinert was an announcer and newscaster in 1937 at WSBA, York, Pa. He later joined Baltimore's WMAR-TV, and became one of Ed Sullivan's early announcers on the CBS-TV *Toast of the Town* variety series.

STEVENSON, BOB. *Announcer*. **Series:** *The Adventures of Philip Marlowe* (ca. 1948–1950); *Broadway is My Beat* (1950); *Earn Your Vacation* (1949); *The Jack Smith, Dinah Shore, Margaret Whiting Show* (1950); *Jeff Regan, Investigator* (1948); *Leave it to Joan* (1949–1950); *Let George Do It* (1951–?); *Life with Luigi* (1948–1954); *Lights Out* (1943); *The Lineup* (1951); *The Lucky Strike Program Starring Jack Benny* (1951); *Our Miss Brooks* (1948); *The Oxydol Show* (1950); *The Phil Harris–Alice Faye Show* (ca. 1948–early 1950s); *Pursuit* (1951–1952); *The Rochester Show* (1950); *Rocky Jordan* (ca. 1948–1950); *Romance* (1950–1951); *Suspense*; *Yours Truly, Johnny Dollar* (1950–1951).

As of 1937 Bob Stevenson was both a news analyst and sportscaster at New York's WHN. His ongoing gigs included General Mills baseball broadcasts, *Gridiron Smoker*, *Latest News at the End of the Day* and Socony-Vacuum baseball broadcasts.

STEWART, JAY CLEVE (born Jay Fix). b. Sept. 6, 1918, Summitville, Ind.; d. Sept. 17, 1989, Los Angeles, Calif. *Announcer, Emcee*. **Series:** *The Carnation Family Party* (master of ceremonies, 1950–1951); *Duffy's Tavern* (1940s); *The Great Gildersleeve* (1949–ca. 1950); *Jay Stewart's Fun Fair* (master of ceremonies, 1949, 1950–1951); *June's My Girl* (1948); *Meet the Missus* (master of ceremonies, mid to late 1940s); *The Open House* (1943–1946); *Surprise Package* (master of ceremonies, 1950); *Take It or Leave It* (1940s); *That's a Good Idea* (1945); *That's Life* (1946–1947); *Truth or Consequences* (ca. 1950s); *What's Doin', Ladies?* (master of ceremonies, 1946–1948); *The Wizard of Odds* (master of ceremonies, ca. 1949–ca. 1953).

Jay Fix, who would rename himself Jay Stewart in 1943, had a newspaper route while attending school at Summitville, Ind. He also worked as a counselor in a summer band camp and took a job as a soda jerk, helping make the ice cream he dispensed. He played the saxophone at nine years of age and emceed floor shows at 14. Before he was 16 he enrolled at DePauw University, Greencastle, Ind., but subsequently transferred to Indianapolis' Butler University.

Fix worked his way through school conducting dance bands and playing the sax. Upon his graduation in 1939 he won an audition at Terre Haute's WBAW and began working there as an announcer. The following year he shifted to Cincinnati's WLW. In 1941 he answered the call of Uncle Sam but was back at WLW a short time later (in November 1941) after a medical discharge. Hearing, in 1943, that there was a scarcity of radio announcers on the West Coast, Fix departed WLW again, landing a spot with CBS in Hollywood. At that juncture he permanently changed his name to Jay Stewart.

For a few weeks during the 1950–1951 television season he produced and presided over the Saturday morning ABC children's stunt series *Fun Fair*. Stewart is better recalled by more people, however, as the announcer and sidekick to emcee Monty Hall on the daily game show infused with wild costumed excitement, *Let's Make a Deal*, on NBC-TV (1964–1968) and ABC-TV (1968–1976). Stewart announced for several other audience participation gigs on the tube, too, including:

It's Anybody's Guess (1977 on NBC, again paired with emcee Monty Hall); *The Joker's Wild* (1977–1986 in syndication, with host Jack Barry and, in 1984, Bill Cullen); *Joker! Joker!! Joker!!!* (1979–1981 in syndication, also with Barry); and *Sale of the Century* (1983–1988 on NBC, with master of ceremonies Jim Perry).

STONE, DAVID P. b. Oct. 27, 1901, Savannah, Ga.; d. Aug. 31, 1995, Minneapolis, Minn. *Announcer, Producer.* **Series:** *Grand Ole Opry* (1939–1940).

The Museum of Broadcasting Hall of Fame noted that—while David Stone didn't sing or play a guitar—"no one did more to promote country music in the Upper Midwest than popular radio and television personality David Stone." Before he got into broadcasting, Stone was employed in machine shops, then theater management, starting his radio career in the 1920s at Nashville's WLAC. He shifted his loyalty to WSM later and by 1928 was an announcer and co-producer of the soon-to-be legendary, world famous *Grand Ole Opry*. While WSM's 50,000 watts carried the program to listeners in 37 states, Canada and Mexico, Stone was on hand in 1939 when NBC began to beam the show nationwide. It would continue doing so for 18 years.

Leaving Music City, U.S.A. in 1940, nonetheless, Stone took a post at Minneapolis–St. Paul's KSTP, where he was hired to inaugurate, host and produce a country music and comedy feature, ultimately assigned the name of *Sunset Valley Barn Dance*. The show played to full houses at dance halls, auditoriums, county fairs and other venues throughout its geographic territory and was heard by millions tuning in to KSTP. The performances established the careers of multiple local country musicians and resulted in a number of spin-off broadcast series such as *Hymn Time, Main Street* and *Sunrise Roundup*.

Eight years after its inception on radio, the barn dance was added to KSTP-TV's early schedule. Meanwhile, Stone presided over a midday series, *County Road 5*, too, and persisted as KSTP farm director until he retired at 85 in 1986. He was inducted into the Museum of Broadcasting Hall of Fame in 2002, seven years following his death.

STONE, GEORGE. *Announcer.* **Series:** *The Art Van Damme Quintet* (ca. 1945–1946); *Crime on the Waterfront* (1949); *Easy Money* (1946); *The Fleischmann Hour*, aka *The Rudy Vallee Show* (ca. 1934–1936); *Grand Marquee* (1946–1947); *Highway Harmonies* (1953); *A Life in Your Hands* (1952); *Lights Out* (mid 1940s).

STORM, JOHN. b. Aug. 1, ?, Burchard, Neb. *Announcer.* **Series:** *Dangerous Assignment* (1949, 1950–1954); *Hawthorne's Adventures*, aka *Hawthorne Show* (ca. 1949–ca. 1950); *Inheritance* (1954–1955); *A Johnny Fletcher Mystery* (ca. 1948); *The Man Called X* (1950); *Music and the Muse* (1949–1950); *The New Adventures of Nero Wolfe* (1950–1951); *Noah Webster Says* (ca. 1947–1948, 1950); *One Night Stand* (1951); *Prelude to Dusk* (1951); *Richard Diamond, Private Detective* (1949); *The Roy Rogers Show* (1952); *The Time, the Place and the Tune* (1948); *The Thirteenth Juror* (1949–1953).

John Storm was employed by NBC in Los Angeles for 32 years, 1937–1969.

STOUT, REX. b. ca. 1887; d. Aug. 27, 1975. *Emcee, Commentator.* **Series:** *Our Secret Weapon* (host, 1942–1943); *People's Platform* (visiting scholar, 1943).

Beginning in 1934 Rex Stout inspired the mystery novels of Nero Wolfe and, ultimately, *The Adventures of Nero Wolfe*. Between 1943 and 1951, the aural series—fawned over by legions of admirers who still fondly recall it—appeared on a trio of radio chains while consuming an aggregate of less than three years of air time in broken segments. For seven months in 1981 the hour-long detective drama subsequently appeared on NBC-TV starring William Conrad as its hero.

Stout, himself, didn't participate in any of the broadcasts with the eccentric fictional comfy chair-bound sleuth; he seemed satisfied to conceive it, and by the time it appeared on radio he was already on the ether anyway. He had his hands in several enterprises, in fact: he was chairman of the Writers War Board which functioned as a clearing house to mobilize journalists in support of the war effort. Stout was an envoy of Freedom House, yet another patriot-promoting enclave. He hosted a little known series on radio, 1941's *Council for Democracy*. In 1944 he lampooned the membership of the Radio Writers Guild for its perceived "white Protestant Anglo-Saxon" overindulgence.

A pundit characterized Stout as an outspoken critic of racial prejudice, yet that declaration seems inconsistent with one he is quoted as stating on the air in September 1942: "I am willing to grant to any grown German one right and only one, the right to a decent burial." According to a reporter, he had come to believe that the main obstacle to peace was "an inherent antidemocratic trait of the German national character." The German people as a race, he felt—not Adolf Hitler acting alone—was guilty of events in their land and for their nation's aggression across Europe. Stout believed U.S. citizens must be persuaded to see the correctness of his vision.

Meanwhile, at least two attempts were made during the Second World War to mock the well-oiled party-line machinations of the Axis powers, holding them up for contempt to American ears. Stout introduced the first feature on CBS, a quarter-hour on Sunday nights, *Our Secret Weapon*; it was soon followed by *Troman Harper, Rumor Detective* on MBS, a quarter-hour on Sunday nights beginning only four months after Stout debuted. (Success frequently breeds success.)

A staff tuned in to the fabrications via shortwave radio dispensed by the propagandists every week, reproducing the best ones in hard copy for Stout. He picked about 150 of the best ones and passed them along to series writer Sue Taylor White. She verified them before working with Stout on scripting the show. On the air, an interlocutor read them aloud in rapid-fire delivery, frequently in derisive German, Italian or Japanese inflection. Stout countered the statements just as quickly as they were dispatched. A small group of thespians portrayed Hitler (Paul Luther), Hirohito (Ted Osborne) and Mussolini (Guy Repp). Occasionally major addresses given in other dialects were included in pithy narratives to make emphatic points.

STRAWSER, NEIL. b. 1927, Rittman, Ohio; d. Dec. 31, 2005, Washington, D.C. *Correspondent, Newscaster.* **Series:** *CBS News on the Hour* (anchor-correspondent, 1952–1986); *CBS World News Roundup* (anchor-correspondent, 1952–ca. 1986); *The World Tonight* (correspondent, 1952–1986).

Neil Strawser graduated from Oberlin College in 1951 and afterwards earned a master's degree at George Washington University. He served with the U.S. Naval Reserve and was a radio disc jockey and local news anchor before joining CBS News in 1952 as an editorial research assistant. Over the next 34 years—to 1986 when he left to become Democratic spokesman for the House Budget Committee—Strawser's star rose at the Washington bureau of CBS and he became one of its busiest and most respected journalists.

A couple of decades later, CBS historian Gary Paul Gates assessed the situation at CBS in D.C. at the dawn of the 1970s: "Clustered behind the pacesetters in the Washington bureau [whom Gates identifies as John Hart, Marvin Kalb, Roger Mudd, Dan Rather, Daniel Schorr and Eric Sevareid] was a hustling herd of correspondents who jockeyed with each other for good assignments [including reporters like Fred Graham, George Herman, Robert Pierpoint]. Among the old guard, those who had been around since the 1950s or earlier and whose best years were behind them, there was Neil Strawser, the 'voice of Washington' back in the days of the Doug Edwards show [1948–1962]. By 1970, Strawser (like Edwards himself) was working primarily in radio."

Possibly more than any other CBS-Washington staffer of that era, Strawser concentrated on radio more than on television. He anchored the network's four-day continuous radio coverage following President John F. Kennedy's assassination in November 1963 as well as its radio reporting of the Watergate hearings and NASA space launches prior to 1987. Strawser wasn't limited to radio by any means; in the late 1950s and early 1960s he frequently appeared on the weeknight quarter-hour telecasts of *Douglas Edwards with the News*. In 1962 he was distinguished as the only television reporter to be admitted into the Guantanamo Bay Naval Base during the Cuban missile crisis. As a result he witnessed the departure of the freighters carrying nuclear missiles returning to Russia. On several occasions he contributed to CBS-TV's *Face the Nation* public affairs series.

All of it led some industry insiders to respectfully dub him "the voice of Washington." In that capacity Strawser aired numerous reports from Congress and federal agencies, particularly on a couple of major weekday radio series: *CBS World News Roundup* in the morning with Dallas Townsend in the anchor chair and *The World Tonight* with Douglas Edwards performing that duty. Strawser sometimes substituted for Townsend during the week and regularly filled his indispensable chair on Saturday mornings. He also anchored weekend *CBS News on the Hour* broadcasts for many years.

As a sideline, Strawser concurrently narrated legions of Encyclopedia Britannica educational films screened in thousands of school classrooms around the country. He retired from the House Budget Committee in 1994.

STUART, ALLAN. *Announcer.* **Series:** *The Voice of Broadway* (1941–1942, ca. 1944).

Allan Stuart was a disc jockey at New York's WJZ in 1952.

SUMMERALL, GEORGE ALLEN (PAT). b. May 10, 1930, Lake City, Fla. Series: CBS sportscasts (1962–1993); *Pat Summerall on Sports* (ca. 1962–1993).

Pat Summerall won the Florida state tennis championship and All-State basketball honors before playing college football from 1949 to 1951 at the University of Arkansas. Following his graduation in 1953, for a decade he played professional football in the National Football League, mostly as a placekicker. The Detroit Lions drafted him in 1952; he broke his arm that year and sat out the remainder of the season. Traded in 1953 to the Chicago Cardinals, Summerall played for four years in the Windy City and then went to the New York Giants (1958–1961). He appeared on CBS Radio in 1960 and by 1962 he joined the network, airing Giants' games on a part time basis. Two years later he became a full time broadcaster for CBS, working NFL telecasts, doing sports features for CBS Radio and providing sports updates for the web's New York flagship outlet, WCBS-AM.

In addition to football, Summerall picked up golfing and tennis assignments across a 32-year association with CBS. In 1994 the Fox network stunned virtually everyone by outbidding CBS for the NFC broadcast rights. Fox immediately took steps to insure that Summerall and his partner John Madden, who had been paired since 1981 as lead announcing team, would continue their duties without interruption. The duo persisted through 2001 when Summerall retired and Madden joined ABC. Fox lured Summerall back for another season in 2002, alongside Brian Baldinger, and then he slipped back into retirement.

In the spring of 2004 Summerall, a recovering alcoholic, experienced successful liver transplant surgery. A few months hence—while ESPN regular announcer Mike Patrick recovered from heart surgery—Summerall called several 2004 preseason and early regular season NFL games. Over an enduring career, meanwhile, Summerall was in the broadcast booth of 26 Super Bowls, more than any other announcer. Ten of those broadcasts were on CBS Radio; the remaining 16 were split between CBS-TV and Fox Television.

SWAYZE, JOHN CAMERON. b. April 4, 1906, Wichita, Kan.; d. Aug. 15, 1995. *Newscaster, Correspondent.* **Series:** *John Cameron Swayze and the News* (newscaster, 1947–1948, 1951–1953); *Monitor* (correspondent, ca. 1955–ca. 1958); *Who Said That?* (panelist, 1948, 1949, 1950). **Aphorisms:** *Glad we could get together; Hopscotching in the world of headlines; It takes a licking but keeps on ticking.*

John Cameron Swayze intended to become an actor and, consequently, studied drama in New York City before enrolling at the University of Kansas. To pay his bills he took a job as a reporter on a small Kansas City radio station. Following graduation, his livelihood was immediately derived by being a columnist and drama critic for *The Kansas City Journal*.

Swayze started newscasting and analyzing over Kansas City's KMBC as early as 1935. By 1937 he moved to rival station WHB but by 1940 he was back at KMBC, primarily as a newscaster-commentator. However, still harboring a need for some public adulation, when he acquired a few opportunities to expand into other areas he seized them. In 1941, for instance, he hosted a weekly half-hour game show on KMBC, *Pun and Punishment*, which sought to "glorify the American pun." Extemporaneously, a handful of continuing personalities derived imaginative witticisms to assist the contenders in figuring out secret words that could help them win cash and merchandise gifts. Swayze resigned his post at KMBC for the final time in 1943 to swim in a larger fish tank.

Joining NBC in New York, he gained a slot in the radio newscast rotation. Perhaps because of his demonstrated interest in game shows, nonetheless, he was appointed permanent panelist for the guesser *Who Said That?* that developed into both radio and television incarnations (Swayze was with the show continuously on NBC-TV from 1948 to 1951).

The nascent development of the nightly news programs on contemporary broadcast television included Swayze almost from their core. Tim Brooks and Earle Marsh meticulously recounted details of that embryonic chapter:

> In February 1948, NBC began a Monday–Friday evening news show called the *Camel Newsreel Theatre*. It was only 10 minutes long, and was not much different from *Esso Newsreel*, which it succeeded, but it was the genesis of the *Camel News Caravan* which took its place a year later [1949]. When that happened, John Cameron Swayze, one of the announcers behind the newsreels, moved in front of the cameras and became an 'anchorman.' The sponsor [R.J. Reynolds Tobacco Co.] was so nervous about this radical departure from the traditional newsreel concept of TV news that it insisted on including fashion shows and other light features to maintain visual interest and attract female viewers. These were soon phased out, but the background music—another holdover from newsreels—remained until the mid-1950s, as did the film narration by a second, newsreel-style announcer. Nevertheless John Cameron Swayze became America's best-known individual newscaster. His nightly sign-off, "Glad we could get together," was one of early television's most familiar phrases. Swayze was essentially a newsreader, however. By the mid-1950s television had become a news-gathering force in its own right, and NBC (feeling pressure from CBS) felt it necessary to put someone with more field experience in front of the cameras. So in October 1956 Swayze was replaced by Chet Huntley and David Brinkley.

For those telecasts Swayze habitually wore a flower on his lapel. Each evening after delivering the major portion of the news, he allowed, *Hopscotching in the world of headlines* as he leaped across a myriad of bulleted items. In 1958 Swayze jumped ship and went over to competitor ABC where—for two full years, 1961 and 1962—he and a couple of virtual unknowns, Bill Lawrence and Al Mann, triple-hosted the web's early evening television newscast Monday through Friday. Before leaving NBC-TV, however, Swayze co-hosted (with Don Goddard) *Watch the World*, a current events show for kids (1950); was quizmaster for *Guess What Happened*, a current events game lasting three weeks (1952); emcee of *Sightseeing with the Swayzes*, aka *Vacationland America*, including films of his family on journeys around the nation (1953); host-narrator of the dramatic anthology *Armstrong Circle Theater* (1955–1957); dispatched travel news on the weekday daytime *Home* show once a week; and was a regular contributor on *The Steve Allen Show* (1957–1958).

Before departing NBC, Swayze slipped over to CBS to appear on the premiering panel guessing game *To Tell the Truth* (Dec. 18, 1956). His inaugural assignment at ABC-TV was as master of ceremonies for the pithy game show *Chance for Romance* which lasted only a few weeks (fall 1958). He presided over yet another travelogue, *It's a Wonderful World*, in syndication (1963). Swayze capped off his TV career hosting two weeks of focusing on television news for the PBS series *Media Probes* (1982).

His newscasting and game show credits notwithstanding, Swayze is probably remembered by more Americans instead for wearing—and seemingly constantly plugging—the Timex wristwatch, a purportedly indestructible timepiece. *It takes a licking but keeps on ticking* was a catchphrase that made him famous after the watch was run over by a bulldozer or remained under water for 36 hours in TV commercials. Viewers loved it (the Timex motto fell from the lips of legions) and sales of the commodity soared. Parenthetically, on one occasion Swayze's commercial went dreadfully awry on live network television, no less. As part of its continuing marketing campaign, Timex was underwriting *The Steve Allen Show*. A wristwatch was attached to what appeared to be a diminutive washing machine. After having been vibrated, sloshed and spun, the watch ultimately quit working. Swayze attempted to recover: "Next week," said he, "the test will work." To which Allen inquired, "What makes you think they're going to be with us next week?"

Late in his career Swayze also finally got to appear in a quartet of motion pictures. He narrated the crime drama *Inside Detroit* (1956); played an uncredited role in *A Face in the Crowd* (1957); was a TV commentator in *The Boston Strangler* (1968); and performed in a small part in *When Nature Calls* (1985). By then a half-century had passed since the public initially heard his voice on the air.

SWEENEY, WARREN. *Announcer.* **Series:** *The CBS Radio Workshop* (1957); *The Columbia Workshop* (1940); *The Couple Next Door* (1957–ca. 1960); *The FBI in Peace and War* (ca. 1944–ca. 1958); *God's Country*, aka *The Burl Ives Show* (1942); *Hear it Now* (1950); *Here's to Veterans* (ca. 1940s); *Let's Pretend* (1952–1954); *Major Bowes and His Original Amateur Hour* (ca. mid 1940s); *News of the World* (newscaster, 1940–1944); *Our Gal Sunday* (1944–?); *The Pet Milk Show* (host-narrator, 1948–1950); *The Philadelphia Symphony Orchestra* (ca. 1953–ca. 1957); *The Radio Forum* (1948); *The Radio School of the Air* (ca. 1940s); *The Raymond Scott Show* (ca. 1940–1944); *Saturday Night Serenade* (ca. early 1940s–1948); *The Second Mrs. Burton* (late 1950s–1960); *Wings of Song*; *World News Today* (1944–1945); *The World Today* (1940–ca. 1942); *Yours Truly, Johnny Dollar* (ca. 1961–1962).

In 1933 announcer Warren Sweeney left Baltimore's WMAL for Washington's WJSV, the CBS-owned outlet in the nation's capital. He departed WJSV in 1939 when he joined the announcing staff at CBS headquarters in New York.

TAUB, SAM (born Samuel Sidney Life). b. Sept. 10, 1886, Brooklyn, N.Y.; d. July 11, 1979, Brooklyn, N.Y. *Sportscaster.* **Series:** *Madison Square Boxing Bouts* (1944–1945).

As a youngster Sam Taub developed a lifelong passion for boxing. He trudged for miles to read blow-by-blow accounts of major fights posted on a bulletin board that *The New York Evening Journal* maintained. He got a job in the advertising department of *The New York Morning Telegraph* and was advanced to secretary to the editor and publisher within a couple of months. He earned extra income assisting sports columnist Alfred Henry Lewis and fight reporter Bat Masterson. Taub covered boxing matches at small clubs and—when Masterson died—was appointed to replace him, a job he held for three decades.

Taub first aired a general sports program over Newark's WOR in 1922. Yet he treated it as nothing more than a lark until a chum informed him he had actually heard him over a crystal set. Taub's first boxing event on the ether occurred in 1929 over WJZ. His network debut didn't occur until 1932, however, when he assisted NBC's Graham McNamee with a bout pitting Max Schmeling against W.L. (Young) Stribling. Taub was a sports commentator over New York's WHN by 1937 and WMGM from 1948 to 1952. WHN carried his *Madison Square Garden Boxing Bouts* between 1940 and 1945 with NBC providing some national coverage in that epoch. Before his broadcast career ended, Taub estimated that he had announced in excess of 7,000 bouts from preliminaries to championship exhibitions.

TAYLOR, HENRY JUNIOR. b. Sept. 2, 1902, Chicago, Ill.; d. Feb. 24, 1984, New York, N.Y. *Commentator.* **Series:** *Your Land and Mine* (news analyst, 1945–1956).

In 1942 Henry J. Taylor, correspondent for the North American Newspaper Alliance and the Scripps-Howard Syndicate, returned from Europe and began broadcasting over New York's WHN. In 1943, after the Blue chain's ties to NBC were severed, Taylor joined the Blue (soon afterward renamed ABC) as a news commentator, possibly limited in those days to the New York outlet. No evidence has surfaced to suggest he held a regular news timeslot on that web prior to 1948.

A single sponsor, General Motors, underwrote his quarter-hour analysis continuously and successively on three networks thereafter. On MBS from 1945 to 1948 Taylor was heard twice a week, Monday and Friday evenings. When he moved to ABC in 1948 his program aired only on Monday nights. That pattern persisted after he transferred to NBC in late 1954. Taylor was branded an arch conservative and protested vigorously against big government spending and socialists, real and imagined. He was particularly drawn to economic and social concerns.

He left the air in December 1956 when he was picked by President Dwight D. Eisenhower for an appointment as ambassador to Switzerland. Taylor's service extended from May 9, 1957 to Feb. 28, 1961, after which he returned to journalism, penning a column for United Features Syndicate. He also authored *An American Speaks His Mind* (Doubleday, 1957) and *Men and Moments* (Random House, 1966).

TEARLE, CONWAY (born Frederick Levy). b. May 17, 1878, New York, N.Y.; d. Oct. 1, 1939, Hollywood, Calif. *Announcer.* **Series:** *Streamlined Shakespeare,* aka *The Shakespeare Circle,* aka *Shakespeare Festival* (narrator, 1937; reprised in 1950).

Conway Tearle found radio—or it found him—only a couple of years before he died. On the ether he focused on an area he knew well, Shakespearean dramas. Until then he had spent his life on the stage and in silent and talking pictures. His parents were a jazz musician, Jules Levy, and stage actress, Marianne Conway. They divorced while their offspring was still young. Conway married Osmond Tearle, a British Shakespearean actor and theater manager. For 17 years, from the time he was 10 years of age, the boy was raised to manhood and lived in England. Although he was a scion of one of England's most prominent theatrical families, the youth's professional debut nevertheless occurred as a boxer at age 16 in a London prizefighting ring. He soon earned an enviable distinction as "The Boy Wonder" before abandoning that fixation for the stage. He was familiar with the environment, of course, having been exposed to his stepdad's venue where he was alternately billed as Frederick Levy and Frederick Conway. Finally, he settled on the appellation Conway Tearle for himself.

Following a successful tour with a Shakespearean repertory company Tearle returned to London seeking more substantial roles. Invariably he was told by directors that he was too young to be entrusted with pivotal characterizations, however. To counter it, he advanced his age by eight years and forever after was listed in *Who's Who* at the wrong age—although he won all sorts of important roles thereafter. He returned to his native America in 1905 and that same year made his Broadway premiere in *Abigail.* After appearing in more than 20 stage productions in England and America, in 1910 Tearle turned to silent films and ultimately to "talkies."

Tearle's most famous movies were branded "women's pictures" where he meticulously performed as a dashing hero or ardent romantic. His more notable silent films included *Helene of the North* (1915); *The Foolish Virgin* (1916); *The Common Law* (1916); *Stella Maris* (1918); *A Virtuous Vamp* (1919); *She Loves and Lies* (1920); *The Eternal Flame* (1922); *Lilies of the Field* (1924); and *Dancing Mothers* (1926). Among his sound films were *Klondike Annie* and *Romeo and Juliet* (both 1936).

THOMAS, LOWELL JACKSON. b. April 6, 1892, Woodington, Ohio; d. Aug. 29, 1981, Pawling, N.Y. *Newscaster, Commentator.* **Series:** *Headline Hunters* (co-host, 1929); *Lowell Thomas and the News,* aka *Literary Digest Topics in Brief* (newscaster, 1930–1976). **Aphorisms:** *Good evening, everybody...*; *So long until tomorrow!*

In his lifetime Lowell Thomas was the most enduring daily newscaster in radio, airing continuously—with the exception of a week in late 1945—from Sept. 29, 1930 to May 14, 1976, when he signed off his long-running series for the last time. A pundit identified him as "the reigning philosopher king of radio news," characterizing Thomas as "an intrepid reporter who went where the news was." He continued: "If Lowell Thomas wasn't there to witness it, it wasn't worth hearing about." He was also labeled "a genial potentate of the news." A radio historiographer, meanwhile, observed, "Thomas was the straightest of newsmen: he was neither a commentator of the [H.V.] Kaltenborn school nor a pundit like [Elmer] Davis." Said Maurice Zolotow in *Coronet*: "He neither views with alarm like [Walter] Winchell nor views with gaiety like [Gabriel] Heatter ... he doesn't offer social messages or uplift; he never gives the impression that he has inside information like Drew Pearson, yet his rating as a newsman has consistently been either first, second, or third over the years." A cohort expressed: "He [Thomas] has no opinions, and his only enemies are rattlesnakes, cannibals, Fascists, and Communists ... but even these he will rarely condemn outright." Sweeping those classifications aside, nonetheless *Variety* branded the veteran broadcaster a "conservative" reporter as contrasted with some of his more "liberal" contemporaries.

Although born in Ohio, from 1900 to 1907 Thomas resided at Victor, Colo., a gold-mining outpost where his physician-surgeon dad practiced medicine. Printer's ink entered the boy's veins while he was young: in 1902, when he was just 10, he delivered not only a local paper that he would one day edit but also *The Denver Post* to local concerns, including saloons, gambling parlors and brothels of the red light district. He completed his delivery route before heading to school every morning. The lad also joined a newsboys' union, signaling an enterprising, business-minded spirit which he exhibited throughout his life.

In 1907 the family returned to the Buckeye State where he attended high school, played quarterback on the football squad and won first prize in a public speaking competition. His award could hardly be believed, however—he was elevated to captain of the football team! A succession of odd jobs (feeding cows, stoking furnaces and operating a laundry) helped him pay his way through the University of Northern Indiana at Valparaiso. In just two years he earned both bachelor's and master's degrees before returning to Colorado to live. Thomas attempted pick-and-shovel mining there before signing on with *The Cripple Creek Times* as a reporter. Not long afterward, he was hired as the 19-year-old $95-a-month editor of *The Victor Daily Record*, the paper he folded and delivered as a youngster. As its only staffer, he covered local prize fights, brawls, shootings and operas. Within a year, he moved to the hamlet's *other* newspaper, *The Victor News*, when its owner offered to boost his income.

Thomas's hometown journalistic grounding paid off. When he decided to leave Victor in 1912 at 20 and earn a couple of additional degrees at the University of Denver, *The Denver Post*—which he had also carried a decade earlier—put him on its staff. Following that stopover, he went to the Windy City where at night he attended Kent College of Law and by day worked alongside fellow reporters Floyd Gibbons, Ben Hecht, Ring Lardner, Charles MacArthur and Carl Sandburg at *The Chicago Evening Journal*. "I chased fires with Carl Sandburg," said Thomas. Having developed a severe case of wanderlust which was to remain with him for a lifetime, Thomas made a couple of trips to Alaska, piling up adventures along the way and developing photographic essays for future lecture tours. He went East to study constitutional law at Princeton University and was concurrently appointed to the faculty to teach public speaking.

In his twenties Thomas organized expeditions to the arctic and went to the battleground front lines in Europe during World War I. One of his quests was to create a pictorial history of Allied servicemen. He went still further in 1918 by visiting Germany during its revolution. His life was dotted by legions of subsequent journeys overseas, providing fodder for more than 50 volumes. Thomas's travels with T.E. Lawrence across the Arabian Desert netted his first and perhaps best remembered tome, *With Lawrence in Arabia* (Century, 1924). An unquenchable Thomas harbored an ambition "to know more about this globe than anyone else ever has." His insatiable appetite for travel suggested that he probably came very close to realizing his dream if indeed he didn't fulfill it.

Before the mid 1920s, he was appearing sporadically on radio to discuss his experiences. One of those early visits to the microphone—although not the first—occurred on March 21, 1925, over Pittsburgh's legendary KDKA. His topic was "Man's First Flight around the World." Thomas was aboard an Army aircraft that flew from the east to west coasts in this country, with its crew completing a global tour. For an hour, meanwhile, he chatted extemporaneously about the mission.

John Dunning reports what happened a few years later:

When William S. Paley of CBS learned that *Literary Digest* was parting company with its ace newscaster, Floyd Gibbons, on NBC, he quickly arranged an audition with Thomas in the hope of luring the sponsor to his network. The *Digest* people were impressed with Thomas but had commitments to NBC, putting Paley in the position of scouting for the enemy. CBS was given small solace, allowed to carry the show to the West Coast while Thomas was heard on the Blue Network in the East and Midwest. This lasted only about six months, and NBC emerged with the entire program in 1931. Thomas's popularity was immediate and vast: he was carrying a Crossley rating of 18.9 in 1932, while other newsmen didn't even register in the polls.

Thomas ventured on the air with a casual, unassuming *Good evening, everybody....* He left it Monday through Thursday nights with *So long until tomorrow!* and on Friday nights with *So long until Monday!* The catchphrases caught on with many Americans and inspired two autobiographical works—*Good Evening Everybody: From Cripple Creek to Samarkand* (William Morrow, 1976) and *So Long Until Tomorrow: From Quaker Hill to Kathmandu* (William Morrow, 1977). His radio scripts were largely the work of writer Prosper Buranelli and drama critic Louis Sherwin.

Thomas was assigned the prestigious weeknight dinner hour of 6:45 P.M. Eastern Time in 1930 when he aired over the NBC Blue chain. He was shifted to the NBC Red web in 1945 and again kept that same favorable quarter-hour two years hence when Procter & Gamble agreed to underwrite him provided he switched to CBS. He was still occupying that coveted timeslot when he left the air for the final time in 1976. For many years near the end of his reign he normally broadcast directly from a studio at his private estate at Pawling, N.Y., 100 miles north of New York City. There, even in his eighties, he was still skiing down winter's snow-covered slopes. Thomas seldom missed a broadcast even when he traveled; he simply reported from whatever global vantage point had currently caught his fancy. He returned to radio in 1979 airing a syndicated feature, *The Best Years*, about elderly luminaries who achieved stunning victories late in life.

In the Depression-riddled early 1930s NBC news chief Abe Schecter's secret weapon against the competition was Thomas, a man who Schecter said was gifted with "a million dollar voice but not a nickel's worth of news." Schecter was the sole newsgathering department at NBC in those days with a lot riding on his shoulders. Yet he performed magic every day, equipped with just a telephone. He reached governors, senators, cabinet secretaries and generals by identifying himself as being from "the Lowell Thomas office," a celebrated moniker seemingly known by everybody. Once in a while a determined Schecter had to throw in a couple of free passes to a Rudy Vallee broadcast or dole out other favors. Despite those, Thomas and Schecter frequently beat the print media to important stories at a time when the papers were desperately trying to paint electronic journalism as a suspect, biased and unreliable source of news.

When the humorous yarns meted out by irascible radio comic Henry Morgan failed to go over, he urged his listeners to turn their dials to Lowell Thomas, who was on the air in the same quarter-hour, to see if they could derive a bigger laugh there.

In the meantime Thomas purportedly telecast the first news program on the small screen in 1939 and appeared on many subsequent video series. When the Federal Communications Commission permitted commercialized programming to invade television's landscape effective July 1, 1941, the NBC-TV outlet in New York, WNBT, went on the air at 7 P.M. that day with Thomas reading the *Sunoco News*. In the late 1950s he presided over a collection of televised specials featuring some of the far-flung locales he traversed. Some of those were repeated in the summer of 1964 for an hour on Tuesday nights on CBS-TV as the travelogue *High Adventure with Lowell Thomas*. In 1966 the newsman hosted a similar feature, that time in syndication, *The World of Lowell Thomas*. Late in his life the Public Broadcasting System offered viewers a panoramic album of documentaries under the umbrella *Lowell Thomas Remembers*. Yet when the tables were turned on him and he became the focus of a program instead of running it, he clearly didn't like it. "This is a sinister conspiracy!" Thomas cried after host Ralph Edwards surprised him as the subject of NBC-TV's *This is Your Life* once in the 1950s. The stunned guest refused to join in the spirit of the merriment or even proffer a grin during the tribute. It was, regrettably, not one of the show's finest hours—or, for that matter, Thomas's either.

Few radio newscasters achieved his level of success, or even came close. Over his lifetime Thomas received 30 honorary doctorates, broadcasting's Peabody Award and countless added honors including election to five halls of fame. Museums complimented him in Colorado and Ohio. A mountain range in Antarctica was named for him along with an arctic island, schools in both the Himalayas and on Long Island plus the law school communications center at the University of Denver.

When his program moved to CBS in 1947, Procter & Gamble paid the bills and is believed to have paid Thomas $2,000 per broadcast for his 15-minute newscasts. His compensation increased significantly with 20 annual lectures at $2,000 each, 10 magazine articles for major periodicals and a new book contract every year, plus narrating two Fox Movietone newsreels shown in theaters weekly (1935–1952) at $1,500 each ($3,000 per week). He also engaged in several successful sideline business enterprises that didn't require his day-to-day involvement. A little math suggests his income may have approached $2 million annually in its peak years. It wasn't a shabby haul for a kid that delivered newspapers to a mining village when he was only 10.

THOMAS, PETER. *Announcer.* **Series:** *Dream Time* (1948); *Young Doctor Malone* (late 1950s–1960).

On the popularly accepted "day radio drama died," Nov. 25, 1960, as CBS divested itself of the final few soap operas still on the air—having arrived three decades earlier—Peter Thomas signed off one of the handful of durable dramas then biting the dust with this soliloquy: "This is Peter Thomas. As the current series of *Young Doctor Malone* comes to a close, we leave Jill on the eve of her wedding day happy in the knowledge that Scotty's mother at last has given her blessing. As for Jerry, the weeks that lie ahead will be challenging ones as he must resume the responsibilities of directing the clinic. But with the encouragement, love and support of Tracy, Jerry will go forward in new paths of service." Organ up and out.

While Thomas arrived late in Radioland, he developed a highly lucrative career in television that extended into the 21st century. He narrated legions of documentaries (e.g., *How the West was Lost* for Discovery TV in 1991, 1993) and mystery dramas (e.g., *Forensic Files* for Court TV from 2000) and provided voiceovers for numerous commercials and public service announcements.

THOMPSON, DOROTHY. b. July 9, 1894, Lancaster, N.Y.; Jan. 30, 1961, Lisbon, Portugal. *Commentator.* **Series:** *Dorothy Thompson Commentary* (commentator, 1937–1941, 1942, 1943, 1944, 1945).

While a student at Syracuse University pursuing journalism, where she earned a bachelor's degree in 1914, Dorothy Thompson—the daughter of a Methodist minister—became a suffragist. She labored tenaciously to establish a woman's right to vote and received a paycheck for her work in publicity and promotion from the New York Woman Suffrage Party. Even then she was giving hints of the kind of crusading scribe she would be forever afterward. (Years later, a pundit depicted her as "a force of nature and hell on wheels.") When the Suffrage Amendment passed, Thompson moved to other PR posts, eventually linking with the National Social Unit Organization pushing social rights, particularly focusing political awareness on the slums.

She decided to ply her craft in Europe beginning in autumn of 1919 after the First World War ended. Thompson interviewed a number of prominent travelers en-route as the ship plowed the Atlantic and turned those interviews into articles for the Jewish Correspondence Bureau. Subsequently, the industrious neophyte dispatched freelance pieces to *The Philadelphia Public Ledger*; became the Vienna correspondent of *The Chicago Daily News*; and supplemented her income as a publicist for the American Red Cross. In 1924 *The Philadelphia Public Ledger* and *The New York Evening Post* tendered a full time position as their regional bureau chief, based in Berlin. Significantly, Thompson was the first of her gender to be appointed a foreign bureau chief. Meanwhile, back home, other papers were picking up what she had written, giving her some notoriety and prestige beyond those two newspaper markets. Perhaps even more impressively, she received the Nobel Prize for literature in 1930 for her sterling efforts.

Thompson had interviewed many key leaders of the continent by then but the one she most wanted remained absolutely elusive. At last, in 1931, after five years of trying she gained the one-on-one session she coveted—with Adolf Hitler at his Berlin headquarters. She was only beginning to catch a glimpse of the awful range of Hitler's power but—when her desire to tell an audience about him coincided with his desire for international attention—she was available. "He had a message for the world," she said, "and so he was ready to see me." Thompson turned that material into the volume *I Saw Hitler* and recalled it later in other forms of print and on the air.

A paraphrase from another of her books, *Let the Record Speak*, helps convey the environment: "As one of only a few female journalists in the early 1930s stationed abroad, Thompson frequently risked her own safety to report vigorously on the rise of Nazism and the German arms buildup. Eventually, Hitler saw that her reports posed a threat to his plans, and he had her removed from Germany in 1934." She was, in fact, the first American correspondent to be expelled from Nazi Germany. When orders came to deport her on Aug. 25, 1934, she had only 24 hours to get out or face incarceration.

Returning to America, Thompson went on the lecture circuit, informing Americans of the threat posed by Nazism and Fascism. She joined *The New York Tribune* in 1936 and began writing a thrice-weekly column titled *On the Record* which was soon syndicated elsewhere. Her working relationship with the *Tribune* continued satisfactorily until 1941, incidentally, after she publicly endorsed Franklin D. Roosevelt for a third term as president and was promptly terminated by the New York journal. It didn't matter to her; by then the column was appearing in more than 200 other papers.

The newspaper column's spread (persisting 22 years), a recurring monthly column in *The Ladies' Home Journal*, several published books, lectures and more invitations to speak at various functions than she could possibly honor (she turned down 700 in just one week in 1937) quickly brought Thompson to the forefront of the radio networks. CBS invited her to become a regular speaker on its chain. She declined, yet—when NBC asked her to be a commentator during the quadrennial conventions of the political parties in the summer of 1936—Thompson readily accepted. Her articulate and perceptive expressions resulted in NBC proffering a contract for a weekly series of commentaries. She said "yes" again. "This radio work and the column combined with her notoriety as the only female journalist to be thrown out of Nazi Germany, propelled Thompson to national fame," assessed a critic. She was soon contributing articles to additional imposing periodicals. By 1939 *Time* magazine ran her picture on its cover and labeled her the second most popular woman in America, just behind first lady Eleanor Roosevelt.

Her first weekly commentary aired on NBC on Aug. 6, 1937 and others followed every Friday night in quarter-hour installments. Five months later she was also airing a second commentary on Tuesday nights on the NBC Blue chain. Over the next eight years, with minimal time-outs for filling other engagements, Thompson usually broadcast in 15-minute segments although for several months in 1938–1939 she was given a half-hour. She alternated between NBC, NBC Blue/ABC and MBS and was sponsored most of the time. A pundit observed, "Thompson's particular strength was her ability to analyze the historical moment, placing events within their political context and describing their impact for a vast audience.... Fueled by the lessons she'd learned as a fiery speaker on the lecture circuit, Thompson's explosive style on radio goaded her audience to learn about and take action to stop the Nazi menace and other atrocities." In her peak years she attracted five million listeners with her perspectives on current events while simultaneously reaching another 10 million readers with her columns and articles.

She received a gold medal from the National Institute of Social Sciences for distinguished service to humanity in 1938. Thompson became the model for "Tess Harding," the chic and sexy globetrotting foreign correspondent and newspaper columnist originally played by Katharine Hepburn in the 1942 movie *Woman of the*

Year. The tale was reprised in the Broadway musical *Applause* with Lauren Bacall in the key role. In the meantime, following the Second World War, Thompson took up the cause of refugees worldwide. Her sense of righteousness was centered in the Middle East, especially during the formative years of Israel as a nation. After she relinquished her popular newspaper column in 1958 she continued consulting informally with many of her broadcasting comrades. Married three times and divorced twice (including from second husband-novelist Sinclair Lewis), she spent the Christmas holidays in 1960 with family members at Lisbon when her health suddenly deteriorated rapidly. After a few weeks, she died there before she was able to return home.

Thompson was the author of 10 volumes: *The New Russia* (H. Holt, 1928); *I Saw Hitler* (Farrar and Rinehart, 1932); *Once on Christmas* (Oxford University Press, 1938); *Refugees: Anarchy or Organization?* (Random House, 1938); *Let the Record Speak* (Houghton Mifflin, 1939); *Listen, Hans* (Houghton Mifflin, 1942); *Let the Promise Be Fulfilled: A Christian View of Palestine* (American Christian Palestine Committee, 1946); *The Developments of Our Times* (Stetson University Press, 1948); *The Crisis of the West* (University of Toronto Press, 1955); and *The Courage to Be Happy* (Houghton Mifflin, 1957). A trio of works has been written about the author: *Dorothy and Red* by Vincent Sheean (Houghton Mifflin, 1963); *Dorothy Thompson: A Legend in Her Time* by Marion K. Sanders (Houghton Mifflin, 1973); and *American Cassandra: The Life of Dorothy Thompson* by Peter Kurth (Little Brown, 1990).

THOR, LARRY (born Arnleifur Lawrence Thorsteinson). b. Aug. 27, 1916, Lundar, Manitoba, Canada; d. March 15, 1976, Santa Monica, Calif. *Announcer.* **Series:** *Broadway is My Beat* (actor, 1949–1954); *The Carnation Family Party* (1950–1951); *The Clyde Beatty Show* (early 1950s); *The Green Lama* (1949); *Rocky Jordan* (1948–1950); *Suspense* (ca. early 1950s).

While Larry Thor spoke only Icelandic until age seven and ended his formal education with high school, one couldn't tell it based on where his career eventually took him. Prior to radio, Thor's work history included farming, ranching, construction, three years with the Canadian cavalry, another three with Princess Patricia's light infantry and then radio while waiting for a mining job application approval! Although he started out singing gratuitously over Flin Flon's CFAR (Flin Flon is a mining-lumbering hamlet in western Manitoba), Thor was soon making $70 a month as the outlet's total writing staff. He got into announcing three years hence at Timmins, Ontario's CKGB, followed by a stint newscasting at Toronto's CKCL. He moved to Montreal next where he reported for the CBS International Service. During less than two years there he also narrated industrial films, short subjects and special features.

Moving to Hollywood, Thor initially linked with KFAC as an announcer, and was quickly snapped up by KMPC as a newscaster. CBS signed him as an announcer in 1948 and—for the next few years, at least—his future was set.

THORGERSEN, EDWARD. b. June 19, 1902, Elizabeth, N.J.; d. Dec. 22, 1997, Wolfeboro, N.H. *Announcer, Sportscaster, Emcee.* **Series:** *The A & P Gypsies* (1927–ca. 1930); *B.A. Rolfe and His Lucky Strike Dance Orchestra*, aka *Saturday Night Party*, aka *The Goodrich Silvertown Orchestra* (ca. 1930–ca. 1933); *Cities Service Concert* (ca. 1927–ca. 1930); *Ed Thorgersen Sports Commentary* (sportscaster, 1939); *The Elgin Football Revue* (host-interlocutor, 1936–1937); *Happy Wonder Bakers* (1927–1931); *Literary Digest Topics in Brief*, aka *Lowell Thomas and the News* (1930–?); *Planters Pickers* (1929–ca. 1930); *Universal Safety Series* (1927–ca. 1928); *Women's International League for Peace and Freedom* (1930).

Ed Thorgersen joined NBC shortly after its inception and in the fledgling dual chain's earliest years was one of its most prominent staff announcers and sportscasters. He was used extensively for commercials and covering special events and regularly turned up presenting dance orchestras and added musical features. Thorgersen was the first of several interlocutors to introduce newscaster Lowell Thomas on his long-running weeknight series premiering on Sept. 29, 1930. On March 1, 1932 Thorgersen was one of four

NBC announcers (others: George Hicks, Ezra McIntosh, Charles O'Connor) transmitting breaking news of the kidnapping of the Lindbergh infant. They reported from a makeshift "studio" in a Hopewell, N.J. restaurant.

Meanwhile, also in the early 1930s, Thorgersen acquired the handle "Thundering Ed," the result of shouting the Lucky Strike cigarette commercials on a dance band series, a technique he acknowledged was ordered by sponsoring American Tobacco Co. He expressed his strong displeasure for the notoriety that resulted. After Thorgersen was picked to narrate the sports segments of the weekly Fox Movietone newsreels screened in theaters across the land, he addressed his unwelcome "fate" publicly in the October 1933 issue of *Radioland*: "I'm through with radio forever. It was impossible to live down the work I did on the radio program. I was a national joke and it got tiresome. I like my present job and I'm going to stick with it."

His statement to the contrary notwithstanding, after his departure from NBC and the passage of time, the ex-air personality cooled down. By 1937, while still reporting for Fox, Thorgersen rejoined NBC and quickly became a permanent fixture on a program he introduced initially: he appeared on *Lowell Thomas and the News* each Monday and Friday night during the football season while also broadcasting daily during the World Series that autumn (1937). Not long afterward, he shifted his allegiance to the recently formed MBS network where he immediately became a sportscaster and commentator of some established repute. Thorgersen was no longer identified as "Thundering Ed," of course, although many listeners and industry insiders probably hadn't forgotten that sobriquet. During the early 1940s he delivered a half-dozen quarter-hour newscasts weekly over New York's WOR, a key station in originating Mutual programming.

TICE, J. OLIN, JR. b. Aug. 23, 1919, Savannah, Ga.; d. Jan. 8, 1998, Blythewood, S.C. *Announcer.* **Series:** *The Galen Drake Show* (1953–1956); *Mr. Keen, Tracer of Lost Persons* (relief announcer, 1953, 1954); *There's Music in the Air* (1953).

In the 1930s and early 1940s Olin Tice seemed to "collect" radio stints in the Carolinas. He announced at WAIM, Anderson, S.C.; WFBC, Greenville, S.C.; WIS, Columbia, S.C.; WCOS, Columbia, S.C.; WDNC, Durham, N.C.; and WBT, Charlotte, N.C. The year Tice landed in Charlotte (1943), he was summoned to WTOP (formerly WJSV), the CBS owned-and-operated station in Washington, D.C. Shortly thereafter, he transferred to CBS in New York. His service there was temporarily put on hold in 1944 when Uncle Sam called him to the Army. Tice returned to CBS following the war.

TILLMAN, JOHN. b. November 1916, Clio, Ala. *Announcer, Emcee.* **Series:** *A Bouquet for You* (1946–1947); *The Columbia Ensemble* (1942); *The Columbia Workshop* (ca. 1950s); *The Danny O'Neil Show*, aka *Singing in the Morning* (1946–?); *Forecast* (1940); *Fun with Dunne* (1943); *The Larry Carr Show* (1946); *Marriage for Two* (1949–1950, ca. 1951–1952); *Matinee at Meadowbrook* (host, 1941); *Meet the Music* (1941); *The Pause That Refreshes on the Air* (1943); *Press Association Dispatches* (1939); *The Story of Mary Marlin* (ca. 1940s); *The Stradivari Orchestra* (1946); *Time to Remember* (1946–1947); *Walter Gross and His Orchestra* (1941); *What Are We Fighting For?* (1942); *Winner Take All* (1946–ca. 1949).

Radio Mirror intimated that John Tillman was already a professional performer before he graduated from Alabama's Barbour County High School. At 16 the youth sang to the accompaniment of his mom at the studio organ over Dothan's WAFG, where he was also a staff announcer. Subsequently, he went off to college in Atlanta but didn't quite finish. Tillman took a job at WSB, combining studies with studio time for the next four years. But shortly before his graduation with a bachelor's degree, WHAS in Louisville, Ky., summoned him to a full time post that blended news commentary and master of ceremonies. He put the degree on the back burner.

In 1939, during his tenure in Louisville, Tillman cut some audition tapes and forwarded them to CBS. Within six weeks he was working for the web in New York. He was entrenched in several assignments, in fact, until 1943 when Uncle Sam tapped him for a different type of service. Returning to CBS from the Army in 1946, Tillman picked up where he left off with a full plate of chain-fed series. Shortly after he got back, he also decided to enroll at New York University at night and finally finish the degree that had eluded him a decade earlier.

Despite his flair in both announcing and hosting national radio series, meanwhile, there apparently is no evidence that Tillman shifted his talent into network television opportunities as the newer medium emerged in the late 1940s and 1950s. While he may have performed on TV in New York City, if his professional abilities extended to the tube it seems they were limited to local appearances.

TINNEY, CAL. b. Feb. 2, 1908, Pontotoc County, Okla.; d. Dec. 2, 1993. *Emcee, Actor, Newscaster.* **Series:** *The Cal Tinney Show* (disc jockey, 1952–1953); *If I Had a Chance* (master of ceremonies, 1938–1939); *The March of Time* (actor, 1932–?); *Robinson Crusoe Jr.* (actor, 1934–1935); *Show Boat* (actor-comic, ca. 1932–1937, ca. 1939–1941); *Sizing Up the News* (newscaster-commentator, 1941–1944, 1945–1946); *Stop Me if You've Heard This One* (visiting panelist, 1939–1940; permanent panelist, 1947–1948); *Vanity Fair* (comic, 1937); *Youth vs. Age* (quizmaster, 1939–1940).

A pundit labeled Cal Tinney "a sort of latter-day Will Rogers." He was, indeed, for he hailed from that venerable wit's home state of Oklahoma, entertaining audiences by dispensing sufficient doses of barnyard humor to amuse folks tuning into his antics in diverse genres (comedy, disc jockey, games, juvenile adventure and news). Tinney imitated Rogers on at least one occasion, playing the famous droll intellect in an episode of *Cavalcade of America*.

Raised on a farm in the Sooner State, he selected newspaper reporting as his line of work after high school, chasing stories as distant as Europe and Asia. Back home in Oklahoma, he launched his own paper. By 1932 he was plugging that journal on Tulsa's KVOO, which offered him his initial exposure to broadcasting. The paper itself folded but in the meantime Tinney had discovered a new professional career. He subsequently turned up on network radio later that year (1932) on *The March of Time*.

In New York City he gained a reputation as a talker on the Maxwell House *Show Boat* and *Vanity Fair*. He began his "light" newscast on local radio in 1940 and gargantuan mail response carried it to Mutual, which beamed it on 74 outlets beginning Aug. 4, 1941. A reviewer observed, "Although Tinney's humor was best remembered, his commentary was often pointed and hard. He took on Westbrook Pegler in Charlie Chaplin's defense, calling Pegler's story on Chaplin 'one of the unfairest, meanest little pieces of journalism in our time.'"

In his initial network run over MBS, Tinney was heard for a quarter-hour three nights weekly. That changed to Monday through Friday evenings when he shifted to ABC from 1945 to 1946. Meanwhile, he launched a local New York series in 1941 over WMCA, *Call for Cal Tinney*, in which he took telephone calls from listeners for a quarter-hour on Wednesday nights. Many of his inquiries surrounded local and state happenings.

For a year, 1948–1949, one of his mirthful radio game shows carried over on NBC-TV, *Stop Me if You've Heard This One*, with Tinney in tow as a permanent panelist. A decade later, on June 10, 1959, he performed in an episode of *Bat Masterson* on NBC-TV, portraying a U.S. marshal. Tinney also narrated a couple of movies—*Roaming the Emerald Isle* (1934) and *The Lone Star State* (1948)—and he played in a third as Clyde Hamilton Baker in *The Missouri Traveler* (1958).

TOMLINSON, EDWARD. b. Sept. 27, 1892, Stockton, Ga.; d. data unknown. *Commentator.* **Series:** *Edward Tomlinson News and Comments* (commentator, 1940–1945, 1946–1949); *The Other Americans* (commentator, 1935–1936); *What's New in South America?* (commentator, 1938).

Edward Tomlinson was a Blue network commentator on Latin American affairs who frequently used his platform to communicate his abiding conviction that South America was of critical significance to the United States. Yet his early ambition was to be a concert pianist so for eight years he studied music. He attended Georgia Normal College and completed his education at the University of Edinburgh (Scotland). A couple of years' service during the First World War was split between American and British forces. In that period he was requested to deliver some educational talks on British staff operations, his first lectures but not his last.

Subsequently, Tomlinson was published in *Colliers, Crowell* and other leading periodicals and penned syndicated newspaper articles. He traversed the United States and Canada on multiple lecture tours, was named official lecturer on South America by the League for Political Education and traveled extensively on that continent. He broadcast from various Pan-American conferences over NBC, was aboard the first passenger aircraft to cross the Andes Mountains and described for network listeners the maiden voyage of the first clipper ship from Miami to Buenos Aires in 1936.

TONKIN, PHIL. *Announcer.* **Series:** *High Adventure* (1947–1949, 1950, 1953–1954); *Murder by Experts* (1949–1951); *The Private Files of Matthew Bell* (1952); *Scotland Yard's Inspector Burke* (1947); *Sing for Your Supper* (1949).

TOWNSEND, DALLAS S, JR. b. Jan. 17, 1919, New York, N.Y.; d. June 1, 1995, Montclair, N.J. *Newscaster.* **Series:** *CBS News on the Hour* (anchor, ca. 1955–1985); *CBS World News Roundup* (anchor, 1956–1961, 1963–1982); *The World Tonight* (anchor, 1961–1963).

After graduating from Princeton University in 1940, Dallas Townsend enrolled in the Columbia University School of Journalism. He served with the U.S. Army during the Second World War as a communications officer in Japan and in other Pacific locales. On his return to the States, Townsend became news editor at New York's WQXR but served only briefly before jumping to CBS in 1941 to begin a career that would last 44 years. He was news editor and correspondent there but, more impressively, he anchored one of the network's two major daily news series—the *CBS World News Roundup* each morning from the mid 1950s to the early 1980s with the exception of a couple of years in the early 1960s. During that span he anchored CBS's other major daily news show, *The World Tonight*. At various times he could be picked up dispatching the *CBS News on the Hour*.

Throughout that epoch Townsend informed Americans about many major events affecting their lives, including reports from the national political conventions (between 1948 and 1984); providing election coverage; plus eyewitness news from space launches, atomic tests, international peace conferences and presidential inaugurations. For his efforts Townsend received an Alfred I. duPont–Columbia University Award in Broadcast Journalism and a George Foster Peabody Award for broadcasting excellence. In 1983 the duPont selection panel observed, "No other newsman in our day has had a broader acquaintance with news nor communicated it with more economy and precision."

TREMAYNE, LES. b. April 16, 1913, Balham, London, England; d. Dec. 19, 2003, Santa Monica, Calif. *Actor, Announcer, Emcee.* **Series:** *The Abbott Mysteries* (actor, 1946); *The Adventures of the Thin Man* (actor, 1943–1946); *Author's Playhouse* (actor, ca. 1941–ca. 1945); *Betty and Bob* (actor, ca. 1930s); *The Bob Crosby Show* (1940s–ca. 1950); *The CBS Radio Mystery Theater* (actor, ca. 1974–ca. 1982); *The Chicago Theater of the Air* (ca. 1940s); *Cloak and Dagger* (actor, 1950); *The Collier Hour* (actor, 1930); *Cousin Willie* (actor, 1953); *The Dreft Star Playhouse* (actor, 1943–1945); *The Edward Everett Horton Show* (1945–1946); *The Falcon* (actor, late 1940s); *The First Nighter* (actor, 1936–1943); *The Fog Lifts* (actor, ca. 1930s); *The Ford Theater* (actor, 1947–1948); *Grand Hotel* (actor, 1933–1938, 1940); *Heartbeat Theater* (actor, 1956–?); *Hildegarde's Raleigh Room* (1944–1947); *I Love a Mystery* (actor, 1940s); *Jack Armstrong, the All-American Boy* (actor, 1930s, 1940s); *The Jackie Gleason–Les Tremayne Show* (co-host, 1944); *Joyce Jordan, Girl Interne*, aka *Joyce Jordan, M.D.* (actor, ca. 1938–1940s); *Lonely Women* (actor, 1942–1943); *Ma Perkins* (actor, 1930s, 1940s, 1950s); *The MGM Theater of the Air* (actor, 1952); *Movietown Radio Theater* (actor, 1951–1954); *Night Court of the Air* (1936); *The Old Gold Program* (1934); *One Man's Family* (actor, ca. 1950s); *The Radio Reader's Digest* (host, 1947–1948); *Real Stories from Real Life* (actor, ca. 1944–ca. 1947); *Romance and Rhythm* (1941); *The Romance of Helen Trent* (actor, 1930s, 1940s, 1950s); *The Second Mrs. Burton* (actor, ca. 1950s); *The Six Shooter* (actor, 1953–1954); *That's Rich* (actor, 1954); *Wendy Warren and the News* (actor, late 1940s–ca. mid 1950s); *The Woman in My House* (ca. 1951–ca. 1959); *Woman in White* (actor, ca. 1940s).

At three years of age Les Tremayne debuted in show business as a silent film thespian, appearing with his mom, actress Dolly Tremayne. He entered Chicago radio in 1930 after community theater, vaudeville and amusement park experience. His first nationwide program was a bit part in *The Shadow of Fu Manchu* on *The Collier Hour*. After he became a busy radio actor, he played in the 18-month Broadway run of *Detective Story*. He performed in 33 Hollywood films, including *The Blue Veil* (1951); *Francis Goes to West Point* (1952); *The War of the Worlds* (1953); *Susan Slept Here* (1954); *A Man Called Peter* (1955); *The Lieutenant Wore Skirts* (1956); *North by Northwest* (1959); *Goldfinger* (1964); *Starchaser: The Legend of Orin* (1985); and *Attack of the B-Movie Monster* (2002).

His television credits included recurring roles on a trio of daytime serials, a single primetime series and voiceovers for an animated cartoon: *One Man's Family* (1954–1955, NBC); *Ellery Queen* (1958–1959, NBC); *Shazam!* (1974–1977, CBS); *One Life to Live* (1987, ABC); and *General Hospital* (1988–1991, ABC). In addition, Tremayne played in more than 50 solo parts on a large contingent of video drama, comedy and variety shows. A sample follows: *The Millionaire* (1955, CBS); *The Jack Benny Program* (1958, CBS); *Perry Mason* (1958, 1960, 1961, 1963, 1964, 1966, CBS); *Wagon Train* (1960, NBC; 1963, 1964, ABC); *Mr. Ed* (1961, 1965, CBS); *The Andy Griffith Show* (1962, CBS); *Bonanza* (1962, 1970, NBC); *The Alfred Hitchcock Hour* (1964, CBS); *The Beverly Hillbillies* (1964, CBS); *The Virginian* (1965, 1966, NBC); and *The Dukes of Hazzard* (1982, CBS).

Tremayne and his second spouse, radio soap opera heroine Alice Reinheart (Chichi Conrad on *Life Can Be Beautiful* and active on many other series), enjoyed an extended run hosting *The Tremaynes*, a breakfast talk-show six mornings a week over New York's WOR. Tremayne, meanwhile, returned to the microphone in the 1970s for appearances on *The CBS Radio Mystery Theater*.

The veteran thespian was a lifelong champion of radio as an essential dramatic medium. It weighed on him heavily when the aural medium waned in the 1950s. The unfortunate result, he affirmed, was that the end did not have to arrive. He observed that radio drama in other nations continued airing after the advent of video. Vast audiences, including convalescents, the aged, the sight impaired and all who missed "those days" were simply left mired in an abysmal swamp, he insisted.

In some radio surveys Tremayne was dubbed the listeners' favorite dramatic actor. He was also picked as one of the two most identifiable voices in America during the early 1940s, listed directly after President Franklin D. Roosevelt. Having appeared on 45 broadcasts weekly in the 1930s, he estimated that—across a six-decade career—he performed on 30,000-plus radio and television shows.

TROUT, ROBERT (born Robert Albert Blondheim). b. Oct. 15, 1908, Washington, D.C.; d. Nov. 14, 2000, New York, N.Y. *Newscaster, Commentator, Correspondent.* **Series:** *All Things Considered* (contributor, ca. 1994–2000); *The American School of the Air* (1930s–?); *Bob Trout and Cedric Adams and the News* (newscaster, 1952–1953); *Calling America* (host, 1943); *CBS World News Roundup*, aka *News of the World* (correspondent, 1938–ca. 1950s); *Chevrolet Spotlights the News* (newscaster, mid 1950s); *Columbia Presents Corwin* (himself, 1944); *The Columbia Workshop* (ca. late 1930s, 1940s); *European News Roundup* (news anchor, 1938–ca. 1939); *Feature Story* (host-narrator, 1945–1946); *Headlines and Bylines* (correspondent, 1937–1938); *Headlines and History* (host, 1944); *History Behind the Headlines* (commentator, 1937); *The Kate Smith Show*, under varied appellations (ca. 1930s); *Kentucky Derby* (sportscaster, 1935, 1936, ca. 1937, ca. 1938); *The News of Europe Direct*, under multiple monikers (anchor, 1939–1940); *The People Act* (narrator, 1952); *Professor Quiz* (1936–1941); *Robert Trout and the News* (newscaster, 1937, 1938–1939, 1941); *Robert Trout with the News Till Now* (1946–1947); *Saturday Night Serenade* (1940s); *This is London* (correspondent, 1941); *Who Said That?* (moderator, 1948, 1949, 1950); *The World Today*, aka *The World Tonight* (anchor, 1940–?).

While writing held at least some fascination for him in boyhood, radio journalist Robert Trout didn't plan on a career in broadcasting or even reporting while growing up. Dreaming his way through Washington's Central High School and branded "a lazy student" there, he envisioned for himself a life of travel and ease that could provide fodder for books he would turn out some day. While he sailed to Europe one summer as a cabin boy on a passenger liner, almost all of the discretionary funds he acquired in his teen years were derived by soda jerking at a drug store and driving a District of Columbia taxicab. Yet Trout was destined to earn a reputation in radio's formative years that wouldn't be eclipsed until one of his protégés subjugated him (and everybody else). Despite his fate, Trout remained steadfast, solid as a rock in radio journalism, spending most of his career with a single employer that surely witnessed not only talent and ability but also his commitment and an abiding sense of responsibility. It was something that his high school teachers probably didn't see in his years with them.

Trout was a rare talent who introduced entertainment features on the ether while authoritatively delivering the day's current events with a style and grace that not only informed but convinced his listeners. His effectiveness, and the undisputed fact he was on the scene during nearly all of radio's golden age, allowed him to earn numerous distinctions across an enduring broadcasting career. While he missed being one of the legendary "Murrow Boys"—CBS correspondents hired by Edward R. Murrow to serve in Europe during World War II—Trout supplanted Murrow for an extended sabbatical that the network's foreign news chief took from his London outpost as the continental conflagration waged on in 1941.

At the time of Murrow's arrival at CBS in 1935 as director of talks, Trout was unequivocally the network's premier newscaster, and for a few years thereafter. He had begun work as a handyman at a small Alexandria, Va., station (WJSV) in 1931 that was purchased by CBS in October 1932. Thereby, he preceded Murrow with CBS for three years. When the regular newscaster failed to show up to read the news one day at WJSV, Trout was pressed into service. That seemingly insignificant incident altered the course of his life and gave him a genuine focus, apparently for the very first time. Indeed, it was Trout who later taught Murrow—with no newspaper or wire experience whatsoever and only negligible airwaves exposure to his credit—everything he knew about broadcasting.

Both, coincidentally, were born six months apart and arrived at CBS in New York in 1935. Trout was initially at the chain's flagship station, WABC. Murrow, meanwhile, was hired by CBS owner-chairman William S. Paley and Murrow was soon to become the network's—as well as Paley's—fair-haired boy for a couple of decades. Trout took him under his wing and instructed him in mike technique: he claimed he developed his own trademark style by viewing the microphone as a telephone; when he broadcast news and comments, Trout believed he was speaking to someone he knew waiting attentively at the other end.

Trout was hailed for so much more than teaching electronic journalism's first superhero, however. It's been substantiated, for instance, that he was broadcasting's first anchorman, gaining the designation when CBS launched its *European News Roundup* on March 13, 1938. In New York, Trout introduced verbal reports from multiple correspondents placed around the continent, offering a format that has been reprised by every radio and television chain since. Returning home, he kept an epic vigil on D-Day June 6, 1944 (indefatigably anchoring the news through the night to 10 A.M., then being relieved for nearly a dozen hours by CBS daytime programming—mostly soap operas—and John Daly and Douglas Edwards handling the anchor desk until he returned; regrettably, some documentaries portray Trout as never leaving that desk in 24 hours, not quite the case).

He also pulled long stints on V-E Day May 8, 1945 and V-J Day Aug. 15, 1945. On the latter occasion, believing the Japanese were about to surrender, Trout remained at CBS for four days. The phone call he was waiting for from the White House arrived the evening of Aug. 14. Trout was later cited for delivering the most enviable line of those tumultuous years—"This, ladies and gentlemen, is the end of the Second World War."

He introduced most of President Franklin D. Roosevelt's talks from the White House and was celebrated for being the first to apply the popular epithet by which those occasions were (and still are) referenced: *Fireside Chats*. The appellation embodying the casually delivered exchanges originated with WJSV manager Harry Butcher, who proposed it because FDR spoke from the Diplomatic Reception Room furnished with a fireplace. Thus, as millions of citizens tuned in, it was as if the chief executive was right by people's home firesides, speaking one-on-one, Butcher reasoned. The idea clicked and Trout introduced it to the common man's everyday vernacular.

Trout made such a favorable impression on FDR (in 1933 the web dubbed him Columbia's "presidential announcer") that Roosevelt occasionally delayed his speeches to see how the newsman would handle the situation. FDR knew full well that he had a reputation for displaying an innate gift of improvisation. CBS's Paley allowed that Trout could talk extemporaneously for a couple of hours if a situation warranted it. Trout was "the most extraordinary ad-libber on the air," a radio historian affirmed. Said another: "His polish and stamina and ad-libbing won him the nickname 'Iron Man of Radio.'" Trout, himself, attempted to explain it: "You just start talking and you keep talking until the second-hand tells you it's all over. Then you give the cue, like this—Bob Trout speaking, this is the Columbia Broadcasting System."

While Trout introduced a plethora of amusement features, he also had many opportunities to hone his skills as a professional newsman. By 1936, for all practical purposes, he virtually covered the Democratic and Republican national conventions singlehandedly. In that pioneering epoch he used a microwave transmitter captured in a walking cane and a wrist watch mike. Strapped to his back was a power amplifier in a leather case. The following year, 1937, Trout went to Europe to provide CBS's coverage of a couple of major events: the coronation of George IV of England; and the controversial marriage in France of the Duke of Windsor—who relinquished the British throne—and Wallis Simpson, a U.S. citizen from Baltimore, Md.

Trout, as anchor, inaugurated a debuting quarter-hour weekday program in 1940, *The World Today* (later, *The World Tonight*). In reality the series began in September 1939, however, under several monikers including *The News of Europe Direct*. Its launch was prompted by the Nazi invasion of Poland. Trout was the anchor from the start. He was temporarily replaced in that role by John Charles Daly beginning in December 1941 after being summoned to London to fill in for Murrow, who returned to America for an extended sabbatical that included a lecture tour.

Trout traveled a topsy-turvy road following the war, nonetheless. Sometimes his career held promise; at other times, it appeared shot. Thankfully for him there were more favorable times than the other kind. When Murrow transitioned upstairs in 1946 as Paley's hand-picked vice president of news and public affairs, an administrative post that its occupant quickly and unmistakably detested, Trout was awarded the network's foremost weeknight quarter-hour newscast. It was a spot that had been carefully crafted by Murrow. As the anchorman presided over *Robert Trout with the News Till Now*, available at his call were live reports and observations from any of 35 CBS correspondents and stringers strategically scattered around the globe. The effort was lauded as "the showpiece of the CBS News lineup" as well as "the most expensive daily news program produced up to that time."

Yet, in 1947, when Murrow threw in the towel upstairs, that prestigious quarter-hour was snatched from Trout's hands without so much as an apology (according to published sources) and given to Murrow, who preferred it to his off-air overseer-policymaking role. It left Trout with not a lot to do and a whole lot of time on his hands. Suddenly, the pasture looked greener elsewhere. Before long, after more than 15 years, he left CBS for rival NBC. Trout turned up there moderating the live quiz-panel show based on current events *Who Said That?* one night weekly in primetime on NBC-TV. He remained at the program's helm until that run left the air in February 1951. That summer, in July and August, he hosted *America Speaks*, a weekday half-hour forum that purported to tell "the American story" to NBC-TV viewers.

By the spring of 1952, however, his wounds apparently healed, Trout was back at

CBS where he moderated a televised public affairs series, *Presidential Timber*, on Friday nights in primetime. In 1957 the network assigned him to anchor *World News Roundup*, a Sunday afternoon newscast. He received a similar nod for *The CBS Saturday News* in 1959, a half-hour matinee newscast. Trout occupied that chair through 1962.

After Walter Cronkite was picked to succeed Douglas Edwards as CBS-TV's nightly news anchor in 1962, there was no question that Cronkite would preside over CBS's coverage of the political conventions a couple of years hence. (Cronkite contributed at the 1952 and 1956 conventions. He anchored the 1960 event.) But when CBS was supremely trounced in the ratings by Chet Huntley and David Brinkley on NBC during the 1964 Republican conclave in San Francisco, Paley was furious. He ordered a new approach for the upcoming Democratic gathering in Atlantic City. From the network's Washington bureau he plucked a bright, youthful correspondent whose star was rising, Roger Mudd, and paired him with the polished radio vet, Robert Trout. They would become joint anchors for that critical episode on the East Coast.

Network news biographer Gary Paul Gates penned an assessment some 14 years later:

> In August 1964, Trout was at last being given his big chance—and at Cronkite's expense. At fifty-five, Trout knew this would also be his last chance [to inherit the anchor chair of the web's most coveted prize, *The CBS Evening News*]. A lean, fastidiously groomed man with a thin mustache and a courtly manner, Trout was something of a living legend to his younger colleagues. He had covered every political convention on radio for CBS since 1936.... Yet, like so many other big names on radio, Trout had trouble making the transition to television.... [In the late 1950s and early 1960s, he anchored local evening news over New York's WCBS-TV.] When it came to major assignments on the network level, Trout was generally passed over, at least in part because his swarthy [dark complexioned] looks were held against him. [Producer] Don Hewitt ... said that he thought Trout looked like "an Armenian rug merchant."

The upshot of the convention pairing was that CBS laid another egg as Huntley-Brinkley repeated its earlier success. As a result, Cronkite was restored to his place of eminence; Mudd was to have another chance for consideration upon Cronkite's retirement in 1981; and Trout—with an impressive record of sterling achievements—was overshadowed. He wouldn't have another opportunity as grand. It represented his last hope to become the kind of headliner in network television that he was in radio. For a while he was a special correspondent for the network, based in Madrid. By the late 1960s, however, he was living in semiretirement in Spain, although he contributed some infrequent stories to ABC, including a report with Peter Jennings on bullfighting.

After his wife of 56 years, Catherine, died in 1994, Trout sold the home they shared for 20 years in Madrid and returned to New York to reside on Manhattan's west side. Retiring in 1996, he still contributed to *All Things Considered*, a National Public Radio feature. "His last years at CBS were spent in almost total eclipse, a rather melancholy fade-out for the man who had once tutored Ed Murrow and had helped shape the early standards of broadcast journalism," Gates remembered.

TRUE, HAROLD. b. April 1, 1891, Michigan; d. Feb. 15, 1973, Fort Lauderdale, Fla. *Announcer.* **Series:** *The Lone Ranger* (1933–ca. 1940).

George W. Trendle inspired *The Lone Ranger* and many employees reported to him as a result of the fact that he owned the series. Some resented the success he enjoyed, however, including initial narrator and WXYZ staff announcer Harold True. He remained embittered in his later years over the fact Trendle profited so enormously while the others connected with the show were essentially shut out.

In addition to his network assignment, True was heard by Detroit area listeners over a couple of local stations in a variety of formats, to wit: *Michigan Reporter* and *Tomorrow's Headlines* (1937–1938, WXYZ); *Town Talk* (1939, WXYZ); *Harold True Sports* (1940, WXYZ); *Town Talk* (1942–1944, WWJ); *News by True* (1945–1947, WWJ).

TUFELD, DICK. b. Dec. 11, 1926, Los Angeles, Calif. *Announcer.* **Series:** *The Amazing Mr. Malone* (ca. late 1940s, early 1950s); *Falstaff's Fables* (1950); *Space Patrol* (1950–?).

Dick Tufeld studied drama at Chicago's Northwestern University before launching a career in radio, television and film. His role model, he said, was Ralph Edwards. Tufeld narrated the 1976 motion picture *Tunnel Vision*. But his greatest impact on show business was in television where he announced more than a dozen series: *Surfside 6* (1960–1962, ABC); *The Gallant Men* (1962–1963, ABC); *The Judy Garland Show* (1963–1964, CBS); *Hollywood Palace* (1964–1970, ABC); *Time Tunnel* (1966–1967, ABC); *Celebrity Sweepstakes* (1974–1976, NBC); *Don Adams Screen Test* (1975, syndication); *The Jim Stafford Show* (1975, ABC); *The Fantastic Four* (1978–1979, NBC); *Spider-Woman* (1979–1980, ABC); *Thundarr [sic] the Barbarian* (1980–1982, ABC); *Spider-Man and His Amazing Friends* (1981–1982, NBC); and *People Are Funny* (1984, NBC).

Nonetheless, the ex-radio announcer is undoubtedly best recalled for voicing the role of a robot on CBS-TV's *Lost in Space* from 1965 to 1968. Tufeld was the voice of the robot in the 1998 *Lost in Space* movie, too. In spite of the fact that a tumor subsequently paralyzed one of his vocal cords and removed his ability to speak, after surgery Tufeld was able to talk again naturally. He milked the role of the robot once more, articulating it in an episode of *The Simpsons* on Fox TV in February 2004.

TURNER, JESSE GRANDERSON (GRANT). b. May 17, 1912, Baird, Texas; d. Oct. 19, 1991, Nashville, Tenn. *Announcer.* Series: *American Ace Coffee Time* (1948–1949); *Grand Ole Opry* (ca. 1947–1957); *Hank Williams Health and Happiness Show* (1949).

Growing up near Abilene, Texas in 1928 Grant Turner performed as "Ike and His Guitar" over that city's KFYO. Although he was still in high school, Turner began announcing for the station the same year. While he majored in journalism in college and worked for newspapers in Louisiana and Texas in the 1930s, he returned to broadcasting at Longview's KFRO in 1940. He moved to a Sherman, Texas, station shortly afterward, and in 1942 took a job at a Knoxville, Tenn. station. On June 6, 1944, D-Day, as the Allies invaded Europe during the Second World War, Turner—having ridden a bus all night to Nashville—won an audition at WSM. He was soon introducing several pre-dawn features such as *Lester Flatt and Earl Scruggs*. Within a few months, however, he was assigned to Grand Ole Opry founder George D. Hay's announcing staff.

In the late 1940s Turner got lucky again, winning what he called the "big prize"—the half-hour portion of that legendary show beamed to the nation every Saturday night over the NBC Radio network. By the early 1950s the segment was heard by 10 million listeners via 170 local stations. The NBC segment, underwritten by the R.J. Reynolds Tobacco Co. for Prince Albert pipe smoking tobacco, was the only half-hour of the four-and-a-half-hour marathon broadcast that was scripted and rehearsed in advance for timing each week, incidentally.

Turner, meanwhile, was eventually labeled "the voice of the Grand Ole Opry." While announcing cohorts introduced other segments of the popular country music series, he was assigned to additional half-hour and quarter-hour portions, as well as the live audience *Friday Night Frolics* (later, *Friday Night Opry*) on WSM. From the mid 1950s until 1977, Turner presided over the *Midnight Jamboree* for an hour after the *Opry* signed off, a live stage show that aired weekly from the Ernest Tubb Record Shop in downtown Nashville (and later near Opryland, U.S.A.). For many years he also conducted *Opry* warm-up shows on the stage of Ryman Auditorium prior to the Saturday night performances. During those hours he played country records and interviewed some of the entertainers scheduled to appear later.

Turner was interlocutor for countless more music-variety features aired by WSM and sometimes transmitted by NBC or in syndication. At the time of his death he was reportedly the only announcer-disc jockey to have been elected to the Country Music Hall of Fame, having received the honor a decade earlier in 1981. He was one of three original members of the Country Disc Jockey Hall of Fame, so named in 1975.

TUTTLE, ROGER. *Announcer.* **Series:** *College Bowl Quiz* (1953–1955); *Crime and Peter Chambers* (1954); *The Duke University Glee Club* (1950); *The Eternal Light* (1947–?); *Stars in Jazz* (1953); *X-Minus One* (ca. 1955–ca. 1958).

A native of Massachusetts, Roger Tuttle attended Duke University and during the Second World War served in the U.S. Navy with the Amphibious Corps in the South Pacific. His professional career carried him to NBC in New York where he devoted more than 40 years to radio and television broadcasting. He introduced the big bands of Tommy Dorsey, Guy Lombardo, Lawrence Welk and many others and was a permanent member of the debuting *Today* show cast with Dave Garroway hosting.

For five years Tuttle introduced Dr. Joyce Brothers. He announced Chet Huntley's coverage of the NASA space missions. He also turned up as the "voice" of numerous television series including *The Andy Griffith Show*; *Law and Order*; *Matlock*; and *Miami Vice*.

TYSON, CICELY. b. Dec. 19, 1933, Harlem, New York. *Emcee.* **Series:** *The Sears Radio Theater*, aka *The Mutual Radio Theater* (hostess, 1979–1981).

Cicely Tyson didn't do much in radio but she still holds the distinction of being the last woman to preside over the final dramatic anthology on commercial network radio. When CBS attempted to capitalize on a nostalgic wave sweeping the country in the 1970s, she was picked as hostess of the weekly love-hate drama night (Thursdays) on *The Sears Radio Theater*. After a year the show shifted networks, becoming *The Mutual Radio Theater*, where it persisted nearly two additional years. In its hosting rotation, Tyson—the only female so honored—was flanked by Lorne Greene on Monday nights (westerns); Andy Griffith on Tuesday nights (comedies); Vincent Price on Wednesday nights (mysteries); and Richard Widmark on Friday nights (adventures).

Originally discovered by a photographer for *Ebony* magazine, Tyson became a fashion model gracing the pages and covers of slick periodicals. At 24, she appeared in her first film and then performed in the celebrated CBS-TV drama *East Side, West Side* (1963–1964), giving her career a tremendous infusion. Ultimately she played roles in 82 movies on television and in theaters between 1957 and 2005. From 1961 to 2005 Tyson also turned up in guest appearances on another 25 television shows, sometimes as herself and on other occasions in lead or character parts.

UTTAL, FRED. b. 1908, New York, N.Y.; d. Nov. 28, 1963. *Emcee, Announcer.* **Series:** *The Al Jolson Program* (1942–1943); *The Army-Navy Game*, aka *Army-Navy House Party* (1942–1943, 1944); *As the Twig is Bent* (early 1940s); *Big Sister* (1936–ca. early 1940s); *Buck Rogers in the 25th Century* (ca. 1930s, 1940s); *Cavalcade of America* (1943); *Consumer Quiz* (quizmaster, 1940–1942); *Detect and Collect* (quizmaster, 1945); *Dollars for Breakfast* (ca. 1944); *The Esso Marketer* (1936); *The George Jessel Show*, aka *For Men Only* (1939–1940); *Guy Lombardo and His Orchestra* (1946); *The Jerry Lester Show* (ca. 1941–ca. 1942, 1943–1944); *Kelly's Courthouse* (master of ceremonies, 1944); *Laugh with Ken*, aka *The Ken Murray Rinso-Lifebuoy Program* (1936); *Lois Long and The Three Suns*, aka *Shopping Talk* (1944–1945); *Martin Kane, Private Eye* (ca. 1949–1952); *Melody Puzzles* (quizmaster, 1937–1938); *Mr. District Attorney* (1951); *Money-Go-Round* (1944); *Music Fights Infantile Paralysis* (1946); *Nick Carter, Master Detective* (1945); *The Paul Whiteman Show* (ca. 1937–1939); *Radio Guide's Court of Honor* (1936–1937); *Radio Reader's Digest* (1947); *This is Holloran*, aka *The Stan Lomax Show* (1944–1945); *What's My Name?* (master of ceremonies, 1939); *Yes or No* (1944); *You and Your Security* (1949); *You're the Expert* (master of ceremonies, 1941).

For six months in 1951 Fred Uttal was moderator of an ABC-TV primetime celebrity panel series, *Q.E.D.* that attempted to solve mystery stories submitted by home viewers.

VAN, LYLE. b. Sept. 10, 1904, Troy, N.Y. *Newscaster.* **Series:** *Lyle Van and the News* (newscaster, 1943–1944, 1945, 1948–1951).

While growing up in Baltimore, Lyle Van was a soloist in the boys' choir of Old St. Paul's Episcopal Church. That helped him acquire his initial radio exposure a few years hence. After graduating from prep school Van headed to Key West, Fla. where he attempted to make a haul in a real estate frenzy. That didn't happen; instead, he lost what little cash he had and went to work as a U.S. deputy marshal, mainly arresting bootleggers. His duties required him to travel infrequently to the Atlanta federal penitentiary to transport prisoners.

On one visit, before leaving town Van auditioned at WSB where he landed a job as an on-air vocalist. A short while later he drifted out of radio to open a retail store. But he lost his shirt on that deal, too. Realizing that he was better at performing than just about anything else, he applied at Atlanta's WGST. The station hired him for the post of program director. Sometime afterward, in 1934, he went to New York and won a tryout for the announcing staff at NBC's Radio City. Eventually Van concentrated most of his efforts in newscasting, initially at NBC and by the mid 1940s for the MBS network, where he persisted into the early 1950s.

VANDERCOOK, JOHN W. b. April 22, 1902, London, England; d. Jan. 6, 1963, Delhi, N.Y. *Newscaster, Commentator, Emcee.* **Series:** *John W. Vandercook* (newscaster-commentator, 1940–1941, 1945–1946, 1953–1955); *John W. Vandercook Air Age News of the Day* (commentator, ca. 1940s); *News of the World* (newscaster, 1940, 1941–1946); *Rebuttal* (moderator, 1950).

"The most elegant voice on the U.S. air" declared *Time* magazine in 1944 in branding author-globetrotter-newsman John W. Vandercook, who led a charmed life. The electronic-focused commentator descended from a proud and dynamic journalistic heritage. His mom, Margaret W. Vandercook, was the author of hundreds of books for girls. At the time of his birth in England, John's dad, John F. Vandercook, was a press association's European manager. With some other parties, the senior Vandercook was to be instrumental in establishing United Press International, one of the major wire services. He also became its first president. In 1919, after the family returned to the U.S., the son graduated from St. Paul's School, Garden City, N.Y. He enrolled at Yale University but dropped out after a year. "There were too damn many Republicans," he explained.

For a year the younger Vandercook performed in a handful of bit parts on Broadway and at other venues. Next he pursued newspaper work with *The Columbus Citizen*, *The Washington News* and *The Baltimore Post*. None of it satisfied him for long. In 1923 he became assistant editor of Macfadden Publications; in 1924, he was feature editor of *The New York Graphic*. Still seeking his ultimate spot, Vandercook decided to veer off the beaten path and see the world, publishing his eyewitness accounts in books and periodicals. In the 15 years that ensued, the bearded Vandercook traveled to some 73 nations, retelling his adventures in print through text and photographic essays, becoming a sought-after author. "He lived the life kids dream of," chronicled author Irving Fang. "He and his wife walked across hundreds of unmapped miles of West Africa. They penetrated the jungles of New Guinea to discover a tribe of head-hunting cannibals who had never seen a white man. They explored unvisited islands in the Solomons and Fijis."

In the meantime an unexpected opening allowed Vandercook to stumble into radio where he perhaps made his most celebrated contributions. He was jawing with an NBC vice president one day in 1940 as word reached them that the Allies had signed a pact to launch some bases in the West Indies. For 15 years Vandercook was a frequent journeyman there, considering it one of his "specialties." He went into a radio studio that same evening to appear on NBC's *News of the World* at 7:15 P.M. For most of the next half-dozen years he did the same thing six nights a week.

Vandercook's observations were impressive to NBC officials and he was promptly offered a contract. While he was decidedly liberal, he spoke authoritatively. He injected some firsthand knowledge into news commentaries about the places he had visited that were strategic battlegrounds or which had particular bearing on the Second World War. Typically, Vandercook was an integral part of NBC's reporting lineup on D-Day on June 6, 1944. "He fearlessly expressed his view of the news and his journalistic philosophy that included a strong dislike of censorship," a critic advised. Added another: "Contrary to the thinking of some commentators, Vandercook expressed the thought that he was amazed by the freedom of radio, saying that no one interfered with anything he wanted to say."

While he left radio for a time during the late 1940s, Vandercook returned in the 1950s. Initially he presided over a pithy MBS feature. But before long he was again providing his insightful news commentaries, that time on ABC, where he was underwritten by the CIO.

VANOCUR, SANDER. b. Jan. 8, 1928, Cleveland, Ohio. *Correspondent.* **Series:** *CBS World News Roundup* (correspondent, ca. 1954); *NBC News on the Hour* (correspondent, 1957–1971).

In 1950 Sander Vanocur earned a bachelor's degree in speech and political science from Northwestern University before enrolling in the London School of Economics for postgraduate study. He then launched a journalism career in 1954, reporting on the London staff of *The Manchester Guardian*. While in London he worked for United Press, CBS News and the North American Service of the British Broadcasting Corp. Returning to the U.S. in 1955, Vanocur became a city staff reporter for *The New York Times*. He quit two years hence to join NBC News, where he gathered and aired current events for 14 years. During that tenure he was the chain's White House correspondent, national political correspondent, Washington correspondent for NBC-TV's *Today*, contributing editor to the nightly *Huntley-Brinkley Report* and host of *First Tuesday*, a monthly magazine on NBC-TV (1969–1970).

At the 1964 political conventions, the Huntley-Brinkley team anchored NBC's coverage while Roger Mudd and Robert Trout did the same for CBS. A seasoned Huntley-Brinkley duo easily carried the day. Contributors like Vanocur helped them do it; he scored an upset by corralling Lyndon B. Johnson for a long, spontaneous interview immediately following Johnson's nominating acceptance address. As the nation's chief executive departed from the convention hall, CBS producer Bill Leonard intercepted him, petitioning in an imploring manner, "Will you wave up to Mr. Trout and Mr. Mudd, sir? You've waved to everybody else." The president courteously turned to the CBS anchor booth and waved hello. But for Mudd-Trout it was goodbye, their singular opportunity to fill such a critical slot having self-destructed in their faces.

In their book on the Edward R. Murrow journalistic legacy, Stanley Cloud and Lynne Olson observed: "It is almost axiomatic that the more an institution breaks faith with those who built it, the more it sanctifies them. When it suits their purposes, CBS News's modern executives and journalists pretend that theirs is still the network of Edward R. Murrow and the Boys. It isn't." Cloud and Olson, writing in the mid 1990s, quoted Vanocur, fleetingly a CBS correspondent in the 1950s: "It drives me up the wall when I hear people at CBS invoking the name of Murrow. Most of them couldn't carry his typewriter.... CBS is now like a cult. They're pagans praying to idols. They invoke these deities to justify their present base claims. In a funny way, they're schizophrenic—they both want to illuminate and erase the tradition."

Following his NBC experience, Vanocur taught briefly at Duke University, Durham, N.C. His career subsequently carried him to *The Washington Post* as television editor and critic (1975–1977) and then to ABC News (1977–1992) as chief diplomatic correspondent, senior correspondent in Buenos Aires and anchor of *Business World*, video's first regularly scheduled commerce feature (1986–1992). From 1995 to 2002, Vanocur anchored a couple of History Channel programs: *Movies in Time* and *History's Business*.

Most recently he headed a Santa Barbara, Calif. full service communications and consulting firm. Vanocur also appeared in a half-dozen motion pictures: *The Gang That Couldn't Shoot Straight* (1971); *Raise the Titanic* (1980); *Dave* (1993); *Without Warning* (1994); *Street Fighter* (1994); and *Weapons of Mass Distraction* (1997).

VAN VOORHIS, WESTBROOK (aka Hugh Conrad). b. Sept. 21, 1903, New Milford, Conn.; d. July 13, 1968, New Milford, Conn. *Announcer, Commentator.* **Series:** *The Great Adventure* (narrator, 1951); *The March of Time* (narrator, 1937–1939, 1942–1945); *Westbrook Van Voorhis* (commentator, 1943–1945). **Aphorism:** *Time marches on!*

Westbrook Van Voorhis was labeled "The Voice of Doom" for the sober manner in which he introduced *The March of Time* when he was with that program: *Time marches on!* Humorist Jim Backus, an announcer during his own show business start, called Van Voorhis "the most thunderous of them all" and claimed the mere mention of Van Voorhis's name "stayed eagles in their flight." Backus proclaimed: "His voice could shatter a shaving mug at twenty paces." Another cohort affirmed that Van Voorhis possessed "the voice of God."

In the 1930s Van Voorhis joined the CBS staff in New York which assigned him to a variety of programming, including assisting with the web's coverage of the 1936 Kentucky Derby from Louisville. By the following year he left for NBC, initially affiliating with the Blue and then the resulting ABC chain.

Van Voorhis enjoyed several opportunities in television, too. He narrated *Crusade in Europe*, a *Time*-sponsored documentary carried for six months by ABC in 1949. In the summer of 1951 he presented the NBC spy thriller *The Door with No Name*. He hosted a revival of his most memorable radio series for a few weeks in 1952 on ABC-TV, *The March of Time through the Years*. In 1954 Van Voorhis interviewed prominent U.S. industrialists for the syndicated video documentary *Mr. Executive*. For six months in 1957 he presided over a half-hour anthology series of suspense dramas on NBC-TV, *Panic!* Some of those same programs, plus some new ones, were aired under the title *No Warning!* in a five-month period in 1958 on the same network, again with Van Voorhis announcing.

For about 15 years Van Voorhis also narrated movie documentaries for *Time* magazine. He did the same for innumerable instructional films about service in the armed forces. In each of his formats audiences found his vivid descriptions of the impact of the Great Depression, World War II and the postwar industrial period compelling.

VENABLES, ROBERT. b. April 4, 1907, Woodstock, Ill.; d. July 1985. *Announcer.* **Series:** *The Whistler.*

In 1941 Bob Venables was a newscaster at Chicago's WGN.

VINES, LEE L. b. April 23, 1898, Texas; d. Dec. 28, 1987, Merced, Calif. *Announcer.* **Series:** *Bouquet for You* (1946–1947); *Cabin B-13* (1948–1949); *The CBS Radio Workshop* (ca. 1956–1957); *County Fair* (1945–1950); *Dr. Standish, Medical Examiner* (1948); *Harry James and His Music Makers* (1945); *The Janette Davis Show* (1948); *King's Row* (narrator, 1951–1952); *Rate Your Mate* (1950, 1951); *The Sears Radio Theater* (actor, 1979); *Stepping Out* (1950); *Studio One* (ca. 1947–1948); *Suspense* (actor, 1961); *Theater of Romance*, aka *Romance* (host, 1944–ca. 1946); *Time for Love* (1953–1954); *Up for Parole* (1950).

In 1940 Lee Vines was the newscaster for WIP, Philadelphia's *Newspaper of the Air* which was heard for a quarter-hour four nights weekly. As radio began to ebb for him he lucked into one of the most enduring assignments on television: for three decades he introduced the *Hallmark Hall of Fame* on a trio of networks—NBC (1952–1978), PBS (1979–1982) and CBS (1983–1984). From 1954 to 1956 Vines also announced the daily *Robert Q. Lewis Show* on CBS-TV.

Furthermore, from 1948 to 1990 (even beyond his death) Vines had the good fortune of appearing on more than a dozen other television series, sometimes in uncredited or voiceover roles, but still seen or heard there. They included: *We, the People* (1948); *Beat the Clock* (1950); *What's My Line?* (1950); *Hallmark Hall of Fame* (1951); *It's News to Me* (1951); *The Name's the Same* (1951); *Balance Your Budget* (1952); *Sing Along with Mitch* (1961); *Password* (1961); *Picture This* (1963); *The Last of the Curlews* (1972); *Hong Kong Phooey* (1974); *The Mary Tyler Moore Show* (1975, 1977); *Rhoda* (1976); and *Cheers* (1990).

VON ZELL, HARRY. b. July 11, 1906, Indianapolis, Ind.; d. Nov. 21, 1981, Calabasas, Calif. *Announcer, Emcee, Actor.* **Series:** *The Adventures of Ellery Queen* (actor); *The Aldrich Family* (1939–?); *The Amazing Mr. Smith* (1941); *Baby Snooks* (ca. 1940s); *Behind the Mike*, aka *Nothing But the Truth* (1940–1942); *Ben Bernie, the Old Maestro* (ca. late 1930s, ca. early 1940s); *Birdseye Open House*, aka *The Dinah Shore Show* (1941–1942, 1943–ca. 1946); *The Botany Song Shop* (1950–1951); *Bright Star* (1952–1953); *Burns and Allen* (sporadic announcer, 1942–1950); *Chicken Every Sunday* (actor, 1949); *Command Performance* (actor, 1945); *The Eddie Cantor Show*, aka *It Can Happen to You* (1940–1946, 1950s); *The Fabulous Dr. Tweedy* (actor, 1946–1947); *Fifteen Minutes with Bing Crosby* (1931–1932); *The Frank Fontaine Show* (1952); *The Fred Allen Show*, aka *Town Hall Tonight* (1936–1942); *Goldenrod Revue* (1933); *The Gulf Screen Guild Theater* (1939); *The Gulf Show*, aka *Will Rogers Show* (1933–1935); *Hobby Lobby*; *Honolulu Bound*, aka *The*

Great American Tourist, aka *The Phil Baker Show* (ca. 1935–1939); *Joan Davis Time* (1945–1947); *Joe and Vi* (1931–1934); *Leave it to Joan* (actor, 1949–1950); *The March of Time* (narrator, 1931–1933); *Meet the Missus* (master of ceremonies, ca. 1944–ca. 1950); *Modern Minstrels* (interlocutor, 1935); *Music by Gershwin* (1934); T*he Old Gold Hour*, aka *The Paul Whiteman Show* (1929–1930); *Quizzer's Baseball* (master of ceremonies, 1941); *Silver Theater* (1943–?); *The Smiths of Hollywood* (actor, 1946); *Stoopnagle and Budd*, aka *The Minute Men* (1934, 1936–1937); *Time to Smile* (1945–1946); *Truth or Consequences* (co-master of ceremonies, 1944); *Wednesday with You* (1945); *We, the People* (ca. late 1930s–?); *Whispering Jack Smith* (1932–1933, 1934–1935).

"Giggles" was Harry Von Zell's nickname while he was in high school. It would serve him well throughout his professional career. His dad was a sports reporter as the son launched into high school at Indianapolis. Before he graduated, however, they were living at Sioux City, Iowa. Then the Von Zells moved to California where the high school grad enrolled at UCLA. He was a member of drama and music organizations there and—until an injury sidelined him—played college football. Von Zell attempted several lines of work, including winning a few matches in the boxing ring. He was a bank messenger, a payroll clerk for the Los Angeles and Salt Lake Railroad and—as the result of a fluke—sang over the air while accompanying himself on the ukulele when he visited a small radio station at Inglewood, Calif., KMIC.

Other singing engagements followed on the ether. Von Zell joined KMIC in 1926 (one source specifies 1927) in a blended role as announcer-vocalist-producer-writer. His star rose swiftly. By 1928, he was announcer and program director at San Diego's KGB, a much larger outlet; in 1929, he was in Los Angeles at KTMR. Not long afterward, he replaced Ted Husing as Paul Whiteman's announcer. Airworthy notoriety lay directly in his path. Von Zell followed Whiteman back East and joined CBS. In 1930 he added some commentary to broadcasts made by Admiral Richard E. Byrd while Byrd was on his celebrated expedition to the South Pole. In 1931 he introduced singer Bing Crosby to radio audiences for the first time.

Von Zell's most memorable, and embarrassing, moment in broadcast history also occurred in 1931 when he stated to legions tuning into CBS: "I give you now the president of the United States, Hoobert Heever." Years later, he told radio historian Chuck Schaden it wasn't an actual presentation of the president himself (as numerous documentarians recorded it), but the last line of a protracted reminiscence of the public servant's life and career. "I must have mentioned in that opening the name of Herbert Hoover no less than twenty times," he stated. "I was very young at the time ... and was very nervous." At the end of the occasion, an extended birthday tribute, Von Zell goofed, mangling the president's moniker. The announcer recalled, "I thought that whatever career might have been a potential in my life began and ended right there in that one incident." While he achieved a well heeled, durable career, the incident dogged Von Zell until his death and is still somewhat mockingly recalled by vintage radio enthusiasts.

In 1935 Von Zell took himself out of everyday broadcasting while working on the radio production staff of Young and Rubicam, one of the major advertising agencies. There he wrote copy, planned productions, produced, directed, announced and performed. Returning to the air full time Von Zell quickly found his strict announcing assignments dwindling; instead, he had more chances to "perform" as a straight man or in comedy sketches with name celebrities like Fred Allen; Phil Baker; Ben Bernie; George Burns and Gracie Allen; Eddie Cantor; Joan Davis; Dinah Shore; and others of their stature. His role was indeed evolving, preparing him for screen activity. He also portrayed the important character of the announcer-straight man on the *Burns and Allen* show on CBS Television (1951–1958) and on the succeeding *George Burns Show* on NBC-TV (1958–1959). It was a part he flaunted on several radio series. In 1959–1960 he was a regular in the cast of *The George Gobel Show* on CBS-TV, too. Von Zell provided the play-by-play commentary on NBC-TV's *Celebrity Golf* series in the 1960–1961 season, a program hosted by golfer Sam Snead.

In the four decades between 1935 and 1975, Von Zell turned up in 27 motion pictures, mostly of the B-movie variety. He often portrayed himself or a radio announcer, or was a film's narrator. Among his features: *Radio Rhapsody* (1935); *How Doooo You Do!!!* (1945); *Till the End of Time* (1946); *Radio Romeo* (1947); *Radio Riot* (1949); *Ma and Pa Kettle Back on the Farm* (1951); *I Can Get It for You Wholesale* (1951); *You're in the Navy Now* (1951); *Call Me Mister* (1951); *Son of Paleface* (1952); and *Boy, Did I Get a Wrong Number!* (1966). Von Zell played an announcer in a single made-for-TV movie in 1975, *Ellery Queen*.

WAGNER, MURRAY. *Announcer.* **Series:** *Double or Nothing* (ca. early 1950s); *Meet Miss Sherlock* (1946, 1947); *Tell it Again* (1948–1949).

Before handing over the *Double or Nothing* quiz show each weekday to Walter O'Keefe, announcer Murray Wagner exuberantly introduced the inveterate master of ceremonies as the "man of the half-hour," and added, "here he is—your paymaster of ceremonies" before bellowing: "OK, O'Keefe!" The epigraphic business was met on cue by thunderous studio audience applause.

WALD, JOHN. *Announcer, Newscaster.* **Series:** *Confession* (1953); *The Eddie Bracken Show* (1945); *Fibber McGee and Molly* (1953–1956); *Frontier Gentleman* (1958); *The Great Gildersleeve* (1947–1949); *The National Lampoon Radio Hour* (cast member, 1972–1976); *NBC Presents: Short Story* (ca. 1951–1952); *The Richfield Reporter* (newscaster, 1939–?); *The Six Shooter* (1954); *Summerfield Bandstand* (1947).

WALDECKER, FRANK. b. Feb. 3, 1902; d. January 1967, Dearborn Heights, Mich. *Announcer.* **Series:** *A Date with Duchin*, aka *The Eddy Duchin Show* (1947); *Pitching Horseshoes* (1941); *Postcard Serenade* (1945); *Treasury Varieties* (1942–1943); *Twenty Questions* (ca. late 1940s, ca. early 1950s).

WALLACE, MYRON (MIKE) (born Myron Leon Wallik). b. May 9, 1918, Brookline, Mass. *Announcer, Actor, Emcee.* **Series:** *All Around the Town* (co-host, 1951–1952); *The Chez Show* (co-host, 1951); *The Crime Files of Flamond* (actor, 1948); *Crime on the Waterfront* (actor, 1949); *Curtain Time* (actor, 1945–1948); *Fact or Fiction* (host, 1946–1947); *The Green Hornet* (1940–1941); *The Guiding Light* (1941–1942); *A Life in Your Hands* (1949–ca. 1951); *The Lone Ranger* (1940–1941); *Ma Perkins* (1941–1942); *Mike and Buff's Mail Bag* (co-host, 1954); *Road of Life* (1941–1942); *Sky King* (late 1940s, early 1950s); *The Spike Jones Show* (late 1940s); *Weekday* (co-host, 1955–1956); *You Bet Your Life* (commercial spokesman, 1947–1950).

Had an immigration officer not misunderstood the pronunciation of the surname when checking his family in at the U.S. border after their arrival from Russia several years before, Myron Wallik might have been known by that moniker today. But the federal agent wrote down "Wallace" instead and the family adopted it as their legal name. Myron Wallace focused on dramatics, public speaking and the student newspaper at Brookline High School, interests he still pursued as an octogenarian. He also played violin in the orchestra and was captain of the tennis team. Upon his graduation, in 1935 he enrolled at the University of Michigan where an uncle was on the faculty. To pay for his schooling, the young Wallace waited tables and washed dishes and was employed by the National Youth Administration, a Roosevelt-era public education assistance plan.

In the meantime he cultivated an interest in radio after visiting the campus station. At a music camp one summer Wallace instructed a course in radio broadcasting. He earned a bachelor's degree from Michigan in 1939 and was subsequently employed by a small Ann Arbor station; then he graduated to stations WASH and WOOD at Grand Rapids as a $20-a-week announcer, continuity writer and salesman. The following year, 1940, he left for the more prosperous WXYZ in Detroit. That station produced several epic dramas beamed nationally (*The Challenge of the Yukon, The Green Hornet, The Lone Ranger*, et al.) and offered him his first network exposure.

Within a year Wallace made the gargantuan leap to Chicago where he was hired as the $150-a-week interlocutor for *Road of Life*. In his spare time he was a news writer and announcer for the station owned by *The Chicago Sun*. (While in the Windy City he changed his handle from Myron to Mike.) He was inducted into the U.S. Navy in 1943 and served as a communications officer.

Returning to Chicago in 1946 Wallace joined WMAQ as a news reporter. Later that decade he delivered lip-smacking pitches for Derby's Peter Pan peanut butter in between acts of the late afternoon juvenile adventure serial *Sky King*. The announcer was so charmed by the stock market during that epoch that it wasn't uncommon to find him on the telephone with his stockbroker, who briefed him of current activity after which Wallace made buying and selling transactions. So caught up was he in his passion that—on at least one occasion—he almost missed a performance of *Sky King* by reducing the time between telephone activity and live broadcast to literal seconds. The director must have held his breath!

At the middle of the 20th century, on Tuesday through Sunday nights from 11:15 P.M. to 1 A.M., Wallace and his then-wife, the glamorous Italian-born actress Buff Cobb, conducted a husband-and-wife talk show over Chicago's WMAQ Radio. They also played record requests received by telephone from listeners. Between 11:30 P.M. and 1 A.M. in 1951, furthermore, NBC carried the program. Called *The Chez Show*, it originated from the Sapphire Bar of Chicago's Chez Paris restaurant. After that series Wallace and Cobb left the Windy City for New York where they reprised their chat sessions on CBS's daytime *All Around the Town*, a billboard of New York events (which also ran for a few months in 1951 on CBS-TV), and later *Mike and Buff's Mail Bag*. For the latter, each day the couple considered questions about home life and George Fisher conducted a recorded interview with a Hollywood movie luminary. Simultaneously, Wallace played a leading part in the 1954 Broadway play *Reclining Figure*. He also organized the news department at Dumont Television and anchored a nightly newscast on its New York outlet.

Wallace hosted a couple of TV game shows in this period, too: CBS's *I'll Buy That* (1953–1954) and NBC's *The Big Surprise* (1956–1957). But his career took a perceptibly different turn in 1956 when he signed for *Nightbeat*, a local TV series. "For the first time," confirmed a source, "a television interviewer challenged his guests with difficult questions, and his audience with difficult subject matter. His confrontational, provocative style fascinated the New York public, and while many public figures dreaded answering Wallace's probing questions, they were eager to be seen by his growing audience." The following year he reached a national public for a half-hour in weekend primetime with *Mike Wallace Interviews* on ABC-TV (1957–1958) and from 1961 to 1964 he narrated a popular syndicated *Biography* video documentary. By then his name was becoming a household word outside the Northeast. He signed an exclusive contract with CBS News, which sent him to Vietnam several times across a decade starting in 1962. *The CBS Morning News with Mike Wallace* debuted in 1963 on television and he remained with that format for three years.

But Wallace's defining career move arrived when, with Harry Reasoner, he co-hosted the premiering CBS newsmagazine *60 Minutes* on Sept. 24, 1968. It's a show on which he asked the hard questions of every sitting U.S. president, and many of the world's other principal figures, too, as the decades rolled by. As spring 2006 arrived he at last decided to abandon his firmly entrenched slot on that venerable series retiring before being overtaken by incapacity or death. Wallace is the author of several best sellers, including two autobiographies, *Close Encounters* (William Morrow, 1984), and *Between You and Me: A Memoir* (Hyperion, 2005). His son Chris Wallace followed in his father's footsteps, becoming a television investigative reporter.

WALLINGTON, JAMES. b. Sept. 5, 1907, Rochester, N.Y.; d. Dec. 22, 1972, Arlington, Va. *Announcer, Emcee*. **Series:** *The Adventures of the Thin Man* (1940s); *The Alan Young Show* (1946–1947); *Ben Bernie, the Old Maestro* (1931–1935); *The Big Show* (early 1950s); *Big Six of the Air* (1932); *Blind Date* (1940s); *Blue Ribbon Music Time* (1947); *The Bob Crosby Show* (1950s); *The Carnation Contented Hour* (1948–1951); *Command Performance U.S.A.*; *Cousin Willie* (1953); *A Day in the Life of Dennis Day* (ca. late 1940s); *The Doctor Fights* (1945); *Duffy's Tavern* (ca. 1940s); *The Eddie Bracken Show* (1946–1947); *The Eddie Cantor Show*, aka *The Chase & Sanborn Hour* (1931–1934); *The Fred Allen Show* (1939–1944); *Freedom USA* (1952); *The George Burns and Gracie Allen Show* (ca.

1940–1941); *The Gibson Family* (1934–1935); *The Globe Theater* (actor, 1944–1945); *The Golden Blossom Revue* (1932); *The Jack Kirkwood Show*, aka *Mirth and Madness* (ca. 1943–1946); *The James Melton Show*, aka *The Texaco Star Theater* (1944–1946); *The Jimmy Durante Show*, aka *The Chase & Sanborn Hour* (1933, 1934); *Junior Miss* (ca. late 1940s, ca. early 1950s); *The Life of Riley* (1949–1951); *Listen to a Love Song*, aka *The Tony Martin Show* (1946); *Major Bowes' Original Amateur Hour*; *The Martin and Lewis Show*; *The Mysterious Traveler* (ca. 1940s); *Philco Hall of Fame*, aka *Radio Hall of Fame* (1943–1946); *The Rudy Vallee Show*; *The Sealed Book* (1945); *The Screen Director's Playhouse* (1949–1951); *Sincerely, Kenny Baker* (1945); *Stella Dallas*; *This is My Best* (host-narrator, 1944).

While attending Union College, Jimmy Wallington made a name for himself at Schenectady's WGY in 1928, beginning as a radio vocalist and becoming an announcer afterward. Using shortwave transmission he read some personal communications aloud from family members of the crew of U.S. Navy Admiral Richard E. Byrd (1888–1957) to relatives stationed at a Little America outpost half a world away. The circumstance was during the first (1928–1930) of a half-dozen expeditions that Byrd completed to Antarctica. When the mission ended and the party returned, Wallington met them aboard the ship as it docked in the New York harbor in June 1930. On the air alongside NBC's Graham McNamee, he interviewed several crew members about their lengthy journey. The gala celebration injected notoriety into Wallington's own career and became a legacy of his early years in broadcasting, for which he would be recalled by many historians.

Media critic Leonard Maltin observed, "In that still-primitive era, announcers took microphones aloft in hot-air balloons, underground in caves, and anywhere else that might make for a colorful broadcast." Hence, among Wallington's notable milestones were the first ship-to-ship broadcast; the world's first broadcast from a submerged submarine; and the first from an underwater diving bell in use at sea. Wallington also distinguished himself in other arenas. On dual occasions (in 1933 and 1935) he won the American Academy of Arts and Letters' gold medal for diction given annually to a radio personality for what was perceived to be the best enunciation of the year. (In later years the tribute was appropriated by *Radio Stars* fanzine.) Wallington also introduced President Franklin D. Roosevelt's appearances on NBC and offered word pictures of the record-setting flights of aviator Charles A. Lindbergh.

Wallington may have been responsible for elevating broadcast announcers from non-entities to recognized, integrated cast members, particularly in broadcast variety series. Radio chronicler Gerald Nachman acknowledged: "Sidekick announcers walked a line between hired man and hired gun, laboring in the shadow of the star while taking potshots at him. In time, it became standard on comedy shows to make the announcer part of the sketches, an idea introduced by Eddie Cantor when he had Jimmy Wallington step in as straight man. The concept didn't really carry over into TV except in the case of talk shows, when radio refugees like Steve Allen sparred with Gene Rayburn and bandleader Skitch Henderson, a tradition now considered de rigueur on TV talk-variety shows; the announcer and/or bandleader stooge is in every late-show job description." And to think it may have all begun with Wallington!

In later years that legendary announcer was a voiceover commercial artist on television, ending his career with the Voice of America. A reporter suggests Wallington went back to NBC Radio in 1961 as a recurring participant on *Monitor* but if that happened, it seems to have been missed by the author of the show's biography.

Writing the foreword to aspiring audio interlocutors in Art Gilmore and Glenn Middleton's 1946 treatise, *Television and Radio Announcing*, Wallington observed: "As one of the trail blazers in this fascinating field, I experience a flush of pride in the modern programs which to me seem to reflect the effective union of creative expression and clock-like teamwork.... Of all the departments and jobs in radio..., that of announcing is the one that many of us find the most fascinating and the one which the greatest number of young Americans seem to select as their career.... The faint of heart will give up before allowing themselves a fair chance, but the men and women who will be the successful announcers of tomorrow are those who now have the desire to learn, the perseverance and the will to train and practice for the position they hope to attain."

WALSH, GEORGE. b. Nov. 29, 1917, Cleveland, Ohio; d. Dec. 5, 2005, Monterey Park, Calif. *Announcer, Emcee.* **Series:** *America Calling* (1952–1953); *Cathy and Elliott Lewis on Stage* (1953–1954); *The CBS Radio Workshop* (ca. 1956–ca. 1957); *Escape* (early 1950s); *Gunsmoke* (1952–1961); *Saturday Theater* (host-narrator, 1954–1955); *Scattergood Baines* (late 1940s); *Suspense* (ca. 1954–ca. 1962); *Whispering Streets* (1950s).

"When I was growing up in Cleveland in the 1930s," George Walsh recalled many years later, "radio was like magic. It was like being an astronaut today." Having to give a speech in high school on what he wanted to do in life, Walsh confessed: "I had no idea. I said that I wanted to be on the radio and repeated some lines from radio shows. My instructor gave me a reasonable mark and asked if I would host a floor show and do some impersonations at the prom. They paid me $15 and two tickets to the prom." After that, he continued fine-tuning his act and appeared on local amateur shows on the air, sometimes winning those competitions.

After high school Walsh went to work in a steel mill and performed at church socials in the evenings. When the Second World War began he enlisted in the U.S. Army Air Corps, serving for a quadrennial. "I froze in Munich and decided that when I got out I wasn't going to return to the Cleveland cold," he pontificated.

He took a job at KSWS, Roswell, N.M., in 1946 and stayed put for a while. He wanted more education, however, and finally enrolled at Hollywood's Don Martin School of Broadcasting in 1952. As a consequence KNX hired him as a part time vacation relief announcer on May 26, 1952 at $100 weekly. He stayed 34 years! By every measure, his greatest success was as the voice that introduced *Gunsmoke*, including a decade on CBS Radio and two decades on CBS-TV (1955–1975). Unlike the other unsuccessful cast members of the radio version, he defied the odds, moving seamlessly from the aural to the video incarnation of the epic western.

Meanwhile, after serving at KNX all that time, "By 1986 I was ready to retire," he allowed. "I had had a prostate cancer operation and a heart pacemaker installed." Still, he continued telephoning occasional stories to KNX from his home in Monterey Park, Calif., for years after his retirement. He died of heart failure.

Parenthetically, a radio historiographer noted that the mystery series *Suspense* lived up to its name. During its later years, announcer Walsh breathed the opening signature into the microphone in a memorable, vacillating basso profundo: *And nowwwwww ... another tale well-calculated ... to keep you in ... Sussssspense ...!*

WALTERS, JOE. *Announcer.* **Series:** *The Adventures of Philip Marlowe* (ca. 1948–ca. 1950); *Broadway is My Beat* (1949–1950, 1951–?); *Bunco Squad* (1950); *Dale Jones and Company*; *I Was There* (1945); *The Lineup* (ca. 1950–ca. 1951); *Rocky Jordan* (1951, 1952–1953).

Joe Walters was a newscaster on local radio early in his professional career, serving San Francisco's KSFC in 1940 and San Diego's KFMB in 1941. He later made his way to the Los Angeles area. He is not to be confused with a prominent radio musician of the period, Joe (Josef) Walters.

WALTON, SIDNEY. b. March 23, 1905, Mississippi; d. Jan. 16, 1958, Los Angeles, Calif. *Commentator, Announcer.* **Series:** *Arthur Tracy, The Street Singer* (1942); *Changing Times* (financial commentator, 1955–1962); *Here's Hollywood* (reporter, 1956); *Voice of Experience* (1933–ca. 1939, ca. 1944); *Whiz Quiz* (1948).

Sidney Walton enjoyed a diverse fling in network radio broadcasting that continued intermittently for three decades. In the course of it he turned up as an announcer, newscaster, impresario, fowl coordinator, disc jockey and commentator on what might have been broadcasting's earliest infomercial. His initial exposure to netcasting transpired in 1933 when he introduced Dr. Marion Sayle Taylor, who dispensed personal advice on *Voice of Experience*. The series persisted throughout the 1930s on CBS, NBC and MBS and was later syndicated. It might have even planted some ideas in Walton's thinking, considering where his career ultimately took him.

In 1940 he delivered a quarter-hour of *Sidney Walton's Music* to the waiting ears tuned to NBC Blue on Saturdays and Sundays. On that show Walton performed everything except the singing, a duty that fell to vocalist Gwen Williams. Otherwise, he was the show's master of ceremonies; conducted the band; directed a group of harmonizing canaries; and—in resonant and imposing tones—pitched cooling systems as an occupation (the show was underwritten by the Air Conditioning Training Corp.). No little effort expended there.

Simultaneously, Walton dispatched the news on a handful of New York City radio stations throughout the 1940s, including WOR, WHN and WINS. Near the end of the decade, he became a WINS DJ, too. He resurfaced in 1948 on ABC Radio introducing the game show *Whiz Quiz* with Johnny Olsen as emcee. But none of what had gone before resulted in his most memorable claim to fame: that wouldn't occur until the mid 1950s when Willard M. Kiplinger was among the first—if not *the* first advertiser—to launch infomercial programming on the ether. He hired Walton as his aural stand-in.

"*Changing Times*, a Kiplinger magazine," as an authoritative-sounding Walton repetitiously reminded aficionados, extolled some proven methods of saving, investing, conducting real estate transactions, handling wills, inheritances, taxes and many other principles of getting ahead. For a quarter-hour on weekend mornings, Walton divulged tips purportedly uncovered by the editors of the periodical backing the show. The series originally appeared on Jan. 23, 1955 and lasted to April 29, 1962, over NBC its first couple of years and MBS thereafter. There was also a quarter-hour television which appeared in some markets throughout the 1960s and early 1970s, seemingly dropped into local schedules on weekends to fill existing holes, paving the way for video infomercials ad nauseam to follow.

In addition to the secrets-packed journal which debuted in 1947—touted as "the nation's first magazine of personal money management" and later re-titled *Kiplinger's Personal Finance Magazine*—Kiplinger, the firm's founder and publisher, also circulated a series of private subscription letters dealing with a diverse range of specialized finance-related topics, family-oriented in scope. In addition, the *Kiplinger Washington Newsletter* is currently hyped as "the most widely read business and economics forecasting publication in the world." On the show one hardly knew where the programming ended and the plugs began, a formula copied by television infomercials today. In reality, *all of it* was advertising.

In the meantime an enterprising Walton had caught on to the concept of making more money by publishing his own financial texts; he turned out a plethora of them in the 1950s and 1960s for a New York outfit, Profit Research Inc. A few titles suggest the scope of his efforts: *How to Legally Avoid Paying Taxes*; *How to Make a Killing in Real Estate*; *How to Make All the Money You Want While Collecting Social Security*; *How to Scheme Your Way to Profit*; *How to Start Getting Rich*; *Pocket Guide to Daily Money-Handling*; *Secrets of Banking and Borrowing*; *Secrets of Speculation*; *How to Get Twice as Much Bank Interest*; *How to Keep from Being Cheated*; and *Plain Language Money Making Book*. It was a far cry from merely directing a few singing canaries.

WARD, PERRY. b. Aug. 18, 1914, Tulsa, Okla.; d. May 29, 1989, Wichita, Kan. *Announcer, Emcee.* **Series:** *Aunt Mary* (1941–ca. 1951); *Duffy's Tavern* (ca. 1940s); *Expectant Father* (host, 1946); *Gaslight Gaieties*, aka *The Gay Nineties Revue* (1944–1945); *Gene Autry's Melody Ranch* (1946); *Jimmy Wakely's Western Song Parade* (1946–1947); *Scramby Amby* (master of ceremonies, 1943, 1944–1945, 1946–1947); *Strange Wills* (1946); *The Theater of Famous Radio Players* (1945); *What's Doin', Ladies?* (master of ceremonies, 1945–1946).

WARREN, CARL. *Announcer, Disc Jockey.* **Series:** *Bobby Benson and the B-Bar-B Riders* (1949–early 1950s); *Dick Kuhn and His Orchestra* (1940); *Guest Time* (disc jockey, 1954–1955); *Hit That Ball* (1939); *Red Benson's Movie Matinee* (1949); *Songs of the B-Bar-B* (1955); *Tex Fletcher* (1951); *Treasury Agent* (1954–1957).

On the Bobby Benson series Carl Warren was known as "Cactus."

WARREN, CHARLES ROBERT. b. Jan. 22, 1917, Plainview, Neb.; d. Dec. 28, 1984,

Santa Clara, Calif. *Announcer, Actor.* **Series:** *Archie Andrews* (ca. late 1940s, ca. early 1950s); *Cloak and Dagger* (1950); *Confidentially Yours* (1950); *Death Valley Sheriff,* aka *The Sheriff* (actor, ca. late 1940s–1951); *Dimension X* (ca. 1950); *The Jane Pickens Show* (1948); *Living 1948–1951* (1948–1951); *Radio City Playhouse* (1948–ca. 1949); *X-Minus One* (mid 1950s).

While he was the composer for the 1945 motion picture *Eve Knew Her Apples,* Bob Warren didn't perform in the big time himself until he completed a stint at Philadelphia's KYW in 1946 as a newscaster. He introduced several aural features originating in New York in the late 1940s. After his radio fortunes began to wane in the early 1950s, Warren took off for the West Coast. By 1952 he was introducing NBC-TV's *This is Your Life.* In 1955 he began a long-running commitment lasting 27 years as announcer for *The Lawrence Welk Show,* 16 years on ABC-TV and 11 more in syndication. The announcer performed similar duties for ABC-TV's *The Girl in My Life* (1973–1974).

WEBER, KARL A. b. March 17, 1916, Columbus Junction, Iowa; d. July 30, 1990, Boston, Mass. *Announcer, Actor.* **Series:** *Arnold Grimm's Daughter* (actor, 1937–1942); *Avalon Time,* aka *The Red Skelton Show* (actor, ca. 1939–1940); *The Barton Family,* aka *The Bartons,* aka *Bud Barton,* aka *The Story of Bud Barton* (actor, ca. 1939–ca. 1942); *Best Plays* (actor, 1952–1953); *Cloak and Dagger* (1950); *Dimension X* (actor, 1950–1951); *Dr. Sixgun* (actor, 1954–1955); *Don Winslow of the Navy* (actor, 1937–ca. 1939); *Girl Alone* (actor, 1935–1941); *The Greatest Story Ever Told* (actor, 1947–1956); *Helpmate* (actor, 1941–1944); *The Inside Story* (actor, 1939); *Inspector Thorne* (actor, 1951); *Kay Fairchild, Stepmother* (actor, ca. 1938–ca. 1942); *Lonely Women* (actor, 1942–1943); *Lorenzo Jones* (actor); *Mr. Keen, Tracer of Lost Persons* (actor, 1946–1954); *Nona from Nowhere* (actor, 1950–1951); *The Romance of Helen Trent* (actor, ca. 1940s, 1950s); *The Second Mrs. Burton* (actor, ca. 1940s, 1950s); *The Strange Romance of Evelyn Winters* (actor, mid to late 1940s); *When a Girl Marries* (actor, ca. 1940s, ca. 1950s); *The Whisper Men* (actor, 1945–1946); *Woman in White* (actor, 1940s); *Words at War* (actor, 1943–1945).

Hoping to become a Broadway actor following graduation from the University of Iowa, Karl Weber paused in Chicago en route to New York. At the insistence of a chum he auditioned for a radio role in the Windy City, won it and stayed put for a half-dozen years before departing for Gotham—appearing on hundreds of shows in the interim. Following his radio escapades and several detours into Broadway productions, the seasoned thespian gained recurring roles on a couple of televised daytime serials, CBS's *Search for Tomorrow* (1955–1956) and NBC's *Kitty Foyle* (1958).

WEBSTER, KURT. *Announcer.* **Series:** *The Johnson Family Singers* (ca. 1946–ca. 1949).

Kurt Webster arrived at Charlotte's WBT in 1946 and—as disc jockey for the *Midnight Dancing Party*—served the first station in the Southeast to operate 24 hours daily, starting in 1944. By playing it so often, Webster singlehandedly revived the Ted Weems rendition of *Heartaches* on that show, a smash recording Weems made in the early 1930s. The second time around it sold a million copies and Weems had to take his band out of retirement due to the record's popularity. Webster was the recipient of a gold record for his work, even coming in for mention by Arthur Godfrey on his CBS morning show.

Webster later was master of ceremonies (from the late 1940s to late 1950s) for a couple of long-running daytime audience participation features on WBT Monday through Friday: the hour-long *What's Cookin'?* with contests and interaction with a large number of studio participants (immediately before Godfrey), and *Strietman Streetman,* a man-on-the-street interview entry (immediately after Godfrey). On Sunday mornings during the last half of the 1940s, Webster presided over a quarter-hour harmony series headlined by the Johnson Family Singers, a clan of a half-dozen gospel vocalists. Among their number was daughter Betty Johnson, who in the 1950s went on to win *Arthur Godfrey's Talent Scouts,* to launch a recording career (*I Dreamed* was her one-hit-wonder in 1956), stage and personal appearance career, and become a regular on Don McNeill's *Breakfast Club* and *The Tonight Show* when Jack Paar hosted it in the early television epoch.

The Johnsons, incidentally, who began on CBS in 1944 originating over WBT, persisted there into the early 1950s, sans Webster.

Webster had worked at WBIR, Knoxville, Tenn., before going to Charlotte. Later he served WAVY, Portsmouth, Va.

WEIGEL, JOHN J. b. 1913, Springfield, Mo.; d. Dec. 12, 2002, Libertyville, Ill. *Announcer.* **Series:** *The Chicago Theater of the Air* (ca. 1940s, 1950s); *Meet the Meeks* (1947–1949).

John Weigel was quizmaster on ABC-TV's *Treasure Quest* for four months in 1949 on which contenders correctly responding to questions about geography were rewarded with expense-paid vacations.

WEIST, DWIGHT. b. Jan. 16, 1910, Palo Alto, Calif.; d. July 16, 1991, Block Island, R.I. *Announcer, Actor, Emcee.* **Series:** *The Adventures of the Thin Man* (ca. 1950); *The Aldrich Family* (ca. 1940s); *Andy Hardy* (actor); *Big Town* (1943–1952); *Buck Rogers in the 25th Century* (actor, 1930s, 1940s); *By Kathleen Norris* (1939–1941); *The Cavalcade of America* (actor, ca. 1940s, 1950s); *Grand Slam* (1946–1953); *Inner Sanctum Mysteries* (1946–1950); *The March of Time* (actor, 1930s, 1940s); *Mr. District Attorney* (actor, 1939); *Official Detective* (ca. 1940s, 1950s); *The Second Mrs. Burton* (actor, 1946–1960); *The Shadow* (actor); *The Texaco Star Theater* (actor, 1940–?); *The Theater Guild on the Air* (narrator-actor, 1940s); *Treasury Star Parade* (actor, 1942–1944); *Valiant Lady* (actor); *We, the People* (host, 1948–1949).

Raised at Scranton, Pa., Dwight Weist penned some sketches for a trio at WAIU in Columbus during his collegiate days at Ohio Wesleyan University. The station manager subsequently auditioned and hired him as an announcer. Weist followed that experience with appearances in stock productions around the Buckeye State, playing a lengthy engagement at the Cleveland Playhouse. New York and network radio were his ultimate goals, nevertheless, and he finally arrived in Gotham, winning spots as an actor or announcer on a myriad of chain-fed series.

Weist's ability to imitate a wide range of ages and accents came to the forefront early in his broadcasting career, gaining for him the appellation "man of 1,000 voices." On *The March of Time*, for instance, a versatile Weist not only appeared as Bruno Richard Hauptmann (the convicted kidnapper of the Lindbergh infant) for nearly two years, he also portrayed Fred Allen; George Arliss; Father Charles Coughlin; Joseph Goebbels; William Randolph Hearst; Adolf Hitler; Fiorello La Guardia; John L. Lewis; George Bernard Shaw; and—as reported by *Radio Guide*—"all three Barrymores, including Ethel." Weist reprised his Hitler impersonation on *Treasury Star Parade* during the war era and his imitation of Fred Allen on *Masquerade*, a local New York show on WABC in the mid 1930s.

In addition to his own airtime duties, the skilled broadcaster co-founded the Weist-Barron School of Television and Commercial Acting in New York City and taught there for 35 years. From 1948 to 1950 Weist hosted *We, the People* for 17 months on CBS-TV and for a few more months on NBC-TV. The feature was a video incarnation of a popular radio series that he and others conducted. Not long afterward, on Sept. 3, 1951, he launched an enduring "career" by introducing CBS-TV's debuting daytime serial *Search for Tomorrow*. He enjoyed permanent economic security from that solitary post for more than three decades, until the drama left CBS three-plus decades hence on March 26, 1982.

Meanwhile, Weist provided voiceovers for radio and television commercials, TV travelogues and Pathe newsreels shown in local cinema houses. He performed in five feature-length movies: *For Your Convenience* (1939); *Zelig* (1983); *The Name of the Rose* (1986); *Nine ½ Weeks* (1986); and *Radio Days* (1987). Between 1945 and 1948 Weist narrated 10 films for a *This is America* movie short series; from 1948 to 1960 he narrated 17 major motion pictures, among them: *This is America: You Can Make a Million* (1950); *The MacArthur Story* (1952); *Magic Movie Moments* (1956); *The Golden Age of Comedy* (1957); *When Comedy Was King* (1960); and *Camps of Death* (1983).

WELCH, NILES. b. July 29, 1888, Hartford, Conn.; d. Nov. 21, 1976, Laguna Niguel, Calif. *Announcer, Actor.* **Series:** *American School of the Air* (1936–?); *The Campbell Playhouse* (1938–ca. 1939); *Columbia Workshop* (actor, 1936–?); *Road of Life* (actor, 1936–?).

When he was only a year old Niles Welch's mom (the surname is sometimes identified as Welsh) carried the boy to France to live. He learned to speak French before English and also became fluent in German. (During the Second World War, incidentally, his ability to communicate in multiple tongues paid off as he appeared on many foreign language broadcasts beamed by the Voice of America overseas.)

Returning to the U.S. from France while he was still a boy, the youth graduated from St. Paul's prep school where he played football; afterwards he enrolled at Yale University. Welch later transferred to Columbia University where—during his senior year—he played the leading role in the annual varsity show. Subsequently he appeared in separate productions on the theatrical stage opposite actresses Miriam Doyle, Edna Hibber and Doris Kean.

Undoubtedly his most prolific impact on show business was in cinematic productions, nonetheless. Starting in the silent screen era and continuing into "talkies," Welch performed in 121 feature-length films, a record eclipsed by few others. Among the B-film titles across more than a quarter-of-a-century that he acted in from 1913 to 1940 were: *One Good Joke Deserves Another* (1913); *Miss George Washington* (1916); *Jane Goes a' Wooing* (1919); *Who Am I?* (1921); *Why Announce Your Marriage?* (1922); *Who Are My Parents?* (1922); *What Wives Want* (1923); *Lying Wives* (1925); *The Substitute Wife* (1925); *Faithful Wives* (1926); *Come On, Tarzan* (1932); *The Constant Woman* (1933); *This Side of Heaven* (1934); *I Believed in You* (1934); *The Count of Monte Cristo* (1934); *The Story of Louis Pasteur* (1935); *Wife vs. Secretary* (1936); *What Becomes of the Children?* (1936); and *The Purple Vigilantes* (1938).

WELLS, RICHARD. b. March 13, 1905; d. February 1968. *Actor, Announcer, Producer.* **Series:** *Aunt Mary* (ca. 1942–?); *Grandstand Thrills* (producer); *Kitty Keene, Incorporated* (actor, ca. late 1930s–1941); *Ma Perkins* (ca. 1930s); *Painted Dreams* (actor, 1933–1934); *The Right to Happiness* (actor, 1940s).

Dick Wells was a true radio veteran, starting as an engineer helping to install KYW while still a student in his mid teens in 1920 at Chicago's Crane Tech High School. He continued working as a radio engineer during subsequent studies at Eureka College, eventually receiving the bachelor of engineering degree from Georgia Tech in Atlanta.

Wells engineered at stations in Rock Island, Ill. and Muscatine, Iowa before turning to announcing at WOC, Davenport, Iowa. He was program manager at a Mexican station, XER, and—with other professionals—organized the Iowa Broadcasting System. After a round-the-world journey in 1930 he joined Chicago's WBBM in 1932 as an announcer. Wells earned a commission in the U.S. Naval Reserve before the inception of World War II.

WESSON, DICK. b. Nov. 19, 1922, Maine; d. April 25, 1996, Riverside, Calif. *Announcer.* **Series:** *Hollywood Open House* (1947–1948); *Invisible Walls* (1950); *Space Patrol* (early to mid 1950s); *Think,* aka *ABC Radio Workshop* (1953).

Dick Wesson, the radio announcer, is occasionally confused with a television and movie actor named Richard Lewis Wesson who was born in Idaho in 1919 and died in California by self-inflicted gunshot in 1979. *That* performer was half of a comedy duo known as The Wesson Brothers (sibling Gene Wesson died in 1975). Richard Lewis Wesson also wrote profusely, including episodes of TV's *The Bob Cummings Show*; *The Real McCoys*; *The Beverly Hillbillies*; *Petticoat Junction*; and more.

The radio Dick Wesson, meanwhile, sustained himself with multiple local audio gigs before hitting the big time. In 1947 he spun turntables on a DJ series, *Platter Patter,* over KALE, Portland, Ore. Three years hence he was a sportscaster at rival Portland station KPOJ. One of his MBS network series, *Invisible Walls,* originated at the latter outlet, in fact. Following his aural-casting experiences, this Wesson, too, got into video, delivering the opening credits for the Walt Disney TV programs following that creative's demise in 1966.

WHITMAN, GAYNE (born Alfred Vosburgh). b. March 19, 1890, Chicago, Ill.; d. Aug. 31, 1958, Hollywood, Calif. *Announcer, Actor, Emcee.* **Series:** *The Arkansas Traveler,* aka *The Bob Burns Show* (ca. 1941–ca. 1942); *The Bell Telephone Hour* (ca. 1940s, ca. 1950s); *Cavalcade of America* (1944–1947); *Chandu the Magician* (actor, 1932–1935); *Eyes Aloft* (host, 1942–1943); *The Greatest of These* (late 1940s); *Lassie* (narrator, late 1940s); *Pacific Story* (narrator, 1943–1947); *Paducah Plantation*, aka *Plantation Party* (1936–1937, 1938–1943); *Strange as it Seems* (host, 1947–1948).

Gayne Whitman sometimes went under the pseudonym Alfred Whitman.

WIDMARK, RICHARD. b. Dec. 26, 1914, Sunrise, Minn. *Actor, Emcee.* **Series:** *Aunt Jenny's Real Life Stories* (actor, 1938–?); *The CBS Radio Mystery Theater* (actor, 1974–ca. 1982); *Ethel and Albert* (actor, 1944); *Front Page Farrell* (actor, 1941–1942); *Gangbusters* (actor, ca. late 1930s, 1940s); *Green Valley, U.S.A.* (actor, 1944); *Home of the Brave* (actor, 1941); *Inner Sanctum Mysteries* (actor, 1941–?); *Joyce Jordan, Girl Interne*, aka *Joyce Jordan, M.D.* (actor, ca. 1938–ca. 1948); *Molle Mystery Theater*, aka *Hearthstone of the Death Squad*, aka *Mark Sabre* (actor, 1943–ca. 1950s); *The Sears Radio Theater*, aka *The Mutual Radio Theater* (host, 1979–1981); *Suspense* (actor, 1953); *Words at War* (actor, 1943–1945).

Growing up in Princeton, Ill., Richard Widmark studied acting while at Lake Forest College, then remained after graduation to teach his major subject to successive undergrads. His first radio work occurred in 1938 when he won a part on the CBS daytime anthology *Aunt Jenny's Real Life Stories.* Five years hence he was on Broadway in *Kiss and Tell.* Four years after that he was in *Kiss of Death*, his first motion picture. That was the launch of a seven-year deal with 20th Century–Fox. Over an enduring career, between 1947 and 2002, Widmark played in 91 films screened in theaters and on television. He also turned up in a handful of guest appearances on television series, always as himself.

Widmark, who had spent much of his early career in radio, returned to it as one of five hosts of the final debuting anthology series (*The Sears Radio Theater*) on a commercial network. Each one introduced the narratives presented on a given night weekly under a particular banner: Monday—Lorne Greene (westerns); Tuesday—Andy Griffith (comedies); Wednesday—Vincent Price (mysteries); Thursday—Cicely Tyson (dramas); Friday—Widmark (adventures). While the revival of dramatic action on the aural ether didn't persist for long, it drew a core contingent that longed for earlier days when similar fare was part of the normal routine, while attracting people of more recent vintage who had never heard drama on radio before.

WILCOX, HARLOW. b. March 12, 1900, Omaha, Neb.; d. Sept. 24, 1960, Hollywood, Calif. *Announcer.* **Series:** *The Adventures of Frank Merriwell* (1934); *Amos 'n' Andy* (1943–1948); *The Amos 'n' Andy Music Hall* (1954–ca. 1960); *Arnold Grimm's Daughter* (ca. 1938–1942); *Baby Snooks* (mid to late 1940s); *Ben Bernie, the Old Maestro* (ca. mid to late 1930s); *Betty and Bob* (1932–ca. 1936); *Blondie* (ca. mid 1940s–ca. 1950); *Boston Blackie* (1944); *The Don Ameche Variety Show* (1940); *Father Knows Best* (ca. 1949–ca. 1953); *Fibber McGee & Molly* (1935–1953); *The Frank Morgan Show* (1944–1945); *The Great Gildersleeve*; *Hap Hazard* (1941); *Hollywood Premiere* (1941); *Ice Box Follies* (1945); *The Kings Men* (1949); *Mayor of the Town* (1940s); *Molle Mystery Theater* (1943–ca. 1948); *Myrt and Marge* (ca. 1931–?); *Niles and Prindle* (1945); *The Passing Parade* (ca. 1940s); *Pennzoil Pete* (ca. 1930–1931); *The Phil Baker Show* (ca. 1933–1935); *Suspense* (1948–1954); *Terry Regan, Attorney at Law* (1938); *Tony Wons Scrapbook* (ca. 1931); *Truth or Consequences* (1946–1954); *The Victor Borge Show* (1945).

Harlow Wilcox hailed from a show business clan. His mom and dad were instrumentalists with Ringling Bros. Barnum & Bailey Circus. His father, a cornet player, eventually became a bandleader. Young Harlow studied voice and acted in and directed amateur theatricals. During his teenage years he left his family to perform on stage, touring Chautauqua circuits. Following college training, Wilcox became a traveling salesman for an electrical equipment manufacturer. A biographer recalled: "That experience taught him to put a product over to listeners. A top commercial spokesman, he had loyal clients who invariably renewed his contract for what formed long and mutually rewarding associations." After five years on the road he was elevated to his firm's sales manager post.

Wilcox was introduced to radio in a 1929 appearance over WGES, a small Chicago station. He joined WBBM the following year and by 1933 was at CBS in New York. A year afterward (1934) he was back in Chicago, having aligned himself with NBC. In the Windy City he formed a lasting friendship with Jim and Marian Jordan, a couple of radio pioneers who were soon to lend their voices to one of the medium's most infamous husband-wife teams, *Fibber McGee & Molly*. When the Jordans departed Chicago for the West Coast, Wilcox didn't hesitate about following them and rejoined the humorous duo in Hollywood.

On *Fibber McGee & Molly* Wilcox was a fixture. Each week at the show's start he ran through the list of performers that invariably ended with "The Kings Men, Billy Mills and His Orchestra and me ... Harlow Wilcox." For nearly two decades he blithely enumerated the attributes of Johnson's Wax—to listeners—and to the McGees. The show and *The Jack Benny Program* (for Jell-O gelatin and Lucky Strike cigarettes with Don Wilson) perfected the integration of the middle commercial into the sitcom storyline. On both series the announcer arrived at midpoint to gush over the respective sponsor's commodity. For his part, McGee saddled Wilcox with the sobriquet "Waxy."

Inevitably the homeowner saw a sales plug on the horizon whenever Wilcox rang the doorbell at the McGee abode at 39 Wistful Vista. Innocently enough, Molly would often feed a straight line to him that simply cried out for a longwinded response extolling the virtues of Johnson's Glo-Coat or another shining product. McGee, in the meantime, was on the verge of cardiac arrest, dumbstruck that his spouse had opened that can of worms: "Oh Molly," he groaned pathetically. "Don't ask him that!" Or, McGee lamented: "Molly! Now you've gone and done it!" Over the studio audience howls, it was all Wilcox needed to break into a soliloquy, waxing ebulliently (pun intended), recounting the countless pluses of polishing floors with a Johnson compound—to McGee's audible chagrin. The latter frequently tried and failed to halt the intrusion while the raucous audience guffaws kept coming. Wilcox and Benny's Wilson may have been the best in the industry in delivering pitches that became part of the good-natured humor of those half-hours. Both got away with it for years.

Just after midnight on March 1, 1932, Wilcox—who wasn't usually deemed a network journalist—broke into a remote dance band program being aired by CBS via WBBM. On that occasion he read a news bulletin noting the Lindbergh infant kidnapping in New Jersey, scoring a coup d'état in dispatching the story first. A pundit observed that the circumstance he reported subsequently evolved into "radio's greatest effort of on-the-spot news coverage up to that time."

In the 1941 feature-length Fibber McGee & Molly movie *Look Who's Laughing*, Wilcox portrayed Mr. Collins. He was a radio announcer in the 1945 film *Screen Snapshots: Number 2, Series 25, Radio Shows*. In addition, in 1953 Wilcox turned up as a reporter on CBS-TV's *You Are There* and played Karl Krauss in a 1956 episode of the syndicated television series *Science Fiction Theater*. Ironically, Wilcox's recorded voice emanated from the 1975 movie *Brother, Can You Spare a Dime?* 15 years following his death.

WILLARD, DICK. b. Jan. 22, 1914; d. Sept. 6, 2000, Taos, N.M. *Announcer, Emcee, Disc Jockey*. **Series:** *Easy Does It* (disc jockey, 1954, 1954–1955); *Mutual Matinee* (disc jockey, 1955–1956); *The Strange Dr. Weird* (1944–1945); *Take it Easy Time* (host, 1945–1946).

Intending to become a vocalist, in his youth a starry-eyed Dick Willard traveled from his home in Binghamton, N.Y. to New York City to seek his fortune. But the city was top-heavy with singers, he discovered to his dismay, and there weren't enough promising opportunities to go around. Sadly he made his way back to the bus station to purchase a return ticket to Binghamton. Just then he spotted a posted notice that the radio station above the bus station was seeking an announcer. He climbed the stairs, landed the job and went on the air, launching a career that was to preoccupy him as an announcer and producer at WOR Radio for the next 44 years.

Beginning in the late 1930s, he was given the assignment of introducing Mary Margaret McBride each weekday as *Martha Deane* on WOR. It was one of the more memorable tasks of his long career.

While he was a "failed singer" in a professional sense, meanwhile, Willard found many chances to hoist a tune otherwise. One reporter observed: "He had a beautiful bass voice; full and rich even into his eighties." Following the years at WOR he narrated programs featuring the band at the parish he attended, Montrose United Methodist Church; he participated in the church choir; he frequently sang solos there and at many other venues (one of his most requested was "I Walked Today Where Jesus Walked"); and he vocalized with a group known as the Harmony Men ensemble. He was proficient in woodworking, also, creating many objects of art which he gave to family and friends. He made the cross that is his church's worship centerpiece.

When WOR held a reunion of former staffers a few years before Willard relocated to New Mexico, he and his wife were invited back. But he had an aversion to returning to New York. To get himself off the hook, he responded: "If you'll send a limousine and put us up at the Waldorf, I'll go." Certain that wouldn't happen, he was surprised on a cold, wet day to look out and see a chauffeured limousine, wheel covers sinking in mud, pulling up to his door. It spoke volumes about the esteem that one station still maintained for one of its long-indentured servants.

WILLIAMS, KENNETH. b. ca. 1915; d. Feb. 16, 1984, Los Angeles, Calif. *Actor, Announcer.* **Series:** *Buck Rogers in the 25th Century* (ca. 1930s); *David Harum* (actor, 1936–1951); *Mr. Keen, Tracer of Lost Persons* (actor, 1948).

Kenny Williams was the "town crier" as well as the announcer on CBS-TV's daytime game show *Video Village* from 1960–1962. In the summer of 1960 the program appeared in a primetime version on CBS-TV, too. Hosts and co-hosts initially were Jack Narz teamed with Joanne Copeland and later Monty Hall linked with Eileen Barton. On ABC-TV's *Shenanigans* weekend game show in 1964–1965, Williams assisted host Stubby Kaye in directing youngsters in a three-dimensional board competition created by Milton Bradley, the show's sponsor. In 1969 Williams introduced host Peter Marshall on NBC-TV's *The Storybook Squares*, a weekend juvenile version of Marshall's popular daytime game show *The Hollywood Squares*. Williams was the announcer of a subsequent syndicated incarnation of *The Hollywood Squares* (1972–1980).

WILSON, DON HARLOW. b. Sept. 1, 1900, Lincoln, Neb.; d. April 25, 1982, Palm Springs, Calif. *Announcer, Actor, Emcee.* **Series:** *The Alan Young Show* (1949); *The Aldrich Family* (actor, 1940s, 1950s); *The Al Jolson Show*, aka *Kraft Music Hall* (mid 1930s); *The Amazing Mr. Smith* (actor, 1941); *Baby Snooks* (mid to late 1940s); *The Bing Crosby Show* (1933–1934); *Chance of a Lifetime* (master of ceremonies, ca. late 1940s–early 1950s); *Command Performance* (1942–ca. 1950); *The Doris Day Show* (1952–1953); *The Ginny Simms Show* (1945); *Glamour Manor* (announcer-actor, 1946–1947); *Good News of 1941* (1940–1941); *Hollywood Mardi Gras*, aka *The Lanny Ross Show* (1937–1938); *Hollywood Spotlight* (1937); *Hollywood Star Theater*, aka *Hollywood Star Preview*, aka *Baker's Theater of Stars* (1947–1950); *Hollywood Theater* (1951–ca. 1952); *The Jack Benny Program* (announcer-actor, 1934–1955, 1956–1958); *The Joe E. Brown Show* (1938–1939); *Light Up Time*, aka *The Frank Sinatra Show* (ca. 1947–1950); *Mail Call* (1942–1950); *Me and Janie* (1949); *Music by Gershwin* (1934); *The Packard Hour* (1937–1938); *Starlight Concert* (1950); *Tarzan* (actor, 1934–1935); *Tim and Irene* (1936); *Tommy Riggs and Betty Lou* (1946); *The Wacky Family* (host-announcer, 1936).

When he was two Don Wilson's family departed Lincoln, Neb. for Denver, Colo. Before he graduated from the University of Colorado in 1923 the youth was a collegiate football star. After trying selling for awhile he and a couple of buddies formed a vocal trio and struck out on the road. The group was lucky enough to impress an underwriter, the Piggly Wiggly grocery chain. Billed as the Piggly Wiggly Trio after that, the threesome toured the western states, performing on behalf of their sponsor.

By the spring of 1927 they secured a permanent slot on San Francisco's KFRC representing the Piggly Wiggly stores. Within a year, nonetheless, they were at Los Angeles' KHJ; they had persuaded the owner of both stations—Don Lee, head of the network bearing his name—and Piggly Wiggly officials to shift them to L.A. for greater exposure. When one member of the group quit, the remaining two (including Wilson) performed as a duet. When his partner left, Wilson quit singing altogether to become a full time announcer, a field he had dabbled in part time already.

A little known fact about Wilson that most people recalling him today have likely forgotten or possibly never encountered is that he was an NBC sportscaster during the network's earliest days. From 1929 through 1937 he provided coverage from the gridiron for the chain's annual New Year's Day Rose Bowl competitions. He also contributed to the 1932 Olympics broadcasts carried by KFI, where he was already chief announcer. NBC convinced him to relocate to the East Coast in 1933 to handle network sports. His replacement as chief announcer at KFI was another budding talent of legendary proportions, Ken Carpenter. When Wilson subsequently returned to the West Coast with comedian Jack Benny's entourage in the mid 1930s, the announcer continued airing West Coast athletic competitions on local radio at $250 per game.

Radio historian John Dunning characterized Jack Benny's durable interlocutor—Wilson's most memorable role—like this: "On April 6, 1934, Don Wilson became the new announcer. Wilson would remain with Benny to the end of the TV show in 1965. His deep, rich voice was one of the show's trademarks, and the role he played—a roly-poly Gargantua—was yet another stretch of Benny's imagination. In reality, Wilson stood a little over six feet and weighed in the mid-220s: hardly the behemoth that Benny would chide with endless fat jokes in the years to come. Wilson also brought to the show a deep belly laugh that could often be heard above the studio audience."

Wilson and a contemporary, Harlow Wilcox of *Fibber McGee & Molly* fame, perfected the assimilation of the middle commercial for their respective sponsors into their best identified series, usually over humorous exchanges with the show's star. Wilson extolled the virtues of Jell-O gelatin desserts and Lucky Strike cigarettes as he bantered with Benny while Wilcox pushed Johnson's wax compounds onto a suspecting Fibber McGee.

Citing other regulars of the Benny ensemble—Eddie (Rochester) Anderson; Mel Blanc; Dennis Day; Phil Harris; Mary Livingston; and Frank Nelson ("Oo-ooooo, would I!")—a critic allowed: "Don Wilson, Benny's announcer, was the only one who always treated him with true respect." Benny claimed he chose Wilson for his unique assignment because "he had a warm voice, he could read a commercial with laughter in his throat, and he proved a great foil to play against." It was said that gags at rehearsal that didn't prompt a hearty guffaw from Wilson were usually tossed out by the show's star.

A handful of radio announcers, including Wilson, were signed by Warner Bros. in 1936 for its Vitaphone subsidiary. Vitaphone produced a string of movie short subjects under the *Our Own United States* umbrella and Wilson and his peers were narrators. Between 1932 and 1953 he turned up in 27 feature-length motion pictures of the B-film variety. Some of those titles included: *Million Dollar Legs* (1932); *Meet the Missus* (1937); *Behind the Mike* (1937); *Radio City Revels* (1938); *Behind the News* (1940); *Swing It Soldier* (1941); *Hi, Neighbor* (1942); *Dangerous Blondes* (1943); *Thank Your Lucky Stars* (1943); *Mardi Gras* (1943); *Radio Stars on Parade* (1945); *Dick Tracy* (1945); *Cinderella Jones* (1946); *The Senator was Indiscreet* (1947); and *Sailor Beware* (1952). Wilson was Benny's sidekick in the televised incarnation of his radio series, *The Jack Benny Program*, on CBS-TV from 1950 to 1964 and NBC-TV from 1964 to 1965. Wilson also appeared with vocalist Dennis Day in a nostalgic stage spectacular, *The Big Broadcast of 1944*, as the pair played venues around the nation in the 1960s. Meanwhile, Wilson's fourth spouse, actress Lois Corbet, specialized in mothers on radio's *Baby Snooks*; *A Date with Judy*; and *Meet Corliss Archer*.

WILSON, WARD. b. May 22, 1903, Trenton, N.J.; d. March 21, 1966, West Palm Beach, Fla. *Actor, Emcee, Announcer.* **Series:** *The Aldrich Family* (actor, 1946–1951); *Can You Top This?* (host, 1945–1951, 1953–1954); *Crime Does Not Pay* (actor, 1952); *The Cukoo Hour* (cast member, 1930–1932, 1934, 1935–1936); *The Fred Allen Show* (actor, ca. 1930s, 1940s); *Fred Vandeventer and the News* (ca. 1944–1948, ca. 1951–1953); *The George*

Burns and Gracie Allen Show (actor, ca. 1930s, 1940s); *The Judy Canova Show* (actor, ca. 1940s); *The Phil Baker Show* (actor, 1934–1939); *Philip Morris Playhouse* (actor, ca. 1941–1944, ca. 1948–1949, ca. 1951); *Raymond Gram Swing and the News* (ca. 1930s, 1940s); *The Royal Vagabonds* (host-comic impressionist, 1932–1933); *Stop Me if You've Heard this One* (panelist, 1939–1940); *That's a Good One* (comedian, 1943); *Walter Winchell and the News*; *What's My Name?* (co-host, 1948, ca. 1949); *Winner Take All* (quizmaster).

Before moving to the performing side of radio, Ward Wilson tested lines and rehearsal microphones at NBC as a field engineer. He went on the air as an impressionist, ultimately mastering the voices of more than 80 recognized figures. For one season, 1950–1951, he hosted the ABC televersion of one of his popular radio engagements, *Can You Top This?*

In between and alongside network gigs, meanwhile, Wilson was a sportscaster for a couple of New York stations: WHN (1944–1946) and WMGM (1952–1956). He also regularly appeared on a plethora of amusing features at those outlets. By the 1960s he relocated to West Palm Beach, Fla. where he found a job as sports director for WEAT Radio and Television.

WINCHELL, WALTER (born Walter Winchel). b. April 7, 1897, New York, N.Y.; d. Feb. 20, 1972, Los Angeles, Calif. *Newscaster, Commentator.* **Series:** *The Jergens Journal* (news-gossip reporter, 1932–1948); *Lucky Strike Dance Orchestra*, aka *Dance Hour* (newscaster, 1931–1932); *Saks on Broadway—Speaker Walter Winchell* (news-gossip reporter, 1930, 1931–1932); *Walter Winchell's Journal* (news-gossip reporter, 1949–1957). **Aphorism:** *Good evening, Mr. and Mrs. North America and all the ships at sea ... Let's go to press!*

Walter Winchell dropped out of school in the sixth grade after his father, Jacob Winchel, the operator of a tiny silk emporium, abandoned his family composed of a wife and two sons. Later Walter's mom, Jenny, took off for Virginia with his younger brother Al to live with relatives, leaving Walter in Harlem to be raised by an 80-year-old grandmother. Walter had begun selling newspapers and magazines at age eight. He became very familiar with street gangs, which he quickly joined. When he was 12, the mother of his boyhood chum, George Jessel, who worked at New York's Imperial Theater, persuaded the manager to hire her son, Winchell and another pal, Jack Weiner, as a singing ushers' trio.

The boys soon joined Gus Edwards' "Newsboys Sextet," which included yet another future star, Eddie Cantor; they all toured together for two years. Winchell remained in vaudeville to 1917 when he left for the Navy, although for all of his duty he was stationed in New York City. After his discharge he returned to the stage.

By 1922, however, he was into journalism, hired as a reviewer by *Vaudeville News*. Intermittently Winchell contributed to *Billboard* and in 1924 he settled at *The New York Graphic* where he began to establish a noticeable reputation. By 1929 he moved over to an even better known competitor, *The New York Daily Mirror*, at a reported salary of $500 weekly. Not too pitiable for Great Depression standards! (Actually, things kept improving: two decades later he was earning $16,000 weekly for a 15-minute radio show alone!) He acquired a column that was syndicated to many newspapers which attracted millions of readers who faithfully perused it for more than three decades. The column's success was directly tied to Winchell's unabashed snooping into the private lives of others, yet he brooked no attempt to inquire into *his* personal life, including that of his family. It was one of the many oddities surrounding a man who earned a name by literally being peculiar.

Winchell's baptism on the ether occurred when he presided over a 1929 local series, *New York by a Representative New Yorker*. It was "lively," confirmed a critic. Jumping fully into radio, he soon led off his weekly series in rapid-fire, staccato delivery style by charging: *Good evening, Mr. and Mrs. North America and all the ships at sea ... Let's go to press! ... Flash! ... New York ...* (and then followed a juicy morsel he had saved to top that week's show). "His newscast was an act," wrote reviewer John Dunning. "He was an entertainer, too sloppy and careless to be taken seriously by so-called serious journalists, but far too powerful to ignore." The freewheeling Winchell could make or break a Broadway play, political candidate or stock offering. The sixth grade dropout could react with acumen to international affairs while revealing the most piddling snatches of Hollywood pillow talk. A lot of his material seemed lacking in taste and capitalized on gossip and innuendo. Winchell delivered inside information about the government; business; entertainment; sports; the underworld; and lots more. He was beholden to countless individuals from many walks for tips, yet it's believed he never paid any of them for their services, and certainly not so in cash.

All of this was dispatched in a steady stream of invective, clocked at 215 words a minute and underscored by the chattering keys of a telegraph device which he maneuvered. In a classic journalistic pose, he rested before the microphone sporting a fedora on his head, his tie loosened and his shirt partially unbuttoned, with a script in his left hand and his right hand jiggling the telegraph machine. It was a sight to behold!

Winchell maintained the ability to stay in hot water with somebody much of the time, whether real or imaginary. He and showman Ben Bernie, both ex-vaudevillians—and both fully understanding how to work a crowd—got into one of those pretentious radio feuds that were the rage in the 1930s. The two traded barbs on their own programs back-and-forth before finally declaring a truce. It was in much the same vein as the sparring by Fred Allen and Jack Benny, Bing Crosby and Bob Hope, and W.C. Fields and Charlie McCarthy in the same era—designed to stimulate audience interest in their respective programs. It worked.

More serious was Winchell's issues with Hollywood gossip columnist Louella Parsons, who occupied a quarter-hour Sunday night radio show on ABC immediately following Winchell's (1944–1951). "This unholy alliance began chummily," wrote Dunning, "but hostility soon set in. Parsons was jealous and protective of her West Coast turf, and she would sit tensely through Winchell's show, fretting that he might beat her on some Hollywood item. This he did often enough to keep their relationship chilly." Parsons biographer George Eels noted that when Winchell raided her column for material, "Her hatchet was unsheathed." In 1950 Winchell got into a verbal spat with local New York radio personality Barry Gray. Because Winchell's influence was so powerful, it appeared that Gray's career was permanently ruined, although he recovered and persisted on the air. Meanwhile, Winchell crossed with columnist-broadcaster Ed Sullivan who—according to biographer Irving Fang—"hated Winchell." Their feud burst into the open. "If Winchell showed some small ability to make friends of newspapermen, his skill at making enemies of them showed nothing less than blazing genius," Fang insisted.

Winchell adopted strong positions politically that he expressed readily and which put him at odds with political figures as well as large segments of the public. He strongly favored the liberal policies of President Franklin D. Roosevelt, for instance (he was even credited by some with electing Roosevelt to his third term). But Winchell didn't transfer his Democratic loyalties to Roosevelt's successor, Harry S Truman. In fact, as the years rolled by, he took an aggressive anti–Communist stance and helped Republican Sen. Joseph McCarthy of Wisconsin fan the flames of mistrust of public figures and ordinary citizens who might be Red sympathizers. It was obvious that Winchell's political philosophy then differed sharply with the deep-seated positions he had taken to the end of the Second World War.

A 16-year commercial relationship with the Andrew Jergens Co. left its hallmark commodity, Jergens hand lotion, clearly identified in the public's subconscious with Winchell. Signing off each week, Winchell wished his listeners "lotions of love." According to one industry observer, he became "the most important and powerful reporter in the nation" in the 1930s and 1940s during Jergens' sponsorship. Often reaching the coveted 10 most listened-to shows, Winchell's quarter-hour peaked at 33.1 in the Hooperatings in 1941–1942, an exceedingly high number, and especially so for a news program. The network claimed Winchell had 33 million listeners on his strongest nights.

Nonetheless, he parted company with ABC Radio in 1955, where he had been one of its star lights, particularly so after the net broke away from NBC more than a decade earlier. Winchell joined MBS and continued his news-gossip series there for just over 16 months. As radio began to wane, he went into television. His brash hyperbole was never as popular with the viewers as it was with the listeners, however. From 1952 to 1955 he presided over *The Walter Winchell Show* on ABC-TV and in 1956 on NBC-TV. He returned to ABC-TV in 1957–1958 with *The Walter Winchell File* which continued in syndication through 1958. From 1959–1963 he narrated ABC-TV's gangster melodrama *The Untouchables.*

Broadway's decline was doing a number on his newspaper column, where he was steadily losing readers. By the mid 1960s, that was over for him, too.

Winchell had been instrumental in calling CBS officials' attention to a still-undiscovered Arthur Godfrey, then an early morning DJ over WJSV in Washington, D.C., in the 1930s. In addition, Winchell helped start the Damon Runyon Fund for Cancer Research in 1946, named for his pal, also a scribe. Winchell was that body's unstinting advocate.

"Today," summarized radio historian Luther Sies, "looking back at the period of Winchell's greatest popularity in the 1930s and 1940s, it is hard to imagine the power he possessed and the ruthlessness with which he used it."

WINTERS, ROLAND. b. Nov. 22, 1904, Boston, Mass.; d. Oct. 22, 1989, Engelwood, N.J. *Announcer, Actor, Emcee.* **Series:** *Bright Horizon* (early 1940s); *The Fishing and Hunting Club of the Air* (panelist, 1950); *Gold and Silver Minstrels* (host, 1946–1947); *The Goodwill Hour* (1936, 1937–1944); *The Greatest Story Ever Told* (actor, 1947–1956); *Highways in Melody* (host-commentator, 1940–1948); *Lorenzo Jones* (actor, ca. late 1930s–early 1950s); *The Milton Berle Show* (actor, 1948–1949); *Murder Clinic* (host-announcer, 1942–1943); *My Best Girls* (actor, 1944–1945); *Treasure Hour of Song* (host-narrator, 1942, 1943–1947).

Roland Winters had an active life beyond radio. He appeared as Uncle Chris in CBS-TV's award-winning *Mama* drama in 1951–1952. In the summers of 1952 and 1953 he played secret agent John Randolph in the NBC-TV spy thriller *Doorway to Danger.* Afterwards, from 1953 to 1956, Winters portrayed J.R. Boone Sr. in the CBS radio-to-TV sitcom (video interpretation only), *Meet Millie.* He was Leonard J. Costello in CBS-TV's *The Smothers Brothers Show* (1965–1966), yet another sitcom.

Between 1947 and 1970, Winters also turned up in 40 celluloid productions. They included the 1960 made-for-TV movie *The Iceman Cometh*; six films in which he played Charlie Chan—*The Chinese Ring* (1947); *Docks of New Orleans, The Shanghai Chest, The Feathered Serpent* and *The Golden Eye* (all 1948); and *The Sky Dragon* (1949)—plus 33 more feature-length motion pictures shown in cinema houses. Among those titles: *Cry of the City* (1948); *The Return of October* (1948); *Abbott and Costello Meet the Killer* and *Boris Karloff* (both 1949); *Once More, My Darling* (1949); *Killer Shark* (1950); *The Underworld Story* (1950); *Between Midnight and Dawn* (1950); *The West Point Story* (1950); *Follow the Sun* (1951); *She's Working Her Way Through College* (1952); *Never Steal Anything Small* (1959); *Cash McCall* (1960); *Blue Hawaii* (1961); and *Follow That Dream* (1962).

WITTEN, LOUIS A. *Announcer.* **Series:** *Ed Wynn, the Fire Chief,* aka *The Texaco Fire Chief* (1932–1935); *The Jumbo Fire Chief Program,* aka *Jumbo* (1935–1936); *Texaco Reporters* (1933).

Louis Witten was part owner and announcer at WAAQ, Greenwich, Conn., when it began operating in 1924. He sold his interest two years later and the station moved to Bayshore, Conn. Witten, meanwhile, joined the announcing staff at Newark's WOR in 1926. His decision proved to be providential.

On Sept. 18, 1927 the Columbia Phonograph Broadcasting System (to soon be renamed CBS) was launched. Occupying a couple of rooms in the Paramount Building on Times Square, the new chain contracted with WOR as its originating station for a short while. Maj. Andrew White, the web's manager, signed it on for the first time that Sunday afternoon at 3 o'clock by introducing a 23-piece orchestra. Witten, in the meantime—already in place as a WOR staffer—was appointed the new network's chief announcer. It must have appeared to him as well as to others a case of being in the right place at the right time.

WOOD, CHARLES. b. Nov. 27, 1911, Pittsburgh, Pa. *Announcer.* **Series:** *The Green Hornet* (1936–1937); *The Lone Ranger* (1936–1937).

After addressing a parent-teacher meeting when he was 15, Charles Wood envisioned a speaking or lecture career for himself. He subsequently joined a boys' glee club and became its dramatic reader. That attracted some producers who lined up two years of appearances for him on stage, starting when Wood was just 18. At 20 he sang baritone with a radio quartet. By then he had graduated from a prep school at Mt. Herman, Mass. and was studying dramatics at Muskingham College, New Concord, Ohio. Wood's tutors included eminent speech educator Charles L. Layton and diction and voice production coach William Saal.

Wood won a guest slot at Cleveland's WTAM following a 1934 audition. Returning home to Pittsburgh afterward, he went on a local station in the Steel City. In 1936 he joined Detroit's WXYZ as a news commentator, moving to Cincinnati's WLW in 1937. In the mid 1930s WXYZ and WLW were two of a quartet of powerful, strategically situated stations that formed the MBS chain. At WLW Wood was one of perhaps a dozen men to introduce *Moon River* to late-night audiences. The feature was a widely popular music-and-poetry series aired in the 1930s and 1940s.

For 27 years—from 1949 to 1976—Wood was employed by ABC in New York.

WOODS, CHARLES. b. ca. 1911; d. Nov. 10, 1997. *Announcer, Emcee.* **Series:** *Lone Journey* (ca. 1951–1952); *Strange* (host-announcer, 1955).

Charles Woods delivered the news at a couple of Philadelphia stations, WCAU and WFIL, before departing the City of Brotherly Love for New York's WOR in 1942.

WOODSON, WILLIAM. b. July 16, 1917, Los Angeles, Calif. *Announcer, Actor.* **Series:** *Douglas of the World* (1950s); *Just Plain Bill* (actor, ca. 1940s, 1950s); *This is Your FBI* (narrator, 1948–1953).

Bill Woodson provided the voice of the sheriff on *The C.B. Bears*, an animated feature on NBC-TV in 1977–1978. From 1977 to 1983 he narrated another cartoon series, *Super Friends*, on ABC-TV.

WOOLLCOTT, ALEXANDER. b. 1887, Phalanx, N.J.; d. Jan. 23, 1943, New York, N.Y. *Announcer, Commentator, Emcee.* **Series:** *A Christmas Carol* (host-narrator, annually 1934–1942); *Information, Please* (guest panelist, ca. 1938–ca. 1942); *People's Platform* (visiting scholar, 1943); *Stage Door Canteen* (guest celebrity, 1942); *The Town Crier* (host-commentator, 1930, 1933–1935, 1937–1938).
Aphorism: *Hear ye! Hear ye!*

Alexander Woollcott (spelled Woolcott by some sources) attended Hamilton College and saw service during World War I as a Medical Corps private while reporting for *The Stars and Stripes*. After the war he became a newspaper reporter, lecturer, actor and author. He also acquired an erudite, urbane capacity marking him as an intellect. There were plenty of demonstrated moments during his professional career, nonetheless, in which he seemed to forget the trappings that normally accompanied that esteem as he stepped totally out of character. As a rule Woollcott dressed casually (some called it "sloppy"). At least once he trudged up and down theater aisles clad in a pair of unbuckled, oversized galoshes complementing his relaxed attire, as if thumbing his nose at the fashionably garbed patrons. It bespoke volumes about his arrogant aloofness and "I don't care" unpredictability.

Over his brief lifetime Woollcott was the drama critic of a trio of metropolitan dailies: *The New York Times* (1914–1922); *The New York World* (1925–1928); and *The New York Herald* (1932). It didn't faze him if he became the center of an imbroglio. In 1916 the Schuberts, owners of multiple Broadway theaters, expelled him (and by inference, *The New York Times* itself) from their performing palaces. When the newspaper made it a legal issue, the state court of appeals sided with the Schuberts and Woollcott continued to be an ex-communicant.

When he was later invited to host a network radio series favoring literary topics that also embraced the theater, society, politics and films, Woollcott prompted an explanation from CBS owner-chairman William S. Paley. Despite his selection of the unlikely—not to say risky—choice for a national town crier, Paley concluded: "I saw in him a unique personality. He had a quality I felt would appeal to a mass audience." And it did.

At his peak six million Americans tuned in to hear Woollcott's interpretation of current thought and interviews with intriguing guests. Among that group were Katherine Cornell, Jimmy Durante and Groucho Marx. "For anybody on Broadway, at the mercy of Woollcott's whim..., a request to appear alongside Woollcott amounted to a command performance," critic Gerald Nachman insisted. Woollcott garnered enough power to be viewed as "a one-man show who cast his web wide enough to dragoon friends and colleagues ... to share his microphone" and to consider it an honor. While he was a frequent name-dropper in chatty appraisals of the Great White Way, he could also produce those luminaries in the studio.

Aired town hall style, his series (which was originally known as *The Early Bookworm*) arrived on the ether to the sound of a bell clanging and the admonition: *Hear ye! Hear ye!* Complete with house orchestra conducted by impresario Robert Armbruster, *The Town Crier* and its host became the most influential bookseller in the country. When Woollcott disclosed that he had gone "quietly mad" (his epithet) over a particular volume, sales of that tome soared. *Goodbye, Mr. Chips*, James Hilton's brief 1934 novel, made it to the top of the best-seller list when Woollcott jumped on its bandwagon. It was released as a 1939 motion picture and more recently in DVD, thanks in large measure to Woollcott's persistence. Furthermore, he shamelessly plugged his own wares, seeing his *While Rome Burns* (Grosset & Dunlap, 1934) climb high in the charts, too. Parenthetically, his salary for the radio series grew to a reported $3,500 per broadcast.

His ego was vast, and his scruples sometimes in question. Woollcott went so far as to portray an unflattering caricature of himself in a 1939 road show rendering of George S. Kaufman and Moss Hart's play *The Man Who Came to Dinner*. The broadcaster appeared on stage as Sheridan Whiteside, an irritable, unreasonable figure (a "radio speaker, writer and friend of the great") that Kaufman and Hart derived with Woollcott as their pattern. For an egocentric, playing himself worked very well.

It never bothered him to chastise a guest while he was on the air. (This was the 1930s, recall, many decades before putting the screws to somebody in public became in vogue.) According to *Current Biography*, Woollcott occasionally concluded a dialogue with an interviewee by stating: "You are beginning to disgust me—how about getting the hell out of here?" Jerald Mason, in the February 1935 issue of *Radioland*, observed that Woollcott possessed "just about the worst voice that ever poured itself into an offended microphone." Author Ron Lackmann acknowledged: "Woollcott wielded enormous power in the entertainment industry, as well as its social and political circles. His personal and idiosyncratic criticisms and caustic comments, often a mixture of sentiment and acrimony, could either 'make-or-break' a play, film, or celebrity." Despite the disparagement leveled by others, historiographer Fred MacDonald assessed Woollcott as "a personality that was engagingly rich in charm."

Woollcott was also a member of the charmed circle of witty linguists calling themselves the Roundtable (and encompassing the likes of Franklin P. Adams; Robert Benchley; Heywood Broun; George S. Kaufman; and Dorothy Parker). In the 1920s and 1930s that academic bunch of elitists systematically met at the Algonquin Hotel to recharge their batteries, discussing and cussing common literary interests while provoking sadistic one-upmanship. They also performed separately as guests on *The Town Crier* and other broadcast programs (e.g., *Information, Please*; *People's Platform*; *Stage Door Canteen*, et al.). They collaborated on varied projects, too. Woollcott, for instance, worked with Kaufman in producing a few satirical works examining American film and dramatic creations.

While participating in a live studio performance of *People's Platform* in early 1943, Woollcott collapsed. The program persevered but, a few hours later, he was dead, the victim of a cerebral hemorrhage.

WYNN, DICK. b. April 16, 1909; d. Aug. 24, 1996. *Announcer.* **Series:** *The Count of Monte Cristo* (ca. 1940s); *The Lone Wolf* (1948–1949).

Dick Wynn's surname is spelled by at least one scholar as Winn.

YOURMAN, ALICE. b. Sept. 17, 1907, South Dakota; d. Oct. 28, 2000. *Actress,*

Announcer. **Series:** *The Aldrich Family* (actress, ca. 1940s); *Archie Andrews* (actress, ca. 1943–?); *Ethel and Albert,* aka *The Private Lives of Ethel and Albert (*actress, 1940s); *Hearts in Harmony* (actress, 1940s, early 1950s); *Myrt and Marge* (actress, 1946); *The Right to Happiness* (actress, ca. early 1950s); *Secret Missions* (actress, 1948–1949); *Two on a Clue* (1944–1946); *Young Widder Brown* (actress, ca. 1940s, 1950s).

Alice Yourman studied dramatics in Chicago and made her radio debut in Hammond, Ind. where she performed and produced a local *March of Time* feature. While subsequently living in Mt. Vernon, Ohio she was active in a local Theater Guild. Following her spouse's demise, however, she carried their two youngsters to New York, seeking a career as a thespian in order to support her family.

Like so many other aspirants before her she competed against hundreds of other young women for a few roles, nearly all of those candidates sounding terribly similar. "What do I have to offer that these others don't?" she inquired of herself. Yourman decided that all she possessed to separate her from the rest of the pack was a Midwestern accent. She concentrated on that and—as a result—won parts on a growing number of radio shows. "Her voice has a fresh quality like a prairie breeze," a director testified.

Yourman defied formidable odds, in fact, by becoming one of a minuscule handful of women to introduce a continuing radio series. She was there when the serialized daytime crime narrative *Two on a Clue* premiered and remained as its interlocutor to the day it left the air about 15 months later—a victim of less-than-promising ratings. The fact that she did so put her in a class with only a tiny handful of others in the industry.

When radio began to slip away, she didn't say good-by to her life in show business, nonetheless. She was just getting started, it seemed. Yourman appeared in one theatrical film, *Dirtymouth* (1970), and a second of the made-for-TV variety, *Luke Was There* (1976). She also gave TV daytime serials and a sitcom a whirl, too. From 1953 to 1962 she carried the long-running role of Laura Grant in *The Guiding Light* on CBS-TV. During that time frame she performed in a 1956 episode of that net's *The Phil Silvers Show* and in 1957 she appeared as Anita Borkowitz in the same web's *The Edge of Night.*

Appendix
More Who Spoke Radioese

This Appendix includes additional names of network and syndicated radio personalities within the sweep of announcers, newscasters, sportscasters, showbiz reporters, consultants, emcees, talk show duos and their equivalents who could not easily be accommodated in the body text. They appear below for one of two reasons and possibly both: (1) Too few verifiable data exist on their personal lives and professional careers; (2) Their performances in radio were minor compared with their significant contributions to entertainment and information in other mediums and venues—or in an unrelated line of work. Their names are included here in an attempt to acknowledge their participation in radio and to be as inclusive as possible. Be assured that whatever oversights or shortcomings may be revealed are unintentional and the reader's indulgence is implored. The names below are followed by the genus of radio performance and the network for which it was performed.

Abbey, Jean. Consultant (women) CBS
Abernathy, William (1894–?). Correspondent NBC, NBC Blue, ABC
Adams, Ben. Newscaster NBC Blue
Adams, Cindy (1930–). Host[†] NBC
Adams, John B. Correspondent CBS
Albright, Sidney. Newscaster NBC, MBS
Alcott, Carroll. Correspondent CBS
Allen, Donald. Correspondent ABC
Allen, Ida Bailey. Consultant (cooking) CBS, NBC
Allen, Robert S. Newscaster MBS
Alsop, Stewart (1914–1974). Commentator ABC
Ames, Mary Ellis. Consultant (cooking) CBS, NBC Blue
Anderson, David M. Correspondent NBC
Anderson, Hubert. Correspondent CBS
Anderson, John. Correspondent CBS
Andrews, Bert. Newscaster ABC
Andrews, Ellis. Announcer NBC, NBC Blue
Andrews, Johnny. Host[†] NBC
Aplon, Bill. Announcer NBC
Arden, Robert. Newscaster [*]
Arlen, Jay. Announcer ABC
Arnot, Charles P. Correspondent ABC
Bailey, William (Bill). Announcer NBC, NBC Blue
Balter, Sam (1909–1998). Sportscaster MBS
Bancroft, Griffing. Correspondent CBS
Barbe, Charles. Correspondent CBS
Barber, Fran. Announcer NBC
Barker, Jeff. Announcer Syndication
Barton, Frances Lee. Consultant (cooking) NBC
Bascom, Jon. Correspondent [*]
Bate, Richard. Correspondent ABC
Baylor, David. Correspondent CBS
Beardsley, Len. Correspondent ABC
Bell, Stanley. Announcer CBS, NBC, NBC Blue
Bemis, Elizabeth (1916–2004). Newscaster CBS

[*]Network data unsubstantiated
[†]Individuals designated as Hosts (in the early days, "Communicators") presided over segments of NBC Radio's weekend programming service "Monitor" (1955–1975). Their assignments were diverse and complex: they introduced multiple features of countless persuasions as well as myriads of reports and a profusion of recorded music, and concurrently interviewed legendary personalities and little known figures from legions of disciplines.

Benton, Joseph Nelson (1924–1988). Correspondent CBS
Berkley, Gil. Announcer NBC
Best, Robert. Correspondent CBS
Beutel Jr., William Charles (Bill) (1930–). Correspondent CBS, ABC
Bjornson, Bjorn. Correspondent NBC
Blue, Ira (1909–1974). Sportscaster NBC, NBC Blue
Boler, Murray. Announcer NBC
Boles, Jim. Consultant (home repairs) MBS, NBC, CBS
Bond, Bill. Announcer MBS
Bourke-White, Margaret. Correspondent CBS
Bower, George. Announcer MBS
Bowles, Chester (1901–1986). News Analyst ABC
Bradley, Bruce. Host† NBC
Brandt, William E. (Bill) (1891–1963). Sportscaster MBS
Brennan, Peter. Correspondent NBC
Brenton, William. Announcer CBS
Brinker, Kaye (1915–). Announcer NBC Blue, CBS, NBC
Brinkley, David (1920–2003). Newscaster, Emcee NBC, ABC
Britt, Jim (1911–1981). Sportscaster CBS, NBC, MBS, ABC
Brooks, William. Correspondent NBC
Brophy, Bill. Correspondent ABC
Brown, Mallory. Correspondent CBS
Brown, Philip. Correspondent CBS
Browne, Malcolm. Correspondent ABC
Bryan, Wright. Correspondent NBC
Bryson, John B. Correspondent ABC
Bunce, Bob. Announcer MBS
Butler, Curtis. Correspondent CBS
Butterworth, Wallace. Announcer NBC, NBC Blue, CBS
Byron, George. Emcee, Announcer MBS, CBS
Cain, Myndall. Consultant (fashion) NBC Blue
Caldwell, Erskine. Correspondent CBS
Campbell, Ted. Announcer NBC, Syndication
Caniff, Frank. Newscaster *
Caplan, Bernard. Correspondent ABC
Cargo, Bill. Announcer ABC
Carson, Paul. Showbiz Reporter *
Carter, Winifred S. Consultant (cooking) NBC Blue, CBS, NBC
Casey, Tom. Announcer NBC Blue
Casserly, John. Correspondent ABC
Cassidy, Henry C. Correspondent NBC
Chaplin, William W. (1895–1978). Correspondent NBC
Chapman, Irving. Correspondent ABC
Charles, Henry. Announcer CBS
Cherne, Leo (1912–1999). Commentator MBS
Chorlian, Edward. Correspondent CBS
Church, Wells (1901–1974). Correspondent *
Cioffi, Lou. Correspondent ABC
Clapper, Raymond Lewis (1892–1944). Newscaster-Analyst CBS, MBS
Clark, Herbert. Correspondent CBS
Clark, Robert E. Correspondent ABC

Cochran, Ronald. Correspondent ABC
Coe, Donald. Correspondent ABC
Coffin, Tris. Correspondent CBS
Compton, Ann (1947–). Correspondent CBS, ABC
Compton, Walter (1912–1959). Announcer/Emcee MBS
Congress, Joseph. Correspondent CBS
Cooke, Alistair (1908–2004). Correspondent NBC
Corrick, Ann M. Correspondent CBS
Corum, Martene Windsor (Bill) (1894–1958). Sportscaster NBC
Corwin, Norman Lewis (1910–). Correspondent CBS
Costello, Bill (1898–1971). Newscaster CBS
Coughlin, (Father) Charles E. (1891–1979). Commentator CBS
Crager, Joel. Correspondent ABC
Crandall, Brad (1927–1991). Host† NBC
Cronkite, Walter (1916–). Features Reporter CBS
Crost, Lyn. Correspondent MBS
Cuhel, Frank J. (1903–1943). Correspondent MBS
Cunningham, Bill. Newscaster MBS
Curie, Eve. Correspondent CBS
Cutting, Dick. Announcer CBS
Dady, Ray E. Newscaster MBS, NBC
Dalton, John. Announcer Syndication
Daly, James (1918–1978). Host† NBC
Daniel, Dan. Host† NBC
David, Rex. Correspondent CBS
Dean, Morton (1935–). Newscaster CBS, ABC
Denton, Robert. Newscaster *
Derr, John. Sportscaster CBS
Desmond, Connie (ca. 1907–1983). Sportscaster CBS
Desponey, Rene A. Correspondent NBC
Dickerson, Dean. Newscaster CBS
Dickerson (Whitehead), Nancy (1927–1997). Correspondent CBS, NBC
DiMaggio, Joseph Paul (Joe) (1914–1999). Sportscaster CBS, NBC
Dooley, Edwin B. (Eddie) (1905–1982). Sportscaster CBS, NBC
Douglas, Chet. Correspondent ABC
Douglas, Paul (1907–1959). Announcer, Sportscaster CBS, NBC
Driscoll, Dave. News/Sportscaster MBS
Dudley, Walter Bronson (Bide) (1877–1944). Showbiz Reporter NBC Blue
Duke, Paul Welden (1926–2005). Correspondent NBC, PBS
Dunn, William J. Correspondent CBS
Dunphy, Don (1908–1998). Sportscaster NBC, ABC
Durocher, Leo (1905–1991). Sportscaster ABC, NBC
Eckland, Victor. Correspondent CBS
Ecklin, Erlin. Correspondent CBS
Edwards, Frank. Commentator CBS
Edwards, Webley. Correspondent CBS
Eid, Leif. Correspondent NBC

Eliot, Bruce. Announcer MBS
Eliot, George Fielding (1894–1971). Commentator CBS
Ellers, Richard. Announcer NBC Blue, NBC
Elliott, John. Correspondent ABC
Elliott, Melvin. Newscaster MBS
Elliston, H. B. Correspondent CBS
Elson, Bob (1904–1981). Sportscaster MBS, NBC
Elton, David. Announcer NBC Blue, NBC
Engel, George. Correspondent ABC
Enslen, Neel (ca. 1893–1938). Announcer NBC, NBC Blue
Essen, Bill. Announcer ABC
Evans, John. Correspondent CBS
Evans, Robert. Correspondent CBS
Ewing, Bill. Announcer ABC
Fadiman, Clifton (Kip) (1904–1999). Emcee NBC
Falk, Raymond. Correspondent ABC
Famin, James. Announcer *
Feldman, Arthur S. Correspondent ABC
Field, Noel. Correspondent CBS
Findell, Jack. Correspondent CBS
Finnigan, Bob. Sportscaster ABC
Fischer, Louis. Correspondent CBS
Fisher, George (1910–1987). Showbiz Reporter MBS, NBC
Fisher, John. Correspondent CBS
Fisher, Thornton (1888–1975). Sportscaster NBC
Flaherty, Pat. Correspondent NBC
Flanagan, Pat (1893–?). Sportscaster NBC
Flanner, Janet (1892–1978). Correspondent ABC
Flannery, Harry W. (1900–1975). Newscaster-Analyst CBS, MBS
Fleisher, Wilfred. Newscaster ABC
Fleming, Art (1924–1995). Host† NBC
Fleming, Robert H. Correspondent ABC
Flynn, Bernardine (1904–1977). Commentator CBS
Folster, George Thomas . Correspondent NBC
Foster, Robert F. Correspondent *
Foster, Wilson K. Correspondent NBC
Fowle, W. Farnsworth (1915–). Correspondent CBS
Francis, Arlene (born Arline Francis Kazanjian) (1907–2001). Commentator CBS
Frost, Bill. Announcer MBS
Frutchy, Fred. Correspondent NBC
Fuldheim, Dorothy Violet Snell (1893–1989). Commentator ABC
Fuqua, Stephen Ogden (1874–?). News Analyst NBC, NBC Blue
Gaeth, Arthur. Newscaster MBS, ABC
Gage, Ben. Announcer CBS
Gardner, Hy (1908–1989). Showbiz Reporter MBS, NBC
Garred, Bob (1915–). Newscaster CBS
Garrett, Ray. Announcer NBC
Garroway Sr., David (Dave) (1913–1982). Host† NBC
Gast, Frank. Announcer CBS
Gates, Paul. Announcer NBC, NBC Blue
Gibbons, Gene. Correspondent *
Gibson, Josephine. Consultant (nutrition) NBC Blue, CBS
Gilchrest, Charles J. Newscaster NBC Blue
Gladstone, Henry (1911–1995). Newscaster MBS
Glickman, Marty (1917–2001). Sportscaster NBC
Glover, Herb. Correspondent CBS
Goad, Rex R. Correspondent *
Goode, Mal. Correspondent ABC
Goodman, Julian. Correspondent NBC
Goodwin, Sidney. Announcer NBC Blue, NBC
Goudiss, Mrs. A. M. Consultant (nutrition) NBC Blue
Gould, Barbara. Consultant (beauty) CBS
Gourlay, Doug. Announcer NBC, NBC Blue
Gowdy, Curt (1919–2006). Sportscaster ABC, CBS, NBC
Grange, Harold "Red" (1903–1991). Sportscaster NBC, CBS, MBS
Greece, Roy. Announcer ABC
Greenwood, William. Correspondent *
Gregson, Jack (1915–). Announcer-Emcee NBC, ABC
Griffin, Charles. Correspondent CBS
Grimsby, Roger. Correspondent ABC
Gunn, George . Announcer NBC Blue.
Gunnison, Royal Arch. Newscaster MBS
Haaker, Edwin. Correspondent NBC
Habicht, Hermann (ca. 1893–?). Correspondent NBC, NBC Blue
Hall, Helen (1914–1984). Correspondent NBC, MBS, Syndication
Hall, Monty (born Maurice Halprin) (1921–). Host† NBC
Hall, Red. Announcer NBC
Hand, William. Correspondent NBC
Hard, Ann. Newscaster NBC
Hard, William S. Newscaster-Analyst NBC
Harder, Ralph. Correspondent CBS
Hardin, Harvey. Newscaster CBS, NBC Blue
Harding, Lawrence (Larry). Announcer CBS
Harding, Lester. Announcer NBC
Harmon, Tom. Correspondent ABC
Harper, Larrie. Announcer CBS
Harrington, John W. (1908–). Sportscaster/Announcer CBS
Harriott, Jim. Correspondent ABC
Hart, John (1946–). Correspondent CBS
Hartrich, Edwin. Correspondent CBS
Hartz, Jack. Announcer CBS
Hasel, Joe. Sportscaster CBS, ABC, NBC
Hauser, Gayelord. Consultant (nutrition) *
Hayes, George (ca. 1889–1967). Announcer NBC Blue, NBC
Hayes, Sam (1904–1958). Newscaster NBC
Hayes, William. Host† NBC
Hefler, George (Alvin) (1912–1975). News/Sportscaster MBS
Heidi, Bud. Announcer NBC
Hemmingway, Frank. Correspondent ABC
Henderson, Leon (1895–1986). Commentator NBC Blue, ABC

APPENDIX

Henry, William M. (Bill) (1890–1970). Newscaster-Analyst CBS
Hewson, Isabel Manning. Consultant (buying) NBC, CBS, NBC Blue
Higby, Les. Correspondent ABC
Higgins, Don. Correspondent CBS
Hightower, Bill. Announcer MBS
Hill, Max. Correspondent NBC
Hill, Robert (Bob). Announcer CBS
Hill, Russell. Correspondent CBS
Hillman, William (Bill) (1895–1962). Newscaster NBC Blue, NBC, MBS
Hinde, John. Correspondent ABC
Hodges, Gilbert. Correspondent ABC
Holcomb, Chester. Correspondent CBS
Holden, Jack (1907–?). Announcer NBC, NBC Blue
Holles, Everett. Correspondent CBS
Holmes, George R. (1895–1939). Newscaster NBC
Hooley, John A. Correspondent ABC
Hopper, DeWolf (1858–1935). Emcee-Narrator CBS, NBC Blue
Hopper, Edna Wallace (1864–1959). Consultant (beauty) CBS
Howard, Lisa (1930–1965). Correspondent MBS, ABC
Howard, Ralph (born Ralph Peterson). Correspondent NBC
Hoyt, Waite (1899–1984). Sportscaster NBC
Hughes, John B. (1904–1989). Commentator NBC, MBS
Hughes, Rupert (1872–1956). Commentator NBC
Hughes, Rush (1902–1979). Newscaster, Emcee NBC, NBC Blue, CBS
Hunt, Frazier. Newscaster MBS, CBS
Hurleigh, Robert F. Newscaster MBS
Hurst, Carol. Announcer NBC
Imus Jr., John Donald (1940–). Host† NBC
Ingersoll, Ralph. Correspondent CBS
Isbell, Harold. Announcer CBS
Janssen, Guthrie A. Correspondent NBC
Jaffe, Sam. Correspondent ABC
Jarriel, Tom (1934–). Correspondent ABC
Jayne, David. Correspondent ABC
Jeffreys, Allan. Correspondent ABC
Jenks, Hugh. Correspondent CBS
Jennings, Peter (1938–2005). Features Reporter ABC
Jewett, Edward K. (Ted). Correspondent NBC, NBC Blue
Johnson, Albin. Correspondent CBS
Johnson, Erskine (1910–1984). Showbiz Reporter CBS, MBS
Johnson, Hugh S. (1882–1942). Commentator NBC Blue
Jones, Phil. Correspondent *
Jones, Russell. Correspondent CBS, ABC
Jordan, Frank J. Correspondent *
Jordon, Edward. Correspondent ABC
Julian, Joseph. Announcer MBS
Kalb, Bernard (1922–). Correspondent CBS, NBC, CNN
Kaltenback, Fred. Newscaster *
Kaney, A. W. (Sen). Announcer NBC, NBC Blue
Kasper, Fred. Announcer ABC
Keating, Baxter. Newscaster *
Keirker, William C. Correspondent NBC, NBC Blue
Kelly, Andrew. Consultant (attitude) NBC, MBS, ABC
Kent, Marshall. Announcer, Emcee MBS
Kephart, William. Announcer NBC Blue
Kerr, Walter. Correspondent CBS
Kilgore, James. Announcer NBC Blue, NBC
King, James. Correspondent CBS
King, Perry. Announcer CBS
Kittell, Clyde. Announcer NBC, NBC Blue
Klein, Stewart. Correspondent ABC
Klode, Frank. Announcer NBC, NBC Blue
Knauth, Theodore W. (1885–?). Correspondent NBC, NBC Blue
Knell, Jack. Correspondent CBS
Koppel, Edward James (Ted) (1940–). Correspondent ABC
Koski, Al. Correspondent ABC
Kraft, Norman. Announcer ABC
Kupcinet, Irv (1912–2003). Newscaster-Analyst ABC
Lacy, Ben. Correspondent ABC
LaGuardia, Fiorello H. (1882–1947). Commentator ABC
Lang, William. Newscaster MBS, ABC, CBS
Langdon, Baden. Correspondent ABC
Lanius Jr., Charles Henry (1906–?). Correspondent NBC, NBC Blue
Larrimore, Bob. Announcer MBS
Laurence, Bill. Correspondent ABC
Lawrence, David (1888–1973). Commentator NBC, ABC
Lawton, Fleetwood. Correspondent NBC
Lazard, Sidney. Correspondent ABC
Leader, Anton. Correspondent ABC
Legg, Frank. Correspondent NBC
Leggett, Dudley. Correspondent ABC
Leimert, Timothy. Correspondent CBS
Leitch, Albert. Correspondent CBS
Lennard, Wallace W. Correspondent ABC
Leslie, Chuck. Announcer ABC
Levin, Marlin. Correspondent ABC
Levine, Irving R. (1922–). Newscaster NBC
Lewis, Robert. Correspondent CBS
Lindley, Ernest K. Newscaster NBC Blue/ABC
Linfoot, Victor. Announcer NBC Blue, NBC
Lismann, Bernard. Correspondent ABC
Lister, Morley. Correspondent CBS
Livingston, Joan Hensman (1910–?). Correspondent NBC, NBC Blue
Lochner, Louis Paul (1887–1975). Newscaster NBC
Lodge, Robert. Correspondent ABC
Lomax, Henry S. (Stan) (1899–1988). Sportscaster MBS
Longmire, Cary. Newscaster NBC
Lord, William (Bill). Correspondent ABC
Lowe, Jim (1927–). Host† NBC

Lundberg, Daniel. Correspondent CBS
Lundell, William. Announcer NBC, NBC Blue
Lusinchi, Victor. Correspondent MBS
Lynch, John F. Correspondent *
Magidoff, Robert. Correspondent NBC
Mahon, Jack. Correspondent MBS
Malone, Ted (aka Alden Russell) (1908–1989). Correspondent NBC Blue/ABC
Manion, Clarence E. Correspondent *
Mann, Arthur. Correspondent MBS
Manning, Paul (?–1995). Correspondent CBS
Manning, Tom. Sportscaster NBC
March, Hal (born Harold Mendelson) (1920–1970). Host† NBC
Marrow, Joan. Consultant (beauty) *
Martin, Campbell. Newscaster *
Martin, Murphy. Correspondent ABC
Martyn, Gilbert. Newscaster NBC Blue, ABC
Marvin, Ken. Announcer MBS
Matthews, James. Announcer CBS
May, Herb. Announcer NBC
Mayo, John. Announcer NBC, NBC Blue
McBee, Keith. Correspondent ABC
McCaffrey, John K. M. (1913–1983). Newscaster MBS, NBC, ABC
McCaffrey, Joseph F. (1914–1994). Correspondent CBS, MBS
McCall, Francis C. Correspondent NBC
McCarthy, Frank. Announcer MBS
McCormick, Stephen J. Correspondent *
McCulla, Jim. Correspondent ABC
McDougall, John. Announcer CBS
McEvoy, Dennis. Correspondent CBS
McGee, Frank (1915–1974). Host† NBC
McIntosh, Ezra. Announcer NBC, NBC Blue
McLaughlin, Marya. Correspondent CBS
McMahon, Ed (1923–). Host† NBC
McNally, Ted. Announcer *
McNutt, Paul Vories (1891–1955). Commentator MBS
McVane, John F. (1912–). Correspondent NBC, NBC Blue
Meeker, Kenneth. Correspondent CBS
Meier, G. Lawrence. Correspondent MBS
Menken, Arthur. Correspondent CBS
Meyer, Arnim. Correspondent CBS
Meyer, Larry. Newscaster CBS
Middleton, Glenn Y. Announcer NBC, NBC Blue
Miles, Allie Lowe. Consultant (lovelorn) MBS, NBC Blue
Miley, Jack. Sportscaster NBC
Moats, Alice L. Correspondent CBS
Monks, John. Announcer NBC Blue, NBC
Monroe Jr., William B. Correspondent *
Montgomery, Edward. Correspondent CBS
Montgomery, Robert (born Henry Montgomery Jr.) (1904–1981). Announcer CBS
Moon, Bob. Announcer Syndication
Moorad, George L. Correspondent CBS
Moore, Hal. Announcer CBS
Moore, Thompson. Correspondent CBS
Moore, Walton. Correspondent CBS
Morgan, Robert W. Host† NBC
Morrison, Chester. Correspondent NBC, CBS
Morrison, Fred W. Correspondent *
Morrissey, John W. Correspondent NBC
Morse, Tony. Newscaster *
Morton, Bruce. Correspondent CBS, ABC
Moseley, Sydney (1888–1961). Commentator MBS
Moshier, Bill. Newscaster *
Mosley, Don. Newscaster. *
Mudd, Roger (1928–). Correspondent CBS, NBC
Murray the K (born Murray Kaufman) (1922–1982). Host† NBC
Nash, Eleanor. Consultant (beauty) NBC Blue
Nelson, Barry (born Robert H. Nielsen) (1920–). Host† NBC
Nichols, Leslie A. Correspondent MBS
Niven, Paul. Correspondent CBS
O'Brien, Tom. Correspondent ABC
O'Donnell, John. Newscaster *
O'Donnell, Tim. Correspondent ABC
O'Hara, Neal. Commentator CBS
Oursler, Fulton (1893–1953). Newscaster MBS
Owen, David. Announcer CBS
Page, Alan. Announcer CBS
Painton, Fred. Correspondent CBS
Parker, Wally. Correspondent ABC
Parr, William Grant. Correspondent NBC
Parsons, Harriet (1906–1983). Showbiz Reporter NBC Blue
Paull, Raymond A. Correspondent ABC
Peters, Harold A. Correspondent ABC
Peterson, Elmer. Newscaster-Analyst NBC
Pierce, Jennings. Announcer NBC Blue, NBC
Pope, Ernest. Correspondent CBS
Porter, Roy. Correspondent NBC Blue
Powers, Jimmy. Sportscaster NBC
Prevensen, Herluf (1908–?). Announcer NBC, NBC Blue
Pringle, Nelson. Correspondent CBS
Pryor, Don. Newscaster CBS
Purcell, John. Correspondent CBS
Pyle, John H. Correspondent NBC
Raleigh, John M. Correspondent CBS
Rather, Dan (1931–). Features Reporter CBS
Rayburn, Gene (born Eugene Rubessa) (1917–1999). Host† NBC
Reasoner, Harry (1923–1991). Features Reporter CBS, ABC
Rector, George. Consultant (nutrition) CBS
Reisenberg, Felix. Correspondent CBS
Rendell, Richard. Newscaster ABC
Resautel, Van. Announcer CBS
Revell, Nellie (1873–1958). Showbiz Reporter NBC, NBC Blue
Reynolds, Frank (1923–1983). Newscaster ABC
Reynolds, Quentin (1902–1965). Newscaster MBS
Rhodes, Helen. Announcer ABC
Richardson, Bob. Showbiz Reporter Syndication
Richardson, Stanley P. Correspondent NBC
Rider, Eugene. Correspondent CBS
Riggs, Z. A. Announcer Syndication
Roberts, Clete (born Cletus Haase) (1912–1984). Newscaster NBC Blue/ABC

APPENDIX

Roberts, Cokie (born Coreen Boggs) (1943–). Correspondent CBS, ABC, NPR
Roberts, J. W. Correspondent *
Robinson, (Major) George D. Newscaster *
Robinson, Prescott. Newscaster MBS
Robson, William. Correspondent CBS
Rolfson, John. Correspondent ABC
Root, Waverly. Correspondent MBS
Ross, Merrill. Announcer MBS
Rouse, Gene. Announcer NBC, NBC Blue
Roventini, Johnny (1910–1998). Commercial. Spokesman NBC, CBS, ABC, MBS
Rowen, Lewis (1907–1991). Announcer NBC
Russell, Don (1907–?). Announcer, Emcee NBC, NBC Blue
Runyon, Damon (born Alfred D. Runyan) (1884–1946). Sportscaster NBC Blue
Russell, David. Announcer NBC, NBC Blue
Ryan, Quin (1899–1978). Newscaster MBS
St. Johns, Adela Rogers (1894–1988). Commentator NBC
Sawyer, Billy. Newscaster MBS
Scali, John A. (1924–2001). Correspondent ABC
Scanlan, Dan. Correspondent CBS
Schacht, Al. Sportscaster MBS
Schieffer, Bob (1937–). Features Reporter CBS
Schmidt, Dana. Correspondent CBS
Schoumacher, David. Correspondent CBS, ABC
Schubert, Paul. Newscaster MBS
Schultz, Sigrid (1893–1980). Correspondent MBS
Scott, Ed. Announcer *
Scott, John. Announcer MBS, NBC
Scott, Martha Ellen (1912–2003). Co-Emcee NBC
Scully, Frances. Showbiz Reporter ABC
Seagrist, Robert. Newscaster MBS
Seavey, Hollis M. Correspondent *
Serafin, Barry (1941–). Correspondent CBS, ABC
Sergio, Lisa (1905–1989). Commentator NBC, ABC
Sharpe, Roger. Correspondent ABC
Shaw, Charles. Correspondent CBS
Shaw, Jack. Correspondent MBS
Shayon, Robert L. Correspondent CBS
Sheean, Vincent. Correspondent CBS
Sheehan, Bill. Correspondent ABC
Shollenberger, Lewis W. (1916–1994). Correspondent CBS, ABC
Siler, Bert. Correspondent MBS
Slanton, John. Consultant (beauty) NBC
Slater, Bill (1902–1965). Sportscaster CBS, MBS
Slocum Jr., William. Correspondent CBS
Slosberg, Merwin. Correspondent NBC
Smith, Carlton. Announcer NBC, NBC Blue
Smith, Harry. Correspondent CBS
Smith, Larry. Commentator NBC
Smith, Lester. Newscaster MBS
Snow, Leida. Correspondent ABC
Sokolsky, George. Showbiz Reporter ABC
Sorensen, Clarence. Correspondent CBS
Souder, Edmund L. Correspondent ABC

Sparks, Jeff. Announcer NBC Blue, NBC, MBS
Spence, Bob. Correspondent CBS, MBS
Stadler, Glen. Correspondent CBS
Stanley, John. Newscaster MBS
Stanton, Andrew. Announcer CBS
Stark, Hal. Announcer CBS
Steele, John. Correspondent MBS
Steele, Ted (1918–1985). Host[†] NBC
Stephanie, Diane. Showbiz Reporter *
Stevens, Carlyle. Announcer CBS
Stevens, Frank. Correspondent CBS
Stevenson, James. Newscaster NBC
Stevenson, Kent. Correspondent CBS
Stewart, James. Correspondent CBS
Stewart, Virginia. Showbiz Reporter NBC Blue
Stowe, Leland (1899–1994). Newscaster Blue/ABC, MBS
Sullivan, Edward Vincent (1901–1974). Showbiz Reporter CBS, ABC
Sullivan, Paul (1908–1986). Newscaster CBS
Tannehill, Raymond. Correspondent ABC
Taylor, Edward. Correspondent CBS
Taylor, Marion Sayle. Consultant (advice) CBS, NBC, MBS, Syndication
Taylor, Tony. Host[†] NBC
Templeton, Joe. Correspondent ABC
Terrett, Courtney. Correspondent CBS
Tillman, John. Correspondent CBS
Tobey, Evelyn. Consultant (fashion) NBC
Tompkins, Phil. Announcer MBS
Totten, Harold O. (Hal) (1901–?). Sportscaster NBC, CBS
Tramont Jr., Charles B. Announcer NBC, NBC Blue
Treanor, Tom. Correspondent NBC
Tremaine, Frank. Correspondent CBS
Truman (Daniel), Margaret (1924–). Co-Emcee NBC
Tucker, John Bartholomew (1930–). Host[†] NBC
Tunis, John R. (1889–1975). Sportscaster NBC Blue, NBC
Twiss, Clinton E. (Buddy) (1904–1952). Announcer NBC, NBC Blue
Unger, Stella Garfield (1904–1970). Showbiz Reporter MBS, NBC
Utley, Clifton (1904–1978). Commentator NBC
Utley, Fran (ca. 1904–2001). Newscaster CBS
Utley, Garrick (1939–). Correspondent NBC, ABC, CNN
Vale, David. Correspondent CBS
Valery, Bernard. Correspondent CBS
Van, Lyle. Newscaster MBS
Van Deventer, Fred (1903–1971). Newscaster MBS
Van Horn, Arthur. Announcer MBS
Van Loon, Hendrik Willem (1882–1944). Commentator NBC
Van Sickle, James. Announcer Syndication
Vincent, Scott. Correspondent ABC
Vinick, Nell. Consultant (beauty) CBS, MBS
Wahl, Jim McDonald. Correspondent NBC
Waldrop, Robert. Announcer NBC, NBC Blue
Walker, Danton MacIntyre (1899–1960). Showbiz Reporter MBS

Walker, Hal (1933–2003). Correspondent CBS, ABC
Wallace, Edward E. Correspondent NBC
Wallace, Forrest P. . Announcer NBC, NBC Blue
Ward, Arch (1896–1955). Sportscaster MBS
Ward, Paul. Correspondent CBS
Warner, Albert L. Newscaster-Analyst CBS, MBS, ABC
Warren, Charles. Correspondent *
Wason, Betty. Correspondent CBS
Watson, George. Announcer., Newscaster NBC, NBC Blue, ABC
Wayne, David (1913–1995). Host[†] NBC
Weaver, Hank (1916–1964). Announcer., Sportscaster CBS, NBC
Weeks, Joe. Announcer CBS, NBC
Wells, Linton. Correspondent CBS
Welles, Sumner (1892–1961). Commentator MBS
Wheeler, George. Correspondent NBC
Wheeler, Jackson. Announcer., Newscaster CBS
White, Ed. Announcer *
White, William L. Correspondent CBS
Whiteside, Arthur (?–1978). Announcer MBS
Wile, Frederic William (1873–1941). Commentator NBC Blue, CBS
Wilkins, Ford. Correspondent CBS
Williams, Oswald M. Correspondent ABC
Williams, Spencer. Correspondent CBS
Williams, Wythe. Newscaster MBS
Wills, W. R. (Bud). Correspondent CBS
Wilson, Big (born Malcolm John Wilson Jr.) (1924–1989). Host[†] NBC
Wilson, Marilyn. Announcer ABC, NBC, CBS
Wilson, Stanley. Correspondent CBS
Wilson, Sven. Correspondent CBS
Wingate, John. Newscaster *
Winter, William. Correspondent CBS
Winters, Ray. Announcer NBC, NBC Blue, MBS
Wismer, Harry (1911–1967). Sportscaster ABC, MBS, Syndication
Wolfe, John A. Announcer CBS
Wolff, Bob. Sportscaster CBS, MBS, NBC
Wolfman Jack (born Robert Smith) (1938–1995). Host[†] NBC
Wood, Harrison. Commentator ABC, MBS
Wood, Milton. Announcer NBC Blue, NBC
Woodyat, Phil. Correspondent CBS
Worthen, Thomas. Correspondent CBS
Wright, Larry. Announcer MBS
Young, John S. (1903–1976). Announcer NBC, NBC Blue, CBS
Young, Murray. Correspondent MBS
Young, Robert. Correspondent ABC
Young, Russ. Announcer CBS, NBC
Young, Thomas Shaw. Announcer NBC
Young, William. Announcer NBC

Bibliography

Anderson, Arthur. *Let's Pretend: A History of Radio's Best Loved Children's Show by a Longtime Cast Member.* Jefferson, N.C.: McFarland, 1994.

Ansbro, George. *I Have a Lady in the Balcony: Memoirs of a Broadcaster.* Jefferson, N.C.: McFarland, 2000.

Barnouw, Erik. *The Golden Web: A History of Broadcasting in the United States, 1933–1953.* New York: Oxford University Press, 1968.

_____. *The Image Empire: A History of Broadcasting in the United States, From 1933.* New York: Oxford University Press, 1970.

_____. *A Tower in Babel: A History of Broadcasting in the United States, Vol. 1—to 1933.* New York: Oxford University Press, 1966.

Bresee, Frank, and Bobb Lynes. *Radio's Golden Years: A Visual Guide to the Shows and the Stars.* Hollywood, Calif.: Frank Bresee Productions, 1998.

Brooks, Tim, and Earle Marsh. *The Complete Directory to Prime Time Network TV Shows 1946–Present.* 4th ed. New York: Ballantine, 1988.

Buxton, Frank, and Bill Owen. *The Big Broadcast, 1920–1950.* 2nd ed. Lanham, Md.: Scarecrow Press, 1997.

Campbell, Robert. *The Golden Years of Broadcasting: A Celebration of the First 50 Years of Radio and TV on NBC.* New York: Scribner's, 1976.

Castleman, Harry, and Walter J. Podrazik. *505 Radio Questions Your Friends Can't Answer.* New York: Walker, 1983.

Chase, Francis, Jr. *Sound and Fury: An Informal History of Broadcasting.* New York: Harper & Brothers, 1942.

Cloud, Stanley, and Lynne Olson. *The Murrow Boys: Pioneers on the Front Lines of Broadcast Journalism.* Boston: Houghton Mifflin, 1996.

Cox, Jim. *The Daytime Serials of Television, 1946–1960.* Jefferson, N.C.: McFarland, 2006.

_____. *Frank and Anne Hummert's Radio Factory: The Programs and Personalities of Broadcasting's Most Prolific Producers.* Jefferson, N.C.: McFarland, 2003.

_____. *The Great Radio Audience Participation Shows: Seventeen Programs from the 1940s and 1950s.* Jefferson, N.C.: McFarland, 2001.

_____. *The Great Radio Soap Operas.* Jefferson, N.C.: McFarland, 1999.

_____. *Historical Dictionary of American Radio Soap Operas.* Lanham, Md.: Scarecrow Press, 2005.

_____. *Mr. Keen, Tracer of Lost Persons: A Complete History and Episode Log of Radio's Most Durable Detective.* Jefferson, N.C.: McFarland, 2004.

_____. *Music Radio: The Great Performers and Programs of the 1920s through Early 1960s.* Jefferson, N.C.: McFarland, 2005.

_____. *Radio Crime Fighters: Over 300 Programs from the Golden Age.* Jefferson, N.C.: McFarland, 2002.

_____. *Say Goodnight, Gracie: The Last Years of Network Radio.* Jefferson, N.C.: McFarland, 2002.

DeLong, Thomas A. *Radio Stars: An Illustrated Biographical Dictionary of 953 Performers, 1920 through 1960.* Jefferson, N.C.: McFarland, 1996.

Duncan, Jacci, ed. *Making Waves: The 50 Greatest Women in Radio and Television as Selected by American Women in Radio and Television, Inc.* Kansas City: Andrews McMeel, 2001.

Dunning, John. *On the Air: The Encyclopedia of Old-Time Radio.* New York: Oxford University Press, 1998.

Fang, Irving E. *Those Radio Commentators!* Ames: University of Iowa Press, 1977.

Fox, Ken, and Maitland McDonagh, eds. *TV Guide Film and Video Companion, 2004.* New York: Barnes & Noble Books, 2003.

Gates, Gary Paul. *Air Time: The Inside Story of CBS News.* New York: Harper and Row, 1978.

Gilmore, Art, and Glenn Y. Middleton. *Television and Radio Announcing.* 3rd ed. Hollywood, Calif.: Hollywood Radio, 1949.

Goldin, J. David. *The Golden Age of Radio: The Standard Reference Work of Radio Programs and Radio Performers of the Past.* Sandy Hook, Conn.: Radio Yesteryear, 2000.

Grams, Martin, Jr. *Gang Busters: The Crime Fighters of American Broadcasting.* Arlington, Va.: Kirby Lithographic, 2004.

Hart, Dennis. *Monitor: The Last Great Radio Show.* San Jose, Calif.: Writers Club Press, 2002.

Harvey, Rita Morley. *Those Wonderful, Terrible Years: George Heller and the American Federation of Television and Radio Artists.* Carbondale: Southern Illinois University Press, 1996.

Hickerson, Jay. *Necrology of Radio Personalities.* Hamden, Conn.: Jay Hickerson, 1996. Plus supplements 1–5: 1997, 1998, 1999, 2000, 2002.

_____. *The Third Revised Ultimate History of Network Radio Programming and Guide to All Circulating Shows.* Hamden, Conn.: Presto Print II, 2005.

Higby, Mary Jane. *Tune in Tomorrow; or, How I Found the Right to Happiness with Our Gal Sunday, Stella Dallas, John's Other Wife, and Other Sudsy Radio Serials.* New York: Cowles Education, 1966.

Hurst, Jack. *Nashville's Grand Ole Opry: The First Fifty Years, 1925–1975.* New York: Harry N. Abrams, 1989.

Hyatt, Wesley. *The Encyclopedia of Daytime Television: Everything You Ever Wanted to Know About Daytime TV But Didn't Know Where to Look! From American Bandstand, As the World Turns, and Bugs Bunny, to Meet the Press, The Price Is Right, and Wide World of Sports, the Rich History of Daytime Television in All Its Glory!* New York: Billboard, 1997.

Johnson, Kenneth M. *The Johnson Family Singers: We Sang for Our Supper.* Jackson: University Press of Mississippi, 1997.

Lackmann, Ron. *Same Time ... Same Station: An A-Z Guide to Radio from Jack Benny to Howard Stern.* New York: Facts on File, 1996

MacDonald, J. Fred. *Don't Touch That Dial! Radio Programming in American Life from 1920 to 1960.* Chicago: Nelson-Hall, 1991.

Maltin, Leonard. *The Great American Broadcast: A Celebration of Radio's Golden Age.* New York: Penguin Putnam, 1997.

McLeod, Elizabeth. *The Original Amos 'n' Andy: Freeman Gosden, Charles Correll and the 1928–1943 Radio Serial.* Jefferson, N.C.: McFarland, 2005.

McNeil, Alex. *Total Television: The Comprehensive Guide to Programming from 1948 to the Present.* 4th ed. New York: Penguin Books, 1996.

Nachman, Gerald. *Raised on Radio: In Quest of The Lone Ranger, Jack Benny, Amos 'n' Andy, The Shadow, Mary Noble, The Great Gildersleeve, Fibber McGee and Molly, Bill Stern, Our Miss Brooks, Henry Aldrich, The Quiz Kids, Mr. First Nighter, Fred Allen, Vic and Sade, The Cisco Kid, Jack Armstrong, Arthur Godfrey, Bob and Ray, The Barbour Family, Henry Morgan, Joe Friday and Other Lost Heroes from Radio's Heyday.* New York: Pantheon Books, 1998.

National Broadcasting Co. *The Fourth Chime.* New York: A. Colish, 1944.

Paulson, Roger C. *Archives of the Airwaves.* Vol. 1. Boalsburg, Pa.: BearManor Media, 2005.

_____. *Archives of the Airwaves.* Vol. 2. Boalsburg, Pa.: BearManor Media, 2005.

Poindexter, Ray. *Golden Throats and Silver Tongues: The Radio Announcers.* Conway, Ark.: River Road Press, 1978.

Robinson, Marc. *Brought to You in Living Color: 75 Years of Great Moments in Television & Radio from NBC.* Hoboken, N.J.: Wiley, 2002.

Schaden, Chuck. *Speaking of Radio: Chuck Schaden's Conversations with the Stars of the Golden Age of Radio.* Morton Grove, Ill.: Nostalgia Digest Press, 2003.

Sies, Luther F. *Encyclopedia of American Radio, 1920–1960.* Jefferson, N.C.: McFarland, 2000.

Slide, Anthony. *Great Radio Personalities in Historic Photographs.* Vestal, N.Y.: Vestal Press, 1982.

Stedman, Raymond William. *The Serials: Suspense and Drama by Installment.* Norman: University of Oklahoma Press, 1971.

Summers, Harrison B., ed. *A Thirty-Year History of Programs Carried on National Radio Networks in the United States, 1926–1956.* New York: Arno Press and *The New York Times,* 1971.

Swartz, Jon D., and Robert C. Reinehr. *Handbook of Old-Time Radio: A Comprehensive Guide to Golden Age Radio Listening and Collecting.* Metuchen, N.J.: Scarecrow Press, 1993.

Terrace, Vincent. *Radio Programs, 1924–1984: A Catalog of Over 1800 Shows.* Jefferson, N.C.: McFarland, 1999.

TV Guide, Editors of. *TV Guide: Guide to TV.* 1st ed. New York: Barnes & Noble, 2004.

Ware, Susan. *It's One O'Clock and Here Is Mary Margaret McBride: A Radio Biography.* New York: New York University Press, 2005.

Index

The A&P Gypsies 52, 69, 270, 291
Abbott, George 166
Abbott and Costello Junior Youth Foundation 230
The Abbott and Costello Kids' Show 187
The Abbott and Costello Show 33, 84, 186, 209, 212, 220, 250
The Abbott Mysteries 294
The ABC Morning News 6
ABC Mystery Time 82
ABC News 11, 178, 201, 218
ABC Radio Workshop 312
The Abe Burrows Show 98
Abie's Irish Rose 5, 42, 63, 80, 87, 104, 228, 234
About Faces 8
Academy Award Theater 48, 176
Academy of Motion Picture Arts and Sciences 207
Ace, Goodman 38
Ace gasoline 73
Adams, Franklin P. 321
Adams, Mason 87
Adams, William Perry 5–6
Add a Line 210
Adelaide Hawley Show 129
Adelaide Hawley's Women's Page 15
The Adele Clark Show 165
Adopted Daughter 195
The Adrian Rollini Trio and the Lenny Herman Quintet 237
Adventure Incorporated 186
Adventure Parade 140
Adventure Theater 32, 120
The Adventurer's Club 214
Adventures by Morse 25
Adventures in Rhythm 169
Adventures in Science 108, 163
The Adventures of Bill Lance 114, 151, 152, 186, 187
The Adventures of Captain Diamond 250
Adventures of Charlie Chan 254
Adventures of Christopher London 234
The Adventures of Dick Cole 177
The Adventures of Dick Tracy 175, 176, 186, 262
The Adventures of Ellery Queen 10, 58, 72, 79, 123, 167, 181, 217, 220, 234, 239, 303
The Adventures of Father Brown 120, 132, 148, 275
The Adventures of Frank Merriwell 14, 39, 43, 313
Adventures of Frank Race 109, 250
Adventures of Gracie 113
The Adventures of Leonidas Witherall 56
The Adventures of M. Hercule Poirot 87
The Adventures of Maisie 15, 87, 186, 187, 193, 209, 212
Adventures of Michael Shane 132
The Adventures of Mr. Meek 5, 187
The Adventures of Nero Wolfe 21, 79, 87, 217, 228
The Adventures of Ozzie and Harriet 17, 274
The Adventures of Philip Marlowe 15, 72, 79, 212, 228, 234, 250, 280, 308
The Adventures of Rin Tin Tin 200
Adventures of Sam Spade 152
Adventures of Sam Spade, Detective 187, 234
The Adventures of Sherlock Holmes 16, 98, 125, 179, 275
The Adventures of Superman 30, 63, 70, 98, 152, 165, 166, 175, 176, 186
The Adventures of Terry and Ted 53
The Adventures of the Abbotts 43, 106, 125
The Adventures of the Falcon 66, 86
The Adventures of the Red Feather Man 98
The Adventures of the Scarlet Cloak 213
The Adventures of the Thin Man 57, 125, 134, 233, 237, 294, 306, 311
The Adventures of Topper 166, 233
The Affairs of Ann Scotland 212
The Affairs of Anthony 193
The Affairs of Peter Salem 217
The AFRS Story 179
Against the Storm 57, 88, 200, 277

Agence Havas 51
Agronsky, Martin 6–7, 50
Agronsky at Large 7
The Air Adventures of Jimmy Allen 230
Air Conditioning Training Corp. 309
A.L. Alexander's Goodwill Court 56
A.L. Alexander's Mediation Board 86
The Al Jolson Program 300
The Al Jolson Show 250, 315
Al Pearce and His Gang 42, 65, 113, 212, 234
Al Pearce Show 113, 212, 239
The Al Trahan Revue 188
The Alan Courtney Show 68
The Alan Young Show 90, 250, 306, 315
The Aldrich Family 48, 86, 224, 262, 303, 311, 315, 316, 322
Alec Templeton Time 206
Alex Dreier, Man on the Go 85
Alex Dreier News and Comments 85
Alexander, Hi 235
Alexander, Jane 142, 223
Alexander, Joan 31
Alfred I. DuPont Award 197, 294
The Alfredo Antonini Orchestra 166–167
Alias Jane Doe 180
Alias Jimmy Valentine 37, 104
Alibi Club 106
Alka-Seltzer 125, 254
Alka-Seltzer Time 164
Allan Jackson and the News 148
All Around the Town 305, 306
All Night Showcase 178
All Sports Program 185
All-Star Western Theater 250
All Things Considered 295
Allbritton, Louise 62
Allen, Edward 8
Allen, Fred 112, 134, 135, 221, 311, 318
Allen, Gracie 213
Allen, Herb 8–9
Allen, Mel 9–10, 22, 89, 139
Allen, Robert S. 225
Allen, Steve 307
Allstate Insurance 236

INDEX

Almanac de Gotham 98
Amalgamated Broadcasting System 45
Amanda of Honeymoon Hill 58, 65, 106
The Amazing Mr. Malone 108, 109, 298
The Amazing Mr. Smith 212, 217, 303, 315
The Amazing Mr. Tutt 250
The Amazing Mrs. Danbury 212
Ameche, Don 10, 11
Ameche, Jim 10–11
Ameche Academy of Broadcasting 11
America Calling 308
American Academy of Arts and Letters 70, 128, 166
American Academy of Arts and Sciences 17
American Ace Coffee Time 299
American Agent 185
The American Album of Familiar Music 13, 26, 58, 167, 195
American Broadcasting Co. (ABC) 116, 180
American Cancer Society 98, 244
American Cancer Society 98
American Cultural Expeditions 59
American Federation of Radio Artists (AFRA) 31, 39, 64, 129, 130, 132, 145, 179, 192, 223, 240
American Federation of Television and Radio Artists 84, 110, 123, 210, 240
American Film Institute 41
The American Forum of the Air 86
American Foundation for the Blind 201
American Guild of Radio Announcers and Producers 166
American Home Products 99, 123
An American in England 202
An American in Russia 172
American Melody Hour 37, 90
American Novels 214
American Portraits 117
The American Radiator Musical Interlude 188
The American School of the Air 163, 202, 295, 311
American Tobacco Co. 27, 37, 58, 237, 292
America Today 133
American Women 46
Americans at Work 163
America's Town Meeting of the Air 58, 69, 117, 121, 134, 165, 244, 245
The Ammident Show 113
Amos 'n' Andy 25, 58, 109, 130, 131, 153, 264, 313
The Amos 'n' Andy Music Hall 10, 313
Anchors Aweigh 218
Anders, Bill 11

Anderson, Bob 11
Anderson, Eddie (Rochester) 316
Anderson, Jack 136
Anderson, Larry 89
Anderson, Orval 11
Anderson, Sherwood 246
Andre, Pierre 67
Andre Kostelanetz-Tony Martin Show 262
Andrew Jergens Co. 223, 318
Andrews, William John 12–13
The Andrews Sisters Eight-to-the-Bar Ranch 26, 193
The Andy Devine Show 84
Andy Hardy 311
Andy Russell Show 250
ANETA (Dutch news agency) 257
Annenberg Center for Health Sciences 86
The Anniversary Club 7
Ansbro, George 13–14, 104, 129, 191
The Answer Man 195
Answer Please 87, 229
Anthony, Allen C. 14
Antoine, H. Jon (Tex) 14
Arabesque 165, 248
Arch Oboler's Plays 217
The Archibald MacLeish Program 200
Archie Andrews 20, 86, 120, 132, 266, 310, 322
Archie Bleyer and His Orchestra 181
Archinard, Paul 14–15
Are These Our Children? 106
Are You a Genius? 58
The Arkansas Traveler 274, 312
Arlen, Margaret 15
Arlington, Charles 15–16
Arliss, George 311
Armbruster, Robert 321
Armchair Adventures 114, 193
Armed Forces Radio Service 15, 27, 28–29, 86, 102, 171, 232
Armen, Kay 119, 123
Armour & Co. 53, 189
The Armour Hour 122
Arms, Russell 77
Armstrong Circle Theater 238
Armstrong of the SBI 153, 214, 230
The Armstrong Theater of Today 48, 93, 166
Army Camp Program 118
The Army Hour 9, 42, 43, 134, 232, 277
The Army-Navy Game 300
Army-Navy House Party 300
The Army Show 118
Arnaz, Desi 247
Arnold (bread) 87
Arnold, Jack 132
Arnold Grimm's Daughter 11, 167, 200, 230, 274, 310, 313
Around the World with Libby 16
Art Baker's Notebook 17, 18
Art Linkletter's House Party 270
The Art of Living 122

The Art Van Damme Quintet 281
The Arthur Godfrey Digest 111, 181
The Arthur Godfrey Roundtable 181
Arthur Godfrey's Talent Scouts 48, 49, 111, 112, 310
Arthur Godfrey Time 111, 181
Arthur Smith and the Crackerjacks 61
Arthur Tracy, the Street Singer 308
As the Twig Is Bent 86, 208, 244, 300
Ask-It Basket 57, 70, 264
Ask Me Another 269
Associated Press 28, 29
Associated Press Best Radio Award 114
Associated Press—One Hundred Years of News 178
Association of Radio News Analysts 156
At Home with Faye and Elliott 10, 247
At Home with Music 193
At the U.N. 103
Atlantic City Headliners Club 203
The Atlantic Family on Tour 264
Atlantic Spotlight 113, 117, 265
Attorney at Law 200
Atwater-Kent Auditions 188
The Atwater-Kent Hour 58, 188
The Atwater-Kent Summer Series 188
Auction Quiz 46, 80
Aunt Jemima 44, 193
Aunt Jenny 49
Aunt Jenny's Life Stories 262
Aunt Jenny's Real Life Stories 102, 104, 244, 246, 262, 263, 313
Aunt Mary 48, 187, 193, 227, 309, 312
Author, Author 165
Author Meets the Critics 20, 119, 266
Author's Playhouse 126, 193, 294
Author's Quiz 165
Autry, Gene 21, 48, 244
Avalon Time 117, 161, 310
The Avengers 13
Averback, Hyman J. 15–16
Avery, Gaylord James 16
Avon 87
Aylesworth, Merlin H. 190

B.A. Rolfe and His Lucky Strike Dance Orchestra 291
Babbe, Owen Miller 16
Babbitt, B.T. 37
Babbitts Best 37
Bab-O 37, 242
Baby Snooks 163, 239, 303, 313, 315
The Baby Snooks Show 7, 65, 152, 209, 234, 235
Bach, Alwyn E.W. 16–17
Bachelor's Children 114
Back Talk and Small Talk 98
Backstage Wife 8, 11, 31, 32, 37,

46, 51, 58, 59, 75, 153, 167, 177, 187, 193
Backus, Jim 302
Baer, Max 245
Bailey, Jack 8, 17, 89
Baker, Art 17–19
Baker, Donald 19, 86
Baker, Eugene Lock 19
Baker, John 128
Baker, Josephine 119
Baker, Phil 235
The Baker's Broadcast 117
Baker's chocolate 276
Baker's Theater of Stars 315
Baldinger, Brian 283
Baldwin, Bill 19–20
Balinger, Art 20
Ball, Donald 20
Ball, Lucille 199, 247
Bancroft, Griffin 258
Bandwagon Mysteries 56, 84
Banghart, Charles Kenneth 20–21
Bankhead, Tallulah 246
Bannon, Jim 21
Barbas, Samantha 221
Barber, Walter Lanier (Red) 21–23, 147, 189, 190
Barbree, Jay 202
Barett, Rona 96
Barker, Bob 89
Barnes, Patrick H. 23
Barnet, Charlie 13
Barnouw, Erik 136
Barrett, Ray 23
Barrie Craig, Confidential Investigator 200, 217, 219
Barry, Jack 23–24, 281
Barry, Norman 24
Barry & Enright Productions 93
Barry Cable TV 24
Barry Cameron 90
Barry Gray on Broadway 119
Barrymore, John 5
Bartell, Harry 25
Bartlett, Thomson 25–26, 72, 196
Barton, Eileen 315
Barton, Francis C. (Frank) 13, 26
The Barton Family 310
The Bartons 230, 310
Baruch, Andre 26–27, 89, 97
Baruch, Bernard 191
Baseball Hall of Fame 76, 107
Baseball Quiz 21
Baseball Round Table 170
Bate, Frederick B. 14, 27–28, 215
Battle of the Sexes 66, 117
Battle Stations 66
Baugh, Tom 263
Baukhage, Hilmar Robert 28–29, 103, 113
Baukhage Talking 28
Baxter, George 29
Bayer 37
Beat the Band 193, 227
Beat the Clock 216
The Beatrice Kay Show 149
The Beatrice Lillie Show 71

Beatty, Morgan 29–30, 101, 254, 255
Beaumont, Martin 166
Beck, Jackson 30–31
Beck, Max 30
Becker, Sanford George 31
Beemer, Bruce Bill (Brace) 31–32
Beggar's Bowl 252
Behind Prison Bars 118
Behind the Front Page 125, 133
Behind the Headlines 138
Behind the Mike 117, 180, 188, 303
Behind the Scenes 179
Behind the Screen Chatter 249
Behind the Story 184
Behlen, Ann Denton 42
Believe It or Not 30, 37, 86, 117, 120, 123, 188
Bell, Alexander Graham 10–11
Bell, Joseph 32
The Bell Telephone Hour 178, 313
Ben Bernie, the Old Maestro 46, 303, 306, 313
The Ben Bernie Show 89, 262
The Ben Bernie War Workers' Program 46
Benaderet, Bea 21, 157
Benchley, Robert 321
Bennett, Bern 32
Bennett, Constance 199
Bennett, Lois 37
Bennett, Sen. Phillip 225
Benny, Jack 102, 166, 316, 318
The Benny Goodman Show 63, 79, 140, 220
Benny Meroff's Revue 23
Benson, Courtney 32–33
Benton & Bowles 251
Bergen, Edgar 11, 21, 235
Bergman, Eddie 162
Berle, Milton 119, 235
Berlin, Irving 119
Bernie, Ben 318
Bernstein, Carl 226
Bert Lahr Show 234
The Best Bands in the Land 135
Best in Business Award 218
Best of All 20
Best Plays 62, 78, 310
Best Sellers 200
The Better Half 250
Betty and Bob 11, 43, 44, 69, 102, 132, 294, 313
Betty Clarke Sings 175
Betty Crocker 129
Betty Crocker Cooking School of the Air 129
The Betty Crocker Magazine of the Air 90
Between the Bookends 58
Beulah 123, 127, 212
The Beulah Show 150
Beyond Tomorrow 200
The Bickersons 140, 149, 193, 235
Big Band Remotes
The Big Break 248
Big City Serenade 95
The Big Guy 32, 62, 241

Big Moments in Sports 165
The Big Show 134, 306
Big Sister 10, 30, 32, 33, 57, 63, 65, 166, 200, 217, 228, 234, 280, 300
Big Six of the Air 306
The Big Story 58, 87, 125
Big Town 5, 32, 65, 86, 153, 212, 311
Bilbo, Sen. Theodore 224
Bill Clifford and His Orchestra 106
Bill Downs and the News 83
Bill Goodwin Show 113
Bill Gwinn Show 122
Bill Rogers and the News 244
Bill Stern Sports 108, 277
The Bill Stern Sports Review 277
The Billie Burke Show 78, 193
Billsbury, Rye 33
Billy and Betty 157
Billy Swift, Boy Detective 113
The Bing Crosby Chesterfield Show 54, 55
The Bing Crosby Show 167, 237, 315
Bingman, Frank 33–34
Bingman, Madelyn 33
Biography in Sound 20, 103, 122, 214
Birds Eye Open House 209, 235, 303
The Bishop and the Gargoyle 32
Bits of Hits 127
Bivens, William C. 34
The Black Castle 80
Black Legion 226
Black Night 82
Blackstone Plantation 117, 159, 217
Blackstone, the Magic Detective 159
Blaine, James Ralph 34
Blair, Frank 34–35
Blanc, Mel 162, 316
Blattner, Buddy 77
Blind Date 250, 306
Bliss, Edward, Jr. 206
Block, Martin 35–36
Blondie 113, 209, 228, 313
The Blubber Bergman Revue 235
Blue Coal Radio Revue 248
Blue Ribbon Music Time 306
Blue Ribbon Town 152, 212
Boake Carter 277
Boake Carter and the News 55
The Bob and Ray Show 66
Bob Burns Show 235, 274, 313
The Bob Crosby Show 48, 140, 176, 294, 306
Bob Elson on Board the Century 244, 246
The Bob Hawk Show 90, 170, 177, 276
Bob Hite and the News 139
The Bob Hope Show 15, 17, 69, 103, 156, 212, 234, 264, 277
Bob Stanton Sports 275
Bob Trout and Cedric Adams and the News 295

INDEX

Bobby Benson and the B-Bar-B Riders 26, 91, 148, 163, 186, 195, 262, 309
Bobby Benson's Adventures 56, 186, 195
The Bobby Doyle Show 172
Boehlert, Eric 174
Boettiger, Anna 246
Boland, Mary 43
Bold Venture 193
Bolton, Joseph Reeves, II 36
Bond, David Ford 36–37, 236
Book Talk 97
Boone, Forest E. 37–38, 252
Boone, Pat 181
Booth, Edwin 211
Borden Special Edition 58
Borden's Home News 133
Boston Blackie 90, 166, 217, 313
Boston Pops Orchestra 117, 122
The Botany Song Shop 303
A Bouquet for You 177, 292, 303
Bowles Advertising 100
Box Score Review 266
Box 13 55, 234
Boxing Bouts 277
Boyd, Malcolm 261
Bradley, Elene 39
Bradley, Milton 315
Bradley, Truman 38–39
Brandt, Lynn 39
Brandt, Melville S. 39
Brandt, Sam 39–40
Brave Tomorrow 87, 134
Breakfast at Sardi's 52, 186, 210, 229
The Breakfast Club 46, 51, 82, 95, 148, 164, 178, 188, 202, 213, 214, 242, 310
Breakfast in Hollywood 42, 52, 186, 210, 229, 230
Breakfast with Breneman 42, 229
Breakfast with Dorothy and Dick 92, 97, 161
Breakfast with the Fitzgeralds 97
Break the Bank 63, 163, 164, 216, 220, 266
Breckinridge, John C. 40
Breckinridge, Mary Marvin 40–42, 203
Breckinridge Public Affairs Center 42
Breckner, Gary C. 42, 96
Breen, Tom 67
Breezing Along 215, 234, 248
Brenda Curtis 98, 239
Brenthouse 7, 103, 141, 142
Bresee, Frank 18, 96
Brewster, Barbara 171
Brickert, Carlton 42–43
Bride and Groom 186, 210
Briggs, Donald P. 43–44
Bright Horizon 166, 177, 214, 217, 319
Bright Star 303
The Brighter Day 33, 233, 244, 277
A Brighter Tomorrow 125, 133
Bringing Up Father 186

Brinkley, David 104, 146, 298
Brinkley, John D. (Jack) 44
British News Service, Ltd. 138
Broadway Hits 52
Broadway Is My Beat 11, 15, 25, 79, 177, 280, 291, 308
Broadway Matinee 10, 21, 217
Broadway Talks Back 149
Brock, Harry 81
The Broken Wing 71
Brokenshire, Norman Ernest 44–46, 249
Brooks, Geraldine 207
Brooks, Ned 275
Brooks, Tim 284
Brothers, Dr. Joyce 300
Broun, Heywood 191, 321
Brown, Cecil 7, 46, 104, 203
Brown, Clarence J. Jr. 42
Brown, Himan 180
Brown, Jim 46
Brown, Robert Vahey 46–47
Brown, Theodore David 47
Browning, Charles 47–48
Browning, Douglas 48
Brownstone Theater 30
Brundage, Hugh E. 48
Bryan, George 48–49, 181
Bryan, Mary 66
Bryant, Geoffrey 49
Buchenwald 264
Buck, Louis 49
Buck Rogers in the 25th Century 71, 81, 102, 152, 244, 300, 311, 315
Bud and Joe Billings 176
Bud Barton 310
Buddy Weed Trio 123
Buell, Bruce Norton 49–50
Buffalo Broadcasting Corp. 193
Bughouse Rhythm 50, 69, 230
Bulldog Drummond 47, 197, 217, 239, 262
The Bullock's Show 193
Bunco Squad 308
Burdett, Winston Mansfield 7, 50, 83, 154, 167, 203
Burke, Merle 60
The Burl Ives Coffee Club 48
The Burl Ives Show 125, 285
Burnett, Carol 165
Burns, Bob 235, 243
Burns, George 213
Burns and Allen 303
The Burns and Allen Show 38, 65, 81, 85, 113, 137, 147, 165, 209, 212
Busse, Henry 162
The Busy Mr. Bingle 30
Buttermilk Kid 216
Buxton, Frank 103, 189, 197, 279
By Kathleen Norris 102, 214, 217, 311
By Popular Demand 30, 63
Byington, Spring 153
Byrd, Admiral Richard E. 93, 304, 307
Byron, Ward 50–51

Cabin B-13, 200, 303
Cable News Network 258
Café Istanbul 200
The Cal Tinney Show 293
Calamity Jane 212
California Caravan 25, 49, 187
California Melodies 98, 113, 169
Call for Music 140
Call the Police 151, 269
Callaghan, Jack 51
Callas, Maria 183
Calling All Cars 30, 175, 193
Calling All Detectives 227
Calling America 122, 224, 295
Calmer, Edgar (Ned) 51
Camay 22, 160
Camel Caravan 48, 113, 140, 211, 212, 220
Camel Comedy Caravan 212
Camel Screen Guild Players 250
Cameo Comedies 177
Campana Serenade 58
Campbell, H. Allen 31
Campbell, Kay 264
Campbell, Robert Maurice 51
Campbell Condensed News 232
Campbell Playhouse 58, 102, 137, 141, 239, 264, 311
The Campbell Room 58
Campbell Soup Co. 222, 265
Campbell Soup Orchestra 128
Campbell's Tomato Juice Program 147, 212
Can You Top This? 79, 80, 233, 276, 316
Canada Dry Ginger Ale Program 136
The Canada Dry Program 58
Canadian Broadcasting Company 33
Candid Microphone 105, 120, 141, 239, 254
Candid Woman 103
Candy Matson 179
Canham, Edwin D. 52
Canham Views the News 52
Cannon, John 52
Cantor, Eddie 93, 220, 235, 307, 317
Capitol Cloakroom 259
Capone, Al 254
Captain Flagg and Sergeant Quirt 266
Captain Midnight 11, 12, 114, 193, 196, 230
Caravan 147
Caravan Theatre 39
The Career of Alice Blair 29, 159
Carefree Carnival 57
Carey, Harry 238
Carl Hohengarten's Orchestra 26
Carlin, Phillips 52–53, 147
Carnation Co. 228
Carnation Contented Hour 200, 227, 306
Carnation Family Party 280, 291
Carnegie, Dale 53
Carnegie Hall 122
Carney, Art 150

INDEX

Carney, Don 23, 36, 53–54
Carnival of Music 60
Carnival with Bernie West 266
Carol Kennedy's Romance 163
Carolina Calling 60, 61
Carolina Hayride 60, 61
Caroline's Golden Store 44, 177
Carpenter, Kenneth L. 13, 54–55, 96, 123, 316
Carroll, Bob 215
Carson, Johnny 213, 265
Carson Robison Trio 176
Carson Robison's Buckaroos 66
Carstensen, Vern 55
Carter, Gaylord 131
Carter, Harold Thomas Henry (Boake) 55–56
Carter Family 61
The Carters of Elm Street 11
Caruso, Carl 56–57
The Cascade of Stars 215
Case, Nelson 57, 215
The Casebook of Gregory Hood 25, 30, 170, 187
The Cases of Mr. Ace 153
Casey, Crime Photographer 30, 71, 139, 181, 217, 239
Cass Daley Show 230
Castro, Fidel 161
Catch Me If You Can 48
Cathy and Elliott Lewis on Stage 308
Cavalcade of America 5, 25, 32, 33, 49, 63, 77, 87, 114, 125, 133, 151, 154, 170, 177, 182, 187, 251, 270, 274, 277, 300, 311, 313
Cavalcade of Music 120
CBS D-Day Coverage 164
CBS Is There 74, 98, 180
CBS Morning News 202, 255, 256
CBS Morning News Roundup 143, 148
CBS News 46, 50, 59, 93, 100, 123, 129, 135, 148, 154, 158, 168
CBS News on the Hour 282, 294
CBS Presents Red Barber 21, 48
CBS Radio Mystery Theater 30, 32, 33, 93, 94, 120, 121, 175, 180, 187, 200, 217, 294, 313
CBS Radio Workshop 25, 80, 101, 124, 139, 152, 213, 228, 285, 303, 308
The CBS Saturday News 7
CBS Sportscasts 283
CBS Views the Press 141
CBS Weekly News Review 48
CBS World News Roundup 50, 51, 61, 83, 87, 88, 125, 135, 143, 154, 158, 172, 180, 202, 203, 259, 264, 266, 271, 282, 294, 295, 302
Cecil Brown and the News 46
Cedric Foster News and Commentary 101
Ceiling Unlimited 187
Cellini, Joseph 121
Central City 49
Central Piedmont Community College 34

Cesar Saerchinger Interviews 252
Challenge of the Yukon 31, 32, 102, 139, 193, 208, 220
The Chamber Music Society of Lower Basin Street 50, 58, 70, 122, 185
Chambers, Ernest 85
Champion Roll Call 120
Chance of a Lifetime 163, 239, 315
Chancellor, John 35
Chandu the Magician 72, 140, 160, 199, 313
Chaney, Lon 161
Changing Times 308
Chaplain Jim 13, 132, 176
Chapman, Bruce 195
Chappell, Ernest (Chappie) 58, 125, 131, 204
Charis foundation garments 222
Charles Collingwood and the News 61
Charles F. McCarthy and the News 185
Charlie and Jessie 57
Charlie Chan 217
Charlie Lung 109
The Charlie Ruggles Show 181
Charlie Stark Music Shop 276
Charlie Wild, Private Detective 244
The Charlotte Greenwood Show 25, 212
The Chase 62, 132, 200
Chase, Ilka 199
Chase and Sanborn 85
The Chase and Sanborn Hour 7, 103, 153, 212, 306, 307
The Checkerboard Fun Fest 49
Cherington, Wood, and Roper 248
Chesterfield Dance Show 248
Chesterfield Presents 248
Chesterfield Quarter Hour 165
Chesterfield Quarter-Hour 239
Chesterfield Supper Club 9, 35, 50, 81, 117, 234
Chesterfield Time 35, 81, 153
Chesterfields 252
Chet Huntley and the News 145
Chevrolet Program 128
Chevrolet Spotlights the News 148, 172, 295
The Chez Show 305, 306
Chiang Kai-shek 155
The Chicago Civic Opera 70
Chicago Defender 82
Chicago Opera Co. 18
Chicago Rail Fair 26
Chicago Theater of the Air 140, 151, 193, 200, 294, 311
Chick Carter, Boy Detective 63, 120, 230
Chicken Every Sunday 303
Chickie 269
The Children's Hour 79, 81, 89, 123
Children's stories in song 176
Childs, Marquis 125
The Chilquot Club Eskimos 52

Chips Davis, Commando 63
Chodorov, Stephen 243
The Choice of a Lifetime 239
The Choraliers 165
The Chordettes 181
Christian Science Monitor 19, 52, 125, 126
Christian Science Views 52
A Christmas Carol 320
Christy, Ken 230
The Chrysler Air Show 163
Cimarron Tavern 139
Cincinnati Drama School 33
Cinderella Incorporated 78, 181
The Cinnamon Bear 137, 209
The Circle 103
Circus Days 117
The Cisco Kid 30, 33, 73, 182, 193
Cities Service Band of America 37
Cities Service Concert 236, 291
Cities Service Oil Co. 37
The Cities Service Orchestra 188
The City 114
City Desk 43, 49
City Hospital 52, 217, 251
Claghorn, Senator Beauregard 77
Claney, Howard 58–59, 215
Clara, Lu and Em 80, 122, 163, 200, 250
Clark, Dane 87
Clark, Harry 59
Clarke, Mae 66
Classical Music for People Who Hate Classical Music 122
Claude Thornhill and His Orchestra 165
Claudia and David 166, 276
Clear All Wires 71
The Clem McCarthy Sports Show 185
Cliché Club 120, 160
Cliff Edwards Show 13
Cloak and Dagger 30, 294, 310
The Clock 165
Close, Upton 59–60
Close-Ups of the News 59
Cloud, Stanley 40, 41, 56, 116, 158, 173, 179, 203, 255, 257, 261, 264, 268, 273, 302
Club Fifteen 264
Club Good Cheer 235
Club Matinee 82, 164
Club 1300 90
The Clyde Beatty Show 30, 228, 291
Coast to Coast on a Bus 13, 70, 79
Cobb, Buff 306
Cobb, David 49
Cobwebs and Nuts 162
Coca-Cola Hour 67
The Coke Club 199, 248
Cole, Frederick B. 60
Cole, Grady 60–61
Colgate 195
Colgate House Party 128
Colgate-Palmolive Co. 163
Colgate-Palmolive-Peet 208, 224
Colgate Sports Newsreel 108, 277

INDEX

Collector's Item 100, 112
College Prom 37
The Collier Hour 5, 32, 37, 158, 165, 234, 244, 294
Collier Radio Hour 6, 244
Collier's Radio Review 165
Collingwood, Charles Cummings 61–62, 135, 154, 156, 173, 179, 203, 264
Collins, Fred 62
Collins, Joseph Martin (Ted) 62–63
Collins, Jud 49
Collins, Ray 235
Collyer, Clayton (Bud) 31, 63–64, 72, 196
Colonel Humphrey Flack 86
Columbia Broadcasting System 21
The Columbia Ensemble 292
Columbia Phonograph Broadcasting System 147, 249, 319
Columbia Phonograph Co. 63
Columbia Pictures 21
Columbia Presents Corwin 25, 30, 77, 79, 102, 117, 168, 180, 187, 200, 250, 266, 295
Columbia Symphony Orchestra, New York 19
Columbia Workshop 19, 31, 43, 59, 102, 163, 168, 181, 197, 200, 220, 244, 248, 285, 292, 295, 311
Combs, George Hamilton, Jr. 64
Come On, Let's Swing 156
Come on In ... It's Art Linkletter's House Party 270
Comedy of Errors 17, 227
Command Performance 9, 54, 65, 81, 182, 187, 215, 303, 315
Command Performance U.S.A. 306
Communism—U.S. Brand 48
Community Chest 98
The Community Sing 81
Concert Time 122
Confession 193, 305
Confidentially Yours 122, 310
Connee Boswell Presents 185
Conner, Nadine 66
Conoco Presents 158
Conover, Hugh 65
Conrad, William 281
The Conrad Nagel Show 206
Considine, Robert Bernard 65, 172
Consolidated Press Association 28
Constance Bennett Calls on You 170
Consumer Quiz 300
Conte, John 65–66
Conti Castille Show 86, 115
Continental Celebrity Club 74
Conway, Marianne 286
Cook, Lou 66
Coolidge, Calvin 44, 190, 243
Cooper, Edwin 66
Copeland, Joanne 315

Copenhagen Royal Theatre 39
Corbet, Lois 316
Cork, Barbara 21
Cornell, John 66
Cornell, Katherine 246, 321
Coronet Quick Quiz 148
Coronet Storyteller 193, 228
Correll, Charles 130
Corwin, Norman 119, 168
Cosmo Tune Time 159
Costello, John Patrick Michael Joseph (Jack) 66–67
Cott, Ted 67–68
The Coty Playgirl 244
Coughlin, Father Charles 311
Could Be 181
Council for Democracy 282
Count Basie and His Orchestra 213
The Count of Monte Cristo 15, 215, 229, 321
Counter Intelligence Corps 154
Countess Olga Medlolago Albani 136
Country Club of the Air 81
Country Disc Jockey Hall of Fame 73, 299
Country Music Hall of Fame 132, 299
Country Time lemonade 141
County Fair 17, 79, 90, 156, 303
The Couple Next Door 11, 44, 101, 124, 285
Court of Human Relations 81, 215
The Court of Missing Heirs 77, 102
Courtney, Alan 68
Courtney Record Carnival 68
Cousin Willie 193, 209, 294, 306
Coward, Noel 79
Cox, Wally 77
Craig, Gordon A. 267
Cravens, Kathryn C. 68–69
Crawford, Joan 223
Cream of Wheat 6
Creeps By Night 30
The Cresta Blanca Carnival of Music 106
The Cresta Blanca Hollywood Players 33
Crime and Peter Chambers 62, 120, 299
Crime Cases of Warden Lawes 125
Crime Classics 15, 25, 170, 228, 250, 266
Crime Doctor 57, 152, 187, 215, 239
Crime Does Not Pay 316
Crime Fighters 164
The Crime Files of Flamond 72, 305
Crime Is My Pastime 215
A Crime Letter from Dan Dodge 148
Crime on the Waterfront 281, 305
Criminal Case Histories 118
Criminal Casebook 34, 57, 217
Crisco 233, 263
Crisco Radio Newspaper 143, 149, 164

Crisis in War Town 98
Cronkite, Walter 62, 83, 88, 167, 261, 262, 264, 298
Crooked Square 217
Crook's Cruise 114
Croom-Johnson, Austin Herbert 159
Crosby, Bing 35, 55, 93, 123, 211, 223, 304, 318
Crosby, Cathy Lee 69
Crosby, John 96, 174, 246
Crosby, Louis 69
Cross, Milton John 13, 69–70, 79, 140
Crossword Quiz 120
Crothers, Sherman (Scatman) 162
The Croupier 72
Crow, Phil 176
Crowley, Matthew 70–71
Cubberly, Dan S. 71
Cugat, Xavier 13, 220
Cugat Rhumba Revue 220
The Cukoo Hour 316
Cullen, William Lawrence 71, 196, 199, 208, 281
Culver, Howard 40, 72
Cummings, Robert 49
Cunningham, Bob 72
The Curley Bradley Show 177
Curley Bradley, the Singing Marshall 114
Current Events 154
The Curt Massey-Martha Tilton Show 177
The Curt Massey Show 127, 177
Curtain Time 114, 140, 305
Curtis, Don 76
Cut 57
Cutrer, Thomas Clinton (T. Tommy) 72–73

Daddy and Rollo 186
Dahlstead, Dresser 73–74
Daily Dilemmas 23
Dale Jones and Company 308
Dalhart, Vernon 176
Daly, John Charles 13, 51, 87, 146, 297
Daly, John Charles, Jr. 74–75
Damon Runyon Fund for Cancer Research 319
The Damon Runyon Theater 55, 79, 234
Damrosch, Walter 132
Damrosch School of Musical Arts 70
Dan Harding's Wife 24, 120
Dance Barn 167
Dance Hour 317
D'Angelo, Carlo 152
Danger Is My Business 269
Dangerous Assignment 281
Dangerously Yours 30
Daniels, Bebe 24
Daniels, Paul 30
Danny and August 30
The Danny Kaye Show 77, 152, 209, 212

The Danny O'Neal Show 292
The Danny Thomas Show 193
Darlan, Jean 179
Darrow, Mike 208
Darts for Dough 11, 114
A Date with Duchin 305
A Date with Judy 25, 113, 170, 187, 193, 212
Dave Garroway Show 57, 82, 127, 230
David, Don 75
David Amity 32
David Harding, Counterspy 107, 127, 149, 167, 175, 237, 244, 266
David Harum 37, 43, 127, 186, 315
David Rose Show 215
David Schoenbrun and the News 255
Davis, Elmer 46, 156, 286
Davis, Janet 181
Dawson, Stuart 75–76
Day, Dennis 316
Day, Doris 127
A Day in the Life of Dennis Day 26, 209, 274, 306
D-Day, Omaha Beach 179
Dealer in Dreams 114
Dean, Dizzy 76–77
Dean, Jay Hanna 76–77
Deane, Martha 183
Dear Abby 25
Dear John 8, 251
Dear Mom 46, 193, 196
Death Valley Days 30, 49, 73, 129, 136, 163
Death Valley Sheriff 310
December Bride 150, 234
Defense Attorney 11, 25, 72
The Defense Rests 72
DeHaven, Gloria 135
Deis, Carol 243
Delmar, Kenneth H. 49, 77
DeLong, Tom 197
DeMille, Cecil B. 269
Dennis King 162
Denton, Robert 78
Dentyne 87
Derby's Peter Pan peanut butter 306
DeRose and Breen 175
Design for Listening 127
Destiny's Trails 186
Detect and Collect 300
Detroit Civic Symphony 128
Devine, Andy 231
Dewey, Thomas E. 37, 85, 156
Dial Dave Garroway 127, 230
Dial Douglas 81
The Diary of Fate 187
Dick Daring, a Boy of Today 43
Dick Daring's Adventures 43
Dick Dunham and the News 86
The Dick Haymes Show 180
Dick Kuhn and His Orchestra 309
Dick Tracy 71, 107, 121, 134
Dillinger, John 231
Dimension X 30, 62, 71, 78, 120, 180, 187, 200, 217, 219, 237, 310

The Dinah Shore Show 17, 38, 140, 209, 235, 303
Disney, Walt 92
Dixie Circus 52
Dixie Cups 77
The Dixieland Music Shop 48
Dixieland Song Shop 140
Dixon, Robert R. 78
Dixon, Tom 78–79
Dizzy Dean 76
Dizzy Dean Baseball, Inc. 77
Dizzy Dean Museum 77
The Dizzy Dean Show 200
Do You Know the Answer? 68
Do You Want to Be an Actor? 103
Dobkin, Lawrence S. 79
Doc Barclay's Daughters 30
Doc, Duke and the Colonel 126
Dr. Christian 25, 26, 109, 110, 182, 192
The Doctor Fights 106, 306
Dr. Gino's Musicale 122
Dr. I.Q. 109
Dr. I.Q. Jr. 14
Dr. I.Q. the Mental Banker 14, 26, 84, 140, 230
Dr. Kildare 152
Dr. Lyon's tooth powder 8, 37
Dr. Norman Vincent Peale 122
Dr. Paul 228
Dr. Sixgun 62, 120, 310
Dr. Standish, Medical Examiner 303
Dr. Wynne's Food Forum 214
Doctors Today 82, 188
Dollar a Minute 113
Dollars for Breakfast 300
The Don Ameche Show 38, 193
The Don Ameche Variety Show 212, 313
Don Ameche's Real Life Stories 217
Don Carney's Dog Chats 53
Don Dowd 82
Don Goddard and the News 111
Don Hollenbeck and the News 141
Don Irwin's Orchestra 24
Don Lee Network 17
Don Martin School of Broadcasting 308
Don Winslow of the Navy 177, 310
Donald, Peter 79–80
Donald Duck cartoons 17
Donaldson, Daniel Jones 80
The Donna Reed Show 170
Don't Forget 70
Don't You Believe It 235
Doorway to Life 187
The Doris Day Show 150, 250, 315
Dorothy Dix on the Air 238
The Dorothy Gordon Show 197
Dorothy Kilgallen's Diary 135
Dorothy Lamour Show 153
Dorothy Thompson Commentary 289
Dorsey, Jimmey 13
Dorsey, Tommy 13
Dot and Will 104, 105
Double or Nothing 60, 69, 128, 140, 142, 163, 305

The Doug Browning Show 48
Dough Re Mi 122
Douglas, Don 80
Douglas, Gilbert 108
Douglas, Hugh 80
Douglas, Paul Fleischer 80–82
Douglas Edwards and the News 87
Douglas of the World 320
Dowd, Donald M. 82
Down Lover's Lane 208
Downey, Morton 276
Downs, Hugh Malcolm 35, 82–83
Downs, William R. Jr. 83–84, 203
Doyle, James 84
Doyle, Mirian 312
Dragnet 7, 8, 25, 94, 109, 170, 187, 192, 193, 228
Drake, Galen 84–85
Drake, Ronald 85
A Dream Comes True 88
Dream Time 289
Dreamboat 150, 172
Dreams of Long Ago 63, 166, 176
Dreft 233
Dreft Star Playhouse 193, 218, 294
Dreier, Alex 85–86
Dreier Comments 85
The Drene Show 38, 235
Drew Pearson 224
Drew Pearson Comments 224
Duchin, Eddie 13
Dudley, Bernard 19, 86
Dudley, Richard Allen 86
Duffy's Tavern 9, 17, 159, 163, 193, 215, 234, 250, 280, 306, 309
Duke of Windsor 297
Duke University Glee Club 299
Dulles, John Foster 261
Dunbar, Russ 86
Duncan Sisters 252
Dunham, Dick 86
Dunne, Frank 86
Dunne, Steve 89
Dunning, John 96, 131, 147, 154, 155, 156, 173, 189, 197, 209–210, 228, 278, 287–288, 316, 317, 318
Dunninger 245
Dunninger Show 237
Dunninger, the Mentalist 167, 175, 237
Dupont Zerone Jesters 81
Durante, Jimmy 321
Duz 64, 233

Eagleton, Thomas 136
Earl Godwin and the News 112
Earl Wilson's Broadway Column 81
Early, Steve 28
The Early Bookworm 321
Early Morning Roundup 178
Earn Your Vacation 150, 280
East of Cairo 32, 187
Eastman, Carl 87
Easton, John 87
Easy Aces 13, 30, 37, 38, 81, 177, 239

INDEX 340

Easy Does It 314
Easy Money 281
Echoes of Cairo 32, 187
Ed East and Polly 48
Ed Fleming and the News 99
Ed Herlihy and the News 134
The Ed Sullivan Show 57
Ed Thorgersen Sports Commentary 291
Ed Wynn Show 233
Ed Wynn, the Fire Chief 186, 188, 319
The Eddie Albert Show 162
The Eddie Bracken Show 21, 185, 266, 305, 306
Eddie Cantor Camel Caravan 164
Eddie Cantor Pabst Blue Ribbon Show 164, 187
The Eddie Cantor Show 25, 164, 209, 220, 234, 303, 306
The Eddie Duchin Show 305
Eddy, Nelson 102
The Edgar Bergen and Charlie McCarthy Show 7, 19, 21, 54, 57, 85, 113, 153, 182, 212, 228
The Edgar Bergen Hour 137
The Edward Everett Horton Show 294
Edward McHugh 88
Edward P. Morgan and the News 196
Edward R. Murrow and the News 58, 78, 93, 154, 158, 202, 255, 256, 264
Edward Tomlinson News and Comments 293
Edwards, Douglas 51, 62, 74, 87–88, 100, 105, 146, 173, 272, 282, 283, 298
Edwards, Gus 317
Edwards, Ralph Livingstone 18, 88–90, 147, 251, 288, 299
Edwin C. Hill Commentary 138
Edwin Canham Sports 52
Eels, George 318
E.I. Dupont 87, 125, 270
Eigen, Jack 215
Eileen Barton Show 164
Einstein, Albert 246
Eisenhower, Dwight D. 37, 85, 202, 279, 286
Eisenhower Medical Center 86
El Lobo Rides Again 170
El Producto 87
Eleanor and Anna Roosevelt 211, 244, 246
Eleanor and Elliott Roosevelt 245, 247
Eleanor Roosevelt 117, 245
The Electric Hour 114
Elgin Adventurer's Club 108
The Elgin Football Revue 291
Ellen Randolph 151, 187
Ellery Queen 211
Elliot, Win 90
Elliott, Bob 60
Elliott, Lawrence K. 90–91
Elliott Roosevelt Commentary 247
Ellis, Rita 84

Elmer Davis 75
Elmer Davis and the News 75
Elmo Roper 248
Elsa Maxwell's Party Line 169, 182, 188
Elson, Bob 190
Emerick, Robert E. 91
Emerson, Faye 127, 247
Emerson radios 247
Emil Vandis and His Orchestra 167
Emily Post 229
Emily Post Institute 230
Emphasis 6
Encore 20
Encore Theater 114
Encores from the Bell Telephone Hour 178
Endorsed by Dorsey 250
Energine 37
Engle, Holland E. 91–92
Enna Jettick Melodies 16
Eno Crime Club 244
Enright, Dan 24
Epstein, Sam and Beryo 122
E.R. Squibb Co. 243
The E.R. Squibb Program 188
Eric Sevareid and the News 259
Ernie Pyle Memorial Award 168
Escape 25, 79, 114, 123, 186, 228, 234, 308
Escape with Me 214, 219
The Esso Marketer 300
Esso News 13
The Eternal Light 14, 78, 79, 108, 277, 299
Ethel and Albert 13, 60, 125, 137, 175, 237, 265, 313, 322
The Ethel Merman Show 217
Ethel Park Richardson 176
European News Roundup 295, 296
Evangeline Adams 248
Evans, Bergen 238
Evans, Franklyn 92
Evans, Richard L. 92
The Eve Young Show 219
An Evening with Romberg 106
Events and Trends of the Week 59
The Eveready Hour 157, 234, 242
Everett, Ethel 214
Everly Brothers 170
Eversharp Penman 208
Everybody Wins 239
Everybody's Music 208
Everyman's Theater 7
Everything for the Boys 180
Everything Goes 228
Ex-Lax 240
Expectant Father 309
Exploring the Unknown 26, 148
Eyes Aloft 7, 313

The Fabulous Dr. Tweedy 58, 137, 303
Faces in the Window 214
Fact or Fiction 305
Fadiman, Clifton 121
Fairey, Wendy 116
The Falcon 32, 66, 86, 134, 149, 241, 294

Falkenburg, Eugenia Lincoln (Jinx) 92–93, 97, 191, 199
Falstaff's Fables 234, 298
Family Skeleton 177, 193
Family Theater 19, 169, 182, 187, 193, 211, 215
Famous Fortunes 129
Famous Jury Trials 87, 117, 151, 163, 167, 195
Fang, Irving E. 56, 60, 101, 126, 138, 174, 268, 301, 318
Fantasies from Lights Out 120
Faraway Hill 39
Farrell, Glenda 207
Farren, Jack 93
Farren, William Anthony 93
Farrington, Fielden 93–94
Fashions in Rations 78
Fates, Gil 75, 161
The Fat Man 148, 165, 175
Father Knows Best 100, 193, 227, 313
Faultless Starch Time 95
Faye, Alice 235
The FBI in Peace and War 26, 30, 43, 213, 277, 285
FBI Washington 13
Feature Page 179
Feature Story 295
Federal Communications Commission 14
The Felony Squad 8
Feminine Fancies 97
Fenneman, George 94–95, 271
Ferguson, Franklyn 95
Ferraday, Lisa 135
Ferrer, Jose 246
Fibber McGee and Molly 182, 192, 209, 211, 305, 313, 314
Fidler, James M. 95–96, 115, 142, 222
Field, Norman 66
Fields, W.C. 318
Field's Minstrels 196
Fifteen Minutes with Bing Crosby 303
Finders Keepers 266
Fireside Chats 245, 297
Fireside Recitals 188
First Anniversary of the United Nations 180
The First Hundred Years 151
The First Line 46
First Love 206
The First National Hour 165
The First Nighter 10, 19, 33, 42, 43, 79, 80, 122, 132, 156, 188, 193, 200, 227, 230, 294
The First Piano Quartet 122
First Use of the Famous NBC Chimes 53
Fish Pond 90, 185, 254
Fisher, George 306
The Fishing and Hunting Club of the Air 175, 319
Fiske, Minnie Maddern 153
The Fitch Bandwagon 50, 66, 73, 100, 103, 127, 156, 208, 212, 234, 235

Fitzgerald, Ed 92, 96–98
Fitzgerald, Ed and Pegeen 92, 191
Fitzgerald, F. Scott 115
Fitzgerald, Margaret Worrall (Pegeen) 92, 98
The Fitzgeralds 92, 97, 98
Fitzmaurice, Michael T. 98–99
Five Minute Mysteries 30, 98
Five Star Theater 176
Flannery, Harry W. 272
Flash Gordon 234
Flashgun Casey 71
Fleet Motion Picture Office 130
Fleetwood, Harry 99
The Fleischmann Hour 234, 281
The Fleischmann Yeast Hour 164, 189
Fleming, Art 104, 219
Fleming, Edward J. 99–100
Fleming, James F. 99, 100
Flight with Music 266
Florida Calling 196
Floyd Gibbons 108
Floyd Gibbons and the News 108
Floyd Mack and the News 178
Fluffo 22
The Flying Red Horse Tavern 164
Flywheel, Shyster & Flywheel 209
The Fog Lifts 294
Foley, Red 170
Fontanne, Lynn 235
Foote, Cone & Belding 76, 128
For Men Only 300
For the Record 108
For Your Approval 104
Forbes, Donald Telfer 100
Ford, Benjamin "Whitey" 169
Ford, Gerald R. 124, 275
Ford, Henry 242
Ford Bond Productions 37
Ford C. Frick Award 107, 139
Ford Show 123
The Ford Summer Theater 93
The Ford Sunday Evening Hour 38
Ford Theater 57, 200, 217, 234, 294
Forecast 179, 292
Forest Lawn Cemetery, Los Angeles 18
Forever Ernest 152
The Forgotten Frontier 40
Forman, Bill 100–101
Forster, Roger 101
Fort Laramie 25, 71, 79, 228
Forty-Five Minutes in Hollywood 220
The Forty Million 241
Foss, Joseph 101
Foster, Cedric W. 101–102
Foster, Phil 119
Foster, Stuart 84
Four Star News 28, 189, 277
Four Star Playhouse 162, 209
Fox Movietone 52, 60, 96, 289, 292
Foy, Fred 102
Framer, Walt 71, 145, 224
Francis, Arlene 45, 83, 235

Franco-American 265
Frank, Carl 102
Frank, Reuven 146
Frank Crummit and Julia Sanderson Show 117, 159
The Frank Fontaine Show 303
The Frank Luther Show 176
The Frank Morgan Show 65, 209, 313
Frank Sinatra in Person 113
The Frank Sinatra Show 38, 170, 193, 315
The Frankie Lane Show 193
Fraser, John Gordon (Jack) 102–103
Fray and Braggiotti 114
Frazer, John 103
The Fred Allen Show 77, 79, 89, 90, 111, 129, 147, 234, 239, 250, 303, 306, 316
Fred Vandevanter and the News 316
Fred Waring Glee Club 123
The Fred Waring Show 34, 65, 81, 164, 248
Frederick, Pauline 103–104
Fredericks, Dirk 104
Fredericks, Don 104
Freedom House 281
Freedom USA 137, 306
Freeman, Florence 88, 104–105
Frick, Ford 185
Friday Is a Big Day 219
Friday Night Follies 73
Friday Night Frolics 299
Friendly, Fred W. 205
Friends of Old Time Radio 13, 99
Friendship Town 53, 176
The Frigidaire Frolics 177
From Hollywood Today 109
Frommer beer 195
Front and Center 109, 153
Front Page Farrell 90, 99, 123, 313
Front Page Parade 117
Frontier Gentleman 25, 71, 79, 150, 228, 305
Frontier Nursing Service (FNS) 40, 42
Frontier Town 101
Frontiers of Science 144
Fu Manchu 74
Fun in Swing 234
Fun in Swing Time 265
Fun with Dunne 292
Funny Side Up 77, 124, 220
Funt, Allen 105, 112, 165, 246
Furlough Fun 156, 274
The Future of Cancer Research 170

Gabriel Heatter Comments 125
Gabriel Heatter News and Comment 133
Gabriel Heatter Show 125
Galbraith, John 106
The Galen Drake Show 84, 292
The Gallant Heart 72, 187, 230
Gallop, Frank 106, 276
Gambling, John A. 241

Game of the Day 76, 165
Game of the Week 76
Gandhi, Mahatma 155
Gangbusters 16, 32, 87, 101, 102, 106, 107, 120, 124, 149, 166, 180, 217, 258, 276, 313
Garagiola, Joseph Henry 107, 145
Garden, Mary 190
Garden of Tomorrow 208
Gardiner, Donald 107–108
Gardner, Hy 172
Garroway, Dave 35, 127, 214, 300
The Garry Moore Show 164, 228
Garry Moore Variety Show 250
Gary, Arthur 108
Gaslight Gaieties 309
Gates, Gary Paul 56, 88, 146, 256, 257, 261, 272, 282, 298
Gateway to Hollywood 42, 212
Gaulle, Charles de 256
The Gay Mrs. Featherstone 193
The Gay Nineties Revue 163, 309
G.E. Circle 151, 270
Geddes, Esther 192
Gene Autry's Melody Ranch 69, 123, 177, 182, 192, 212, 309
General Electric 214, 270
The General Electric Program 108
The General Electric Show 54, 55
The General Electric Theater 54
General Foods Corp. 51, 56, 169, 277
The General Mills Hour 218
General Mills, Inc. 129, 228, 280
General Motors 87, 125, 270, 285
General Motors Concerts 70, 122, 158, 208, 270
Geneva Research Center 116
Gentleman Adventurer 104
George, Sen. Walter 224
The George Burns and Gracie Allen Show 192, 193, 235, 306, 317
George D. Hay Foundation 132
George D. Hay Music Hall of Fame Theater 132
George Foster Peabody Broadcasting Award 23, 46, 62, 74, 88, 104, 173, 205, 218, 294
George IV 297
George Hamilton Combs News and Commentary 64
George Heller Gold Lifetime Membership Card Award 31
George Hicks and the News 136
The George Jessel Show 50, 300
George Jessel's Jamboree 58
The George O'Hanlon Show 234, 250
George Olsen and His Orchestra 219
George Putnam and the News 232
George VI 27
Gervasi, Frank 203
Get Rich Quick 34, 216
Get That Story 179
Get Together 216
G.I. Journal 274
Gibbons, Edward 108

INDEX

Gibbons, Floyd 287, 288
Gibbons, Jim 28
Gibbons, Raphael Floyd Phillips 108–109
Gibney, Hal 94, 96
Gibney, Harold T. 109
The Gibson Family 5, 145, 187, 244, 307
The Gibsons 187
The Gillette Community Sing 81
Gilmore, Art 109–111, 131, 203, 307
The Ginny Simms Show 114, 315
Girl Alone 43, 46, 120, 177, 310
Give and Take 46, 163
Glade, Earl J. Jr. 111
Glamour Manor 17, 187, 192, 215, 218, 315
Gleason, Jackie 34, 150, 172, 216
Glenn, John 264
The Glenn Miller Orchestra 213
The Glenn Miller Show 81
The Globe Theater 307
The Gloom Chasers 68, 239
Go for the House 48, 163
Go Get It 36
Goddard, Don 74, 111, 284
Godfrey, Arthur Morton 34, 45, 91, 111–112, 161, 181, 183, 310, 319
God's Country 48, 285
Godwin, Earl 112–113
Goebbels, Joseph 311
The Gold and Silver Minstrels 47, 319
Gold Is Where You Find It 100
The Goldbergs 63, 100, 123, 130, 131, 153, 163, 195, 239, 241, 244
Golden Blossom Revue 307
Golden Days of Radio 19, 109
Golden Mike Award 114
Golden Theater Group 123
Goldenrod Revue 303
Golder, Harry 113
Good, Pamela 51
Good Diction Award 17
Good News 163
Good News of 1938/1939/1940 145, 234
Good News of 1941 315
Goodman, Benny 13, 220
Goodman Repertory Co. 43
Goodrich, B.F. 40
The Goodrich Silvertown Orchestra 52, 291
Goodrich Sports Review 278
Goodson-Todman Productions 93
The Goodwill Hour 102, 319
"Goofy" voiceovers 17
Gordon, Bert 235
Gordon, Don 114
Gordon, Joyce 87
Gordon, Ruth 82
Gordon MacRae Show 262
Gore, Al, Jr. 73
Goren, Charles 85
Gosden, Freeman 130
The Gospel Singer 88

Goss, Frank B. 114
Gould, Jack 146
Goulding, Ray 60
Gowdy, Curt 77
Grace, Roger M. 233
Gracie Fields Show 113, 123
Gracie Fields Victory Show 113
Grady Cole and the Johnson Family 60
Grady Cole Center 61
Grady Cole Show 60, 61
Graham, Ethel Briggs 114
Graham, Frank 114–115
Graham, Fred 282
Graham, Sheilah 115–116, 142, 221
Grainger, Percy 128
Gramps 186
Grams, Martin, Jr. 258
Granby's Green Acres 170
Grand Central Station 10, 29, 30, 117, 123, 125, 134, 163, 166, 193, 200, 217, 239
Grand Hotel 10, 43, 227, 294
Grand Marquee 10, 281
Grand Ole Opry 49, 72, 73, 131, 169, 281, 299
Grand Slam 311
Grandin, Thomas B. 41, 116–117, 203
Grandma Travels 120
Grandstand Thrills 312
Grant, Lee 81
Grant, Peter 117
Grant, Taylor 117–118
Grant Advertising, Inc. 14
The Grape Nuts Program 85
Grapevine Rancho 266
Graser, Earl 32
Grauer, Ben 87, 106, 246, 261
Grauer, Bennett 117–118, 136
Grauman, Sid 95
Gray, Barry 118–119, 318
The Great Adventure 302
The Great American Tourist 304
The Great Atlantic & Pacific Tea Co. (A&P) 270
The Great Day 163
Great Day for Music 178
Great Decisions 7
The Great Gildersleeve 7, 21, 54, 84, 87, 137, 192, 239, 274, 280, 305, 313
The Great Gunns 11, 193, 200
Great Moments in History 163
Great Novels 201
Great Plays 201
The Great Talent Hunt 47
The Greatest of These 313
Greatest Sports Thrills 165
The Greatest Story Ever Told 199, 208, 310, 319
Green, Harry 234
Green, Maury 233
The Green Hornet 87, 93, 94, 102, 127, 128, 139, 185, 208, 219, 229, 305, 320
The Green Lama 25, 79, 291
The Green Valley Line 219

Green Valley, U.S.A. 208, 217, 313
Greene, Lorne 119–120
Greenway, Isabella Selmes 41
Griffis, William 120
Griffith, Andrew Samuel 120
Griffith, Andy 119
Griffith, Lester Lee 120–121
Grimes, Tammy 121
Grodin, Charles 214
The Grouch Club 17, 171
The Grummits 79
Guedel, John 18, 95, 270
Guest Star 65, 77, 90, 187, 199, 213, 215, 233, 234
Guest Time 309
The Guiding Light 8, 63, 101, 122, 193, 200, 201, 218, 227, 230, 242, 305
Guiterman, Richard L. 214
Gulf Headliner 123, 242
The Gulf Headliners 32
Gulf Oil Corp. 243
The Gulf Screen Guild Show 65
The Gulf Screen Guild Theater 65, 303
The Gulf Show 303
Gulf Spray Presents 79
The Gumps 88
Gunn, George 121
Gunsmoke 25, 33, 72, 79, 90, 94, 187, 228, 250
Gunther, John Joseph 121–122
Guy Lombardo and His Orchestra 23, 300
Guy Lombardo Time 26
Gwinn, Bill 122

Hackett, Buddy 77
Hal Kemp and His Orchestra 153
Hale, Arthur 122
Haleloke 181
Haley's 37
Hall, Monty 128, 213, 280, 281, 315
Hall, Radcliffe 122
Hall, Tom T. 170
Hallmark Hall of Fame 114, 303
Hallmark Playhouse 114, 123
The Halls of Ivy 54, 187, 234
Halsey, Stuart & Co. 157
Halsey Stuart Program 157
Hamilton, Gene 122–123
Hancock, Don 123
Hangen, Welles 104
Hank Williams Health and Happiness Show 299
Hanlon, Thomas, Jr. 123–124
Hannes, Art 124
Hannibal Cobb 120, 217
Hanson, Oscar B. 53
Hap Hazard 164, 313
Happy Island 30, 186, 233
Happy Jim Parsons 156
The Happy Rambler 156
Happy Trails 69, 79, 228
Happy Wonder Bakers Trio 176, 291
Harden, Frank 196
Harding, Warren 133

The Hardy Family 8, 186
Harkness, Richard C. 124
Harkness of Washington 124
The Harold Peary Show 170
Harold Teen 11, 193
Harold True Sports 298
Harper, Troman 124–125
Harrice, Cy 125
Harriman, Averell 62
Harris, Phil 316
Harry James and His Music Makers 303
Harry James and His Orchestra 220
The Harry James Show 34
Harry Marble and the News 180
Harsch, Joseph Close 104, 125–126
Harshbarger, Dema 142
Hart, John 282
Hart, Moss 321
Hart, Schaffner and Marx Trumpeters 137–138
Hartz, Jim 35
Hartzell, Clarence L. 126
Harv and Esther 234
The Harvest of Stars 123
Harvey, Paul 72, 126–127, 203, 279
Hashknife Hartley 180, 184
Haskell, Jack 127–128
Hatos, Stefan 127–128
Hauptmann, Bruno Richard 133, 258, 311
Have Gun, Will Travel 25, 72, 79, 80, 228
Havrilla, Alois 128–129
Hawley, Adelaide Cumming 129
Hawley, Mark Hiram 129–130
Hawthorne House 109
Hawthorne Show 281
Hawthorne's Adventures 151, 281
Hay, Bill 58, 130–131
Hay, George Dewey 131–132, 299
Hay, Jacob 275
Hayden Planetarium 209
Hayes, Helen 245
Hayes, Linda 69
Hayes, Peter Lind 97
Healy, Mary 97
Hear It Now 21, 141, 202, 205, 285
Hearst, William Randolph 133, 222, 311
Hearst's International News Service 267
The Heart of America 98
Heartbeat Theater 33, 192, 193, 200, 209, 228, 234, 294

Hearthstone of the Death Squad 124, 313
Heart's Desire 7, 48
Hearts in Harmony 134, 322
Heartthrobs of the Hills 63, 157, 166, 176
Heatherton, Ray 86
Heatherton House 86
Heatter, Basil 134
Heatter, Gabriel 133–134, 286
Hebrew National 201
Hecht, Ben 287
Hecker's Information Service 163
Hedda Hopper 212
The Hedda Hopper Show 86, 141
Hedda Hopper's Hollywood 17, 141, 212
Heel Hugger Harmonies 16
Heinz Magazine of the Air 5, 88, 90, 115, 163
The Helen Hayes Theater 48, 106
Helen Hiett News 137
Helen Holden, Government Girl 34
Hello Mom 109
A Helping Hand 123
Helpmate 66, 310
Hence, Carleton 87
Henderson, Skitch 307
Henning, Paul 20
Henry Adams and His Book 23
Henry Duffy Players 38, 113, 163
The Henry Morgan Show 20, 77, 117, 134, 147, 148, 164, 197, 198, 248, 262
Her Honor, Nancy James 98, 102, 106
The Herb Oscar Anderson Show 237
Herb Sheldon Show 266
Herb Shriner Time 164
Here Comes Elmer 212
Here Comes McBride 20
Here's Hollywood 308
Here's Morgan 19, 20, 147, 148, 164, 197, 198
Here's to Romance 10, 164
Here's to Veterans 82, 164, 220, 285
Heritage 148
Herlihy, Ed 134–135, 197
Herlihy, Walter F. 135
Herman, George 7, 135–136, 256, 282
The Hermit's Cave 101, 127, 128, 192, 219
Hersholt, Jean 110
Hi Jinx 262
Hibber, Edna 312
Hicks, George Francis 136–137, 292
Hicks, John 137
Hiestand, John (Bud) 137
Hiett, Helen 137
Higby, Mary Jane 276
High Adventure 56, 140, 170, 294
High Places 63
Highroads to Health 30
Highway Harmonies 281
Highway Patrol 98, 187

Highways in Melody 319
Hilda Hope 57
Hildegarde 58, 63, 122, 262
Hildegarde's Raleigh Room 294
Hilgemeier, Edward, Jr. 207
Hill, Edwin Conger 137–138
Hill, George Washington 38, 237
Hillbilly Heartthrobs 63, 166, 176
Hillman, William 138–139
Hilltop House 31, 33, 43, 106, 164, 208
Hilton, Bob 89
Hilton, James 321
The Hinds Honey and Almond Cream Program 38
Hines, Eleanor 15
His Honor, the Barber 180
History Behind the Headlines 295
A History Book Wired for Sound 30
Hit That Ball 309
Hit the Jackpot 48, 277
Hite, Bob 139
Hitler, Adolf 143, 155, 253, 267, 282, 290, 311
Hits and Misses 167
Hoagy Carmichael Show 156, 170
Hobby Lobby 78, 102, 159, 265, 303
Hodges, Russell Patrick 139–140
Hodiak, John 96
Hoffman, Harold 258
Hoffman, Howard Ralph 140
Hogan, George 140
Hogan's Daughter 239
Holbrook, John F. 140
Holcombe, Harry John 140–141
Holland Housewife 230
Hollenbeck, Don 141
Hollywood Airport 254
Hollywood Barn Dance 123
Hollywood Bowl Concert 227
Hollywood Byline 274
Hollywood Calling 15
Hollywood Hotel 212, 221, 222, 223
Hollywood in Person 17
Hollywood Jackpot 77
Hollywood Mardi Gras 315
Hollywood Mystery Time 84
Hollywood Nights 176
Hollywood on the Air 95, 96
Hollywood Open House 10, 312
Hollywood Players 33
Hollywood Playhouse 10, 38, 69
Hollywood Premiere 221, 223, 313
Hollywood Preview 179, 187
Hollywood Searchlight 227
Hollywood Showcase 113, 114, 141, 170
Hollywood Soundstage 80
Hollywood Spotlight 315
Hollywood Star Playhouse 11, 25, 152, 212
Hollywood Star Preview 315
Hollywood Star Theater 315
Hollywood Startime 42, 152, 157, 212
Hollywood Theater 315

INDEX

Hollywood Tour 73
Hollywood Walk of Fame 221, 233
Hollywood with Irene Rich 249
Home Circle 151
Home Is What You Make It 20, 117
Home of the Brave 313
Home on the Range 208
Home Sweet Home 13
The Hometowners 8
Honest Harold 170
Honeymoon in New York 134, 144, 164, 266
The Honeymooners 16
Honolulu Bound 303
Honor the Law 209, 266
The Hoosier Commentator 95
Hoosier Hot Shots 227
Hoot'nanny 244
Hoover, Herbert 69, 147, 225, 226
Hoover, J. Edgar 69
Hop Harrigan 30, 71, 237
Hope, Bob 26, 93, 318
Hopper, DeWolf 141
Hopper, Edna Wallace 141
Hopper, Hedda 96, 115, 141–143, 221, 223
Hopper, William 142
The Horace Heidt Show 140
The Hormel Program 137
Horn and Hardart Children's Hour 81, 88–89, 134, 135
Horton, Edward Everett 66
Hot Copy 82
The Hotpoint Holiday Hour 193
Hottelet, Richard C. 143, 203, 271
The Hour of Charm 57, 106, 187, 233, 239, 265, 277
The Hour of St. Francis 187
The Hour of Smiles 250
House by the Side of the Road 5
House Ethics Committee 258
House in the Country 32, 63, 151
House of Melody 109
House Party 18
Houseboat Hannah 19
Housewives Protective League 84
Houston, Mark 143
How To 170
How to Get the Most Out of Life 229
How to Win Friends and Influence People 53
Howard K. Smith News and Comment 271
Howard Thurston, the Magician 42
Howe, Quincy 143–144, 156
Howell, Wayne 144
How'm I Doin? 220
How's the Family? 11
Hubert, Harold 87
Hudson, Tom 144
Hull, Warren 145, 224
The Human Side of the News 138
Humanizing the News 232
Hummert, Frank and Anne 8, 11, 14, 37, 51, 59, 99, 242

Huntley, Chet 145–147, 162, 298, 300
Husing, Edward Britt (Ted) 52, 109, 147–148, 185
Huss, Pierre 203
H.V. Kaltenborn Comments 154
Hymns of All Churches 177, 227
Hymn Time 281

I Deal in Crime 73
I Devise and Bequeath 72, 194
I Fly Anything 66, 94
I Love a Mystery 7, 21, 25, 73, 179, 187, 294
I Love Adventure 73, 187
I Love Lucy 150
I Packed My Trunk 217
I Sustain the Wings 144
I Want a Divorce 8
I Was There 145, 179, 308
Ice Box Follies 212, 313
Idelson, Bill 126
If I Had a Chance 293
I'll Never Forget 23, 176
Ilson, Saul 85
Imperial Time 262
In Care of Aggie Horn 82, 126
In Town Today 180
In Your Name 215
Incredible But True 214
Indictment 213
Information Please 19, 22, 37, 58, 70, 117, 121, 134, 149, 236, 237, 247, 251, 320
Inheritance 281
Inner Sanctum Mysteries 14, 134, 180, 201, 244, 311, 313
Inside News from Hollywood 269
The Inside Story 310
Inside Story of Names That Make the News 138
Inspector Thorne 310
Institute of International Education 203
Interchurch World Movement 183
Interesting Neighbors 103
Interesting People 53
International Academy of Television Arts and Sciences 67
International Brotherhood of Teamsters 73
International News Service (INS) 6, 46, 108, 138, 160
International Radio-Television Society 168, 218
Into the Light 79
Invisible Walls 312
Invitation to Learning 143
Iowa Broadcasting System 312
Ipana 87
Irene Beasley 81
Irene Rich Dramas 109, 114, 134, 193, 251
Irish, Jack 148
Irving, Charles 148
It Can Be Done 43
It Can Happen to You 303
It Could Be You 122
It Happened in Hollywood 65

It Happened in 1955 265
It Happened in the Service 7
It Happened Last Night 81
It Pays to Be Ignorant 239, 277
It Pays to Be Married 127
It's a Great Life 186, 209
It's a Living 7
It's a Man's World 162
It's a Woman's World 245
It's Always Albert 48
It's Higgins, Sir 132, 237
It's Our Turn 82
It's the Barrys 23
It's the Tops 134
Ivory soap 57, 233
Ivory Soap Program 239

J. Walter Thompson agency 168, 263
Jack and Cliff 186, 214, 266
The Jack & Gene Show 171
Jack Armstrong, the All-American Boy 10, 33, 38, 52, 81, 95, 172, 177, 188, 193, 230, 294
The Jack Benny Program 33, 37, 38, 58, 77, 81, 128, 136, 192, 209, 237, 251, 265, 315
Jack Bundy's Album 266
Jack Bundy's Carnival 266
The Jack Carson Show 15, 153, 228, 265
Jack Frost Melody Moments 128, 129
Jack Frost sugar 129
The Jackie Gleason–Les Tremayne Show 294
Jack Haley Show 145
Jack Haskell 127
Jack Johnstone's Dramas 152
The Jack Kirkwood Show 19, 266, 307
The Jack Lestser Show 172
Jack Okie's College 113
The Jack Paar Show 15, 209, 251
The Jack Pearl Show 106, 187, 234
The Jack Pepper Show 30
The Jack Smith, Dinah Shore, Margaret Whiting Show 280
Jack Smith Show 123
Jack Webb Show 106
Jack's Place 137
Jackson, Allan Harry 148–149
Jackson, Jay 149–150
Jacobs, Johnny 150
James, Dennis 150–151
James, Harry 34
James, Hugh 151
James, Owen 151
The James and Pamela Mason Show 26
The James Melton Show 307
Jan August Show 239
Jane Ace, Disc Jockey 219
Jane Arden 104, 159, 201
Jane Endicott, Reporter 123
The Jane Froman Show 147
The Jane Pickens Show 14, 134, 144, 310
The Janette Davis Show 303

Jarvis, Al 35
Jay Sims and the News 269
Jay Stewart's Fun Fair 66, 280
J.B. Mennen Co. 268
The Jean Shepherd Show 179
The Jeddo Highlanders 70
Jeff Regan, Investigator 114, 187, 193, 209, 229, 277, 280
Jefferson Patterson Park 42
Jeffreys, Anne 66
Jell-O 316
The Jell-O Program Starring Jack Benny 182, 210
Jenner, Sen. William 225
Jennings, Peter 273, 298
Jergens 118, 142
The Jergens Journal 118, 151, 317
The Jerry Lester Show 300
Jerry of the Circus 192
The Jerry Wayne Show 79, 186, 262
Jessel, George 45, 317
Jewett, Edward K. (Ted) 151–152
Jewish Telegraph Agency 257
Jim Backus Show 114, 127, 265
Jim Doyle and the News 84
The Jimmy Dorsey Show 266
The Jimmy Durante Show 228, 307
The Jimmy Durante Show–Garry Moore Show 228
Jimmy Edmondson Show 266
Jimmy Fidler 95, 109
Jimmy Fidler in Hollywood 42, 95
Jimmy Wakely's Western Song Parade 309
Jingo 215, 234, 248
The Jo Stafford Show 150, 193
The Joan Davis Show 33
Joan Davis Time 170, 304
Joe and Ethel Turp 30
Joe and Vi 304
The Joe Dimaggio Show 23, 30, 47, 148
The Joe E. Brown Show 315
Joe Mooney Quartette 165
Joe Palooka 147, 234
The Joe Penner Show 21, 113, 140
John B. Kennedy–Edwin C. Hill News 138, 158
John B. Kennedy News 158
John Cameron Swayze and the News 283
John Charles Thomas 211
The John Conte Show 65, 66
John Gordon Fraser and the News 103
John Gunther Comments 121
John MacVane and the News 178
John Nesbitt and the News 211
John Steele, Adventurer 179
John W. Vandercook 301
John W. Vandercook Air Age News of the Day 301
Johnny Fletcher 113
A Johnny Fletcher Mystery 113, 151, 281
Johnny Long and His Orchestra 219

Johnny Lujack of Notre Dame 230
Johnny Mercer Show 150
Johnny Mercer's Music Shop 212
Johnny Modero, Pier 23 169
The Johnny Morgan Show 66, 237
The Johnny Olsen Show 216
Johnny Olsen's Get-Together 216
Johnny Olsen's Luncheon Club 216
Johnny Olsen's Rumpus Room 165, 216
Johnny Presents 57, 152, 239
John's Other Wife 71, 100, 104, 166, 244
Johnson, Betty 84, 310
Johnson, Edward 152
Johnson, Kenneth M. 61
Johnson, Lyndon B. 83, 302
Johnson & Johnson 87
The Johnson Family 184
Johnson Family Singers 61, 310
The Johnson Family Singers 310
Johnson's Glo-Coat 314
Johnson's wax 316
Johnstone, Jack 152
Jolson, Al 55, 93, 223
Jonathan Kegg 153
Jonathan Trimble, Esquire 109, 182
Jones, Candy 280
Jones, Dean 85
Jones, Rep. Robert F. 226
Jones Piano House, Fort Dodge, Iowa 16
Jordan, Jim 314
Jordan, Marian 314
Jordan, Max 27, 152
Joseph C. Harsch Commentary 125
Josephy, Helen 183
Journal of Living 175
Joy 22
Joy, Dick 152–153, 207, 212
Joyce Jordan, Girl Interne 42, 239, 241, 277, 294, 313
Joyce Jordan, M.D. 42, 63, 98, 217, 233, 277, 294, 313
Jubilee 274
The Judge 71, 79
Judge Perkins 141
Judy and Jane 44, 140, 193
Judy Canova Show 114, 162, 212, 228, 274, 317
Judy, Jill and Johnny 220
Juke Box Jury 150
Jumbo 319
The Jumbo Fire Chief Program 319
June's My Girl 234, 280
Jungle Jim 71, 77, 167, 237
Junior Junction 172
Junior Miss 48, 150, 307
Just Between Us 179
Just Entertainment 101, 123
Just Plain Bill 26, 33, 37, 49, 63, 66, 93, 134, 167, 208, 219, 320
Juvenile adventure series 71
Juvenile Jury 23, 24, 90

KaDell, Carlton 131, 153
The Kaiser Traveler 125
Kalb, Marvin 275, 282

Kalischer, Peter 153–154
Kaltenborn, Hans Von 28, 75, 101, 106, 154–156, 253, 286
Kaltenborn Edits the News 29, 106, 122, 154
Kanin, Garson 81
Kansas City Opera Company 161
Kaplow, Herb 104
Karloff, Boris 231
Kate Hopkins, Angel of Mercy 57, 63
The Kate Smith Hour 75
The Kate Smith New Star Revue 76
The Kate Smith Show 26, 62, 220, 295
Kate Smith Speaks 46
Kathryn Cravens Broadcasts the News 68, 69
Kathy Godfrey Show 139
Katie's Daughter 20, 86
Kaufman, George S. 321
Kaufman, Irving 156
Kay Fairchild, Stepmother 153, 167, 193, 310
Kay Kyser's Kollege of Musical Knowledge 35, 101, 117, 137, 186, 212, 274
Kaye, Stubby 315
Kean, Doris 312
Keating, Larry 156–157, 162
Keaton, Buster 20
Kebbe, Charles 99
Keech, Kelvin Kirkwood 157
Keep It Dark 277
Keeping Up with Rosemary 208
Keeping Up with Wigglesworth 71
Kellogg 167, 181
Kelly, Grace 92, 119
Kelly, Pat 9
Kelly, Patrick Joseph 157–158, 251
Kelly, Tom 145
Kelly's Courthouse 80, 167, 262, 300
The Kemtone Hour 167
The Ken Banghart Show 20, 66
The Ken Murray Rinso–Lifebuoy Program 300
The Ken Murray Show 42, 57
Kendrick, Alexander 154, 158, 257
Kennedy, Arthur 246
Kennedy, John B. 158–159
Kennedy, John F. 84, 149, 161, 197, 202, 205, 264, 272, 282
Kennedy, John Milton 159
Kennedy, Tom 24, 208
Kennedy, Willard A. 159
Kenneth Banghart and the News 20
Kent, Alan Bradley 159–160
Kent, George 190
Kent, Rosemary 182
Kenton, Stan 162
Kentucky Derby 295
Kentucky Music Hall of Fame and Museum, Renfro Valley 169

Kerr, Deborah 115
Kiernan, Walter 160
Kiernan's Corner 160
Kilgallen, Dorothy May 92, 97, 160–161, 166, 191, 199
Kilgallen, Jim 160
Kinard, J. Spencer 92, 161
King, Delmer Randolph 161–162
King, Dennis 162
King, Edward 162
King, Jean Paul 162–163
King, John Reed 163–164, 196, 249
King, Joseph 164
King, Margaret 224
King, Walter Woolf 164
King, Wayne 57, 178
King Features Syndicate 138
King for a Night 212
The King's Men 212, 313
King's Row 303
Kiplinger, Willard M. 309
Kirby, Durward 164–165, 181
Kirby, Gene 165
Kirby, Grover C. (Kleve) 165
Kitty Foyle 9, 63
Kitty Keene, Incorporated 44, 80, 153, 312
Klauber, Ed 41
Knickerbocker Playhouse 19, 193
Knight, Frank 165–166
Know Your NBCs 211
Kollmar, Richard 92, 97, 161, 166, 191
Kools 60
The Korn Kobblers 68
Kovacs, Ernie 8
Kraft Foods 135
Kraft Music Hall 37, 54, 55, 134, 167, 223, 237, 276, 315
Kramer, Harry 166–167
Kramer, Mandel 102
Krueger Sports Reel 185
Krupa, Gene 13
Krupp, Roger Thurston 67, 167–168
Ku Klux Klan 226
Kuralt, Charles Bishop 168–169, 218

Lackmann, Ron 321
Ladies Be Seated 34, 48, 121, 127, 196, 216, 237
Ladies Fair 91, 114, 196
Lady Be Beautiful 7
The Lady Esther Screen Guild Theater 38, 193
Lady Esther Serenade 212
The Lady Next Door 79
La Frano, Anthony J. 169
La Gallienne, Eva 201
La Guardia, Fiorello 311
Lahr, Bert 243
Lair, John 169–170
Lamour, Dorothy 52, 96
The Land of the Lost 98
Landis, K.M. 147
Landon, Alf 248
The Landt Trio 239

Lange, Jim 150
Langley, Ralph 170
Langston, Murray 89
Lanham, Gene 159
The Lanny Ross Show 34, 57, 163, 265, 315
Lansing, Mary 210
La Prade, Ernest 53
Lardner, Ring 287
La Rosa, Julius 112
The Larry Carr Show 292
Larry Clinton's Musical Conversations 136
Larry Lesueur and the News 78, 172
Lassie 177, 193, 313
Latham, John Jackson 170
Latting, Robert 170
Laugh and Swing Club 197
Laugh Doctors 197
Laugh with Ken 42, 300
Lavender and New Lace 237
Lavender and Old Lace 265
Law West of the Pecos 69
Lawford, Peter 20
Lawrence, Bill 284
Lawrence, Jerome 18
Lawrence, Jerry 170
Lawrence, Morton 170
Lawrence, T.E. 287
The Lawrence Welk High Life Revue 47
The Lawrence Welk Show 47
Lawyer Q 150
Lawyer Tucker 123
Layman, Zora 177
Layton, Charles L. 320
Lazy Dan, the Minstrel Man 156
League of Nations 59
Leave It to Bill 113
Leave It to Joan 212, 280, 304
Leave It to the Girls 26, 92, 141, 160, 186, 198
Lee, Don 315
Lee, Thomas 66
Lee, William 217
The Lehn and Fink Serenade 16
Leighton, Bernard 84
Leith Stevens Harmonies 195
Leitzel, Lillian 133
LeMaire, Charles 164
Lemond, Robert W. 170–171
Leo Reisman and His Orchestra 245
Leonard, Bill 302
The Leopold Stokowski Show 67
Les Brown Orchestra 127
Les Brown Orchestra 127
Lesch Silver Co. 53
Lescoulie, Jack 16, 171–172, 216
Lester, Jack 172
Lester Flatt and Earl Scruggs 299
Lesueur, Lawrence Edward 56, 88, 172–173, 179, 203, 264, 268
Let George Do It 25, 87, 137, 182, 187, 280
Let Yourself Go 239
Let's Be Charming 23
Let's Be Lazy 196

Let's Dance 13, 53
Let's Go Nightclubbing 219
Let's Laugh and Get Acquainted 109, 275
Let's Play Reporter 78
Let's Pretend 5, 48, 285
Let's Talk Hollywood 15
Letterman, David 238
Lever Brothers 223, 263
Levine, Irving R. 104
Levy, Jules 286
Lewis, Alfred Henry 285
Lewis, Fulton, Jr. 173–174
Lewis, John L. 311
Lewis, Robert Q. 181, 241
Lewis, Sinclair 246
Leyden, Bill 213
The Life and Love of Dr. Susan 176
Life Begins 239, 241, 265
Life Begins at Eighty 23, 24, 186, 239
Life Can Be Beautiful 30, 31, 57, 63, 78, 87, 89, 103, 123, 132, 134, 166, 233, 277
A Life in Your Hands 153, 188, 214, 230, 281, 305
The Life of Mary Sothern 30, 166, 239
The Life of Riley 48, 54, 209, 212, 234, 307
Life Savers 199
Life with Luigi 170, 177, 234, 280
The Lifebuoy Program 250
The Lifebuoy Show 235, 274
The Light of the World 5, 100, 193, 200, 201, 217
Light Up Time 315
Lights Out 132, 170, 180, 280, 281
Li'l Abner 126, 164
Lillie, Beatrice 71
Lincoln, Abraham 40
Lincoln Highway 187
Linda's First Love 26, 101
Lindbergh, Charles 190, 215, 245, 258, 292, 307
Lindlahr, Victor Hugo 175
Lindley, Ernest K. 138
Lindsley, Charles Frederick 175
The Lineup 15, 16, 71, 187, 280, 308
The Linit Bath Club Revue 147, 239
Linkletter, Art 18
The Lion's Eye 229, 277
Liquid Joy 233
Listen 9
Listen, America 122, 224
Listen to a Love Song 307
Listening Post 63, 200
Literary Digest 165
Literary Digest Topics in Brief 286, 291
Little Herman 80
Little Known Facts about Well-Known People 53, 140
Little Ol' Hollywood 7
Little Orphan Annie 11, 26
The Little Things in Life 244
Live Like a Millionaire 186, 211

Live-on-tape mystery dramas 180
The Lives of Harry Lime 217
Living 1948 108
Living 1948, 1949, 1950, 1951 117
Living 1948–1951 310
Livingston, Mary 316
Log Cabin Jamboree 145
Logan, Barbara 231
Lois Long and The Three Suns 300
Lombardo, Guy 13, 57, 130
Lombardoland, U.S.A. 217, 248
Lone Journey 57, 132, 164, 197, 277, 320
The Lone Ranger 31, 32, 87, 102, 113, 127, 128, 139, 193, 219, 229, 298, 305, 320
The Lone Wolf 11, 321
Lonely Women 193, 227, 294, 310
The Longines Symphonette 165, 166
Longines Symphonette Society 166
Look Your Best 266
Looking Over the Week 158
Lora Lawton 20, 37, 98, 233
Lord, Phillips H. 214, 258
Lorenzo Jones 175, 239, 310, 319
Louella Parsons 193, 221
Louella Parsons Show 84, 113, 274
Louis, Joe 279
Love, Andy 159
Love Letters 178
Love Notes 117
Love Story Theater 10
Lovejoy, Frank 153
Lowe, Donald Herbert 175
Lowe, Jim 47
Lowell Thomas and the News 13, 57, 151, 165, 167, 286, 291
Lowther, George 175–176
L.S. Rothschild (firm) 87
Lucas, Paul 207
Lucky Strike 27, 38, 237, 252, 292, 314, 316
The Lucky Strike Dance Orchestra 58, 317
The Lucky Strike Hour 58
The Lucky Strike Music Hall 70
The Lucky Strike Program Starring Jack Benny 280
Luden's Novelty Orchestra 16
Luke Slaughter of Tombstone 228
Lum and Abner 19, 42, 69, 114, 122, 126, 167, 177, 212, 265
Luncheon at Sardi's 140
Luncheon at the Waldorf 176, 220
Lund, John 176
Lunt, Alfred 235
Luther, Frank 176–177
Luther, Paul 177, 282
Luther Brothers 176
Luther-Layman Singers 176
Lux Radio Theater 10, 25, 32, 54, 77, 79, 98, 109, 123, 140, 159, 164, 182, 192, 206, 209, 215, 223, 251
Lycons 37
Lyle Van and the News 300

Lyon, Ben 24
Lyon, Charles Albert 177

Ma and Pa 265
Ma Perkins 33, 44, 46, 80, 193, 229, 294, 305, 312
MacArthur, Charles 287
MacArthur, Douglas 7, 154
MacCormack, Franklyn 177–178
MacDonald, J. Fred 204, 205, 321
Macfadden Publications 301
Mack, Floyd 178
Mack, Nila 6
MacKenzie, Murdo 55
MacLaughlin, Don 258
MacVane, John F. 178–179
Madame Sylvia of Hollywood 104
Madden, John 283
Madelline Carroll Reads 86
Madison Square Boxing Bouts 285
Madison Square Garden Boxing 194
The Magic Key 70, 117, 158, 245
Magic Key of RCA 109
Magic Rhythm 140
The Magnificent Montague 219, 241
Mail Call 65, 235, 315
Main Street 281
Main Street Sketches 53
Maisie 186
Major Bowes' Original Amateur Hour 52, 67, 89, 123, 181, 189, 195, 215, 262, 285, 307
Make Believe Ballroom 35, 178
Make-Believe Town, Hollywood 72, 150, 218
Make Your Music 233
Makers of History 209
Mallie, Theodore A. 179
Maltin, Leonard 15, 18, 81, 89, 110, 188, 189, 213, 219, 228, 307
The Man Behind the Gun 30, 177
A Man Called Jordan 79
The Man Called X 25, 114, 152, 170, 187, 212, 281
The Man from Homicide 11, 79
The Man I Married 30, 63, 201, 217, 228, 265
Manhattan at Midnight 10, 79, 234
Manhattan Gazette 105
Manhattan Maharajah 13
Manhattan Merry-Go-Round 13, 37, 167, 176
Manhattan Mother 201, 239
Manhattan Parade 111
Manlove, Dudley D. 179
Mann, Al 284
Manners, Dorothy 223
Manning, Charles Knox 179–180
Manning, Tom 136
Mantovani, Annunzio Paolo 66

Marble, Harry W. 15, 180
March of Dimes 99
March of Dimes Victory Program 180
The March of Time 5, 30, 77, 79, 87, 102, 127, 128, 147, 151, 166, 187, 201, 244, 293, 302, 304, 311, 322
Margaret Arlen 15, 180
Marie, the Little French Princess 26
The Mariners 181
The Mario Lanza Show 19
Mark Sabre 101, 313
Mark Trail 30, 71, 237
Mark Warnow Orchestra 26
The Marlin Hurt and Beulah Show 212
Marlowe, Julia 5
Marlowe, Marion 181
Maroon, Fred J. 261
The Marriage 78, 120
Marriage Club, Inc. 57
Marriage for Two 292
Married for Life 104
Mars, Inc. 14
Marsh, Earle 284
Marshall, E.G. 180
Marshall, George C. 195
Marshall, Peter 315
Martha Webster 43, 239, 265
Martin, Freddy 162
Martin, H. Gilbert 180
Martin, Jeff Frank, Jr. 180
Martin, Judith "Miss Manners" 230
Martin, Tony 16
The Martin and Lewis Show 7–8, 134, 144, 150, 194, 250, 307
The Martin Block Show 35
Martin Kane, Private Eye 300
Marvin, Anthony 181
Marvin Miller and the News 194
Marvin Miller, Storyteller 194
Marx, Groucho 94, 271, 321
Marx Brothers 252
Mary and Bob's True Stories 248
Mary Margaret McBride 183
Mary Pickford Dramas 212
Mary Small 63
Mary Small Show 262
Masefield, John 253
Mason, Ella 214
Mason, Jerald 321
Masquerade 43, 153, 172, 227, 229
Master of the Bow 252
Masterson, John 211, 246
Masterson, Paul C. 181
Mather, John E. (Jack) 182
Matinee at Meadowbrook 220, 292
Matinee in Rhythm 235
Matinee Theater 30, 180
Matthews, Grace 33
Maudie's Diary 195
Maxwell, Elsa 182–183, 245
Maxwell, Marilyn 66
Maxwell House 105, 293

Maxwell House Coffee Time 42, 65, 113, 234, 235
Maxwell House Melodies 250
Maxwell House Show Boat 42, 145, 251
Maxwell House Summer Show 235
Mayer, Louis B. 223
Mayor of the Town 153, 180, 313
McBride, Mary Margaret 15, 183–184, 314
McCall, Don 184
McCarthy, Charles F. 185
McCarthy, Charlie 11, 318
McCarthy, Clem 185, 279
McCarthy, Jack 185
McCarthy, John 185–186
McCarthy, Joseph R. 6, 141, 174, 205–206, 224, 226, 268, 318
McClain, Jimmy 14
McCormick, Robert K. 104, 186
McCoy, Jack E. 186
McCrary, John Reagan (Tex) 92, 97, 191–192
McCullough, Dan 186
McDonald, Arch 139
McDonnell, Craig 186
McElhone, Eloise 186
McElroy, Jack 186
McGarry and His Mouse 87, 220
McGee, Frank 35, 104, 147
McGeehan, Patrick Joseph 186–187
McGovern, John 187
The McGuire Sisters 181
McIntire, John Herrick 187–188
McIntosh, Ezra 292
McKee, Robert 188
McKellar, Sen. Kenneth 224
McLeod, Elizabeth 130
McMahon, Ed 265
McNamee, Graham 44, 52, 128, 136, 147, 188–191, 236, 243, 278, 285, 307
McNeil, Alex 106
McNeil, Don 82, 202, 242, 310
McVey, Tyler 192
Me and Janie 194, 315
Meadows, Jayne 199
The Meal of Your Life 248
The Meaning of the News 125
Meeder, William 277
Meet Corliss Archer 54, 127, 137, 180, 250, 265, 266
Meet Joe Public 17
Meet Me at Porky's 109, 209
Meet Me in St. Louis 132
Meet Millie 33, 170
Meet Miss Sherlock 305
Meet Mr. McNutley 187, 265
Meet Mr. Meek 187, 262
Meet Mr. Morgan 198
Meet Tex and Jinx 92, 191
Meet the Champions 171
Meet the Dixons 262
Meet the Meeks 8, 311
Meet the Missus 17, 26, 196, 280, 304

Meet the Music 292
Meet the Press 103, 117, 274
Meet the Songwriters 175
Meet Your Match 196
Meet Your Navy 164
Meikle, Pat 26
The Mel Allen Show 9
The Mel Blanc Show 234
Mel Torme Show 163
Melodies Organistic 123
Melody and Madness 145, 179, 265
Melody Highway 70
Melody Lane with Jerry Wayne 79
Melody Promenade 120
Melody Puzzles 134, 300
Melody Roundup 84
Melody Treasure Hunt 36
Melton, James 243
Mendenhall, Rachel 69
Meneghini, Giovanni Battista 183
Merchandise Mart, Chicago 122
The Mercury Summer Theater 10, 239
The Mercury Summer Theater of the Air 58
Mercury Theater 102
Mercury Theater on the Air 58, 77, 138, 154, 187, 262
Meredith, Burgess 207
The Meredith Willson–John Nesbitt Show 211
Meredith Willson's Music Room 20
Merrill Mueller News Commentary 201
The Merry Life of Mary Christmas 180
The Metropolitan Auditions on the Air 175
Metropolitan Echoes 136
Metropolitan Life Insurance Co. 149
Metropolitan Opera 70
The Metropolitan Opera 70
The Metropolitan Opera Auditions on the Air 58, 70, 117, 152
Metropolitan Opera Company 152, 251
Metz, Stuart Blim 193
Meyer, Mrs. Eugene 245
Meyer the Buyer 49, 81, 234, 244
Meyers, Edward Theodore 193
Meyerson, Bess 199
MGM Screen Test 65
MGM Theater of the Air 87, 294
Michael, Ed 104, 193
Michael, Jay 193
Michaels, Lorne 219
Michigan Reporter 298
The Mickey Mouse Theater of the Air 137
Mid-Century Broadcast 180
Middlesex Transportation Co. 258
Middleton, Glenn Y. 111, 307

Midnight Dancing Party 310
The Midnight Flyer 11
Midnight Jamboree 299
Midstream 19, 194
The Mighty Casey 224
The Mighty Show 201
Mike and Buff's Mail Bag 167, 305, 306
Miles Laboratories, Inc. 125, 254
Military Analysis of the News 29
Milkman's Matinee 171
Miller, Dean 229
Miller, Glenn 13
Miller, Marvin 80, 193–195
Millett, W. Arthur 195
Millions for Defense 189
The Milt Herth Trio 66
Milton Berle Show 30, 106, 148, 239, 319
Milton Cross Opera Album 70, 235
The Mindy Carson Show 219
Miner, Jan 219
The Minute Men 304
Minute Mysteries 163
The Miracle of America 179
Mirth and Madness 266, 307
Mirth and Melody 151
Miss America Pageant 221
Miss Pinkerton, Inc. 109
The Missus Goes a-Shopping 163
The Missus Goes to Market 26, 196
Mr. Ace and Jane 239
Mr. Aladdin 11
Mr. and Mrs. Blandings 212, 275
Mr. and Mrs. North 20, 117, 164, 217, 276
Mr. Chameleon 48, 58, 167
Mr. District Attorney 49, 117, 129, 134, 266, 300, 311
Mr. Feathers 43, 91
Mr. Keen, Tracer of Lost Persons 13, 43, 48, 67, 91, 99, 100, 104, 117, 132, 167, 193, 244, 275, 292, 310, 315
Mr. President 66, 175
Mitchell, Albert 195
Moawski, Ivan 228
The Modern Adventures of Casanova 25, 234
Modern Cinderella 167
Modern Minstrels 304
Modern Romances 186, 214, 252
Molle Mystery Theater 86, 201, 262, 313
Mommie and the Men 233
Monday Merry-Go-Round 37
Monday Morning Headlines 107
Money-Go-Round 300
Monitor 9, 21, 23, 29, 34, 39, 47, 65, 82, 100, 103, 106, 107, 117, 122, 124, 144, 160, 197, 201, 219, 220, 254, 283, 307
Monitor Views 52
Monroe, Bill 275
Montgomery Ward 12, 14
Moon Dreams 140, 194

Moon River 47, 82, 117, 141, 178, 320
Moonlight Savings Time 170
Moonlight Serenade 81
Moore, Garry 165, 181
Moore, Tom 196
The Morey Amsterdam Show 30, 148
Morgan, Edward P. 196–197
Morgan, Henry 44, 197–199, 288
Morgan, Raymond 199
The Mormon Tabernacle Choir 92, 111, 161
Morning Almanac 276
Morning Edition 23
Morning News Roundup 122
Morrison, Bret 199–200
Morrow, Don 87, 200
Morse, Carlton E. 13
Moss, Arnold 87, 200–201
Mother Knows Best 145, 224
Mother o' Mine 276
Motion Picture Relief Fund 207
Mottola, Tony 277
Movie Quiz 17
Movietown Radio Theater 294
Mowrer, Edgar Ansel 203
The Moylan Sisters 175
Mrs. Miniver 87, 201
Mrs. Roosevelt Meets the Public 245
Mrs. Wiggs of the Cabbage Patch 13
Mudd, Roger 256, 282, 298, 302
Mueller, Merrill F. 201–202
Mullaly, John C. 228
Murder and Mr. Malone 109
Murder at Midnight 98, 102, 199
Murder by Experts 294
Murder Clinic 165, 319
Murder Is My Hobby 215
Murder Will Out 157
Murphy, Pat 67
Murphy, Robert Leo 202
Murray, Jan 213
Murrow, Edward R. 7, 27, 40, 41, 50, 51, 61, 74, 75, 78, 83, 87, 101, 109, 116, 117, 127, 135, 143, 146, 154, 156, 158, 164, 173, 181, 202–206, 253, 255, 256, 257, 259–260, 264, 267, 268, 272, 296, 297
Murrow, Janet 116
Murrow Boys 40, 41, 46, 50, 51, 61, 62, 83, 87, 116, 143, 149, 158, 173, 203–205, 255, 257, 260, 271
Museum of Broadcasting Hall of Fame 281
Music America Loves Best 77
Music and Manners 197
Music and the Muse 281
Music and the Spoken Word from the Crossroads of the West 92, 111, 161
Music Appreciation Hour 122, 132

Music Box Theater 123
Music by Gershwin 304, 315
Music City, U.S.A. 73
Music Depreciation 169
Music Fights Infantile Paralysis 300
Music from Hollywood 153
Music from the Heart of America 127
Music Millions Love 91
The Music of Andre Kostelanetz 91
Music Tent 48, 104
Music That Endures 11
Music Through the Night 99
Music You Want 67
Musical Americana 70
Musical Bouquet 200
The Musical Clock 237
Musical Cruise 23
Musical Matinee 186
Musical Memories 43
Musical Millwheel 80
Musical Mock Trial 58, 89, 262
Musical Mysteries 90
Musical Romance 95
Musical Varieties 237
Musicana 219
Musicomedy 70, 262
Mussolini, Benito 155
Muted Rhythm 109
Mutual Broadcasting System (MBS) 22, 31, 46, 56, 64, 179
Mutual Chamber Music Concert 137
Mutual-Don Lee network 66
Mutual Matinee 314
Mutual News 15, 84, 101, 270
The Mutual Radio Theater 72, 109, 119, 120, 209, 228, 300, 313
My Best Girls 19, 262, 319
My Favorite Husband 25, 170
My Friend Irma 33, 56, 150, 170, 212, 234
My Good Wife 65
My Little Margie 250
My Mother's Husband 186
My Secret Ambition 152
My Silent Partner 86
My Son and I 26, 276
My Son Jeep 16, 62
My True Story 32, 57, 214, 237, 244
Myra Kingsley, Astrologer 163
Myrt and Marge 26, 30, 46, 71, 98, 132, 163, 177, 217, 234, 248, 265, 313, 322
Mysteries in Paris 187
Mysteries of the Crooked Square 217, 250
The Mysterious Traveler 30, 56, 86, 91, 170, 200, 217, 307
Mystery File 160
Mystery in the Air 30, 49, 72, 250
Mystery Is My Hobby 49
Mystery of the Week 57, 87, 233, 277
Mystery Theater 30, 77, 101, 217

Nachman, Gerald 96, 183, 197, 209, 242, 245, 307, 321
Nagel, Conrad 206–207
Name That Tune 144
Name the Movie 194
Name the Place 117, 215
Names of Tomorrow 109
Narz, Jack 207–208, 315
Nash Program 108
National Academy of Television Arts and Sciences 52, 74
National Academy of Vocal Arts 118
The National Air Travel Club 199
National Amateur Night 48, 49
National Barn Dance 125, 131, 169
National Baseball Hall of Fame 22–23
National Broadcasting Company 12–13, 190
National Carbon Co. 244
National Cash Register Co. 41
National Emergency Council 64
The National Farm and Home Hour 28
National Football League 190
National Geographic Society 59
National Headliners Club 28, 83, 136, 137
National Lampoon Radio Hour 305
National Life and Accident Insurance Co. 131
National Players 163
National Public Radio 23, 104, 143, 214
National Rifle Association 264
National Social Unit Organization 289
National Space Society 83
The Naval Air Reserve Show 10, 234
NBC Artists Service 59
NBC Bandstand 127, 133, 220
NBC Inaugural Gala 242
NBC News 14, 27, 46, 85, 118, 121, 122, 134, 152, 201, 215, 219, 254
NBC News on the Hour 6, 124, 302
NBC News Roundup 124, 178
NBC Pacific Coast Network 13
NBC Presents: Short Story 187, 275, 305
NBC Radio Theater 144
NBC Sports 39
NBC Star Playhouse 176
The NBC Story Shop 185, 186
NBC Summer Symphony 122
The NBC Symphony Orchestra 57, 58, 78, 118, 122
The NBC University Theater 79, 194, 275
The NBC University Theatre 109
The NBC War Telescope 178
Neal, Floyd 208
Neal, Harold (Hal) 208
Nebel, Long John 119

Ned Calmer and the News 51
Ned Jordan, Secret Agent 139, 185, 219, 229
Neely, Henry Milton 208–209
Neighbor Nell 175
The Nellie Revell Show 175
Nelson, Frank 209–210, 316
Nelson, John 186, 210–211, 246
Nelson, Wayne 211
Nelson Eddy Show 152
Nesbitt, John Booth 211
Never Too Old 18
The New Adventures of Nero Wolfe 25, 275, 281
The New Adventures of Philip Marlowe 25
New Business World 136
The New Carnation Contented Hour 57
New Deal on Main Street 54
The New Junior Junction 172
The New Old Gold Show 8, 152
The New Penny 32
New York by a Representative New Yorker 317
New York Lighting Electric Stores News 167
New York Operatic Guild 181
The New York Philharmonic Orchestra 86, 106
The New York Philharmonic Symphony 70
The New York Philharmonic Symphony Orchestra 149, 165, 201, 211
New York Yankees 22, 76, 107
New York's World Fair 181
Newell, Lloyd 92
Newell-Emmett advertising 159
The Newlyweds 217
Newman, Edwin 104
News and Rhythm 25, 26
News and Views from the Show World 94
News by Hicks 136
News by True 298
News for Women 230
The News from Europe 49
News from the Nation's Capitol 28
News Game 20
News Here and Abroad 138
News of Europe 40
The News of Europe Direct 295, 297
News of the Week in Industry 187
News of the World 29, 59, 108, 122, 149, 178, 180, 254, 285, 295, 301
News of Tomorrow 103, 193
News Roundup 137, 138
News Through a Woman's Eyes 68
Newsbreak 29
Newsmark 218
Newspaper Enterprise Association 183
Newspaper of the Air 140
Newsweek 6

Next, Dave Garroway 127
Nick Carter, Master Detective 98, 127, 137, 230, 300
Night Cap Yarns 114
The Night Club of the Air 46
Night Court of the Air 294
Night Editor 19
Night Life 139, 214
Night Watch 71
Nightbeat 25, 79, 236
Nightline 125, 126
Niles, Kenneth L. 96, 212
Niles, Wendell Edward, Sr. 212–213
Niles and Prindle 212, 313
Nimitz, Chester 130
The 1937 Radio Show 36
The 1957 March of Dimes Galaxy of Stars 98
Niven, David 96
Nixon, Richard M. 233, 258, 264
Noah Webster Says 103, 175, 281
Nobel Prize 290
Noble, Ray 57
Nobles, Charles A. 213
Nobody's Children 159
Noel, Dick 213
Nolan, Jeanette 188
Nona from Nowhere 37, 310
Nordine, Ken 214
Norris, Kathleen 214
North American Newspaper Alliance 28, 103, 139, 285
Norville, Deborah 7
Nothing But the Truth 180, 303
Novins, Stuart 7
Now Hear This 31, 67
Now It Can Be Told 262
Nutrition, health and diet 175

Oboler, Arch 119
O'Brien, Joe 87, 214–215
O'Connor, Bob 215
O'Connor, Charles Peter 215, 292
O'Connor, Rod 215–216
O'Dare, Kitty 68
Odd Side of the News 276
Of All Things 133
Official Detective 26, 148, 186, 217, 311
The O'Flynn 248
O'Hara 109
O'Keefe, Walter 126
The Old Curiosity Shop 248
Old Fashioned Revival Hour 48
The Old Gold Comedy Theater 21
The Old Gold Hour 48, 147, 304
Old Gold Party Time 123
The Old Gold Program 21, 294
The Old Gold Show 21, 194
The Oldsmobile Program 147
Olin, Bob 119
Olivio Santoro 237
Olney Theatre Summer Playhouse, Maryland 21
Olsen, Johnny 196, 216–217
Olsen, Penny 216

Olson, Lynne 40, 41, 56, 116, 158, 173, 179, 203, 255, 257, 261, 264, 268, 273, 302
Omar, the Mystic 192
Omar the Swingmaker 13
On Broadway 30, 244
On Stage 25, 187, 209
On Stage America 48, 94
On Stage Everybody 216
On the Line with Considine 65
On the Road with Charles Kuralt 168
On Your Mark 63
Onassis, Aristotle 183
One Foot in Heaven 187
One Man's Destiny 86
One Man's Family 12, 13, 26, 54, 79, 90, 126, 187, 192, 194, 228, 294
One Man's Opinion 160
One Night Stand 217, 281
One Thousand Dollar Reward 239
The O'Neills 89, 134, 186, 187, 217, 228
The Open Door 104, 201
Open House 26, 280
Opry House Matinee 49
Opry Star Spotlight 73
The Orange Lantern 32, 187
O'Reilly, Bill 7
O'Riley, Jack 217
Orphans of Divorce 37, 208
Orson Welles' Radio Almanac 152
Ortega, Santos 49, 87, 217–218
Orwell, George 120
Osborne, Ted 282
Osborne Brothers 170
Osgood, Charles 57, 218
The Osgood File 218
O'Sullivan, Terry 218–219
The Other Americans 293
The Other Generation 197
Our Gal Sunday 89, 94, 99, 163, 167, 187, 195, 217, 276, 285
Our Miss Brooks 150, 170, 250, 274, 280
Our Secret Weapon 125, 177, 281
Out of the Deep 51, 275
Ovaltine 12
Over Our Coffee Cups 245
Overseas Press Club 50, 83, 154
Owen, Bill 103, 189, 197, 279
Owen, Ethel 194
Oxydol 21, 80
The Oxydol Show 280

Paar, Jack 161, 183, 310
Pacific Pioneer Broadcasters 84, 110, 192
The Pacific Story 109, 313
The Packard Hour 158, 315
Packard Mardi Gras 54
Paducah Plantation 123, 313
Pages of Romance 187, 234
Painted Dreams 230, 312
Paley, William S. 41, 56, 112, 129, 204, 243, 253, 256, 268, 273, 288, 296, 297, 320

Pall Mall 58, 125
Palmer, Betsy 199
The Palmolive Beauty Box Theater 163, 166, 250
The Palmolive Community Sing 156
Palmolive Hour 52, 128
Pan American Coffee Co. 246
Pancho and His Orchestra 111
Parallel 20
The Paramount Hour 162
The Paramount Playhouse 162
The Paramount-Publix Hour 162
The Paramount-Publix Radio Hour 162
Paramount Theater, New York 19
Pardo, Donald George 86, 219, 229
The Park Avenue Penners 113
Parker, Dorothy 321
Parker, Frank 181
Parker, Rollon 219–220
The Parker Family 59, 151
Parks, Bert 123, 145, 196, 220–221
Parligras, Natalia 116
Parsons, John 222
Parsons, Louella 96, 115, 142, 221–224, 318
Parties at Pickfair 200, 212
Party Time at Club Roma 8
Pasadena Playhouse 25, 66
The Passing Parade 54, 65, 177, 206, 211, 313
Passmore, Matthew 257
Pastels in Rhythm 127
Pat Barnes 23
Pat Barnes and Barbara Show 23
Pat Barnes Barnstormers 23
Pat Barnes in Person 23
Pat Novak for Hire 92, 94, 106
Pat Summerall on Sports 283
Pathé News 22, 128, 129, 311
Patrick, Mike 283
Patterson, Jefferson 41
Patton, Gen. George S. 79
Paul, Ralph 145, 224
Paul Douglas, Sports 81
Paul Harvey News and Comments 126
Paul White Radio-TV News Directors Association Award 104
Paul Whiteman Orchestra 122, 159
Paul Whiteman Presents 113
Paul Whiteman Show 48, 81, 104, 147, 237, 300, 304
Paul Whiteman's Musical Varieties 164
Pauline Frederick and the News 103
Paulson, Roger C. 96
The Pause That Refreshes 86, 91
The Pause That Refreshes on the Air 67, 292
Payroll Savings Plan 90
PDQ Quiz 42
The Peabodys 72

Pearl Harbor 14, 28, 74, 85–86, 126, 136, 216, 272
Pearson, Andrew Russell (Drew) 210, 224–227, 287
Pearson, Fort 227
Pearson, Dr. Paul 225
Pearson, Ted 227
Pearson Foundation 226
Peck, Gregory 115
Pegeen Prefers 98
Pegler, Westbrook 225, 293
Pelletier, Vincent 227–228
Penner, Joe 21
The Penny Singleton Show 180
Pennzoil Pete 313
The People Act 295
People Are Funny 8, 18, 134, 142, 193, 215
People's Platform 281, 320
The People's Rally 158
People's Vote 114
Pepper Young's Family 5, 21, 22, 35, 98, 104, 159, 160, 193, 277
Pepsi-Cola 159
Pepsodent 131
The Pepsodent Show 277
The Pepsodent Show Starring Bob Hope 113
Perrin, Victor Herbert 228
Perry, Jim 281
Perry Como Show 277
Perry Mason 43, 71, 78, 87, 159, 217, 244, 277
Persico, Joseph E. 205
Person to Person 7
Personal Column of the Air 103
Pet milk 73
The Pet Milk Show 134, 285
Pete Kelly's Blues 94, 228
The Peter Donald Show 79, 150
The Peter Lind Hayes Show 49, 127
Peter Quill 194
Petrie, George 49
Petrie, Howard 228–229
Petrova, Olga 43
Petruzzi, Jack 229
Pfeiffer, Robert O. 229
Pfizer, Beryl 103
The Phil Baker Show 42, 89, 123, 304, 313, 317
Phil Harris and Alice Faye Show 101, 182, 209, 280
Phil Rizzuto's Sports Caravan 238
Phil Spitalny Show 265
Philadelphia Opera Society 208
Philadelphia Symphony Orchestra 285
Philco Concert Orchestra 147
Philco Corp. 55
Philco Hall of Fame 113, 307
The Philco Hour of Theater Memories 208
Philco Radio Hall of Fame 65, 79, 89, 113, 237
Philco Radio Hour 147, 208
Philco Radio Time 54, 55, 237
Philco Summer Hour 217

Philip Morris Follies of 1946, 50, 239
Philip Morris Night with Horace Heidt 101
Philip Morris Playhouse 10, 20, 57, 63, 140, 152, 187, 234, 239, 317
Philip Morris Playhouse on Broadway 149, 164
Philip Morris Presents 215
Phillips 37
Phillips, Irna 217
Philo Vance 30
Phone Again Finnegan 212
The Phrase That Pays 47
Piano Playhouse 70, 175
The Piano Troubadours 156
Piastro, Mishel 166
Pick a Date with Buddy Rogers 13
Pick and Pat 81, 250
Pickens Party 134, 144
Pickens Sisters 243
Pierce, Carl Webster 229
Pierpoint, Robert 204, 256, 282
Pierre Andre Show 12
Piggly Wiggly 315
Pilat, Oliver R. 226
Pipe Dreams 234
Pitching Horseshoes 305
Plantation Jubilee 177
Plantation Party 123, 177, 313
Planters Pickers 291
Platter Patter 312
Play Broadcast 194, 255
Plays for Americans 182
Pleasure Island 23
Pleasure Time 81
Plummer, Amanda 121
Plummer, Christopher 121
Poetic Melodies 123, 177, 178
Poetry-reading 178
Poet's Gold 248
Poindexter, Ray 106, 130, 150, 203
Point Sublime 109
Policewoman 86, 135
Polk, George 158, 257
Pond's beauty products 245–246
Pond's Program 245
Pontiac 14
The Pontiac Show 147
Popeye the Sailor 30, 157
Portia Faces Life 42, 43, 67, 217, 233
Portraits of Life 18
Post, Elizabeth Lindley 230
Post, Emily 229–230
Post, Peggy Grayson 230
Post, Wiley 243
Post Broadcasting System, Hawaii 168
Post Grape Nuts Flakes 195
Postcard Serenade 305
Pot o' Gold 18, 67, 118, 266, 277
Potluck Party 17
Powell, Dick 222, 223
Powell, Kenneth C. 230

INDEX 352

Powers Charm School 135
Prelude to Dusk 281
Prentiss, Ed 230
Presby, Arch 162, 230–231
Presenting Boris Karloff 121
Presenting Charles Boyer 15, 275
Press Association Dispatches 292
Press Club 194
Press Radio News 164
Pretty Kitty Kelly 63, 71, 166
Price, Vincent Leonard, Jr. 119, 120, 231
Prince Albert tobacco 299
Prince Charming 216
Pringle, Bess 263
The Private Files of Matthew Bell 294
The Private Files of Rex Saunders 20
The Private Lives of Ethel and Albert 60, 175, 237, 265, 322
Procter & Gamble Co. 21, 22, 57, 64, 89, 125, 233–234, 236, 263, 288, 289
Professor Puzzlewit 157
Professor Quiz 111, 122, 295
Promenade Concerts 122
Proudly We Hail 20, 206
Prudential Family Hour 106
The Prudential Family Hour of Stars 38, 152
Pull Over, Neighbor 18
Pure Oil Co. 124
Purple Heart 114
Purple Heart Theater 187
Pursuit 19, 280
Purvis, Melvin 231
Putnam, George Arthur 231–232
Putnam, George Carson 232
Putnam, George Frederick 232–233

Q.E.D. 48
Quaker Puffed Wheat 48
Queen for a Day 17, 19, 143, 227
Quick as a Flash 30, 90, 106, 125, 200, 217, 239
Quicksilver 46
Quiet Please 58, 98, 170, 193
Quincy, Bob 61
Quincy Howe and the News 143
Quincy Howe Comments 143
Quinn, Carmel 181
Quint, Bernard 122
Quixie Doodles 234
The Quiz Kids 19, 51, 95, 164, 167, 196, 227
Quizmasters
Quiz of Two Cities 63, 91, 98
Quizzer's Baseball 304

Raby, John 276
Racing Scratches 185
Radio Almanac 182
Radio City Party 158
Radio City Playhouse 62, 237, 310
Radio Correspondents' Association 174

Radio Digest 131
The Radio Edition of the Bible 199
Radio Enthusiasts of Puget Sound 25
Radio feuds 318
The Radio Forum 285
Radio Guide 56, 69, 75
Radio Guide's Court of Honor 300
Radio Guild 223
Radio Hall of Fame 36, 102, 218
Radio Hall of Fame 22, 65, 79, 89, 122, 217, 307
Radio History of the War 30
Radio-Keith-Orpheum Hour 189
Radio Life Magazine 28
Radio Mirror 69, 91
Radio Press International 64
Radio Reader's Digest 80, 127, 149, 166, 180, 206, 211, 233, 294, 300
Radio Revels 156
The Radio School of the Air 285
Radio stations: CFAR, Manitoba 291; CKCG, Timmins, Ont. 291; CKCL, Toronto 291; CKLW, Detroit 48; KABC, San Antonio 255; KALE, Portland, Ore. 312; KARK, Little Rock, Ark. 73; KBBQ, Burbank 15; KBOI, Idaho 111; KCBQ, San Diego 48; KCEE, Tucson 11; KCIJ, Shreveport, La. 73; KCKN, Kansas City, Kan. 21; KCMJ, Palm Springs 153; KCOP, Los Angeles 170, 233; KDAY, Los Angeles 48; KDKA, Pittsburgh 23, 71, 139, 237, 242, 287; KDON, Monterey, Calif. 252; KDYL, Salt Lake City 20; KECA, Los Angeles 18, 170; KEFM, Chicago 153; KEHE, Los Angeles 17, 21, 48, 103, 153, 170; KEJK, Beverly Hills 187; KENO, Las Vegas 163; KEX, Portland, Ore. 19, 134; KFAB, Lincoln, Neb. 16; KFAC, Los Angeles 50, 79, 153, 171, 209, 291; KFI, Los Angeles 18, 21, 33, 48, 54–55, 57, 123, 146, 148, 168, 170, 251, 316; KFKX, Hastings, Neb. 130; KFMB, San Diego 308; KFML, Denver 101; KFON, Long Beach 57; KFOX, Long Beach 84, 114, 153; KFRC, San Francisco 9, 48, 98, 113, 169, 315; KFRO, Longview, Texas 299; KFSD, San Diego 17; KFSO, San Francisco 20; KFVK, Sacramento 113; KFWB, Los Angeles 15, 20, 35, 109, 114, 170; KFYO, Abilene, Texas 299; KGB, San Diego 17, 48, 232, 304; KGER, Long Beach 57; KGFJ, Los Angeles 171; KGO,

San Francisco 13, 20, 57, 94, 157; KGW, Portland 109, 134, 146, 231; KGY, Olympia, Wash. 71; KHJ, Hollywood 15, 17, 19, 21, 33, 42, 48, 56, 66, 79, 113, 140, 169, 212, 216, 233, 243, 315; KHQ, Spokane 146; KID, Idaho Falls 216; KIEV, Los Angeles 233; KJR, Seattle 212; KKGO, Los Angeles 79; KLAC, Los Angeles 35; KLEE, Houston 73, 255; KLO, Ogden, Utah 216; KLX, Oakland 12; KMBC, Kansas City, Mo. 161, 283, 284; KMIC, Inglewood, Calif. 304; KMOX, St. Louis 21, 69, 107, 114, 194; KMPC, Beverly Hills 15, 42, 48, 101, 134, 188; KMTH, Los Angeles 16; KMTR, Hollywood 38, 168, 209; KNUZ, Houston 73; KNX, Hollywood 10, 39, 42, 62, 69, 84, 109, 114, 115, 123, 146, 153, 171, 179, 250 308; KNXT, Los Angeles 232; KOA, Denver 209; KOIL, Omaha 20, 72; KOL, Seattle 109; KOLO, Reno 130; KOY, Phoenix 71, 181; KPLC, Lake Charles, La. 73; KPLM, Palm Springs 211; KPLS, Los Angeles 233; KPO, San Francisco 92, 157; KPOJ, Portland, Ore. 312; KPRC, San Francisco 89, 227; KQV, Pittsburgh 188; KRKD, Los Angeles 48; KRLA, Los Angeles 233; KROW, Oakland 89; KRUX, Phoenix 48; KSAN, San Francisco 179; KSFC, San Francisco 308; KSFO, San Francisco 109; KSL, Salt Lake City 216; KSO, Des Moines 239; KSSC, Grand Junction, Colo. 19; KSTP, St. Paul 11, 168, 202, 232, 281; KSWS, Roswell, N.M. 308; KTAB, San Francisco 109, 168; KTHS, Hot Springs, Ark. 149; KTLA, Los Angeles 170; KTLN, Denver 101; KTMR, Los Angeles 304; KTRH, Houston 255; KTSA, San Antonio 48; KUPD, Phoenix 48; KUSC, Los Angeles 79; KUTA, Salt Lake City 216; KVAN, Vancouver 236; KVOD, Denver 101; KVOO, Tulsa 126, 241, 243, 293; KVOR, Colorado Springs 69; KWIK, Burbank 207, 250; KWK, St. Louis 14, 68, 194; KWKH, Shreveport, La. 20; KWSC, Pullman, Wash. 109, 203; KXYZ, Houston 73, 255; KYA, San Francisco 170; KYW, Chicago 185, 241, 310, 312; WAAB, Boston 101;

INDEX

WAAT, Newark 220; WABC, New York 6, 20, 45, 63, 66, 81, 97, 112, 128, 163, 166, 249, 269; WABD, New York 31; WAFG, Dothan, Ala. 292; WAGA, Atlanta 49; WAGF, Dothan, Ala. 87; WAHG, Long Island 155; WAIM, Anderson, S.C. 292; WAIR, Winston-Salem 107; WAIU, Columbus, Ohio 122, 311; WASH, Ann Arbor 305; WASI, Cincinnnati 22; WASK, Lafayette, Ind. 62; WATT, Jersey City 150; WAVY, Portsmouth, Va. 311; WAYS, Charlotte, N.C. 168; WBAB, Atlantic City 199; WBAL, New York 99; WBAP, Fort Worth 265; WBAW, Terre Haute, Ind. 280; WBBM, Chicago 26, 38, 72, 114, 127, 168, 177, 196, 243, 269, 312, 314; WBEN, Buffalo 235; WBET, Boston 147; WBIC, Bay Shore, N.Y. 46; WBIR, Knoxville 311; WBMC, Detroit 102; WBNS, Columbus, Ohio 149; WBNX, New York 30; WBRE, Wilkes-Barre, Pa. 224; WBT, Charlotte 31, 34, 61, 139, 168, 292, 310–311; WBYN, Brooklyn 45; WBZ, Springfield, Mass. 16–17, 56, 175, 213, 215, 228; WBZA, Boston 17, 78, 213; WBZA, Springfield, Mass. 228; WCAE, Pittsburgh 193; WCAH, Columbus, Ohio 20; WCAU, Philadelphia 14, 45, 55, 56, 117, 170, 180, 198, 276, 320; WCBD, Chicago 239; WCBR, Goldsboro 15; WCBS, New York 21, 99, 144, 218, 283; WCCO, Minneapolis 216; WCFL, Chicago 178; WCKY, Covington, Ky. 139; WCOL, Columbus, Ohio 149; WCOP, Boston 199; WCOS, Columbia, S.C. 292; WCSC, Charleston 34; WDAF, Kansas City, Mo. 266; WDBO, Orlando 11; WDCR, Hartford, Conn. 23; WDNC, Durham, N.C. 92, 276; WDOD, Chattanooga 49; WDSU, New Orleans 73; WEAF, New York 44, 52, 59, 97, 111, 128, 136, 155, 159, 184 189, 198, 232, 243, 251, 276; WEAT, West Palm Beach, Fla. 317; WEBC, Duluth 11, 184, 198; WEBO, Marquette, Mich. 242; WEEU, Reading, Pa. 276; WEGM, Chicago 140; WENR, Chicago 23, 24, 39, 165, 172, 178, 227; WEW, St. Louis 80; WFAA, Dallas 11; WFBC, Greenville, S.C. 34;

WFBH, New York 45; WFBM, Indianapolis 164; WFBR, Baltimore 90, 112; WFIL, Philadelphia 48, 159, 170, 320; WGAR, Buffalo 49; WGBS, Miami 68; WGES, Chicago 314; WGHO, Kingston, N.Y. 184; WGMS, Washington, D.C. 218; WGN, Chicago 11, 12, 20, 23, 31, 72, 91, 100, 108, 126, 127, 130 148, 195, 216, 250, 255, 303; WGR, Buffalo 47, 250; WGST, Atlanta 220, 301; WGY, Schenectady, N.Y. 122, 250, 270; WHA, Madison, Wisc. 99; WHAM, Rochester 278; WHAS, Louisville 14, 37, 149, 292; WHB, Kansas City, Mo. 283; WHBF, Rock Island, Ill. 55; WHBQ, Memphis 48; WHDH, Boston 135; WHDL, Olean, N.Y. 124; WHET, Troy, Ala. 87; WHN, New York 11, 22, 30, 64, 147, 148, 168, 170, 185, 198, 285, 309, 317; WHO, Des Moines 17, 235; WHP, Harrisburg, Pa. 271; WHT, Chicago 23, 75; WHUD, Peekskill, N.Y. 215; WHYN, Holyoke, Mass. 78; WIBA, Madison, Wisc. 100; WIBO, Chicago 24, 75, 249; WICC, Bridgeport, Conn. 122; WIL, St. Louis 177, 194; WILL, Urbana 149; WIND, Gary, Ind. 139, 169, 252; WINS, New York 23, 30, 44, 90, 111, 139, 165, 185, 241, 309; WINZ, Miami 68; WIOD, Miami 68, 134, 275–276; WIP, Philadelphia 170, 208, 276, 303; WIS, Columbia, S.C. 34, 65, 292; WISN, Milwaukee 26; WITH, Baltimore 86; WJDX, Jackson, Miss. 73; WJJD, Chicago 11, 153, 169; WJKS, Gary, Ind. 227; WJLB, Detroit 128; WJQS, Jackson, Miss. 73; WJR, Detroit 90; WJSV, Washington, D.C. 34, 45, 65, 74, 91, 112, 285, 296, 319; WJXN, McComb, Miss. 73; WJZ, New York 44, 52, 70, 97, 103 123, 128, 141, 147, 155, 158, 159, 160, 161, 191, 198, 283; WKAT, Miami Beach 54, 119; WKAZ, Charleston, W. Va. 48; WKBW, Buffalo 49, 250; WKRC, Cincinnati 33; WKZO, Kalamazoo, Mich. 126, 149, 250; WLAC, Nashville 281; WLIT, Philadelphia 82; WLOE, Boston 74, 135; WLOK, Lima, Ohio 82; WLS, Chicago 11, 44, 169; WLTH, Brooklyn 240; WLW, Cincinnati 14, 22, 31, 33, 47, 48, 82, 117, 141,

149, 161, 163, 165, 169, 178, 269, 280, 320; WMAC, New York 198; WMAK, Buffalo 129; WMAL, Washington, D.C. 6, 28, 29, 45, 112, 113, 121, 138, 285; WMAQ, Chicago 24, 39, 82, 85, 130, 131, 165, 177, 227, 306; WMAZ, Chicago 131; WMC, Memphis, Tenn. 73, 149; WMCA, New York 48, 54, 68, 97, 103, 105, 111, 119, 133, 139, 171, 185, 214–215, 240, 276, 293; WMEX, Boston 90; WMGM, New York 47, 90, 198, 240, 285, 317; WMT, Cedar Rapids, Iowa 229; WMYQ, Miami 48; WNAC, Boston 101, 198, 243, 262; WNBC, New York 14, 23, 45, 47, 72, 97, 99, 124, 215; WNCN, New York 99; WNEW, New York 30, 31, 34, 35, 36, 45, 47, 65, 67, 68, 69, 150, 159, 167, 170; WNJR, Newark 129; WNOE, New Orleans 73, 172; WNRC, Greensboro, N.C. 211; WNYC, Brooklyn 67, 98, 181; WOC, Davenport, Iowa 312; WOL, Washington, D.C. 34–35, 138, 139; WOOD, Grand Rapids, Mich. 121, 305; WOR, New York 15, 19, 22, 23, 31, 36, 44, 45, 54, 59, 68, 78, 84, 86, 91, 97, 98, 103, 119, 122, 128, 133, 134, 137, 140, 155, 159, 160, 161, 170, 179, 183–184, 186, 195, 198, 241, 252, 269, 270, 285, 292, 309, 314–315, 319; WOV, New York 68, 159; WOW, Omaha 16, 19; WPAC, Patchogue, N.Y. 45–46; WPAT, Paterson, N.J. 129, 241; WPCH, New York 240; WPEN, Philadelphia 55; WPG, Atlantic City 45, 199; WPTF, Raleigh 15; WQAM, Miami 68; WQXR, New York 99, 143, 144, 294; WRAL, Raleigh 15, 185; WRBU, Gastonia, N.C. 34; WRC, Washington, D.C. 21, 28, 29, 45, 107, 111, 113, 121, 124, 136; WRCA, New York 21, 97; WREC, Memphis 73; WRHM, Minneapolis 168; WRLT, Florida 21; WRR, Dallas 195; WRUF, Gainesville, Florida 22; WSAI, Cincinnati 66; WSB, Atlanta 87, 292; WSBA, York, Pa. 280; WSKB, McComb, Miss. 73; WSLI, Jackson, Miss. 73; WSM, Nashville 49, 73, 281, 299; WSOC, Charlotte 34; WSUL, Iowa City 55; WTAG, Worcester, Mass. 78, 86; WTAM, Cleveland 122, 177,

320; WTCN, Minneapolis 216; WTHT, Hartford 101; WTIC, Hartford, Conn. 44; WTMA, Charleston, S.C. 144; WTMJ, Milwaukee 114, 216, 242; WTNT, Nashville 86; WTOP, Washington, D.C. 260, 292; WVEC, San Luis Obispo, Cal. 216; WVNJ, Oakdale, N.J. 47; WVOM, Boston 59; WVP, Newark 155; WWDC, Washington, D.C. 199; WWJ, Detroit 242, 298; WWL, New Orleans 11, 165; WWSW, Pittsburgh 71; WXYZ, Detroit 31, 87, 94, 102, 113, 128, 185, 220, 298, 305, 320; XER, Mexico 312
The Radio Theater 231
Radio Writers Guild 282
Raffetto, Michael 21
Raffles 25
The Railroad Hour 194, 227
Raising Your Parents 70
Raleigh and Kool Program 103
The Raleigh Cigarette Program 38
The Raleigh Cigarette Program Starring Red Skelton 187, 215
The Raleigh Room 63
Ralph Bellamy Stock Co. 17
Ralph Edwards Productions 90
Ralph Morrison and His Orchestra 214
Ralph Norman and His Orchestra 120–121
Rambling with Gambling 241
Rangers Quartet 61
Rate Your Mate 303
Rather, Dan 154, 167, 261, 282
Rawson, Ronald W. 233–234
Ray Anthony and His Orchestra 213
The Ray Bolger Show 228
The Ray Noble Show 15
Rayburn, Gene 171, 229, 307
Raye, Martha 66
Raylin Productions, Inc. 83
Raymond Gram Swing and the News 187, 317
Raymond Paige Show 262
Raymond Scott Show 285
Rayve shampoo 195
RCA Radio Theater 144
RCA Victor Show 20, 77, 125
Reagan, Ronald 7, 26, 223
Real Folks 16
Real Stories from Real Life 294
The Realsilk Program 138
Reasoner, Harry 62, 167, 273, 306
Rebuttal 211, 301
The Red Barber Show 21
Red Barber Sports 48, 123
Red Barber's Club Room 21
Red Benson's Movie Matinee 309
Red Feather Roundup 187
Red Lacquer and Jade 252
Red Ryder 8, 25, 109, 153, 187, 266

The Red Skelton Show 38, 140, 161, 187, 192, 194, 215, 310
Reddy, John 211, 246
Reddy, Tom 234
The Redhead 132
Reed, Florence 43
Reed, Theodore Alan 234–235
Reed, Toby 235
Reese, Pee Wee 77
Refreshment Time 199
Reichman, Joe 162
Reimers, Edwin W. 235–236
Reinheart, Alice 295
Reisman, Leo 245
Rendevous with Ross 248
Renfrew of the Mounted 87, 89, 220
Renfro Valley Barn Dance 169
Renfro Valley Sunday Mornin' Gatherin' 169
Renwick, Katherine 235
Report to the Nation 74, 164, 259
Repp, Guy 282
Request Performance 265
Reserved for Garroway 127
The Rest of the Story 126
Results, Incorporated 215
Reunion 220
Reunion of the States 18
Revelers Quartet 243
Revere All-Star Revue 235
Rexall Summer Show 101
Rexall Summer Theater 228
Reynolds (metals) 87
Reynolds, Frank 273
RFD America 66, 82
Rhapsody in Rhythm 109
Rhee, Syngman 154
Rhythm at Eight 147
Rhythm on the Road 78
Rhythm Road 237
Rhythmic Melodies 178
Rice, Glen 188
Rice, Grantland 236, 279
Rice, Howard 54
Rich, John 104
Rich Man's Darling 195
Richard C. Hottelet 143
Richard Diamond, Private Detective 15, 101, 152, 162, 215, 275, 281
Richard Harkness and the News 124
Richardson, Ethel Park 177
Richfield Country Club 118
Richfield Reporter 100, 145, 305
Rickles, Donald Newton 236
Rico, Lionel 237
Riggs, Glenn 237
Riggs, Lee Aubrey "Speed" 37, 237–238, 252
The Right Thing to Do 229
The Right to Happiness 32, 65, 98, 151, 153, 194, 230, 233, 312, 322
Rinso 10
Ripley, Joseph S. 238
Ripley, Robert L. 255
The Risë Stevens Show 69

The Rising Sun Show 91
Ritchie, Jean 170
Rizzuto, Philip Francis 9, 238
R.J. Reynolds Tobacco Co. 299
RKO-General Corp. 169
The RKO Theater of the Air 189
Road of Life 49, 57, 63, 71, 80, 89, 120, 153, 194, 200, 229, 233, 305, 311
Road to Danger 126, 200
Robbins, Charles 104
Robert Benchley Show 265
The Robert Burns Panatella Show 165, 217
Robert McCormick and the News 186
The Robert Merrill Show 78
Robert Q. Lewis 20–21
The Robert Q. Lewis Show 30, 124, 266
Robert St. John and the News 254
The Robert Shaw Chorale 21
Robert Trout and the News 295
Robert Trout with the News Till Now 295, 297
Roberts, Bruce 261
Roberts, David Kelley, Jr. 239
Roberts, Ed 239
Roberts, Howard 9
Roberts, Ken 87, 239–241
Roberts, Nancy 241
Roberts, Nicole 241
Roberts, Peter 241
Roberts, Tony 241
Robertson, Chris 257
Robinson, Alvin 241–242
Robinson, Max 273
Robinson Crusoe Jr. 293
Robison, Carson J. 176
The Rochester Show 280
Rock 'n' Roll Dance Party 32
Rockabye Dudley 86
Rocky Fortune 162, 182
Rocky Jordan 79, 280, 291, 308
Roen, Louis Bernard 242
Roger Kilgore, Public Defender 120, 217
Rogers, Ginger 125
Rogers, Will 51, 190, 242–244
Rogers, William 244
Rogers of the Gazette 25, 79, 170, 228, 250
Rogue's Gallery 56, 84
The Rollickers 208
Romance 25, 71, 79, 80, 106, 114, 215, 217, 250, 277, 280, 303
Romance and Rhythm 294
Romance Isle 53
The Romance of Helen Trent 11, 94, 123, 153, 194, 200, 230, 294, 310
Romance of the Ranchos 114, 170, 187
Romance, Rhythm and Ripley 10
Ronson, Adele 244
Roosevelt, Eleanor 58, 69, 105, 129, 244–246, 290
Roosevelt, Elliott 246–248

Roosevelt, Franklin Delano 6, 28, 56, 60, 64, 74, 103, 107, 112, 117, 124, 138, 151, 224, 245, 264, 290, 295, 307, 318
Roosty of the AAF 109
Roper, Elmo 248
Roper Center for Public Opinion Research 248
Rose of My Dreams 86, 91
Rosemary 5, 78, 87, 98, 134, 214
Rosemary Clooney Show 150
Roses and Drums 5
Ross, David 248–249
Ross, Norman 249–250
Roundup of War Reports 138
Rountree, Martha 274, 275
Rovetini, Johnny 57
Rowan, Roy A. 250
Roxy and His Gang 52, 70
Roy, Michael 250
The Roy Rogers Show 20, 69, 79, 187, 194, 209, 228, 274, 281
Royal, John F. 27, 278
Royal Crown Revue 189, 234
Royal Gelatin Hour 38, 102, 141, 189, 234
The Royal Vagabonds 317
Rubinoff, David 11
Rubinoff and His Violin 11
Rudd, Hughes 167
The Rudy Vallee Show 38, 102, 114, 141, 144, 189, 194, 212, 234, 276, 281, 307
Ruffner, Edmund Birch (Tiny) 250–251
Ruick, Melville 251
Russ Hodges, Sports 139
Russert, Tim 275
Rusty Draper 250
Ruth, Babe 245
Ruysdael, Basil 38, 238, 251–252

Saal, William 320
Sabin, Robert Cook 252
The Sad Sack 152
Saerchinger, Cesar 252–253
Safer, Morley 167
The Saint 15, 25, 79, 152, 153, 275
St. George, Dorian 253–254
St. John, Robert 85, 254–255
Saks on Broadway—Speaker Walter Winchell 317
Salant, Richard 262
Sally's Furriers 215
Sally's Movieland Review 215
The Salt Lake City Tabernacle Choir 161
Salute to Saturday 232
Salute to Youth 118
Sam 'n' Henry 130
Sam Pilgrim's Progress 187
Sammy Kaye Show 122, 149
Sammy Kaye's Sunday Serenade 13
Sandburg, Carl 287
Sandham Prize for Extemporaneous Speaking 118
Sara's Private Caper 180, 209

Sarnoff, David 273
Satan's Waitin' 114
The Saturday Morning Vaudeville Theater 10
Saturday Night Bandwagon 91
Saturday Night Party 291
Saturday Night Revue 47
Saturday Night Serenade 5, 285, 295
Saturday Night Swing Club 9, 81, 140, 147
Saturday Theater 308
Savage, Guy 255
Savage, Henry W. 251
Save the Children Foundation 104
Scattergood Baines 80, 91, 167, 194, 276, 308
Schaden, Chuck 20, 304
Schaefer Revue 67
Schaefer Star Revue 21
Schafer, Natalie 116
Schecter, Abe 288
Scherer, Ray 104
Schieffer, Bob 7, 135
Schmeling, Max 285
Schoenbrun, Daniel 204
Schoenbrun, David 158, 255–256, 257
Schorr, Daniel 158, 256–258, 282
Schorr, Lisbeth 257
Schwartz, David 150
Schwarzkopf, H. Norman, Sr. 258–259
The Scorpion 217
Scotland Yard's Inspector Burke 275, 294
Scout About Town 91, 119, 224
Scramby Amby 157, 309
Screen Actors Guild 223
Screen Director's Guild 176
Screen Director's Playhouse 176, 187, 307
Screen Guild Playhouse 206
Screen Guild Theater 65, 250
Screen Test 65
Scripps-Howard Syndicate 285
The Sea Hound 48
The Sealed Book 307
Sealtest Sunday Night Party 118
Sealtest Variety Theater 109, 153
Sealtest Village Store 15, 144, 234
The Search That Never Ends 277
The Sears Radio Theater 72, 109, 119, 120, 187, 192, 194, 197, 209, 228, 300, 303, 313
Second Honeymoon 193, 220
Second Husband 26, 79, 132
The Second Mrs. Burton 59, 151, 186, 285, 294, 310, 311
Second Sunday 103
Secret City 126
Secret Missions 322
Selby Shoe Co. 245
Señor Ben 118
Sensation and Swing 136
Sergeant Preston of the Yukon 31, 102, 193

Sergio, Lisa 103
The Series Radio Theater 231
Serutan 175
Service to the Front 46
Service with a Smile 118
Sesno, Frank 169
Seth Parker 136
Sevareid, Arnold Eric 116, 135, 149, 167, 203, 206, 259–262, 264, 272, 282
Seven Front Street 224
Seven Star Revue 147
Seventy-Six Revue with Conrad Nagel 206
Seymour, Dan 249, 262–263
Shadel, Willard R. 263–264
The Shadow 26, 30, 31, 33, 56, 77, 87, 102, 123, 175, 179, 200, 217, 234, 239, 248, 265, 311
The Shakespeare Circle 286
Shakespeare Festival 286
Shakespeare Festival Players 201
Sharbutt, Delbert Eugene 131, 264–265
Shaw, George Bernard 253, 311
Shaw, Stan 171
Shaw, Winnie 215
The Sheaffer Parade 165
Sheen, Bishop Fulton J. 67
Sheilah Graham 115
Sheldon, Herbert H. 265–266
Shell Chateau 223
Shepard, Robert L. 266
Sheppard, Dr. Sam 161
The Sheriff 43, 163, 310
Sherlock Holmes 8, 25, 32, 65
Sherry, Bob 266
Sherwood, Bob 96
Shieffer, Bob 167
Shields, Frederick 266
Shipley, Bill 266
Shirer, William L. 41, 116, 125, 156, 181, 203, 266–269
Shirley, Tom 269
Shirley Temple Time 38
Sholtz, William 245
Shoot the Moon 63
Shopping Talk 300
Shor, Toots 247
Shore, Dinah 52
Shoshani, Michael 53, 157
Shouse, Jouette 41
Show Boat 42, 104, 208, 244, 251, 293
The Show Goes On 124
Show Stoppers 179
The Show Without a Name 228
Showtime 274
Shriner, Herb 243
Sidney Bernstein Theater, London 19
Sidney Hillman Foundation Award 197
Sidney Walton's Music 309
Sies, Luther F. 103, 119, 144, 156, 189, 203, 225, 259, 319
Signal Carnival 103
The Silent Men 275
The Silver Eagle 126, 214

INDEX

Silver Eagle, Mountie 10, 21, 66, 126, 140, 172, 214, 230
Silver Summer Revue 70, 262
Silver Theater 17, 25, 63, 65, 152, 167, 206, 304
Simms, Hal 269–270
Simms, Lu Ann 181
Simpson, Wallis 297
Sinatra, Frank 113, 223, 252
Sincerely, Kenny Baker 307
The Sinclair Headliner 270
Sinclair oil 270
Sing Along 239
Sing, America, Sing 18
Sing for Your Dough 19
Sing for Your Supper 294
Sing It Again 124, 262
Singin' Sam 111, 265
Singing Cinderella 163
Singing in the Morning 292
The Singing Story Lady 46
Singiser, Frank 270
Singo 13
The Six Shooter 25, 79, 109, 152, 234, 294, 305
The Sixty-Four Dollar Question 162
The $64,000 Question 144
Sizing Up the News 46, 293
Skelly News 85
Skelton, Red 39, 117, 162, 235
The Skip Farrell Show 172
Skippy Hollywood Theater 113
The Sky Blazers 57
Sky King 11, 153, 163, 172, 214, 305
Skyline Roof 59
Slater, Bill and Tom 140
Slattery, Jack H. 270–271
Sleep No More 118
Sloan, Ted 185
Sloane, Everett 87
The Slumber Hour 70
Smilin' Ed and His Buster Brown Gang 194, 230, 231
Smith, Arthur Robert 261
Smith, Ed 271
Smith, Howard Kingsbury, Jr. 7, 203, 256, 260, 262, 271–274
Smith, Jack 26
Smith, Kate 63, 76, 183, 245
Smith, Verne 274
The Smiths of Hollywood 192, 304
Smoke Dreams 196
Snead, Sam 304
Snow Village Sketches 86, 140
Snyder, Tom 26
So Proudly We Hail 21
So the Story Goes 179, 211
So This Is Radio 106, 201
So You Think You Know Music 23, 49, 67, 163
Soap operas 44, 71, 105
Society Girl 30, 67
Society of Professional Journalists 65
Society to Preserve and Encourage Radio Drama, Variety and Comedy (SPERDVAC) 110

Socony-Vacuum 280
The Soldier Who Came Home 90
Soldier's Wife 33
Soldiers with Wings 109
Somebody Knows 114, 152
Somerset Maugham Theater 162, 200
A Song Is Born 157
Song of the Stranger 200
The Song of Your Life 58
The Song Shop 265
The Song Writing Machine 217
Songs by George Bryan 49, 262
Songs by Morton Downey 164, 248
Songs by Sinatra 113, 193
Songs of a Dreamer 19
Songs of Jerry Wayne 262
Songs of the B-Bar-B 309
Sothern, Edward 5
Sound Off 48
Southern Cruise 212
Southwest Broadcasting System 95
Space Patrol 194, 298, 312
The Spade Cooley Show 170
Spargrove, William 274
Sparring Partners 160
The Sparrow and the Hawk 98, 181
Speak Up, America 227
Speak Your Mind 72, 126
Special Agent 91, 104, 170
Special Investigator 23, 217
Speed Gibson of the International Secret Police 182, 233
Speed Show 108
Spencer, Edith 263
Spend a Million 62
Spic 'n' Span 233
Spike Jones Show 137, 152, 250, 305
Spin to Win 145
The Spirit of '41, 74
Spivak, Lawrence E. 274–275
Spoon River Anthology 201
Sports Central USA 90
Sports Daily 9
Sports Scraps 278
Sports Stories 236
Sports Today 277
Sportsman's Quiz 19
Sportsmen's Club 277
Spotlight Bands 250
Spotlight on America 232
Spotlight Review 152, 164
Spry shortening 263
S.R.O. 48, 186
Stage Door Canteen 63, 320
Stahl, Leslie 7
Stairway to the Stars 237
Stalin, Joseph 196
Stan Kenton and His Orchestra 106
The Stan Lomax Show 300
Standard Oil Co. 251
The Standard Symphony 109
Stang, Arnold 77, 197
Stanley, Don 275

Stanley, John 275
Stanton, Frank 88, 261
Stanton, Robert S. 275–276
Stapleton, Jean 214
The Star and the Story 235
Star for a Night 81, 151
Star Performance 193
Star Time with Dorothy Kilgallen 160
Stark, Charles 276–277
Stark, Richard S. 277
Starlight Concert 315
Starlight Serenade 86, 265
The Starlighters 234
Starr of Space 66
Starring Boris Karloff 121
Stars and Starters 23
Stars for Defense 90, 220
Stars in Jazz 299
Stars in Khaki 'n' Blue 67
Stars in the Air 150
Stars of Melody 16
Stars Over Hollywood 21, 109, 114, 179, 187, 194
State Fair Concert 251
Steinbrenner, George 9
Stella Dallas 37, 58, 67, 79, 98, 106, 167, 201, 208, 307
Stephenson, Robert Robinson 277
Stepmother 123
Stepping Out 31, 303
Sterling, Leonard G. 277
Sterling Drugs Inc. 37
Stern, Bill 23, 93, 127
Stern, Henry William 277–280
Steve Allen Show 150
Stevens, Lee 280
Stevenson, Bob 280
Stewart, Jay Cleve 280–281
Stewart, Martha 230
Stewart, Paul 235
Stiles, Hallie 243
Stone, David P. 281
Stone, George 165, 281
Stoopnagle and Budd 26, 59, 68, 89, 239, 304
Stop Me If You've Heard This One 47, 262, 293, 317
Stop or Go 193
Stop That Villain 17, 194
Stop the Music! 48, 123, 127, 220
Stories of Escape 165
Storm, John 281
The Story Behind the Headlines 252
The Story of Bess Johnson 43
The Story of Bud Barton 310
The Story of Dr. Susan 33
The Story of Ellen Randolph 187
The Story of Holly Sloan 228
The Story of Joan and Kermit 177
The Story of Mary Marlin 5, 38, 42, 46, 57, 63, 79, 121, 200, 201, 292
The Story of Sandra Martin 170
Stout, Rex 124, 281–282
The Stradivari Orchestra 67, 292

Straight Arrow 33, 72
Strange 320
Strange as It Seems 128, 153, 187, 276, 313
The Strange Dr. Karnac 60
The Strange Dr. Weird 314
The Strange Romance of Evelyn Winters 86, 91, 132, 310
Strange Wills 72, 194, 309
Strawser, Neil 282–283
Streamlined Shakespeare 286
The Street Singer 248
Stribling, W.L. (Young) 285
Strictly from Dixie 137
Strictly Personal 132
Strietman Streetman 310
Strike It Rich 19, 71, 145, 224
String Symphony 122
Stroke of Fate 160, 217, 237
Strolling Songsters 175
Struthers, Jan 247
Stu Erwin Show 163
Stuart, Allan 283
Stuart, Mary 148, 218
Studebaker 20
The Studebaker Champions 118, 147, 248
Studio One 98, 303
Sullivan, Brian 66
Sullivan, Ed 280
The Summer Family Hour 106
Summer Hotel 81, 262
Summer Stars 220
Summerall, George Allen (Pat) 283
Summerfield Bandstand 305
Sunday Dinner at Aunt Fanny's 164
Sunday Down South 49
Sunday Evening News of the World 224
Sunday Evening News Roundup 137, 178
Sunday Evening Party 276
Sunday/Friday with Dave Garroway 100, 230
The Sunday News Desk 185
Sunday News Highlights 232
Sundial 91, 112
Sunkist Farms 142
Sunkist Growers 222, 223
Sunrise Roundup 281
Sunrise Serenade 102
Sunset Valley Barn Dance 281
The Sunshine Hour 234
Superman 200
Superstition 34
Surprise Package 280
Surprise Serenade 82, 114
Suspense 15, 25, 32, 38, 79, 98, 176, 177, 180, 187, 193, 212, 228, 280, 291, 303, 308, 313
Sussman, Barry 226
Sutton, Vida Ravenscroft 140
The Swan Soap Show 113
Swanson, Gloria 96
Swayze, John Cameron 21, 88, 283–285
Sweeney, Warren 285

Sweeney and March 15, 170, 228
Sweeney and March Show 123
Sweet River 140, 230
Sweetheart soap 86, 246
Swift Garden Party 162
Swing, Raymond Gram 156, 203
Swingshift Frolics 216
The Sylvan Levin Opera Concert 179
Symphonies Under the Stars 187

T-Man 170
Take a Break 220
Take a Good Look 8
Take a Note 197
Take a Number 148, 266
Take It Easy Time 314
Take It or Leave It 15, 31, 212, 239, 248, 280
Take Me Back to Renfro Valley (song) 169
A Tale of Today 42, 230, 274
Talent Search, Country Style 23
Tales of Fatima 98
Tales of the Texas Rangers 15, 25, 33, 109, 180
Tales of Willie Piper 90, 148
Talk with Irene Rich 249
Talk Your Way Out of It 79
Talmadge, Eugene 226
Tapestries of Life 18
Tareyton 87
Tarzan 15, 153, 187, 193, 209, 266, 315
Taub, Sam 285
Taylor, Elizabeth 142, 223
Taylor, Henry Junior 285–286
Taylor, Dr. Marion Sayle 308
Tearle, Conway 286
Tearle, Osmond 286
Ted Cott Award 67
Ted Husing 147
Ted Husing's Bandstand 148
Ted Husing's Sportslants 147
The Ted Lewis Show 211
Ted Mack's Original Amateur Hour 150
Teentimers Canteen 144
Teentimers Club 65, 144
Telegraphed news reports 12
The Telephone Hour 21, 152
Tell It Again 150, 194, 305
Ten-Two-Four Ranch 100
Tena and Tim 11, 140
Tennessee Ernie Ford Show 213
Tennessee Jed 32, 187
Terkel Time 127
Terminex Show 163
Terrace, Vincent 197
Terrace Gardens, Chicago 24
Terry and the Pirates 47, 48, 63, 79, 157, 175, 176
Terry Regan, Attorney at Law 10, 227, 313
Tex and Jinx 97, 262
Tex Fletcher 309
Texaco 87
The Texaco Fire Chief 188, 319

Texaco Reporters 319
Texaco Star Theater 10, 66, 90, 106, 148, 163, 307, 311
Texas Co. 146
Thanks for Tomorrow 134
Thanks to America 275
That Brewster Boy 194
That They Might Live 58
That's a Good Idea 280
That's a Good One 134, 317
That's Life 280
That's My Pop 123
That's Rich 11, 209, 234, 250, 295
Theater Five 32, 94, 102
Theater Guild Dramas 77
The Theater Guild of the Air 77
Theater Guild on the Air 45, 136, 249, 311
The Theater of Famous Radio Players 194, 309
Theater of Romance 123, 303
Theater of Today 166
Theater U.S.A. 234
There Was a Woman 121
There's Always a Woman 179
There's Music in the Air 292
These Are Americans 146
These Are Our Men 5, 67, 89
They Burned the Books 187
Think 312
Think Fast 64, 186
The Third Man 217
The Thirteenth Juror 281
Thirty Minutes in Hollywood 58
This Amazing America 46
This Could Be You 122
This Day Is Ours 9, 19, 30, 217
This Fabulous World 85
This I Believe 202
This Is Bing Crosby 54, 55
This Is Galen Drake 84
This Is Holloran 300
This Is Hollywood 86, 141, 212
This Is Jazz 104
This Is Judy Jones 8
This Is Life 194, 227
This Is London 61, 75, 138, 172, 202, 259, 264, 295
This Is My Best 187, 274, 307
This Is My Song 122
This Is My Story 141, 182
This Is Nora Drake 71, 148, 239
This Is Our Enemy 98, 201
This Is the Story 179, 230
This Is the Truth 180
This Is Your FBI 25, 49, 70, 102, 157, 217, 320
This Is Your Life 20, 89, 140
This Life Is Mine 98, 181, 208
This Moving World 8
This Small Town 87, 134
Thomas, Danny 119
Thomas, John Charles 19
Thomas, Lowell Jackson 29, 59, 60, 101, 135, 151, 156, 286–289, 291
Thomas, Norman 133
Thomas, Peter 289

INDEX

Thomas Cook & Sons 21
Thomas Jefferson 201
Thompson, Bobby 139
Thompson, Dorothy 103, 289–291
Thor, Larry 291
Thorgersen, Edward 291–292
Those Good Old Days 23
Those Sensational Years 172
Those We Love 153
Those Websters 126, 148, 177
Three Beaus and a Peep 84
Three City Byline 115
Three for the Money 63
The Three Musketeers 209
Three Ring Time 113
Three Sheets to the Wind 54
Three Star Extra 151
Three's a Crowd 163
Thurston, the Magician 42
Tibbett, Lawrence 252
Tice, J. Olin, Jr. 84, 292–293
Tide 22, 277
Tillman, John 292–293
Tim and Irene 189, 234, 265, 315
Time for Crime 215
Time for Love 303
The Time of Your Life 189
The Time, the Place and the Tune 281
Time to Remember 292
Time to Shine 248
Time to Smile 164, 304
Times a-Wastin' 63
Timex 284–285
The Timid Soul 30
Tinney, Cal 243, 293
Toasties Time 234, 235
Tobacco auctioneers 37–38
Today at the Duncans 209, 210
Today with Mrs. Roosevelt 245
Today's Children 126, 165, 192, 194, 218, 227, 230, 242
Today's the Day 91–92
Tom Corbett, Space Cadet 30, 31
Tom, Dick and Harry 8
Tom Mix Ralston Straight Shooters 95, 114, 121, 175
Tomlinson, Edward 293–294
Tommy Bartlett's Ski, Sky and Stage Show, Robot World and Exploratory 26
The Tommy Dorsey Playshop 169
Tommy Dorsey Show 212
Tommy Dorsey's Orchestra 103
Tommy Riggs and Betty Lou 113, 114, 181, 182, 248, 250, 262, 315
Tomorrow 26
Tomorrow's Headlines 107, 298
Tone, Franchot 96
Toni Arden Show 164
Tonight 26
Tonight at Hoagy's 156–157
Tonight on Broadway 147, 239
Tonkin, Phil 294
Tony and Gus 251
The Tony Martin Show 101, 307
Tony Marvin and the News 181

Tony Wons Scrapbook 313
Too Many Cooks 94
Top of the News from Washington 173
Top Secret 62
Top Secrets of the FBI 91, 231
Tops in Sports 101, 165
Tops in Town 80
Torme Time 163
Toscanini, Arturo 86
Tovrov, Orin 80
The Town Crier 81, 320
Town Hall Tonight 89, 250, 303
Town Talk 298
Townsend, Dallas S. Jr. 283, 294
Trammel, Miles 60
Transradio 50
Traub Co. 248
Travis, Merle 170
Treasure Hour of Song 86, 251, 319
Treasury Agent 31, 127, 217, 309
The Treasury Hour 189, 211
Treasury of Music 65
Treasury Salute 67, 220, 266, 277
Treasury Star Parade 42, 79, 81, 91, 153, 206, 211, 311
Treasury Star Salute 206
Treasury Varieties 305
Trebek, Alex 208
Treet Time 194
Tremayne, Les 294–295
The Tremaynes 295
Tremendous Trifles 136
Trendle, George W. 298
Tribute to George Gershwin 208
Troman Harper, Rumor Detective 124, 282
Trotsky, Leon 196
Trotter, John Scott 55
The Trouble with Marriage 80
Trout, Robert 51, 56, 74, 101, 164, 181, 203, 295–298, 302
True, Harold 298
True Adventures of Junior G-Men 231
True Detective Mysteries 86, 151, 224, 234
True or False 216, 237
The True Story Hour with Mary and Bob 58, 81, 147, 248
True Story Time 118
The Truitts 230
Truman, Harry S. 85, 139, 156, 168, 224, 248, 318
Truman, Margaret 191
Truth or Consequences 9, 18, 54, 63, 89, 105, 134, 170, 177, 239, 274, 280, 304, 313
Tufeld, Dick 298–299
Tune-Up Time 262
Turn Back the Turntables 237, 266
Turner, Grant 49, 73
Turner, Jesse Granderson 299
Turner, Ted 258
Tuttle, Roger 299–300

The 1280 Club 68
20th Century–Fox 34, 171
Twenty-First Precinct 101, 124
Twenty Questions 148, 149, 305
Twenty-Six by Corwin 43, 77, 106
Twenty Thousand Years in Sing Sing 32, 118, 157
Two for the Money 164
Two on a Clue 322
Two Seats in the Balcony 208
Tyson, Cicely 119, 120, 300

Ulric, Lenore 43
Uncle Charlie's Tent Show 244
Uncle Don 23, 36, 53, 119, 122, 165, 197, 208
Uncle Don Institute of Child Guidance and Recreation 54
Uncle Ezra 125, 126
Uncle Jim's Question Bee 32, 262
Uncle Walter's Doghouse 177, 194
Under Arrest 47, 87, 93, 186
The Unexpected 187
U.N. Correspondents Association 104
The United Nations Today 180
U.S. Committee for UNICEF 83
U.S. Information Agency 205
U.S. Steel 27, 45, 87, 136
U.S. Steel Hour 77, 136
United Textile Manufacturers 180
Universal News Service 108
Universal Safety Series 291
University of Chicago Round Table 245, 246
University of the Air 203
Up for Parole 180, 303
Utley, Garrick 275
Uttal, Fred 48, 300

Vacation Serenade 118
Vacation with Music 67, 134
Valiant Lady 5, 104, 105, 186, 195, 201, 217, 234, 311
Vallee, Rudy 142, 190, 235
Vallee Varieties 144, 234
Van, Lyle 300–301
Vanderbilt, Gloria 69
Vandercook, John F. 301
Vandercook, John W. 156, 254, 255, 301
Vandercook, Margaret W. 301
Van Doren, Charles 104
Vanity Fair 115, 200, 245, 293
Vanocur, Sander 302
Van Voorhis, Westbrook 302–303
Variety Fair 91
The Variety Show 147, 239
The Vaughn Monroe Show 250
V.D. Radio Project 136
Venables, Robert 303
Vendig, Irving 277
The Vera Vague Show 151
Vic and Sade 46, 89, 100, 126, 134, 148, 167, 177, 227, 237, 239

Vic Damone Show 104
The Vicks Open House 145
Victor Borge Show 163, 239, 313
Victor Lindlahr 175
Victory Parade of Spotlight Bands 250
Viennese Nights 208
Vines, Lee L. 303
Viorst, Judith 257
Vitaphone 316
A Voice in the Night 47
Voice of America 74, 173, 180, 205, 312
Voice of America 39, 118
The Voice of Broadway 160, 283
Voice of Experience 308
Voice of Firestone 122, 151, 189, 251
Voice of the Army 98, 220, 277
The Voice of Vic Damone 217
Voices and Events 100
Vonn, Veola 210
Von Zell, Harry 38, 303–305
Vox Pop 67, 102, 118, 145, 153, 167, 189
The Voyage of the Scarlet Queen 15

The Wacky Family 315
Wagner, Murray 305
Wain, Bea 27, 97
Wake Up America 121, 170, 213
Wald, John 305
Waldecker, Frank 305
Walk a Mile 90, 170, 224, 238
Walker, Bob 159
Walker, Henry 11
Walker, Larry 61
Wallace, Chris 275, 306
Wallace, Myron (Mike) 305–306
Waller, Theodore 137
Wallington, James 140, 306–308
Walsh, George 308
Walter Gross and His Orchestra 292
Walter Winchell 109
Walter Winchell and the News 317
Walter Winchell's Journal 118, 125, 151, 277, 317
Walters, Barbara 35, 273
Walters, Joe 308
Walton, Sidney 308–309
Waltz Time 13, 58
Wander (firm) 12
Wanted 62
Ward, Perry 309
Ware, Susan 184
Waring, Fred 34
Warner Brothers 145
Warner Brothers-Capricorn Records 48
War of the Worlds 77, 102
"The War of the Worlds" 262
War Town 98
Warren, Carl 309
Warren, Charles Robert 309–310

Warrick, Ruth 214
Washington Merry-Go-Round 224
Washington Report 125
Washington Week 256, 258
Wason, Betty 50
Watch and Win 8
Watch the World Go By 112
Watergate 257–258
Waterloo Junction 126
Waters, Ethel 191
Watson, George 67
Way Down Home 42
Wayfaring Stranger 48
Wayne Howell and the News 144
Wayne Howell Show 144
The Wayne King Show 127, 177
Wayside Cottage 5
WBBM Nutty Club 47
We Are Always Young 277
We Are Four 271
We Deliver the Goods 39, 72
We Love and Learn 86, 87, 94, 208, 242, 244
We Take Your Word 141
We, the Abbotts 187
We, the People 49, 123, 133, 172, 245, 262, 304
Weaver, Pat 100
Weaver of Dreams 252
Webb, Chick 13
Webb, Jack 8, 94
Weber, Karl A. 310
Webster, Kurt 61, 310–311
Webster, Maurie 96
Wednesday with You 304
Weekday 160, 305
Weekend 134, 160
Weekly War Journal 138, 178
Weems, Ted 310
Weigel, John J. 311
Weist, Dwight 311
Weist-Barron School of Television and Commercial Acting 311
Welch, Niles 311–312
Welcome to Hollywood 42
Welcome Travelers 10, 25, 26, 72, 127, 142, 196, 214
Welcome Valley 43
Welk, Lawrence 232
Welles, H.G. 262
Welles, Orson 77, 130, 223, 247, 262
Wells, Richard 312
Wendy Warren and the News 32, 87, 88, 104 105, 151, 295
Wesson, Dick 312
West, Mae 85
Westbrook Van Voorhis 302
Western adventure series 182
Western Newspaper Union 28
Western Radio Institute 12
Westin, Av 273
Westinghouse Corp. 93, 165
The Westinghouse Program 211
The Westinghouse Sunday Concert 211
Weston, Paul 234

What Are We Fighting For? 292
What Makes You Tick? 13, 125
What's Cookin'? 310
What's Doin', Ladies? 280, 309
What's My Line 43, 74, 160
What's My Name? 102, 163, 239, 300, 317
What's New? 10
What's New in South America? 293
What's on Your Mind 42
What's the Good Word? 125
What's the Name of That Song? 122
What's the Score? 122
What Would You Have Done? 67, 118
Wheatenaville Sketches 57
The Wheel of Fortune 217
When a Girl Marries 13, 21, 39, 98, 106, 107, 151, 162, 166, 212, 276, 277, 310
Where Have You Been? 67
The Whisper Men 262, 310
The Whisperer 236
Whispering Jack Smith 304
Whispering Streets 71, 102, 124, 308
The Whistler 15, 72, 89, 101, 151, 152, 170, 187, 194, 236, 303
White, Andrew 147, 319
White, Betty 207
White, Clarence 41
White, J. Andrew 52, 189
White, Martha 73
White, Paul 27, 75, 116, 125, 156, 272
White, Sue Taylor 282
White Fires of Inspiration 114
The White Owl Program 165
The White Owl Smoker 139
White Owl Sports Smoker 9
Whitehall 1212 237
Whiteman, Paul 50, 55, 183, 195
Whitley, Ray 177
Whitman, Gayne 312–313
Whiz Quiz 216, 308
Who Dun It? 78, 217
Who Knows? 152
Who Said That? 154, 197, 241, 283, 295, 297
Widmark, Richard 119, 120, 313
Wilcox, Harlow 131, 313–314
Wild Bill Hickok 177, 179, 182, 192
Wiley, Lee 245
Wilkinson, Ellen 203
Will Osborne and His Orchestra 219
The Will Rogers Program 242
The Will Rogers Show 32, 52, 242, 303
Willard, Dick 314–315
William Hillman 138
William Hillman and Bill Henry 138
William L. Shirer 266
William L. Shirer Commentary 266

Williams, Alexander 183
Williams, Gwen 309
Williams, Kenneth 315
Willie Piper 90, 185
Willkie, Wendell 124
Wilson, Dick 45
Wilson, Don Harlow 96, 210, 314, 315–316
Wilson, Doreen 45
Wilson, Earl 172, 247
Wilson, Ward 316–317
Wilson, Woodrow 112
Win Your Lady 10, 200
Winchell, Walter 96, 101, 118, 119, 142, 156, 221, 223, 225, 233, 286, 317–319
Wings of Destiny 114, 153, 194
Wings of Song 285
Wings Over America 187
Winner Take All 32, 63, 292, 317
Winning in the West 109
Winslowe, Paula 66
Winters, Roland 319
The Witch's Tale 30
Witten, Louis A. 319
The Wizard of Odds 84, 280
WLS Barn Dance 131
Wolfe, Edwin 220
The Woman 163
Woman from Nowhere 8, 193
The Woman in My House 177, 295
Woman in White 82, 170, 177, 194, 200, 218, 230, 295, 310
A Woman of America 30, 106
Woman of Courage 87
Women's International League for Peace and Freedom 291
Wons, Tony 243
Wood, Charles 320
Woods, Charles 320
Woodson, William 320
Woodward, Fred C. 226
Woodward, Robert 226
Woollcott, Alexander 320–321
Words at War 30, 67, 98, 217, 310, 313
Words in the Night 248
World Adventurers 108

The World Is Our Beat 143, 255, 256
World News Parade 59
World News Roundup 61, 255, 256, 259, 264, 266, 271
World News Today 40, 94, 100, 285
World News Tonight 180, 255, 256, 259, 264, 266, 271
World News with Robert Trout 51, 83, 255
World Now 117
The World Today 74, 143, 202, 285, 295, 297
The World Tonight 50, 143, 149, 154, 158, 172, 282, 294, 295, 297
The World of Nordine 214
The World's Biggest Make Believe Ballroom 35
The World's Great Novels 21, 172, 188, 214
The World's Most Honored Flights 199
Worrall, Margaret 97
W.R. Grace Co. 214
Wright, Stewart 25
Wrigley, William J. 268
WSM Barn Dance 131
Wu Pei-fu 59
Wynn, Dick 321
Wynn, Ed 45, 190
Wynne, Dr. Shirley 214

X Minus One 30, 32, 62, 67, 120, 217, 219, 299, 310
The Xavier Cugat Show 220

Yarns for Yanks 193
Years of Crisis 202
Yes or No 300
You and Your Security 300
You Are There 30, 51, 74, 141, 143, 180, 193, 239
You Bet Your Life 94, 270, 305
You Can't Take It with You 266
You Were There 215
Young, Agnes 263
Young, Thomas Shaw 17

Young & Rubicam 76
Young Doctor Malone 31, 102, 148, 233, 289
Young Hickory 121
Young Love 137, 250
Young Man with a Band 262
Young Widder Brown 13, 14, 32, 63, 104, 105, 322
Your All-Time Hit Parade 37, 237
Your Crossword Quiz 230
Your Dream Has Come True 274
Your Family and Mine 5, 37, 79, 102
Your Gospel Singer 103
Your Happy Birthday 251
Your Hit Parade 26, 35, 37, 38, 77, 127, 145, 237, 251, 252, 265
Your Hit Parade on Parade 251
Your Hollywood Reporter 95
Your Home Beautiful 266
Your Land and Mine 285
Your Lover 176
Your Lucky Strike 180
Your News Parade 138
Your Radio Reporter 134
Your Radio Theater 275
Your Richfield Reporter 122
Your Song and Mine 26, 91
You're the Expert 265, 300
Your Tropical Trip 150
Your Voice of America 179
Yourman, Alice 321–322
Yours for a Song 86, 115
Yours Truly, Johnny Dollar 5, 25, 30, 71, 79, 124, 152, 176, 177, 217, 228, 250, 277, 280, 285
Youth Opportunity Program 101
Youth vs. Age 57, 151, 293
Yvette Sings 118

The Zane Grey Show 101, 228
The Zane Grey Theater 21, 228
The Zerone Program 81
Ziegfeld Follies of the Air 163, 234, 242
Zolotow, Maurice 286

www.ingramcontent.com/pod-product-compliance
Lightning Source LLC
Chambersburg PA
CBHW081536300426
44116CB00015B/2650